VICTOR CONSIDERANT
AND THE RISE AND FALL OF
FRENCH ROMANTIC SOCIALISM

Victor Considerant in 1848. Lithograph by Lafosse. Photo from Cabinet des Estampes, Bibliothèque Nationale.

Victor Considerant
and the Rise and Fall of French Romantic Socialism

JONATHAN BEECHER

University of California Press

BERKELEY   LOS ANGELES   LONDON

An earlier version of chapter 1 and a small part of
chapter 2 have been published as "Victor Considerant:
The Making of a Fourierist," in Richard Bienvenu
and Mordechai Feingold (eds.), *In the Presence of the
Past: Essays in Honor of Frank Manuel* (Amsterdam:
Kluwer, 1991), 93–120. A portion of chapter 10 has been
published in a French translation by Michel Cordillot as
"Vieux Monde et nouveau monde. La Révolution de 1848
vue par Victor Considerant," in *Cahiers Charles Fourier*,
10 (December 1999), 17–26. A small part of chapter 13
and most of chapter 14 have been translated into French
by Michel Cordillot and published as "Une Utopie
manquée au Texas: Victor Considerant et Réunion,"
in *Cahiers Charles Fourier*, 4 (1993), 40–79.

University of California Press
Berkeley and Los Angeles, California

University of California Press, Ltd.
London, England

Library of Congress Cataloging-in-Publication Data

Beecher, Jonathan.
    Victor Considerant and the rise and fall of French romantic
socialism / Jonathan Beecher.
        p.   cm.
    Includes bibliographical references (p.) and index.
    ISBN 0-520-22297-0 (cloth : alk. paper)
    1. Considerant, Victor, 1808–1893.   2. Socialists—France—
Biography.   3. Utopian socialism—France—History—
19th century.   I. Title.

HX704.C7 B44 2001
335'.0092—dc21
[B]
                                    00-028717

Manufactured in the United States of America
9 8 7 6 5 4 3 2 1 0

10 9 8 7 6 5 4 3 2 1

⊗ The paper used in this publication meets the minimum requirements
of ANSI / NISO Z39 0.48-1992(R 1997) (Permanence of Paper).

For Merike, David, and Lembit
"Meil on tore koos."

CONTENTS

Illustrations follow page 266.

PREFACE

The first glimmer of an idea for this book came to me long ago, when I was taken to visit the Colonie Sociétaire at Condé-sur-Vesgre, the site of the first effort made to create a community based on the ideas of the great utopian thinker Charles Fourier. The soil was sandy and the vegetation scrubby; I could see why Fourier's original followers found it difficult to farm this land. Near the entrance stood some impressive and venerable pine trees, however, and even a few sequoias. The latter, I was told, were "les Texas"—some of them apparently grown from seedlings brought back from Texas by Fourier's follower Victor Considerant in 1869 at the conclusion of his fifteen-year exile in America.

Victor Considerant's name was familiar to me. I knew him as Fourier's most important disciple, a man who had devoted himself for decades to the creation of a movement aimed at the spread and implementation of Fourier's ideas. I knew him also as one of the handful of individuals who had created socialist journalism and who advanced socialism as an ideology and a movement in the 1840s. Considerant had been active in radical politics in 1848 as one of the leaders of the democratic and socialist left but then had dropped out of sight, or at least my sight. I knew dimly that Considerant had spent many years in America after the collapse of the Second French Republic. This vivid reminder of his American experience planted in me the idea of someday getting to know the story of his Texas years and putting it together with what I already knew about his activities as a Fourierist, a socialist journalist, and a 'forty-eighter.

During the years that followed, as I worked on a long intellectual biography of Charles Fourier, my curiosity about Considerant grew. He had not fared well at the hands of some of the leading Fourier scholars. Indeed, it seemed to me that he had been made into a scapegoat by many who believed that Fourier had been poorly served by his followers. He was criticized for having published some of Fourier's manuscripts in adulterated form and having suppressed others, notably the extraordinary sexual utopia, *Le Nouveau monde amoureux*, first published by Simone Debout-Oleskiewicz only in 1967. Considerant was also charged with having watered down Fourier's theory, stripping it of its playful utopian vignettes and its "mathematical poetry" and turning it into a prosaic socialist scheme for the organization of labor. Finally, in some quarters he was attacked for having concentrated the energies and resources of the Fourierist movement on reformist political activities that Fourier himself would have scorned.

These charges against Considerant, some of which had originally been made by dissidents within the Fourierist movement itself, I found impossible to deny. The first article I ever published presented a passage from one of Fourier's manuscripts that had been censored by Considerant and his colleagues when the manuscript was published in August 1848. Still I found myself dissatisfied by the attacks on Considerant. After all, it was Fourier himself, and not one of his followers, who initiated the effort to present his doctrine in a form palatable to the bourgeois politicians and businessmen whom he hoped to interest in his ideas. The attacks on Considerant also seemed to discount the fact that his interest in Fourier's doctrine was not that of a scholar or an archivist but that of an activist who did in fact manage to rescue Fourier's ideas from the obscurity into which they would otherwise have fallen and who gave them a new life, albeit a different life than that with which Fourier himself had endowed them.

It seemed to me that Considerant's attempts to recast Fourier's ideas in terms appropriate to the needs of the social movement that he had created posed a number of interesting questions in the history of ideas. Furthermore, thinking about Considerant not as a Fourierist but rather as an early socialist activist, I found myself impressed by his energy and by the sheer range of his activities and relations. In his role as leader of one of the major socialist *écoles*, or movements, of the 1840s, Considerant wrote thousands of letters, hundreds of newspaper articles, and dozens of pamphlets and brochures; he undertook lecture tours all over France, Belgium, and

French-speaking Switzerland; he was the host and master of ceremonies at countless banquets, soirées, public meetings, and private gatherings of the faithful; he made time to write a three-volume work that proved to be one of the major doctrinal writings of the early socialist movement; and along with all of this he was the founder, fund-raiser, editor, and chief writer for a series of newspapers and journals, including a daily paper that lasted for almost ten years. Though he may indeed have been responsible for watering down Fourier's theory, he seemed to be a fascinating and significant figure in his own right.

Now, after having spent more than a decade in close contact with Victor Considerant, I have gained a keen sense of his flaws and limitations. I should say, however, that I continue to like and even admire the man. I also feel a powerful sense of kinship with him and, more generally, with other naive and idealistic social reformers and political visionaries of his generation. One of my main impulses in writing this book was to try to understand how and why these people could have made such a mess of the opportunities they had in 1848. Nonetheless, the book is written out of sympathy and a desire to deepen and enrich our understanding of a generation of thinkers and political activists who have long been treated with (at best) amused condescension. My attempt to be even-handed in my treatment of Considerant does not reflect any coolness or indifference on my part, but rather my (possibly old-fashioned) sense that this is how history should be written.

I knew in the 1960s that the sources for a biography of Considerant were abundant. The Fourierist papers at the Archives Nationales in Paris included folders of Considerant's correspondence, drafts of unpublished works, and a substantial archive of letters exchanged by the disciples of Fourier over a period of more than sixty years. All of this constituted a much richer array of unpublished sources than those I had in writing Fourier's biography. But there was more to come. In 1976, with the publication of Russell M. Jones's article, "Victor Considerant in America," I became aware of the existence at the Ecole Normale Supérieure, where I had spent two years, of another major collection of Considerant material. The Fourier and Considerant papers had originally been kept at the Ecole Normale; and after World War II, when they were transferred to the Archives Nationales, a dozen cartons had apparently been overlooked and left in an attic at the Ecole Normale.

When I began to concentrate my energies on this book in the mid-1980s, it turned out that the sources were even richer than I had imagined. Librarians at the Ecole Normale unearthed another carton. Considerant's police dossier at the Archives Générales du Royaume in Brussels turned out to contain several hundred items, giving a surprisingly down-to-earth picture of his life during his five years of exile in Belgium. I found other rich files on Considerant at the Paris Prefecture of Police, the army archives at Vincennes, and the papers of Frédéric Dorian at Saint-Etienne. At the same time, my friends in Franche-Comté—notably, Jean-Claude Dubos and Michel Vernus—were doing work on Considerant's Franc-comtois connections that I found fascinating. Dubos and I began to correspond regularly, and he alerted me to the discovery of new sources—including yet another important collection of Considerant letters that has now been acquired by the Bibliothèque Municipale de Besançon.

Given the wealth of the sources, it seemed to me that I had an opportunity to take a different approach to Considerant than I had taken in writing Fourier's biography. In approaching Fourier, I found that the sparseness of the biographical sources and the sheer originality of his thinking made it important for me to situate his ideas in their intellectual context. My focus in the Fourier biography was on the development, revelation, and initial response to a unique utopian vision. In writing on Considerant, however, I found myself considering a person who was much more actively involved than Fourier in the life of his time and who was definitely not an original thinker. Considerant was first and foremost a journalist who devoted much of his early life to popularizing Fourier's ideas and building a movement around them. He led a long and eventful life that included participation in the three great political revolutions of the nineteenth century—1830, 1848, and the Paris Commune of 1871. He maintained continuing, if not always friendly, ties with most of the other early socialists, and he had at least occasional contact with a long list of romantic writers, including Nodier, Lamartine, Sainte-Beuve, Nerval, and Alexandre Dumas *père*.

In reading and thinking about Considerant, I soon realized that what was most interesting about his life was not so much what made it unique but rather what he had in common with other members of his generation. Gradually then, I settled on the idea of a biography of Considerant that would focus on his links with other 'forty-eighters and, more broadly, with the romantic generation of which he was a part. I hoped such a biography would help me to address a number of questions. How was it that a thinker as spectacularly eccentric as Charles Fourier managed to find a significant following among people as conventional and intellectually earth-bound as were the majority of his disciples? If early French socialism is not helpfully characterized as "pre-Marxist" (or pre-anything), what did stand at the center of the thinking of Considerant and his socialist contemporaries? How can one explain the blending in their thought of religious longings and faith in science? Why did radical thinkers and activists of Considerant's generation, who rose to positions of power and influence in 1848, accomplish so little? How could they be swept from the scene so quickly? And what, if anything, did they learn from the debacle of 1848–1851? Did Considerant and other radicals of his generation ever manage to recover their intellectual bearings after the defeats of this period? Finally, what can be learned from Considerant's long stay in America and his unsuccessful attempts to make utopia rise out of the sagebrush and chaparral of West Texas about the extraordinary appeal of mid-century America to European democrats and its corrosive effects on their ideologies and visions? I cannot say that this book gives a full answer to any of these questions. Still, I hope that the story I have told will shed some light on all of them.

Now that I am done, it pleases me to reflect upon the help and encouragement I've received along the way. A fellowship from the John Simon Guggenheim Foundation and a University of California President's Fellowship in the Humanities made it possible for me to write almost half of this book during a splendid eighteen-month sabbatical in 1988–1989. The rest was done in summer vacations and with the help of grants from the University of California Faculty Senate Research Committee and the American Philosophical Society. I am grateful to all.

Given the way I work, which involves total immersion in primary sources both printed and manuscript, I owe much to the help I've received from librarians and archivists across America and in Europe. The staff of the McHenry Library here at UCSC has been wonderful to me over the years; and I am particularly grateful for the extraordinary efforts of several generations of interlibrary loan librarians from Joan Hodgson and Betty Rentz to Julia Graham. I also want to thank the staff of the Bibliothèque of the Ecole Normale Supérieure, especially its director, Pierre Petitmengin, and also Madame Dauphraigne, for their kindness and help to me over many years. I have always looked forward to working at the library of the Ecole Normale—not only for its wonderful collections and calm ambiance but also for the personal attention of Monsieur Petitmengin and his staff.

I would like to express my thanks for the special help I've received from Madame Solange Vervaeck of the Archives Générales du Royaume at Brussels, from Madame Richard and Madame Waille at the Bibliothèque Municipale de Besançon and from Valerii Nikolaevich Fomichev at the Russian State Archives of Social-Political History in Moscow. I have also benefited from many kindnesses on the part of librarians and archivists at the Archives Nationales, the Bibliothèque Nationale, the Bibliothèque Historique de la Ville de Paris, the Archives Historiques de la Guerre, the Archives de la Préfecture de Police de la Seine, the Bibliothèque Municipale de Salins, the departmental archives at Saint-Etienne, the Baker Library at Dartmouth College, the Green Library at Stanford University, and the Widener, Kress, and Houghton Libraries at Harvard University. I owe a particular debt to Pierre Mercklé both for sharing with me an early version of his excellent inventory of the Considerant papers at the Ecole Normale and for our numerous conversations during his months here at Santa Cruz on Considerant, Fourier, and the sociology of utopia.

Over the years many of my colleagues at the University of California, Santa Cruz, have listened to me talk about Victor Considerant and have provided encouragement and helpful criticism. I'm especially grateful to Bruce Thompson, Mark Traugott, Tyler Stovall, Buchanan Sharp, John Dizikes, Peter Kenez, Robert Berkhofer, Gary Miles, Cindy Polecritti, Gail Hershatter, Terry Burke, Lynn Westerkamp, and David Sweet. I also owe much to Naomi Andrews, not only for her work as my research assistant but also for numerous exchanges of ideas.

Among colleagues outside Santa Cruz who have been helpful in various ways and from whom I have learned much, I would particularly like to thank Richard Bienvenu, Joseph Butwin, Daniel Field, Christopher Johnson, Temma Kaplan, Betje Klier, Kristin Ross, Francis Sartorius, William Sewell, and John Womack. I want to thank colleagues who have sent me material that bears on this book: Paul Crapo and Donald Reid in this country, Michel Cordillot in Paris and Auxerre, Hans Moors in Amsterdam, Marc Vuilleumier in Geneva, and the late Mirella Larizza Lolli in Milan. I also want to express my gratitude to Jean and Monique Adam for the warmth of their welcome on the occasion of my return to the Colonie Sociétaire at Condé-sur-Vesgre and for their continuing friendship.

There are three individuals to whom I owe special intellectual debts. Gareth Stedman Jones's work on utopian socialism has helped me understand where I am going. T. J. Clark has now moved on to other things, but his work on Courbet and Franche-Comté continues to inspire me. Norman O. Brown, who understands the utopian mentality from the inside, gave my biography of Fourier a critical reading that helped define the questions that lie behind the writing of this book. I am grateful to all three of them both for their work and for their comments on mine.

I would like to express my thanks to a number of historians of nineteenth-century America who have given me helpful advice and have broadened my understanding of the issues raised by this book. Robert Agnew, Laurence Veysey, and Alfred Habegger were all helpful at an early stage. I am particularly grateful to Laurie Robertson-Lorant for her guidance and encouragement and for her wonderful contextualist biography of Herman Melville, which has renewed my confidence in the kind of work we both aspire to do. Most especially I want to thank Carl Guarneri, who read my "American chapters" careful and critically, who has shared research notes and archival finds with me, and who has for some years now been a generous and discerning fellow traveler in the history of Franco-American utopianism. I also owe a continuing debt of gratitude to my colleagues in the Berkeley French Historians' group, which Susanna Barrows has made such a lively and convivial center of intellectual exchange for many years now. My thanks go to Susanna, to Ted and Joby Margadant, Keith Baker, Karen Offen, Carla Hesse, Kathy Kudlick, Lou Roberts, Mark Traugott, and Tyler Stovall for their thoughtful comments on ten chapters of this book and for their continuing camaraderie.

The greatest debt I have incurred in the writing of this book is to my friends in Paris and Besançon. Although Guy and Brigitte Vourc'h and Michel Cotté have now passed away, I will never forget their kindness, affection, and generosity. Nor will I forget that of Colette Cotté, who continues to be my host, my friend, and my guide in the Paris we both love. I am grateful to the whole Vourc'h family—especially Catherine Vourc'h-Drubigny—for their friendship and hospitality over four decades now.

I also owe a big debt of gratitude to my friends in Franche-Comté: François Lassus, Michel Cordillot, Chantal Guillaume, and Louis Ucciani of the *Cahiers Charles Fourier;* to Michel Vernus, from whom I have learned much about the history of the book and the history of Franche-Comté; and above all to Gaston Bordet and Jean-Claude Dubos. I am grateful to Gaston and to his late wife Nicole Bordet for making me feel "at home" in Franche-Comté—for hikes in the hills above Ornans, for guided tours of Besançon, Poligny, Arbois, and Salins, and Alphonse Jobez' forges de Syam, for discussions of Proudhon and Lamennais and Henri Guillemin, for a memorable 14 juillet at Pugey, and for introducing me to that most redoubtable of eaux-de-vie from the Jura mountains, *la gentiane.* My debt to Jean-Claude Dubos is no less great. He has been my guide through the labyrinth of Franc-comtois history, genealogy, and culture, his knowledge of which is equaled only by his extraordinary generosity in sharing with others his archival finds, his ideas, and his work in progress. My thanks go to him for his help, his many kindnesses, and his hospitality during my visits to Besançon over the past dozen years.

Finally, I want to thank the three people to whom this book is dedicated, Merike Lepasaar, David Beecher, and Lembit Beecher. The boys have grown up with this book, and Merike has lived with it as well as with me. They shared my first foray into Victor Considerant's Texas: together we retraced the route taken by Considerant and Albert Brisbane from Fort Smith to the Trinity River; we looked for traces of Reunion in West Dallas and for the Considerants' house outside San Antonio; and we camped in Lost Maples State Natural Area on land Considerant once owned just north of what is now Utopia, Texas. But we have shared much more than the trip to Utopia. Their love, encouragement, and companionship have brightened my life.

The Problem of Romantic Socialism

This book is an attempt both to tell the story of a life and to deepen our understanding of early French socialism—what used to be known as "pre-Marxist" or "utopian" socialism and what I have chosen to call "romantic socialism." Thus, whereas my principal aim has been to present as rich and nuanced an account as possible of the personal and political experience of Victor Considerant, I have hoped in doing so to shed light on the collective experience of Considerant's generation, more particularly those members of his generation—Saint-Simonians, Fourierists, early feminists, independent prophets of a better world—who constituted the first groups and movements that called themselves socialist.

Some historians of socialism—Benoît Malon, for one—have attempted to trace its history back to antiquity, to the Athens of Solon and the Croton of Pythagoras, or to the ascetic Jewish sect of the Essenes near the Dead Sea.[1] Others have found elements of socialism in the egalitarian strivings that seem to have marked human history since the earliest societies. As a self-conscious movement and ideology, however, socialism came into being in the romantic period. The first self-proclaimed socialists were contemporaries of Hugo, Delacroix, and George Sand; and the word *socialisme* itself was first used in the early 1830s. One of the earliest uses of the term was in an article by Pierre Leroux that was published in 1834 in the *Revue encyclopédique.* "I am the first to have made use of the word SOCIALISM," wrote Leroux later. "It was a neologism then, a necessary neologism. I invented the word as a contrast to 'individualism,' which was beginning to be widely used." Although others had actually used the term before Leroux, he was right to claim that he gave the word currency and right also that at its beginnings socialism was explicitly contrasted to egoism and individualism. This contrast was to be a fundamental feature of what I call romantic socialism.[2]

I

Early French socialism has long been misunderstood as a kind of "curtain raiser" to Marxian socialism. It has been viewed mainly in economic terms, as a reaction to the rise of industrial capitalism and a rejection of the prevailing liberal theory that the best and most natural economic system places no restraints on the individual's pursuit of private gain. Of course, early French socialism did have an economic dimension, but the early socialists' criticism and remedies were not only economic. They were writing out of a broader sense of social and moral disintegration. They believed that the French Revolution and early industrialization had produced a breakdown of traditional associations and group ties, that individuals were becoming increasingly detached from any kind of corporate structure, and that society as a whole was becoming increasingly fragmented and individualistic. Their ideas were presented as a remedy for the collapse of community rather than for any specifically economic problem.

The romantic socialists wanted a society bound by ties of love and affective solidarity. Though their plans for the organization of such a society differed, they shared a sense that the institutional arrangements of the new order must be based on cooperation rather than competition, on solidarity rather than egoism. They also shared a belief in the peaceful transformation of society; thus, with few exceptions they rejected violence and coercion. They had no desire to see their ideas imposed by terror or political revolution. In any case, they believed that this would not be necessary. For they counted on support from members of the privileged classes. In that respect they were social optimists, and their optimism was rooted, ultimately, in their belief in the existence of a common good—their belief that there was no fundamental or unbridgeable conflict of interests between the rich and the poor. What they wanted was a society organized around this common good, around the generous impulses of its members and the devotion of the individual to the whole.[3]

The romantic socialists shared this belief in a common good with the Enlightenment *philosophes,* but they rejected two shibboleths of the radical Enlightenment: atheism and materialism. The idiom of these early socialists was a religious idiom; almost all of them were theists, and many of them traced socialism's roots to early Christianity. As for materialism, it is striking by its absence from the philosophies of these thinkers. Indeed, the materialist tradition—running from Lucretius to LaMettrie to Helvétius and on to Marx and Engels—had no attraction for most of them. The arguments, explanations, and categories that they found appealing referred not to material but to final causes, not to empirical but to ideal realities. In criticizing the rapacity and greed of early capitalism, they adopted not the language of political economy but rather that of Lamartine, who, writing in 1834, described his contemporaries as confronted by the choice between "the idea of morality, religion, and evangelical charity" and "the idea of egoism in politics."[4]

If the romantic socialists used religious language, most of them also presented their thought as an exact science—a science of social organization that would allow human beings to turn away both from sterile philosophical controversy and from the destructive arena of politics and to resolve in scientific fashion the problem of social harmony. Indeed, one of the striking features of their thought is that, whereas they constantly presented their theories as rooted in the discovery of the true laws of nature and society, they also frequently spoke in the tones of religious prophets. For them the laws of nature were also the laws of God, and the new science was the true religion. This blending of science and religion, prophecy and sociology, was one of the hallmarks of their thinking.[5]

Romantic socialism as here defined emerged in France in the early 1830s in the writings of Pierre Leroux, Philippe Buchez, Victor Considerant, Flora Tristan, Constantin Pecqueur, and many of the lesser followers of Saint-Simon and Fourier. Its representatives belonged to a common generation, which was roughly that of Victor Hugo and Alfred de Musset, *enfants du siècle*—born during the Directory or under Napoleon, educated under the Bourbon Restoration, and entering public life around 1830. Like most of the writers and poets of the age, the romantic socialists lived in the shadow of the French Revolution. They believed that their great task was to reconstruct social and intellectual order in a world turned upside down by the Revolution. They shared with other romantic thinkers a sense that the revolutionaries had destroyed both a social system and a system of belief but had left little in its place. They described themselves as living in an intellectual and moral "vacuum" and believed that their task was to fill this vacuum—to work out a new doctrine or "faith" that would serve to unify society, exalt sentiments of affection, and replace antagonism with association.[6]

Just as the July Monarchy was the great period for many of the romantic poets and novelists—Hugo and Lamartine, Vigny and Musset, Balzac and Stendhal—it was also the great period of romantic socialism. Between 1830 and 1848 a socialist press emerged, a dozen major doctrinal works were published, and many new socialist groups and movements appeared. At the same time, romantic socialism merged with other ideologies of the democratic left, and a common credo took shape. This credo included a faith in universal (male) suffrage and in the collective wisdom of "the people," a belief that the differences between classes and nations were not irreconcilable, and a philosophy of "peaceful democracy," which assumed that if politicians would only appeal to the "higher" impulses of "the people," a new era of class harmony and social peace might begin.

It was in 1848—with the overthrow of the July Monarchy in France and of repressive police states in much of the rest of Europe—that socialists and republicans at last had their chance at power. In France a democratic republic was proclaimed and a provisional government (including the socialist Louis Blanc) was empowered to set up a program of National Workshops that would guarantee all citizens the right to work. (This had been the great demand of the socialists, most forcefully articulated by Louis Blanc and Victor Considerant.) Thus the spring of 1848 was a time of great hopes that were often expressed in religious and apocalyptic language. It soon became evident, however, that the Provisional Government, which was dominated by moderates hostile to socialism, was neither willing nor able to give adequate support to the National Workshops. Then, when elections were held in April, Paris voted to the left, but the provinces voted solidly conservative. The problem confronting the radicals was that the vast majority of newly enfranchised voters were peasants, who were often illiterate, totally lacking in political experience, and quite content to let priests and gentry make decisions for them.

After the elections, a conflict developed between Paris and the provinces and between the conservative majority in the National Assembly and the more radical democrats and socialists. In June 1848 the government, along with the conservative majority in the Assembly, decided to get rid of the National Workshops, which were expensive and were attracting thousands of unemployed workers to Paris. This decision precipitated an armed insurrection by the Parisian poor. Barricades went up in the working-class quarters; and the National Guard, regular army, and Mobile Guard units found themselves confronted by an army of fifty thousand insurgents. Only four days later, after some of the bloodiest streetfighting Paris had ever known, did the government regain control of the city.

The popular insurrection of June 1848 shattered the dream of the romantic socialists and other radicals that a "democratic and social republic" might usher in a new age of class harmony. After the insurrection was crushed, the socialist program of "peaceful democracy" ceased to have any real political meaning. The left made subsequent efforts to regroup and to find a following among the peasantry. These efforts, as we shall see, had considerable success, but the final result of the revolution of 1848 was to deal a mortal blow to the high-minded and generous humanitarian aspirations of the romantic socialists. By the end of 1851, most of them had been thrown into exile and left with their public lives—and in many cases their beliefs—shattered.

"Socialism is dead," wrote Louis Reybaud in 1854. "To speak of it is to pronounce its funeral oration." In retrospect, such reports of socialism's demise seem, as Mark Twain would have said, greatly exaggerated. What *was* dead in 1854, however, was a certain kind of socialism. Never again would the generous, conciliatory, humanitarian, romantic socialism of the 1840s command the support that it had in the spring of 1848. Never again would the religious rhetoric of 1848 enjoy the same resonance. The invocation of Jesus Christ as the "first socialist" and of the revolution itself as a "religious" transformation that would regenerate society soon began to seem dated. A generation later Benoît Malon could speak with exasperation of the "accoutrements of religiosity" and the "neo-Christianity" that had "poisoned" the "socialist revival" of the Second Republic.[7]

II

It has not been easy for modern historians of socialism to write convincingly and without condescension about the pre-1848 period. We are distanced from the romantic socialists by the hyperbole and vagueness of their language, by their persistent idealism, by their propensity for religious and metaphysical speculation, and above all, perhaps, by their confident expectation of the coming of a new world consistent with their ideals. We are also distanced from them by the fact that their illusions (as we would say) were destroyed so rapidly and completely by the events of 1848–1851. By the end of the Second Republic, their faith in universal male suffrage as a vehicle of change had come to seem ludicrous, and their humanitarian and religious rhetoric had fallen completely out of style. Just a few years later, in 1855, Alexandre Erdan could give the romantic socialists prominent billing in his "survey of the religious eccentricities of our time." And when a number of them returned from exile in the late 1860s, they were regarded as relics of a bygone era—the *vieilles barbes,* or "old codgers," of 1848.[8]

During the 1870s and 1880s, Marxism emerged as *the* great ideology of the European left; the eclipse of romantic socialism was complete. Friedrich Engels' *Socialism: Utopian and Scientific,* which was originally published in 1878 as a portion of Engels' polemic against the German philosopher Eugen Duhring, relegated these thinkers en masse to the status of "utopian" precursors of "scientific" socialism. Engels' treatment of the original triumvirate of utopian socialists—Saint-Simon, Fourier, and Robert Owen—was sympathetic; and Engels paid particular tribute to Fourier as a remorseless critic of the "material and moral misery of the bourgeois world" and as a thinker whose "imperturbably serene nature" made him "assuredly one of the greatest satirists of all time." As for the element of "fantasy" in the writing of the utopian socialists, Engels claimed that it was "unavoidable" at a time "when capitalist production was as yet so little developed" and the proletariat "as yet incapable of independent political action." However, Engels concluded that "we need not dwell a moment longer upon this side of the question" since it "now belongs wholly to the past."[9]

With regard to the second generation of the early socialists—the followers of Saint-Simon and Fourier and their contemporaries—Marx and Engels had already made their position clear in the *Communist Manifesto.* Although the early utopians were "in many respects revolutionary," their disciples had "in every case formed mere reactionary sects." Not recognizing the historical development of the proletariat, they "held fast to the original views of their masters." They constantly sought "to deaden the class struggle and to reconcile class antagonisms." Dreaming of the experimental realization of their social utopias, they were "compelled to appeal to the feelings and purses of the bourgeois." In the end, they differed from the reactionary critics of bourgeois society only by their "more systematic pedantry, and by their fanatical and superstitious belief in the miraculous effects of their social science."[10]

For more than a century, scholarly discussion of early French socialism remained within the parameters set by Marx and Engels. A clear contrast was established between the "scientific" or "forward-looking" aspects of early socialism and the "utopian" or "fantastic" elements. The early socialists were seen as "precursors" whose intellectual inadequacies could best be understood as the outcome or reflection of a "transitional" moment in history and whose "contributions" to socialism were assimilated by Marx and Engels. Thus G. D. H. Cole could write of Fourier that there was much in his writings that was "fantastic" and even "plainly mad," but it was "unnecessary to dwell on these fantasies" since they had "no connection with the essence of his teaching." Fourier was, if properly understood, "a serious social thinker who contributed much of permanent value." Likewise George Lichtheim, although vastly more nuanced and better informed than Cole, could insist that Fourier's "quaint notions" on cosmology and his "grotesque fantasies" had no relation to either his social criticism or his vision of the good society. Indeed, the whole point of Lichtheim's influential *Origins of Socialism* was that socialism was a "movement which had to emancipate itself from inherited illusions before it could attain consciousness of its true nature."[11]

The problem with this approach to early socialism is that it was both teleological and reductionist. It was teleological in the sense that it interpreted early socialist thought as a series of fragmentary, disconnected intuitions pointing to a future, still undisclosed, theory. It was reductionist in the sense that it treated the development of socialism as a "reflection" of the growth of the working-class movement while discounting their repeated claim that they represented not a class but all humanity.[12]

What is lost in such interpretations is, first of all, a sense of the coherence and inner logic of the romantic socialists' thought. To treat their doctrines as grab bags of "brilliant anticipations" and "archaic fantasies" is to deny oneself insight into the connections that *they* saw between their cosmologies and their visions of the good society, their religious ideas and their social criticism. What is also lost is a sense of context—an understanding of how their views represented plausible responses to their world and their experience. Romantic socialism was, as I have already suggested, the creation of a particular age and a particular generation. Central to the experience of this generation was a sense of the need to find new bases for social and intellectual order after the dislocations of the revolutionary and Napoleonic periods. In their minds, the need for community and the need for religion were closely linked. Many of them came to regard shared religious beliefs as essential to knitting the fabric of an otherwise divided society. It is no coincidence that most of the major romantic socialist thinkers presented themselves as the founders of new religions as well as new societies. Almost all of them shared with Victor Considerant the belief that "the essential feature of any religion" was "to *rally* or *bind* men together."[13]

One final problem created by the "grab-bag approach" to the romantic socialists is that it limits our ability to see them whole or to bring them back to life. I believe that one of the principal tasks of the historian is, as Michelet put it, to "resurrect" the past—to "rekindle ashes long cold." I understand that any historical recreation or "resurrection" of the past must be accomplished in terms of conventions and categories and in a language that belong to us, not the age we are studying. In that sense the historian's work is always a work of translation. But this does not mean that we have no access to the past—that it will always be a closed book to us. Nor does it mean that we are condemned to wander aimlessly in a world of words. Few of us now share Michelet's confidence in the historian's ability to grasp "the inmost thought" of a whole epoch or people. Nonetheless, I believe— and perhaps this is why I am particularly drawn to biography—in our ability to deepen, enrich, and in a sense give life to our understanding of the past through the close scrutiny of individual lives. Here I am attempting to shed some light on the thought and experience of the first socialists by showing how one of their number made sense of his world and tried to change it, how he responded to the collapse of the democratic and socialist left after 1848, how his views changed over time, and how they did not change.[14]

PART I

Roots

1

Franche-Comté and Family

Although Victor Considerant became a Parisian by adoption and later an American citizen, he never forgot that he was a native of Franche-Comté. And although he made his reputation as the chief exponent of an ideology that minimized the importance of birthplace, family, and local tradition, his own ties with the land of his birth and his family were strong. Franche-Comté was a rugged, heavily forested region on France's eastern frontier. It was a region of mountains, trout streams, sawmills, small wood-burning forges, and dairy farms famous for their traditions of cooperative cheese production. Much of Franche-Comté was high plateau country, physically isolated and almost inaccessible in winter, and its inhabitants had long possessed a reputation for independence and fierce devotion to their local liberties. The name "Free County" was of late medieval origin and harked back to their struggle for independence from the French, the Burgundians, and the Habsburgs. Franche-Comté had been under the domination of all of these before it was definitively integrated into the kingdom of France by Louis XIV.[1]

The town of Salins, where Considerant was born on October 12, 1808, had been the second city of the province at the time of the French conquest. Even then, however, its population was under six thousand, and it was not much bigger in Considerant's time. Still it was, and remains, a lovely town—stretched out along the narrow valley of a normally placid river, quaintly named "La Furieuse," and overlooked by vineyards, forts, and great rocky promontories on either side. As the name suggests, Salins was the site of a saltworks, one of the oldest and best known in the east of France during the Old Regime. But it was also, like the neighboring towns of Arbois and Poligny, a city of wine producers—the *vignerons* whose quarter, le Matachin, with its casks, vaulted cellars, and fifteenth-century houses, was to be celebrated, long after Considerant had left the region, by his younger admirer, the writer Max Buchon.[2]

Considerants had been living at Salins for three generations prior to Victor's birth. A Jacques Considerant, who first appears in the local records around 1740 as a *manant* (laborer), subsequently worked at a variety of jobs ranging from bookbinder to *marchand fripier* (junk dealer) and *teneur de billiard* (billiard parlor operator). His son, Victor's grandfather, Jean-Claude Considerant (1748–1813), was a modest bookseller and bookbinder who was driven into bankruptcy in 1782 and finished his life as a worker in the Salins saltworks. Victor's father, Jean-Baptiste Considerant (1771–1827), was also involved in the book trade. He ran a printing shop for many years and also served as town librarian before becoming a professor at the Collège de Salins in 1812. He never became rich and was not well known outside of Salins. Unlike his forebears, though, he became an important, and ultimately revered, figure in the cultural life of his birthplace.[3]

Considerant's mother, born Suzanne Courbe, was also a native of Salins. Although she was the daughter of a notary, her few surviving letters show her to have been poorly educated, if literate. Her dowry seems to have been modest—the Considerants were never rich—but she was related through her mother to two of the wealthiest and most influential families in the Jura, the Gréa and Jobez families. Both were large landowners with close ties to the world of the ironmasters of Franche-Comté, and this was to prove important to Considerant in the 1830s and 1840s, when he was seeking support for the ideas of Charles Fourier and for his own efforts to enter politics.[4]

Considerant's parents were married in 1790, and he was the youngest of four surviving children. Although the others—two girls and a boy—were much older than he, his relations with all three were warm and affectionate. He had a special fondness for his sister Justine, who was almost old enough to be his mother, having been born in 1794. Married and widowed at a young age, Justine took a second husband in 1826. This was Henry Palas, the manager of a small wire-making factory (*tréfilerie*) in Montarlot. In one of his earliest surviving letters, Considerant wrote a friend of the relative affluence of this new brother-in-law:

He has a fixed income of a thousand francs. He also has a big house with all the rooms and outbuildings you could ask for in the country-side. There's a cow-shed, a stable, a hayloft, etc., plus gardens and or-chards around the house, plus fields and meadows nearby, plus wood for his own use and workers from the forge at his disposal.[5]

All this seemed like affluence indeed to the young Considerant, whose fam-ily took in boarders to make ends meet and whose father's highest salary as a teacher was 750 francs a year.

In 1827, after the birth of their son Jules, Justine and her husband left Montarlot and settled in Poligny, where Palas went into business as an iron merchant. In later years Considerant's trips to Franche-Comté usually in-cluded a visit with the Palases; and he was to maintain a warm, if sporadic, correspondence with Justine until her death in 1880 at the age of eighty-six. Considerant was also to keep in touch with his other sister, Julie, who died a spinster in the 1860s, and with his brother Gustave (also called "Bon-homme"), who served for many years as professor of mathematics at the Collège de Saumur.[6]

I

The most important influence in Considerant's early life was his father. Jean-Baptiste Considerant was by all accounts an extraordinary person, at once a modest and extremely learned man and a man of high principles who could lament "the *sottises* in the novel of my life."[7] After his death his friends spoke of him as a character out of Plutarch, a "giant among pyg-mies." But the course of his life did not flow smoothly. He was educated, like his son Victor, at the Collège de Salins, where he was said to have shown a special love for Latin and Greek. In time he also mastered Italian and Spanish, and his English was good enough for him to publish transla-tions of John Gay. He welcomed the French Revolution; and in 1792, after the invasion of French territory, he joined the first battalion of volunteers from the Jura, eventually becoming its quartermaster. After his release from the army, he set himself up as a printer at Salins; and in 1797 he was also appointed town librarian. This was a modest position—his salary was just four hundred francs a year plus lodgings at the Collège—but during the next ten years he won a considerable local reputation both for his eru-dition and for his personal generosity. In 1810 he was enlisted by Jean-Jacques Ordinaire, first rector of the Académie de Besançon, to help estab-lish a university at Besançon, but after two years he was eager to return to Salins. In 1812 he was appointed professor of humanities at the Collège de

Salins, where he came to be revered as a teacher of legendary eloquence and probity. For fourteen years he provided his students with what the principal of the Collège described as a model of learning and virtue. But his last few years as a teacher were clouded by the tightening hold on education exercised throughout France by the most reactionary elements within the Catholic Church.[8]

In politics, Jean-Baptiste Considerant was a liberal; in religious matters, a freethinker and a Voltairean. As he grew older he became increasingly skeptical and disabused. He had initially supported the French Revolution but was turned against it by the Terror. He was initially sympathetic to Napoleon but was shocked by his despotism as emperor. He expected little from the Restoration, and Victor recalled long afterward that on the return of the Bourbons his father had spoken of quitting France and emigrating with a few friends to the banks of the Ohio River in America. He wrote a friend in September 1815 that he had once believed that "patriotism, order, justice, and humanity would eventually overcome all the petty passions," but "the experience of twenty years" had taught him that each new regime would only repeat "all the excesses and all the crimes" of its predecessors. He was no more attracted to an idealized past than he was to the regimes and rulers of his own time. The spectacle of human cruelty, however, never ceased to revolt him.[9]

Jean-Baptiste Considerant was a passionate, impulsive man—a man of deep convictions and quixotic urges. In 1798 he went all the way to Rome to defend army comrades unjustly brought to trial for having denounced the graft of Masséna and the other French generals in Italy. Ten years later, on the eve of Victor's birth, he again abandoned his wife and family to rejoin the army as private secretary to General Mouton in Spain—only to return home after a few months because he found "the bloody spectacle" of the French intervention in Spain so repellent. His friend Charles Weiss, the Nestor of early nineteenth-century Franche-Comté, said of him: "I have never seen a man more eloquent than he when his speech was inspired by a generous feeling coming from his heart." In a volume devoted to the "unrecognized moments and forgotten glories" of Franche-Comté, Charles Nodier, who knew him well, could pay tribute to the dedication, courage, and learning of Jean-Baptiste Considerant, whose literary work and personal qualities had never received adequate recognition because "a noble lack of ambition that is characteristic of a certain type of Franc-comtois" had "distanced him from all the paths to wealth and glory."[10]

The qualities that his contemporaries found most striking in Jean-Baptiste Considerant were his generosity and his selflessness. What made him in their eyes a "hero of antiquity" was his readiness, like that of the virtuous republicans of old, to identify his own interests with those of the community and the nation. The most impressive example of this was the story, repeated often after his death, of his heroic conduct during the great fire of 1825 that destroyed much of Salins. Organizing his students with the help of his elder son Gustave, who was also on the faculty, he managed to save the Collège and also most of the books in the town library while allowing his home and his printing shop to burn. Charles Nodier, who visited Salins immediately after the fire, wrote later that tales of Considerant's virtue and courage "echoed over the ruins of Salins." [11]

Much of the correspondence of Jean-Baptiste Considerant has survived. It conveys a vivid sense not only of the character of the man but also of the values he inculcated in his children. He scorned honors, decorations, and titles; he refused a soldier's pension on the ground that others were more deserving; and he never ceased being angered by signs of moral cowardice and hypocrisy. His letters to his wife were also full of instructions about the children and little sermons on morality. "I note with pleasure," he wrote in 1809, "that Bonhomme [Gustave] and his sisters are conforming to my desire to have them work. Be sure to encourage this taste in them. Take care that they never acquire a taste for dissipation. This would be the scourge of their honor and of their future existence." [12]

Jean-Baptiste Considerant's letters are one of the few sources we have concerning his son's earliest years. The impression they give is that Victor was a happy child, made much of by the family, full of "gaiety and pranks," but also frequently sick. In 1814, when Victor was six, he almost died of a childhood illness; and we have a letter that gives moving expression to his father's sense of relief at the boy's recovery:

> My fine and dear comrade, death has given up its prey, but all we still have is just a poor little mummy who looks like he belongs to the other world much more than to this one. Our poor Victor, after three weeks of grief, delirium, prostration, and anguish, he is back among the living. A few rays of life are already playing in his eyes; a hint of a smile creeps over his pale lips. How many backward steps has he been obliged to take to regain this vale of tears.

Then the father added, thinking of the trials of his own life: "If he is not going to be any happier than me, then he has made a big mistake." [13]

Despite his father's anticlericalism, Victor was raised as a Catholic and took his first communion at the age of ten. This does not necessarily mean that his mother was devout: it would have been a risky gesture for any teacher in a Restoration college to refuse to raise his child within the Church. In any case, Considerant ceased to think of himself as a member of the Church well before he reached adulthood. The persecution of his father by the Church was only the last straw. Indeed, his father wrote a friend in 1824 that Victor was "very much alarmed by the furies of the priests." In January and February of the following year the sixteen-year-old boy was probably already a scornful bystander when the city of Besançon was taken over by the celebrants of one of the most spectacular of the Restoration's Catholic "missions"—grotesque exercises in public piety that involved huge religious processions and extravagant acts of collective penance. Considerant's compatriot, Pierre-Joseph Proudhon, was later to speak of the Mission of 1825 as having inspired his "first doubts" about the teachings of the Catholic Church. But Considerant's own first doubts had been awakened much earlier. A few months after his first communion in 1818, the bishop of his diocese had come to Salins to perform the sacrament of confirmation. Considerant recalled that the bishop arrived "with a train of lackeys, a retinue," which was "an unprecedented sight" in the little town of Salins. The next day the bishop gave a superb sermon on "the value of poverty, humility, and suffering and the need to scorn the riches of the world." The bishop was so eloquent, however, that he left the ten-year-old Considerant at first confused and eventually "shocked" and "scandalized" by "the contradiction between his sermon and his retinue." [14]

Between 1816 and 1824 Considerant attended the Collège de Salins. He was remembered as a good student and "a charming boy, open, affectionate, a quick learner, a boy on whom great hopes were placed." [15] He does not seem to have been particularly engaged by his schoolwork, however; fishing and exploring the countryside were more appealing. A few years later he could describe himself as having been "a child of freedom" who "ran around as he pleased all over the countryside, in town, in the streets, even on the roofs of the houses." And in *Destinée sociale* he was speaking from his own experience when he wrote that children were not intended "to spend eight years of their youth indoors, bending wanly over grammar books, text books, Greek and Latin books, performing tedious tasks that they find neither useful nor agreeable, covering their fingers with ink, silently and gravely wearing out the bottoms of their pants on their school benches." His own interests as a boy were more practical, utilitarian, and even scientific.

> I remember very well that as young children at the Collège . . . we had very pronounced and useful vocations. I remember that we even pooled

our modest resources in order to purchase small tools, saws, axes, planes, shovels, picks and rakes, hammers and anvils. We worked steadfastly and with great pleasure on our gardens and groves. . . . We forged, filed, and finished knives. One of us became an excellent cutler. We constructed water wheels and little pumps with leather valves and brass springs that worked marvelously well.

Considerant and his comrades did not lack intellectual curiosity, but they were more interested in "explanations drawn from physics, chemistry, and natural history that related to our mechanical constructions" than in obscure points of French history or Latin grammar.[16]

When Considerant came to take his examinations for the bachelor's degree in August 1824, he did very well in the humanistic disciplines that constituted the core of the curriculum. If his performance in Greek was only "adequate," he received grades of "good" in Latin, rhetoric, and philosophy, and "fairly good" in history, geography, and science. What he really cared about was science and mathematics. Thus it was decided that he should complete his secondary education in Besançon, studying advanced mathematics with Professor Delly and doing the work in science necessary to qualify for admission to the Ecole Polytechnique, the greatest scientific school in France.[17]

Considerant arrived in Besançon in the fall of 1824. He was made welcome by friends of his father's such as the Thelmiers and the Delacroix family, whose sons Alphonse, Albert, and Emile became good friends. For two years, he later recalled, he and Alphonse Delacroix were almost inseparable. From the start he also saw much of the family of Clarisse Vigoureux, whose son Paul had boarded with the Considerants in Salins. Considerant spent the next two years at the Collège Royal de Besançon, registered as an *externe* and studying advanced algebra, physics, and chemistry. He did well enough that at the end of his first year he had already passed two of the three examinations necessary for admission to Polytechnique; the third he easily passed in his second year.[18]

These were exciting years for Considerant. He discovered in himself a love of knowledge—especially scientific knowledge—that he was to carry with him to the grave. And he formed new friendships. One that endured was with Alphonse Tamisier from Lons-le-Saunier, who was to take the same path as Considerant to the Ecole Polytechnique and then to Metz. A future Fourierist and army officer and later a civil engineer, Tamisier was to serve as a legislator under both the Second and Third Republics. Fifty years later he was still writing "mon cher Siderant" in terms of undiminished affection.[19] But much the most important friendship established by

Considerant during these years was with the family of Paul Vigoureux: his mother Clarisse, and his sisters Claire and Julie. It was in their house that Considerant discovered Fourier and met his future wife.

II

When Considerant arrived in Besançon in 1824, Paul's mother, Clarisse Vigoureux, was just thirty-five, but she had already been widowed for seven years. Her husband had died tragically in 1817, committing suicide after being subjected to apparently unfounded attacks concerning his probity as a businessman. Clarisse Vigoureux, whose hair had turned white within a month after her husband's death, was left with three young children and a sizable fortune. Entrusting the fortune to the care of her brother, Joseph Gauthier, a wealthy ironmaster, she devoted herself to the upbringing of her children. Claire, the oldest (born in 1809), was apparently her favorite. Her younger daughter Julie (born in 1812) posed few problems. But Paul (born in 1811) was an undisciplined boy and a slow and recalcitrant learner. Clarisse was unable to do much with him herself. Therefore around 1820 she sent him to board with the Considerants while attending the Collège de Salins. It was also because of her problems with Paul that Clarisse Vigoureux began making inquiries concerning alternative modes of education. During the summer of 1821 or 1822, while she and the children were visiting her brother Joseph at his country estate, she had discussed problems of education with one of his friends. This was Just Muiron, a functionary at the Besançon Prefecture who had become an enthusiastic partisan of the ideas of the still-unknown utopian thinker, Charles Fourier. Muiron told Clarisse Vigoureux that, at that moment, a book by Fourier was being published in Besançon that described a new, noncoercive method of education that she should know about. It was called the *Traité d'association domestique-agricole.*[20]

Although Clarisse Vigoureux did not make personal contact with Fourier until several years later, she read his book while it was still in proof— first the chapters on education, and then the whole book. She was overwhelmed. In it she found much more than an attractive new method of education. She also found a theory of social organization, a natural philosophy, and even a theodicy that helped her make sense of the shocks and disappointments of her own life. As she wrote later, "This great book opened up for me the horizon of a new world in which the goal of life was revealed to me." She saw in Fourier's theory a "new holy ark" in which "everything

[was] prepared to render a hitherto sterile and dreary life happy and enriching."[21]

This was Clarisse Vigoureux's state of mind at the time of Considerant's arrival in Besançon. She had discovered a "new holy ark" that consoled her for her losses and gave a meaning to her life that it had not previously possessed. A reserved and some thought haughty person who had lived in relative isolation since her husband's death, she was no doubt eager to talk about her discovery. In Considerant she had an ideal interlocutor—a bright, thoughtful, and remarkably responsive boy who was a good friend of her son but who possessed qualities of feeling and intellect utterly lacking in Paul. There was naturally no exchange of letters between Considerant and Clarisse Vigoureux as long as both were living in Besançon, and there is little evidence on which to construct an account of the early development of their relationship. What seems clear is that although Victor and Paul remained close friends throughout this period, their friendship had little of the intensity that came to characterize the relationship between Victor and Paul's mother. The tone of the letters that the two did exchange starting in 1826 leaves no doubt that in Victor Considerant Clarisse Vigoureux found an ideal son, and in Clarisse Victor found a mother no more affectionate perhaps than his own, but a mother with whom he could share and discuss a much wider range of ideas and feelings. What is also clear is that the mediating presence in this relationship—the means by which it became articulate—was the theory of Charles Fourier. The thirty-five-year-old widow and the sixteen-year-old schoolboy studied and discussed Fourier together; and at the end of the boy's two years in Besançon, he had come to count himself—along with Clarisse Vigoureux and her friend, the deaf functionary, Just Muiron—as one of Fourier's most zealous admirers. Considerant could write later, in discussing the early development of the Fourierist movement, that at the beginning Fourier had just three real partisans: "a deaf man, a woman, and a schoolboy."[22]

Considerant's ties with Clarisse Vigoureux were not exclusive. It is evident, again from their correspondence, that his closeness with her did not diminish his continuing affection for his own mother. It is also evident that whatever erotic impulses he may have felt with regard to Clarisse Vigoureux were safely sublimated into feelings of affection for the family as a whole, especially for the two girls. Indeed, he fell in love with the older daughter, Claire. She was just fifteen when Considerant met her; and her death two years later makes her a shadowy figure in the surviving sources. However, we do have a thinly veiled sketch of the relationship in a story written by the young Considerant in 1831. In it, Claire appears as a "gentle, timid, and tender-hearted" person whose "celestial" grace and "angelic" kindness had a "magical" influence on him, calming and giving focus to his restless disposition and tumultuous inner life.[23]

These two years at Besançon were a time of intellectual and above all emotional awakening for Considerant. Yet the larger world intruded. And its intrusion was particularly painful as far as Victor's father was concerned. During Victor's second year at the Collège de Besançon, Jean-Baptiste Considerant was informed that he would have to give up his teaching position at the Collège de Salins and accept a transfer to Sarlat hundreds of kilometers away. This punitive transfer was not a complete surprise. In 1821 a royal ordinance had placed every college in France under the supervision of the bishop of its diocese "in order to provide religious and moral guidance to youths naturally prone to be seduced by apparently generous and noble theories." In 1823 the liberal Constitutional priest, Father Racle, had been replaced as principal of the Collège de Salins by a conservative ultramontanist whose goal, in Jean-Baptiste Considerant's words, was to turn the college into "a little seminary." The following year the elder Considerant was denounced to university authorities as a "Jacobin" and a teacher of "impiety." Finally, early in 1826, when word of his transfer came, Jean-Baptiste Considerant simply refused to go. He wished to remain in Salins, he said, and he would give up teaching altogether rather than allow himself to be sent to the other end of France. Ten years earlier he had already written his friend Thelmier: "From now on I'm going to stay in my hole, and I wish to be buried in my own cemetery. I cling to the bones of my ancestors like an American Indian."[24]

We can glimpse Victor's reaction to his father's dismissal from a letter he wrote to Clarisse Vigoureux from Salins during the Easter vacation of 1826. He was writing, he said, not because he had promised to do so, but because writing her was "almost a need for me."

> From the day I arrived almost all serious conversations that I have heard have focused on an evil or on the effects of evil. What troubles me most is the exasperation of my father. He tries to appear calm, but this apparent tranquillity hides an agitation that breaks through from time to time. His thoughts are constantly pursuing him. You are aware of the strength of his deepest feelings. The intensity that they have for him, and their continual concentration on . . . the spectacle of constantly renewed injustice, makes me fear for his health. Why must it be that those powers whose development ought to bring happiness to

their possessor, burn him up more than they help him? How eager I am to see the end of our world's disorder!

Victor went on to observe that his father was refusing to ask for help in gaining reinstatement. He would not write his friend Jean-Jacques Ordinaire in Paris because he had detected in Ordinaire "a hint of egotism." In any case, the town council of Salins had already lodged an official protest, which had been rejected. Now, Victor wrote, the college itself was "on the brink of ruin." His family would have to cease taking in students as boarders. His older brother Gustave, who taught mathematics at the college, was likely to lose his certification. The only member of the family who seemed to have any future was now Victor himself. "I am full of hope," he wrote. "My father has high hopes for me too, and that pleases me very much. It calms the irritation produced in him by the sight of injustice and the arbitrary exercise of power."[25]

Jean-Baptiste Considerant lived long enough to see his son gain admission to the Ecole Polytechnique, but not much longer. He died on April 27, 1827, during Victor's first year at the Ecole. His funeral was the occasion not only for a remarkable outpouring of grief and admiration, but also for bitter attacks on the "hypocritical malevolence" of the religious and civil authorities, who, in depriving this "Socrates" of his teaching position, had driven him to the grave.[26] His son was always to cherish his memory.

III

The Ecole Polytechnique, which Considerant entered in the fall of 1826, was founded in 1794 to train army officers and military engineers. It had always been more than a military school, though. Its original faculty members were some of the finest mathematicians and scientists in France, and from the beginning the curriculum went far beyond courses in engineering and military strategy. Rather the emphasis was on basic mathematics and science. Students were admitted to Polytechnique only after passing rigorous entrance examinations; and during their two years at the school they took courses in advanced geometry, physics, and chemistry, as well as engineering and warfare. The aim was to give students a sufficient grounding in mathematics and theoretical science that they might be able, with further training, to do first-rate work in a variety of fields in the applied sciences. Although the system involved a kind of intellectual force-feeding that many students found brutal, it worked. In its first two decades the

Ecole Polytechnique became one of the most admired scientific schools in Europe, training hundreds of young men for government service, not only in the army but also in many branches of the civil administration.[27]

Under the restored Bourbon monarchy, the Ecole Polytechnique underwent reorganization and political attacks, and it acquired a new generation of faculty. Still, it retained both the prestige and the esprit de corps of the early years. A special slang was cultivated at the Ecole, and the "old boy network" that had already begun to develop among graduates of Polytechnique under Napoleon became more fully elaborated under the Restoration. Two other features of life at Polytechnique that changed relatively little after the fall of Napoleon were the staggering workload and the regimentation. In 1804 Napoleon had imposed barrack residence and military drill on all Polytechniciens, and these remained requirements in Considerant's time. Living at the school as *internes*, the Polytechniciens slept within its walls, took their meals together, studied together, drilled together, and were only allowed out on Sundays and for a few hours on Wednesdays.[28]

Considerant had looked forward to attending the Ecole Polytechnique with high anticipation. For a bright young man of modest provincial background, admission to the Ecole meant the beginning of a new intellectual and social life, and it was almost a guarantee of a successful career. Soon after his arrival in the fall of 1826, though, Considerant was describing the school as a "prison" and life in it as "slavery." He wrote a family friend during his second year:

> Who will save me from these ridiculous rules! I have often cried out in my fury against the discipline here and the despotic beating of our drums. It's hard for a child who was born free to be in prison at the age of twenty when until the age of eighteen he was running all over the countryside, in town, on the streets, and even on the roofs of the houses.[29]

Considerant's situation at the Ecole Polytechnique was the more difficult in that, during the course of his first year, within the space of barely three months, he lost both his beloved, Claire Vigoureux, and the father whom he idolized. Each of these deaths was extremely painful for him. Together they were devastating.

Judging from Considerant's letters to Clarisse Vigoureux, the deaths of Claire and of his father threw him into a state of anguished reflection on evil and its causes and on the tragic inability of the living to make contact with the souls of the dead. He found some consolation in Fourier's doctrine, and even in Fourier's writings on metempsychosis, which gave him hope that, once "this monstrous civilization" was overcome, it would be possible to establish "communications with those who are in a higher world." Still, he was tormented by the distance that separated him from his loved ones, both living and dead. "I go to sleep at night," he wrote Clarisse Vigoureux, "only after having thought a long time about you, about my mother, and about those whom we have lost. During the day I often share the gaiety of my comrades. But I am not happy."[30]

Gradually Considerant became caught up in his work and the life of the Ecole. He complained about his health and about the food, and he wrote Clarisse Vigoureux that he found the "ceaseless" study of mathematics "brutalizing." Nonetheless, he applied himself to the work. He made friends easily and was not troubled by the hazing normally inflicted on first-year students. In fact, in December 1826, shortly after his arrival, he learned that he was one of five entering students whom the second-year students proposed to award a scholarship covering the cost of room, board, and uniforms. Considerant declined the scholarship, arguing that there were others more needy than he. "The resources of my family would not by themselves have permitted me to the attend the Ecole," he wrote, but he was able to borrow money. In writing Clarisse Vigoureux about this, he marveled that, although he had not talked of his family's difficulties to anyone at Polytechnique, his comrades were aware not only of the losses the Considerants had suffered in the great fire of 1825 but also of his father's persecution by the ultras.[31]

During the last years of the Bourbon monarchy, the Ecole Polytechnique became known as a "redoubt of liberal ideas," and it was easy for the son of Jean-Baptiste Considerant to identify himself with the opposition to Charles X. Considerant participated in a collective student protest of repressive measures taken by the government against the Ecole, and his already strong interest in Fourier's theory did not prevent him from describing himself, in a letter to a friend of his father's generation, as a "twenty-year-old liberal."

> We talk politics here all the time. Every day we smuggle in newspapers like the *Constitutionnel* and the *Courrier*. We discuss peace and war, we fight the Turks, we denounce their good friends the English, we discuss the laws proposed to our representatives, etc. . . . and if you will permit me a serious reflection, I would say that while we are young and passionate, it's true, we are all attached to representative government. We want a monarchy, but one with free institutions that are in harmony with a great and liberal nation.

Politics was not the only diversion of the Polytechniciens. Bawdy novels were smuggled in along with the *Constitutionnel*. There were also all-night conversations and the elaborate practical jokes that became known as *canulars*. All this provided some solace from "the integral calculus and other sciences that are not very rich in pleasures, at least for the common run of martyrs."[32]

Considerant never ceased to complain in his letters about the intellectual force-feeding that went on at the Ecole Polytechnique—the discipline, the coercive teaching methods, and the cloistering of the students. Like most of his comrades, he looked forward with particular relish to their moments of liberty—the *jours de sortie* that enabled them to get out from behind the bars of their "prison." Sunday was their free day, and Considerant learned to make the most of it. Often he spent part of the day writing letters to his family and friends. He also occasionally joined his comrades for trips to *bals publiques* and *fêtes* in the villages on the outskirts of Paris. As he wrote Clarisse Vigoureux in July 1828 while he was studying for his final examinations:

> Last Sunday . . . I went out to Sceaux, where I knew I would find several students from my division. I found them in the pretty park at Sceaux. It was the day of the village *fête,* and my comrades began the dancing early because there was no time to lose. They got the little peasant girls dancing. I joined them. But after three contra-dances we left. . . . There were hardly any other cavaliers at that time . . . so the dancing had to stop.[33]

On most Sundays, though, Considerant stayed in Paris and went calling on a fairly extensive network of Franc-comtois, friends of his parents for the most part, who lived in Paris.

Although Considerant's parents were not wealthy, they were well connected, and during his two years at Polytechnique Considerant got to know several of the most important figures in the political and cultural life of Franche-Comté. His closest ties were with two families of Franc-comtois *notables* to whom he was related through his mother: the Gréa and Jobez families. Desiré-Adrien Gréa (1787–1863) was a wealthy landowner who had a large estate at Rotalier in the Jura and whose father François-Augustin Gréa (1742–1824) was the uncle of Considerant's mother.[34] Emmanuel Jobez (1775–1828) was one of the most important ironmasters in Franche-Comté and the uncle of Gréa's wife. In 1827 and 1828 Jobez, who was then a member of the Chamber of Deputies, made Considerant welcome in his household, where he was treated almost as a member of the family. Considerant also saw much of Gréa, who was to succeed Jobez as deputy after the latter's accidental death in September 1828. Although he was not a man of ideas, Gréa had some interest in Fourier's doctrine, and he was fond of Considerant. Indeed, in 1825, after the disastrous fire at Salins, he had offered to subsidize Considerant's education.[35]

During his years at Polytechnique, Considerant also began a lifelong relationship with the family of the writer, Charles Nodier, whose salon at the Bibliothèque de l'Arsenal served as a gathering place for writers and artists from Franche-Comté. Considerant's father had been close to Nodier for many years. Nodier had visited the Considerants in Salins and, by his own account, had "often held [young Victor] on his knees." Considerant had been reluctant to call on him because he knew that in his last years his father had "stopped seeing Nodier, whose character he did not approve of." When Considerant finally did call on the Nodiers, however, he was received with great warmth. "I went by myself to see them last Sunday," he wrote Clarisse Vigoureux:

> I was made to feel right at home. Madame Nodier exudes a kindness that is consistent with all the good things I had heard about her, and her husband has a Franc-comtois nonchalance that is charming in a Parisian salon. . . . He insisted that I come again and often. Why must it be that a man of such talent should not have a good character? Again, it's Civilization that spoils everything.

It was at the Nodier salon that Considerant met another Franc-comtois, a "defender of Civilization, a great preacher of progress," whom Considerant described as a "counter-pivot of Charles Fourier." This was the celebrated professor Théodore Jouffroy. Considerant found him vain and long-winded. "He is as pedantic as Monsieur Fourier is simple," he wrote soon after this meeting. "I didn't tell him my name. All I did was listen to him talk. Oh really, people like that are strange."[36]

Another Franc-comtois whom Considerant got to know at this time—possibly through Nodier—was Charles Magnin (1793–1862). A native of Salins and a friend of Considerant's father, Magnin was a librarian at the Bibliothèque Royale who also served as theater critic for the important journal *Le Globe*. Although Magnin was a friend of the pompous Jouffroy, Considerant found him far more appealing; and despite the fifteen-year difference in their ages a long-lasting friendship developed between them. While at the Ecole Polytechnique, Considerant saw Magnin fairly often and attempted both to interest him in Fourier's ideas and also to enlist his help in publicizing a protest of the Polytechniciens against the government.[37]

Considerant's two years at the Ecole Polytechnique were important for him in many respects. They gave him a solid foundation in mathematics and science, which he was to draw on for the rest of his life. They also enabled him to establish contacts. Long after his resignation from the army, Considerant remained in touch with a network of graduates of the Ecole Polytechnique and also with two of the most distinguished figures in the French army, the marshals Bugeaud and Soult, both of whom took a liking to Considerant at an early point in his career. At the same time the opportunity to get out occasionally from behind "the grills of my prison" and to explore Paris left Considerant with a love of the French capital that he was never to lose. "I miss Paris with all my heart," he wrote Charles Magnin from Metz in August 1829. "I had such good, such agreeable acquaintances there. I could easily have met other people whom I very much desire to meet. . . . In that great center of movement life is really life. There is ten times more intensity there than in our stagnant [provincial] cities. Ah, never come to live in the provinces!"[38]

There is one other respect in which Considerant's years at the Ecole Polytechnique were important to him. As Friedrich Hayek and others have argued, Polytechnique offered its students much more than a solid grounding in the sciences and an opportunity for social and intellectual advancement. The school also instilled in them a strong sense of optimism about the powers of the human mind and the utility of science. Students graduated from Polytechnique with a faith in man's ability to utilize the methods of science to harness and control the forces not only of nature but also of society. The strength of this faith varied, of course, from one individual to another, but they all shared the belief that problems of social organization could be solved in basically the same way as problems in the building of a road or a bridge. This belief in the efficacy of scientific planning and "social engineering" was to be most dramatically exemplified by the Saint-Simonians.[39] However, it was also to become essential to Considerant's outlook. Throughout his life, Considerant retained a faith in progress and a belief that the application of scientific knowledge to social problems was the key to progress. In this respect, as in several others, Considerant's attitudes were decisively shaped by his years at the Ecole Polytechnique.

IV

In September 1828 Considerant passed his final examinations at the Ecole Polytechnique. He ranked in the middle of his class, and this was good enough to allow him to go on to do advanced work at the military school of his choice.[40] Thus in the fall of 1828, having received his appointment as *sous-lieutenant-élève* in the Corps of Engineers, he entered the Ecole d'Application d'Artillerie et du Génie Militaire de Metz as one of thirty-two Polytechniciens in the entering cohort of engineers.

The Ecole d'Application de Metz actually included two separate schools, a school of military engineering and a school of artillery. Students at both schools were normally graduates of the Ecole Polytechnique, but their work here was more specialized. Required courses included topography, geology, surveying, and permanent field fortification as well as frequent time-consuming projects in military drawing. "We have lots of work to do here," Considerant wrote during his second year. "It is the courses on permanent fortification and the drawing for these courses that keep us busiest. Until five o'clock our days are completely full. There are six hours of required drawing to be done in the classrooms, and then there are exercises, maneuvers or riding lessons."[41] While in training, students at the Ecole d'Application were also required to participate in elaborate exercises in siege warfare in which fortified positions were subjected to artillery barrages that an American visitor from West Point could describe as impressive but also "mortifying" because of their superiority to contemporary American military maneuvers. To Considerant, however, they were entertainments. "This evening we are having a night session," he wrote Paul Vigoureux in the fall of 1829. "We will begin by firing cannons and big siege guns from four o'clock until nine. Then we will finish up by firing rockets, signal flares, fireballs, etc. The sky is clear and the session will be delightful. So far I've had a wonderful time listening to all that noise."[42]

Discipline at Metz was less strict than at Polytechnique. Students were allowed out in the evenings; they could dine in town if they wished and go to the theater and read what they wanted. Initially Considerant took little advantage of his new freedom. He wrote that in Metz he had begun to "feel once again the old thirst for learning" that had motivated him as a student in Besançon and that he had lost during his "two years of slavery" at Polytechnique. So he preferred to work. In any case, the local theater company was unimpressive, he wrote Clarisse Vigoureux, and he was not yet "known" in the town.

> Every evening there are dances to which a certain number of students always go. As for me, I still don't know anyone here; and I am waiting impatiently for the letters [of introduction] that will open a few doors for me. Almost a month has gone by now during which I have seen no one but my comrades. I'm not used to this monotonous style of life.

In due course the letters arrived and the doors opened. A year later Considerant was writing in a very different vein.

> There is not a town in France, I think, in which people dance as much as they do here in Metz during the winter. . . . Every night there are two, three, sometimes four balls and dance evenings. . . . Besides all these private parties we dance at the Prefecture on Thursdays, and every Saturday there is a ball at the City Hall to which everyone comes. Those are the best ones. The rooms are huge, and when there is a double row of ladies all around the two big ballrooms it makes a magnificent spectacle. There is always a large number of officers there, and the variety of the uniforms adds to the effect created by the whole. . . . There are so many men at every ball that it is extremely rare for a woman to be left a wallflower. So all the ladies from out of town are delighted.

In the end, none of this made much difference to Considerant. Increasingly the frenetic social life in Metz came to seem empty to him. By the middle of his second year he could write that the dancing and the parties "do not prevent me from finding the life I lead detestable."[43]

What depressed Considerant about his life in Metz was in part simply the boredom and routine of peacetime army life. In writing friends in Franche-Comté, he adopted tones foreshadowing those of Vigny and Musset, cursing the fate that had caused him to miss out on the French military expedition to Algiers. He found himself falling into a state of "apathy," and he lamented the fact that in Metz "all our days are like one another." Of his prospects in the army he wrote, "The only thing that I desire, the only pleasure that [the army] could give me, is a war." At the same time he found it increasingly difficult to be so far away from Paris.[44] In a letter of February 1830 to Charles Magnin, he described Paris as "the object of all my desires. . . . I cannot stand the prospect of being employed indefinitely as an engineer in some corner of France. If my work makes a slave of me, it will be the torment of my life." A few months later, in a letter to Clarisse Vigoureux, he was asking himself whether his discontent might not spring from some deeper inner source.

> At one time I believed that I would be happy at the Ecole Polytechnique; at Polytechnique I supposed that I would find happiness here in Metz; and now that I'm here the past sixteen months have convinced me that life in Metz is dull and monotonous. For a long time I blamed my condition as a soldier for the dark colors in which my life was painted. But now I have begun to think that most of my problems come from *me* rather than from *my circumstances*. After all I have many comrades who are not at all discontent. What the world calls "experi-

ence of life," which is something that the old Romans and their admirers have always valued so highly, seems to me to be a sad and useless thing, a brutalizing and destructive thing.

In June 1830, Considerant could write that his work at the Ecole had become more satisfying to him. "I don't mean to say that it makes me happy," he wrote, "but at least it absorbs me." Still, it depressed him to think of making a career as a military engineer, and now he found himself equally depressed by the "bad faith" and pettiness of political controversy under Charles X. "For the past month I haven't read a line in a journal," he wrote Clarisse Vigoureux. "The politics, the disputes, the ridiculous pretensions of the ultras and the liberals fill me with boredom and disgust."[45]

The Revolution of July 1830 briefly drew Considerant out of the state of torpor into which he had fallen by the end of his second year in Metz. Despite his earlier expressions of disgust at the pretensions of both ultras and liberals, he reacted with joy at the first reports of revolution at Paris. In the night of July 29 a placard appeared on the walls of the Hôtel de Ville in Metz: "Charles X was King by virtue of the Charter that he had sworn to support. He has violated his oath. We must refuse to pay taxes. Long live the Nation." The next day all kinds of rumors spread. The prefect of the Moselle, the comte de Vendeuvre, had just returned from a trip to Trèves, and liberals accused him of having gone to plot with the Prussians against France. Considerant later wrote proudly that, in order to get the National Guard to arm itself, he had urged his comrades to spread rumors that the Prussians were attacking. Subsequently he helped organize demonstrations against Bourbon sympathizers—including the commander of the Ecole d'Application—and participated in the removal of Bourbon flags and insignia from public buildings. In recounting all this to Clarisse Vigoureux a few days later, Considerant described himself as having "a hundred times more physical strength and health than a week ago." He only regretted that there had not been "a little battle" that would have given him the opportunity to distinguish himself.[46]

Considerant's euphoria did not last long. He was sickened by the "rush for spoils" that followed the installation of the July Monarchy, and he found the new Chamber of Deputies "pitiful." Soon his old discontents returned, and with them his doubts about a military career. Thus in late September 1830 he formally requested a leave of absence from the Ecole d'Application. At the same time he wrote a long letter to a high army officer—probably Marshal Soult—asking for help in securing a position as a tutor in science. Possessing no wealth of his own, he explained, he was reluctant to take work that might be demeaning for a Polytechnicien. He did not wish to "fall from the rank in society" that he had acquired, and thus he hoped to tutor "an individual from a distinguished background." Considerant went on to describe his situation and prospects.

> In many respects my situation pleases me. It would please me much more if, instead of the prospect of having to bury myself in some corner of France, I could look forward to several years of military action just as soon as I joined my regiment. However that may be, my present circumstances are thwarting a very powerful need which I feel in myself and which is impelling me to devote myself to certain studies and certain intellectual labors. My work here is thwarting that need by taking up too much of my time and by keeping me away from Paris, where it would be easier and more possible for me to gratify this need.

Although the language is vague, it is clear that the studies Considerant wished to undertake in Paris concerned the doctrine of Charles Fourier.[47]

Considerant's request for leave was not granted, and he spent the fall of 1830 working hard in Metz preparing for the examinations that would complete his studies at the Ecole d'Application. In December he wrote Clarisse Vigoureux that he was "stuffed like a cannon ready to fire" with mathematics, science, military tactics, and strategy. Finally, on January 10, 1831, after passing his examinations, he was formally commissioned second lieutenant in the Second Regiment of Military Engineers. Then at last he was given a furlough—just a few weeks, but long enough to go to Paris to see Clarisse and Julie Vigoureux and also Charles Fourier. In late January he attended a public lecture given by Fourier in an attempt to arouse interest in his doctrine. The lecture was not a success. Considerant wrote a friend shortly afterward, "Although Monsieur Fourier's thought is rich in ideas and insights, he does not know how to present them."[48]

One result of Considerant's absorption in Fourier's theory was that he increasingly saw himself as estranged, not only from the army but also from his compatriots. He was reminded of this estrangement in mid-February, shortly before his return to Metz, when he paid a brief visit to Salins to see his family. In his blue, red, and black uniform he felt like an exotic creature from another world. The townspeople were impressed by the uniform, but since he had in the past made no secret of his admiration for Fourier and his ideas, he knew that many of them regarded him as a madman. Even relatives such as his Aunt Dupuy thought that he was "absolutely crazy." He had friends like the Thiebauds, Auguste and Mariette, who "understood" Fourier's system and "desired its application," but they were a minority. Thus he tried to keep a low profile at Salins.

I have resolved to say nothing at all, and I am sticking to my resolution as much as I can. However, I am not the object of attacks as contemptible as before, so far as [Fourier's] system is concerned. People still think of me as a madman, but my uniform and my "rank in the world" add something respectable to my folly.

Considerant added that his brother Gustave, who was a teacher at the Collège de Salins, did not benefit from an impressive uniform. He was regarded "almost as a terrorist" at Salins because he had "taken the liberty of not having complete confidence in the Chamber and the government."[49]

Considerant himself lacked confidence in the Chamber and the government. He made that clear in March, shortly after returning to his regiment, when he joined dozens of his fellow officers in signing a statement publicly supporting the Association Nationale, a liberal organization hostile to the conservative ministry of Casimir Périer. Created with the nominal aim of preventing another Bourbon Restoration, the Association Nationale was in fact a rallying point for opponents of the July Monarchy. It had been conceived in Metz, but by March 1831 it had attracted support from liberal politicians, government functionaries, and career army officers in half the departments in France. At the end of the month, however, the Périer government passed legislation forbidding all state functionaries and army officers from joining it and threatening to punish those who had already done so. Thus on April 20, just a few weeks after his return to Metz, Considerant and many of his fellow officers were placed on unpaid leave for an indefinite period.[50]

Considerant was delighted to be able to return to Paris so quickly. This time he found a job teaching mathematics in a private school run by a former student of his father's. This school, the Institut Barbet, was located on the impasse des Feuillantines and specialized in preparing students for the Ecole Polytechnique, Saint-Cyr, and other *grandes écoles*.[51] Considerant apparently shared an apartment on the rue de Vaugirard with Paul Vigoureux and enjoyed an independent bohemian life—"an artist's life lived among artists"—that he later looked back on fondly. At the end of the year he described this life to Claude-Victor Thelmier in the accents of a Rastignac recalling his own beginnings.

This period of independence was one of the happiest of my life. Just imagine your crazy young man perched on the roof of a coach with one of his friends and setting out for Paris with no other resources than a hundred francs in his pocket, but more joyous and more full of laughter on this occasion than if he had received the citizen's crown that adorns with such dazzling, stunning, suffocating luster the gracious and sublime head of Louis Philippe, the chosen ruler of the sovereign people, who are dying of hunger all over wealthy France. Indeed, what happiness not to know what is going to become of one. What happiness to say: Here I am finally dependent on myself alone and without the crutch of a profession to support me. I have been disinherited by my paternal government. It's all up to me then, to me with my twenty-two years, to me alone. By all the saints that protect me, I swear that I will manage.[52]

During these three or four months Considerant was in touch with the Nodiers. He was a regular at their salon, and in late August he dined with them and a group including the poet Antoine Fontaney, the critic Sainte-Beuve, and Nodier's collaborators Alphonse de Cailleux and Baron Taylor. With the help of Paul Vigoureux, Considerant also created a circle of young people—"artists and others"—whom he managed to interest in Fourier's ideas. This group, which included the Bisontin Victor Coste and the *Centraliens* André Morlon and Henri Delprat, was Considerant's first Fourierist study circle.[53]

One result of this brief bohemian period in Considerant's life is that he became a published author of fiction. His short story "Un Pressentiment," which appeared in the October 1831 issue of the *Revue des deux mondes*, was a veiled account of his relationship with Claire Vigoureux and of his "presentiment" of her tragic death at the age of seventeen. One contemporary reader described it as a "charming" story; however, its publication in an important Parisian literary journal alongside Alfred de Vigny's "Docteur Noir" probably owed something to connections Considerant had established at Charles Nodier's salon. For one of the founders of the *Revue des deux mondes*, Alexandre Bixio, who had become a good friend of Considerant, was a regular at Nodier's weekly receptions at the Arsenal.[54]

Considerant loved Paris and would have been happy to prolong his stay indefinitely. However, his "charming" life in the capital came to an end in September, when Marshal Soult ordered all the young officers who had been compromised by their support of the Association Nationale back to their regiments. Considerant was received coolly in Metz: his commanding officer evaluated him as "lacking zeal" and "unable to do exercises in campaign and siege fortification."[55] Still, Considerant's general morale was much improved because he was extremely successful, on his return to Metz, in interesting his fellow officers in Fourier's ideas. Indeed, most of his energies during the fall and winter of 1831–1832 went into the organization of a Fourierist study group in Metz. This was the beginning of a new career for Considerant.

2

The Making of a Fourierist

Victor Considerant first made his mark in French intellectual life as a disciple of the utopian socialist thinker Charles Fourier and a popularizer of Fourier's ideas. More than any other individual, Considerant was responsible for the fact that Fourier's theories of association and attractive work, which had been conceived in the immediate aftermath of the French Revolution, finally found an audience a generation later in the vastly different intellectual climate of the early July Monarchy. One of the main concerns of this biography will be to take the measure of Considerant's engagement with Fourier's thought—his discovery of Fourier, his assimilation and reformulation of Fourier's ideas, and his attempts in his middle and later years to stake out positions of his own. But to begin with, something must be said about Fourier himself.

I

Charles Fourier stands out, even among thinkers in the utopian tradition, both for his radical break with existing philosophies, customs, and institutions and for the luxuriant detail of his descriptions of the ideal society. He was the nineteenth century's complete utopian. A psychologist who celebrated the passions as agents of human happiness, he carried to its ultimate conclusion the rejection of the doctrine of original sin, which had been a hallmark of utopian thinking ever since the Renaissance. A visionary who foresaw an age in which sea water could be turned into lemonade, he had a faith in the power of human beings to shape their own world that was remarkable even in the age of Napoleon.

Like other early nineteenth-century utopian prophets, Charles Fourier was a major figure in the intellectual reaction to the French Revolution. With Henri Saint-Simon and Auguste Comte and with the counterrevolutionary theocrats Louis de Bonald and Joseph de Maistre, he was one of a group of thinkers whose main concern was to find their intellectual bearings in a world torn apart by the French Revolution. Like Saint-Simon, Comte, Bonald, and Maistre, Fourier was acutely aware of the inadequacy of the Enlightenment's worldview in the face of the problems confronting Europe in the aftermath of the Revolution. In his opinion, as in theirs, the Revolution not only wiped out the aristocratic and feudal social order but also revealed the bankruptcy of the Enlightenment confidence in human reason, progress, and equality. The Revolution, in Fourier's view, was the *coup d'essai* of the Enlightenment *philosophes*—an experiment whose failure demonstrated that their "torrents of political and moral enlightenment" were "nothing more than torrents of illusions."[1]

Hostile to the *philosophes,* Fourier and his contemporaries were Napoleonic in their own intellectual ambitions. Rejecting the empirical and critical traditions of the Enlightenment, they attempted to construct vast systems and formulate general theories to fill the intellectual and spiritual vacuum of the postrevolutionary period. What this meant for Fourier, as for Saint-Simon and his follower the young Auguste Comte, was the construction of a universal system, a unitary or total science based on a single law that would be equally valid for the physical and social worlds.

There were two keystones to Fourier's system. One was a conception of human nature, the other a conception of God. In his conception of human nature, Fourier rejected the *philosophes'* view of all humans as essentially similar in nature and equal in rights in favor of a view emphasizing human uniqueness and diversity. In his opinion the human mind was not a blank slate: all human beings were born with innate dispositions and propensities. The most fundamental of these propensities Fourier called the passions. These were basic instinctual drives "given us by nature prior to any reflection." They varied from one individual to another and could not be permanently altered or suppressed; they were "persistent despite the opposition of reason, duty, prejudice, etc." Much of Fourier's writing consisted of attempts to work out a classification of these drives. There were twelve cardinal passions, he argued. The five "luxurious" passions expressed the cravings of the five senses. The four "affective" passions derived from people's social needs: friendship, love, ambition, and familism (or parenthood). Most important of all were the three "distributive" or "mechanizing" passions—so named because their free expression was essential for the gratification of the other nine: the Cabalist, or intriguing, passion; the Butterfly, or passion for change and variety; and the Composite, the passion for a mixture of physical and spiritual pleasures. Taken together, these passions served as the building blocks for a rich gamut of 810 personality types.[2]

Fourier's conception of God was in some respects quite conventional for its time and in other respects radically idiosyncratic. Like many of the eighteenth-century deists, he accepted the argument from design: he believed that the perfectly harmonious Newtonian universe was itself proof of the existence of an infinitely wise creator. Fourier's speculations on the properties of the deity, however, took him far beyond the deists' wildest dreams. He believed that divine providence was necessarily complete—that a God possessing such attributes as perfect goodness and infinite wisdom could not have failed to make some provision for the terrestrial happiness of his children. God was bound, in other words, by His very nature to have devised a "social code" for the organization of life on earth and the harmonious interaction of the passions.

The main task that Fourier set himself as a social theorist was to define the contours of a new world consistent with God's plan—a world in which the full and free expression of the passions would constantly serve to promote concord and social unity. Fourier's great intellectual breakthrough came in 1799. From this point on he believed himself in possession of the "key" to his total science. Not only had he established the necessity of a divine social code. He had also discovered the principles on which it would be possible to explain "the plans adopted by God" in assigning "passions, properties, forms, colors, and tastes" to everything that existed in the animal, vegetable, and mineral kingdoms. His total science thus included much more than an account of God's plans for the harmonious organization of society. It also encompassed a theory of history tracing the thirty-two stages in the earth's eighty-thousand-year life span, a cosmogony describing the origin of the universe and the copulation of planets, a theory of metempsychosis accounting for the migration of souls between material and "aromal" worlds, and a science of "universal analogy" uncovering correspondences between the human passions and all the phenomena of nature.[3]

Throughout the Napoleonic period and much of the Bourbon Restoration, Fourier devoted himself unstintingly to developing his initial insights

and fleshing out his theory. His major works always contained some discussion of the esoteric branches of the doctrine: the cosmogony, the theories of metempsychosis and universal analogy. They also included an elaborate critique of the fraud, waste, exploitation, and instinctual repression
that characterized life in modern "civilization" (a pejorative term for Fourier). But they were principally organized around descriptions of his ideal
community, called the Phalanx. Fourier always imagined the Phalanx in a
rural setting. Ideally, he wrote, it would be situated on a square league of
land. The terrain would be hilly, the supply of water plentiful, and the climate suitable for the cultivation of a wide variety of crops. Visitors would
be struck by the elegance and sheer vastness of the central building, or Phalanstery. This was to be a huge structure, somewhat reminiscent of Versailles, colossal in its outlines but adorned with "a multitude of colonnades,
domes, and peristyles." Its lodgings, workshops, meeting rooms, and banquet halls would be built to accommodate roughly 1,600 people. Fourier
was particularly proud of one architectural innovation, the "street gallery,"
which would enable people to travel quickly from their rooms to public
halls and workshops without ever exposing themselves to the elements.

Fourier's plans for his ideal community focused particularly on the intrigues, rivalries, and alliances that would develop within what he called
"passionate" groups and series—small groups and series of groups in
which people of different ages, classes, and passions would come together
to work and play in conditions carefully calibrated to ensure that the gratification of individual desire led to collective happiness. Fourier also devised
a system of communal childrearing and education in which children would
be encouraged from an early age to develop vocations consistent with their
instinctual (or "passional") endowment. He wrote a whole treatise (not
published until 1967) on the amorous institutions and practices that would
emerge in a society in which people were free to act out all their sexual desires, even those most maligned in contemporary society. In the "new
amorous world," wrote Fourier, "no one capable of love" would ever "be
frustrated in his or her desire," and this guarantee of amorous gratification
would serve as the basis for the development of a world of subtle and complex human relationships that would only become possible once basic human needs were satisfied.[4]

The other central element in Fourier's utopian vision—along with his
evocation of a "new amorous world"—was the idea of "attractive work."
Fourier believed that work was not necessarily boring or stultifying and
that under the right conditions it could become a source of pleasure and
a means of self-expression for every man and woman. The goal was to or-

ganize society in such a way that the necessary work would be done not out of a sense of duty or obligation but at the urging of the passions. To achieve this, Fourier believed it would be necessary to grant a *minimum*—a guaranteed minimum income—to all members of the community, whether they worked or not. This "social minimum" would be supplemented by the educational system, which would allow children to develop whatever skills and aptitudes were natural to them. Short work sessions would keep people from being tied down to a single job. The competition of work groups would stimulate productivity. For those jobs (like garbage collecting and latrine cleaning) that were truly repulsive, Fourier had a unique solution. Recognizing that most young children are passionately attracted to filth and excrement, he devised a corps called the Little Hordes, whose task it would be to clean toilets, collect garbage, and disinfect butcher shops. "Less decorative than useful," this group of dirty children would serve the community at the same time that they gratified their love of filth.[5]

Much of Fourier's writing on the organization of the ideal community was addressed to a particular individual whom he called "the founder." This was the still unknown benefactor who would provide the capital necessary to set up the first trial Phalanx according to Fourier's precise specifications. He initially believed that if the trial were to succeed, all the institutions of the Phalanx would have to be perfectly adapted to the dictates of the passions. The ideal size of the Phalanx, 1,620 members, was dictated by the 810 personality types. In order to satisfy the demands of the passion for change, no single activity could last more than two hours. There would also be a vast network of titles and offices, which were largely decorative but still useful as rewards for people who were ambitious or cabalistically inclined.

In his mature years Fourier made a few concessions. He came to believe that a "reduced trial" might be made with as few as four hundred members. He also suggested that his contemporaries might work their way gradually into the ideal (or "Phalansterian") social order through a series of modest experiments in association, such as the creation of credit institutions, collective kitchens, and producers' associations. Such small-scale experiments in association would serve to accustom people to cooperation rather than competition, he argued, and thereby pave the way for bolder ventures.

II

One of the ironies in the history of the spread of Charles Fourier's ideas is that although Fourier himself eventually became convinced that the only

way he could gain support was to purge his theory of its esoteric cosmogony and its elaborate metaphysical foundations, his earliest disciples
were in fact attracted to his doctrine precisely by the cosmogony and metaphysics. Fourier's first real disciple, Just Muiron, came upon Fourier's doctrine at a moment of spiritual crisis. Deaf since childhood, Muiron had, by
his own account, fallen at the age of twenty-five into a state of loneliness
and depression in which his soul was mastered by "a deadly disgust and a
universal skepticism." Reading theosophists like Swedenborg and Saint-
Martin helped put him back on the right track, but it was only in meditating upon Fourier's first work, the *Théorie des quatre mouvements*, that
Muiron found true peace of mind. He felt that he at last "understood the
causes of evil and error" and that he "was going to learn the *sense* and *purpose* of everything."[6]

Like Muiron, many of Fourier's other early disciples were dabblers in
the occult sciences who were attracted as much, or more, by his providen-
tialism, cosmogony, and theory of metempsychosis as by his economic
ideas and social theory. Even those like Clarisse Vigoureux who turned to
Fourier for specific forms of guidance or consolation found in his thought
more than they were looking for. Clarisse Vigoureux first read Fourier in
the hope of finding guidance on how to educate her children, but her reading revealed to her "the purpose of life" and "the horizon of a new world."[7]

Since Victor Considerant has often been regarded as a popularizer who
purged Fourier's thought of its esoteric elements, reducing it to a scheme
for the organization of labor, it is worth emphasizing that he too was initially attracted by the noneconomic aspects of Fourier's doctrine. Fourier's
theory of metempsychosis, providentialist metaphysics, and writings on
the theodicy question all engaged the young Considerant's imagination. In
1826 and 1827 he found consolation in Fourier's doctrine for the deaths of
his father and of Claire Vigoureux and derived hope from Fourier's vision
of a future world where the living and the dead might be reunited. At the
same time, however, the young Considerant was also entranced by what he
regarded as the rigorously scientific and "mathematical" character of Fourier's thought. For him, Fourier's doctrine had the appeal of an exact science
that would place the study of human nature and human motivation on as
firm a footing as that of physics or astronomy.

Considerant's first introduction to the doctrine came in the fall of 1824,
when he had just turned sixteen. Freshly arrived at Besançon to prepare for
the Ecole Polytechnique, he was, as we have seen, the first person with
whom Clarisse Vigoureux was able to share her new-found enthusiasm for
Fourier's ideas. Some sense of what these ideas meant to the young Consi-

derant may be gained from his long letter of May 1826 to Clarisse's son, Paul. In it, Considerant attempts to explain the foundations of Fourier's thought to the younger Paul without any reference to Fourier's ideal community, the Phalanx, or to his economic ideas. Instead, all the emphasis is on Fourier's critique of philosophy, his psychological views, and above all his arguments concerning the nature of the deity and the necessity of a "divine social code."

For Considerant, the initial attractiveness of Fourier's system lay in part in the fact that it offered both an explanation and a cure for the individual suffering and social ills that had scarred human history up to his own time. "Who is the author of evil?" he asked rhetorically. It was not God but man himself, with his reliance on the contrivances of human reason, who was the cause of evil. But "human reason has been judged," wrote Considerant. "The errors of the legislators have been demonstrated" since all their laws had done nothing to ensure human happiness. "We must have no pity," wrote the seventeen-year-old Considerant, "for all the systems of the legislators and philosophers." What was needed, he argued, was the discovery of a plan of social organization consistent with the "intentions" of the deity. Can we really suppose, he asked, that God could have created all the elements and impulses of our social world—passions, tastes, and attractions—without also creating a "code" of laws governing their proper interaction? Such an assumption was obviously insulting to God: it reduced Him to the status of a distracted and incompetent carpenter, capable of gathering construction materials for a house without ever drawing up plans.

Fourier's great insight, in Considerant's view, was to recognize that the surest guide to the study of the human passions was furnished by the physical sciences. If the movements of matter were governed by the laws of gravitational attraction, Fourier argued, the movements of the passions must be determined by an analogous form of "passionate attraction." Fourier's accomplishment was to work out the laws of this new science of passionate attraction. This was a science of human motivation that included an elaborate classification of the basic human drives or passions and a description of the institutional framework within which these drives could attain their proper or predestined ends. It was this "scientific" argument for passionate attraction that Considerant attempted to explain to Paul Vigoureux in his letter of May 1826. The assumption on which the whole theory rested, Considerant wrote, was that the passions were *meant* to be harmonized and that, once institutions were organized in a manner consistent with God's plan, all human beings would lead a life rich in physical and emotional gratification. God's laws were not based on constraint but on attraction and pleasure. Merely to recognize this was in itself a source of immense delight. Thus in expounding Fourier's ideas to his friend, Considerant could hardly contain his own emotion. "I am sure that I have spoken to your heart," he wrote. "I am sure that you share the sweet emotion, the feeling of happiness in which I am engulfed at this moment."[8]

What made Fourier's doctrine particularly appealing to Considerant, what engaged his imagination, was its rigorously scientific and "mathematical" character. This aspect of the theory was foremost in the account he gave of it to his friend Charles Magnin in 1829, at the end of his first year in Metz.

> Systems, ideal republics, all the conceptions of a philosophical imagination, fall before a rigorous, mathematical science. Once man is analyzed and once the passions are defined, classified, and discovered to tell the truth, one can grasp the riddles they pose and the ends they seek. Then we know the conditions necessary for [the creation of] the social mechanism we are looking for. . . . This is the procedure followed by any exact science; it is that of a mathematical problem. The formula is an admirable expression of the accordance of the laws of harmony in the material sphere and in the social sphere.[9]

So while the young Polytechnicien found consolation in Fourier's theories of metempsychosis, what really excited him about Fourier's doctrine was its claim to bring a scientific understanding of human nature and society, and thus to replace philosophy with science.

III

In Besançon, Considerant had already begun to think of himself as a partisan of Fourier's doctrine. At the Ecole Polytechnique he became a proselytizer. "From the time of his arrival," recalled a friend, "Victor Considerant talked to his comrades about a theory which he had, so to speak, breathed in with the air of his birthplace." While at Polytechnique Considerant also got to know Fourier himself. The man was not easily approachable; even his oldest disciple, Just Muiron, was scarcely on intimate terms with him. Still, by the time of his graduation from Polytechnique, Considerant could speak of Fourier with affection as well as respect. In July 1828, when Fourier had gone to Besançon to oversee the publication of the *Nouveau monde industriel*, Considerant asked Clarisse Vigoureux to "give Monsieur Fourier all the homage that his genius merits, and tell me the interesting things that you learn from him." Then he added: "Ah, if I were still in Franche-Comté, how happy I would be. I think he would be obliged to use the rod on his disciple as did the ancient Greeks. Fortunately he doesn't carry philosophy that far."[10]

At the Ecole Polytechnique Considerant's "Fourierism" (the word did not yet exist) was still broad and undogmatic. He had no trouble reconciling it with a lively interest in Mesmerist doctrines of animal magnetism. Thus in December 1826, as he was getting to know Fourier, Considerant wrote an admiring letter to—and apparently called on—Joseph-François Deleuze, a professor of natural history at the Jardin des Plantes who was one of Mesmer's leading French followers. While at Polytechnique Considerant also made a study of works by and about Robert Owen. In November 1829, having read the first ten issues of the Saint-Simonian journal the *Organisateur,* he was able to speak with enthusiasm about the "powerful ideas" of the developing Saint-Simonian movement. In the *Organisateur,* he wrote Clarisse Vigoureux, "there are pages that I would believe written by one of us." There were even Fourierist neologisms. But it was not likely that the Saint-Simonians were plagiarizing Fourier "because everywhere there is an instinctive awareness of the need for social change."[11]

It was during Considerant's years in Metz (1828–1832) that his commitment to Fourier's doctrine took on a dogmatic and exclusive character. He began to see himself as a member of an *école* or movement, as the defender of a "cause," and as one of the guardians and exponents of a new "science." Others saw him in a new light, too. Armand de Melun, who visited Metz in August 1829, later recalled that Considerant "was already conspicuous . . . for his eccentric ideas and his grotesque doctrines, which people made fun of even while they admired the seriousness of his convictions and the confused aspirations of his philanthropy." Two years later Considerant himself could write to Fourier from Metz: "We all have our nicknames here, and mine is 'Phalanstery.'"[12]

Until 1830, Considerant's major "writings" in support of Fourier's ideas consisted of voluminous letters to friends like Paul Vigoureux and Charles Magnin. But in March 1830 Considerant published an article on Fourier in a small Parisian literary journal called *Le Mercure de France au XIXe siècle.* This article, a detailed analysis of Fourier's *Nouveau monde industriel,* was actually the first sympathetic and well-informed account of Fourier's ideas to appear in any Parisian journal. It presented the book as "the fruit of thirty-seven years of meditation and labor" and credited Fourier with at last having discovered the "science" of social organization. Even Fourier's critical writing was praised by Considerant as a contribution to scientific understanding. "He has created," wrote Considerant, "the natural history of the vices of our social world."[13]

One would expect the appearance of this article to have delighted Fourier. Judging from a letter Fourier later wrote to the journal's editor, however, his joy was less than complete: "Monsieur Considerant . . . is a highly zealous disciple," he wrote, "but one who often falls into the common error of mixing the sophisms of the philosophers with my theory. I found in his article thirty-five errors of this sort, every one of which could have required a refutation."[14]

Fourier was obviously a hard man to please, but Considerant was undaunted. Throughout his years in Metz he kept up a running correspondence with Fourier, plying him with questions about the fine points of the doctrine and urging him to devote his time and energy to the publication of a full doctrinal treatise. At the same time Considerant worked hard at awakening interest in Fourier's ideas among his friends and acquaintances. He made a special effort with Charles Nodier, and in August 1831 he reported to Clarisse Vigoureux that he had gotten Nodier to take a look at Fourier's *Nouveau monde industriel.* Unfortunately, Nodier had "an obsession" that prevented him from fully appreciating Fourier. "He believes that man stands outside the general plan of creation, that he is destined to a state of confusion, disorder, and evil. In his eyes this is a sign of the grandeur of man." Considerant observed derisively that this was "the idea of a poet in a time of social conflagration."[15]

Considerant had more success with his comrades in Metz. In September 1831 he embarked on a series of half a dozen lectures on Fourier's system to a select audience of his friends. "I consider these lectures very important," he wrote Fourier, "because if I succeed with fifteen of my comrades, the others will be won over quickly; and next year, as these officers are dispersed all over France, they will serve our cause in spreading our science." The lectures were a great success. After the first, which dealt with "the series as the unique and necessary law of creation," Considerant reported triumphantly to Clarisse Vigoureux that all his listeners had recognized the "fecundity" of Fourier's law of the series, and one of them had told him that he would be "crushed" if the argument of the subsequent lectures proved less rigorous than the first. At the end of the lecture Considerant's colleagues congratulated him "like an orator coming down from the rostrum," and he could boast that "this meeting was a big event in our military world" and that "now the Phalanstery is regarded as something well thought out and well contrived." He added that he had "shuddered" at Fourier's difficulty at finding supporters in Paris when he saw "how easy it is to present the discovery in a free and attractive manner." Two weeks later Considerant remained jubilant. "I've had five sessions already," he wrote

Fourier. "People understand you here, and your name is pronounced with admiration." [16]

When he gave his first lectures in Metz, Considerant was still a few days short of his twenty-third birthday. His grasp of Fourier's ideas was by his own account imperfect, and he was still learning how to speak in public, but the lectures marked the beginning of a new career for him. It soon became apparent both to Fourier's other disciples and to Considerant himself that he was able to present Fourier's ideas to the general public far more convincingly than was Fourier himself. Considerant could translate Fourier's ideas into the romantic idiom of the 1830s, giving them a resonance they had previously lacked.

IV

Until the end of 1831, the Fourierist "movement" consisted of just a handful of individuals. Most of them were from Besançon, and the three leading figures were all socially marginal—"a deaf man, a woman, and a schoolboy," as Considerant put it. The transformation of this small band of disciples into an important social movement was extraordinarily swift. By the end of 1832 the number of Fourier's followers had swelled into the hundreds, and they included deputies and doctors, professors and Polytechniciens. They had now created their own journal; they had begun to receive attention in the Paris press; and they were embarked on a campaign to raise money to finance the establishment of a trial Phalanx according to Fourier's specifications.

These developments did not take place in isolation. The emergence of a Fourierist movement was part of a broad social and political awakening that touched many facets of French life during the first few years of the July Monarchy. This awakening, which was made possible in part by the loosening after 1830 of long-standing restrictions on the press and on the freedom of association, had multiple dimensions. It was marked by the revival of republicanism as a significant force in French political life, by a new radical consciousness among French industrial workers, and by the emergence among the urban bourgeoisie of a new consciousness of the social problems caused by industrialization and rapid urban growth. Together, these developments provided the context for a variety of new social movements, all seeking to define and resolve the problems caused by the rise of the new industrial society. Fourierism was one of these movements; another was Saint-Simonism.

The Saint-Simonians, whose thinking was loosely inspired by the social philosopher Henri Saint-Simon (1762–1825), were brilliant but troubled young men and women who saw themselves as living in a society in which traditional social bonds had collapsed. They were eager for a faith that would give their lives direction and purpose, and they regarded Saint-Simon as the prophet of a new world in which science and love might collaborate to bring about the material and moral regeneration of humanity. In 1830, having constituted themselves formally as a "church," they began to devote themselves to missionary activity, organizing groups of "preachers" to circulate throughout the provinces expounding their social gospel. One such group came to Metz in the fall of 1831, and Considerant was impressed by the fluency of their principal speaker, Jules Lechevalier, as well as by the size and diversity of the audience. "There was a huge crowd in the auditorium," he wrote Clarisse Vigoureux. "It was open to everyone. . . . The greasy bonnet of the cook shined next to the elegant hat of the lady; decorated generals could be seen along with common soldiers and woodcutters."[17]

Like other organized religions, the Saint-Simonian Church had its schisms and heresies. These culminated, at the end of 1831, in a great schism that tore the church apart. Many of the young men and women who abandoned Saint-Simonism at that time, finding themselves unable to live without some faith, joined the ranks of the Fourierists. Two of the most important "converts" to Fourierism from Saint-Simonism were the Polytechnicien Abel Transon and the former law student Jules Lechevalier. Both were gifted writers and speakers, and in the winter and spring of 1832 each published articles and gave public lectures on Fourierism that were important both in winning over wavering Saint-Simonians and in giving Fourierism intellectual respectability in the eyes of the public at large. Thus the breakup of the Saint-Simonian Church helped create a climate favorable to the rapid growth of Fourierism.[18]

Considerant was more a witness to than a participant in these events. He played a role (along with Just Muiron) in the conversion to Fourierism of Jules Lechevalier, with whom he had long conversations in Metz in the fall of 1831; and the huge crowds drawn by the Saint-Simonians inspired Considerant to embark in December on a new lecture series of his own at the Hôtel de Ville in Metz. Having invited "the prefect, all the authorities, the ablest women, members of the bourgeoisie, and officers from the army garrison," he could boast that his audience was sure to be "stylish and brilliant." However, Considerant necessarily missed Lechevalier's triumphal series of public lectures in Paris in February and March of 1832; and he could only participate at a distance in the intense discussions that went on in Paris concerning the future direction of the Fourierist movement. Feeling increasingly isolated in Metz, he applied for a furlough that would enable him to spend at least a few weeks in Paris. On March 14 his application was granted, and ten days later he was on his way to Paris.[19]

The big activity that drew Considerant to Paris in the spring of 1832 was the creation of a Fourierist journal. For several months Considerant had been discussing the matter by letter with Fourier. Convinced that the Saint-Simonians were a band of hypocritical plagiarists ("scientific Cossacks plundering and making travesties of the ideas of others"), Fourier believed he needed a journal both to expose their misdeeds and to publicize his own ideas. Considerant, who did not regard the Saint-Simonians as plagiarists, nonetheless believed that a journal comparable to the Saint-Simonian *Globe* could provide the Fourierists with an invaluable forum for the presentation of their ideas. "Our journal should be purely scientific," he wrote Fourier.

> It should not have to bother about day-to-day events. It should come out once a week and be eight pages long. At least half of it should always be devoted to the publication of the elementary method on which you are working now. Whenever you wish, the whole journal should be devoted to your writing. We will utilize the space that remains to speak about the need to organize association and to provoke public discussion on the subject. Only later, and after due preparation, will we turn to [Fourier's theories on] the study of man.[20]

Back in Paris in late March, Considerant discussed the journal at length not only with Fourier but also with Lechevalier and Transon. He also helped raise funds and establish a headquarters for the journal, which would serve as a meeting place for the disciples. By the end of April an office had been rented on the rue Joquelet, near Brongniart's new Paris Bourse. With it came a large reception room and a small adjoining apartment, which became Fourier's new residence.

Considerant's stay in Paris was marked by high hopes and a frenzy of activity. At the outset he lodged with Paul Vigoureux, now a student at the Ecole Centrale d'Industrie, who was renting an apartment on the rue Vieille du Temple. But he had little time to spend with his friend for he quickly got caught up both in Fourierist activities and in volunteer work at a medical center established in the Faubourg Saint-Antoine to treat victims of the cholera epidemic that raged at Paris. In a letter dated May 1 he spoke of the forthcoming journal, the new office, a brochure he intended to publish, a series of lectures he planned to give to students from the Ecole Polytechnique, and a long article he had just written—a "thorough analysis" of Fourier's system originally intended for the *Revue des deux mondes*.

"I simply cannot leave Paris at this time," he wrote. "We must concentrate all our efforts to make this moment decisive." Considerant was expected to return to his regiment in Metz by May 7, but he managed to get his furlough extended. He knew he could not go on receiving furloughs indefinitely and might eventually have to resign his army commission. He was reluctant to do so not because he worried about giving up his career but rather because he believed the uniform was useful to him. "It gives me access to certain people," he wrote, "among others students and graduates of the Ecole [Polytechnique]." But in "six or eight months," he added, "all these problems will have disappeared." In a year at most Fourier's system would be put to the test through the creation of a trial Phalanx, and this would be "the signal for the greatest revolution that can occur on the face of the globe."[21]

V

The new journal, which first appeared on June 1, 1832, was initially called *Le Phalanstère*. (After three months the name was changed to *La Réforme industrielle ou le Phalanstère*.) It was a weekly of eight large two-column pages. Its subtitle was "Journal for the foundation of an agricultural and manufacturing Phalanx associated in work and housekeeping," and its editors described it as "devoted to making known the advantages of domestic and agricultural association and the means discovered by Monsieur Fourier to create such an association." The journal's aim was both to provide a forum for the elaboration of Fourier's ideas and to rally support for the establishment of a trial Phalanx. The first issue included an introductory statement, drafted jointly by Considerant and Lechevalier, which insisted that Fourierism was not merely a set of abstract ideas. Instead it brought "a FACT to people eager for facts and realities." Thus the first issue of the *Phalanstère* stressed the realization of Fourier's ideas. Fourier himself contributed a long programmatic statement on the trial Phalanx; the rest of the issue was given over to the publication of the official statutes of the two shareholding companies. One of them, a Society for the Foundation of an Agricultural and Industrial Phalanx, was intended to raise a capital of four million francs for the trial Phalanx. The other, a Society for the Publication and Propagation of the Theory of Charles Fourier, sought to raise thirty thousand francs for the publication of the journal and of writings by Fourier and his followers.[22]

Despite the professed desire of Fourier's disciples to concentrate on practical matters, little was said in the early numbers of the *Phalanstère* concerning the actual establishment of a trial Phalanx. In fact, most of the articles published during the first six months—including those by Considerant, Lechevalier, and Transon—were broad restatements of Fourier's main ideas. The chief contributor was Fourier himself. At least a third of each issue consisted of essays by Fourier on particular aspects of the theory, ranging from architecture to cosmogony. He had little to say about contemporary politics, but he did use the journal as a platform from which to launch attacks on "sophists" and "philanthropic comedians" such as Saint-Simon, Owen, and their disciples. In this respect he was indefatigable. Almost every issue contained a new article on the "secret designs" of the Saint-Simonians, the "mindlessness of the philosophers," or the "war of the four rebellious sciences against the four faithful sciences."

Shortly after the appearance of the first issue of *Le Phalanstère*, Considerant's furlough expired and he had to return to Metz. There he renewed his efforts to proselytize among his fellow soldiers, and on June 18 he could already report that about fifteen of his comrades wished to subscribe to the new journal. "Enthusiasm is very high in Metz," he wrote Clarisse Vigoureux, adding that his comrades were now talking of resigning their commissions once the trial Phalanx was on its feet. Two weeks later Considerant remained ebullient. He announced that he was about to be inducted into the Masonic lodge in Metz, and he boasted that if he could persuade its members to purchase shares in one of the new Fourierist societies, the lodges of Nancy, Pont-à-Mousson, and Sarreguemines would surely follow suit.[23]

Still, Considerant felt isolated in Metz. He had to get back to Paris. In late June he addressed a formal request for a year's furlough to the minister of war, Marshal Soult, adding that if this could not be granted he would have to resign. The request was granted, and on July 19 Considerant wrote Lechevalier jubilantly about this "proof" that the government was "far from looking unfavorably on our efforts." By the end of July he was back in Paris.[24]

For almost a year Considerant was absorbed by work on *Le Phalanstère*. In the fall of 1832 he published a long series of articles entitled "Societary Theory" setting forth the main elements of the doctrine. In other articles he showed how Fourier's thought might help resolve specific social and economic problems such as the overcrowding of the cities and the unrest among the miners at Anzin and the silk weavers at Lyon. He also wrote articles on contemporary journalism, applauding the growing independence of provincial journals vis-à-vis the traditional "lordship" of the Paris press and exhorting journalists to turn away from "sterile and dangerous discussions on governmental forms" to focus instead on "problems of industrial and social reform." At the same time Considerant supervised the journal's administration and arranged for the collaboration of a number of young army officers—including Alphonse Tamisier, Allyre Bureau, Hippolyte Renaud, and Albert Guillemon—whom he had known at Polytechnique and in Metz. Their contributions were uneven in quality, but the young men shared a desire to reach a wide audience by focusing on Fourier's basic economic ideas and referring as little as possible to his cosmological and sexual views, or even to his theory of passionate attraction.

The disciples' efforts bore some fruit. After just a few weeks of publication they could boast of having received "a fairly large number" of expressions of support from former Saint-Simonians. They also noted that Fourier was getting some attention in the provincial press. But the success of the *Phalanstère* should not be exaggerated. Its press run never greatly exceeded one thousand, and its total number of subscribers was probably fewer than half that.[25] In any case, the disciples were preaching to the converted. Despite their desire to reach a wide audience, most of their articles could not have made sense to someone not already familiar with Fourier's thought.

Considerant's collaborators recognized the journal's limitations. One of the more outspoken, the Polytechnicien Nicolas Lemoyne, bluntly described it as "indigestible."[26] Most found it too dry and too exclusively theoretical to be of any use in arousing interest in Fourier's ideas among outsiders. According to many of the disciples, though, there was another, graver, problem: Fourier's contributions to the journal. Even his oldest and most loyal disciple, Just Muiron, had little confidence in Fourier's ability to make his ideas attractive, or simply accessible, to a wide audience. To Considerant, Fourier's limitations as a popularizer of his own ideas seemed obvious, and his letters to Clarisse Vigoureux were full of complaints about the damage Fourier was doing to his own cause. "In the eighteenth issue," he wrote, "you will receive an article on the emancipation of journalists. In that article you will recognize all of his inanity as a journalist. That article is really stupid." To propose duchies and hereditary principalities as rewards for sympathetic journalists was to demonstrate an "ineptitude" as great in its way as was Fourier's brilliance as a creator. "He is really killing the journal and discrediting us all."[27]

Fourier's disciples often complained about his contributions to the *Phalanstère*. They deplored his outbursts against the Saint-Simonians. They were also disturbed by his unexplained theoretical allusions and bizarre terminology. One of them wrote to Fourier anonymously,

> In the last number of the *Phalanstère*, you address yourself to the capitalists. You want them to bring you their money . . . and you talk to them about "tribes" and "choirs" and "internal" and "external" rivalry, about the "three sexes," and about "simple" and "compound" impulsions, etc., etc. To understand all these things one has to read your works. But you know very well that the capitalists have not read them.

No less offensive to many of the disciples was Fourier's "extravagance" as a polemicist and the "vulgarity" of his tone when he was making his best effort *not* to be obscure. Eventually almost all the disciples came to agree with the views expressed by Considerant in October 1833 as he looked back on the *Phalanstère's* first year: "We needed a great deal of courage to keep on moving ahead with an awareness of the permanent harm [Fourier] was doing to the doctrine by his articles in the journal."[28]

Given these feelings, it is not surprising that Fourier and the disciples were frequently at odds. Indeed, the tension between them seems to have existed from the beginning of their collaboration on the *Phalanstère*. In the very first issue the editors printed a note apologizing for Fourier's insistence on accompanying his initial programmatic statement with an elaborate "tableau" of the fifteen different "degrees or stages" of association, which could only be understood by initiates. In July 1832, after Fourier had written an exceptionally vituperative article on the Saint-Simonians, Lechevalier and Transon published a categorical rejection of his position. Again in September, after Fourier had published an article on his cosmological theories, the editors found it necessary to point out solemnly that "the art of associating in industry, agriculture, and domestic life is independent of the phenomena of creation and of everything that may be happening on the surface of the other planets."[29]

Fourier himself does not seem to have been greatly troubled by these disavowals. The important thing for him was to be able to speak his mind; if the disciples didn't like it, they could say so. Fourier was more disturbed by the tendency of some of his disciples to write about the Phalanx as if it were simply an experimental farm. Throughout the summer and fall of 1832 he kept complaining about the "watering down" of his theories and the "Saint-Simonian prejudices" that crept into the writings of his followers. They in turn continued to fear that his more outlandish ideas, his "bad taste," and his aggressiveness in polemic would alienate potential supporters.

In the fall of 1832 a series of particularly bitter confrontations took place between Fourier and his disciples. The root of the trouble seems to have been Fourier's fear of being "enslaved" by his followers. For over twelve years he had been receiving money from Just Muiron and Clarisse Vigoureux. By 1832 they were virtually supporting him, and there were times when he couldn't stand the thought of it. He found it even harder to tolerate Considerant's attempts to edit his writing. In November he turned on Considerant, who wrote Clarisse Vigoureux a long and bitter letter at the end of the month.

> You speak about divisions among us. Well, my God, there haven't been any [for some time]. . . . As for Monsieur Fourier, we simply let him alone. Do you know that he has twice become furious at me? On the first occasion, however, I behaved so gently that the gentle Transon, who was there, could not understand why I didn't send that bitter and unjust man packing. The cause of the second scene was simply that I told him in front of other people that it would not be worthy of him to write the kind of "amusing" articles that he said he wished to write for the journal. I have taken the utmost care to avoid having disputes with him. I speak to him very rarely and always with the greatest gentleness. If he says the opposite, he is lying and that's all there is to it.

Considerant went on to observe bitterly that he was "very glad" to report that Fourier had taken a dislike to him, for Fourier was "the very essence of injustice, jealousy, and . . . ingratitude." To be disliked by such a man was "an indication that one has done something for the Phalansterian movement." [30]

The letters containing Fourier's side of the story have been lost, but we can gain some sense of it from a letter written to him by Clarisse Vigoureux in early December.

> Just why do you seem so sad and discontent at a time when we have such high hopes? For a year things have been going better than any of us could have hoped. [Yet] you seem dissatisfied with all your disciples; you find fault with Victor. . . . Poor Victor, I once saw you acting so unfairly toward him that I want to tell myself that the same thing is happening again today. . . . But what distresses me most is the pain and sadness that you feel. This weighs on my heart and almost on my conscience as if we were imperiously charged with the responsibility of making you happy until the moment when the human race has accepted you as its master.

Clarisse Vigoureux told Fourier that his ideas were "too lofty" for his critics to comprehend and that he could not descend to their level "without losing the dignity that is necessary for success." She also tried to dispel his suspicion that the disciples wished "to keep [him] away from the journal."

No doubt she was speaking in good faith, but still Fourier's suspicion was well founded. Early in 1833 the journal's editors announced a series of editorial changes, one aim of which was precisely to reduce Fourier's role.[31]

Seeking to make the journal less sectarian and to reach a wider public, Considerant and his colleagues expanded it from eight to twelve pages and announced that they would be publishing fewer articles on large doctrinal questions and more on the application of Fourier's theory to specific social problems. They began to print book reviews and to take stands on current debates in medicine, education, and agriculture. At the same time they attempted to place limits on the space available to Fourier and to subject him to the same deadlines as everyone else. Fourier's response was simply to ignore these limitations. He continued to write articles that filled a third to a half of the journal, to make major changes on the proofs at the last moment, and to rely on catchy, attention-getting phrases and advertising techniques that his disciples regarded as vulgar. Increasingly in the spring and summer of 1833 he also devoted large portions of his articles to attacks on the "errors" and "Saint-Simonian formulas" of his own disciples. In March, for example, Fourier filled one-third of an issue with an attack on his disciple Charles Pellarin and on "the kind of service that is rendered by certain bumbling friends who are assassinating me while they think they are improving my reputation."[32]

The disciples' public response to all this was mild, but in fact they were fed up. After June 1833 Considerant and Abel Transon ceased to write for the *Phalanstère*. In August Considerant summed up the feelings of many of the disciples when he called for the suspension of publication. "It is of the utmost importance," he wrote, "that Fourier should cease to have the means to publish articles by which he is destroying both himself and his theory in the eyes of the public."[33]

Le Phalanstère did not cease publication in August 1833. It was made a monthly and continued to appear as such through February 1834; however, it ceased to be the organ of a movement. For it was abandoned by the disciples, and during the last six months its articles—which bore such rousing titles as "The Scientific Poltroons," "Mystification of the Sirens of Progress," and "Commercial Speculation Offering a Net Profit of 300% in Six Months"—were all by Fourier. Meanwhile Considerant and his fellow disciples turned their attention to other matters—notably, the attempt to create a trial Phalanx, which had been announced in the first issue of the journal but which (like the journal) was in trouble by the summer of 1833.

VI

From the time he first fell under Fourier's spell, Considerant had always believed that Fourier's distinctiveness as a social thinker lay in the fact that his ideas were meant to be put to experimental verification. He believed that the main goal of any Fourierist movement or organization should be the promotion of an *essai*—the creation of a trial Phalanx. He stated this clearly in the first issue of the *Phalanstère*, and in his private correspondence he was equally emphatic. "You see that we are moving forward," he wrote Julie Vigoureux on May 1, 1832, "and I am not taking back any of my predictions. Next year we will make the experiment."[34]

When Considerant got back to Paris in late July 1832, he joined the efforts already under way to purchase the land needed for the trial. Fourier had specified that ideally the land should be located not far from Paris. Such land proved expensive, however, so the search was widened. Properties were considered in Normandy, Touraine, the Vendée, and even Les Landes. All were either infertile or too costly. Finally land was found near Paris at a reasonable price. Considerant went out to inspect it in late September, and soon afterward a tentative agreement was reached with Dr. Alexandre-François Baudet-Dulary, a deputy from Seine-et-Oise, and with Joseph-Antoine Devay, the owner of a farm at Condé-sur-Vesgre, southwest of Paris near the forest of Rambouillet. Devay agreed to accept shares in the Founding Society in lieu of cash payment for the farm; and Baudet-Dulary, a man of wealth and influence who took Fourier's ideas far more seriously than any potential "founder" who had yet emerged, agreed to provide the funds needed to purchase adjoining land and make initial improvements. There was an informal understanding that the venture would be presented to the public as the creation of a "model agricultural colony" and that Fourier would be kept out of it during the initial phases.[35]

The choice of a site was announced by Baudet-Dulary in November. In two articles in the *Phalanstère* Baudet-Dulary observed that Condé was going to represent a retreat from the initial specifications. The community would be organized "*insofar as possible* according to the method of Charles Fourier." Its size would be reduced to six hundred people and the working capital to 1.2 million francs. Since the term "Phalanstery" had sometimes been judged "bizarre," the community would be called simply a "Societary Colony."[36] Jules Lechevalier spelled out the meaning of these changes in another article that distinguished between the work of "the theorists" and that of "the executors." "In our prospectus we asked for executors," wrote Lechevalier dramatically. "They have appeared." Now it was their turn to "put into practice what they have found to be immediately realizable in the theory of Charles Fourier." Baudet-Dulary and Devay had "modified the original act according to the dictates of reality." Lechevalier concluded by observing that in the negotiations over the execution of his ideas, Fourier himself had been "just as agreeable, just as accommodating . . . as he is firm and inflexible in theoretical calculations. 'I am the pilot,' he says. 'I will show you the solutions to be sought, the pitfalls to be avoided. After listening to my advice, you will be free to act as you wish.'"[37]

Fourier's attitude toward the experiment at Condé was actually rather less than accommodating. This came as no surprise to Considerant. Already in September 1832 he had asked Clarisse Vigoureux not even to speak of Condé to Fourier because he was "sure to make trouble." By November he could write that Baudet-Dulary and Devay were "masters of their fortunes" and had "every right" to modify Fourier's plans "in any way they think necessary to bring in shareholders." Considerant continued:

> Monsieur Fourier must not be an absolute master in selecting different types of industry and agriculture. That would, on the contrary, be a very bad thing because, as far as practical matters are concerned, he has ideas that are entirely false and even ridiculous. His manias can do us a great deal of harm. Ah, my God, don't we have an understanding of the Phalanstery? Don't we know that the tasks to be performed in the trial Phalanx must be as attractive as possible in themselves? And if Monsieur Fourier wrongly imagines that such and such a job is repugnant or attractive in itself when experience proves the contrary, are we necessarily obliged to accept the erroneous ideas that have become lodged in his head?[38]

In November 1832 Fourier had not yet given up on Condé. He had, however, begun to adopt a rather detached attitude toward the colony. The following month, while Baudet-Dulary and Devay were attempting to raise money, Fourier coolly began to discuss in the journal the desirability of establishing *multiple* trial Phalanxes.[39]

Considerant remained in Paris throughout the winter of 1832–1833. His main preoccupation was still the *Phalanstère* and, more generally, what he had come to refer to as the work of "propagation"—spreading and popularizing Fourier's ideas by means of lectures and articles. Considerant made several visits to Condé, however; and in December 1832 he could write that sixty hired workers were clearing the land and readying it for spring planting.

> For some time a small army of laborers belonging to three neighboring villages and divided into three companies has taken up positions on the

land of the colony. More than sixty men are scattered about and exe-
cuting preparatory tasks. They are digging drainage ditches, cutting
briars, and burning their roots. Meanwhile wagons are crisscrossing
the fields and restoring to productivity soil that contemporary society
ought to be ashamed of leaving sterile when it is cluttered with such
a large number of starving people.[40]

By February two hundred workers were engaged at Condé, and the progress reports that appeared regularly in the *Phalanstère* continued to be optimistic. Then, toward the end of March, Joseph Devay had to publish a
long article refuting various "calumnies" concerning the infertility of the
soil at Condé as well as "salon gossip" that members of the colony were
"practicing free love with bacchantes." In addition, Baudet-Dulary reported on March 15 that because of difficulties in his own attempts to buy
land adjacent to Devay's property, he had only managed to submit his formal request for government authorization of a joint-stock company with
limited liability on March 1. There was no chance that authorization would
be granted prior to March 21, the scheduled opening date.[41]

Baudet-Dulary's decision to postpone the colony's official opening was a
blow to many of Fourier's followers. These people would have been even
more distressed if they had known what was really going on. For Baudet-
Dulary had come to believe that Considerant, Lechevalier, and Fourier
himself were all "quite prepared to sacrifice the colony to the journal,
which is all they really care about." Furthermore, he and Devay were actually confronted by difficulties far more serious than those mentioned in
print. The most pressing problem was a lack of capital. Baudet-Dulary and
Devay were attempting to create a joint-stock company with a capital of
1.2 million francs. There remained over 900,000 francs to be collected, and
the value of the shares actually purchased between May 1, 1832, and
March 1, 1833, totaled just 10,750 francs. In order to pay the workers who
were clearing and cultivating the land at Condé, Baudet-Dulary had already drawn heavily on his personal funds.[42]

Finally, at the end of May 1833, Baudet-Dulary announced to the public that the Societary Colony was in serious trouble and that he had decided
to assume full responsibility for the whole enterprise. "It is less a question
now of realizing the magnificent promises of the theory," he wrote, "than
of yielding some result, however feeble it might be." Two weeks later the
definitive text of the agreement constituting the "first Societary Colony"
was published in the *Phalanstère*. Fourier's ideas were watered down even
more than in the provisional agreement published the previous November,
and a note by Baudet-Dulary stressed the modest and pragmatic character

of his approach. "I announce nothing absolute. I am not beginning with 600 colonists but with 150 workers, of whom 60 are now lodged and fed in the first buildings of the future colony." Henceforth Fourier's role was to be that of an "indispensable advisor" but one without any formal responsibilities or powers. Fourier was in fact anything but pleased with the new arrangements. It seemed to him that he was simply being denied a voice in the affairs at Condé, and in his letters to Just Muiron he railed against the "dictatorship" of Baudet-Dulary and the "incompetence" of the architect Baudet-Dulary had chosen.[43]

During the hot summer months of 1833, while Fourier was fretting about Baudet-Dulary, Considerant and Transon went to Condé to try to rescue the colony. They were joined by friends of Considerant like Paul Vigoureux and the young Frédéric Dorian from Montbéliard, and by such Fourierists as A. Maurize, Alphonse Morellet, a Captain Gerardin from Besançon, Adolphe Brac de La Perrière from Lyon, and the Spanish republican Joaquin Abreu. Some of these individuals, like Brac de La Perrière, were well-to-do young gentlemen from the provinces; others were engineers with degrees from the Ecole Polytechnique; Abreu was a middle-aged former navy officer. But all of them joined in the work of clearing land, plowing, and planting fruit trees that had been started in the spring by day laborers hired by Baudet-Dulary. There was also much construction to be done. The architect, of whom Fourier and others were fiercely critical, was forced to leave in late July. Still, work continued on the temporary lodgings that he had started. The construction of a brickworks was undertaken on the banks of the Vesgre. And on a promontory overlooking the rest of the property, construction began on a wing of the future Phalanstery.

On July 19 Jules Lechevalier could write in the *Phalanstère* of the "great activity" displayed by "our most dedicated associates" at Condé. On the spot, though, the situation looked less encouraging. Despite the hard work, few really knew what they were doing at Condé; and as the summer wore on, tension arose between the hired workers and the middle-class disciples. At the very moment when Lechevalier's optimistic progress report was appearing in the journal, Considerant, who described himself as "dropping with fatigue," wrote a letter to Charles Pellarin in Paris lamenting the chaotic state of affairs at Condé and urging Pellarin not to bring visitors to the colony. Those who did come were struck not only by the disorganization but also by the gloom and complete absence of enthusiasm at Condé.[44]

By mid-August it was clear that nothing significant could be accomplished that summer. A huge amount of money had been spent, apparently to little purpose. True, hundreds of trees had been planted and the vegetable garden was thriving despite the summer's dryness. The old mill on the property had been repaired and enlarged; a brickworks had been established; and a complex of farm buildings had been created with "lodging for sixty people, common rooms, a blacksmith's and wheelwright's workshop, a carpenter's and cabinetmaker's shop, and immense stables."[45] But all this was meant to serve a community that could not come into being without much more money than Baudet-Dulary and all of Fourier's other disciples possessed.

On August 12 Considerant decided to leave Condé. He informed Baudet-Dulary that he would happily travel the length and breadth of France to raise money, if only he could convince himself that the Societary Colony was not a "bottomless pit." But now he had lost all hope. Four days later a brief note appeared on the back page of the *Phalanstère* over Fourier's signature.

> The preparatory work at the Colony of Condé-sur-Vesgre having undergone delays, the mechanism of attractive industry cannot be activated [at this time]. Since the summer season is already well advanced, and since the inauguration cannot take place outside the months of planting, the inauguration is postponed until next spring. Meanwhile work will be continued and the beginnings will be so much the easier in May of 1834.

Despite Fourier's efforts to put a good face on things, there was a mood of frustration and finger-pointing among his disciples. Some blamed Fourier, others blamed the architect, still others blamed Baudet-Dulary, whom Considerant described as a man who "keeps on making mistakes . . . not every day but every hour of the day." As for Fourier, he had lost all hope in Condé. Thus he turned his attention elsewhere; and in a series of articles published in the *Phalanstère* he developed his ideas for a children's Phalanx, an experiment in association that might be organized cheaply and rapidly with five hundred children under the age of twelve.[46]

On September 22, 1833, the first general assembly of the shareholders of the Societary Colony was held at Condé. Fourier took the day-long trip from Paris to attend. Considerant, Transon, and Muiron also came. Out of a total of forty-eight shareholders, however, only thirteen managed to be present. The main business of the meeting was a long and gloomy report by Baudet-Dulary. Tracing the stages in the life of the colony, he noted that his own attempt to set up a shareholding company with a working capital of 1.2 million francs was still far from realization. The total sum gathered came to 378,000 francs, and of that amount by far the greater part was his own contribution. "With such feeble resources," he observed, "we have not been able to create a Phalanstery."[47]

This meeting at Condé was neither an end nor a beginning as far as the life of the Societary Colony was concerned. Within a few months the disciples had launched a new campaign to raise funds to establish a children's Phalanx the following year. This project, which would involve 250 children, was to cost a mere 250,000 francs. Even this sum proved to be more than the disciples could raise. In 1836 the society formed by Baudet-Dulary was legally dissolved. The property at Condé-sur-Vesgre remained in his hands, but he took it upon himself to reimburse in full all the other shareholders. In the final reckoning his losses amounted to 487,000 francs.[48]

3

Fourierist Leader

By the fall of 1833, Considerant had given up on the two projects he and his colleagues had so enthusiastically embarked upon some eighteen months earlier. The effort to create a Phalanx at Condé was moribund, having been abandoned by Fourier himself as well as by most of his disciples. The journal was still being published, but only as a monthly; and Considerant no longer regarded it as a significant vehicle for the spread of Fourier's ideas. After a year and a half of close collaboration with Fourier, Considerant, along with most of the other Parisian disciples, had concluded that the man was impossible to work with. They all resented Fourier's dogmatism and intransigence—what Considerant called his "arid and exclusive nature"[1]— and they found him crude and inept as a popularizer of his own ideas.

As a result, in the last months of 1833 Considerant and some of his colleagues struck off on their own. Without ceasing to consider themselves Fourier's followers, they began to create a Fourierist movement independent of Fourier himself. Leaving Fourier to do whatever he wanted with the journal, Considerant, Jules Lechevalier, and Adrien Berbrugger embarked on speaking tours of the provinces. Between August and December 1833, Considerant lectured to large audiences at Montargis, Orléans, Houdan, and Besançon; Lechevalier spoke at Rouen, Bordeaux, and Nantes, and Berbrugger at Lyon, Dijon, and Besançon. On these tours, which they sometimes described in Saint-Simonian fashion as Phalansterian "missions," they downplayed Fourier's effort to present his theory as a science and a profit-making scheme, a practical and experimentally verifiable theory of industrial organization that would yield a profit to shrewd investors. Instead, they tried to awaken the public's generous and humanitarian impulses. "We must . . . make our appeal above all to the social sentiments," explained Considerant. "We must present the work at Condé as a tentative venture in high philanthropy rather than a pure business speculation, and [we must] interest people through their love for the public welfare . . . rather than through their selfish interest." [2]

Considerant spelled out the reasons for this change in approach in an important twenty-page letter written from Montargis to his cousin Adrien Gréa on October 10, 1833. Here Considerant offered a detailed critique of the Fourierists' activities over the previous sixteen months and an analysis of the new directions the movement might take. The first and most important step was to terminate Fourier's connection with the effort to spread his ideas. Fourier should devote himself to work on his incomplete theoretical treatise, Considerant maintained, leaving "propagation" to his disciples.

In founding the journal in June 1832, began Considerant, and in seeking Fourier's help and advice in all their activities, the disciples had attempted to rally around Fourier and to march with him as their leader. Some of them already knew that "he would be of little help in the work of propagation." Nevertheless the effort to work with him had been worth making and had, no doubt, yielded significant results. First of all, the publication of the *Phalanstère* had given Fourier the satisfaction, after "thirty-four years of torment," of "being at last able to make his voice heard by the public." Secondly, by bringing Fourier's theory into the public domain, the disciples had given him a guarantee that his ideas could never be stolen from him. They had thus done something to allay the "miser's mania" that led him to regard "everyone who approached him" as a potential plagiarist. Finally, wrote Considerant, the attempt to work closely with Fourier had given the disciples credibility and demonstrated their good faith. They were now free to work independently of Fourier—to attempt to spread his ideas (or some of them) without being hindered by his criticism.

Considerant went on to describe the different tactics the disciples might have adopted in seeking a wider audience. The first course, the one they had actually followed, was to stress the "scientific and industrial" aspects of Fourier's doctrine—to treat the creation of the Phalanx as a controlled experiment designed to verify a scientific hypothesis. The second tactic was one the disciples might have adopted had it not been completely foreign to Fourier's "arid" and "glacial" nature. This would have been to emphasize the "social idea" in Fourier's thought and to appeal to the generous impulses of the public, "the love of the collective good and of humanity." The third approach was the "religious, moralizing, and pontifical" approach. This was the approach of the Saint-Simonians, who had created a sect and sought to "moralize the people," placing themselves at the top of the pontifical hierarchy. Finally, there was the deceptive approach. The Fourierists might have disguised their theory, "hiding from the public the fact that we possessed a complete system, that we were armed from head to foot and ready for battle."

Neither of these last two possibilities satisfied Considerant. Furthermore, he wrote, they were unthinkable under Fourier's leadership. As for the second, the appeal to the generous impulses, it was attractive to the "ardent and young natures of the disciples but antithetical to Fourier's mentality. Thus they had been wise to stress initially the "scientific and industrial" aspects of the doctrine. By presenting themselves as the exponents of an empirically verifiable science, they had been able to gain respect and to offer a serious alternative to the facile liberalism of 1830 and the windy preaching of the Saint-Simonians. Now it was time to change tactics and to adopt "a warmer social appeal."

Considerant described the imminent "new phase in the propagation of the doctrine." The *Phalanstère* had awakened or reinforced interest in Fourierism among groups of disciples in cities like Lyon, Dijon, and Besançon. The task now was to link these provincial groups and coordinate their activity through the establishment of a center in Paris and the creation of a new journal. Lecture series should also be organized and speakers sent out through the provinces. Fourier's role henceforth would be to work toward the completion of a comprehensive theoretical treatise.[3]

While Considerant was outlining his thoughts about the new directions to be taken by the Fourierist movement, he had already begun to put them into practice. He was at Montargis, on the first leg of a speaking and fundraising tour. Although he found the city "brutish and hair-raisingly sluggish," he assured Gréa that Montargis would "cough up several thousand francs for the Phalanstery." Not all of his time was devoted to proselytizing and fund-raising, however. The summer's activities had exhausted Considerant, and he complained of headaches and general prostration. During his several weeks' stay in Montargis he at last got to rest. He was lodged on a hill overlooking the city in a medieval castle belonging to Baroness Lydie Vassal Roger. Madame Roger, an adept of magnetism and theosophy and a former protégé of Fabre d'Olivet, had sought out Fourier in Paris and had remained in correspondence with him. An eclectic like many of Fourier's early admirers, she saw "significant analogies between his doctrines and those of Fabre d'Olivet"; and during Considerant's stay there was much conversation about the *illuminati*, about "unpublished and secret" manuscripts left by Fabre d'Olivet at his death, and about the two years she had spent as a member of his "sanctuary."[4]

Considerant moved on to Orléans in mid-October. Warned on his arrival about the mercantile character of the city, he at first planned merely to get acquainted with a few potential recruits and backers. His initial contacts were fruitful enough, though, that he decided to hold a public meeting at the Hôtel de Ville. An audience of two hundred turned out for his first lecture. Within two weeks—although still troubled by headaches—he had given five lectures and written two articles for *Le Loiret*, the largest journal in the department. Although he complained to Clarisse Vigoureux that the city was egoistical and unlikely to yield much money, he was satisfied with his efforts as a publicist. One thing he lacked, however, was a succinct exposition of Fourier's doctrine to supplement his lectures. He wrote at the end of October that he was torn between the desire to carry his message west along the Loire to Tours and Nantes and the urge to halt his "mission" briefly to produce a concise, readable summary of the doctrine.[5]

In late November Considerant was on the road again—this time bound for Besançon. By mid-December he had given five public lectures, and he wrote that he was "making as much headway as could be expected in Besançon." He had presented Fourier's theory in a sufficiently engaging manner that it was "no longer good taste to laugh at it and make fun of it." Indeed, a few people were now "enchanted" by Fourier—the painter Auguste Charpentier, for example, and a number of women. Considerant appreciatively quoted one of them, a Madame Coladon, to the effect that "only crazy people, women, and the young" could fully appreciate Fourier. But the reaction of the solid male citizens of Besançon—"*le commerce et les perruques*," as Considerant put it flippantly—was skeptical at best. By his own account, they found him "brash" and "presumptuous" to lecture them at his age in such a "cocksure" tone and with his "air of mathematical certainty."[6]

In fact, it was not only stuffy old lawyers and businessmen who found Considerant brash and cocksure. Just Muiron also found the young man frivolous, flighty, lacking in "fixity, perseverance, and poise," and—worst of all—not sufficiently concerned with fund-raising. His lectures had "moved people, touched their hearts," and "awakened their intellects," but, complained Muiron, had "no material results." Considerant had not even raised enough money in Besançon to pay the thirty francs it cost to rent a hall. "I just don't understand our young people who talk with everyone and do not persuade anyone to give a centime!" What's more, instead of working on his popularization of Fourier's ideas, Considerant was now talking about writing a novel! "I find him too much of an *artist*," commented Muiron dryly.[7]

His lectures completed, Considerant set off on foot with his friend Victor Coste for his home at Salins. He planned to spend a few weeks with his mother, resting and working on his brochure—and his novel. Shortly after their arrival at Salins, Considerant and Coste were joined by the new Fourierist Adrien Berbrugger, who had just completed two successful lecture series at Lyon. Considerant then took his friends on several long hikes through the Jura. He and Berbrugger had time to discuss the successes and disappointments of the previous year and also to make grandiose plans for future lecture tours all over the East and North of France. Considerant also spoke with enthusiasm about his various writing projects. His brochure on Fourier's theory had now assumed substantial proportions. So had his novel, which he described to Clarisse Vigoureux as a didactic work— "a novel that is not a novel"—to be published anonymously under the title *Le Livre jaune*. His theme would be "the absurdity of the life and functions of the individual household considered as the unique social destiny of women." The story would begin with a marital dispute in which the husband complained about overcooked meat while the wife dreamed about attending a course of Fourierist lectures. Considerant made no great claims for this *bluette*, but he observed that by working on it during the day and on his "serious brochure" at night, he was learning how to write quickly.[8]

Two months later, at the beginning of March, Considerant was no longer talking about his novel and was scaling down the ambitious lecture tour he had discussed with Berbrugger. His health had been poor. He suffered from headaches and lethargy, and he complained about the lack of stimulation and "unbelievable sluggishness" in Salins. "My mother is always good and intelligent," he wrote, "but these people of Salins in general and my beloved uncles and aunts in particular are so limited and insufferable that I am on the outs with almost everyone." Still, he was encouraged by his progress on the brochure, which was now approaching book length. Previously, he wrote Clarisse Vigoureux, he had never been able to stick to long writing projects; he found them "difficult for my character, which doesn't like being tied down." But now he was enjoying the work, and it was going well.[9]

Throughout the spring and summer of 1834, Considerant worked at a fever pitch and in a state of mounting euphoria. In April he was still complaining about intermittent headaches, but he talked optimistically about raising money for a new journal to take the place of "our modest and solid *Phalanstère.*" He also reported that he had completed the first draft of his book. His friends Auguste and Mariette Thiebaud and Charlotte Bally had helped him copy the manuscript, and he was almost ready to take it to Besançon for printing. A few weeks later he wrote from Besançon that he was already correcting proof and reading passages to his friends: "People here like it. . . . They say: 'This is the book that we've needed.' It will be clear, easy to understand and to read. . . . Despite the carelessness of the writing, which is due to the speed with which I have been working, it is written with the contemporary reader in mind." Considerant wanted to be done with the book so that he could turn to other tasks: fund-raising for the journal, and organizing a system of correspondence to link Fourierists all over France.[10] In fact, the process of printing and binding lasted all summer, and with last-minute additions the printed text ran to well over five hundred pages. This was a lot considering his avowed aim to "give a fairly brief, clear, and relatively complete explication" of Fourier's theory—all the more so since this turned out to be only the first of three volumes. But *Destinée sociale* was certainly clear, and it was written with verve and enthusiasm.

Considerant brought the same enthusiasm to the book's distribution. When it came off Louis Sainte-Agathe's press in mid-September, Considerant drew up a "plan of attack" for contacting potential reviewers in Paris. With Just Muiron's help, he obtained prepublication pledges from thirty-five subscribers. He dispatched 150 copies to a dozen friends who had agreed to serve as his agents in provincial towns from Montbéliard to Bayonne.[11] Sales were relatively brisk, and the Breton Fourierist Théodore Pouliquen was speaking for many when he described the book as the best and most useful introduction to Fourier's thought. Considerant's colleagues were delighted; Fourier himself was not displeased; and sales did not suffer two years later when (to Considerant's delight) Pope Gregory XVI had it placed on the Index of Forbidden Books.[12]

In commenting on the first volume of *Destinée sociale*, the librarian Charles Weiss, a friend of Nodier and an influential figure in the cultural life of Franche-Comté, noted that the book was written with "a sufficiently remarkable talent" that Besançon's centrist journal, *L'Impartial* (edited by Just Muiron) could praise it "without compromising its party." Weiss added that the book nonetheless would not succeed in Franche-Comté, "a land of good sense in which systems are not accepted until experience has demonstrated their advantages." Weiss was exaggerating the conservatism of his compatriots: Considerant's list of subscribers included many members of the local establishment. It might be more accurate to say that *outside* Franche-Comté *Destinée sociale* met with considerable resistance from the *notables* and other influential members of society. However, the work did attract attention among the young and among those who were already to some degree alienated from the society and politics of the early July Monarchy. In the end it proved to be so much more accessible and popular than any of Fourier's works that there is more than a grain of truth in Hubert Bourgin's description of *Destinée sociale* as "the first exposition of Fourierism that counts in the history of ideas." [13]

II

Despite the success of *Destinée sociale,* the years 1834–1836 were difficult ones for the Ecole Sociétaire, as the Fourierists now called themselves. With the failure of the Condé experiment and the journal's collapse, the life seemed to go out of the Fourierist movement. This was also a difficult period for Considerant personally—a period of soul-searching and false starts. There were some memorable moments—a night of "luminous cosmogonical and religious conversation" in 1835, for example, when Considerant and his friends Désiré Laverdant, Charles Dain, and Eugène d'Izalguier glimpsed images of higher realms and experienced "the transcendent enthusiasm of high harmony." [14] But the question of Considerant's future kept intruding. Did he really wish to give up a promising military career to devote himself to a cause that many now regarded as hopeless? For a long time he was able to postpone a final decision by requesting renewed furloughs, but these became increasingly difficult to obtain. In the fall of 1835 Considerant's request was only granted thanks to the personal intervention of the minister of war, Marshal Maison, and a warm letter of recommendation from General Bugeaud. [15] Then, in February 1836, he was notified that there would be no more furloughs and that he could expect to be assigned to Bayonne on his return to the army. Now he had to make a choice. In the summer of 1836, Considerant submitted his resignation. Henceforth his own future was identified with that of the Fourierist movement. [16]

Considerant's main accomplishment during the mid-1830s was the publication of the first volume of *Destinée sociale.* This was only the first volume, though, and after the euphoria of September and October 1834, when he was distributing the book and drawing up his "plan of attack" for the conquest of the Paris press, he found it difficult to get back to work on the second volume. He also found it hard to get started on the fund-raising and other preliminary work for the new journal. As early as the spring of 1834, he was already fantasizing about the "brilliant editorial staff" he would gather and the money he would raise from friends in Franche-Comté. He was convinced that the journal would be launched "in a few months," but the months passed, and he kept running into obstacles. In the first place, not everyone shared his desire to produce a journal that would reach out to the general public. For Just Muiron, Alphonse Tamisier, and others, the most important function of the journal would not be to make "converts" but to promote discussion among the existing disciples.[17] Then, in the fall of 1835, with the passage of the notorious "September laws" on the press, censorship was tightened and the *cautionnement,* or deposit, required to start a paper in the capital was doubled. Considerant had to begin again the process of fund-raising. He found himself under increasing strain, and during the winter and spring of 1836 he was plagued by headaches and insomnia. His friends began to worry about a physical breakdown. They feared that in trying to organize the journal and act as leader of the Ecole Sociétaire Considerant had undertaken a task beyond his means.[18]

Despite his physical problems, Considerant did manage to produce two substantial pieces of writing in the winter of 1835–1836. The first was a long and fiercely provocative attack on Christianity and Christian asceticism, which he delivered as a speech at a historical congress held at the Hôtel de Ville in December 1835. In this speech, Considerant insisted on the distinction between the teaching of Jesus Christ and historical Christianity. "Unfortunately," he declared, "Christianity as it has existed in fact and in history has enunciated doctrines fatal to humanity, and since these illusory and fallacious doctrines lead in a direction opposed to that desired by Jesus, it is necessary to refute them if one seeks the same objectives as Jesus."[19]

In Considerant's view, the message of Jesus was a message of unity and love. "What did Jesus want?" he asked. "He wanted to unite people with each other, and to unite them all with God. Jesus wanted nothing else. As he said, 'Love God and your fellow man. That is all the law. It is the law and the prophets.'" What Jesus could not provide was "A VERITABLE MEANS of establishing the reign of love among men." It had been left to Fourier to discover such a means. If Jesus of Nazareth returned to earth today, Considerant asserted, "he would immediately make himself a disciple of Fourier of Besançon."[20]

Considerant's discussion of historical Christianity was no less provocative. He asserted that Christianity was "a religion of slaves made by slaves." The main concern of its theologians had been "to formulate the dogma that declares human nature impotent and depraved." This "perverse idea" was, according to Considerant, pagan in origin, "prior to Christianity," and "had concerned Christ very little." Christ had preached a "doctrine of love and charity," and it was only after the death of Christ—presumably in the writing of Christians such as Saint Paul and Saint Augustine—that the "older Eastern dogma" of innate corruption had "fatally slipped into Christianity."[21]

Considerant's argument that Christian dogma represented a betrayal of the teachings of Jesus was made largely in historical terms; it was in historical terms also that he concluded his speech. Arguing in a manner reminiscent of the Marquis de Condorcet that the whole history of human progress had been "accomplished through the negation of Christian dogma," Considerant described history itself as "the overwhelming struggle of the genius of humanity against the antihumanitarian dogma on which Christianity pivoted." Unlike Condorcet, however, Considerant recognized that the attempts of the human race to free itself from the shackles of Christian dogma had an inner as well as an outer dimension. The cause of progress, in his view, was "the permanent revolt of humanity against the Christian in the heart of the Christian."[22]

This speech caused an uproar. It was wildly applauded by what one journal described as a claque of "forty or fifty bearded young men," but it left most of the audience "stupefied." The organizer of the congress, the Christian socialist Buchez, refused to publish it or to permit any discussion of Considerant's positions. Catholic journals denounced it, and Just Muiron complained about Considerant's lack of prudence. Fourier himself wrote letters to the newspapers attempting to distance himself from Considerant. "I am not responsible for what I have neither said nor written," wrote Fourier. His theory was (in his words) "purely industrial" and had "no relation to the controversies of religious sects," which were "the seeds of civil war."[23]

Considerant tried to put a good face on all of this. He wrote Fourier that the free publicity would ultimately benefit the Ecole Sociétaire; and he published a letter in the *Journal de Paris* responding vigorously to the "odious attacks" of the Catholic *Gazette de France* "directed against me and against a doctrine that it calls Fourierism." Yet the net effect of Considerant's speech was to divide Fourier's followers and to compromise his doctrine in the eyes of the public. When the speech appeared in print a year later, a few disciples wrote Considerant to express their delight, but the more typical response was that of Hugon Reydor of Geneva, who wrote that it was "quite simply a blunder and a frivolous act."[24]

If the impact of Considerant's speech at the Hôtel de Ville was largely negative, his second substantial work of this period had little impact of any kind. This was a 150-page brochure published anonymously, *Nécessité d'une dernière débâcle politique en France.* This brochure was an attack not on Christianity but on all established political parties and on the whole tradition of political journalism that had developed in France since the fall of Napoleon. The brochure's aim was to demonstrate that the quarrels of monarchists, republicans, and partisans of the *juste milieu* were rooted in a misunderstanding of the possibilities of politics. The real aim of politics, Considerant argued, and the only appropriate starting point for an authentic political science, was the search for a common good. This search would have to be carried on in the realm of production, and it would necessarily involve experiments with various forms of economic association. The sterile conflict of political factions and "stupid chatter" of the existing political press could only delay the discovery of a theory of association consistent with the common good. After an extensive critique of political faction in general, and the Parisian political press in particular, Considerant concluded with a brief and, he hoped, tantalizing discussion of the theory of association proposed by the "Ecole ou le Parti Sociétaire."

When this brochure appeared in March 1836, Considerant wrote the Paris prefect of police, requesting permission to have it sold on the street in front of the Chamber of Deputies, the Chamber of Peers, and the Stock Exchange. He said his aim was to demonstrate that political quarrels were pernicious and that public energies should be brought to bear on "the agricultural and industrial questions that are the keys to wealth, well-being, order, and true liberty." He added that because he had attacked the political press of all parties, he had no hope of getting publicity for his brochure in the journals. Thus he was forced to sell it on the street and to adopt a "flamboyant" title. He assured the prefect of police that his quarrel was not with the existing government but with the whole system of party politics.[25]

Considerant's conciliatory words made little difference. His brochure passed unnoticed. Late in 1836 he published a second edition under a slightly different title, but by then he himself had lost interest.[26] For in July 1836 his journal finally began to appear. At the same time the unhappiness of many of the provincial disciples with his leadership of the Ecole Sociétaire culminated in the emergence of a dissident movement that began to challenge Considerant on a wide variety of issues.

III

Ironically, the first dissident was Just Muiron, Fourier's first disciple. As early as 1833 Muiron was filling his letters to Clarisse Vigoureux with complaints about Considerant's erratic work habits and nonchalant attitude toward administrative problems. "I am afraid," he wrote, "that our Victor may be completely unsuited to running a large operation, especially a journal." The methodical Muiron was particularly unhappy about Considerant's failure to draw up a set of detailed plans for the Societary Colony at Condé before seeking to raise money from the public. Muiron was also eager to see formal arrangements made to establish a correspondence network among isolated provincial disciples. The Fourierist movement needed a unity and cohesion, he believed, that Considerant was either unwilling or unable to give it.[27]

Early in 1835 Muiron submitted to Considerant and Clarisse Vigoureux a set of proposals for the revitalization of the Ecole Sociétaire. Apparently they took the form of a "draft circular" to be sent to all disciples, a letter designed to initiate a fund-raising campaign, and the establishment of a "Phalansterian correspondence," which would enable Fourierists all over France to keep in regular contact. Considerant had no time to give to Muiron's proposals. He sent back a long and testy reply reminding Muiron of everything he had done for the Fourierist movement over the previous eighteen months and asking Muiron, in essence, not to bother him with further suggestions. Muiron replied with a long letter of his own, striking a pose of injured innocence and insisting that he had not meant to criticize Considerant but only to help respond to the widespread "clamor and complaints" concerning "the state of torpor and inanity into which the Phalansterian group was plunged."[28]

A year later Muiron returned to the charge. In June 1836, after repeatedly chiding Considerant for his inactivity, Muiron drew up an elaborate set of statutes for a "Phalansterian Union," which would establish formal ties between Fourierists all over France. This Union would be hierarchically organized; its functions would include raising money to support Fourier and to finance a trial Phalanx; and its center would be located in either Paris or Besançon, depending on whether or not Considerant was willing to serve as its director. Muiron had his statutes privately published and then sent them out to a number of his oldest friends within the movement. In due course he received expressions of support from about forty of the disciples, including Charles Pellarin and Hippolyte Renaud in Besançon and large groups of Fourierists in Lyon and Strasbourg. Muiron also sent a copy to Fourier, asking for his opinion. "All your disciples," explained Muiron, "urgently feel the need of a bond between them, an affiliation that would make possible coordinated and unitary action."[29]

Fourier was not impressed by Muiron's proposal, which he dismissed as "extremely sterile." Considerant even less so. He wrote Clarisse Vigoureux contemptuously of Muiron's desire to "distribute colors and ranks" among Fourier's disciples and to "constitute a center of action in Besançon." He also apparently accused Muiron of "declaring war" on him and trying to undermine his efforts to rally support for the new journal, *La Phalange*, the first issue of which appeared on July 10.[30]

Muiron was not one to give up easily however. On August 14 he wrote a long letter to Considerant attempting to explain his position. Fourier's theory was "a faith," he argued, and no faith can endure without "an assembly of the faithful." Such an assembly had begun to take shape in 1832 and 1833 with the publication of *Le Phalanstère* and the *essai* at Condé. If these efforts had failed, Muiron wrote, it was because the assembly was not yet "sufficiently formally constituted." All the other Phalansterians were agreed on this. None of them, except for Considerant himself, could imagine it possible "to preach association without practicing it, insofar as this is possible in contemporary civilization." Muiron observed that the Phalansterian Union would support Considerant in his work on the new journal. "Only," he noted ominously, "it will express the wish, I presume, that your attacks against certain dominant prejudices . . . might take a more diplomatic form." Muiron added that he was preparing a circular to be distributed to all supporters of a Phalansterian Union "in order to inform them of your opposition to their desires and of how you intend to prevent their realization."[31]

This letter was more than Considerant could stand. He was exhausted by his efforts to bring out the first four numbers of *La Phalange*. Still, he dropped everything, and for "five days and nights" at the end of August he devote himself to writing what turned out to be a 123-page response to Muiron. Considerant wrote this letter "with a tired brain, with fever in my body, and with pain in my heart." His main point was clear enough: the attempt to define and codify all activities and relations within the Ecole Sociétaire would have a stultifying effect on the whole enterprise. It was both vain and dangerous, he argued, to seek "to constitute a union by an appeal, by a charter, and by statutes, before having taken the action capable of guiding and maintaining the union." Considerant believed that publishing the new journal and creating a lively group of Parisian Fourierists would ultimately do much more than drawing up a set of statutes to create a true union among Fourier's disciples. He criticized Muiron bitterly for his distracting barrage of "vain, tiresome, and inopportune" queries and criticisms. "For two whole years," he wrote Muiron, "you have not stopped wrangling, pestering, and bothering Madame Vigoureux and me [with your obsessions] without having produced an iota of productive accomplishments." Considerant concluded with brutal frankness, attributing Muiron's meddlesomeness to a general "incompetence in personal relations" that resulted from his deafness. "Just, you lack a sense. Unfortunately, you only have eleven passions. You are not a complete person, and despite your intelligence . . . you could not participate in the ranks of the active members of a Phalanx." [32]

At about the same time Clarisse Vigoureux wrote a long letter of her own to Muiron, making many of the same points more tactfully. Criticizing Muiron for having lent his name to the opposition to Considerant, she urged him to stop "plaguing" Considerant with unwanted advice and criticism. "Among all of us Considerant is the only person capable of championing our ideas effectively. I beg you . . . not to pester . . . this man who has burned his bridges and who is in the forefront of the struggle for the salvation of humanity." Recognizing that Muiron's interventions may have been prompted by the desire to regain a lost preeminence within the Fourierist movement, Clarisse Vigoureux assured him that his contributions to the movement would never be forgotten. Neither Muiron nor anyone else in the movement had a magnetism equal to that of Considerant. At the same time no one could forget the crucial role Muiron had played in befriending Fourier, seeing to the publication of his works, and initiating the first group of disciples to Fourier's science. [33]

Muiron was persuaded by Considerant and Clarisse Vigoureux not to pursue his proposal for a Phalansterian Union. On September 25 he somewhat grudgingly promised that he would send out no more circulars, and he informed his friend Hugon Reydor in Geneva that Considerant had "edified" him. This did not put an end to the movement of dissidence, however. For the problems Muiron had pointed out were real. Above all, Fourier's provincial disciples had a strong and unsatisfied desire to keep in closer touch with each other and with the plans and activities of the movement's Parisian leaders. As Wladimir Gagneur wrote to Considerant in August 1836:

> Give us some sign of life. At least tell us, or have someone else tell us, how many subscribers you have, what are your financial resources, your plans, etc. Just Muiron has good reason to associate us, because you must admit that the *Parisian monopoly* lords it over the poor provincials in every way. It's not exactly encouraging to be kept in the dark about your plans and your hopes. [34]

Throughout the fall of 1836, many other provincial disciples wrote Considerant in support of Muiron's proposal. Some of them were not aware that Considerant opposed it. Others knew but favored the proposal anyway. Still others supported Considerant but asked him to find his own way of giving substance to the idea of a Phalansterian Union. Finally, and particularly galling to Considerant, there were a few Fourierists—notably Brac de La Perrière, Morellet, and Hugon Reydor—who tried to compel Considerant to circulate among all the disciples a detailed justification of his own conduct and a precise explanation of his reasons for rejecting the idea of a Phalansterian Union.[35]

This last intervention was made possible because Muiron broke his promise of silence and told La Perrière about Considerant's confidential letter. Considerant soon discovered this. Immediately he dispatched a bitter letter to Muiron denouncing La Perrière as an "idle gossip" and an "intriguer" and raging at Muiron's duplicity or weakness. "Well, my dear Just, it was written that you would make me drain the cup down to the very last dregs. . . . It is always from you and your initiatives that misfortune and unhappiness come." Considerant proposed that he and Muiron jointly issue a circular letter giving the background of the dispute and announcing its resolution. Muiron would agree not to pursue his "untimely" proposal of a Phalansterian Union. On their side Considerant and "the Paris group" would create some kind of a center in the capital and would open a register of all people who wished "to give their active support to the effort of Phalansterian propagation and realization." This agreement was signed on October 10, 1836, and shortly thereafter it was apparently circulated among the disciples.[36] Having surmounted the first challenge to his authority as leader of the Ecole Sociétaire, Considerant was now, for a time, free to concentrate on the new journal.

IV

The first issue of *La Phalange. Journal de la Science Sociale* finally appeared on July 10, 1836. It was a substantial journal: each issue contained thirty-two double-columned pages, and the first issue included a feuilleton and rubrics on "politics" and "art and literature" as well as "social science." All of this reflected Considerant's desire to get beyond the sectarianism of *Le Phalanstère* and to create a popular journal that could mold public opinion. As he wrote early in 1836, he wanted a journal that would "grapple with contemporary questions" in politics, science, industry, and aesthetics. Eventually he hoped to supplement it with a monthly review devoted to longer doctrinal studies.[37]

Considerant's main problem in his efforts to find funding was that many

Fourierists had a narrower vision. Most of Muiron's wealthy friends, for example, wanted a journal that would avoid controversial political questions; Muiron himself kept arguing that the journal had to remain relatively bland and circumspect in order to find financial backers. Finally, Considerant did succeed in raising the money he needed to get the journal started. A 5,000 franc contribution from Clarisse Vigoureux was helpful, as were 2,500 francs from Frédéric Dorian and 1,500 francs each from Joseph and François Devay. Ironically, it was Just Muiron who proved to be Considerant's most valuable ally, raising 13,500 francs, more than half of the necessary 25,000 franc *cautionnement*, in loans from wealthy spinsters from Franche-Comté.[38]

La Phalange represented a compromise between Considerant's vision and that of Muiron and his friends. Despite Considerant's disclaimers, it *was* a sectarian journal, the principal aim of which was "the teaching of an organized science." Nonetheless, many of the disciples were delighted by it. Jaenger of Colmar praised its "openness and simplicity" and saw it as opening "a new period of progress" for the Ecole Sociétaire. "The first two numbers of *La Phalange* have fully satisfied me," he wrote. "We are done with the dogmatic and severe manner of the old *Phalanstère*." Writing from the heart of rural Brittany, Pouliquen of Landivisau was also happy about the new journal, "which we have been waiting for with such impatience." Given the shortage of printed matter of any kind in Brittany, he wrote, the journal was sure to be helpful in the work of propagation. Even this devoted follower of Fourier noted his friends' complaints about the journal's "lack of variety," the "dogmatic tone" of its articles, and the need for an occasional bit of levity, though. Others were harsher in their criticism. The museum director Constantin Prévost of Toulouse complained that *La Phalange* was so full of "bluster" that it was impossible to tell from reading it much about the real state of the Ecole Sociétaire. In a similar vein, the Polytechnicien Hippolyte Renaud reminded Considerant that in and of itself the journal did not satisfy the dissidents' demands for a center.[39]

Such comments did not trouble Considerant. He believed that the journal was reaching a wider and more sophisticated audience than its predecessor. "*La Phalange* is doing well in what's called the thinking world," he wrote. "It is read in Paris; it gets talked about; people agree on the talent of the editors and the scientific and social importance of the subjects treated." Before long, *La Phalange* might well attain a "unique position in the periodical press ... a philosophical standing analogous to that of the old *Globe*." And Considerant spoke of Fourier with cavalier, almost cynical detachment: "Père Fourier is fine. He has given us an excellent article for the next number. . . . Furthermore, you will find that articles by him, announced in advance and presented as extracts taken from the sanctuary, make a fine impression."[40]

Despite Considerant's optimism, the journal's first few months were difficult. It was often late; correspondence with subscribers and contributors was not maintained; and there was a lack of coordination among the principal collaborators. In founding *La Phalange*, Considerant had created a four-member editorial committee that was in theory responsible for the "laborious" work of revising and editing articles and handling editorial correspondence. In fact, Considerant did most of the work himself; and in a letter of August 5, 1836, he described himself as "overwhelmed" by work on the journal. The editorial committee did not function regularly because most articles were handed in too late for formal review. A proposed advisory committee for reading manuscripts never met. Considerant was, in any case, dubious about the value of such committees. He felt they were a waste of time, often serving as forums for "perfectly trivial discussions." In his view, the Ecole Sociétaire simply lacked "competent, trained, and tested" individuals who might work on the journal on a regular basis.[41]

During the first year of the journal's existence, Considerant continued to do the lion's share of the writing and editorial work. At the same time he was absorbed by many other activities. In December 1836 he gave a series of public lectures in Chartres, and in January 1837 he opened a weekly lecture series on "la science sociale" at the Athénée Royale in Paris. He also continued to work on the second volume of *Destinée sociale*. In the midst of all this Considerant had neither the time nor, apparently, the desire to honor his pledge to Muiron about creating a center that would coordinate the efforts of provincial Fourierists. In August 1836 he published an article in *La Phalange* suggesting that the journal, as a rallying point and a "central and unitary organ," already filled the functions of the center that Muiron hoped to create.[42] There was something to this. The offices of *La Phalange* on the rue Jacob quickly became a meeting place for Parisian Fourierists, and there were weekly dinners at the restaurant Tavernier in the Palais Royal. However, Considerant made no effort to establish a correspondence network among the provincial disciples. Nor did he encourage the efforts of Baudet-Dulary and Madaule to breathe new life into the colony at Condé. Thus, although nearly all the disciples regarded *La Phalange* as an important contribution to the revival of the Fourierist movement, there was some grumbling about Considerant's failure to consider other initiatives.

It was in reaction to this grumbling, and to the prodding of Just Muiron, that Considerant finally published an article in *La Phalange* in July 1837 announcing the opening of a fund drive to raise ten thousand francs to cover the cost of drawing up plans for a trial Phalanx. The response was enthusiastic: pledges totaling well over ten thousand francs were received in just a few weeks. Nevertheless, some disciples were unhappy about the fact that all the money was to be used simply to draw up plans and print a brochure. Others wondered whether this initial appeal was simply a delaying action on Considerant's part, in Emile Poulat's words "a bone thrown to the impatient." There was reason to wonder. For in acknowledging a contribution from a provincial disciple, Considerant wrote that money could be more usefully spent on the journal than on plans for a trial Phalanx, since "the trial still seems a long way off."[43]

By this time Muiron's criticism of Considerant was beginning to seem moderate. If his Phalansterian Union had gotten nowhere, other dissident groups had emerged. In Toulouse, Constantin Prévost announced the creation of a "Union Harmonienne," which, he claimed, had the support of Fourierist groups at Lyon and Bordeaux. Already in June Prévost had addressed an open letter to all Fourierists, denouncing the "sluggishness" of the movement and inaugurating a published exchange of letters that was to go on for several years as *La Correspondance harmonienne*. Seeking to create "closer spiritual ties" among the disciples, Prévost's initiative was something that Muiron had been advocating for over two years.[44]

Other dissidents were based in Besançon, where Dr. Edouard Ordinaire, a friend of Muiron's and the son of a childhood friend of Fourier's, took the lead in founding an Institut Sociétaire. This organization, whose directors also included Eugène Tandonnet, Henri Fugère, and Hugh Doherty, represented another effort to overcome the "sterile isolation" of Fourier's partisans. Bitterly critical of what they considered Considerant's arbitrary and authoritarian leadership, the founders of the Institut Sociétaire announced that only when links were established between the most isolated of Fourier's followers would the Ecole Sociétaire be "truly constituted."[45]

A final symptom of dissatisfaction within the Ecole Sociétaire came in July, when *La Phalange* published a notice concerning a "Société André" created by a commercial broker along ostensibly Fourierist lines. So many readers expressed an interest in this project, which they took for an officially sanctioned effort to realize Fourier's ideas, that Considerant was obliged to send out a special circular explaining that the only legitimate Fourierist effort of "realization" was the Societary Colony at Condé.[46]

The opposition to Considerant came to a head in the summer of 1837. In July the members of the Institut Sociétaire attempted to enlist Fourier's support. Fourier's initial response was encouraging. Although he had dismissed Prévost's Union Harmonienne as divisive, he agreed to cooperate with the organizers of the Institut Sociétaire and even to provide them with theoretical guidance. On July 20, however, when members of the Institut Sociétaire met with Fourier, he told them that he had changed his mind. Having discussed the matter with Considerant, Fourier now thought it best to bring the dissidents to a meeting with Considerant at which he, Fourier, would serve as mediator.[47]

The meeting took place on July 31. Fourier, who was in fact a dying man, did what he could to bring the two sides together. The dominant voice at the meeting was not his, however, but that of Considerant, who managed to pack the meeting with his supporters. Thus Ordinaire and his allies had to make their case before a largely hostile audience. Their main complaints against Considerant were that he was trying to do everything himself, that he lacked administrative skill, and that he had alienated many of Fourier's original followers with his brusque and dictatorial ways. Ordinaire maintained that he had always been a friend of Considerant and an "admirer of his perseverance and talent" and that he had long refused to listen to Considerant's critics. But experience had convinced Ordinaire that the critics were right, that Considerant was a poor administrator and organizer and not "sufficiently conciliatory to rally people around him." Tandonnet's criticisms were similar. Praising Considerant's gifts as a writer and his "great logical powers," Tandonnet maintained that "talent as a writer is not enough to direct a great movement." What was needed was to reorganize the Ecole Sociétaire in such a way that, while Considerant continued to edit the journal, the tasks of fund-raising and administration were placed in more capable hands. The journal would then become not merely an end in itself but rather "the center and pivot" of a whole range of activities, including an attempt at the "realization" of Fourier's theory.[48]

Considerant was unyielding. He rejected the proposed reorganization on the ground that among the Fourierists it would be impossible to find "six people capable of participating on a committee." He went on to contrast his own long-standing dedication to the movement with the dilettantism of his critics.

> On one side there is a man who for fifteen years has dedicated himself to propagating the doctrine, who has always been on the breach, who has sacrificed his captain's epaulets. That man, Messieurs, is Considerant, is me. On the other side there are a few people who have so far done little or nothing for the cause and who are protesting against me. The question is whom do you wish to follow.

Considerant invited the dissidents to work with him on his terms, adding that if they persisted in trying to create an Institut Sociétaire he would oppose them "with all his strength and with all the means at his disposal."[49]

Not long after this meeting, probably at Considerant's prodding and perhaps with his help, Fourier composed, or copied, a declaration expressing his full support for "the direction given to our propaganda by my disciple and friend, Victor Considerant": "I have never believed," Fourier wrote, "that it could be right and proper to establish another center of action than the existing center for which the journal *La Phalange* is the organ. . . . I strongly disapprove of any scission, and I invite all the partisans of my doctrine to rally around the work proposed by Considerant."[50] This declaration, which may in fact have been written for the dying Fourier by Considerant, was to be Fourier's last word on the dissidents. But it was not their last word, or Considerant's. In August the supporters of the Institut Sociétaire published a thirty-two-page brochure, *Aux Phalanstèriens*. Here they stated their views, described the regulations of the Institut Sociétaire, and summarized the discussions that took place during the meeting of July 31. A few weeks later Considerant and his allies published their own account of the meeting in a *Lettre confidentielle aux membres de la réunion du 31 juillet en réponse à une brochure intitulée "Aux Phalanstèriens."* Denouncing Ordinaire and his colleagues as schismatics, Considerant gave a full account of his own reasons for opposing the creation of "a Phalansterian society with statutes, affiliations, deliberations, diplomas, etc." His main point was that any premature attempt at formalizing the organization of the Ecole would only serve to promote self-absorption and intrigue. Far from strengthening the ties that bound the Fourierists together, such an effort would "excite rivalry, stimulate vanity, create friction and new obstacles." The real unification of the movement could only come, Considerant argued, through the absorption of the whole group in the work of community-building.[51]

V

Considerant's quarrel with the dissidents of the Institut Sociétaire continued into the fall of 1837. In September they published a *Réponse confidentielle* to his *Lettre Confidentielle* in which they called for the opening of a subscription to provide for Fourier in his old age. This was a disingenuous gesture since for many years Clarisse Vigoureux and Just Muiron had been discretely but effectively supporting Fourier. But Considerant and his allies did not have the opportunity to pursue the argument. For on October 10, 1837, Fourier died.

Fourier's death did not come as a surprise. For several months it had been apparent that his digestive system was breaking down, and then in September he suffered a stroke that left him partially paralyzed on the right side. By the end of September Fourier had virtually ceased to eat, and he refused access to his apartment to anyone but a cleaning lady who looked in on him occasionally. On the morning of October 10 she found him dead at his bedside. She called Clarisse Vigoureux and Considerant, who closed Fourier's eyes, arranged for the making of a death mask, and notified his one surviving sister.[52]

One consequence of Fourier's death was at least temporarily to mute the quarrel between Considerant and the dissidents and to give Considerant an opportunity to act as the unquestioned leader of the Ecole Sociétaire. It was he who organized the funeral ceremony held at Fourier's grave in the Montmartre Cemetery, and he who delivered the eulogy comparing Fourier's life and death to the coming and crucifixion of Jesus Christ. It was he who edited the black-bordered number of *La Phalange* that appeared immediately after Fourier's death with an account of his last days and a call for the collection of materials for an official biography. Finally, it was also Considerant who, just eleven days after Fourier's death, was named (along with Clarisse Vigoureux) joint heir of the large collection of unpublished manuscripts that Fourier had originally left to Just Muiron.[53]

In all of this there was little question about Considerant's right to assume leadership of the Ecole Sociétaire. A few dissidents did complain about the Catholic burial given to Fourier, but the greater number of Fourier's disciples spontaneously rallied around Considerant and looked to him to provide leadership following Fourier's death. "Henceforth it is on you that all our hopes rest," wrote one of them. "Now you are called, my dear Victor, to take over the legacy of Fourier," wrote another. "It is up to you to continue the great work of the master." The most complete expression of support for Considerant at this time, however, came from a group of disciples who saw him as the guardian of what they themselves referred to as the "orthodox" interpretation of Fourier's doctrine.

> Now that Fourier is no longer in our midst, it is of the highest importance to preserve the doctrine in all its purity, all its orthodoxy. Now Monsieur Considerant seems to us to be the disciple who has most carefully studied the theory and who knows it best today. Therefore we think that it is up to him to give shape and impetus to the Ecole Sociétaire.

The conclusion these disciples drew was that "the right to criticize the acts of the center should not be granted to other groups."[54]

Of course, the dissidents were not happy with this sort of language. One of them, Edouard Ordinaire, wrote a scathing attack of Considerant that included a parody of his "papal" pretensions: "I am to Fourier what Mohammed was to God, what Saint Peter was to Jesus Christ. I hold the keys to the Kingdom of Phalansterian Harmony. I am your pope." More typical of the views of Fourier's disciples, however, were the sentiments expressed by Jaenger of Colmar, who voiced complete support for Considerant and deplored the effect the schism was having on the Fourierists' efforts at outreach.[55]

In fact, the schism within the ranks of the Fourierist movement was far from over. It persisted well into the 1840s as various groups of provincial disciples continued to criticize Considerant for giving inadequate support to new attempts to realize Fourier's ideas, for failing to publish the manuscripts left by Fourier, and for his management of the journal, *La Phalange*. The periodical *Correspondance harmonienne*, which continued to appear for several years after Fourier's death, served as a rallying point for the dissidents, and in 1840 it was still publishing letters that characterized Considerant as a "trickster," the "pasha of the Ecole," and a "golden tongue with a grocer's soul."[56] In the mid-1840s a new cohort of critics emerged who focused for the most part on other issues, and by this time most (though not all) of the original dissidents had returned to the fold. Finally, many of them were won back by personal appeals from Considerant and by the movement's continued growth under his direction. Even the vituperative Edouard Ordinaire was reconciled with Considerant, and in 1844 Ordinaire could congratulate his former antagonist on the success of his new daily paper: "The influence of *Démocratie pacifique* spreads from day to day and wins over the most rebellious people."[57]

4

Marriage and Politics

On February 16, 1838, barely four months after Fourier's death, Victor Considerant and Julie Vigoureux signed their marriage contract. Witnessed by Julie's brother Paul, the contract specified that her mother was to provide a dowry of forty thousand francs, but that the dowry was to remain in Julie's control—it was not to become joint property.[1] Shortly thereafter, in a brief civil ceremony at the *mairie* of the Xe *arrondissement*, Victor and Julie became husband and wife. He was at that time twenty-nine years old, and he had, by his own account, loved her and been loved by her "for more than ten years."[2]

Why did Victor and Julie wait so long to get married? Even in a century famous for its long engagements, ten years was a long wait. There were no economic barriers since Clarisse Vigoureux was in a position to help the couple set up housekeeping at any time. The problem, by Victor's own account, was that he had lacked maturity. "I would have married her on graduating from the Ecole Polytechnique if I had felt myself mature enough."[3] For her part, Julie may have been unsure of Victor's love. According to Julie's cousin Clarisse Coignet, Julie's older sister Claire had been Victor's first love. After her death Julie, who was just fourteen years old, became Victor's confidante. "After having shed many tears together, they consoled each other, and little by little they became attached to one another by feelings that deepened as time passed and that led them eventually to marriage."[4]

What Clarisse Coignet's account leaves out is that, so far as one can judge from his early correspondence, Considerant initially had a far more intense relationship with Julie's mother than with Julie herself. Most of the letters he wrote ostensibly to both of them during his twenties seem actually to have been written to Clarisse Vigoureux; and in these letters he often referred to Julie as a "child." Julie might well have wondered just where she fit in—the more so since by all accounts Victor was a handsome and even "seductive" man.

In fact he did love her, and he rapidly came to depend on her. Her health was never very good, but early in the marriage it became clear that Julie's role would be to support her husband—to do everything possible to smooth his path and create good working conditions for him. The couple changed apartments often: not until they were both past sixty did they remain in a single apartment for more than a few years. Yet Julie always managed to make a nest for herself and her husband—to organize their lives efficiently, see to her mother's needs, and maintain quiet in the house when the nocturnal Victor was sleeping all morning after a long night of writing.

Julie's cousin Clarisse, who saw much of the Considerants during the early years of their marriage, described their life at this time as busy but remarkably harmonious. Julie's days were divided between her domestic responsibilities, her own work as a painter, and the entertaining she was obliged to do as the wife of the leader of the Ecole Sociétaire. Still she found time for occasional outings and trips to museums with her cousin. Clarisse Vigoureux, who was now living with Julie and Victor, spent long hours in her room, reading, writing, and dreaming. Victor, absorbed by the affairs of the Ecole during the day, often worked late at night on an article or correspondence. They would all come together over dinner, though, where the meals were frugal but the conversation lively, and where Victor reported on his struggles in the Fourierist cause. Much later Julie's cousin could recall the evening when Victor returned exuberant after a long talk with the novelist Alexandre Dumas. He said he was convinced that Dumas was now "three-quarters" converted to Fourierism. "I am afraid," observed Clarisse Coignet dryly, "that the fourth quarter never materialized."[5]

I

At the time of his marriage, Victor Considerant's career as a journalist, organizer, and activist lay largely ahead of him; his political views were to undergo major changes during the next dozen years. But he had already found his own voice as a writer. This is not a bad point, therefore, to pause in our narrative and try to get to know Considerant better. What sort of person had he become by his thirtieth year? How did he appear to others? What can we say about his inner psychological development?

The earliest known portraits of Considerant date from the 1840s. They show a tall, strapping man, erect in his bearing, full of vitality, with a direct, piercing gaze. He appears to be something of a dandy, carefully if not always conventionally dressed, and obviously proud of his ample *moustaches gauloises*. Acquaintances commented on his distinctive "presence" —his grace of movement and his brusque, soldierly manner. His handshake was firm and he looked people in the eye. He was also described as a voluble talker—a warm and persuasive public speaker and a lively, responsive, and tireless conversationalist.

To the American journalist Charles Dana, Considerant was youthful and athletic in appearance, about six feet tall, and lithe and nimble in his movements. His features were "rather large but still delicate and intellectual," and he had about him a "manly elegance" suggesting "activity and outdoor exercise rather than the unhealthy confinement of the man of letters." There was "ease and dignity and cordiality to his manner," which made him easy to get to know and to talk with. Dana was also impressed by Considerant's eloquence as a public speaker.

> His fine person, graceful manner and intellectual face, make it a pleasure to see him ascend the tribune. His voice, though pitched upon a rather high key, is rich and musical, and his elocution distinct and artistic. He speaks with facility and, as he grows excited by his subject, with eloquence. He addresses the intellect rather than the sentiments, but always with a richness of diction which gratifies the imagination.

Dana added, however, that Considerant was "not a popular speaker, and would convince a class of students or of intellectual men much more certainly than he would carry off the applause of a club."[6]

Dana's sketch is vivid but distant and a bit too respectful. Fortunately we have another, more intimate picture of the man—a nuanced, penetrating, and critical picture drawn by a woman who first got to know him around the time of his marriage. This was Julie's cousin, Clarisse Coignet (*née* Gauthier), who was to write the first biography of Considerant. Although never a "Fourierist" properly speaking, Clarisse Coignet was a steadfast friend of Victor and Julie, and she was able to appreciate his qualities without being blinded by his faults. Like others who knew Considerant as a young man, she insisted on his physical attractiveness, his "seductiveness." She described him as a tall, thin, and "supple" man with flowing chestnut hair and a "luminous glance." There was grace in his movements and a "natural elegance in his attitudes." He dominated his contemporaries, she wrote, by the simplicity of his bearing and "the sheer attractiveness of his nature." Coignet went on, however, to describe Considerant's caste of mind as "full of contrasts."

> The ability to generalize and to abstract, the taste for philosophy and science, were joined in him with the imagination of an artist and the enthusiasm of a believer. The scientific studies of his youth, and mathematics, which was especially appreciated then, turned him more to abstraction than to observation. Thus he espoused Fourierism somewhat in the manner of the old dialecticians who were more rigorous and skillful in their argumentation than certain of the correctness of their starting point. Instead of deriving his doctrine from human nature, he considered human nature in the light of the doctrine, completely missing the infinite complications, the spontaneity, the vanity, the contradictory motives that make it difficult to integrate human beings within any artificial scheme.

Coignet saw this blindness to human complexity as giving Considerant the fluency that made him a persuasive speaker. Once embarked on an argument or a speech before a sympathetic audience, he could rise to heights of eloquence, and "his sincerity, his warmth, his enthusiasm" would "carry away" an audience. Then came a gentle barb: "In the provinces especially he won ovations."[7]

Clarisse Coignet gives us the portrait of a man whose eloquence and "élan" were made possible in part by his intellectual dogmatism and his blindness to complexity. She also stresses his sheer tirelessness in argument. Noting that Considerant never lacked antagonists within the Fourierist movement, she describes him as someone who would defeat his intellectual adversaries simply by outlasting them.

> With his vibrant voice and passionate dialectic [Considerant] would dominate discussions and would finish by crushing his adversaries, if only by exhausting them. This spontaneous and youthful ardor, which could also be haughty and curt, would sometimes bring charges of despotism on Considerant. But . . . with Considerant doctrinal pride was so disengaged from personal pride that he was easily forgiven. Once an argument was over, his authoritarian bearing would vanish. He would become much less a schoolteacher than the servant of an idea, a worker alongside other workers, giving of himself unstintingly, without seeking personal triumphs or personal advantage.

Thus, in Clarisse Coignet's view, Considerant was at once intellectually despotic and emotionally generous. Tireless and uncompromising in argument, he was naive and effusive in his ordinary human contacts. "In personal relations," she wrote, "no one was more straightforward, more open, more cordial." He was childlike in his directness, his capacity for affection — and his lack of tolerance for the lies and stratagems of the adult world.[8]

Not everyone appreciated Considerant's simplicity and bluff directness. Some people found him overbearing. And his difficulties with dissidents within the Fourierist movement stemmed as much from personality clashes as from ideological differences. The deterioration of Considerant's relations with Just Muiron, for example, owed less to any disagreement concerning the interpretation of Fourier than to Considerant's disgust with Muiron's meddlesome carping and Muiron's resentment at Considerant's peremptory and cavalier dismissal of *all* his ideas. After Fourier's death the two patched up their relationship, but in their letters to Clarisse Vigoureux each kept complaining about the other: Muiron about Considerant's lack of tact and administrative skill, and Considerant about Muiron's sententiousness and narrow sectarianism. In the 1840s a new source of conflict emerged, as Muiron began to demand remuneration for the money he had spent publishing Fourier's works and helping support him during his last years. Considerant found these demands "shameful" and "unworthy" of Muiron. Others including Baudet-Dulary, Arthur Young, and above all Clarisse Vigoureux had made great sacrifices without complaint. Muiron, however, lacked their high-minded and self-sacrificing devotion to the cause. "He has always imagined that the propagation [of the doctrine] ought to be a lucrative affair for him." What Considerant found particularly galling was that Muiron himself was wealthy and thoroughly bourgeois in his tastes and aspirations. "We have no right," wrote Considerant later, "to give charity to the sole individual among us who has a personal fortune and whose only dependent is a natural daughter whom he recently married off to a rich man. He boasts about it. It's disgusting!"[9]

Despite his difficulties with Muiron, it is clear that Considerant had a remarkable gift for forming and maintaining friendships. Within the Fourierist movement he inspired particularly intense loyalty and admiration among those whom he had introduced to Fourier's ideas. "My dear Victor," wrote François Cantagrel in dedicating his first book to Considerant, "you initiated me into the societary theory. You guided my first steps in the study of this sublime science of which you are the most brilliant interpreter." Désiré Laverdant, who often disagreed with Considerant on political and religious matters, remained constant in his gratitude and affection for the man who, as he later put it, had rescued him from "the night of skepticism" by introducing him to Fourier's ideas. Considerant's greatest admirer within the movement, though, was the Polytechnicien Allyre Bureau. One of Considerant's earliest "converts" to Fourierism and one of the most dedicated and selfless members of the Ecole Sociétaire, Bureau always looked up to Considerant with the admiration of a younger brother. Considerant often took Bureau's friendship for granted and treated him cavalierly, but Bureau never wavered in his loyalty to Considerant, even when it meant sacrificing the well-being of his wife and family.[10]

Considerant had equally strong and lasting personal relations with a number of men who were on the margin of the Fourierist movement or whose active participation in it was short-lived. Some of these, like the Polytechnicien Alphonse Tamisier, were natives of Franche-Comté. Others, like the future minister Frédéric Dorian, the architect César Daly, and the Breton journalist Jules Benoît, had dabbled in Fourierism as young men but remained lifelong friends and admirers of Considerant. Considerant also maintained close ties throughout his life with several comrades from the Ecole Polytechnique who never shared his ideas but appreciated his idealism and candor. One of these was Michel Chevalier, who met with Considerant often and could write him with warmth and affection long after he had disavowed his own Saint-Simonian past.

What about Considerant's relations with women? Here the evidence is thin. We know that in addition to being sympathetic in principle to the emerging women's movement, Considerant got on well with a number of its most articulate representatives. Unlike many of his male contemporaries, he did not feel threatened or intimidated by the intelligence of a Flora Tristan or a Cristina Belgiojoso. We also know that he was considered a handsome and dashing man. He knew it, too. At the age of twenty he could write rather smugly of sweeping "the little peasant girls" off their feet at a summer fête at the Parc des Sceaux. Ten years later (a week before his marriage!) his friend Jules Benoît could tease him about his taste for variety in women. He does not seem to have been a Lothario. But we do know that during his long "engagement" to Julie he had at least one brief affair—with the self-taught seamstress Désirée Véret. It may not have amounted to much, but she remembered it vividly sixty years later.[11]

As a young man, Considerant was frequently invited out. From his first years at Paris, while a student at the Ecole Polytechnique, he was made welcome at Charles Nodier's salon at the Bibliothèque de l'Arsenal. Through the Nodiers he gained access to the Parisian world of arts and letters. In

August 1831 we find him, not yet twenty-three years old, dining at the Arsenal in the company of the poet Antoine Fontaney, the critic Sainte-Beuve, and Nodier's collaborators Alphonse de Cailleux and Baron Taylor. In March 1833 he turns up—along with Lerminier, Ballanche, Sainte-Beuve, de Vigny, and Baron d'Eckstein—at a reception given by the young (and still liberal) Montalembert. Ten days later he appears dressed as the dey of Algiers at the spectacular costume ball given for seven hundred guests by Alexandre Dumas with the collaboration of a group of artists including Delacroix, Barye, and Grandville. At the same time, and on a more regular basis, Considerant frequented the Sunday evening receptions held by Geoffroy de Saint-Hilaire in his apartment near the Jardin des Plantes, where "young writers, poets and artists" like David d'Angers, Alphonse Esquiros, Hugo, and Musset "mixed by candle-light with distinguished white-haired savants."[12]

Considerant retained his contacts with the fashionable world of arts and letters throughout the July Monarchy. His "sharply etched features" were often seen at the elegant salon of the playwright Virginie Ancelot in the Chaussée d'Antin, where he rubbed shoulders with legitimist journalists, Polish and Russian expatriates, and an odd assortment of dandies, deputies, and eccentrics. His contacts with the great literary giant of the period, Balzac, were apparently limited to two unsuccessful attempts to solicit contributions for *La Phalange* and *La Démocratie pacifique*. However, he established relatively close personal relations with two of the most popular novelists of the time, Alexandre Dumas and Eugène Sue, both of whom published fiction in Fourierist journals. Eugène Sue eventually became closely identified with the Fourierist movement. If Considerant never did manage to win over Dumas, the two remained friends. In 1843 we find them both invited to a dinner party at the home of their mutual friend Alexandre Bixio, where another guest, a still unknown diplomat named Camillo Cavour, noted with pleasure that Considerant "speaks with much energy against the radicals."[13]

Other literary acquaintances of Considerant included the poets Petrus Borel, Gérard de Nerval, and Leconte de Lisle. Nerval, who disparagingly referred to Considerant in 1850 as "merely a vice-prophet," the Omar to Fourier's Mohammed, was only a casual acquaintance.[14] But Leconte de Lisle, the future Parnassien poet, was for two years an active participant in the literary life of the Ecole Sociétaire. Between 1845 and 1847 he published more than twenty poems in the Fourierist journals, and he briefly served as literary editor for *Démocratie pacifique*. He was more exacting than Considerant on matters of style, however, and he soon got fed up and resigned. Already in 1846 he could describe Considerant and his associates as "the most honest and good-hearted members of the Parisian press" but also "the most ignorant of art." Leconte de Lisle cared enough about Considerant, however, to stay in touch after the latter's exile and to send him a copy of *Poèmes antiques* in 1852.[15]

Considerant's most significant literary friendships during the July Monarchy were with the poet Lamartine and the Italian patriot, Princess Cristina Belgiojoso. For a few years in the early 1840s Considerant and Lamartine were political allies, Considerant supporting the poet's attempts to create a new "parti social," and Lamartine giving his endorsement to Considerant's candidacy for elective office. More long-lived was Considerant's friendship with Princess Belgiojoso, who became well known in the 1840s for her beauty, her talent as a writer, and the intensity of her commitment to Italian unification. She became an ally to Considerant in his attempts to widen the audience for the Fourierist newspaper, *Démocratie pacifique*, writing articles, buying shares, and soliciting contributions for the newspaper from her friends, one of whom was Balzac. Considerant in turn came to her aid in 1845 by arranging for the purchase of some of her property in Lombardy when it was in danger of confiscation by the Austrian authorities.[16]

Normally gregarious, effusive, and even seductive, Considerant took pride in his relations with some of the best-known writers and artists of his time. One final facet of his personality, however, remains to be noted. As he grew older he became increasingly susceptible to long periods of withdrawal and depression, which sometimes alternated with interludes of euphoria and frenzied activity. It was during the winter months and long cold spells that Considerant most often fell into these periods of depression. Clarisse Coignet was a witness to more than one of them.

> How many times during the cold and rainy season I saw him stretched out on a sofa, sluggish, immobile, silently watching the smoke from his cigarette swirl in the air, or following the changing colors and the slow movements of a certain chameleon, his pet and his friend. A particular sympathy united them: the intense dislike of the cold.[17]

So Considerant's state of mind, his morale, and also his physical health, were directly dependent on the weather and the seasons. In times of warm, sunny weather he was normally vivacious, active, and optimistic about the world. But in the winter he was often sick, and he would sometimes fall into a state of lethargy so deep that not even Julie could do much to get him out of it.

This psychological portrait of Considerant (drawn from Clarisse Coignet's observations) is born out by his correspondence. Among his earliest letters, dating from his student years, we find numerous complaints about sore throats, fevers, headaches, and spells of lassitude and depression, in which both his physical health and his state of mind are clearly and repeatedly linked to the weather and the seasons. Throughout most of the 1830s and 1840s, Considerant led a life that often left him in a state of near exhaustion. For more than fifteen years his regular routine as a journalist kept him up much of the night working on newspaper articles, meeting deadlines, and maintaining a voluminous correspondence. Although he sometimes slept through the morning, he was constantly run down, and periodically he simply had to stop everything. Considerant's late nights and alternating periods of lethargy and concentrated work were more symptoms than causes of his problems, though. What ailed him, in modern terms, was a specific form of manic depressive illness. With his frequent winter fall into gloom and lethargy and withdrawal, he had many of the symptoms of what psychologists now describe as seasonal affective disorder. His susceptibility to this particular form of bipolar disorder was to last all his life, and it was to be marked by periods of winter depression and withdrawal at times so debilitating that Julie simply had to look after him.[18]

II

Julie Considerant was herself plagued by ill health—heart palpitations and respiratory problems—during much of her adult life. Victor's early letters to her are full of admonitions to avoid tiring herself, and she seems to have found both writing and travel difficult. On the other hand, she found painting a constant source of pleasure. Her work was good enough to win praise from accomplished painters like Jean Gigoux, and she managed to supplement the Considerants' income through the sale of gouaches, pastels, and cameos in malachite.

Everyone who knew Julie was impressed by her strength of character. She was not a striking beauty. Clarisse Coignet noted that even as a young woman she never had the delicate and harmonious features or the elegance of her mother. She did, however, have a warmth, a graciousness, and a quiet seriousness that many people found irresistible. Physically, Coignet described her as "a very Comtois type with prominent cheekbones and somewhat irregular features but tall, slender, shapely" with "lovely blond hair that softened the lines of her face." She had a lively, curious mind, a strong capacity for empathy, and vigorous inner resources.[19]

Some of Julie Considerant's inner strength may have come from the fact that she had to learn how to cope with the experience of loss at an early age. Her father died by his own hand when she was not yet five, and her older sister Claire died suddenly just ten years later, leaving her and her mother absolutely devastated. Clarisse Vigoureux never got over the loss of her eldest child. According to Clarisse Coignet, Claire's death threw her mother "into a state of despair," and this "weighed long and heavily" on Julie, who "often spoke of her youth as having been spent in a state of mourning and tears."[20]

For Julie the summers were happier times. Almost every year in July or August she and her mother and her brother Paul left their gloomy gray stone house on the rue du College in Besançon to spend a month or two at Montagney, the country estate of her mother's brother, Joseph Gauthier. By the early 1820s Joseph Gauthier had become a man of great wealth and status in Franche-Comté. The operator of several dozen iron foundries, Joseph Gauthier was a solitary, taciturn, and enormously hardworking individual who rose early, spent his days in his study or out inspecting his *forges,* and gave his wife a free hand in running the family estate. Clarisse Vigoureux, who was devoted to her brother, believed she understood him better than his wife did. She was probably right. For Virginie Gauthier (*née* Génisset) was a totally different person from her husband Joseph. Outgoing and talkative, she loved to entertain. Her daughter later recalled that in summertime there were often twenty places set for dinner at Montagney and that Virginie Gauthier never tired of organizing parties and outings—"trips by boat and by horse-drawn carriage with refreshments and often full dinners in the middle of the countryside, dancing parties, games, charades, speechmaking, readings, and above all plays, everything from Scribe to Victor Hugo, that the talented Madame Gauthier knew how to put on so well."[21]

It was during a visit to Montagney that Victor Considerant's relationship with Julie Vigoureux blossomed into love. In September 1828, just after taking his final examinations at the Ecole Polytechnique, he came to spend a few weeks at Montagney with Julie and Clarisse Vigoureux. Julie's sister Claire had died early the previous year; and Victor and Julie took long walks in a countryside suffused with memories of Claire. Victor wrote shortly thereafter that he *needed* to speak with Julie about her sister and that he felt Claire's presence almost palpably as that of a "divine influence" enveloping him and Julie and her mother. "I saw her everywhere," he recalled. "In the fields . . . in the air, I heard her voice." Julie, whose sense of loss was unremitting, kept asking, "Why did she leave us?" Victor did his best to explain, with the help of Fourier's theories of immortality and metempsychosis, that Claire was still with them, and watching them, from a higher and happier place. So they consoled each other; and as they did so, the bonds between them deepened. "I only desired one thing," he wrote, "and that was for my soul to join with that of Julie." Finally, on the night before Victor left, he and Clarisse Vigoureux had a long talk; and it appears from a somewhat cryptic letter written by Victor the next day with "all your words of yesterday ringing in my heart" that Clarisse Vigoureux had brought him to the recognition that his long-standing affection for Julie had become love.[22]

Victor and Julie apparently considered themselves to be engaged to be married from this time on. Of course Julie was just sixteen years old; and Victor, who turned twenty in October 1828, was not to consider himself "mature" enough to marry for another ten years. During the first years of their long engagement, if that's what it was, Julie must have been well aware that Victor's first love had been her sister and that his relations with her mother were, at the outset, both more intense and more adult than his relations with her. Gradually, though, she acquired self-confidence, becoming first an equal partner in the relationship and eventually the stronger partner in the marriage.

Like Victor, Julie had the gift of friendship. In the Archives Nationales there is a huge collection of letters addressed to her over half a century by her childhood friend Justine Demesmay. They show her ability to inspire and maintain an extremely close friendship with someone whose life experiences and attitudes were radically different from her own. She also had warm and rich relations with women of greatly differing ages. Aimée Beuque, a contemporary of Julie's mother, once wrote Julie that she cherished her friendship "because the immense difference in our ages has never mattered to you." Julie was also a sister both to her contemporary Marie Nodier and to her cousin Clarisse, who was eleven years younger.[23]

Both Victor and Julie adored children, and one of the great disappointments of their life together was that they did not have children of their own. They tried, and it would seem from veiled references in their correspondence that Julie may have had a miscarriage early in their marriage, and that she blamed herself for "not having had confidence" in Victor sooner.[24] They eventually became reconciled to childlessness, and during their travels in the 1850s and 1860s they seem to have found surrogate children wherever they lived—notably in Barvaux, Belgium, in the early 1850s, and in San Antonio, Texas, in the late 1860s. In San Antonio they virtually adopted as their daughter a young girl named Christine Bruck, whom they taught French and who remained in contact with them long after their return to France.[25]

Both Victor and Julie knew how to talk language that children understood. One of the most touching letters Victor ever wrote was an evocation of what life in the Phalansterian merchant marine might be like, addressed to the ten-year-old son of his Belgian friend Philippe Bourson. For her part, Julie always took pleasure in the company of children and brought such gentleness, tact, and insight to her relations with them that Marie Nodier could call her "the mother of all children."[26]

III

Considerant's marriage did not take him away from the life of the Ecole Sociétaire. His resignation from the army in 1836 had of course represented a choice to devote himself full time to the affairs of the Ecole. Considerant was able to live in a way consistent with this choice, however, largely because he married a woman who shared his commitment. In 1842, when it seemed that he would have to take a job outside the movement in order to support Julie and her mother, Julie adamantly rejected the idea. "Don't you see, your whole life ought to be dedicated to the cause," she told him. "I would go hang myself right away if I thought that I was leading you astray."[27]

Following his marriage, Considerant's absorption in the activities of the Ecole Sociétaire only increased. In 1838 and 1839 he did the bulk of the writing and editorial work of *La Phalange*. He also played a leading role in the social activities of the Ecole, holding meetings and receptions at the offices of *La Phalange* on the rue Jacob, and presiding over Wednesday evening dinners at a restaurant in the Palais Royal. Long afterward, a participant in these dinners recalled the atmosphere of informal camaraderie that Considerant managed to create.

> We would meet around six o'clock in the galérie d'Orléans of the Palais Royal. From there we would go to the restaurant Tavernier, run by a man from Arbois, where a large room was reserved for us in the back of the restaurant. Anyone who had simply been introduced by a comrade was welcome to take his place around the table, where a very simple dinner was served at a cost of two francs a person. Victor Considerant took his place at the head of the table and generally kept the conversation moving along. With his erect bearing, his long red mustaches, his equable and intelligent face, he put everyone at ease. The

conversation turned not on politics but on the progress of the Ecole Sociétaire, on our plans for the future and our needs of the moment.[28]

Evidently Considerant's leadership of the Ecole Sociétaire was now taken
for granted—at least by the Parisian Fourierists.

The two years immediately following Considerant's marriage were a
difficult period both in his own life and in that of the Ecole. The bitterness
left by the schism of 1836–1837 lingered, and the *Correspondance harmonienne* founded by the dissident Constantin Prévost had degenerated
into a vehicle for what one of Considerant's allies described as "arrogant
posturing." The Ecole was also plagued by financial problems: the journal
was losing money, and a year after Fourier's death his funeral and burial
expenses had not yet been paid. Ordinarily Clarisse Vigoureux would have
helped take care of such debts, but owing to business losses suffered by her
brother, she was no longer able to contribute much. Thus in September 1838 Considerant had to make a series of embarrassed personal appeals
for funds to wealthy friends of the Ecole.[29]

Considerant's personal problems in the years 1838 and 1839 were
closely related to the difficulties facing the movement as a whole. The
struggles with the dissidents had left him bitter and depressed. "I've had to
put up with worries and expenses and miserable displays of human vanity
instead of the aid and succor I was expecting," he wrote Pierre Paul Jaenger
of Colmar. He claimed that the experience had cost him both his health and
his confidence in human nature. Even more upsetting were personal attacks from people within the Fourierist movement whose egoism made it
impossible for them to comprehend a disinterested or generous act. "With
people like that," he wrote, "you are either a lunatic or a golddigger. They
cannot understand anything that is noble and beyond their reach. It is always a petty or trivial motive, such as they themselves have in their hearts,
that they take for the cause of acts that they cannot otherwise comprehend." These people were whispering that Considerant's "phalansterian
zeal" was feigned—merely a mask that he had worn while pursuing Julie
Vigoureux's fortune. What they didn't know was that, in marrying Julie, he
had insisted that her dowry remain in her hands.[30]

Considerant's refusal to lay claim to Julie's dowry was a gesture made in
good faith. Still it is clear that his marriage was in other ways financially
advantageous to him. For one thing, it enabled him to begin to think of
running for elective office. Under the July Monarchy the right to stand for
election to the Chamber of Deputies was limited to men over thirty who
paid at least five hundred francs a year in taxes. It was possible, however,

for candidates to make special arrangements to meet the tax requirement. In 1831, for example, Etienne Cabet's election to the Chamber was made possible by the transfer to his name of property actually owned by a friend of his Parisian patroness. It appears that Considerant benefited from a similar arrangement in 1839 and that his initial forays in electoral politics were made possible first by a grant of property from Clarisse Vigoureux and later on by similar grants from several wealthy ironmasters from Franche-Comté.[31]

For some time prior to his marriage, Considerant had been receiving financial support for his Fourierist activities from Clarisse Vigoureux and possibly also from a group of ironmasters known to her and to her brother Joseph Gauthier. In 1836 she contributed 5,000 of the 25,000 francs necessary as a *cautionnement* for the journal *La Phalange*. At the same time her son Paul had written a dozen *maîtres de forges* in the Jura asking them to subscribe to the journal. Two years later, when Considerant turned thirty, he wrote his friend Frédéric Dorian exultantly that, as the possessor of a notarized delegation of property from his mother-in-law, he was now eligible to stand for the Chamber of Deputies and that he had learned of a possible vacancy in Dorian's own electoral college of Montbéliard.[32]

IV

Parliamentary elections under the July Monarchy were normally intimate affairs where a few hundred wealthy electors in each district gathered to listen to the candidates, to drink, dine, gossip, bargain, and finally vote. The leading candidates were generally local *notables*, and the atmosphere was one of conviviality laced with intrigue. Local prefects and subprefects frequently attempted to "manage" elections, but as both Balzac and Stendhal showed in their fictionalized accounts of elections under the July Monarchy, this was not easy to do in districts where the wealthiest property owners were both independent and influential. It was even harder to do on those rare occasions (like the election of 1839) when political debate focused on national, rather than local, issues.[33]

The elections of March 1839 have been described as "the most bitterly fought of the July Monarchy." They pitted the conservative Molé government against a coalition including the two arch rivals Guizot and Thiers, the moderate reformer Odilon Barrot, and the legitimist Berryer. Both sides used every available means of pressure and persuasion. On instructions from the Interior Ministry, prefects dismissed office holders known to support the Coalition, and the government made full use of the subsidized press. Special election issues of *Le Journal des débats* and *La Presse,* both of which received money from the government's *fonds secrets,* were circulated throughout France as ministerial manifestos. In these newspapers the Coalition was accused of unleashing "the spirit of revolution" and of menacing the Charter of 1830 in the name of Henri V or Brutus. "Having legalized anarchic passion," thundered the *Journal des débats,* "it remains for them to unleash it upon your property, your industries, your families."[34]

On its side the Coalition, which cloaked its own conservatism in radical rhetoric, attempted to mount a coordinated campaign. It formed committees, held rallies, and published pamphlets attacking the "ministry of lackeys" and its "pusillanimous" foreign policy and comparing Louis Philippe with Charles X and Molé with Polignac. It sent out a circular letter to officials all over France warning them that support of the ministry might jeopardize their future. In a number of cases Coalition supporters also used, or at least tolerated, physical intimidation, encouraging crowds to attack prefects and government supporters.[35]

Victor Considerant threw himself into this election campaign. He attended meetings, gave speeches, and got endorsements. Imitating the strategy of the major candidates, he published a special issue of *La Phalange* that included a manifesto to be circulated among electors. In this manifesto, "Peace or War: To France and to the Electors," Considerant denounced the Coalition as an anomalous assemblage of incompatible elements intoxicated by their own bellicose rhetoric and united only by their desire to humiliate the king and overthrow the Molé government. Staking out an independent position for himself as a "new man" who stood outside the "dangerous rivalries" of the past, Considerant attacked the whole tenor of political discussion in France. What relation could there possibly be, he asked, between the prosperity and happiness of nations and "the narrow ideas and vain passions that have been stirring things up for so long in our legislative assemblies"? There was nothing to hope for from "the cloudy, pretentious, and puritanical phraseology of Monsieur Guizot" any more than from the sonorous and empty abstractions of the republicans or from "the tricolored eloquence of Monsieur Thiers," who "sprinkled the Chamber with his bellicose images." Spades and plowshares and the tools of the forge created the wealth of nations, and in the modern world these should be given the honors that past ages extended to the instruments of war. Why waste time on petty parliamentary intrigues, wrote Considerant, when we should be increasing the productivity of our fields and factories, developing the sciences and the arts, giving work to the unemployed, and creating a decent life for those in need?[36]

Considerant's only problem in running for election was deciding where to be a candidate. His first thought was to run in the *arrondissement* of Poligny, where he was well known. But Poligny already had a deputy, a professor of physics, Claude Pouillet, who had no intention of stepping down. Considerant also explored the possibility of presenting himself at Colmar, where he had numerous friends and allies. Though few of them were electors, he went there anyway—only to discover that the reelection of the incumbent deputy, Golbéry, was viewed as certain. A local journalist noted that Considerant's "sudden appearance at Colmar" had "surprised everyone" and that this "self-proclaimed defender of popular interests" had "inundated" the town with copies of his special issue of *La Phalange*. Fortunately, observed the journalist, the electors of Colmar had too much good sense to be taken in by this outsider's "pretensions": they recognized his candidacy as a ministerial ploy to try to erode the support of a pro-Coalition deputy.[37]

It was at Montbéliard that Considerant mounted his most serious effort. There the incumbent deputy, Silas Tourangin, had apparently decided to withdraw, thus creating what Considerant regarded as a golden opportunity. Throwing himself into the fray, he dispatched a volley of letters to Frédéric Dorian and other influential friends. He obtained letters of endorsement from Michel Chevalier and others. On her side Clarisse Vigoureux wrote letters, paid visits, and lobbied in support of her son-in-law's candidacy. Considerant soon learned that Silas Tourangin had not withdrawn and that most of the local *notables* whom he had hoped to win over were committed to Tourangin. Still his hopes had been raised, and in late February he drew up a special electoral manifesto and traveled to Montbéliard to participate in the electoral meetings. Since Tourangin was a supporter of the Coalition, Considerant angled for the endorsement of the prefect and the government. Apparently he got it. On election day, March 2, a pamphlet appeared ridiculing the candidacy of "Considerant the phalansterian [who is] today the candidate of the ministry and the prefecture at Montbéliard." Considerant himself took an upbeat view of the situation. On March 1 he wrote Julie that he had "maneuvered masterfully" to create a situation where, if Tourangin failed to win an absolute majority on the first round, he could present himself as a compromise candidate.[38]

In fact, Tourangin won easily. Announcing his defeat to Julie, Considerant attributed it to spitefulness on the part of his enemies, "the Tourangistes."

> It became a matter of vanity and cabalistic intrigue. These last few days
> when my candidacy became serious and acquired supporters, the Tou-
> rangistes got scared and began to act with incredible maliciousness. . . .
> They ridiculed my mustache and the Phalanstery, and finally I finished
> with 21 votes. Silas [Tourangin] had 103 and Bourgon 46.

Considerant consoled himself with the thought that his twenty-one votes
were cast by electors whose "intelligence and superiority" were uncon-
tested and that "the more intelligent Tourangistes" were prepared to support him when and if Silas Tourangin resigned.[39]

In the aftermath of Considerant's electoral defeat, an astute family
friend wrote Julie Considerant that she could not understand why Victor
had stood for election at Montbéliard "where he had no chance" rather
than Colmar or Poligny, where he was known. She observed that Victor did
not yet understand how much work it took to get elected deputy. "You have
never mixed electoral porridge," she commented wryly, adding that she
hoped Victor wasn't too discouraged. He wasn't. He was already looking
forward to the next election. "I am no more of a deputy now than I was before," he told Julie, "but I am deputyable."[40]

In barely a year, however, Considerant's political future was to be called
into question. His wife's uncle, Joseph Gauthier, was obliged to declare bankruptcy, and with his bankruptcy, the fortune of Clarisse Vigoureux, which
had permitted Considerant to stand for election, vanished into thin air.

V

By 1830 Clarisse Vigoureux's brother, Joseph Gauthier, had become known
in Franche-Comté as the "Napoleon of the ironmasters." He had won this
reputation by building up an empire of some two dozen ironworks, which
was at its height the largest metallurgical enterprise in Franche-Comté.
Specializing in the production of iron wire, Joseph Gauthier's forges were
all of the old-fashioned wood-burning kind. This was not surprising, given
the abundance of forests in the department of Haute-Saone, where most of
the ironworks were located. What *was* distinctive about Joseph Gauthier's
way of doing business is that, unlike other ironmasters in Franche-Comté,
he did not own the forges that he ran. Rather, he leased them. As Jean-
Claude Dubos has shown in his masterful study of the Gauthier family fortune, Joseph Gauthier chose not to tie up his capital in land and buildings.
By leasing his ironworks, he was able to run more of them—and to expand
his empire more rapidly—than if he had purchased them outright. What

he does not seem to have considered was that when bad times came, he might need something else beside his reputation and skill in order to obtain credit. The purchase of a few ironworks would have slowed the expansion of his empire, but it would have given him collateral in time of need.[41]

The cause of Joseph Gauthier's downfall was twofold. He was, first of all, one of many casualties of a general crisis in the metallurgical industries that made itself felt beginning in 1837. But Joseph Gauthier's problems were compounded by the fact that at just this time he was attempting to introduce new production techniques—notably the use of green, undried wood—which made his iron harder to market. As a result, in 1838, with the slowing of demand, he lost 600,000 francs; and the following year his losses reached a million francs. Paul Vigoureux, who had been employed by his uncle since 1834 as a traveling inspector, was one of the first to recognize how bad the situation was; in 1839 he advised his mother to withdraw from the partnership with her brother. Paul proposed that he, his mother, and his other uncle, Claude-François Gauthier, form a company of their own. After some hesitation, Clarisse Vigoureux decided to stay with Joseph.[42]

Although Joseph Gauthier was not a man who permitted intimacy, his sister Clarisse had always admired and even idolized him in a sense. She also trusted him completely, never questioning his business judgment or asking for an accounting of his handling of her money. Following her husband's death, she had entrusted him with the management of her fortune and her children's inheritance, but the partnership between them had never been formalized. Joseph Gauthier had simply added his sister's money to his own capital without giving her or the children anything resembling collateral. As Paul Vigoureux wrote long afterward, Joseph Gauthier could have guaranteed the security of his sister and her children simply by buying a particular piece of property in their names. This was not in keeping, however, with the business practices of a man who "like all kings, thought only of himself."[43]

Clarisse Vigoureux and her children needed no guarantees as long as Joseph Gauthier prospered, but by the fall of 1840 his situation had become desperate. A host of creditors were threatening him with legal action, and his debts approached half a million francs. (Interestingly, and despite his subsequent denials, one of the creditors who took legal action against Joseph Gauthier and helped drive him into bankruptcy was Paul Vigoureux.) For a time Gauthier appears to have hoped that wealthy friends of Considerant would loan him the money he needed to avoid bankruptcy, and on November 7 Considerant did write Joseph Gauthier's banker that he was having some success in securing loans for the Maison Gauthier, but by then it was too late. On October 31 Joseph Gauthier had to stop payment on his debts.[44]

On December 19 a family gathering took place at Besançon. Considerant attended, representing both his wife and his mother-in-law. The day before the meeting he wrote them that neither he nor Julie's other uncle, Claude-François Gauthier, had any real idea of the state of Joseph Gauthier's finances, but he was hopeful. "It seems that the inventory will show a favorable balance, and that most of the creditors are willing to wait." A week later he remained optimistic that a friendly settlement could be reached. In fact, Joseph Gauthier's creditors had lost patience. They descended on him, and on January 20, 1841, he was officially declared bankrupt. Julie's fortune and that of her mother were gone.[45]

Bankruptcy proceedings continued through the spring and summer of 1841. They were particularly time-consuming because Joseph Gauthier's holdings were widely dispersed and had never been properly inventoried. In the meantime Considerant took stock of the situation. Realizing that he was now the sole means of support for both his wife and his mother-in-law, he considered the possibility of returning to the army engineering corps. One well-meaning friend wrote Julie that Victor should offer to write for the conservative *Journal des débats;* she had been told that the *Débats* paid ten thousand francs a year. More seriously, Victor considered the possibility of returning to the Ecole Polytechnique to take a part-time job as its librarian. He knew that the job was open and that by tradition it usually went to a graduate of Polytechnique with literary qualifications. Thus he sent a formal letter of application to the commander of the Ecole. In a more personal letter to one of the commander's colleagues, he described his state of mind following Joseph Gauthier's bankruptcy.

> We have lost our fortune—*completely.* The fortune of my mother-in-law and my wife, which was considerable, has been lost, down to the last centime, in Monsieur Gauthier's industrial disaster. . . . This ruin wouldn't make much difference to me, because it is not my nature to worry about money. But you can imagine that the situation of my mother-in-law and my wife . . . has left me in a state of cruel anxiety. Of course I am able to hide my worries, but you will understand that I cannot conceal from myself just how precarious my position is. . . . Thus I am seeking a position that would give me a *minimum* and would secure the existence of those whose fate is linked to mine.

The position at the Ecole Polytechnique was not offered to Considerant. Nor did he attempt to reenter the army. In the end he did not have to find a paying job outside the Fourierist movement. Instead, he soon began to draw a salary of six thousand francs a year from the movement itself. This was enough for him to support Julie and her mother in comfort if not luxury.[46]

In due course Clarisse Vigoureux received a modest inheritance from her second brother, Claude-François Gauthier, who died in 1850. Thus, prior to their emigration to America, Victor, Julie, and Clarisse never lived in conditions approaching penury. Still, Joseph Gauthier's bankruptcy forced them to lower their expectations and took away the economic security that Clarisse's fortune had provided. For Clarisse herself the loss of this fortune was a devastating psychological blow. Having been a major source of support to the Fourierist movement, she could not reconcile herself to being supported by others. Thereafter she spent much of her time in her room, withdrawn and silent. "She never complained," recalled Clarisse Coignet much later, "but her worried features, and sometimes a painfully hidden sigh, betrayed the inner burden she was bearing." For Julie's brother Paul, Joseph Gauthier's bankruptcy was also a calamity. He was to spend the rest of his long life bemoaning the loss of his inheritance, blaming others, and seeking to reclaim—from his mother, his sister, and his brother-in-law— bits of the fortune of which he felt he had been unjustly deprived. What is more significant for us is that Victor and Julie were *not* devastated. Neither of them succumbed to bitterness or self-pity. The loss of Julie's mother's fortune did not in any way alter their feelings about her, each other, or the world.[47]

VI

The cessation of Clarisse Vigoureux's financial support was a blow to the Fourierists. For more than a decade Madame Vigoureux had played a crucial role in subsidizing the movement. She had helped support Fourier during his last years; she had provided a large part of the funds for the publication of the first two Fourierist journals; and she had given Considerant the guarantees that had enabled him to quit the army and devote all his energies to the movement. After 1840 she was no longer able to do any of this. Still the movement survived. For just as the Maison Gauthier was falling into bankruptcy, a new benefactor appeared on the scene—a benefactor able, at least for a time, to subsidize the Ecole Sociétaire more lavishly than Clarisse Vigoureux ever had.

This new benefactor was a rich English expatriate named Arthur Young, who made contact with Considerant in the spring of 1840. A resident of Antwerp at the time, Arthur Young had been introduced to Fourier's ideas by the Belgian Fourierist Zoé Gatti de Gamond. He is best remembered as the sponsor of the abortive Fourierist experiment at Cîteaux in Burgundy in 1841 and 1842. His principal desire from the outset of was to subsidize an experiment in applied Fourierism. Initially, Considerant managed to persuade him that no such experiment could succeed without first strengthening the Fourierist journal and articulating a system for the "propagation" of the doctrine. Thus, in June 1840, Arthur Young made a verbal commitment to contribute 350,000 francs to the Ecole Sociétaire over the next few years.[48]

As it turned out, Arthur Young was not able to honor his pledge in its entirety. Still, by November 1841 his actual contributions already totaled 230,000 francs. This was enough to give the Ecole Sociétaire a financial security it had never previously enjoyed. Young's support also made possible four significant changes in the organization of the Ecole. The first was the creation, as of June 15, 1840, of a joint shareholding company "for the propagation and realization of the Societary Theory" under the direction of Considerant and Amédée Paget. According to its statutes, this company had two goals: the "propagation" or spread of the doctrine; and its "experimental realization" through the creation of a model community. A second change made possible by Young's largesse was the conversion of the journal *La Phalange* into what Considerant described as a "quasi-daily" paper. Previously published just twice a month, it began to appear three times a week as of September 2, 1840. A third change was the payment of an annual stipend of six thousand francs to Considerant for his work as director of the journal and leader of the Ecole Sociétaire. The final new development in the life of the Ecole was the transfer of its offices—and of Victor and Julie's residence—from their relatively modest quarters on the rue Jacob to an elegant and far more spacious *hôtel* at 6, rue de Tournon. This move, which took place at the beginning of September 1840, opened a new chapter in the life of the Ecole Sociétaire.[49]

PART II

Socialism

5

Journalist and Lecturer

Although the 1840s began badly for Victor Considerant, this was to prove the great period of his life, his "marvelous decade." Forced by Joseph Gauthier's bankruptcy to find new sources of financial support for his movement, he did so. In the process he and his colleagues created an elaborate organization—a shareholding company, a publishing house, a network of provincial bookstores and lending libraries, a stable of lecturers, and a daily newspaper. The cornerstone of it all was the newspaper. Founded in August 1843, *La Démocratie pacifique* was one of the first socialist dailies; and its creation changed the character of what Considerant and his colleagues had come to call the Ecole Sociétaire. The Ecole never entirely lost its sectarian ambiance, but during the 1840s the narrow group of disciples became a broadly based social movement.

Considerant's life during the 1840s was completely bound up with this effort of outreach. He lectured widely on Fourierism; he published numerous popularizations of Fourier's thought; he participated in a host of fund-raising activities. Continuing to run for political office, he was finally successful in 1843. Most centrally, though, he was involved in the day-to-day work of getting out a daily newspaper.

I

The July Monarchy marked a turning point in the history of French journalism. During this period something resembling modern mass journalism began to take shape. The most significant development was Emile de Girardin's creation of *La Presse* in 1836. This was a daily paper that cost just forty francs a year—half the customary price—and derived much of its revenue from advertising. Other Paris dailies soon adopted Girardin's formula; between 1836 and 1845 the circulation of the twenty principal Paris dailies doubled, from 73,000 in 1836 to 148,000 in 1845.[1] At the same time, as competition for readers increased, new features like the serial novel were introduced, and the *fait divers* became a more significant part of each day's "news."

These developments influenced Victor Considerant's thinking about the role of journalism in the propagation of Fourier's ideas. In creating *La Phalange,* his intention had been to produce a literary and philosophical journal that would shape contemporary opinion as the original *Globe* had done in the last years of the Restoration. In fact, *La Phalange* never came close to conquering the influence or the audience that Considerant hoped for. Circulation remained low, and few publishable articles were submitted by anyone outside the small group of Parisian Fourierists. In April 1837 Considerant cut the number of issues from two to just one a month. Still, the number of subscribers never rose above 1,300. In order to create the illusion that the journal was being read outside the movement, Considerant and his colleagues had to distribute copies gratis to libraries, reading rooms, and other journals.[2]

In 1838 and 1839, most of the writing and editorial work for *La Phalange* had to be done by Considerant himself and just one colleague, Julien Blanc. There was simply not enough money to commission articles or to reimburse other colleagues for time devoted to the journal. This problem was alleviated in 1840 thanks to the generosity of Arthur Young; and in September 1840 *La Phalange* became a "quasi-daily paper" appearing three times a week instead of twice a month. In announcing the change, Considerant wrote that the new *Phalange* would be "as varied and complete" as a daily newspaper and that it would reproduce the deliberations of the legislative bodies and high courts while "keeping its readers informed about all the interesting developments in the domains of social economy, domestic and foreign politics, literature, the arts, the sciences [and] philosophy." *La Phalange* would thus "take the place of a daily newspaper."[3] This was wishful thinking. Nonetheless, September 1840 did mark a turning point in Fourierist journalism. After that date the circle of contributors to *La Phalange* widened appreciably; the range of articles broadened; and the journal took on a new character. For the first time, an effort was made to address contemporary political and economic questions and to suggest Fourierist perspectives through the analysis of crimes and court cases and other "calamities of the present social system."

The transformation of *La Phalange* from a bimonthly journal to a "quasi-daily" was followed in August 1843 by the establishment of a real daily, *La Démocratie pacifique*. The new name, which everyone could understand, was meant to signify the end of Fourierist sectarianism and the desire to produce a journal that would be "accessible to everyone" and "not only to the initiates of a school." Of course, the new newspaper never rivaled *La Presse* or *Le Siècle*, but its circulation did go as high as 2,200, and its creation was in a significant sense made possible by the innovations of *La Presse* and *Le Siècle*. In its first two weeks of publication, *Démocratie pacifique* carried ads for insurance companies, seltzer waters, skin preparations, cures for gout and rheumatism, a hair darkener, and Michelet and Quinet's new book, *Des Jésuites*. It also ran its own feuilleton and covered crime under the special Fourierist rubric "faits de subversion." In addition, it carried stock exchange quotations and theater listings and in many other ways mimicked the larger, more widely read dailies.[4]

In its content *Démocratie pacifique* was resolutely contemporary. It ran articles on the debates in the Chamber of Deputies, on the Irish question, on strike movements in the building trades, and on the salt tax. Although Considerant was listed as chief editor, he no longer had to put the journal out single-handedly. In fact, much of the day-to-day responsibility of seeing each issue through the press was assumed by François Cantagrel, who ordinarily served as managing editor. This gave Considerant more time for writing and also for the extensive speaking tours that he undertook in the mid-1840s. His own contributions to the journal covered a wide range of topics. He became increasingly critical of the "sad comedy" of French domestic policies under Guizot, and by 1845 he was outspoken in his denunciation of "the horrors" of the French war of conquest in Algeria. He was also deeply engaged, as was Clarisse Vigoureux, by the Poles' struggle for emancipation from Russian rule. He similarly supported the demands for home rule and freedom of worship of the Irish, who "belong to the British Empire by the same right that Greece belongs to the Ottoman Empire."[5] But his favorite topic was the press itself; and from 1843 to 1847 he wrote dozens of articles, generally polemical in tone, on the misdeeds and venality of the Parisian press—the "fawning" of the *Journal des débats*, the "pasquinades" of *La*

Presse, the stridency of *Le National,* the "cynicism" of Granier de Cassagnac's *Globe* and the Thiersist *Commerce,* and the "sterile and revolutionary democracy" of *La Réforme.*

To make a profit during the July Monarchy, a daily newspaper needed about 4,000 subscribers—3,000 simply to cover costs. Throughout this period barely a third of the two dozen Paris dailies had enough readers to make even a small profit. The others required outside aid. In the case of proministerial journals, this aid often came from the government's *fonds secret.* An opposition journal, on the other hand, had to have a patron or a group of wealthy supporters. Thus Raspail's *Réformateur* (1834–1835) was financed by the republican comte de Kersausie, and in Macon the wealthy Lamartine paid 15,000 francs a year out of his own pocket to subsidize *Le Bien public.*[6]

Arthur Young played the role of patron for *La Phalange* in September 1840, when it began to appear three times a week. By 1843, however, when the *Phalange* gave way to the daily *Démocratie pacifique,* Young's money had been spent, and Considerant and his colleagues had to find some other way of financing the new daily newspaper. They established a joint-stock company, the Society for the Transformation of *La Phalange* into a Daily Journal, which was constituted on June 10, 1843. The company was endowed with an elaborate set of statutes specifying the voting rights of shareholders while giving Considerant full authority in editorial matters.[7]

Considerant hoped that, after a few transitional years, *Démocratie pacifique* would yield a profit. Thus he presented the new daily journal to Fourierists as an attractive investment. Many believed him, and by the end of 1845, 336,000 francs' worth of shares had been sold. Unfortunately, neither Considerant nor anyone else had anticipated just how costly the production of a daily journal could be. Figures for 1845 show that expenses for that year totaled 250,000 francs. Receipts from the sale of subscriptions and individual copies (104,000 francs) and from advertising (8,500 francs) came to less than half this sum. There was no way the difference could be made up out of the interest on the money invested by the shareholders.[8]

So early in 1846 Considerant and his colleagues took another tack. Arguing that their journal was "not a speculation like all the other contemporary journals" but rather "a work of great social charity," they appealed to their readers' generosity. On February 7 a letter went out asking for pledges to a "Societary Fund" (*Rente sociétaire*). It asked that every partisan of Fourier's ideas make a relatively modest monthly payment to the Ecole Sociétaire. If 1,500 Fourierists each contributed 7 francs a month, the annual income would reach 126,000 francs. This would be enough to put the journal out of danger. In addition, the Societary Fund would serve as a powerful form of social cement within the movement. "We live in a corrosive milieu," ran the letter, "a milieu hostile to any form of organization. The Fund is the cement that must unify, join, and associate all the molecules of the moral being which calls itself the Ecole Sociétaire." Those who contributed to the Fund would receive without charge an irregularly published newsletter, the *Bulletin phalanstérien*, which would enable members of the Ecole to keep in close contact with one another.[9]

The response to this initial appeal was encouraging but far from sufficient: after three weeks 437 individuals had pledged 38,760 francs. Thus, on March 4 the directors sent out a second appeal, warning that if pledged annual contributions to the Fund did not reach a total of 100,000 francs soon, the publication of *Démocratie pacifique* would have to cease. This threat was greeted sarcastically by other journals—notably *La Presse*. But it worked. The goal was almost met in a few weeks, and by the end of June 1,440 contributors had pledged 98,689 francs. Of course, money pledged was not money collected, and within a year the Fourierists would be complaining about "the difficulties inherent in a system of collection that involves roughly 24,000 payments each year." But *Démocratie pacifique* survived.[10]

II

Démocratie pacifique was the most ambitious and widely influential of all the Fourierist journals. Still, it was just one element in what Considerant described as "a whole system of techniques of propagation." This system also included other, more specialized journals. There was the theoretical journal, *La Phalange. Revue de la science sociale*, which appeared monthly and bimonthly between 1845 and 1849 and was intended to "give the Ecole a new impulsion toward the regions of science."[11] Long theoretical articles by the disciples were published in *La Phalange*, but its most important function was as a medium for the publication of manuscripts left by Fourier. There was also the *Bulletin phalanstérien*, sent out at no charge to contributors to the Societary Fund beginning in July 1846. This newsletter, which continued to appear irregularly until April 1850, dealt with the inner life of the Ecole and included summaries of meetings, financial statements, and special reports to shareholders. A third publication of a very different sort was the *Almanach phalanstérien*, issued each year between 1845 and 1852. Designed to popularize Fourier's ideas among peasants and workers, these almanachs were successful beyond all expectations. The first, the almanach for 1845, sold 9,000 in the first two weeks after publication and

22,000 copies in all. Thus, as Jules Duval put it, "the new gospel of association" was carried "into huts and palaces alike."[12]

In addition to its periodicals, the Ecole Sociétaire had its own publishing
house and bookstore, the Libraire Sociétaire. By the mid-1840s their list
was extensive. It included not only new editions of Fourier's writings and
Charles Pellarin's widely read biography of Fourier but also influential popularizations of Fourier's ideas such as Hippolyte Renaud's *Solidarité* (1842)
and François Cantagrel's *Le Fou du Palais Royal* (1841). Renaud's book was
their best seller, having sold over 7,000 copies by 1845. The bookstore also
carried the works of friends and fellow travelers such as Eugène Sue and
Flora Tristan. A special effort was made to reach the poor: the Librairie Sociétaire's catalogue of publications regularly listed over twenty works at a
price of one franc or less.[13]

Considerant's *Destinée sociale*, which went through three editions by
1848, contributed to the popularization of Fourier's ideas, but Considerant
also published numerous brochures and pamphlets intended to convey the
rudiments of Fourier's theory to a wide audience. Some of these brochures
were extracts from earlier works: the *Petit cours de politique et d'économie
sociale à l'usage des ignorants et des savants* (1844), for example, was
taken from Considerant's *Débacle de la politique en France* (1836). Others,
such as the *Exposition abrégée du système phalanstérien de Fourier* (1845),
which had sold 2,131 copies by 1847, summarized lectures given by Considerant. All these works could be purchased not only in Paris but also in
the provinces and even abroad through a network of agents in over forty
cities and towns. The volume of sales rose from an annual 10,000 francs in
1843 to almost 60,000 francs in 1846.[14]

The Fourierists spread their "new gospel" not only by print but also by
oratory. By the mid-1840s Considerant and Victor Hennequin were making regular speaking tours of the provinces, seeking both to awaken interest in Fourier's ideas and to strengthen the commitment of those who were
already interested. And every year on Fourier's birthday, a banquet in Paris
was the occasion for speeches and for dozens of toasts. These banquets began modestly as extensions of the Wednesday evening dinners. Soon, however, they attracted hundreds of participants and were moved to a large
rented hall on the rue Saint-Honoré, the Salle Valentino. By the mid-1840s
banquets were being held all over France. Finally, on April 7, 1847, Fourier's seventy-fifth birthday was celebrated in thirty-four French cities and
towns (also New York City, Rio de Janeiro, and Mauritius). At Paris
"nearly a thousand" people gathered at the Salle Valentino to toast Fourier,

Poland, and the emancipation of women and to eat at tables representing each of the thirty cities that had contributed most to the Societary Fund.[15]

The physical center of all this activity was the Fourierist headquarters in Paris, which moved three times during the 1840s. Originally located on the rue Jacob, the Fourierists moved in August 1840 to the more spacious quarters of an old townhouse at 6, rue de Tournon. This *hôtel* provided ample room for a printing press and the journal's editorial offices; there were also living quarters for Victor and Julie and a study for Victor, as well as an elegant salon for large receptions. A visitor described the new headquarters:

> Considerant had rented a big apartment, an old townhouse on the rue de Tournon. . . . Each week the Wednesday dinner was still held at Tavernier's restaurant; but after dinner people moved on to the rue de Tournon, and the evening finished up in the salons of that old *hôtel*. On the ground floor Considerant's study opened out onto the large salon, which was dominated by [Jean Gigoux's] fine life-sized oil portrait of Fourier. It was there, in the midst of clouds of tobacco smoke—because Considerant's only weakness was that to the end of his life he was an inveterate smoker—that the big-wigs of the Phalansterian School held their meetings.[16]

For more than three years this *hôtel* on the rue de Tournon remained the heart of the Fourierist movement. During that time the Wednesday evening receptions became a relatively well-known Parisian social event, attracting artists and writers like Lamartine, Dumas, and Sue, as well as expatriate intellectuals like the German radicals Moses Hess and Arnold Ruge.

For reasons unknown—probably as an economy measure—the Ecole Sociétaire moved into more modest quarters on the rue de Seine in January 1844. In making this move the Considerants traded their elegant lodgings on the rue de Tournon for a sixth-floor apartment. Julie's cousin, Clarisse Gauthier, often visited them there; and long afterward she recalled the warmth of their welcome and the pleasure she took spending mornings talking quietly with Julie while Victor, who often worked late into the night, was still asleep.

> The salon . . . lacked fine furniture, but was large, as is often the case in old dwellings, and full of keepsakes and tastefully arranged art objects: flowers in a vase, bronzes, statuettes, portraits. It was my cousin [Julie] who arranged and took care of all this, because the one servant had enough to do with the heavy cleaning. . . . When Julie's work was done, she would settle down at her easel or workbench and begin to paint a watercolor or else carve a medallion or a brooch in malachite

representing the head of Fourier. This was to be sold for the benefit of the Ecole. "It's my contribution," she would say.

In her memoirs, Clarisse Gauthier also recalled the Wednesday evenings, when the salon on the rue de Seine would come alive.

> In the evening . . . the doors would open and the salon would fill up. The receptions were entirely simple: conversation and a cup of tea. Alongside the members of the Ecole would gather the celebrities of the day, eccentrics of all kinds, prominent people, foreigners, people curious about the leader whose fame was spreading in the outside world. Lively discussions would break out, sometimes between two adversaries . . . sometimes in the fashion of a tournament in which many people would speak, one after another, with Victor always taking the lead. Sometimes the talk would be less sustained and would be carried on in smaller, more intimate groups. But the conversation would always focus on moral and social ideas.[17]

So, the Wednesday receptions lost none of their vitality with the move to simpler quarters.

The last and most splendid of the domiciles of the Ecole Sociétaire was located at 2, rue de Beaune, with another entrance on the quai Voltaire. Situated just across the Seine from the Tuilerie Palace, this was an elegant townhouse, the Hôtel Mailly-Nesles, which became the headquarters of the Ecole and the Considerants' official residence in late September 1846.[18] Visitors were impressed. "You enter by a vast gateway as if you were going into some baronial chateau," wrote Charles Dana in 1848.

> You cross the broad paved court and are in the publication office, which is a scene of business, where four or five persons are constantly occupied; connected with that are some half dozen different apartments. There is the private room of the editors where the work is done; joining that is a large room of a more public character where you see any of them you wish for, and where you are almost sure to find someone writing letters or looking at a book. Next is the library where you find a complete collection of the publications of the School, fortified by scientific and other works of all sorts; farther on is the drawing room where the weekly reunions are held; it is very spacious [and] handsome. . . . The series is closed by the reading room where you always find the journals of the day and generally some half dozen gentlemen discussing them.

The courtyard of the building included a garden that Dana found impressive.

The garden, though not a large one, seems to contain everything delightful. Beds of flowers, graveled walks, thick shrubbery, green turf, tall old trees with most grateful shade, and a swing, leaping bars, etc. for the lovers of gymnastics. You can read, or walk, or talk there as securely as if you were in nature's most retired nook, and never once imagine that you are in the midst of Paris. At evening it is very pleasant to be there: you will generally encounter one or two of our workers taking a moment's rest, and perhaps an Association from the country come up to see the movement in Paris. You are free there from all restrictions, and you can walk by yourself and imagine yourself at home again.[19]

Charles Dana was not the only American to visit the rue de Beaune in 1847 and 1848. Others included Albert Brisbane, the Boston businessman James T. Fisher, the Quaker abolitionist Rebecca Buffum Spring, and the Transcendentalist intellectual Margaret Fuller. Fisher shared Dana's appreciation of the building, the elegant garden, and the "determined-looking" Fourierists, and Rebecca Spring was long to remember the warmth of Julie Considerant's welcome. Margaret Fuller, however, was less pleased by her visit to the rue de Beaune. "The Fourierites . . . are terribly wearisome here in Europe," she wrote in May 1847. "The tide of things does not wash through them as violently as with us." They were too caught up "in the treadmill of the system." Still, she added, "they serve this great future which I shall not live to see."[20]

III

If the written word was the principal means by which the Fourierists spread and fortified the faith, another was the spoken word. Imitating the Saint-Simonian "missions" of 1831 and 1832—the speaking tours by which the "fathers" of the Saint-Simonian Church had attempted to inspire their followers—Considerant, Jules Lechevalier, and Adrien Berbrugger had set off on their own lecture tours during the fall and winter of 1833. In the course of this first "campaign" Considerant discovered that he was indeed a gifted and persuasive speaker. A few years later, when the Ecole Sociétaire was in a position to expand, Considerant set out on a series of speaking tours in the provinces. In 1840 and 1841 he lectured at Versailles, Dijon, Macon, Cluny, and Lyon. In Strasbourg in 1842, after arousing interest in Fourier in a talk at a scientific congress, he went on to give a "course" of six lectures at the Hôtel de Ville. In 1845 he traveled through the north of France, lecturing at Saint-Quentin, Reims, and Mézières on a tour that culminated with an enormously successful series of seven lectures in Brussels. In 1846 he toured the Swiss cantons of Vaud, Neuchâtel, and Geneva, giving well-attended lecture series in Lausanne and Geneva and meeting with active groups of Fourierists in Locle.[21]

Almost everywhere Considerant was warmly received. In some cases, like his lectures at Lille in June and July of 1846, admission was by invitation only, and his main contacts were with local elites or, as the *Journal de Lille* put it, with "men whose theoretical studies [and] thoughtful disposition fit them for the examination of social problems."[22] More often Considerant's lectures were open to the public and attended by large and enthusiastic audiences. Generally he gave half a dozen lectures, presenting the main outlines of Fourier's system and concluding with a session entirely devoted to questions from the audience. At the end of the series a banquet was often held in his honor.

Considerant's audiences consisted largely of well-to-do professional people—lawyers, doctors, teachers, army officers, and journalists, with a sprinkling of students and (especially in industrial centers like Lille and Mulhouse) industrialists and businessmen. In French-speaking Switzerland, however, Fourier's ideas had a following among watchmakers and other artisans. For this reason, and despite Considerant's insistence on his fundamental moderation, he was on one occasion the object of an order of expulsion by the authorities of the canton of Neuchâtel. Significantly, this order, which was issued in the wake of the Genevan revolution of October 1846, was slow in being implemented, and Considerant managed to enlist the support of the French foreign minister—none other than François Guizot—in protesting it.[23]

At the end of his life, Considerant often looked back nostalgically on his lecture tours of the 1840s. He was then at the height of his powers as a speaker, and he almost invariably managed to establish a good rapport with his audiences. They found him eloquent, and local papers abounded in tributes to the "clear, rapid, elegant, and spirited exposition of Monsieur Considerant" and to "his remarkably fluent and lucid delivery." His greatest gifts were clarity and his obvious sincerity, his ability to convey to sympathetic audiences a sense of his own conviction. He was neither trenchant nor witty; according to Clarisse Coignet, he lacked "esprit" as a lecturer. But his "sincere enthusiasm" could inspire audiences. His conviction gave him authority; and wherever he started a lecture series, he often concluded it by filling the largest auditorium in town. Such was the case in 1846 in Geneva, where the *Journal de Genève* devoted a long article to Considerant.

We find in the disciple of Charles Fourier the traits of both the soldier and the apostle. . . . His delivery has nothing pretentious about it. He doesn't care at all about oratorical forms; his speech is not at all studied. He is sufficiently in command of his science to be able to dispense with the rhetorical coloring that too often conceals sophisms. The apostle is evident in the verve and animation of his language and even in a certain volubility. Too many convictions fill this heart and this mind for him to be held back by conventional rules.

The journal went on to assure its readers that if Considerant repeated himself, he did so "without tiring his audience," and that he was "precise and clear above all."[24]

Considerant's greatest success as a lecturer came in Brussels, where in October and November 1845 he gave a series of seven lectures to an audience of over a thousand. On this occasion cabinet ministers, deputies, generals, and high government functionaries all came to hear him speak. His Belgian audience was impressed, as were audiences in France, by his fluent and unaffected manner of delivery. What particularly appealed to the Belgians, though, had more to do with substance than with style. This was his explicit disavowal of republican sympathies and his emphasis on the role that could be played by the upper classes and by established governments in the implementation of Fourier's ideas. Considerant was known to be sympathetic to the July Monarchy—had he not dedicated *Destinée sociale* to Louis Philippe?—and he was also on record as repudiating Jacobin doctrines of popular democracy and territorial expansion. In the newly independent Belgian monarchy, this was just what most members of the establishment wanted to hear from a French social reformer.[25]

In Brussels, as in Lyon and Reims, there already existed a significant group of local Fourierists prior to Considerant's lectures. The group in Brussels included the brothers Félix and Alexandre Delhasse, the brothers Colignon, the journalist Philippe Bourson, and other lawyers, professors, and army officers. But Considerant's success in Brussels was due not only to the efforts of the organized Fourierist group but also to his close personal relations with two of the most influential figures in Belgian public life, Charles Rogier and Edouard Ducpétiaux. Charles Rogier was at a young age one of the architects of Belgian independence. A man of unusual cultivation, a friend of Vigny, Sainte-Beuve, and Michel Chevalier, Charles Rogier became in later life the epitome of the limits of Belgian political liberalism. In the crisis of 1848 he did as much as anyone to resist reform and to save the monarchy. Initially, however, when Considerant first got to know him, Charles Rogier was a man of wide horizons and sympathies.[26]

Long afterward, Considerant recalled their first extended contact, his two-week visit to Rogier at the governor's palace in Antwerp in 1838 or 1839.

> About a dozen years ago I spent two weeks with you, in the manor house you occupied as Governor of Antwerp. In our eighteen-hour conversations by the fire I came to know you intimately. You were then *un homme de coeur*. You were moved by the noblest, truest feelings. You had an admirable understanding of the vanities, the foolishness, and the follies of the contemporary world. You understood the critical state of the world, the imperious needs of modern society, its odious aspects, the urgent necessity of its transformation in a *democratic and social* direction. . . . You spontaneously assured me that if you were to return to power it would only be to begin the great work of social transformation by organizing, under the disguise of another name, a veritable Phalanstery for the families of the workers and employees of your country's railroad system.

Considerant kept in touch with Rogier throughout the 1840s, occasionally poking fun at his friend's pomposity and regretting the withering of his socialist impulses. Still, it is probable that in 1845 Rogier's friendship helped Considerant get a sympathetic hearing from representatives of the highest strata of official Belgian society.[27]

Considerant's other important Belgian connection was the humanitarian social reformer and prison inspector Edouard Ducpétiaux. Ducpétiaux was a wealthy intellectual who began at an early age to write prolifically on the problems of poverty and criminality. His preoccupation with social reform led him eventually to a kind of social catholicism that many Fourierists found distasteful. But in the 1840s he was attracted by Fourierism, and his correspondence with Considerant and François Cantagrel is full of avowals of indebtedness to the Fourierist movement and comments about his own efforts to disseminate Fourierist literature in Belgium. Many of these letters reflect the political timorousness of even "advanced" Belgian thought at this time. In July 1843, for example, Ducpétiaux solemnly advised Considerant not to name his new daily journal *Démocratie pacifique*. "The word 'democracy' can frighten people," he wrote, "even if one adds to it the epithet 'peaceful.' The mere word will suffice to get your journal banned in most German and Italian states." In other letters Ducpétiaux was disarmingly generous in speaking of his debt to Fourier. In sending a copy of his nine-hundred-page treatise *De la condition physique et morale des jeunes ouvriers et des moyens de l'améliorer* (1843), he wrote:

> I have sown here and there a few views of the future, a few aspirations toward an entirely new order of things. These views and aspirations I

owe to the Ecole Sociétaire. My plan of reform is thus, properly speaking, only a transitional project. Unable to gain acceptance for the heroic remedy, I have had to limit myself to proposing palliatives. . . . But I have never lost sight of the final goal toward which, like you, I am aiming.

Until 1848 Ducpétiaux continued to pay tribute to the Fourierists and their "heroic remedy." His enthusiasm waned rapidly, however, after Considerant and his colleagues identified themselves wholeheartedly with the February Revolution and the republic that grew out of it. Other early Belgian Fourierists—notably Félix Delhasse and Hippolyte Colignon—kept the faith, though, and were to remain close to Considerant for years to come.[28]

IV

In addition to his journalistic work and lecture tours, Considerant had one other major preoccupation in the 1840s: electoral politics. He believed that by running for public office he could both draw attention to Fourier's ideas and dissipate the cloud of prejudice and misunderstanding that surrounded them. His abortive candidacy for the Chamber of Deputies in 1839 only served to whet his appetite for public office. In July 1842 he presented himself once again as a candidate for the Chamber of Deputies, this time in the Xe *arrondissement* in Paris. When other, better-placed candidates emerged to challenge the ministerial incumbent, Considerant desisted—but not before publishing his own electoral circular, soliciting (and receiving) the support of Lamartine, and delivering a forceful attack on the Guizot ministry at a meeting of the Electoral College.[29]

According to Considerant's friends, the net effect of his brief candidacy in 1842 was entirely positive. Désiré Laverdant wrote that Considerant's gifts as a speaker, his "vigor" and "forcefulness" in discussion, and his ultimate willingness to step down in favor of another candidate had served to "erase all the ordinary confusions" from the minds of electors. "They know that we are neither republicans nor Saint-Simonians nor communists nor enemies of property. They know that we are entirely independent of parties and devoted to ideas of glory and national honor as well as peace and to ideas of progress as well as moderate conservatism." Considerant's own assessment was just as upbeat. "Let our friends know," he wrote Julie, "that I am now a sober and reliable politician, that my candidacy, my speech to the electoral college of the Xe *arrondissement,* and my disinterested conduct have won me considerable support." Considerant looked hopefully to the future. He thought it "probable" that he would be elected to the Conseil

Général of Paris in the next elections and that this would strengthen his position for a future candidacy for the Chamber of Deputies.[30]

In November 1843 Considerant ran for office again. This time his objective was indeed to win a seat on the Conseil Général representing the same Xe *arrondissement* of Paris. The election "campaign" consisted primarily of a series of public meetings, where the candidates presented themselves and their views to the wealthy Parisians who were the electors of the Xe *arrondissement*. (This Left Bank district included the Quartier des Invalides and the old aristocratic Faubourg Saint-Germain.) Considerant participated in these meetings and won applause for his "practical knowledge" and "the frankness of his explanations." He also published (with A. Perreymond) a series of articles in *Démocratie pacifique* that constituted a kind of platform. In these articles Considerant and Perreymond argued that the time had come to place Paris and its suburbs under a unified administrative system. "The Department of the Seine ought to be considered . . . as a systematic whole," they maintained; and the public works projects that were carried out in piecemeal fashion by the commune, the department, and the state "ought to be combined and centralized." To make this possible, the Conseil Général would have to play a more active role in planning and implementing urban development projects. If anyone doubted the need for a unified administrative system, he should simply consider the "appalling spectacle" presented by the Parisian suburbs, the world beyond the old Paris customs wall. "It's a chaos of eroded fields, bumpy roads, broken rocks, stagnant water, arid wastes, and overgrown gardens; it's a mess of shacks, factories, and buildings of all sorts scattered about in the most disorderly manner imaginable."[31]

During the election campaign of 1843, Considerant was attacked by the governmental *Journal des débats* for his "democratic daydreams" and ridiculed by the republican *National,* which described his ideas as "as clear as the ocean of lemonade predicted by Fourier." However, he received the support of Lamartine's *Bien public* and of two journals representing the dynastic opposition, *Le Siècle* and *La Patrie.* Furthermore the Legitimists, who were practicing a *politique du pire,* threw their support to Considerant—a fact that the prefect of the Seine, Rambuteau, found particularly galling since Considerant "hid neither his desires nor his hopes." In the end, he was elected on the second ballot, the second of three successful candidates in a field of thirteen, with 643 votes out of 1,264 cast.[32]

Considerant's election to the Conseil Général de la Seine was regarded by other Fourierists as more than a personal triumph. "For you, for me, and for all of us," wrote one of them, "your election is a sign . . . of progress that must bear fruit in generations to come." For another correspondent it was "a great victory won by our fine and noble cause . . . an immense step forward in public opinion." These correspondents were right to see Considerant's victory as a triumph for the Fourierist movement. A sign of the movement's growing respectability, it also gave Considerant a public forum and the opportunity to get a hearing for concrete applications of Fourier's ideas to contemporary needs and problems. Thus, during his five years on the Conseil Général, Considerant made a whole series of proposals concerning everything from old age assistance and the care of orphans to the beautification of Paris. He also called for the adoption of a progressive income tax, which would shift the burden of taxation from the lower classes to land owners and wealthy entrepreneurs.[33]

Two issues of particular concern to Considerant during these years were the fortification of Paris and the development of a national railroad system. The debate over Paris's fortification became heated in 1840, when the threat of war reinforced the position of influential politicians like Adolphe Thiers, who had for some time been calling for the construction of a wall and a ring of forts around Paris and its suburbs. Considerant strongly opposed the idea. This was not because he believed, as some did, that the fortifications had no strategic value. On the contrary, he recognized their military usefulness. Nonetheless, he shared the view of many radicals—Cabet, Pecqueur, and Dézamy, for example—that the "secret aim" of the government in proposing to fortify Paris was to "crush and control" the capital—to enable the government to put down any popular insurrectionary movement coming from within the city. Considerant also criticized fortification on the ground that it would open an arms race in Europe. His principal argument was broader, however, and rested on a vision of France as endowed with a "peaceful and organizing" mission. If France was to play a "powerful and glorious" role in the modern world, he believed, it could only be through "extending to our neighbors a friendly hand."[34]

The second issue that particularly engaged Considerant's attention during his years on the Conseil Général was the debate over the construction and financing of France's railroad network. Initially, Considerant had been skeptical (as were Thiers and many others) of the benefits of railroad transportation. In a pamphlet entitled *Déraison et dangers de l'engouement pour les chemins de fer* (1838), he argued that there were many projects "much more productive, more urgent [and] more precious for the nation" than the construction of railroad lines. "Before seeking to associate the North and the South, the West and the East," he wrote, "we need to learn how to associate masters and workers in France, the wealthy and the poor, capital with labor and talent." Within a few years, however, he changed his tune. Like many former Saint-Simonians and other recent graduates of the Ecole Polytechnique, Considerant came to be fascinated by the possibilities opened up by the railroad, which he saw as "a new and powerful means of communication, sociability, and industry." For that very reason—because of the railroad's potential as an instrument of peaceful communication and exchange—he argued that the choice of routes and the whole process of railroad construction in France should not be left to private initiative. Indeed, the private development of a railroad network in France would be "one of those acts of extreme immorality and transcendent folly that tarnish forever whole periods of history." What was needed, he believed, was a system of state ownership and development that would give "the people, the entire nation" effective control over the railroads.[35]

In the end, and after a national debate in which Lamartine led the opposition to privatization, the Chamber of Deputies adopted a government-sponsored plan that gave private investors just about everything they wanted. The development of a French railroad system was carried out under private management and for private profit but with the government agreeing to provide subsidies, land grants, and low-interest loans and to pay for the construction of bridges, tunnels, and railway stations. For Considerant, all of this was a bitter pill to swallow—the more so in that the government's encouragement of private investment was followed by a speculative "railroad mania" that lasted two years and culminated in several spectacular bankruptcies. "Is France for sale?" he asked in a bitter editorial in *Démocratie pacifique* in June 1844. Was the railroad network, which could become a vital organ of France and an agent of her social and economic transformation, to be sold off in pieces to "a pack of cosmopolitan bankers and speculators drawn from all countries by the rush for spoils"? Then why not sell off the other resources, institutions, and traditions of France and force the nation back into "the most shameful of feudalisms, that of the strong-box, the high and low financiers, and the gentlemen of the bank and the bourse."[36]

V

One dimension of Fourierist activity in the 1840s that did *not* engage Considerant's energies was the concern with what came to be known as "la réalisation"—the attempt to create some form of association, whether a model community or a modest consumers' cooperative, that would in some measure "realize" or confirm Fourier's utopian plans. After the failure of the

Societary Colony at Condé-sur-Vesgre in 1834, many of Fourier's follow-ers—especially Muiron and others associated with the various dissident groups of 1836 and 1837—were eager to try again. The decade that fol-lowed Fourier's death was marked by more than a dozen French experi-ments in applied Fourierism.[37] These experiments were initiated for the most part by provincials, like the dissident Lorraine doctor Arthur de Bon-nard and the remarkable Lyonnais silk manufacturer Michel Derrion, who stood outside or on the margins of the "official" Ecole Sociétaire. There were some individuals, however, who remained in close contact with Con-siderant—like Madaule and Dr. Baudet-Dulary—who were eager to renew the effort of "realization."

Considerant himself was dubious about all these ventures in applied Fourierism. For him the failure of the effort at Condé had been instructive. It had convinced him that the resources of the Ecole should not be thrown into another *essai* until everything was ready. Repeatedly in the 1840s, when asked to consider proposals in practical Fourierism, Considerant re-sponded by invoking the lessons of Condé-sur-Vesgre—"the fortunate failure of Condé"—which had served, in his view, to "open the eyes" of the Fourierists, to make them aware of possible difficulties, and to change their "blind enthusiasm" into a "reflective enthusiasm." Condé had made it clear, he argued, that certain conditions would have to be met before the leader-ship of the Ecole could feel justified in engaging its resources in a major "ef-fort de réalisation." Plans would have to be drawn up; capital would have to be raised (four million francs for "the easiest and cheapest of the *decisive* verifications" of Fourier's theory); and a group of competent and trustwor-thy managers would have to be formed. Finally and most importantly, nothing should be undertaken until the Ecole itself had conquered an un-assailable position in the intellectual world—a position strong enough to defend itself and its doctrine against the criticism that an *essai* was sure to provoke.[38]

Some Fourierists found Considerant's arguments on these points dis-ingenuous. To argue that nothing should be done until the Ecole had con-quered an unassailable position was effectively to put off any effort at "re-alization" for years. Furthermore, in his efforts to create a widely read daily newspaper, Considerant seemed actually less concerned to mobilize re-sources for an *essai* than to further his own political ambitions. Some of his critics, like Charles Pellarin, who ceased to play an active role in the move-ment in 1846, felt that Considerant's preoccupation with his own career had led him to betray the trust they had placed in him. Jules Duval was proba-bly speaking for many others when he wrote much later that, by imposing impossibly stringent conditions, Considerant had in fact turned the idea of a trial Phalanx into an unrealizable utopia. "The ideal was magnificent, dazzling; it exalted forms of devotion that included the most touching self-sacrifice. But it remained completely elusive in the heaven of imagination, without ever coming down to the ground of reality."[39]

During the 1840s, French Fourierists made two major attempts to bring the ideal down to earth through the creation of trial communities. The first was Arthur Young's community at Cîteaux in Burgundy; the second was the Union Agricole of Saint-Denis de Sig in Algeria. Both of these ventures were too important for Considerant to ignore. As we have seen, Arthur Young was initially persuaded by Considerant to devote much of his sizable fortune to subsidizing *La Phalange,* but Young soon became impatient at Considerant's emphasis on the word as opposed to the deed. He also found some of Considerant's articles on political and religious questions offensive to his own beliefs as a British subject and a devout Christian.[40] Not surprisingly Young soon began to look for other ways to spend his money. During the winter of 1840–1841, he and Considerant exchanged letters concerning the possible purchase of the lands and remaining buildings at Condé-sur-Vesgre. Nothing came of this exchange—partly because Considerant and the Fourierists were unable to produce for Young plans that would serve as the basis for a new initiative at Condé.[41]

Then, in February 1841, a Belgian Fourierist who had been connected with the dissidents of 1836, Madame Zoé Gatti de Gammond, managed to interest Young in the idea of converting the land around the old Cistercian abbey at Cîteaux in Burgundy into the setting for a community modeled in some respects on Fourier's ideas. In March Young visited Cîteaux and decided to make a down payment on the property. The total cost of the abbey, along with five hundred acres of arable land, was 1.5 million francs. Young expected that two-thirds of that amount would come from other investors.[42]

Considerant was alarmed, to put it mildly, at Young's eagerness to tie up his whole fortune in the venture at Cîteaux. He knew that this would mean the end of Young's subsidies to the *Phalange.* He also feared that the failure of the effort at Cîteaux, which he judged inevitable given Young's inexperience, would compromise the Fourierist movement as a whole, but he was unable to talk Young out of his idea. In the summer of 1841, Young assumed personal direction of activities at Cîteaux, and in the fall the first "colonists" began to arrive. According to Young's plans, the community at Cîteaux was to draw only on some of the "industrial or economic" branches of Fourier's theory. Workers would be guaranteed a "minimum" of food, clothing, and lodging, and income would be distributed according to each individual's contribution in work, talent, and capital. In return, each participant would pledge to Young himself "the fidelity of a brother and the obedience of a son."[43]

While Arthur Young kept busy at Cîteaux, Considerant wrote him a steady stream of letters dealing with the financial problems of the journal and the need for funds to cover its costs. Diplomatic at first, these letters became increasingly shrill and hectoring. Soon Considerant was threatening Young with legal action and warning that if funds were not soon forthcoming, the Fourierists would have to sell off their holdings at Condé-sur-Vesgre and suspend publication of the *Phalange*. At the same time he advised Young that it would be necessary, in the interest of the movement, to publish in the *Phalange* a formal disavowal of the Cîteaux venture. On December 19, 1841, the following statement appeared in the journal: "The operation of Cîteaux is not being carried on under the direction of *La Phalange*. This does not prevent *La Phalange* from keenly desiring its success." The phrasing was tactful, but the message was clear.[44]

Considerant's desire to distance himself and the movement from Cîteaux was well justified. By the spring of 1842, competent observers agreed that the venture had "no chance of success." The main problem was that the "colonists" Young had brought in consisted largely of Parisian artisans unable to do the farm work required at Cîteaux. To get crops planted and vines tended properly, Young had to hire local workers. By the beginning of 1843, the main group of ninety-nine *sociétaires* was supported by a staff of sixty-eight wage laborers, gardeners, and domestics.[45] Young's resources were rapidly depleted, and the investors he had hoped to attract never appeared. Unable to meet mortgage payments, Young lost control of the property in 1846. Early that year Considerant once again publicly disavowed Young's activities at Cîteaux, but this time in stronger language:

> Neither at Cîteaux nor anywhere else has there ever been . . . a test of the Harmonian theory or anything like a test. Far from having participated in the enterprise at Cîteaux, . . . Monsieur Considerant did everything he could to dissuade the generous promoter. Finally, this venture seemed so unlikely to resolve experimentally the question of the Phalanx that, despite [our] feelings of esteem and affection [for Arthur Young], the Ecole refrained entirely from giving the slightest gesture of support to it.[46]

This was Considerant's last word on Cîteaux.

The second major effort in practical Fourierism during the 1840s was the attempt to create a Fourierist community in Algeria. The initiative for this effort came largely from the active group of Fourierists at Lyon. These included two doctors, Fleury Imbert and François Barrier, the lawyer Alphonse Morellet, and several merchants, Félix Beuque, Eugène Dumortier, and César Bertholon, as well as a wealthy land owner from Vienne, Jacques Reverchon. Others interested in the venture included several army officers from Franche-Comté, notably Hippolyte Renaud. These were the core of a group of thirty-three "founding members" who in December 1845 formed a shareholding company called the Union Agricole d'Afrique. The aim of this company was to develop a large tract of land near Saint-Denis du Sig in western Algeria, midway between Oran and Mascara.[47]

Dr. Barrier drafted an elaborate set of statutes for the Union Agricole d'Afrique. These included a long preamble emphasizing that the community to be established would only bear a limited resemblance to the most modest of Fourier's communal schemes. An effort would be made to promote "the solidarity of interests between capitalists and workers" and to replace "the system of *morcellement*" with "the advantages of unity in the organization of work, economy in production and consumption, justice in distribution, and constructive rivalry in the participation of each individual in the common work." This would be enough, Barrier maintained, to make the community a model for the peaceful colonization of Algeria and for the gradual integration of the Algerian and French populations.

> Colonization should be carried out on new bases. It should become national and social: national in adding to the glory and the strength of France; social in bringing the light of civilization to a barbarous country where it will serve the cause of humanity and progress. But to retain this dual character, colonization should take place without the unjust oppression of the native population. Within certain limits the Arab element should be respected and considered as placed under the tutelage of France. Instead of seeking the destruction of this element, as some have not hesitated to think and say, [the French] should seek the means to absorb it and to put it to work through the fusion of interests.

Instead of displacing the Arabs and driving them into the barren interior of their own country, Barrier argued that in the long run it would be wiser, as well as more humane, to create new communities in Algeria that would attract the indigenous population.[48]

The promoters of the community at Saint-Denis du Sig managed to get the support of the military commander of the province of Oran, Lamoricière. They also got a sympathetic hearing from the nominal head of the government, Considerant's old protector, Marshal Soult. At the same time, the ex-Saint-Simonian pope, Prosper Enfantin, who had been deeply involved in schemes for the development of Algeria for over a decade, published a laudatory article on the venture in his journal *L'Algérie*. The proposed community at Sig was, in his words, "an enterprise that appears to combine all the elements of success, the morality and the knowledge of the men involved, together with the advantages of the site and the wisdom of the plan."[49]

In the end, the Union Agricole d'Afrique was a disappointment. In one form or another the community of "Sigville" lasted for decades, but it never even approximated the dreams of its founders. The main problem was a lack of capital. While the statutes had called for a capital of a million francs, less than 400,000 was actually raised. Still, the prospects seemed good enough in 1846 that Considerant could write two relatively positive articles in *Démocratie pacifique* on "the societary principle in Algeria." He took pains in these articles, however, to emphasize that although the founders of Sigville had been influenced by Fourier's economic ideas, they were not seeking to test or verify Fourier's theory of social organization. Sigville was merely a "transitional operation," the failure of which would in no way compromise Fourier's theory.

> If at Sigville instead of simply making a venture in colonization by borrowing from the Societary Doctrine the principle of association, its founders had attempted to make a test of the system of the series, if they had tried to organize an experimental Phalanx, we would have been careful not to compromise the Ecole and the Theory by giving them any support whatsoever. When the time comes to make an experimental test of the Theory, and we hope it will be soon, we will need the support of all the energies of the Ecole. And it will not be in Africa but in the region of Paris, in proximity to the greatest center of activity and publicity and within reach of all the resources of modern society, that this difficult and decisive experiment will be made.[50]

Ironically in the light of this letter, when Considerant finally did give his full support to an experimental test of the theory, it was in Texas. But this was only after the June Days of 1848 and December 2, 1851.

6

"Social Science"

Victor Considerant's reputation as a theorist of socialism rests largely upon one major treatise and a few pamphlets. The treatise, *Destinée sociale*, was originally published in three volumes between 1834 and 1844. The most important of the pamphlets, the *Manifeste politique et social de la Démocratie pacifique*, first appeared in August 1843 as an introductory issue of the Fourierists' daily journal. It was reprinted in 1847 with a few additions as *Principes du socialisme. Manifeste de la démocratie au XIXe siècle.* Other major pamphlets include: *Bases de la politique positive. Manifeste de l'Ecole sociétaire* (1841), and the *Exposition abrégée du système phalanstérien de Fourier* (1845). Most of these works were presented as popularizations or extensions of the thought of Charles Fourier. All were written hastily in the midst of Considerant's other activities as a journalist, lecturer, fundraiser, and Fourierist *militant*. Even in the treatise the style is colloquial and the tone informal: Considerant banters with his readers, quotes from recent newspapers, and apologizes for the excesses and errors of earlier works. Still, taken as a whole, these works add up to a substantial body of writing. And despite Considerant's self-appointed role as a guardian of Fourierist orthodoxy, they can be seen as representing a point of view distinct from Fourier's.

Interestingly, these works were all first published before Considerant began to identify himself as a socialist. He did occasionally refer to *socia-*

listes and *socialisme* in his writings of the July Monarchy.[1] Like Pierre Leroux, however, who gave the words currency in French, Considerant initially used them to refer to the ideas of others. Prior to 1847 he generally
described himself as the exponent of a *science sociale*. The main tenets of
this science derived from the work of Fourier, but Considerant ordered,
clarified, and simplified Fourier's thought, emphasizing those points that
seemed to have contemporary resonance and omitting or downplaying
whole aspects of Fourier's thought—notably the speculations on love and
cosmogony—that he feared would offend, shock, or mystify his readers.
This effort to soften and cleanse Fourier's thought was evident both in Considerant's social criticism and in his discussion of the ideal community that
Fourier called the Phalanx.

I

A continuing theme in Considerant's critique of what he, like Fourier, referred to pejoratively as "civilization" was the sterility of modern political
thought. Much political thought was in his view simply an attempt to con-
fer legitimacy on existing institutions or to represent narrowly conceived
interests. Even among oppositional thinkers the focus on political rights
obscured the more basic need to guarantee subsistence and the right to
work. The main problem with contemporary political thinking, though,
was its divisive and adversarial character. It set people at odds with one another, whereas the point was to find common ground—"to associate interests and unite people."[2]

Of all the problems that the political theorists avoided, the most pressing, according to Considerant, was the problem of poverty. We live in a
world, he wrote, where the vast majority of people lack the means to support themselves adequately, a world where appeals to duty, love of country,
and the respect owed authority only serve to justify ever more extreme
contrasts of wealth and poverty. Why should this be? Why, given the immense progress of science and industry, should the masses still be "so badly
clothed and housed, so poor, so crude of speech, so hungry"?[3]

Considerant's analysis of the roots of poverty focused on the two great
flaws of modern civilization: the organization of commerce and the organization of work. The proper function of commerce was to distribute goods
and to serve as an intermediary between producer and consumer. Instead
of playing this modest role, that of a valet, however, the merchant acted as
lord and master with regard to both producer and consumer. The merchant
"despoiled" society through his control of necessary goods, through huge

profits, speculation, hoarding, falsification, and fraudulent bankruptcy. Considerant called him a "parasite" nourished by the labor of the productive classes and a "vampire . . . sucking up the wealth and the blood of the body social."[4]

In 1834 Considerant could describe "the mercantile system" as "the great wound" of modern civilization. Not only was it a major cause of poverty; it was also the source of a variety of social vices due to the role it played in narrowing the horizons of contemporaries, reinforcing their greedy and selfish impulses, and concentrating their energies on the pursuit of profit at the expense of everything else.

> The mercantile spirit spreads corruption and egoism throughout society. It erodes, corrodes, and destroys the national spirit; it reinforces all the low, egoistic, and perverse impulses; it denigrates everything that is noble and great; it weighs and measures art and poetry by its own scales and standards. The only kind of book it understands is an account book; it views man as no more than a machine which counts, calculates, adds, and subtracts. . . . It atrophies all human feelings by giving monstrous development to egoistic greed.[5]

If anyone doubted the role played by commerce and the mercantile spirit in destroying the sense of solidarity and of a common good, Considerant noted, it was only necessary to recall the behavior of many Parisians during the cholera epidemic of 1832. The rich isolated themselves in their fancy quartiers, while merchants and pharmacists made great profits from the sale at outlandish prices of drugs (some of which they knew to be useless) reputed to provide protection against the epidemic.[6]

If one cause of poverty was a faulty system of distribution, another was a system of production within which almost all work was either useless or unappealing. Vast sums were spent to maintain armies and police forces that created nothing. Robbers, prisoners, and prostitutes were of course equally unproductive, but so were judges, lawyers, administrators, customs inspectors, and philosophers, as well as bankers, shopkeepers, and merchants. Ironically, some of the least productive members of society were showered with the most honors. Others—prostitutes, beggars, and criminals—were treated with contempt and wrongly held responsible for the lives they led.[7]

Even when work was genuinely productive, it was almost never done efficiently or with enthusiasm. In contemporary "civilized" society there was nothing appealing about productive work. Indeed, one of the fundamental, defining features of modern civilization was "industrial repugnance," or the loathing of industrial work. The only stimulus that drove people to work in modern societies was hunger. "It is indigence alone," wrote Considerant, "that can condemn and force man to work." The modern worker was "a veritable slave," and as long as productive work remained an ordeal it would be avoided. No one would willingly choose to join the "vast herd of *beasts of burden*" who could be seen "deformed, ravaged by sickness, and bent over their furrows or workbenches as they prepare the refined food and the sumptuous pleasures of the upper classes."[8]

A word that often appeared in Considerant's analyses of the ills of civilization was *morcellement* (fragmentation, subdivision). The economic and social order was fragmented, according to Considerant, and this division or fragmentation was another cause of poverty. In the sphere of agriculture the system of smallholding and *morcellement* kept much of France's huge peasant population in a state of dire poverty. "*Morcellement* impoverishes, ruins the soil," wrote Considerant. "It causes the degeneration of breeds of animals. . . . It multiplies tasks, periods of idleness, and lost time. It prevents the introduction of good scientific methods of farming due to the combined influence of routine, ignorance, lack of capital, etc."[9] If *morcellement* was the besetting vice of agricultural production, it was even more obviously a characteristic feature of both production and consumption within the household economy.

A long tradition running from Aristotle down to the political economists of the nineteenth century tended to dismiss as trivial any discussion of the organization of work within the household. Considerant, however, regarded the question as vital. "Social reform is completely dependent," he wrote, "on the question of the organization of the household." His main point was that the household was an incredibly inefficient economic unit. In a village of 2,000 inhabitants there were likely to be at least 400 kitchens, 400 dining rooms, and 400 cooks. Furthermore, each of these 400 cooks would spend much of her day doing the marketing for her family, then doing the laundry, then the housecleaning. All of these tasks could be done much more efficiently by a much smaller number of specialists using modern equipment and working for the village as a whole.[10]

Considerant believed that there was an even more significant drawback to an economic system organized around the household. This was the role that it forced on women. In dividing society up into a significant male sphere (the market) and an insignificant female sphere (the household), political economists seemed to assume that "woman was made intentionally and uniquely to cook dinner, mend breeches, and make babies." Only by calling into question traditional assumptions concerning the household economy would it be possible, Considerant argued, to begin "to resolve the immense problem of the social liberty of women and of the emancipation of the female genius." It would also be necessary, of course, to free women from the constraints imposed by the "perpetual and indissoluble marriage tie." For this to happen, women would have to acquire the right to initiate divorce proceedings on the same grounds as men.[11]

As the foregoing suggests, Considerant's critique of *morcellement* took him far beyond the economic realm. Indeed, he regarded his society as marked in *all* its aspects by division, disorder, confusion, anarchy, and constant conflict. Climb up one of the towers of Notre Dame de Paris, he wrote, and you will be struck by the "spectacle of disorder," the "frightful architectural mess," that Paris itself presents. The Gothic clutter and disorganization of the capital, with its dark, winding streets, jumbled rooftops, and hodgepodge of architectural styles, was a mirror of the "social anarchy" that prevailed within the city, with its overcrowding, disease, and corrosive effect on human solidarity.[12]

Considerant's reflections on the fragmentation and disorder of contemporary society culminated with a critique of what he called the "intellectual anarchy" of the modern age. Just as the economy and society were the site of constant discord and conflict, he argued, so too was the world of ideas. For more than a century the intellectual world had been "a tumult of contradictory ideas." Divided into factions, sects, and coteries, people had lost their sense of common bonds and interests. They formed parties based on doctrines that never represented more than a narrow and fragmentary interest. These parties were constantly tending to dissolve into "splinter groups" organized around "ideological stupidities, empty words, and theories so ephemeral and narrow that they cannot crop up without exciting the hostility of other such theories."[13]

One of the most striking symptoms of the intellectual anarchy of the modern world was the role the press had come to play in contemporary society. Almost every political faction and social group now had its own journal, and each of these journals simultaneously inflamed and fed off the struggles of the group it represented. Most of these journals showed their colors in their titles: thus alongside the "journal of monarchic interests" there was a journal of "democratic interests," and alongside the journal of "new interests" there was a journal of "old interests." When a journal concealed its partisan perspective under some "charlatan title" like "journal of progress" or "good sense," no one was fooled. What each journal offered was special pleading for the interests of its particular constituency and callous disregard for the well-being of society as a whole.[14]

Within a divided and conflict-ridden world, Considerant argued, success went to those who most effectively asserted their own particular interests. A premium was placed on egoism—whether that of individuals, sects, parties, or classes. Philosophical doctrines emphasizing the individual's pursuit of happiness and religious doctrines offering the possibility of individual salvation only served to reinforce the reigning egoism by throwing "every individual into an isolated and egotistical search for *his own* particular happiness." In this fragmented and contentious society, appeals to "live for others" or to practice charity necessarily rang false. People led separate lives and the individual was left "like it or not, to the deadly boredom of isolation and the stupefying dullness of solitude." Around each individual civilization traced "a narrow circle of egoistical interests, devoid of links to those outside the circle."[15]

One consequence of the premium placed on the egoistic pursuit of individual interests in July Monarchy France was the enormous prestige attached to wealth, however shady the means by which it had been acquired. Considerant discerned no more fitting symbol for the culture of the period than the figure of Robert Macaire, the sleazy speculator and promoter brought to life on the French stage by the talented actor, Frédéric Lemaître, and in the press by the caricatures of Daumier.

> Has there ever been a period of French history more venal, more mercantile, more abundant in sharp business practices, more immoral than our time? And this in spite of all the moral ostentation and buffoonery with which we are inundated. . . . Isn't Robert Macaire now standing before us in all his glory? Hasn't he moved out of the low quarters in which he once lived to set himself up in a mansion with horse and carriage? Who does not respect, bow to, and venerate Robert Macaire?[16]

In a world that worshipped Robert Macaire there was something almost comic about appeals to generous impulses or a common good. Everything about the society worked to atrophy the sense of a shared destiny or participation in a common enterprise. "There are no more generous affections and social sentiments," wrote Considerant. "Love of country is no more than a term that serves to cover up partisan intrigue, to conceal the plots of ambitious people."[17]

So, Considerant's picture of contemporary France was that of an egoistic and individualistic culture that had its roots in "a social organization that *divides* people instead of *uniting* them."[18] What was needed, then, was reflection on the problem of social organization itself.

II

Victor Considerant generally presented his critique of contemporary society within a historical context. In *Destinée sociale* the historical framework was provided by Charles Fourier's elaborate classification of the four periods of "social infancy" (Edenism, Savagery, Patriarchy, Barbarism) and the four stages of "Civilization" from Childhood to Decrepitude.[19] In most of Considerant's later works, this broad framework was quietly jettisoned. Modern history, as he came to see it, was the story of the movement from traditional aristocratic and warlike societies to democratic societies based on labor, science, and industrial development.

Ancient societies, according to Considerant, were organized around war and sustained economically by slavery, "the most complete, most inhuman, and most barbarous system of the exploitation of man by man."[20] Free men, whether plebeians or patricians, made war and consumed goods produced by slave labor. Feudal society was similar in kind to the slave societies of antiquity; it was still organized around the making of war. The main difference was that the feudal economy was organized around serfdom, a somewhat less brutal form of exploitation than slavery.

It was through developments in science and industry and through changes in the organization of labor, through "the slow but irresistible conquest of force by intelligence, of the genius of war by the genius of creation," that a new order gradually emerged within the heart of feudal society. The key moment in the emergence of this new order was the French Revolution, with its abolition of feudal distinctions and its recognition of the equality of all citizens before the law. "The epoch of '89 marked in the history of humanity the great separation between the old order and the new, between the right of force and the right of labor, between aristocratic right, the right of conquest perpetuated by birth, and democratic rights, common law, the right of all to all."[21]

So important a turning point did the Revolution seem to contemporaries, Considerant wrote, that it was widely believed at the time that it had, in and of itself, "founded and established" the new order. This was "a grave error." Outside the realm of politics, where the Revolution had been creative, almost all its work was destructive. It had overthrown the last vestiges of a feudal order founded on war and on the privilege of noble birth. It had proclaimed the principle of the equality of all citizens, and it had created institutions of representative government and education that gave some substance to the democratic idea. But the failures of the Revolution in the social and economic spheres were no less clear than its political accomplishments. In particular, the Revolution had "left the whole industrial order without organization, without direction, and without any form of control." It had overthrown the guild system without replacing it with a better system for the organization of work. It had turned the whole domain of the production and distribution of wealth into a realm of "industrial anarchy" based on "competition without limit and without control." Ironically, however, the consequence of "free" competition, more often than not, was the crushing of small producers and the establishment of powerful monopolies in many different branches of industry.[22]

As a result of all these developments, and despite the legal abolition of privilege and the proclamation of equality before the law, the actual structure of society remained hierarchical and aristocratic. Those who were born in poverty almost always died in it; those who were born to wealth generally managed to pass it on to their descendants. Contrary to the egalitarian principles of the French Revolution, the fact of the matter was that high political, industrial, and financial positions, and almost all high places in administration and the liberal professions, were monopolized by members, and often familial dynasties, of the upper and middle classes, while "arduous, unrewarding, loathsome, unsteady, miserably paid work remains the permanent lot of lower-class families."[23]

Whatever political changes the Revolution had made, it brought no structural changes to economic and social life. Indeed, one of the principal features of the postrevolutionary period was "the rapid and powerful development of a NEW FEUDALISM, of *industrial and financial* feudalism that is taking the place of the noble and military aristocracy of the Old Regime." After the great "explosion" of 1789, after the destruction of feudal property, the guild system, and the old political order, the old aristocracy seemed gone forever. Under the new conditions of industrial and commercial freedom, however, a new aristocracy was emerging, as the wealthiest and best-educated members of society came to occupy the most important places and claim the scarcest resources. This new aristocracy already dominated politics and imposed its will on the government. Writing in 1843, Considerant found numerous contemporary examples of "the infeudation of the government to the new aristocracy." Private companies ran canals (often built with government aid) like fiefs, leveling tolls and controlling the movement of goods according to their whims. In overseeing the development of a national railroad system, the government had repeatedly promoted the interests of the big financiers, "the great and all-powerful vassals of the Bank."[24]

Considerant went on to describe the structure of postrevolutionary society in terms that anticipate those of Karl Marx. Society was coming to be divided, he wrote, into two classes: a ruling class that possessed capital and the instruments of labor; and a class of destitute proletarians. The proletarian majority lived in a state of absolute dependence on the capitalists, obliged to sell their labor power for a meager wage. These two classes were in a constant state of conflict. Indeed, the workshop had become a "battlefield" where capital and labor engaged in a mortal struggle. The conditions of the struggle were "monstrously unequal," though, and in modern societies the domination of capital was becoming ever more apparent. One of the consequences of that domination was the reduction of increasing numbers of proletarians into a state of "collective servitude." Another consequence was the crushing of the middle classes: "the gradual crushing of small and middle-sized property, industry, and commerce under the weight of big property, under the colossal wheels of big industry and big commerce."[25]

Under the system of "free or anarchic competition," conflict took place not only between classes but also within them. Considerant stressed the systemic nature of the conflict: it was not something that people sought or willed; it was forced on them by circumstances. Constrained to seek work every day to feed their families, they had no choice but to sell their labor cheaply. When the supply of workers was plentiful, as it usually was, free competition obliged them to accept starvation wages. The employers' position was similar. "The competition of the masters among themselves forces each one of them, *however humane he might be,* to pay the most meager wages" because there was no other way to compete with other employers. Free competition was thus an "odious mechanism" that broke "all the laws of justice and humanity" and constantly tended to drive wages down, creating a "permanent state of war" pitting labor, machines, and capital against each other.[26]

Writing in the mid-1840s, Considerant emphasized that the polarization of society was creating a dangerous and potentially explosive situation. Neither the working poor in France nor the French bourgeoisie would tolerate the sort of treatment that their English and Irish counterparts had had to endure. Indeed, in England the growth of the Chartist movement had been accompanied by the development of "social hatred" of a "frightening intensity." "It is certain," wrote Considerant in August 1843, "that the movement of European societies is toward social revolution and that we are headed toward a European Jacquerie." Life in the most advanced industrial societies had become "a veritable Hell" for most of the population, and the threat of class war was constant. To avoid revolution a better form of social and economic organization would have to be found.[27]

In this context, questions that Considerant had been asking for more than a decade took on increased urgency. Didn't the human race have another "social destiny" than the violence and hatred of revolution? Were humans placed on earth and created social beings only to tear each other apart and devour each other like ferocious beasts? Could people only unite with one another for the purpose of fighting other groups? "Shouldn't we rather believe," Considerant asked, "that if we can unite fractiously and temporarily in groups and parties for the labors of war, we are called, one and all, to unite in a permanent union for the great accomplishment of peace, work, and happiness?" Was it not possible for human beings to organize around their common interests and to consider as their goals "the realization of the harmony of interests, the fusion of classes, the rallying of all human powers"? It was with these questions in mind, and in formulating this goal, that Considerant turned from social criticism to the elaboration of his social science.[28]

III

In all his major works of the July Monarchy, Considerant presented himself as the proponent of a new science of man and society—a science that defined once and for all the nature of man, stipulated the ends of life, the "destinies" for which human beings were created, and described a new form of social organization consistent with man's needs and the development of his faculties. This science was premised on a set of assumptions about human nature completely opposed to those of traditional Christianity with its doctrine of original sin and its view of this world as a vale of tears.

For centuries, Considerant observed, philosophers and priests had been preaching their "dismal doctrine that evil is eternal, inevitable, and purposeful; that its source is our very nature, our vicious and corrupt nature, that deprivation, pain, and tears constitute our earthly lot." But this view was patently false. Not only was it contrary to "the veritable spirit of Christ," who wanted all men to unite and live together on earth as brothers. It was also belied by man's evident success in transforming the natural world, his alleged place of exile, into a "rich and beautiful domain" capable of serving his needs and his pleasures. Christianity treated man as a worm, a weak and dependent creature, condemned to eke out a miserable life on earth and to be the plaything of forces beyond his control. In fact, however, this supposedly miserable creature had proved himself capable of harnessing the forces of nature and building roads, canals, and cities on an initially barren planet.[29]

Man's task on earth, Considerant maintained, was to "manage his terrestrial domain, to act on his planet, to LABOR." Man was to husband and develop the earth's resources, build cities, develop agriculture and industry, and, in so doing, create social institutions adapted to his nature and to the development of his faculties. Considerant never doubted that man was a social animal and that his "destiny" was to live in a society adapted to his needs and expressive of his powers. Nor did he doubt that human beings are creatures of passion, that we are all moved by instinctual drives that are unchanging and stronger than reason. He also believed that work—first of all, the work of creating and maintaining a habitable universe—was an act through which human beings defined themselves and expressed their true natures. He insisted, however, that for work to become an instrument of the fulfillment of man's destiny, it had to be organized in a manner consistent with man's basic penchants and passions.[30]

What were the passions? Considerant noted that in his time the word "passion" had strong negative connotations. This was because modern civilized society only rarely permitted the "harmonic" expression of a passion. More commonly a passion acted upon had negative or "subversive" consequences. Thus he insisted that he used the term in a sense that was "scientific and independent of the acts that [a passion] provokes." Passion for Considerant was the basic force that moved human beings to action.

> Passion is a force; it is the motive force of human nature. It is passion that stimulates and gives movement to our intellectual and muscular powers. It is from passion that all our acts, good and bad, take their origin. The great task of the theory of social destiny is to provide the natural law of the passions.[31]

Following Fourier, Considerant argued that these fundamental instinctual drives could be subsumed within a basic classification of twelve recurring or cardinal passions, each of which was immutable and indestructible.

In civilization, with its repressive moral doctrines and its regime of "perpetual and indissoluble marriage," most of the passions were stifled. The result was only to create a state of "internal war" within every man and woman. This was a war that could never be won, Considerant insisted, and also a war that did not need to be fought. The passions were benign and harmonious if given full and free expression. This was not, of course, the view of the traditional moralists. If they had their way, the human species would not have been endowed with the passions of love, ambition, intrigue, the need for change, or the penchant for luxury. What passions would the moralists have regarded as acceptable? The love of family, no doubt, and also perhaps "a few flaccid and solitary accords of friendship."

> Then they would have gotten us impassioned by resignation, moderation, privation, and what not. All the sentimental, unctuous, or grim harping with which moralism has plagued us ever since our birth. . . . Unfortunately God, who is not saving man for the very moral pleasures of moderation, who has not destined him for a life of privations . . . has prepared for him a future of infinite riches, an ocean of joys.

The moralists would have to resign themselves, then, to taking human nature as it was. Since social forms were changeable and human nature irreducible, moralists and political philosophers would have to focus their attention on changing society. "Reason," wrote Considerant, "must find a social form that can adapt itself to man's passional makeup."[32]

IV

In his novel *Autre étude de femme,* Balzac wrote that the verb *organiser* was "a word of the Empire that contains all of Napoleon." Balzac might have added that this word and its cognates retained their resonance into the July Monarchy. For Victor Considerant, as for many other social thinkers who were born during the empire and only reached maturity after 1830, the word *organisation* was almost a mantra. "The organization of work," "industrial organization," "social organization," "the organization of the Phalanx"—these terms keep recurring in Considerant's prose; indeed, the second part of *Destinée sociale,* the part that follows the critique, is titled simply "Organisation."[33]

What almost all of Considerant's uses of the term *organisation* have in common is the reference to planning and design. Organization for Considerant is the result of conscious effort and direction—not of accident or tradition. Organization does not simply come about; it is produced, guided, and directed. Considerant rarely uses the term *organisation* to refer to bad or inadequate forms of social order. Most commonly the term refers to a rational or scientific structuring of society sufficient to resolve the "social question."

Considerant's characterization of the social question followed from his analysis of the ills of civilized society and his reflections on the passions. It was not merely the problem of poverty that concerned him. It was also the problem of the isolation of people from one another in contemporary society—the competition between them and the collapse of traditional social bonds, the spread of egoism and individualism that disturbed conservatives like Bonald and Balzac as much as radicals. The social question as Considerant understood it was the problem of bringing an end to the fragmentation, conflict, and social divisions of modern society—the problem of creating economic prosperity and social harmony in the place of poverty, conflict, and isolation.[34]

Considerant maintained that in his time two principal solutions to the social question were proposed. One was communism or the community of goods; the other was association. Communism, by which he meant the ideas not of Marx but of neo-Babouvists such as Théodore Dézamy and Jean-Jacques Pillot, involved the forcible creation of community through the expropriation of the property of the rich and the establishment of a society in which most of the resources were collectively owned.[35] Considerant called this the "violent" and "revolutionary" reaction to "the social encroachment and tyrannical domination of capital." It had "the immense advantage of simplicity," and for that reason it had begun to spread among the working class. Considerant, however, believed that the attack on the right of private ownership of property was "a retrograde idea" that would lose its appeal in any society that guaranteed the right to work and placed reasonable limits on the power of the wealthy.[36]

Association, on the other hand, involved cooperation and a measure of collective ownership, but not the enforced equality of communism. What did Considerant mean by the term "association"? In a dialogue entitled "A Phalansterian and the First Comer," he led the reader slowly, by simple steps, to an understanding: "We say that individuals associate when they unite their resources, their capital, and their own powers to accomplish together a task that they could not undertake or that they would accomplish less successfully in isolation." An association, then, was a *voluntary* grouping of individuals whose claims on the goods produced by the association depended on their contribution in capital, labor, and talent. Wealthy members of an association would not be obliged to give up their wealth; at the same time the poorest member was also a shareholder who could speak about "our land, our palace, our castles, our factories." Within an association property was multifaceted—it was both private and collective—and Considerant could speak in glowing terms about the superiority of this system over both the enforced equality of communism and the competitive struggle of capitalism.[37]

The goal of association, Considerant wrote, was "to seek out the arrangements needed to introduce harmony among men and to enable them all to participate in social well-being." To achieve this goal, three conditions would have to be met. The first was a vast increase in the productivity of labor, which would require a more efficient organization of the work force. Work done on farms, in factories and workshops, and in the household would have to be rendered more attractive and done more efficiently. Only by stimulating productivity would it be possible to increase social wealth to the point where the lives of most individuals would cease to consist of endless competition for scarce resources. Only then—once basic needs were satisfied—could a climate be created in which people would be likely to act on the basis of generous rather than narrowly selfish impulses. As Considerant put it, "The harmonic development of the social sentiments has to be founded on a broad base of social wealth."[38]

The second condition for resolving the social question was a more equitable distribution of wealth. This did not mean equality. It did mean a system of remuneration according to which a community's earnings would be divided up among its members according to their contributions in capital, labor, and talent.[39] And it meant a guarantee of the right to work, "the first social right of man, the one that safeguards and embraces all the others." It also meant that if people were unable to work and lacked a comfortable standard of living, the community would undertake to provide them with a guaranteed minimum in food, clothing, and housing, without setting any conditions.[40]

Considerant argued forcefully that granting this economic minimum should precede any effort to widen the availability of education. "There is not and there cannot be," he wrote, "any veritable, solid, and useful education for members of society who are deprived of the necessities." Indeed, "nothing is more deadly," he claimed, "than instruction or education for people placed in these conditions." It was a recipe for social unrest to develop the intellectual faculties of the poor and refine their tastes without giving them the means to satisfy the needs thus created. Indeed, the creation of an educated but hungry population was "the great malady of all advanced civilizations and one of the strongest causes of their political convulsions."[41]

Looking at the question from the perspective not of social order but of individual liberty, Considerant reached similar conclusions. "Liberty," he argued, "will always be a word devoid of meaning as long as common people have not attained well-being." Freedom, legal equality, and political rights mean little to people who are in dire need. "Make revolutions, pass decrees, promulgate constitutions, proclaim any number or kind of republics, nominate whomever you wish as president or consul: you have done nothing for the real freedom of the masses so long as society has not guaranteed to every man, woman, and child a minimum necessary for existence." [42]

The third and most important of Considerant's conditions for the resolution of the social question was the development of a new model of community organization adapted to "the needs and requirements" of human nature. In *Destinée sociale* he called this model simply "the commune." Elsewhere he referred to it by its Fourierist name as "the Phalanx." In either case the plan of community organization was "the cornerstone of the whole social edifice." [43] The commune or Phalanx was not only the site of a society's production and consumption; it was also the institutional setting within which the hitherto discordant human passions would find outlets that were both pleasurable and socially useful.

v

Much of *Destinée sociale* consisted of a detailed description of Considerant's plan of communal organization. What was needed was a square league of land and a population of about 1,800 to 2,000 men, women, and children. The community was to run as a joint-stock company in which members would be issued shares based on their contributions in labor, capital, and talent. For emotional bonding to occur and the passions to find constructive outlets, however, all daily activities had to be organized in small "passional" groups in which people of similar inclinations and aptitudes could interact.

These "passional" groups were the basic building blocks of the collective life of the community. They were purely voluntary gatherings composed of individuals united by common penchants and by affection for each other. Every individual would join a variety of groups, but no one would be forced to join a particular group. Many of these groups were work groups devoted to raising a particular crop or performing a specific set of tasks. There was also to be an elaborate network of educational groups designed to help the young develop their faculties and discover their aptitudes at an early age. [44]

Considerant attached particular importance to the architectural design of his community, drawing up his own plans and illustrations. He described the Phalanstery, or central building, as a "splendid palace" rising out of a sea of gardens, flower beds, and shaded lawns like "a marmoreal island bathing in an island of greenery." It would be a "royal dwelling place" for "a regenerated population." [45]

The Phalanstery was to be the focal point of the community's activities. With its imposing central facade, watchtower, vast inner courtyards, and two huge wings, it would house the workshops, kitchens, dining rooms, studios, and recreation rooms of the community as well as its living quarters. The noisiest workshops would be concentrated at the extreme end of one wing, while much of the opposite wing would consist of lodgings and reception rooms designed to accommodate visitors. The central section of the Phalanstery would be given over to dining and living rooms, a concert hall, and a ballroom on the ground floor, with individual apartments on the upper floors. These apartments would be available at three different rates, but no restrictions on access would exclude even the humblest of "Phalansterians" from any of the community's activities.

Much of this was straight out of Fourier, but on the question of the role of modern technology in the Phalanx Considerant had his own ideas. Fourier always imagined the Phalanx in a rural setting, and the examples of work groups that he cited were invariably drawn from agriculture and usually from arboriculture. His books abounded in accounts of the rivalries and intrigues of apple pickers, pear grafters, and rose growers. Considerant occasionally borrowed his illustrative details and examples from Fourier, and he was capable of waxing eloquent on the "verdant perspectives" of Phalansterian architecture. Still, he made it clear that the Phalanx would be a center of "advanced" industrial activities. Like a true Polytechnicien, he took delight in the conquest of nature by modern technology. Next to the Phalanstery, he wrote, an "industrial city" would rise with its factories, large workshops, and warehouses.

> There, just opposite the Phalanstery, motors and heavy machines deploy their power. They grind, crush, or transform raw materials under their metal components and perform for the benefit of the Phalanx a thousand marvelous operations. [This industrial city] is an arsenal of the active and living creations of human intelligence, the ark in which are gathered all the industrial species added by the creative power of man to the vegetable and animal species, those "machines" invented by the original creator. There all the elements are subdued, all the fluids are controlled, all the mysterious forces are harnessed, all the powers of nature are conquered, all the gods of ancient Olympus are placed under the control of the god of the earth. They are humble servants who obey his commands and proclaim his kingdom.[46]

This paean to man's ability to tame the elements and conquer nature was cast, like similar passages in Marx and (in an ironic vein) Balzac, in a form that suggested a religious transformation. In the new world of the Phalanx, the Olympian gods—and implicitly the Christian God as well—would have to step aside and make way for the "god of the earth," who was man himself.

Considerant's fascination with the possibilities created by technological development is evident throughout his descriptions of the Phalanstery. Taking his readers into the kitchen, he marvels at the great ovens, the glittering utensils, the laborsaving devices. He recounts in detail the process by which heat from the kitchen will be transferred to the greenhouses, baths, and private apartments. Other systems for moving water, preventing fires, and reflecting candlelight are lovingly described. Considerant observes that these systems, which are now employed "in palaces and in a few sumptuous townhouses in France and especially in England," will be made available to all. He asserts that the amenities of the Phalanstery will "universalize comfort and well-being." Since everything in the Phalanstery has been "foreseen and provided for, arranged and organized," man's role will be to "rule as master of water, air, heat, and light."[47]

The central feature of Considerant's account of life in the Phalanx was his description of the organization of work. "In the Phalanx," he wrote, "work in agriculture, in the household, in science, education, and the arts is not carried on in isolation by workers separated from one another and spending their days . . . tied to the same job." Instead work was "performed in short and varied sessions . . . by squads, by *groups* of workers, groups spontaneously and freely formed by people sharing similar penchants and personalities."[48]

Sharing Fourier's belief that work was not a curse and that under the right conditions any job could be made attractive, Considerant described in detail the organization of the groups—and series of groups—within which work would be done in the Phalanx. The point was to create a setting in which people would work at the urging of the passions. The basic "mechanism" that would make this possible was the "passionate series." Following Fourier, Considerant defined this as "a league of various groups, graduated in ascending and descending order, passionately bound together because they share a common liking for some task." Each series was to be divided into a number of groups devoted to special tasks, and membership in any work group was absolutely voluntary. The members of a group had to be "passionately engaged" in their work and not driven to it by motives of "need, morality, reason, duty, and constraint." A series, moreover, was not a bland gathering of men and women with identical tastes and personalities. In fact, the proper functioning of a series depended upon the creation of a sort of ordered discord and rivalry among the groups that composed it. For this reason variety and inequality were essential; each series had to be made up of individuals who shared a common passion but differed greatly in "age, wealth, character, interest, etc."[49]

Since modern industrial work "plunged" the worker into a state of monotony and "nailed" him or her to a dull and unchanging task, Considerant devoted particular attention to the need for varied occupations. This was consistent with Fourier's belief that the "Butterfly"—the need for change and variety—was a basic human passion. To satisfy this need, each Phalanx would have to organize a large number of series. These work series would vary from one community to another, but in any case dozens of series would be necessary to enable each worker to do as many jobs as he or she chose. Eventually every worker would be attracted to at least twenty occupations, and thanks to "Phalansterian" education, all would be capable of laboring productively in each of them.[50]

The members of the Phalanx would never be bored and would always work ardently. However, their enthusiasm for their work would depend on more than gratifying the need for change and variety. The other two distributive passions, the Cabalist and the Composite, had to be brought into play. The Cabalist was the penchant for plots and conspiracies that manifested itself in the intrigues and rivalries of the workplace. Like the Butterfly, it would inspire "extreme ardor" at work, but it would also encourage intimacy among group members and rivalry between groups. Because no one spent all of his or her time in the same group, there was no danger that the competition between groups would become a source of permanent discord.[51]

The third distributive passion was the Composite. Whereas the Cabalist was a calculating passion, a form of "deliberate ardor," the Composite was the free, blind enthusiasm that would emerge when both the spirit and the senses were stimulated. The work of the Phalanx would stimulate the spirit by fostering a sense of fellowship among co-workers. The senses, on the other hand, would be charmed by the excellence of the goods produced by the work groups.[52]

In all of this Considerant followed Fourier closely. Where he differed from Fourier was less in substance than tone. Fourier possessed the inventiveness, playfulness, and delicate touch of a Rococo miniaturist; his accounts of life in the Phalanx were full of vignettes featuring characters like Cleon the sybarite, the vestal Galatea, and Damon the flower fancier. Considerant, on the other hand, generally adopted the earnest, didactic, and somewhat breathless tone of a teacher concerned to convey as clearly and succinctly as possible the main elements of a "social science" that included the blueprint of an ideal society. Fourier's work, with its irony, parody, and flights of fancy, was a kind of utopian poetry, whereas what Considerant offered was socialist prose.

Considerant also differed from Fourier in what he left out. In at least some of his public lectures, Considerant had much to say about the liberation of women and the role to be played by women in the society of the future.[53] In his main published accounts of life in the Phalanx, however, he quickly passed over two of the central concerns of Fourier's "Phalansterians"—love and food. In Considerant's work, Fourier's original vision of passional fulfillment and sexual liberation was reduced to a scheme for the organization of work. Other dimensions of Fourier's thought—his cosmogony and his theories of metempsychosis and universal analogy—were almost totally ignored. Considerant was well aware of this. He acknowledged that there was more to Fourier's thought than his popularizations conveyed, and he promised to make amends. "Questions of high harmony" would find their "natural place" in another volume, he wrote at the end of the second volume of *Destinée sociale,* and these would include a full discussion of "the social position of woman in the harmonic periods." When the third volume appeared, though, it was entirely devoted to questions of education. In 1851 Considerant began to publish articles on cosmogony and religion in *Démocratie pacifique,* but these came to an end after a few months with the closure of the journal.[54]

VI

If the Phalanx represented Considerant's ideal of social organization, it was not his only contribution to the discussion of the social question. His pamphlets and newspaper articles of the 1830s and 1840s also included numerous reformist proposals, most of which involved appeals for state intervention. As has already been noted, he was active in the (ultimately unsuccessful) campaign for extensive government regulation and control over the development of a national railroad system. "The abandonment of the railroads to the monopolistic corporations is the system of the Middle Ages; its exploitation by the state is the system of liberty," he wrote in 1844. "It is necessary that the railroads remain in the hands of the state, which represents all the people. The state is the people, the entire nation; a monopoly exercised by the state is no longer a monopoly. The state is a universal corporation of which all citizens are stockholders."[55]

Throughout the July Monarchy Considerant also carried on an active campaign for the liberalization of French divorce laws and a general improvement in the status of women both within and outside marriage. He called for an end to the "enslavement" of women in marriage, to "the brutal and charnel possession of the body of the woman" by her husband.

What marriage should be, he insisted, was not a rite of submission and domination but "a voluntary union" within which a woman could maintain control of her assets and which she could terminate whenever she wished. Considerant also argued that "women's work," including housework, was just as deserving of compensation as was the labor of a man. He called for legislation to guarantee employment and educational opportunities for women. Only thus, he maintained, could "woman march toward the conquest of her *individuality,* her *social independence.*"[56]

Finally, an insistent theme that ran through much of Considerant's writing in the decade before the 1848 revolution was his call for legislation recognizing the right to work. Repeatedly during the July Monarchy he criticized republicans such as François Arago, who argued that electoral reform was the necessary condition of social change. "We will do much more for the happiness of the lower classes," he wrote, "for their real emancipation and true progress, in guaranteeing these classes well-remunerated work, than in winning political rights and a meaningless sovereignty for them. . . . The most important of the people's rights is the *right to work.*"[57]

Fourier had articulated the concept of the right to work as "the first of the natural rights" as early as 1806. It was only a generation later, though, in 1839, that Louis Blanc and Victor Considerant almost simultaneously gave substance and currency to the concept. Louis Blanc argued in his influential *Organisation du travail* that capitalist competition was "a system of extermination" for wage earners and ultimately "a cause of ruin" for the bourgeoisie. It was the duty of the state, he maintained, to guarantee work and a minimum wage to all its citizens through the creation of a network of "social workshops"—cooperative enterprises to be run by the workers themselves with production and distribution coordinated by the state.[58] Both Considerant's arguments for the right to work and his proposals for its implementation differed from those of Louis Blanc. Considerant argued that the private ownership of property (which he favored) could only be legitimate in a society that guaranteed the right to work to those without property. As for the implementation of the right to work, he maintained that this would require the creation of jobs in state-subsidized "industrial institutions" to be financed, presumably, through income from taxation.[59]

What is interesting about all of Considerant's reform proposals during the July Monarchy is the role he assigned to the state. Considerant dreamed of a world divided into small, relatively self-sustaining communities. He also looked forward to some form of European federation in which the powers of existing nation-states would be greatly reduced. When he made practical proposals for reform, however, he repeatedly turned to the idea of an interventionist state that would use its centralized administrative machinery to plan and control the economic and social life of the nation. This confidence in government regulation was reflected in a proposal, to which he attached great importance, that the July Monarchy create a special Ministry of Progress, "charged with promoting and organizing studies concerning social improvements (and also with promoting the local testing of all proposals)." Such a ministry, Considerant suggested, should include two divisions: a division of "industrial progress" would examine and evaluate technical innovations; and a division of "social progress" would evaluate proposals relative to the social system itself. This idea, which was to bear fruit in popular agitation for a Ministry of Progress in 1848, was one of many instances of the continuing influence on Considerant's thinking of his faith in central planning and government direction of economic development, which he owed in part at least to his years at the Ecole Polytechnique.[60]

7

Among the Early Socialists

One of the more striking political cartoons published in Paris journals and newspapers in 1848 was Bertall's "La Foire aux idées." It shows a group of carnival barkers advertising their wares. On one side we can see Victor Considerant, professor of social prosthesis, luring the crowd into his Phalansteriana with promises of "Guaranteed Happiness." Alongside Considerant, Pierre-Joseph Proudhon advertises a scheme that will do away with property. Facing them, Etienne Cabet invites the crowd to visit his promised land of Icarie. Farther away one sees a shaggy Pierre Leroux and a tiny Louis Blanc hawking their nostrums along with a seller of false teeth and Daumier's corrupt promoter, Robert Macaire. "Hurry," the caption reads, "while there's still time."[1]

This cartoon illustrates a phenomenon that had impressed observers of the Paris scene well before the revolution of 1848. Radical social reformers were divided into sectarian movements or *écoles*, each with its own particular remedy and its own theoretical jargon. Just as the Saint-Simonians had advocated the collectivist and hierarchical organization of production, the Fourierists called for the association of capital, labor, and talent within the Phalanx. Other schemes included the egalitarian communism of the Icarians, the producers' cooperatives of Buchez, the social workshops of Louis Blanc, the state socialism of Constantin Pecqueur, and Proudhon's credit bank. Most of these *écoles* had their own journals, and they competed with one another for the public's attention in a manner not unlike that suggested by Bertall's cartoon. It was out of this competition that romantic socialism emerged. Significantly, however, even though the word *socialisme* had been given currency by Pierre Leroux in 1833, it was only after the 1848 revolution that it came into common usage. As Marie d'Agoult wrote, looking back from the vantage point of the Second Empire: "Until [1848] the radical *écoles* and sects were only considered in isolation under the names 'Babouvism,' 'Saint-Simonism,' 'Fourierism,' etc., without referring them to the common principle that has made it possible to designate them all under the general term of 'socialism.'"[2]

I

Of all the socialist *écoles* that flourished under the July Monarchy the first and the most influential was the Ecole Saint-Simonienne. Many of the Saint-Simonians were, like Considerant, graduates of the Ecole Polytechnique, where they had acquired excellent training in mathematics, science, and engineering, along with a fervent belief in the power of science to solve social problems. They were also seekers who were initially drawn to Saint-Simon not only by his view of science as the key to the material and moral reorganization of society but also, and most importantly, by the vision of social reconciliation suggested by his final work, *Le Nouveau christianisme*, which called for the establishment of a new religion aimed at improving as rapidly as possible the condition of "the poorest and most numerous class."[3]

The heyday of the Saint-Simonian movement was brief. Having come together immediately after the death of the Master in 1825, the Saint-Simonians traversed in a few years the distance from study group to religion and from the celebration of industrial expansion as a panacea for society's ills to a more complex vision of social regeneration. In December 1829 they constituted themselves formally as a "church" under the authority of two "supreme fathers," Prosper Enfantin and Saint-Amand Bazard. The next two years were a period of growth and missionary activity but also of internal conflict culminating in the schism of November 1831, when the followers of Bazard withdrew from the church, while Enfantin reoriented the Saint-Simonian theology, called for a monastic retreat, and initiated the search for a "Female Messiah" that was eventually to take the faithful remnant to Egypt. By 1835 the Saint-Simonian movement had fallen apart. For a few years at the beginning of the July Monarchy, however, the preaching and proselytizing of the Saint-Simonians had considerable resonance in France. In retrospect it is clear that Saint-Simonism played an important role in crystallizing the discontents and aspirations of some of the most talented French writers and intellectuals who reached maturity toward the end of the Restoration. Many of these people were eventually to look back on their Saint-Simonian days with detachment and even embarrassment, but they remained in contact. Some went on to play important roles in banking, commerce, railway construction, and the general economic development of France during the Second Empire.

The emergence of Fourierism as a significant social movement coincided with the breakup of Saint-Simonism. Thus Considerant's first ventures as a Fourierist prophet and publicist took place in a climate of conflict between these two *écoles*. Fourier himself was deeply suspicious of the Saint-Simonians, and in several works dating from the early 1830s he bitterly denounced their "snares and charlatanism." Considerant's views were more nuanced. He criticized the Saint-Simonians for their "retrograde" desire "to resolve the social question in favor of authority as opposed to liberty." He also described their questioning of the right of inheritance as a threat to the concept of private property. Nonetheless, he regarded the Saint-Simonians as trenchant social critics, and he recognized the appeal their ideas might have "in the wretched strata of society."[4]

Considerant got to know Emile Barrault and several of the other Saint-Simonians in the fall of 1830, at the time of a Saint-Simonian "mission" to Metz. He wrote Clarisse Vigoureux soon after that he had attended two of Barrault's *prédications*—"one on women and the other on political events"—and that he found the latter "magnificent." He urged Clarisse Vigoureux, who was then in Paris, to attend some of the Saint-Simonian meetings in their "temple" on the rue Monsigny.

> You will hear men of talent, who are powerful in their critique of modern society and in their hopes for the future. Their conception of social organization is founded on a narrow view of man. They have not appealed to our whole nature. Thus they have made some mistakes. However that may be, you will hear some good things there and you will see that there is more eloquence there than in our pitiful Chamber of Deputies.[5]

In due course Considerant developed fairly close personal ties with several of the Saint-Simonians. One of them, the economist, mining engineer, and future diplomat, Michel Chevalier, was to remain a lifelong friend. And there were two dissident Saint-Simonians, whom Considerant only got to know after the movement's breakup, whom he came to regard with respect if not friendship. These were Philippe Buchez and Pierre Leroux.

Philippe Buchez, who had been a Carbonarist conspirator at the age of twenty-four, subsequently passed through Saint-Simonism and then reverted to Catholicism to become an independent Christian socialist. His lifelong goal was to reconcile Christianity and social progress; and this concern lay behind his efforts as a radical journalist, philosopher of history, and co-editor of the influential *Histoire parlementaire de la Révolution française* (1834–1838). He was also an ardent partisan of the producers' cooperative—one of the founders of the cooperative movement in France. In 1840 a group of his working-class followers founded a journal called *L'Atelier*, which effectively championed the cause of the producers' association for the next ten years.[6]

Buchez and Considerant approached the "social question" from radically different perspectives. Between the asceticism of the Christian socialist and the hedonist psychology of the Fourierist there was a world of difference. Despite his admiration for Robespierre and his role as the founder of the "Catholic-Conventional" school of historical interpretation, Buchez's thought was imbued with an awareness of human sinfulness that was also poles apart from the Fourierist celebration of the passions. Not surprisingly, their initial contacts were hostile. The two crossed swords in 1835 at the historical congress organized by Buchez at the Hôtel de Ville. In 1837, the Fourierist Chambellant criticized Buchez in *La Phalange* for taking "as a point of departure all the errors of Christianity" on sacrifice, the denial of the flesh, and the evils of the passions. Conversely, the editors of *L'Atelier* criticized Fourier's theory of the passions in the light of the Christian doctrine of renunciation: "Christianity seeks to place the flesh under the spirit, and to dominate passion by moral authority." In time, though, Considerant came to respect Buchez as "a man of sincere dedication" whose life had been one of "sacrifice to his ideas, his faith, and humanity."[7]

Considerant took seriously Buchez's lifelong effort to link the Christian tradition to that of the democratic Enlightenment. In 1848 he wrote that Buchez was "not without influence" on the Fourierists' "discovery" that "we Phalansterians are, after all, the Christians of the nineteenth century." Considerant also admired Buchez's effort as a philosopher of history to work out a science of society on the model of the natural sciences. Buchez's *physiologie sociale* could, he believed, yield fruitful insights and analogies concerning the historical development of humanity. Considerant was less taken, however, with Buchez's practical proposals concerning the role that producers' associations might play in enabling workers to share profits and to dispense with the services of merchants and capitalists. Buchez's association was, in Considerant's view, "a little industrial monastery, a little abbey, in which shoes or pots or locks are made." It was "the application of the monastic principle to a monotonous industry"—with the exception that Buchez's idea of association applied only to productive activities and not to the organization of domestic life.[8]

At the heart of the disagreements between Considerant and Buchez lay two different visions of association. For Buchez and his followers, association was to be a feature of production but not of consumption and living arrangements. For Considerant, on the other hand, association was to be integral: it was to apply to all aspects of life. Considerant criticized Buchez for failing to question the viability of the household as an economic unit and for ignoring the economies of scale to be realized through the collectivization of domestic work. The Fourierist vision of association was also meant to include all social classes—to "rally" capital, labor, and talent within a single community. According to Considerant, the possessors of capital were to share profits and to play a significant role in the organization of labor. Buchez and his followers rejected all this. Their associations were open only to workers. They saw their goal as "the complete emancipation of the working classes," and they believed that only through their own efforts could workers free themselves from the "industrial servitude" in which they lived.[9]

Finally, however, Considerant saw Buchez as a significant and influential figure in the emerging socialist movement of the 1840s.

> If Buchez's system is not worth much, if he has an exaggerated fear of Satan . . . he has nonetheless contributed to developing in modern socialism a sentiment of dedication, duty, and self-sacrifice. To be sure, this is not a solution to the social problem, but it is quite compatible with the quest of a broader ideal than his. Although these qualities are not widely appreciated in the old egotistical world . . . they are capable of giving today's socialism a strength that would enable it to triumph.

Considerant could argue that "on balance, the school of Buchez merits sincere respect. It has strengthened the soul of the People. Its austerity is good for times of struggle. Its dedication suits militant socialism." Buchez and his followers were "sincere men" whose austerity and moralism were not a "hypocritical veneer" but a true faith.[10]

A second early refugee from Saint-Simonism whom Considerant eventually came to respect was Pierre Leroux. A founder of the first *Globe* and a friend of Sainte-Beuve, Hugo, and George Sand, Leroux broke with

Enfantin in 1831. He then joined the staff of *La Revue encyclopédique*, where he published a series of important articles characterizing what he regarded as the moral and religious vacuum of postrevolutionary France. Leroux's major theoretical treatise, *De l'humanité* (1840), was not widely read. However, some of its central ideas—notably his belief that Christianity must give way to a more comprehensive "religion of humanity"—found a wide audience through their popularization in the novels of George Sand, whom Leroux served as a philosophical mentor.[11]

After his break with Enfantin, Leroux remained on close terms with a number of the Saint-Simonians, including several who later defected to Fourierism. One of them, Abel Transon, published an influential "succinct exposition" of Fourier's theory in Leroux's *Revue encyclopédique*. Leroux himself was never particularly sympathetic to Fourier's ideas, though. He disliked Fourier's psychological hedonism, his "sensualist" fantasies, and the "materialist mysticism" of his theory of accords. In 1846 and 1847 Leroux published a strange book-length series of "letters on Fourierism," in which he attempted both to refute Fourier's ideas and to demonstrate that many of them were plagiarized from Saint-Simon, Diderot, and Restif de la Bretonne.[12]

Not surprisingly, Considerant's initial relations with Leroux were clouded. Nonetheless, he had been impressed by several of Leroux's early writings; and in 1848, when both were elected to the National Assembly, Considerant came to appreciate Leroux's personal warmth and courage. Leroux was one of the very few members of the Assembly to speak out in behalf of the insurgents of June, and Considerant could write at the end of 1848 that he found Leroux "so good, so full of heart," and so reliable in a time of crisis, that he had come to love him "as a brother."[13]

Finally, Considerant came to regard Leroux as a kind of "egalitarian Saint-Simonian"—a thinker who shared the Saint-Simonians' sense of the need for a new faith but rejected their authoritarianism. He also regarded Leroux as a democrat who articulated forcefully, if not always clearly, the aspirations of romantic socialism. "I have been reading you for eighteen years," he addressed Leroux publicly in 1848:

> No one feels more keenly then you, more religiously than you, the vague and generous aspirations of modern socialism, the need for the realization of the principles of a democratic philosophy. You have often expressed these sentiments with a noble and poetic eloquence. Often, too, you have mixed them in impure water, drawn from all the theological, metaphysical, political, historical, democratic, mystical, and even eclectic sources.[14]

Considerant regarded Leroux's struggles with theology and metaphysics with a measure of ironic detachment, but still he saluted Leroux as a comrade and fellow traveler.

II

A second major current in the early socialist movement was the communitarianism represented by Robert Owen in England and Etienne Cabet in France. Owen, whose career as an industrial reformer dated from the beginning of the century, had become famous by 1820 thanks to the success of his model community at New Lanark, Scotland. Fourier wrote Owen in 1824, hoping to convert him to his own ideas on association. Rebuffed, Fourier turned on Owen and accused him of having compromised the very idea of association with his "diatribes against property, religion, and marriage" and of having hypocritically donned "the mask of philanthropy" in order to win fame and fortune.[15]

Considerant was embarrassed by Fourier's personal attacks on Owen. He wrote Clarisse Vigoureux in 1829 that Owen seemed "rather a man convinced of the excellence of his schemes than a hypocrite taking advantage of the human race." For his part Considerant was intrigued by Owen. He found Owen's conception of human nature superficial, but still he was impressed by Owen's practical achievements at New Lanark. Thus, while still a student in Metz, he made a fairly extensive study of Owen, reading some of his work in English along with French popularizations like Joseph Rey's *Lettres sur le système de la coopération mutuelle* (1828). Later he was to establish personal contact with Owen, whom he met at Paris in 1837 and 1848.[16]

In Considerant's view, Robert Owen had two fundamental insights. The first was that cooperation rather than competition was the key to a better life for all. The second was that good education could produce workers eager to share and cooperate. The two great flaws in Owen's thinking, according to Considerant, were his suppression of private property and his failure to reckon with the passions, attributes, and desires that made each individual unique.

> Proceeding on the assumption that the individual is the result of his education and his natural endowment, and that no one can boast that either is his own personal achievement, [Owen] concludes that there is no such thing as individual worth, and he gets rid of the difficulties of distribution by abolishing the right to the personal ownership of property.

The result would be a comfortable but stultifying way of life.

> Monsieur Owen's idea is to bring together in the same building two or three thousand weavers, *all* weaving from morning to night, eating the *same* food at the same table, putting *all* their goods and *all* their work in *common*, and having the right only to *equal* shares.

For Considerant, the main problem with this communitarian vision was that Owen had identified community with equality.[17]

All of this, according to Considerant, was a rehash of Thomas More's *Utopia*, "adapted to the conditions of an industrial age by an English manufacturer full of gentleness, kindness, and love of humanity, but counting far too much on education and far too little on the inalterable passions." Thus Owenism was "a tendency more sentimental than scientific toward the principle of cooperation and collectivism." It was "the error of a mind lacking in imagination, profundity, and genius, guided by a heart of gold, and deceived by excessive optimism, although endowed with a great practical knowledge of modern industry."[18]

There was a small French Owenite movement. Its members included Jules Gay and Joseph Rey, both of whom also had links with Fourierism. Much more numerous in France than the handful of self-described French Owenites, however, were the Icarians, the followers of Etienne Cabet, whom Considerant rightly regarded as Robert Owen's French counterpart. Considerant noted that Cabet had begun his political career as a radical democrat and became a communist under the influence of Owen during an extended period of exile in England. "Icarian communism," wrote Considerant, "is only Owenism imported . . . and dressed up in French clothing." Cabet's scheme was more legalistic and his rhetoric more stridently democratic than Owen's. The chief difference between the two lay in Cabet's greater emphasis on the centralization of power and the role of the state, both of which were naturally downplayed in a "cooperative conception produced in England, the country of individual initiative par excellence."[19]

Considerant neither had nor sought any personal contact with Cabet, whose egalitarian and communist ideas appealed to workers and artisans but not to the propertied elite whose support Considerant sought in his electoral campaigns. In 1846 and 1847, *Démocratie pacifique* engaged in a lively polemic with Cabet and his followers. The Fourierists' general line was that Cabet's crude and simplistic ideas were at best a starting place, an introduction to the "practical" and "scientific" socialism that Fourier had to offer. In an 1846 article entitled "To Be Done with M. Cabet," Considerant wrote that Cabet's ideas were appealing to "the masses" because of their simplicity but were impossibly vague. Cabet was utterly lacking in the "practical sense" displayed by Robert Owen. As for the Icarian journal *Le Populaire*, Considerant described it as "a faucet of commonplaces that flow out every month at the bidding of Monsieur Cabet."[20]

Considerant's principal objections to Icarian communism focused on Cabet's conception of property and work. In Considerant's view, Cabet had not given adequate thought to the problem of organizing labor within a collectivist framework. Cabet also failed to recognize the universality of the aspiration to private ownership. Considerant wrote:

> We are not communists. We believe that the principle of individual property is a right, a sacred right, without which there can be no lasting and stable society. At the same time we believe that the system of subdivided [*morcélée*] individual property is a bad system, and that in the interest of the proprietors themselves property is destined to pass from the subdivided state to the societary state.

Cabet presented himself as a "benign communist" who opposed the forcible seizure of individual holdings. The problem, as Considerant saw it, was that Cabet's denial of the right of private ownership, which was at the heart of "the communist idea," would lead sooner or later to the "revolutionary suppression of private property."[21]

III

Pierre-Joseph Proudhon, the great anarchist and *bête-noir* of the bourgeoisie during the 1840s, was Considerant's compatriot and contemporary. Born in Besançon in 1809, Proudhon attended the Collège de Besançon at the same time as Considerant; and the two had friends in common—among them Gustave Courbet, Charles Weiss, and even Just Muiron, who in 1832 tried to hire Proudhon as managing editor for his weekly newspaper *L'Impartial de Besançon*. Proudhon knew Fourier's work well: he had studied it more carefully than any other contemporary radical outside the Fourierist movement. Yet he and Considerant were never close. At school they had no contact; and in later life their most significant interactions took the form of pitched battles.[22]

One issue that separated these two Franc-comtois was the question of Proudhon's debt to Fourier. Proudhon was an autodidact and a fiercely independent thinker whose intellectual growth was marked by periods in which he surrendered himself to the ideas of others, then spat out what he could not assimilate and proceeded furiously to criticize everything he had rejected. This was the way Proudhon dealt with Fourier, whose ideas he first encountered in 1829, when, as a twenty-year-old proofreader at the Imprimerie Gauthier in Besançon, he oversaw the printing of Fourier's *Le Nouveau monde industriel*. According to his own account, Proudhon was for six weeks "the captive of this bizarre genius." Before the typesetting was finished, however, he had already begun to entertain his fellow workers with jokes at Fourier's expense.[23]

In later years Proudhon fiercely criticized many of Fourier's ideas. He had no liking for Fourier's "detestable" moral views, his "chimerical" laws of analogy, or the veneration of "Saint Fourier" by his disciples. He dismissed Fourier's metaphysics as "rhapsody and plagiarism," his classification of the passions as "erroneous," and most of his other theories as "so much childish twaddle." But Proudhon was fascinated as well as repelled by Fourier's thought. One of his principal works, *De la création de l'ordre dans l'humanité* (1843), centered on a conception of the series that clearly owed much to Fourier. In 1845 Proudhon could write wryly and provocatively in his notebooks: "I am the only interpreter that Fourier has had up to now."[24]

Proudhon's belief that he had understood Fourier better than Fourier's own disciples gave a bitter edge to his comments on Considerant. In his correspondence, his notebooks, and even his published works, Proudhon described Considerant as a "trickster," a "barking dog," and a "charlatan." Considerant's charlatanism, according to Proudhon, consisted in the fact that he pandered to the public and presented Fourier as all things to all people in order to raise money and recruit new members for his sect. Fourier's Phalanstery was a mansion with many rooms, but to make Fourier's ideas alluring to a wide public, Considerant had to conceal the theory of free love and minimize the doctrine's fundamental immorality.[25]

Equally deceptive, in Proudhon's opinion, were Considerant's writings on property. Considerant and the other Fourierists were wrong to describe themselves as defenders of property. Within the Fourierist Phalanx, the community controlled capital and the instruments of production. Although the property owners were paid interest on their initial investment, they had no control over it: their interest was a "compensation," not an acknowledgment of ownership. According to Proudhon, the system of Fourier deprived property owners of "the greatest pleasure of ownership, the right to dispose of their holdings freely."[26]

The disagreements between Considerant and Proudhon came to a head with the publication by Proudhon in January 1842 of a brochure entitled *Avertissement aux propriétaires, ou lettre à M. Victor Considerant, rédacteur de la Phalange, sur une défense de la propriété*. In this brochure, itself a response to an anonymous *Défense du Fouriérisme,* Proudhon elaborated his own theory of property and argued that attempts to reform or redistribute private property would eventually lead to its destruction. The brochure also included a concerted attack on Considerant, together with the prophecy that he would sooner or later be led by the consequences of his own ideas "to renounce his whims about property and inequality."

> Yes, you yourself, *Monsieur le rédacteur,* will sooner or later desert the Phalanstery. Keep defending your flag, devote yourself tirelessly to propaganda, fight for property, preach free love and family at one and the same time, found colonies, organize series of contrasted groups. [Nevertheless] within five years you will be liberated from the Phalansterian limbo in which your poor soul is languishing.

Proudhon described Considerant as possessing a lively and inquiring mind, a mind "well suited for exact and rigorous science" but temporarily "subjugated by the hallucinations of an ignoramus and a madman." Proudhon concluded his pamphlet by evoking a future in which he and Considerant might be intellectual allies, marching "under the same flag, fighting for the same cause."[27]

Considerant was not convinced. Although he did not reply directly to Proudhon's *Avertissement aux propriétaires,* his later work included a critical analysis of "the socialism of Proudhon" in which charges of deception and mystification were turned back on Proudhon himself. Observing that Proudhon had become the scapegoat of all the enemies of socialism, Considerant argued that Proudhon was in fact much more of an individualist than a communist or communitarian.

> Proudhon intends to allow everyone his property. He has not the slightest desire for a sharing of goods or for a society in which people work and live together. Any arrangement of this sort, any community or association, is horrifying to him. His thought is the most fundamental kind of individualism.

All that Proudhon wanted, according to Considerant, was to terminate the economic role of the parasitical middleman—to create an economic system in which the producers of wealth received all its profits.[28]

In what sense was Proudhon a socialist? Considerant called him a "knotty" and negative socialist. "Proudhon's power," he wrote, "is entirely in his negations." Proudhon's great concern was to emancipate labor from the constraints imposed by capital, but he was hostile to the idea of the organization of labor. Ideas of community, sentiment, passion, combination, and the harmony of human energies had no appeal to him. His aim was to do away with interest and profit and to make credit available to all. What Proudhon failed to recognize was that his credit schemes could only work with the help of a strong state and a strong central bank. "Logic leads Proudhon," wrote Considerant, "whether he likes it or not, in a direction he does not want to go, toward a veritable state communism."[29]

These statements were made late in 1848, at a time when Proudhon was deeply involved in the development of his exchange bank and various other credit schemes. In later writings Proudhon did address some of the questions of social organization that Considerant correctly saw him as evading in 1848, but Considerant never took notice. When the two became involved in a fierce war of words early in 1849, it focused almost entirely on the insurrection of June 1848 and the role each had played during those terrible days. Neither this polemic nor any of Proudhon's subsequent writings caused Considerant to modify his view as to the fundamental contrast between Proudhon's "disheveled, anarchic, [and] destructive socialism" and his own "organizing, conciliating, and pacific socialism."[30]

IV

Flora Tristan was the first of the early socialists to pursue in a systematic way Charles Fourier's insight that in modern societies the oppression of women and the oppression of the laboring classes are closely connected. The natural daughter of a French mother and a Peruvian nobleman who died when she was four, Tristan was brought up in poverty. After a disastrous marriage and a bitter struggle for the custody of her children, she became a writer and a journalist. At thirty-five she published an autobiography that, together with her novel *Méphis*, established her as a major figure in the emerging feminist movement. Her *Promenades dans Londres*, published in 1840, painted a harrowing picture of the life of the London proletariat; and her final and most influential work, *L'Union ouvrière* (1843), was an impassioned call for workers to organize themselves into self-governing unions. In the last year of her life she embarked on a *tour de France*, seeking to rally support for the creation of a workers' union. She died of exhaustion and typhoid fever in 1844 at the age of forty-one.[31]

Flora Tristan's first contact with the Fourierists came in 1835, when she wrote Fourier himself, asking to be put to use. "Every day I become more deeply convinced of the sublimity of your doctrine," she wrote, "and I feel more strongly an imperious need to associate with the people who profess it." In particular she wished to meet "Monsieur Considerant, about whom people have spoken so highly." For the rest of her life she was to keep in close contact with the Fourierists. Fourier's discussion in the *Théorie des quatre mouvements* of the right to work and the "woman question" always remained an inspiration to her. She took his statement that advances in the position of women were the key to all social progress as the epigraph for her last work, the posthumously published *L'Emancipation de la femme, ou le testament de la pariah*.[32]

Flora Tristan came to regard Considerant as her most faithful ally in the socialist camp, but her friendship and admiration were never unqualified. In 1836 she wrote him a long letter in his capacity as director of *La Phalange*, protesting the largely critical tone of the journal and the lack of a clear, concise statement of Fourier's doctrine.

> The science of Monsieur Fourier is, you say, a *truth*. (For my part I only recognize relative truths, not absolute ones.) The mark of truth is to impress everyone with its clarity. I confess to you, Monsieur, that many people, including me, find Monsieur Fourier's science very obscure. . . . I'm sure you can understand that if, in order to be a Phalansterian, you first have to have spent four years at the Ecole Normale and have a thorough knowledge of astronomy, mathematics, physics, etc., etc., and then spend four more years *studying Fourier*. Oh! I'm sure you can understand that in this case very few people are qualified to become *Phalansterians*.

What Flora Tristan wanted above all was a clear statement of the "means of realization" by which the Fourierists proposed to remedy the "innumerable ills" besetting society.[33]

Considerant published this letter in *La Phalange*, praising Flora Tristan as "one of the women who has brought the most love, intelligence, and zeal to the social cause." Subsequently he gave her various forms of support, publishing announcements of her works, advising her on possible reviewers, making a small contribution toward the publication of *Union ouvrière*, and finally publishing extracts from that work in *La Phalange*. On her side, Flora Tristan made a contribution to Considerant's fund-raising appeal of 1837. "I am not a Phalansterian," she wrote, "but the extreme tolerance that I profess permits me to take from each system what seems good and feasible to me."[34]

Some of the letters exchanged by Considerant and Flora Tristan have been lost. These include an angry letter written by Tristan protesting her exclusion, as a woman, from the banquet held in April 1838 on the anniversary of Fourier's birth. It is clear, at any rate, that her initial enthusiasm for Fourier's ideas abated and she eventually came to believe that Fourier had stolen his fundamental ideas from obscure precursors such as the sixteenth-century Italian writer Francesco Doni. Toward the end of her life she also became fed up with the Fourierist rank and file, whom she found excessively prudent, egotistical, and "bourgeois." But she never lost her admiration and affection for her "brother in humanity," Victor Considerant.[35]

A crucial moment for Flora Tristan in her efforts to win an audience came in March 1843, when Considerant published in *La Phalange* substantial excerpts from her forthcoming *L'Union ouvrière*. Considerant wrote that he did not believe the time ripe for Tristan's proposal. The working class did not yet possess a sense of its own collective powers, and "as long as there is not a Common Idea, there cannot be a Party, a Union." He argued, however, that the publication of *L'Union ouvrière* could serve to raise the consciousness of the working class.

> These writings, which speak to the masses about their interests and their rights, are preparations and initiations. If the working classes of the cities and the countryside are still, for the most part, brutalized by ignorance and poverty, there are already in their ranks a considerable number of individuals who thirst for ideas and education and who can tell their brothers about their readings. The proletarian is going through a process of initiation, and it is good that his initiation should take place by contact with big and bold ideas which will develop in him a sense of dignity at the same time as a conception of his rights.[36]

Considerant saluted the appearance of *L'Union ouvrière* as a work likely to awaken both "a sense of solidarity among the pariahs of civilization" and a sense of the need for responsible action on the part of "the ruling classes." At the same time he wrote Tristan a letter praising the Workers' Union as an idea of "much grandeur and power." It was "a utopia" and it needed to be clothed "in a cloak of high social charity and not of revolt," but it would do good.[37]

Flora Tristan was delighted both by Considerant's publication of her text and by his commentary. "Here is an unexpected development!" she wrote in her journal.

> I send out a chapter "On the means of constituting the working class." Considerant writes me a superb letter. He finds my idea lofty, powerful, capable of shedding light on the working of society, and he asks my permission to talk with his collaborators about the publication [of the chapter] that I am asking for. Then four days later, on March 29, he publishes part of it with a very good leader. On the 31st he publishes the rest, almost a chapter. He follows it with an article in which he situ-

ates me among the peaceful socialists. In a word, that's just fine. That evening he writes me a very good and very warm letter, placing his *Phalange* at my disposal. Who could have anticipated this?

Flora Tristan believed that Considerant's support indicated a desire to break with the wealthy bourgeois who had hitherto been the principal backers of the Ecole Sociétaire.

> Considerant has at last recognized that he can do nothing with rich people, that he has made no progress at all in the past eleven years. Finally he has lost patience and, just as I told him seven years ago, he has finally begun to try to rely on the only real power that exists in society, the power of the greatest number. It took my article to get him to do this. He approves in private of my manner of speaking, but he would never have dared to speak like that himself. I believe that the insertion of my chapter in *La Phalange* is going to be an event with momentous consequences for this journal—because by printing the chapter, the journal will find itself committed and forced to move in the same direction. What amuses me is the surprise this must have been for the subscribers, those bourgeois property owners who are accustomed to reading articles in favor of the rich. Their eyes must have popped out of their heads when they saw how I treat property owners!

In Tristan's opinion, the publication of her chapter proved that Considerant was "smarter and more sincere" than his fellow journalists. "I have hope for that man," she wrote. She was convinced that when the time came, he would "abandon the cause of the rich for the cause of the people."[38]

In fact, the transformation that Flora Tristan hoped to see in Considerant would not take place in her lifetime. During her *tour de France*, the resistance and suspicion that she encountered at the hands of the authorities sometimes caused her to reflect bitterly on the quixotic moderation of her "credulous and naive friend, Considerant." For his part, and with the qualifications expressed earlier, he remained her ally and supporter. After her death, in writing her obituary, he pulled out all the stops, describing her as a martyr whose fate served to clarify the nature of the century and the regime. "This bold and powerful dedication, this noble daring, this hard apostolate culminating in a martyr's death were a strange anomaly in an egotistical century that does not comprehend the ardor of a generous faith and that responds to such a faith too often by irony and outrage." This sort of rhetoric came easily to Considerant, but it was deeply felt. In the end, the example of Flora Tristan may have had a more powerful influence on him than did his ideas on the thinking of his "sister in humanity."[39]

V

During the July Monarchy, Paris became a magnet for radical intellectuals from the rest of Europe. The Russian liberal Pavel Annenkov compared the impression Paris produced on his compatriots to that of a desert oasis: "They flung themselves at the city with the passion and enthusiasm of wayfarers coming out of a desert wasteland and finding the long expected fountainhead." The German jurist Eduard Gans similarly evoked the "excitement and tense expectation" aroused by the prospect of a trip to Paris, where "everything" was "important and meaningful." Arnold Ruge could describe himself departing for Paris in 1843 as about to cross "the threshold of a new world." "May it live up to our dreams!" wrote Ruge. "At the end of our journey we will find the vast valley of Paris, the cradle of the new Europe."[40]

What attracted these intellectual expatriates was not only Parisian culture—the theater, the cafés, the salons—though these certainly had their appeal. More important were the freedom and sheer vitality of the French capital. Paris had long been known for its hospitality to foreigners, but during the July Monarchy writers, artists, and intellectuals from the rest of Europe flocked to Paris in greater numbers than ever. There, as Isaiah Berlin has written, "they were neither, as in Berlin, bullied into conformity by the native civilization, nor yet, as in London, left coldly to themselves, clustering in small isolated groups, but rather were welcomed freely and even enthusiastically, and given free entry into the artistic and social salons which had survived the years of monarchist restoration."[41]

The intellectual atmosphere these expatriates entered was hopeful and exalted. They had the opportunity to say and write what they wanted, to inveigh against the old order, to organize, to conspire, and to experience an open fellowship and solidarity inconceivable in Berlin, Warsaw, or Vienna. Each year brought more expatriates, swelling the size of the German, Polish, Russian, Italian, and Hungarian colonies that had formed at Paris. By 1844 the German community alone, which mixed political refugees with a much larger number of artisans, included forty thousand people with their own newspapers, cafés, and reading rooms.[42] The Polish community, which consisted largely of refugees from the unsuccessful revolt of 1830–1831 against Russian rule, was growing even faster.

One element in the scene that awaited intellectual exiles arriving in Paris was the Fourierist headquarters at the rue de Tournon and (later) at the rue de Beaune. Many of them made their way sooner or later to the Fourierists' Wednesday evenings. The Russians Mikhail Bakunin and Ivan

Golovine, the Germans Wilhelm Weitling, Moses Hess, Arnold Ruge, Lorenz von Stein, and Heinrich Heine, the Pole August Cieszkowski, the Italian Giuseppi Bucellati, and the Spanish republican Joaquin Abreu were all visitors during the 1840s, as were intellectual tourists from English-speaking countries, like the Americans Margaret Fuller and Charles Dana and the British Owenite, John Barmby.

Several of the earliest foreign visitors to Fourierist headquarters were political refugees from Poland. One of them, Jan Czynski, who had been a vice president of the Warsaw Patriotic Society, became a Fourierist and took up permanent residence in France. The author of half a dozen Fourierist brochures in French, Czynski also propagated Fourierist ideas in the journals of the Polish emigration. He and Considerant never got along, though, and by the time of Fourier's death Czynski had already identified himself with the dissident faction within the movement.[43] Considerant's relations with the Polish left-Hegelian philosopher August Cieszkowski were smoother. Cieszkowski settled in Paris in 1838, soon after the publication of his influential *Prolegomenon to Historiosophy*. His diary for the winter of 1838–1839 shows numerous visits to the offices of *La Phalange* as well as a pilgrimage to Fourier's grave in the Montmartre Cemetery. Under the influence of Considerant and the Fourierists, Cieszkowski's interests shifted from philosophy to politics and economics. His articles on agricultural credit (written in collaboration with Jules Duval) and on the reform of the French Chamber of Peers both initially appeared in Fourierist periodicals; and he has been seen as a thinker who, in his journalism of the 1840s, attempted to apply Hegelian insights to the concerns of the early French socialists. He and Considerant were to remain in touch after the debacle of 1848.[44]

Like many members of his generation, Considerant became a staunch partisan of Polish independence. In 1831, as a young army officer, he railed in his private correspondence against the brutality of the Russian repression of the Polish insurrection. Fifteen years later, at the time of the Habsburg repression of the Krakow uprising, he helped form a Franco-Polish friendship committee and wrote editorials calling upon the French government to come to the aid of "that heroic nation." In 1848, Considerant became one of the more prominent partisans of Polish independence. With the encouragement of Stanislas Worcell, he helped set up a Society of the Friends of Democratic Poland, charged with "defending the cause of Poland" through speeches and journalism and with "providing material aid to the Polish emigration."[45]

Considerant's relations with radical German expatriates were just as cordial as his relations with the Poles. Moses Hess, who attended a Wednesday evening soirée at the rue de Tournon in March 1843, reported that Considerant spent much of the evening rhapsodizing about Franco-German friendship. Arnold Ruge, whom Hess took to meet Considerant the following August, was warmly received. "Victor Considerant has a weakness for Germans," Ruge wrote later. "Thus I received a favorable reception from him for my plan for a Franco-German intellectual alliance.... But I had against me the fact that the Fourierists thought that I was appealing to violence." In the end Ruge's proposal for a jointly produced *German-French Yearbook* got no support from the French. Apparently Considerant did fear being associated with revolutionaries. Nonetheless, he was quite willing to publish a protest in *Démocratie pacifique* against the attack on the radical press in Germany, which had led to the emigration not only of Ruge and Hess but also Karl Marx, Karl Bernays, and Georg Herwegh.[46]

During 1844 and 1845, Arnold Ruge was a frequent visitor to the Fourierist offices on the rue de Seine. Having studied the works of Fourier and his disciples, Ruge came to regard Fourier as "the father of all the ideas and systems which under the name of 'socialism' now penetrate French society." Ruge could even write that Fourier "plays the same role in France as Hegel [in Germany]: he lends arms to all parties. The conservatives love his polemic against philosophy and revolution, while his critique of civilization, commerce, the family, morality, and politics pleases revolutionaries." At the same time, Ruge appreciated the urbanity and broad-mindedness of Fourier's disciples. "In the salon of *Démocratie pacifique*," he wrote, "it was my pleasure to encounter the real gentility of French society and of refined manners which have nothing pedantic about them. As soon as you enter you are put at ease; there is no constraint there; people read, play chess, hold discussions, talk politics, but always in a high-minded way which presupposes a state of human intercourse not yet revealed to Germany."[47]

Arnold Ruge's delight at the Fourierists' "gentility" might not have been shared by his young colleague, Karl Marx, who arrived in Paris in late October 1843, ostensibly to join with Ruge in resurrecting the *Deutsche Jahrbucher*. In December, Marx and Ruge published a letter in *Démocratie pacifique*, responding to charges that they had falsely identified Lamartine as a would-be collaborator.[48] This letter is Marx's only known contact with the Fourierists, however. During most of his sixteen months in Paris, Marx kept to himself and his work, venturing out only occasionally to probe the world of the Parisian working class and the German émigré artisans. In

March 1844, Marx apparently attended a banquet held by Louis Blanc and the other editors of the socialist journal *La Réforme;* between October 1844 and February 1845 he had an intense personal and intellectual confrontation with Proudhon. There is no evidence, though, that Marx and Considerant ever met.[49] On February 24, 1845, the *Démocratie pacifique* published an article protesting Marx's expulsion from France, but neither that article nor the earlier one protesting Marx's expulsion from Germany left any trace in Considerant's memory. Toward the end of his life, asked when he had first heard of Karl Marx, Considerant replied that it was not until after his return from exile in 1869.[50]

If Considerant was hardly aware of Marx's existence in the 1840s, how important was Considerant to Marx? The sixteen months that Marx spent in Paris between October 1843 and February 1845 were a vitally important period in his intellectual development. During that period Marx discovered the proletariat, became a socialist, and entered into his lifelong partnership with Friedrich Engels. At this time Marx also made an intensive study of French socialism, as he had wanted to do ever since 1842, when he wrote that "to assess the writings of Leroux, Considerant, and above all the sharp-witted Proudhon . . . long and deep study would be necessary."[51] In the course of his own study Marx almost certainly read Considerant's *Manifeste politique et sociale de la démocratie pacifique* (published shortly before Marx's arrival in Paris), parts of *Destinée sociale,* and probably other works as well. In these readings Marx seems to have been particularly engaged by Considerant's critique of bourgeois society and the capitalist economy.

During his Paris period, Marx was only beginning his study of economics. He was just becoming aware, as he later put it, that "the anatomy of civil society is to be sought in political economy." He was also just beginning (in *On the Jewish Question*) to see the relevance of Feuerbach's conception of religious alienation to the understanding of money, the new god of modern commercial society. At this crucial point in his intellectual development Marx may well have been fascinated by Considerant's analysis of the economic anarchy produced by unregulated capitalism and by Considerant's account of "the development of a new feudalism, an industrial and financial feudalism," which was replacing the old landed aristocracy of the Old Regime "through the liquidation and impoverishment of the intermediary classes." Marx must also have been intrigued to see all of this connected to an analysis of the role played by free competition and "an uncontrolled industrialism" in driving down workers' salaries and creating a society divided into "the possessors of the materials and the instruments of labor," on the one hand, and a "class of proletarians stripped of all possessions," on the other.[52]

Considerant's language in the *Manifeste de la démocratie pacifique* of 1843 is at some points so close to that of the *Communist Manifesto* of 1848 that some scholars have described Considerant's work as a significant "influence" on Marx and Engels.[53] A few have even asserted that the *Manifesto* is largely a "paraphrase" or a "translation" of Considerant's pamphlet.[54] The latter claims do not deserve to be taken seriously. At the heart of the *Communist Manifesto* stands an argument concerning the laws of historical change and the historical necessity of revolution, which is not to be found in Considerant. But what about the claims of influence? The issue cannot be definitively resolved. However, it does seem that Considerant's work (along with that of other French socialists, including Pierre Leroux, Louis Blanc, and Constantin Pecqueur) played a role in the initial shaping of Marx's socialist perspective and in convincing the twenty-five-year-old exile that the dehumanization of modern man, which he had previously considered from moral and religious standpoints, could not be understood apart from its economic roots.

VI

The foregoing account of Considerant's relations with other socialist leaders during the 1840s underlines the sectarian nature of French radicalism at this time. Considerant tells us of the affection he felt for some of his comrades on the left. Often, though, his relations with them took the form of combat. He defended Fourier against charges of plagiarism brought by Leroux and Tristan, attacked Cabet for his communistic views on property, and quarreled with Proudhon over just about everything. Of course, these conflicts between socialists and communists of various stripes delighted the conservative and *juste-milieu* press. If Bertall presented the rival socialist leaders as competing sideshow barkers, other cartoonists depicted them as wild animals, prone to attack one another at any provocation.

None of this should cause us to lose sight of the fact that socialism came of age in the 1840s. It was not until 1847 that Considerant began to identify himself as a socialist.[55] Nevertheless, a broadly based socialist movement emerged during the July Monarchy and Considerant helped shape its ideology. His influence on the development of socialist thought was probably greatest in the sphere of social criticism. Considerant did much to popularize a view of contemporary society as riven by class conflict—a conflict not simply of rich and poor but of capitalists and wage workers. His analysis of the "anarchic" character of early capitalist production, the "monopolistic" tendency of the market economy, and the replacement of military feudalism by a new "industrial feudalism"—all of this entered into the general current of French socialist thought.

Considerant also gave the demand for the right to work—first voiced by Fourier at the beginning of the century—a currency that it had never previously possessed. It is no coincidence that when on February 25, 1848, a crowd burst into the Hôtel de Ville and called on the Provisional Government to guarantee the right to work, their spokesman carried a petition drafted by an editor of *Démocratie pacifique*.[56] No one had done more than the Fourierists—and above all Considerant—to put this demand at the top of the political agenda of the left. Considerant's influence as a social critic was felt in other ways as well that were at once more diffuse and more pervasive. Sharing Charles Fourier's inability to accept human suffering as a necessary part of things, Considerant did much in his writings to spread the view that most of the "ordinary" trials of life—hunger, disease, poverty, crime, ignorance, immorality—were not inevitable consequences of the human condition but *social* problems with social solutions.

Another contribution of Considerant's to the development of socialist ideology was to help give the concepts of "association," "community," and "peaceful democracy" the extraordinary resonance they had acquired by 1848. "Communism"—whether that of Cabet or of the neo-Babouvists—became in the 1840s a "specter" strongly associated in the popular imagination with memories of the "agrarian law" and the forcible expropriation of wealth during the French Revolution.[57] It was in response to the invocation of these revolutionary memories that Considerant represented Fourierism as a system that would harmonize the claims of workers and employers, proprietors and the propertyless. These images of harmony and reconciliation—the overcoming of conflict—were central to Considerant's thought. In stressing them, he helped give French socialism the conciliatory character that was so essential to it in 1848.

Hardly less important in shaping early French socialism was Considerant's stress on the religious roots of socialist thought. Early in his career he had repeatedly contrasted historical Christianity, that "religion of slaves, made by slaves," with the message of unity and love preached by Jesus. In the second volume of *Destinée sociale* (1838), he softened his criticism and spelled out more fully his conception of Jesus Christ's message as a message of hope for this world. For Considerant in *Destinée sociale*, the religion of Jesus Christ was a powerful embodiment of the unity and collective feeling that would one day prevail on earth. By the last years of the July Monarchy, his writing had become saturated with religious rhetoric. Muting his earlier critique of Christianity, he wrote in 1847 that modern socialism "is the pure spirit of Christ." Christianity was now "the Great Religion of Humanity," and fraternity and unity were at once "the two revelations of Christ" and "the alpha and omega of social science."[58]

Finally and most importantly, Considerant influenced the development of socialist ideology through his insistent contrasting of the socialist ideal with the existing system of competition, egoism, and individualism. For Considerant, social good did not come from the selfish pursuit of individual happiness but from *dévouement* and the love of humanity—from dedication to a common cause. Thus, in describing his ideal society, he repeatedly emphasized the cooperation, bonding, and deepening of affective ties that would take place within it. As the socialist Henri Brissac wrote much later, one of Considerant's significant contributions was "to awaken altruistic sentiments" among the educated youth of his time. This is a point worth stressing because it suggests a fascinating irony. What Considerant inherited from Fourier was a science of society in which the unfettered pursuit of individual interests was seen as the road to social harmony. What he transformed it into was a democratic and humanitarian creed that sought to awaken generous and high-minded impulses and to build a new social order around "the love of the collective good and of humanity." This appeal to the individual's higher self, capacity for self-abnegation, and love of humanity would not have been congenial to Fourier, but it was essential to the romantic socialism that Considerant helped to fashion.[59]

8

Toward a Radical Politics

The last years of the July Monarchy were a period of transition in Considerant's thought. After years of supporting Louis Philippe and the principle of constitutional monarchy, he finally broke with the government and joined the opposition. He became deeply involved in electoral politics, which he had initially rejected as sterile and meaningless, and became a fierce critic of parliamentary corruption and the elite of bankers, merchants, and land owners that had ruled France since 1830. At the same time he distanced himself from Fourier in significant ways, describing Fourier's theory as a mere "hypothesis" and arguing for the "necessity of constraint and repression," at least in the short term. This chapter considers how and why Considerant's thinking changed so radically in the period 1840–1848.

I

Victor Considerant's relation to Fourier's doctrine was not initially problematic. We have already seen how as a young man he had been swept off his feet by Fourier's thought, which opened up a whole new world to him. What especially excited him was that Fourier seemed to offer both a plausible explanation for the world's ills and a compelling picture of the ideal order intended by God. Fourier's work also combined imaginative power with a "mathematical rigor" that gave the eighteen-year-old Considerant "a new confidence in the future." "You can regard it as an axiom," he wrote Paul Vigoureux in 1826, "that tastes and penchants which exist now, even those which cause the most disorder, can be utilized [in the ideal society] and have been created for that very purpose."[1]

The young Considerant found everything about Fourier's doctrine fascinating. He regarded Fourier as a "genius" who had broken with two thousand years of philosophy to offer a totally new understanding of man and society, the past, and the future, and he made no distinction between the "practical" and "esoteric" aspects of Fourier's doctrine. Indeed, Fourier's initial appeal to Considerant lay largely in areas that were later to be regarded as marginal or esoteric. He was fascinated by Fourier's analogies between the movement of the heavenly bodies and the movement of the passions in the social world. He also found consolation in Fourier's doctrine of metempsychosis for the pain he felt at the deaths of his father and Claire Vigoureux. Thus in his early letters, one finds Considerant seeking to "master" Fourier's doctrine and to "teach" it to friends like Paul Vigoureux and Charles Magnin.[2]

The first real tensions between Fourier and Considerant came in 1832 and 1833, when Considerant and his colleagues attempted to found a journal and build a community based on Fourier's ideas. They soon found that Fourier was difficult to work with and his expectations impossible to satisfy. The clash between Fourier and his disciples was not merely a matter of personality or temperament, though. Considerant and his friends were also separated from Fourier by an intellectual gulf that only grew wider as the years passed. Fourier's view of human nature and human motivation was in some ways very close to that of the psychological hedonists and materialists of the eighteenth century. Considerant, on the other hand, was a romantic who believed that men and women had a "higher self," a capacity for empathy, self-sacrifice, and *dévouement*, for generous and disinterested action, and that it was only by drawing on these qualities that the good society could be established. Although Considerant spoke the language of "passionate attraction" and gratified desire, he gave Fourier's concepts a new meaning. Considerant did not really believe that the unfettered pursuit of individual goals would lead to social harmony. He was constantly appealing to "higher" and generous impulses that Fourier would have disdained.

The intellectual gulf between Considerant and Fourier widened when Considerant embarked on an effort of proselytism in the early 1830s. Quickly he discovered that many of the ideas he found appealing in Fourier's thought did not seem so attractive to others. Eventually he came to believe that the doctrine, as Fourier had expounded it, was simply too strange, too spectacularly eccentric, to have wide appeal. "In its simple and fine nudity," he wrote, "the Societary Theory would have seemed to be just a strange and bizarre conception, unrelated to real and present things, a sterile and inapplicable scheme."[3]

In 1833, when Considerant set out to provide an "elementary exposition" of Fourier's thought that would be "clear and acceptable to the public," he was selective, avoiding extended discussions of Fourier's cosmogony and his theory of universal analogy and drawing a veil over Fourier's sexual fantasies and his radically antipatriarchal vision of a "new amorous world." He presented Fourier as a solemn and responsible humanitarian reformer, and he explicitly argued against a libertarian interpretation of his thought, asserting that "the principle which dominates the conception of Fourier is not the principle of *liberty* but rather the principle of ORDER." He also reformulated many of Fourier's key ideas and concepts, putting them in a more commonplace idiom and a more conventional form. Fourier's "Phalanx" became Considerant's "commune"; Fourier's neologisms—his "pivots," "mixed scales," and "bi-compound accords"—were discretely removed; and Fourier's dry irony gave way to Considerant's earnest moralizing. "I had to *disguise the science*," he wrote, "and without harming the rigor and coherence of the demonstrations and the method, I had to abandon the concise and rather dry forms of didactic language to try to be clear and appealing."[4] This effort to "disguise the science" was characteristic of all Considerant's writing on Fourier's doctrine. He often presented Fourier's ideas as the basis of a science—a "new social science"—but defined that science in a way that removed most of what was strangest and most idiosyncratic.

Considerant's effort to distance himself from the more esoteric and radical aspects of Fourier's thought only increased after 1839, when he began to run for elective office. At electoral meetings he was often asked about his commitment to Fourier's ideas. Did he take seriously Fourier's prophecy that the sea would soon turn into pink lemonade? Did he share Fourier's belief in free love? Were not Fourier's ideas close to those of the communists? In time Considerant worked out answers to these questions. Fourier's theory was "a hypothesis" that he accepted with "the reservation that it be verified by experience." He himself believed "firmly" that the future would confirm Fourier's predictions and vindicate his dreams. Until then he accepted the theory "conditionally."[5] Considerant's reservations about Fourier's thought became even more explicit in 1841, with the publication of *Bases de la politique positive*. In this long brochure, written in his most reassuringly "scientific" mode, Considerant went further than ever before in his effort to allay fears concerning Fourier's psychological radicalism.

> The Societary Doctrine . . . proclaims more strongly than any other doctrine the SOCIAL NECESSITY of the more or less complete sacrifice of the passions and of individual liberty [and] the necessity of constraint and repression . . . as long as the form of society is not sufficiently perfect to harmonize liberty or the desires of individual passion with the dictates of the collective order.

The Ecole Sociétaire sought the full and free expression of the individual passions, Considerant explained, but this could only take place following the "practical verification" of Fourier's "still unrealized" prophecies concerning the establishment of a community in which "the passional liberty of the individual would coincide at all points with the requirements of order."[6]

It has been argued that the publication of the *Bases de la politique positive* in 1841 represented Considerant's "first major theoretical break with pure Fourierism."[7] There is some truth in this. Never before had Considerant gone so far in distancing himself from the radical implications of Fourier's theory of "passionate attraction." What needs to be emphasized here, however, is that while attempting to make Fourier's ideas accessible to a wide public, Considerant never ceased claiming for himself the right to define Fourierist orthodoxy. His enemies felt that Considerant was simply unable to accept criticism and that he perceived any independent voice as a challenge to his own authority within the movement. His own view was that to survive and prosper the Fourierist movement needed a single "center of impulsion and direction," which only he and his associates could provide. He did not seek immunity to criticism, but he insisted that legitimate and fair-minded criticism must accept his claim to "coordinate and unify" the activities of the movement, while illegitimate "denigrating" criticism, which attempted to bypass the center, could only serve as "a seed of dissolution and internal division."[8]

If Considerant was a jealous guardian of Fourierist orthodoxy in his dealings with provincials, he was positively condescending in his relations with foreigners. In his correspondence with American Associationists in 1844, he lectured them about the dangers of prematurely establishing "embryonic associations" and the importance of the Fourierists' Parisian headquarters. He also took his role as guardian of Fourier's papers with the utmost seriousness. In allowing Albert Brisbane to make copies of some of Fourier's manuscripts, he imposed exacting terms: only twenty-four carefully chosen Americans (one-quarter of whom had to be women) were allowed to consult Brisbane's copies.[9]

The American Fourierists took all this in their stride, but in France some reacted bitterly to what they considered Considerant's high-handed and dictatorial control of the movement. They complained that he had become "the pasha of the Ecole," that the Paris center resembled the Vatican and Considerant had made himself into a kind of socialist pope. Charles Pellarin, Fourier's official biographer, withdrew from his positions of leadership in 1845, protesting that Considerant and his associates had turned Fourier's system into a piece of "private property" and that the Fourierist movement had itself become the greatest obstacle to the spread of Fourier's ideas. Flora Tristan noted wryly in 1843 that Considerant was known at Bordeaux as "the king of the democratic phalanx." His close friend Désiré Laverdant claimed to be speaking for others when he wrote Considerant an anguished letter criticizing the "tendency to despotism" in his handling of the affairs of the movement.

> People never find fault with your heart or with the nobility of your goals. . . . You are still loved and honored by all. . . . People accuse you of a lack of leadership. They are right. You think you have done more for us than any other leader would have. Indeed, you are always on terms of friendship and camaraderie with us. That is just the problem. You have never been able to establish relations of [authority and] ambition among us. The result is that leadership becomes difficult whenever it is necessary to move from the tone of equality to the tone of command. Thus you have a strong tendency (it is instinct that inspires you, no doubt) *to act alone after consulting each of us individually.* That is a false and disorderly arrangement. The result is . . . that people now speak of "the journal of Monsieur Considerant."

Unable to delegate authority or to work together with groups of colleagues to establish a consensus, Considerant appeared to many to be an arbitrary and capricious leader.[10]

Some of the opposition to Considerant's leadership focused more on matters of style than substance. Considerant's brusque, military manner had always been offensive to some of his followers.[11] Others found his journalistic writing ponderous, overblown, and at times vulgar. However, most of them also had substantive complaints. In particular, they accused him of having abandoned essential elements of Fourier's doctrine out of a desire to promote his own political career. "The first stone of the Phalanx [is] not laid," wrote Alphonse Toussenel in 1847, but "the center which ought to be taking the initiative" had "lulled itself to sleep in the delights of civilized journalism" and was mainly concerned with getting "its supreme director" elected deputy. Already in 1843, Toussenel noted, Considerant's decision to change the name of the Fourierist newspaper from *La Phalange* to *La Démocratie pacifique* was a straw in the wind—an indication "of a fatal tendency toward the cunning politics of concealing one's own flag and putting on the uniform of the enemy in order to sneak into its camp." For Toussenel, Considerant was an opportunist whose political ambitions explained his willingness to abandon Fourierist principles.[12]

The criticism of Considerant by dissident Fourierists in the 1840s was to find an echo more than a century later in the writings of scholars. Emile Lehouck, for example, described Considerant's thought as "a new doctrine" that took "singular liberties with the original Fourierism." According to Lehouck, Considerant proceeded to "a laicization and an embourgeoisement" of Fourier's thought. Whereas Fourier had made "an extraordinary effort of imagination" to escape contemporary civilized society, "his principal disciple did not cease reintegrating his discoveries into existing society."[13]

One can hardly argue with this criticism. Nor can one argue with the claim made by Lehouck, Simone Debout, and others that in publishing Fourier's manuscripts and reprinting his major works during the 1840s Considerant made significant cuts and omissions. Even Fourier's most conventional treatise, the *Nouveau monde industriel,* was reprinted in 1845 in a bowdlerized version. Virtually nothing was published by Considerant or any of Fourier's other disciples from the manuscript notebooks comprising Fourier's sexual utopia, the *Nouveau monde amoureux.*[14]

This said, two comments are in order. First, in the publishing of Fourier's manuscripts, Considerant's timidity was limited to sexual questions. If he and his colleagues allowed the *Nouveau monde amoureux* to languish in obscurity, they did publish all of Fourier's major writings on cosmogony and the theory of universal analogy. Second, under the circumstances—and given the fact that Considerant's main concerns in the 1840s were creating a social movement and publishing a daily newspaper—his record as editor of Fourier's works and publisher of his manuscripts was surprisingly good. The publication of major texts by Fourier on cosmogony, "the material deterioration of the planet," and "the exponential scale of personality types" (all of which appeared in *La Phalange* between 1845 and 1848) would have been far more likely to compromise than serve Considerant's political ambitions. Far from seeking consistently to "hide the flag" and "sneak" into the "enemy camp," Considerant was guided in his attempts to popularize Fourier's ideas by a sense of his obligation to devote at least a part of the movement's resources to the publication of texts that would convey a relatively full sense of Fourier's thought—even in some of its more eccentric aspects.

II

If Considerant's attitude toward Charles Fourier's ideas changed over the years, so did his attitude toward politics. During the Second Republic he threw himself into the political arena and came to identify himself with a democratic socialist movement committed both to the implementation of major social reforms and to the defense of republican institutions. This represented a departure not only from his earlier views but also from the disdain for politics, especially republican politics, that had always marked Fourier's outlook.

As a young man Considerant had held conventional liberal political positions similar to those of his father. For months after the July Revolution he could still speak confidently about the prospects of "Tricolor France" as opposed to "that inane and cowardly dynasty that we've just gotten rid of." But he soon came to share Fourier's disgust with politics. At the outset of *Destinée sociale* he argued forcefully that the great error of the previous generation had been the belief that social questions could be solved by political means. "Those who seek happiness through politics and constitutional transformations," he wrote, "are pursuing a chimera and dreaming a utopia." Until this error was recognized, Europe would continue to be "agitated by vain revolutions."[15]

Considerant elaborated these views in 1836 in the provocatively titled *Nécessité d' une dernière débâcle politique*. There he adopted a posture of Olympian detachment, criticizing liberals, conservatives, and *juste milieu* moderates alike for their absorption in the intrigues and illusions of politics. The revolution of July 1830, which he had initially welcomed, soon became his prime example of a sterile change in governments without significant social consequences. "The coup on the streets in July was completely political," he wrote, "and could only produce a political result, a constitutional reshuffle, and not a new and better social combination."[16]

Throughout much of the July Monarchy, Considerant kept his distance from conventional political debate and from "all those trivial and forlorn constitutional quarrels" that constituted the political life of the period. He had contempt for the dynastic opposition—or, as he put it, "the Odilon Barrot and *Courrier français* opposition"—"that opposition more hollow than the desiccated skull of a thousand-year-old skeleton, echoing like an empty tomb." But he also distanced himself from the republicans. In 1843 he could speak of "the war that we have been waging for a dozen years against the hateful, violent, and revolutionary doctrines" of the republican *National*. The same year he could urge Lamartine to break with the parliamentary opposition. "You made a mistake in placing yourself on the benches of the opposition," he wrote. "You ought not to be on any bench. That is a place for schoolchildren . . . or for party men." [17]

With regard to contemporary political institutions Considerant often claimed that his stance was neutral. He could accept, and work within, any existing political system. "The Societary Doctrine accepts the republic in America," he wrote in 1841, "constitutional monarchy in France, absolute monarchy in Germany. . . . If a republican government were established in France . . . we would fight its adversaries with the same arguments that we use today against its partisans." [18] Of course France was not a republic; it was a constitutional monarchy. Thus Considerant supported the July Monarchy. He was a monarchist not for doctrinal reasons but because he believed that the existing government, which happened to be a constitutional monarchy, was better suited than any conceivable alternative to provide the "peace and calm" needed for the introduction and implementation of a significant program of social reforms.

If Considerant was a monarchist, however, there was always something idiosyncratic about his monarchism. He was, first of all, a *democratic* monarchist. This position has mystified some commentators, but it was perfectly coherent. For Considerant did not regard democracy as a primarily political ideology. Like his contemporary Tocqueville, though with none of Tocqueville's anxiety, he generally used the term "democracy" to refer not to a political system based on universal suffrage but to a type of society in which the interests of all took precedence over the interests of an aristocratic elite. The granting of full political rights to all citizens should only come, Considerant argued, once education and social reform had created an electorate capable of watching out for its own interests. In his *Manifeste* of 1843 he put it this way:

> The word Democracy does not signify "the government of society by the lower classes"; it signifies "the government and organization of society *in the interest of all,* by the *hierarchical* intervention in each activity by a number of citizens *which will grow with the stages of social development."* The people is not a class; it is the totality of society. And government is not the blind and confused action of incompetents; it is

the intelligent and unitary action of the competent—whose number should constantly tend to increase as a result of social education and the action of government. If democracy was understood in this sense, it was perfectly compatible with constitutional monarchy and with restrictions on suffrage.[19]

Down until 1848, Considerant continued to defend constitutional monarchy. Normally he did so on pragmatic grounds, arguing that under existing conditions only monarchy could provide the stability necessary for serious social reform. At times, however, he argued forcefully that monarchical government had played, and would continue to play, a key role in shaping French national identity.

> France does not wish to set itself up as a republic, and it is entirely correct. Its memories, its traditions, its sentiments, and its national constitution are monarchical. In the present state of society and of Europe, monarchy is a necessary condition for the existence, strength, and unity of France. If the republic had lasted fifty years in France, with all of its discussions and its tremors, it would have reduced us before the end of that time to a state lower than that of poor Poland today. France understands that both by intelligence and by instinct.

Writing in 1844, Considerant conceded that "the monarchical attachments of France are not shining very brightly today." But that, he asserted, was because "the issue of monarchy is complicated by that of bad government."[20]

By the mid-1840s, Considerant still defended constitutional monarchy in principle, but he was becoming increasingly critical of the "bad government" that ruled France, that is, the government led by François Guizot that had emerged after the diplomatic crisis of 1840. He found it difficult to maintain the posture of political detachment that he had recommended in his earliest writings. In 1847, in reissuing his *Manifeste* of 1843, he added a significant footnote to his discussion of the need to get beyond the "old quarrels" of "moribund parties" and to focus on the economic and social questions of the future. "The deplorable and shameful direction given in recent years to the internal and foreign policies of France by the official representatives of the conservative party [has led to] the abandonment of the dignity of France and the principles of the Revolution . . . and the revival of struggles on the terrain of power and pure politics."[21] During the last few years of the July Monarchy, Considerant became increasingly absorbed in political struggles. If he continued to defend constitutional monarchy in principle in 1847, he had in point of fact joined the opposition.

How do we explain Considerant's political evolution? What turned this self-proclaimed supporter of constitutional monarchy against the ministers of Louis Philippe and eventually against the monarchy itself? What drove him into close collaboration with the republicans, whose views he had long dismissed as "hateful, violent, and revolutionary"? Here one point should be emphasized. Considerant was not particularly disturbed (at least prior to 1846) by Guizot's refusal to broaden the suffrage. From the outset of the July Monarchy, French republicans had been calling for the establishment of universal (male) suffrage. Many others had asserted that the right to vote should be extended to a larger proportion of adult males than the 167,000 highest taxpayers enfranchised by the electoral law of 1831. None of this initially mattered to Considerant, who argued repeatedly that the issue of the size of the electorate was a "political hors d'oeuvre" that had no bearing on essential social questions. Indeed, if broadening the suffrage meant enfranchising large numbers of illiterates, it could be positively harmful.[22]

Eventually Considerant was to give his qualified endorsement to the movement for electoral reform, but prior to 1846 the issue did not interest him. What then *were* the roots of his disenchantment with the July Monarchy? Generally speaking, it seems that Considerant came to regard the July Monarchy as a great lost opportunity. In the early 1830s he believed that the ministers of Louis Philippe would be obliged sooner or later to consider "progressive solutions" to the most pressing social problems. Only gradually was this conviction shaken. This is how he put it in 1847:

> As long as the current government of France, which represents the ideas of the upper bourgeoisie, was the object of violent attacks, we did not hesitate to defend it against its adversaries. We did not doubt that, once consolidated and master of the situation, it would prove, at least in a certain measure, to be favorable to the progressive and liberal tendencies that had given rise to it in 1830. Both its duty and its interests dictated this course of action. Things have not turned out that way.

Considerant found it extremely hard to abandon the hopes he had placed in the July Monarchy. As late as 1847, in dedicating the second edition of *Destinée sociale* to Louis Philippe, he could still write that he hoped to see the King "laying the first stone of the first Phalanstery." This may have been little more than a rhetorical gesture; however, there was nothing rhetorical about the "profound grief" Considerant expressed five years earlier in a letter to his wife at the news of the accidental death of the duc d'Orléans, the liberal heir to the throne. Finally, however, the failure of Guizot, Thiers, and the other leading ministers of the July Monarchy to grapple with, or even recognize, the major social problems confronting France in the 1840s convinced Considerant that significant initiatives would have to come from some other quarter.[23]

If Considerant was disheartened by the domestic policies of the July Monarchy, he was equally disappointed by the government's foreign policy. Although he emphatically rejected the expansionism of the republicans, who wished France to annex Belgium and the left bank of the Rhine, he shared their frustration with regard to the "timorous" attitude of Louis Philippe and his ministers toward the European powers. Like many Frenchmen of various political persuasions, he was bitterly disappointed by France's failure to come to the aid of the Poles when they revolted against their Russian masters in November 1830. He was never as sanguine as Louis Blanc about the role a vigorous French foreign policy might play in making over the continent on liberal lines. He did, however, deplore the willingness of Louis Philippe and his ministers to compromise with dictators and to withhold support from movements of national liberation not only in Poland but also in Italy and Spain. He shared the anger of much of the opposition at the marriage alliance established with Bourbon Spain in 1846. This was in his view only a particularly gross example of the government's tendency to form "shadowy alliances with the great antiliberal conspiracy of the aristocracies and the absolutist courts."[24]

So Considerant's dissatisfaction with the July Monarchy came about gradually, and he clung to the distinction between the king and his ministers, the "good" regime and the "bad" government, long after other radicals closer to the republican tradition (such as Louis Blanc and Etienne Cabet) had rejected both. In the end, the "deplorable and shameful direction" given to both foreign and domestic policy proved too much for him to stomach.

III

In one area, Considerant's break with the policies and leaders of the July Monarchy was dramatic. This was the area of French colonial policy—more specifically, French policy with regard to the conquest and colonization of Algeria. French troops had been occupying Algeria ever since the waning days of the Restoration, when a French expeditionary force was sent to Algiers to "punish" the Dey for a slight against the French consul. Considerant, then an officer in training at Metz, initially shared the enthusiasm of most young army officers for the venture. He yearned for "the perils and conquests" that participation in the Army of Africa would bring; he wrote Clarisse Vigoureux that he was attracted even by the fact that many French soldiers could not tolerate conditions in Algeria. "It's better to begin with a difficult campaign than an easy one," he wrote. "As for glory, a Prussian bayonet doesn't give any more than the yataghan of a Kabyle or a Berber."[25]

During his years in Metz, Considerant had established good relations with two military men who were to play important roles in the French occupation of Algeria. One was Marshal Soult, a veteran of the revolutionary and Napoleonic wars who served as minister of war and president of the Council of State during much of the July Monarchy. The other was General (later Marshal) Bugeaud, a crusty, conservative, and at times apoplectic old soldier who was to serve as governor-general of Algeria from 1841 to 1847. Both these men knew and liked the young Considerant and wrote the testimonials to his character that helped him secure repeated leaves of absence from the army early in his career as a Fourierist apostle. Considerant had a simplicity of character and a bluff straightforwardness that both these career army officers appreciated. Bugeaud in particular seems to have been something of a father figure and protector to Considerant in the early 1830s.[26]

Neither of these men was initially much interested in Algeria. Indeed, at the outset of the July Monarchy there was little support anywhere in France for colonizing Algeria or even for extending the French military presence beyond the coastal perimeter. As more troops were sent in to fight Algerian resistance movements, however, and as the cost of maintaining an occupying army increased, the question of the French presence in Algeria became a matter of national honor. Bugeaud himself was one of many who moved from skepticism to strong support for the colonization of Algeria. In due course Bugeaud became known as the advocate of a unique system of military colonies and as the inventor of a particularly brutal type of colonial warfare that involved burning homes and crops in lightning raids on the native Algerian population. During his tenure as governor-general, the number of French troops in Algeria rose to 108,000, a third of the entire French army, and the French extended their control of the coastal regions, without however managing to put an end to Algerian resistance.

Considerant kept in touch with Bugeaud after his resignation from the army in 1836, and the two continued to correspond even when Bugeaud was the effective ruler of French Algeria. Bugeaud's letters to Considerant are full of affectionate insults, justifications of his policies, complaints about the ignorance and incomprehension of radical journalists in France, and challenges casually thrown out. "If you really care about my education," wrote Bugeaud in 1842, "come here and set up a Phalanstery. I promise you a fine piece of land. Come show us something practical; and when I see your community working well, I'll come and imitate you." Until that time Bugeaud would continue to create agricultural colonies in his own way.[27]

During the early 1840s the Fourierist journals, *La Phalange* and *La Démocratie pacifique*, generally supported the French presence in Algeria as an effort to bring European civilization and enlightenment to "the haunts of fanaticism and barbarism." Contributors to *Démocratie pacifique* occasionally criticized Bugeaud, but they also came to his defense against the attacks of "shrill and whining" liberal journals like *Le National*. When Bugeaud was appointed marshal in 1843, *Le National* complained that a man who had made his reputation putting down Parisian insurrections was scarcely deserving of the honor. Considerant replied sardonically by asking whether to have defended one's government at the risk of one's life was really something to be ashamed of. He praised Bugeaud's energy, "superior" military qualities, and "tireless dedication" to French interests as he understood them, but he went on to regret Bugeaud's failure to keep his promise to "aspire in Africa after both conquests of the plow and those of the sword."[28]

In February 1844, an article by Charles Pellarin criticizing Bugeaud's "bellicose system of conquest" brought a fierce response from the governor-general. It was only the following year, though, after Bugeaud had published a lengthy justification of the slaughter by French troops of five hundred Algerians trapped in a cave, that Considerant finally and definitively broke with his former *patron*. In a series of impassioned articles on "the justification of the horrors " perpetrated by the French army in Algeria and on the "odious" character of the war, Considerant denounced Bugeaud and the whole French effort to subdue Algeria by force. The murder of innocent Algerians, he wrote, was only "a *natural, logical,* and *new* consequence of the frightful and stupid system of government adopted for several years in Algeria." Considerant concluded by indicting Bugeaud. "We have for many years," he wrote, "defended . . . Marshal Bugeaud against the attacks of the press." Bugeaud had in particular been wrongly blamed for the massacre of innocent Parisians on the rue Transnonain during the republican insurrection of April 1834. "We have believed," wrote Considerant, that the image of Bugeaud as a murderer, "the man of the rue Transnonain," was a republican myth. "Today we recognize with profound sadness, after eight years of good relations and illusions have been violently dispelled, that what we took for a myth, a creation of passion, was a reality."[29]

So by the summer of 1845 Considerant had broken with Bugeaud and was now bitterly critical of France's Algerian policy. He had not yet given up on the king or on the July Monarchy itself. Still, the political distance that Considerant had traveled since his first foray into electoral politics in 1839 was evident in August 1846 when, while continuing to serve on the Municipal Council of Paris, he stood for election to the Chamber of Deputies in the department of the Loiret. Now he was no longer seeking to present himself as a compromise choice to electors satisfied with neither the ministerial nor the opposition candidate. Instead, he was himself the principal opposition candidate, running with the endorsement of the democratic *Journal du Loiret* and the eminent republican astronomer, François Arago.[30]

Considerant's performance at the main electoral meeting held at Montargis was in the opinion of one liberal elector "a magnificent triumph," but it was not enough to win him the election. In the end he received 91 votes out of 419 cast. This was a respectable showing, given the fact that all over France these elections of 1846 were a great victory for the government.[31] Coming at the end of a three-year period of political calm and economic expansion, the elections turned out to be a last hurrah for the ministry of François Guizot. Within two years, however, the ministry, the king, and the constitutional monarchy itself were all to be swept away in the course of a crisis that transformed the political life of France.

IV

During the last two years of the July Monarchy, France underwent an economic crisis that had multiple dimensions. It began as an agricultural crisis originating in bad weather, crop failure, and high food prices. A bad harvest in 1845 was followed by a worse one in 1846, and this was accompanied by the spread to the continent of the potato blight that had already devastated Ireland. The cost of potatoes, which were now fairly widely consumed in eastern France, increased as much as four times between the spring of 1846 and the spring of 1847. During the same period the price of wheat—and hence the price of bread—doubled throughout France.[32]

The consequence of high food prices in an economy where many people lived on the margin and where bread remained the staff of life was that the amount of money workers and poor peasants had to spend on clothing and other manufactured goods fell sharply. Between 1846 and 1847 the cost of food rose from one-third to two-thirds or even three-quarters of the total income of a family of peasants or artisans. As a result, the domestic market for manufactured goods collapsed, bringing widespread unemployment.

To complicate the situation further, this agricultural crisis was accompanied by a financial crisis of largely independent origin. This was a crisis of credit provoked in part by the mania of railroad speculation and by an overheated economy stimulated by the rapid commercial and industrial growth of the early 1840s. Credit was becoming scarce right when the government had to draw heavily on the assets of the Bank of France to pay for Russian wheat imported in the winter of 1846–1847. The gold reserves of the Bank of France fell from 201 million francs in June 1846 to 47 million in January 1847 when, to the consternation of the business community, the Bank of France raised its discount rate from 4 percent to 5 percent.

Conditions improved in the last few months of 1847: the harvest was better; unemployment fell; and in December 1847 the Bank of France returned to a 4 percent discount rate. Nevertheless the consequences of this crisis were grave. In the cities there was massive unemployment; and in rural France the whole system of cottage industries, which was essential to the survival of the poorer peasants, began to crumble. In the first six months of 1847, peasants and workers who were no longer able to feed their families gathered to rob grain convoys, break machines, and set upon the houses of the rich. Government troops had to intervene in many parts of France. Finally, with the better harvest of 1847, relative calm returned. One of the legacies of the period of crisis and disorder that reached its height in the first six months of 1847, however, was that the elite—the *notables* who remained in control of France—lost confidence in the government's ability to maintain a climate in which business could prosper and to command the respect and obedience of the lower classes.[33]

This loss of confidence was exacerbated in 1847 by a series of political scandals that discredited both the government and the regime and demonstrated to the world at large exactly how the government obtained its parliamentary majorities. In the spring of 1847, during a trial, it was revealed that two former ministers had accepted bribes in exchange for mining concessions. After one of them, Charles Teste, attempted suicide, both were condemned to prison in July 1847. A few months later Guizot himself was accused of having withdrawn 600,000 francs from government funds to pay off a man who had apparently been sold a ministerial job that he never got to hold. At the same time, more routine forms of corruption were brought to light—payoffs to deputies who supported the government, bribes to officials who could influence the awarding of government contracts, and so forth. All of this led both Marx and Tocqueville to use the same image to describe the July Monarchy: the workings of the government, they wrote, resembled those of a joint-stock company, all of whose operations were designed to benefit the principal shareholders.[34]

In the eyes of many of its critics, the main problem with the July Monarchy was its narrow social base. These critics argued that the insistence of Guizot and Louis Philippe on keeping the electorate so small was a major cause of the corruption and the spirit of egotism that festered within the ruling class. Around this issue a negative coalition formed—a coalition of diverse groups united in their opposition to the narrowness of the suffrage. The Fourierists, who had previously expressed no interest in electoral reform, now seized on this issue, too. *Démocratie pacifique* began to publish articles protesting the narrowness of the suffrage, and in October 1846 the journal joined with other opposition newspapers in formally endorsing a proposal for electoral reform.[35]

Finally, in the spring of 1847, the leaders of the parliamentary opposition decided to carry the issue to the country and devised a tactic that would get around the laws against political associations. The idea was to organize banquets in Paris and the provinces that reformist deputies would attend along with electors and local *notables* who could pay an admission price high enough to keep out the unwashed multitude. Since this "banquet campaign" was ultimately to get out of hand, it is important to point out that at its inception its supporters had no thought of overthrowing the constitutional monarchy. On the contrary, their purpose was to save the monarchy by widening its base of support. This was certainly the view of Victor Considerant, who declared at a banquet at Montargis in November 1847: "We wish a reform to ward off the storms of the future."[36]

V

Considerant had many reasons to join the opposition. He could not ignore the government's deafness to calls for social reform, its persistence in a foreign policy based on "shadowy alliances" with the most reactionary regimes in Europe, or the "odious" methods of colonial warfare employed in Algeria by his former mentor, Marshal Bugeaud. All of these policies and positions made Considerant and his colleagues responsive to appeals to join with opponents of the government in the negative coalition that took shape in 1846 and 1847. What pushed them firmly and irrevocably into the opposition, though, was the government's seizure in July 1847 of three separate issues of *Démocratie pacifique* on the charge of "offense to public morality." In the first two cases the condemned articles were excerpts from a novel that the journal was running as a feuilleton. In the third case an article by Considerant provoked the seizure.[37]

Why did the interior minister order the seizure of *Démocratie pacifique*? The novel's allegedly salacious sections were actually no worse than passages that might have been extracted from several other novels then running in installments in more influential and widely read journals. Probably the government wished to send a message to the opposition press as a whole by bringing charges against one of Paris's least influential opposition dailies. In any case, the editors of *Démocratie pacifique* were found guilty as charged. As the paper's managing editor, François Cantagrel was sentenced to a month in jail and ordered to pay a fine of 100 francs.[38]

This episode won *Démocratie pacifique* a notoriety that it had never previously possessed and brought it the support of much of the Paris press. It also released Considerant's previously muted anger and broadened its target to include not only the government but also the regime and the elite—the new "mercantile and industrial aristocracy"—that ruled France under the July Monarchy. In a series of articles published in July and August 1847, Considerant thundered against the egotism and greed of the ruling class. "There are no more generous affections and social ideas," he wrote on July 11.

> Love of country is no more than a name that serves to adorn partisan intrigue, to prettify the plots of ambitious people. . . . The only faculties, activities, and powers that count are those useful in piling up money. Money!! Money!! . . . Everything is for sale; men and consciences just like goods at the market. And men cost less, because someone who has sold himself seven times can still sell himself again.[39]

Considerant's attack on the July Monarchy's ruling class and on the prevailing climate of selfishness and greed reached its climax in August 1847. Pulling out all the rhetorical stops in an article entitled "Une Société qui tombe," he directed his fire at the elite of bankers, wholesale merchants, and wealthy land owners who had ruled France since 1830. What, he asked, had been accomplished in seventeen years by "these hypocritical spokesmen of the bourgeoisie, these princes of the bank, these heroes of speculation?" Exercising control over the government of "a noble nation," they had sought to turn its "generous tendencies" to the advantage of their own "filthy egoism." During the Restoration, representatives of these groups had "raised the banner of progress" and "proclaimed principles of justice and liberty," but these principles were simply weapons used to overthrow the old aristocracy. Once they had gained power for themselves, they exploited it systematically to debase, bribe, and corrupt everyone whose acquiescence they needed to remain in power.

What Considerant focused on in this attack on the elite of the July Monarchy was not the crimes and scandals but rather the state of mind that made the scandals possible. "You have killed all faith," he addressed the ruling class:

> You have sought to snuff out every noble idea, every generous senti-
> ment. You have treated as an enemy everything that could heal people's
> souls, enlighten their minds, warm their hearts. You have sought to
> create a world in which the only legal interests were the gross interests.
> You have disgraced dedication, social passion. You have honored all
> forms of baseness, glorified all forms of cowardice, rewarded all forms
> of depravity that betray . . . the traditions, duties, and sentiments of
> France.

For seventeen years the rulers of France had been "poisoning" French soil with the seeds of greed, individualism, materialism, and "political, social, and religious atheism." Now they were asking why the French had seemingly lost their capacity for self-sacrifice and disinterested action. Appalled at the social world they themselves had created, the Orleanist bourgeoisie rightly feared that their days in power were numbered.[40]

The next day Considerant published an article entitled "Oui, vous êtes responsables!" elaborating on the charges made in "Une Société qui tombe," but this time focusing more narrowly on politics—the Guizot ministry and the political scandals. Supported by a majority that they had created using "all the inventions and tricks of political and social corruption," Guizot and his colleagues had, according to Considerant, "audaciously betrayed" the hopes of the Fourierists and many others. They had "poisoned" France, he wrote. Society had fallen into an "abyss of corruption, vices, demoralization, and crime," and the political elite was quite rightly being held responsible. A "hurricane of scorn" was rising from the depths of the nation; the monarchy itself was in danger; and only the resignation of the Guizot ministry could prevent a catastrophe. "Resign today," Considerant told Guizot, "if you don't wish to drag down society, the crown, and France with you!"[41]

The issue containing "Une Société qui tombe" was seized, and on September 7 the Fourierists found themselves again in court, charged with "exciting the hatred of citizens against different classes of people [and] against the government." The prosecutor described Considerant's article as "the delirium of an imagination nourished on misrepresentations and calumnies." He argued that although *Démocratie pacifique* had long been a harmless purveyor of impractical abstractions, it had recently changed course and was now "definitively committed" to the destruction of existing laws and institutions. In a long and passionate speech, defense attorney Charles Dain reviewed the entire history of the movement, seeking to show that the Fourierists had repeatedly championed "the cause of peace and public order," that they had defended the government with "an almost blind persistence," and that Considerant's charges were similar to those being made by other journalists at a time when "public opinion" was "rising like a single man" to protest the policies and the corruption of the government. After five minutes of deliberation, the jury returned a verdict of "not guilty" on all charges.[42]

The charges brought against Considerant's article and the resulting acquittal cemented the Fourierists' ties with the opposition. The article was widely reprinted, and the jury's verdict was hailed by the opposition journals as a victory for the press as a whole. Much was also made of the fact that *Démocratie pacifique* had long been known for its moderation and its "indulgence" with regard to the government. An editorialist for the liberal daily *Le Commerce* could speak of "the conversion" of *Démocratie pacifique* as dramatic evidence of the spread of opposition.[43]

In the case of Considerant, the word "conversion" may not be too strong. He had always had a substantial capacity for indignation and moral outrage, and his response to the summer's revelations of governmental corruption was predictably passionate. However, he also seems to have been exhilarated by the multiple seizures of *Démocratie pacifique*, by the reaction to his article, and by the sense of participation in a common struggle. Thus, in the late summer of 1847, he flung himself into the activities of the opposition with an energy and a single-mindedness he had never before brought to politics. On September 5 he published a long article on the "Praslin affair"—a spectacular murder-suicide that the opposition seized upon as dramatic evidence of the moral collapse of the Orleanist bourgeoisie. At the same time—and despite his own long record of disinterest in electoral reform—he became caught up in the reformist banquet campaign organized by the opposition to the Guizot ministry.[44]

Considerant participated in at least two major provincial banquets and arranged for a colleague's participation in a third. On September 19 he was one of the principal speakers at the "reformist banquet of Saint-Quentin," where he celebrated the work of the French Revolution as "breaking the entrenched aristocracy, which barred the bourgeoisie's way to political liberty and social dignity." He advised the bourgeoisie that it was time for them "to open their ranks to the people." Otherwise, he warned, if "the people" were denied political rights, if the bourgeoisie retreated behind a "wall of egotism" just as the eighteenth-century aristocracy had, the people might be forced to "break down the wall." On November 23 in Montargis, Considerant celebrated the banquet campaign itself as an "awakening of national sentiment," a "long-repressed explosion of morality and dignity," and "the peaceful and legal insurrection of a public conscience too long and too pro-foundly insulted." [45]

When Pierre-Joseph Proudhon got wind of Considerant's speeches in Saint-Quentin and Montargis (as reprinted in the Paris press), he professed stupefaction. He could not interpret Considerant's "preposterous toast" at Saint-Quentin—his celebration of the French Revolution and the principle of equality—as anything else than a cynical political maneuver. Of Considerant's speech in Montargis, Proudhon wrote: "Considerant is betraying his convictions. After having preached against electoral reform, he supports it because he wants to become a deputy." [46] Considerant was indeed campaigning for election to the Chamber of Deputies. Shortly after the banquet in Montargis, elections were held and Considerant was once again defeated in the Loiret—though by a narrower vote than the previous year. [47] Yet Proudhon was wrong to impute cynical calculation to Considerant. His change of position was sincere, and it was to prove enduring. This enemy of electoral reform had now become a committed partisan of republican government.

PART III

Revolution

9

Revolutionary Springtime

"Vive la République!!!" read the headline of *Démocratie pacifique* on the morning of February 25, 1848. "Honor to the National Guards who by the power of their indignation have brought about the fall of a corrupt monarchy! Honor to the proletarians who shed their blood on the barricades with such heroism! May these two elements of the population remain united." The previous afternoon after two days of street demonstrations in Paris, Louis Philippe had abdicated. By nightfall a republic had been declared and a Provisional Government established. Though dominated by moderates, the Provisional Government also included two radical republicans, Alexandre-Auguste Ledru-Rollin and Ferdinand Flocon, the socialist Louis Blanc, and a worker, Alexandre Martin, known as Albert, who had been active in the revolutionary secret societies of the July Monarchy.[1]

The next day, February 25, under pressure from a huge crowd of workers gathered in front of the Hôtel de Ville, the Provisional Government issued a proclamation pledging itself to guarantee all French citizens the right to work. On February 26, in support of that guarantee, the Provisional Government announced the creation of a program of "National Workshops" to be supervised by the minister of public works, Alexandre-Thomas Marie. Nominally inspired by the scheme of state-sponsored "social workshops" or producers' cooperatives proposed by Louis Blanc, these National Workshops turned out to be no more than a form of temporary poor relief in which unemployed workers were put to work at menial tasks of dubious usefulness. This was not evident at the outset, however. Finally, on February 28 in response to a large-scale demonstration demanding the creation of a ministry of progress or labor, the Provisional Government agreed to create not a new ministry but a "Workers' Commission" to study the problems of France's working population and to arbitrate labor disputes. This Workers' Commission was to consist largely of some two hundred working-class delegates representing various trades. Presided over by Louis Blanc, they would meet in the Luxembourg Palace, the former meeting place of the Chamber of Peers. The commission had no explicit lawmaking powers, and it was soon to be mocked by Karl Marx as a "ministry of pious wishes."[2] In the first week of the republic, though, the creation of this "parliament of work" seemed, like the creation of the National Workshops, to constitute a recognition on the part of the Provisional Government of the importance that the concerns of the working class would have in the life of the new republic.

Victor Considerant was not in Paris to participate in the February Revolution, but through his writings he had helped articulate the ideology of the democratic and socialist left. He had helped give currency to the concept of the right to work; he had initiated the demand for a "Ministry of Progress"; and he had repeatedly insisted on the need to harmonize the interests of workers and employers, rich and poor. But if Considerant had helped to shape the demands of the left in 1848, the events of that year had an even more obvious role in shaping his career. Like other members of the radical opposition to the July Monarchy, he suddenly found himself thrust into a position of power and influence that was new to him. Until February 1848 he had been an outsider—the leader of a sectarian social movement who sought to widen the base of that movement but who was still essentially a critic of the existing social and political order. During the sixteen months that followed, he became a political figure of some influence in France— ridiculed by some, admired by others, but in any case intimately involved in the public life of the nation. The story we have to tell in the next three chapters is the story of what Considerant did with power and how he lost it.

I

In late February 1848, Considerant was in Liège on the first leg of what was to be an extensive lecture tour throughout Belgium. He had already given half a dozen lectures to enthusiastic audiences, and it seemed as though he was going to repeat his triumph of three years earlier at Brussels. The crowd numbered over a thousand most nights, and a reviewer for the *Tribune de Liège* spoke of their "religious attention" and "sympathetic bravos" as "the disciple of Fourier began the exposition of his peaceful science."[3]

News of the abdication of Louis Philippe and the proclamation of the republic reached Liège on the morning of February 25. Considerant immediately cut short his lecture tour. "While the blood of my fellow citizens is flowing for liberty in France," he informed his hosts, "I should not, I cannot give lectures in Belgium."[4] By nightfall he was in Brussels. Instead of continuing directly by train to Paris, though, he attempted to make contact with his friend, Charles Rogier.

Rogier was now Belgium's minister of the interior and the dominant figure in a new liberal ministry. Already he had shown himself to be a far more cautious reformer than most of his political allies had anticipated. Just three weeks earlier he had submitted to the Belgian Chamber of Deputies a very modest package of reform proposals, insisting that he could go no further. Rogier was also, as Considerant well knew, a committed monarchist and a loyal subject of King Leopold I. What Considerant wished to tell Rogier, however, was that the day of monarchies was done and that the greatest service he could render his countrymen would be to persuade the king either to abdicate immediately or else to hold a national referendum on Belgium's future form of government. Although Leopold did in fact discuss with his ministers the possibility of abdication, Considerant's unsolicited advice can hardly have been welcome to Rogier. Apparently he received Considerant briefly and with ironic politeness. Nonetheless, Considerant was not easily discouraged.[5]

During the night of February 25–26, Considerant, who could not sleep, wrote two letters to Rogier that show him in a state of feverish excitement. In the first, written at one o'clock in the morning, Considerant urged Rogier to advise Leopold to abdicate gracefully, thus setting an example for other monarchs. Otherwise, he predicted, "before two o'clock in the afternoon there will be one hundred thousand people in the streets of Brussels, intoxicated with an electric enthusiasm and shouting 'Vive la République!'" At four thirty in the morning Considerant sent off a second letter. In it he described himself as "calm, in a state of luminous and limpid enthusiasm that enables me to see the future as if it were already part of history."

> My dear Rogier, You still have six or eight hours at the very most. . . . Yesterday when I left you, you still had your eyes shut. You must look at the situation as it is. . . . As soon as the French newspapers arrive, inundating Belgium with heroic accounts of the miracle that the people of Paris have just accomplished, an indescribable enthusiasm is going

to take possession of the population. The liberal, official, bourgeois Belgium that constituted yesterday's public opinion and public authority will not weigh an ounce next to the voice of the people, once it has been awakened by the great voice of France.

The victory of peoples over kings had begun in Italy, continued Considerant. Now it would spread from France throughout the West.

The first acts of the Republic will be peaceful acts, acts intended to protect people and property and at the same time to promote individual emancipation, acts bearing the stamp of that magnificent clemency that always follows great deeds of dedication and rapid victories. These acts will conquer for the Republic widespread and enthusiastic support the like of which has never been seen on earth. This is what is going to happen, I tell you.

The world had changed, Considerant insisted. A wind was rising that would "make crowns fall like dry leaves in autumn." The republic would become the form of Europe's governments as it was already that of the American government.[6]

Whatever Charles Rogier may have made of these letters, they are a remarkable expression of 1848 political euphoria. As such, they are not, of course, unique. At the same time in a different part of Brussels, Friedrich Engels was celebrating the revolution in France as a triumph for democracy in all of Europe: "The flames of the Tuileries and of the Palais Royal [sic] are the rosy dawn of the proletariat. If the Germans show a little courage and pride, in four weeks it will be possible to cry out, 'Long live the German Republic!'"[7]

In time Engels was to change his mind about the February Revolution, which he and Marx were later to deride as "the beautiful revolution," a pale, ghostly, and ultimately insignificant imitation of 1789. Considerant's identification with the February Revolution—with its goals and with the hopes it inspired—was to prove enduring. But at the time Considerant and Engels shared the belief that the same revolutionary wind that had toppled the July Monarchy in France would soon bring down the Belgian monarchy of Leopold I. About this, of course, they were wrong. After an initial moment of panic, Leopold I pulled himself together. Having informed his cabinet that he was ready to abdicate if the people wished it, he took steps to deal vigorously with any popular demonstration. The civic guard was mobilized and the army placed on alert. In fact, Brussels was quiet on February 26. The following day the Brussels Democratic Association (of which Marx was a vice-president) held a large but peaceful meeting. That evening a big crowd did gather on Brussels' Grand Place in front of the Hôtel de Ville, but after a few cries of "Vive la République!" it was dispersed by mounted soldiers. Considerant's hundred thousand "indescribably enthusiastic" demonstrators never appeared.[8]

II

When Considerant returned to Paris on February 28, he found the capital in a state of extraordinary effervescence. Every day new political clubs were forming and new newspapers appearing. The walls of the city were plastered with posters of all sizes, shapes, and colors; the boulevards buzzed with activity late into the night; and throughout Paris traces remained of the barricades thrown up on the twenty-third and twenty-fourth. At the Hôtel de Ville, the Provisional Government was just concluding a marathon four-day initial session. Its inability to solve the country's problems by fiat was evident in the long lines of unemployed workers that formed each day in front of the *mairies* of Paris's twelve *arrondissements* and in the appearance of a new flea market on the Champs-Elysées, where the needy and unemployed came to sell their meager possessions. Still, Considerant must have been struck, as were most observers, by the palpable sense of joy and hopefulness that the proclamation of the republic had brought with it. At night, too, Paris had an almost magical appearance, for during the street-fighting most of the city's gas lamps had been broken, and to provide some illumination Parisians put lamps in their windows.

At the rue de Beaune, Considerant found his colleagues at the center of events and reveling in it. They were forming their own club, the United Socialists, which held its first meeting on March 2.[9] Their journal had been among the first in Paris to come out in support of the republic. In a special edition of *Démocratie pacifique* published in the evening of February 25, they had presented themselves as conciliators who could bring together the disparate socialist *écoles* into a single movement. "Until now, *Démocratie pacifique* has been the organ of the Phalansterian movement," Allyre Bureau had written. "In this moment of general conciliation, of universally shared enthusiasm, it hoists its flag and offers it as a rallying point for all socialists."[10] In an influential article in the same issue François Vidal had also sought to specify the relation between the political revolution and the social transformations the Fourierists were seeking.

> Social reform is the end; the Republic is the means. All socialists are republicans; all republicans are socialists. . . . The revolution begun in

1789, almost sixty years ago, had always remained within its first phase, its critical phase. Now it is going to enter its second phase, its organic phase. . . . Let us first begin by reestablishing calm and peace in the city; then without delay we will consider the means of assuring the people the enjoyment and exercise of their rights.[11]

Among these rights, foremost in the eyes of the Fourierists was the right to work. The attempt to give substance to this "first and most sacred of rights" was to be the central element in the Fourierists' political program.

Considerant soon began to issue statements of his own concerning the goals of the new republic. In some of these statements he urged the Provisional Government to approach the problem of the organization of labor more directly. On March 1, for example, he renewed his demand for a Ministry of Progress, which would study the plans for the organization of labor proposed by the different socialist sects and encourage the testing of these plans on the local level. When addressing the general population, Considerant stressed the need for patience, class collaboration, and the careful elaboration of "scientific" solutions to difficult social problems. If the republic was to make a difference, he wrote in an election statement, it would have to "reassure men's minds" and "conciliate their interests."

> The problems that the revolution has to solve are social problems, and social problems can only be resolved by science and by calm and progressive experiments. No plundering, no violence, no blood, no wild and hateful passions! That is our common motto. Let us preach fraternity and love of the public good; let us study the science that teaches us to find practical solutions to social problems. Let us plant good seeds in people's minds and hearts . . . and the great day will come when, as the Gospel and Philosophy predict, all men will be brothers, the day when, as the Prophet has predicted, swords and spears will be changed into plowshares and tools.[12]

With his appeal to the authority of both science and scripture, his invocation of "fraternity" and "the public good," and his fundamental hopefulness about the possibility of nonviolent solutions to social conflict, Considerant gave classic expression in the first days of the republic to a political optimism that was widely shared on the left.

Convinced of the need for reassurance, conciliation, and class harmony, for the avoidance of violence and bloodshed, Considerant and his colleagues very quickly came to regard the leader of the Provisional Government, Alphonse de Lamartine, as the essential figure in the life of the new republic. Considerant saw Lamartine as "the living incarnation of harmony," an individual who could rise above the quarrels of parties and factions and inspire others to do likewise. Within the Provisional Government, he wrote later, Lamartine was the "magnificent expression" of the desire for reconciliation that was almost universally shared in the period immediately following the February Revolution.[13]

Considerant applauded the role Lamartine played at the outset of the revolution in the republic's adoption of the tricolor flag. He shared Lamartine's view that the tricolor was the emblem of the nation and not simply a regime, whereas the red flag "awakened ideas of blood and vengeance." Considerant also praised Lamartine's famous circular of March 4 promising that the French would make no effort to export revolution to other nations. In reprinting this document in *Démocratie pacifique*, he gave it the headline: "Here at Last Is the Word of France." This admiration of Lamartine was not to last, however. One evening in conversation with Lamartine, Considerant learned that as minister of foreign affairs Lamartine hoped to annex for France the Savoie and Nice, while offering Lombardy to Sardinia and returning Venice to Austria as compensation.

Lamartine's willingness to play great power politics shocked Considerant. "This was a revelation," he wrote later. He had "nourished great illusions" about Lamartine. But whereas the poet's speeches shone with the promise of the future, the past governed the thoughts and tendencies of the politician. "Lamartine was lost for the revolution."[14]

Considerant might have been expected to be more sympathetic to Louis Blanc than to Lamartine. Although he supported many of Blanc's specific initiatives and paid tribute to his good intentions, however, Considerant was critical of Blanc's role in the first months of the revolution. Writing in the fall of 1848, he praised Louis Blanc as "the first of the leading republicans to recognize the inanity of pure political reform in and of its own sake." Blanc had understood and forcefully articulated the socialist critique of bourgeois society. In his role as president of the Luxembourg Commission, however, he had shown himself to be intellectually "rigid" and also "somewhat intoxicated" by power. "He frightened society by giving the impression of wishing to impose his egalitarian socialism on it by force." Considerant went on to assert that if ever the mantle of power fell on him, his first concern would be to reassure public opinion that he had no dictatorial ambitions. "I would speak to the public of experimentation, and I would proclaim as the most sacred of rights the insurrection of men's minds against all programs of social reform, starting with my own, that might seek to win over the rural population without being freely accepted by it."[15]

Considerant's reservations about Louis Blanc's exercise of power were based on firsthand experience. Considerant had participated for a few weeks in the sessions of the Luxembourg Commission as one of a dozen or so socialists appointed by Louis Blanc to aid the working-class delegates in their deliberations. He had crossed swords with Louis Blanc on several occasions, arguing against Blanc's positions on the necessity of an egalitarian wage system and on state regulation of convent-work. In each case, Considerant favored a more supple and less intrusive role for the state, but in fact his participation in the work of the Luxembourg Commission did not last long. The commission soon became a forum for the elaboration of Louis Blanc's theories and also something of a political club attempting to promote working-class candidates in the forthcoming elections. By then Considerant had become preoccupied with his own candidacy for the National Assembly.[16]

III

The elections for the National Constituent Assembly, held on April 23, were the first direct national elections held in France by universal male suffrage since 1795. Not surprisingly, they were accompanied by much confusion and acrimony. There was a major controversy concerning the timing of the elections; Considerant was only one of many who subsequently accused the Provisional Government of "immense stupidity" in failing to hold elections as soon as possible after the euphoria of the February Days.[17] There was also confusion about the role of the electoral committees that met all over France to endorse slates of candidates; and there were bitter arguments about the heavy-handed attempts of the interior minister, Ledru-Rollin, to use the powers of his office to secure the election of "right-thinking" republicans and democrats. In the end, however, the efforts of radical republicans like Ledru-Rollin made little difference. In the absence of grass-roots republican traditions or any sort of mass political culture, the result of the elections, almost everywhere in provincial France, was to return to power men who were already "known"—local *notables* or office-holders under the July Monarchy.

From the beginning there was no doubt that Considerant would be a candidate. The only question was where. In the end he allowed his name to be presented in Paris but made his principal effort in the Loiret, where he had old friends and had begun to develop political support as a result of his campaigns for the Chamber of Deputies in 1846 and 1847.[18] In early March he traveled to Montargis to help organize a Democratic Society intended to introduce previously unenfranchised voters to "the study of social issues" and to prepare them for "the real and enlightened exercise of the sovereignty of the people."[19] Within this Democratic Society an electoral committee was formed, and on March 18 a straw vote was taken to endorse two candidates to represent the *arrondissement* of Montargis as part of the democratic slate of eight candidates for the whole department of the Loiret. Considerant finished a respectable second, well behind the moderate republican lawyer Louis-Félix Rondeau, but ahead of the wealthy proprietor and Catholic pamphleteer Cormenin.

On March 19 a similar meeting was held at Orléans, organized by that city's Republican Central Committee. After hearing from almost all of the twenty-six candidates seeking election from the Loiret, the audience took their own straw vote. Although Considerant received fewer votes than several of the area's liberal *notables*, he still finished fifth among the twelve serious candidates; and the *Journal du Loiret* of March 21 described his speech and that of a working-class candidate, a carpenter from Gien named Jules-François Michot, as the two most warmly applauded. A week later another meeting was held in Orléans, this time including delegates from the whole department. At this second meeting both Considerant and Michot came under attack. The worker Michot was accused of communism, drunkenness, and ingratitude toward his parents; Considerant had to answer questions about his purported hostility to private property and about Fourier's critique of marriage. Considerant had little trouble distancing himself from Fourier and setting the record straight about his views on property. He recalled that in his polemics against Proudhon, Cabet, and the Babouvist communists he had repeatedly championed private property, but his working-class ally, Michot, was damaged by the questioning.

As the election approached, Considerant and the other candidates traveled all over the department, speaking at forums organized by the electoral committees of Gien, Sully, Briare, and Pithiviers. These meetings were crowded and contentious, and Considerant was repeatedly put on the defensive. He was attacked so often about Fourier's views that he had to write the *Journal du Loiret* on April 13 stating that he did not accept Fourier's doctrine in its entirety, especially not Fourier's theories on marriage. He was also attacked—both from the right and the left—as a political opportunist, a long-standing monarchist whose conversion to republicanism preceded the revolution by very little. This was not entirely false, but the charges concerning his "communism" were, and these were repeated so often that he finally had a brochure printed up in which he gathered together several dozen citations from his writings showing that he had never been a partisan of anything like the *communauté des biens*.[20]

Despite these attacks, Considerant enjoyed political campaigning. He was good at it. He was a gifted, experienced, and often persuasive public speaker; and his earnestness, enthusiasm, and obvious lack of guile won the sympathies of many listeners who did not share all his views. As Fernand Dieudonné put it in his detailed study of this election:

> The members and delegates of the Central Committee, the members of the republican societies who put Considerant's name on their electoral lists did not see in him the socialist but the democrat. . . . It was not his theories that they wished to send to the Constituent Assembly; it was his talent, his experience in handling social and economic questions. The republicans said so clearly.[21]

Considerant also had prominent allies. He received endorsements from Lamartine, from the mayor of Paris, Armand Marrast, and from the minister of education, Hippolyte Carnot, and his collaborator Edouard Charton. In addition, he won the editorial backing of local newspapers such as the *Loiret* and the *Démocrat du Loing*. More important than these endorsements, though, was the support he received from the newly enfranchised working-class population of Orléans. These workers turned out in large numbers for Considerant's speeches and appearances in Orléans; and their organization, the Reunion of Orléans Workers, strongly supported his candidacy. Thus after the election he made a point of thanking "the working-class population of Orléans, with which I had closer contact than with other parts of the population of the department."[22]

The results of the election in the Loiret were in some respects similar to those in the rest of provincial France. The turnout was heavy—close to 85 percent—even though voters in rural communes often had to travel long distances to reach their polling places. The largest vote-getters were old *notables*—a former baron, a great land owner, an influential lawyer, a former mayor of Orléans—and two had previously served as deputies under the July Monarchy. What was distinctive about the elections in the Loiret, however, was that three of the eight successful candidates were avowed democrats. The seventh was the worker Michot, and the eighth and last of the *élus* was Considerant, who received 34,370 votes out of a total of 73,249 cast.[23]

If Considerant's victory was narrow, it was nonetheless celebrated by Fourierists everywhere as an event of epic significance. Considerant himself was euphoric. We get a glimpse of his excitement in the correspondence of Prosper Mérimée. On May 3, the day before the first meeting of the National Assembly, both Mérimée and Considerant were invited to dinner by the eccentric English M.P. and patron of the arts Richard Monckton Milnes. The other guests at this extraordinary dinner included George Sand, Alfred de Vigny, François Mignet, and Alexis de Tocqueville. According to the amused Mérimée, it was Considerant who dominated the conversation, speaking in a loud voice and pounding on the table "with thoroughly republican manners." Mérimée observed that as Considerant carried on in his "stentor's voice," Tocqueville and Mignet, who were "not used to dining in such company," looked increasingly alarmed.[24]

In his public statements at this time, however, Considerant was eager to present himself as a moderate and a conciliator. In a letter of May 10 to his constituents he wrote that he hoped the fears created among conservatives by his election would soon be dispelled. "I have promised to work for peace, unity, concord, and for the conciliation of all interests and all rights without sacrificing any. I will keep my promise."[25]

The newly elected National Assembly convened on May 4 in a huge and hastily built wooden structure in the courtyard of the Palais Bourbon. Considerant took his place high up on the left near most of the other democrats. The first order of business was to proclaim the establishment of the Second Republic. This was actually done twice—first indoors and then, late in the afternoon, on the steps of the Palais Bourbon, in the light of the setting sun and before an immense throng. Shouts of "Vive la République!" rang out again and again—apparently seventeen times in all. According to some witnesses it was a moment of high emotion. Marie d'Agoult wrote of tears being shed and strangers embracing, but for Tocqueville most of the new representatives were wary and fearful, and the Constituent Assembly had been elected "to face civil war."[26]

There were no parties in the Assembly in any modern sense. Instead, there were loose alliances of representatives, and Considerant joined one of them—the Society of Republican Representatives, which had its headquarters on the rue des Pyramids. This group had about sixty members, including socialists like Louis Blanc and Pierre Leroux, as well as radical republicans such as Théodore Bac, Eugène Baune, and Jean-Jacques Vignerte.[27] Dedicated republicans constituted a minority in the Assembly, though. Of the 880 new *représentants du peuple,* over half were *républicains du lendemain,* who had rallied to the republic out of expediency after the February Revolution. Close to a hundred were unrepentant legitimists (who favored a return to the "legitimate" Bourbon dynasty). Almost two hundred were Orleanists. Only eighty to a hundred had identified themselves as republicans before February; and Considerant noted that the number of those who took seriously the idea of social reform was even smaller.

I hadn't spent forty-five minutes in the midst of my dear colleagues who had clucked and cackled so much about the social question, the social revolution, and the new social order, before I became convinced of the fact that I was sitting right in the middle of an assembly of jays, magpies, and multi-colored parrots. . . . Of the 900 of us who were there, perched on all the benches, there were a good 800 who had repeated the words "social question," "social revolution," "organization of credit," "organization of work," and all the words that the revolution had introduced, just as parrots say everything their masters care to teach them. . . . More than that, these 800 social reformers basically detested socialism and everything that goes with it. Their greatest desire was to smother or crush any conception of social reform.[28]

If the elections of April 23 represented a defeat for the left, its position was worsened by a series of decisions taken by the Constituent Assembly in its first days. The most important of these was the replacement of the Provisional Government by a five-member Executive Commission that excluded radicals such as the socialist Louis Blanc and the worker Albert. This was followed by the creation of a new, more conservative ministry, by the Assembly's overwhelming rejection of Louis Blanc's proposal for the appointment of a new minister of labor and progress, and by Louis Blanc's resignation on May 8 as head of the Luxembourg Commission. There was now talk in the National Assembly about the need to "finish with" the costly experiment of the National Workshops. It rapidly became clear that no significant effort to address social issues was going to come out of the Assembly.

This was the context in which the events leading up to the ill-fated *journée* of May 15 unfolded.[29] Frustrated by the revolution's apparent loss of momentum, a number of radical club members argued that a show of popular force was needed to get the revolution back on track. The occasion that presented itself was the debate scheduled for May 15 on the question of French intervention in support of Polish independence. The cause of Poland, that "martyr-nation," had long attracted support in France, and Considerant himself had written articles protesting the "pusillanimous" policies of Thiers and Guizot with regard to Russian rule in Poland. On the evening of May 11, Considerant attended a large meeting of Polish sympathizers presided over by the liberal marquis Jules de Lasteyrie. When a delegate from the radical clubs urged the meeting to endorse a march on the National Assembly demanding French military intervention in Poland, Considerant joined the majority in opposing the proposal. This was hardly the time, he argued, to try to intimidate the National Assembly with threats of violence. Four days later, on the morning of May 15, the lead article in *Démocratie pacifique* condemned the march as a foolish and ill-timed idea that could disrupt the Assembly and compromise Poland's cause.[30]

The events of May 15 more than justified Considerant's fears. A huge march on the National Assembly did take place, and although the purpose was nominally to deliver a petition in behalf of the Poles, the Assembly was in fact invaded by a great crowd. As the crowd pushed its way into the Assembly, François Raspail attempted to read the petition "in the name of 300,000 men who are waiting at the door," but his voice could scarcely be heard above the tumult. The radicals Armand Barbès and Auguste Blanqui attempted to speak, and then Ledru-Rollin tried unsuccessfully to quiet the crowd. The president of the Assembly, Philippe Buchez, had lost all control of the situation.

Almost all the representatives (including Considerant) were appalled by what was happening, but a few of the radicals saw an opportunity. Mounting to the speakers' rostrum, Barbès began to call out a list of names—apparently the members of a new provisional government. Before Barbès could finish, though, he was interrupted by other speakers with other lists. One such list included Considerant's name along with those of Barbès and Blanqui and the socialists Louis Blanc, Pierre Leroux, and Etienne Cabet. When the tumult was at its height, one of the leaders of the demonstration, a former revolutionary named Aloysius Huber who was subsequently shown to have been employed as a police spy during the July Monarchy, got control of the rostrum and shouted at the top of his lungs: "Citizens, the National Assembly is dissolved!" After more confusion the crowd poured out of the Assembly and the insurgents headed for the Hôtel de Ville, the traditional setting for the proclamation of revolutionary governments in France. Few actually reached the Hôtel de Ville, though, for they were intercepted by troops from the National Guard, who had been called out earlier by Buchez. The Guards rapidly surrounded the Assembly and arrested the remaining insurgents as well as others whose principal crime was to be known as prominent figures on the left.

The abortive insurrection of May 15 played so nicely into the hands of the reaction that it has been argued that the whole thing was a trap—in Henri Guillemin's words, "a well-executed police operation."[31] Be that as it may, the events of May 15 compromised the radical left and got many of its leaders arrested. By nightfall Barbès, Albert, and Raspail were in police custody; Blanqui was in hiding; and the position of Louis Blanc—who had been unwillingly carried in triumph by the insurgents—had been deeply compromised. Considerant himself felt sufficiently compromised that the following day he went before the Assembly to dissociate himself explicitly from the insurrection. "For twenty years," he insisted, "I have devoted my life to spreading throughout society ideas of peace, fraternity, union, and harmony. . . . I have not ceased to combat violence and factionalism in all their forms." Considerant explained that the previous day, during the course of "the saturnalia which we all witnessed, calm and impassive on our benches," he had been approached by "one of those wretched fools" and asked to serve on the insurrectionary provisional government. "Are you crazy?" he had replied. "And who do you take me for? I am here at my post, and my duty would be to get my throat slit rather than accept a proposition like the one you have just made to me." [32]

Considerant's final assessment of the significance of May 15 was more nuanced than the references to "saturnalia" and "wretched fools" suggest. An anonymous article entitled "A Failed Revolution" that appeared in *Démocratie pacifique* on May 16 (which probably reflects Considerant's views even if he didn't write it) draws two lessons. The obvious lesson for proletarians was that "anarchy" was more likely "to compromise their sacred cause than serve it." The lesson for the National Assembly was that their actions were being watched by "the people" and that there were "dangers" in failing to come resolutely to grips with fundamental social issues. [33] A few years later Considerant went further toward justifying the action of the crowd.

> I say bluntly that on May 15 [the Constituent Assembly] was judged—judged by popular sentiment and judged rightly. The eleven whole days that it spent under the flaccid presidency of Buchez, discussing half of a bad set of rules, proved that it was ten thousand meters beneath the level required by interior and exterior circumstances. The party of the old *National* had control over this hybrid gathering. Nothing came out of this assembly, and from the sound that it made the forces of democracy knew very well that nothing was going to come out of it—at least nothing great, broad, fruitful, truly democratic. It was a hybrid. The sign of sterility glittered on its forehead. [34]

By 1851, when he wrote these words, Considerant had come to see the *journée* of May 15 as a demonstration not of the folly of the insurrectionists but of the sterility and incompetence of the Constituent Assembly itself. In May 1848, however, he had not yet given up on the Assembly, and its work still absorbed him.

IV

The first two tasks confronting the Constituent Assembly were the drawing up of a constitution and the need to find some more satisfactory answer than the National Workshops to the problem of unemployment. Each of these tasks became the particular concern of a committee—the Constitutional Committee and the Labor Committee. Considerant was one of the few members of the Assembly who served on both these important committees; and during the months of May and June they took up most of his time and energy.

The Constitutional Committee, which first met on May 19, consisted of eighteen elected members. It was dominated by moderate republicans associated with the *National* such as Armand Marrast and Achille de Vaulabelle and by former members of the July Monarchy's dynastic opposition like Odilon Barrot, Gustave de Beaumont, and Alexis de Tocqueville. Considerant was one of just two democrats on the committee (the other, Lamennais, resigned after a few days), and he was elected only on the third round. His 339 votes were the smallest total received by any of the representatives chosen.

The main task of the committee was to prepare the draft of a constitution that could be discussed by the Assembly as a whole. After a month of almost daily meetings a draft was completed and presented to the Assembly on June 19. In the climate of reaction that prevailed in July and August, though, many of the more liberal and democratic provisions of the original draft were watered down or simply eliminated. A new, more conservative version was presented to the Assembly on August 30, and this was further amended in September and October.[35] Although Considerant played a fairly active role in preparing the first draft, the text of the constitution that was finally adopted by the Assembly on November 4 bore virtually no trace of his influence.

The best-known account of the inner workings of the Constitutional Committee is the bemused and condescending chapter in Alexis de Tocqueville's *Souvenirs* of 1848.[36] There, with typical acerbity, Tocqueville describes the committee as a group of mediocrities of whom "nothing very remarkable was to be expected." The two democrats on the committee—Lamennais and Considerant—are dismissed as "no more than fantastic dreamers," and Considerant is dispatched in one brutal aphorism: "If he was sincere, he should have been put in a mental institution."[37] Of course, if Tocqueville's opinion had been widely shared, Considerant would not have been elected to the committee. In fact, Considerant seems to have been respected for his willingness to compromise and for what his adversary Odilon Barrot described as "a certain moderation in his doctrines, a certain dignity in his bearing, and some caution in his language."[38]

The moderation shown by Considerant as a member of the Constitutional Committee is indeed striking. On many issues he took positions that radical republicans would have found objectionable. He recognized the cogency of Tocqueville's arguments for a bicameral legislature, even if he did not finally support them. After some hesitation he supported the election of the president by the National Assembly rather than by popular vote. "Principles impose the popular election of the president," he observed. "But the education of the people is not complete. We must wait until the people have a greater appreciation of their rights before we let them exercise them."[39]

There were two points, however, on which Considerant was intransigent. The first was the right to work. On May 15, during the invasion of the National Assembly, he had already argued that a decree reaffirming the Assembly's support of the right to work would be "a striking proof" that it was still on the side of the workers. On May 23 he told the Constitutional Committee: "The right to work is properly speaking a conquest of the February Revolution. If this right is not clearly recognized, the workers will think that the revolution has been stolen from them." When Barrot, Marrast, and Gustave de Beaumont argued that the right to work was impossible to guarantee, Considerant held his ground. "For the workers," he asserted, "the whole value of the Constitution will lie in this one expression: the right to work."[40] In the end a cautious affirmation of the right to work was included in the draft of the constitution presented to the Assembly on June 19, and this was pretty clearly a result of Considerant's efforts.

The other issue on which Considerant was adamant was women's suffrage. He had long believed that the degradation of women in contemporary societies could not, and should not, last. Like almost every other male on the democratic left, though, he had never come out publicly in support of women's suffrage. On June 13, 1848, however, he formally proposed to the committee that adult women be given the right to vote. Why, he asked, should an intelligent woman be denied a right exercised by her husband's valet? Why should she be denied all political rights just as she had long been denied all civil rights? As he expected, Considerant was a minority of one on this question. Later he wrote that his proposal was not given the derisive reception he had anticipated. His colleagues seemed to understand that "given absolutely unlimited male suffrage, no reason could be offered to justify the prejudice that formally excludes women from the sphere of political rights." After the vote was taken, he added, one of his conservative colleagues noted wryly that in fifty years no one would understand the denial of the vote to women.[41]

Considerant's support of women's suffrage is worth noting. It came at a time when almost all republicans were ridiculing the women's movement and when even George Sand was scornfully denouncing the proposal of some "exalted women" that she stand for election to the National Assembly. A few years later the influential republican writer, Marie d'Agoult, was to speak condescendingly of "the so-called free women" of 1848 whose zeal outran their talent. In this context Considerant's proposal seems bold and progressive. One can ask how significant a gesture it really was, since Considerant did not pursue the matter, and since throughout the first months of the Second Republic his journal *Démocratie pacifique* had little to say on the question of women's political rights. Still, even as an isolated gesture, Considerant's willingness to give his support to the handful of women who were calling for the vote in 1848 took some courage, and it distinguishes him from virtually every other male radical of his generation. Joined with his support of liberalized divorce legislation and his strong critique of "the regime of perpetual and indissoluble marriage," his advocacy of women's suffrage makes him one of the leading mid-century male feminists.[42]

The second major committee to which Considerant belonged was the Labor Committee, which met for the first time on May 17, taking over some of the functions of the now defunct Luxembourg Commission. Like the Constituent Assembly itself, the Labor Committee was very large—it had over sixty members—and essentially conservative in its composition. It included a number of workers, but few of them were socialist or even republican; and the most influential, Anthîme Corbon, a follower of Buchez who had moved to the right, was described by a colleague as "heart and soul for the reactionary royalist element in the Assembly."[43] Most committee members were either doctrinaire economic liberals or representatives of conservative landed interests.

The dominant member of this committee was the vicomte Frédéric Alfred Pierre de Falloux. Best remembered today for his sponsorship of the pro-Catholic education law of 1850, Falloux came from a staunchly Catholic and royalist background. In the old Chamber of Deputies he had sat among the tiny group of legitimists. He was a shrewd man—intelligent, suave, unfailingly civil, impeccable in his manners, and totally lacking in candor. Tocqueville called him cunning, but added that he possessed "an uncommon and very effective kind of cunning, for he succeeded in believing temporarily the mixture of truth and falsehood that he served up to others."[44]

Although Falloux subsequently described himself as no more than a reporter for the Labor Committee, it is clear from a study of its stenographic minutes that he dominated its deliberations.[45] It is also clear that Falloux played a fundamental role in pushing through the committee a bill calling for the dissolution of the National Workshops. Since Considerant served (along with Falloux and the future Communard Charles Beslay) on a subcommittee appointed to consider the whole issue of the National Workshops, this is an episode that merits close attention.

Even before May 15, the future of the National Workshops seemed bleak. They had come under repeated attack during the election campaign, and on May 13 the Executive Commission had already quietly begun to prepare the way for their dissolution. In the reaction that followed May 15, however, a concerted attack on the workshops was organized, first in the right-wing press and then in the Assembly. On May 17 the minister of public works, Trélat, came before the Assembly to announce that the government now favored dissolution. The workshops were only intended to be a "temporary organization," he argued, and it was time to stop giving workers "disguised charity" for "useless projects." The following day Trélat appeared before the newly created Labor Committee and spoke at length about "the dangers of the workshops" and the need to put an end to "the fiction of labor" that they sustained. At the same time the Labor Committee appointed a subcommittee to make a detailed study of the whole question of the National Workshops. The three members of this subcommittee were Falloux, Beslay, and Considerant.[46]

We have no record of the proceedings of this subcommittee, but we do have the report delivered in its name by Falloux to the Labor Committee on May 25. This report began with a devastating attack on the National Workshops. From the economic standpoint, Falloux argued, the workshops were a disaster. There were "scandalous abuses" in their administration; and since members of the workshops had on occasion turned down offers of employment by private entrepreneurs, the workshops themselves could be characterized as "la grève organisée"—a kind of subsidized strike. From the political standpoint, the workshops were even more dangerous. They were a "rebel camp," a "perpetual menace to public order." Indeed, the threat that they posed to society was growing, as the number of individuals enrolled in the workshops increased "at a frightening rate." Falloux went on to propose three ways of dealing with the problem of the National Workshops, all of which might be put into effect simultaneously: (1) Unmarried workers might be given the option of enlistment in the army or dismissal from the workshops. (2) Workers who were not permanent residents of Paris might be returned to the provinces. (3) Those who remained members of the workshops should be paid piece-wages rather than by the day.[47]

None of these proposals came as a surprise. Similar recommendations had already been discussed within the Executive Commission and even in the Assembly. What was striking about Falloux's report, however, was its stridency. The situation was becoming "more and more perilous," he insisted, and it "must soon be brought to an end." Furthermore, the Executive Commission had shown itself either unwilling or unable to take the appropriate measures. Something had to be done quickly. Falloux did not explicitly urge the immediate dissolution of the workshops. (He left that to others.) However, he did make the point that if the workshops were dissolved, there would not be significant resistance among the workers. "Take what measures you prefer," he told the committee. "We guarantee that we will not encounter serious resistance; and in case we do, let us not be afraid to use force, force without the shedding of blood, but that moral force which belongs to the law."[48]

Falloux later insisted repeatedly that he was as surprised as anyone when the actual attempt to dissolve the National Workshops met with massive resistance. It was a calumny, he claimed, to suggest that he had sought deliberately to provoke a movement of protest that could be used as the excuse for massive reprisals.[49] These claims are hardly convincing. It strains credibility to think that a man as tough-minded and cynical as Falloux could really have believed that "serious resistance" would not develop, or that if it did, it could be put down with "moral force." What is almost equally incredible, however, is that Victor Considerant could have allowed this report—in the name of the subcommittee of which he was a member—to have gone virtually unchallenged. Such is the impression one gets from the published sources. When Falloux had finished, the Protestant minister Coquerel spoke in support of the immediate dissolution of the National Workshops. According to the *procès verbal* or summary of the discussion, Considerant's only contribution to the ensuing debate was to urge what amounted to a brief delaying action, but the full stenographic record leaves a different impression. Considerant did indeed accept the necessity of dissolving the workshops "as they are now organized." However, he argued forcefully for some sort of "guarantees" to be given the affected workers. He proposed that the state offer subsidies to firms (notably those in the construction industry) hiring former members of the National

Workshops. He also urged the passage of legislation that would facilitate the placement of unemployed workers.[50]

The discussion concerning Falloux's report continued within the Labor Committee for two more days, and the manuscript minutes make clear (as the published summary does not) that Considerant became more aggressive in challenging different portions of the report. He accepted charges concerning the "poor administration" of the National Workshops and reiterated his belief that they could not be maintained in their existing form. At the same time he continued to emphasize the importance of finding employment for discharged members of the workshops, and on May 29 he attempted to get a hearing for a draft statement or "program" concerning the rights of workers, which he wished to see appended to any decree on the abolition of the workshops. (He had in fact submitted this program earlier, only to see it shelved by the committee.)

> I remind you that I have submitted a program with the end in mind, which we can all readily appreciate today, of showing the working class that we are concerned about it. The greatest danger that we are running now lies in its mistrust of our intentions. We must do everything possible to make sure that this mistrust is not exploited by outsiders.[51]

Considerant reminded the committee that he could have forced a vote on his proposal. "It was my right to force you to reject it." He did not exercise that right because he had no desire to stir up class antagonism, but he did want his proposal to receive serious consideration. At this point his conservative colleague from the Loiret, the lawyer Louis-Félix Rondeau, interrupted: "Don't go putting utopias in the place of facts." Considerant replied indignantly: "No citizen can say that I'm proposing utopias." "You're proposing one today," responded Rondeau, whereupon the president, Anthîme Corbon, intervened: "Let's spend our time doing something useful." Finally Considerant exploded angrily: "I tell you, it's a sad state of affairs we've reached!" By this time he was shouting. A moment later Considerant apologized for losing his temper, but it was clear that the committee did not regard as "useful" any discussion of workers' rights.[52]

That afternoon, May 29, Falloux presented his report on the National Workshops to the Assembly as a whole, together with a slightly revised set of decrees. Speaking (so he claimed) with "clarity and frankness," he described the members of the Labor Committee as united in their desire to "bring about ameliorations in the situation of workers." There could be no doubt, he said, that the experiment of the National Workshops had failed. The product of labor in the workshops was "derisory," and they engendered "disorder and laziness." The workshops also posed a political threat to the capital; they had become "a center of menacing fermentation." Did this mean that the workshops should simply be dissolved? Not at all, or at least not for the present. Rather the committee proposed the issuance of a decree with three main articles: (1) the replacement of a daily wage by a piece-wage; (2) the encouragement of provincial public works projects that might absorb the excess of laborers in the Paris workshops; and (3) the return of workers who could not prove at least three months' residence in Paris to their provinces of origin. These articles, which were in fact more moderate than the tenor of Falloux's report, were adopted in a decree voted by the Assembly the following day.[53]

The decree of May 30 on the National Workshops was easier to pass than to implement. Funds for public works projects were limited, and it proved difficult to get the reliable census of the Paris workshops that was needed before workers could be relocated. Furthermore, without jobs to send workers to in the provinces, relocation solved nothing. Thus for two weeks the Executive Commission fumbled; and its reluctance to execute the law was reinforced by a growing sense that to start relocating workers at a time of deepening unrest would be to invite disaster.

Then, on June 14, Falloux went on the attack and accused the minister of public works, Trélat, of stalling—intentionally failing to execute the law—possibly for some unavowed political motive. At the same time, through a "swift and subtle series of moves," Falloux maneuvered the question of the National Workshops out of the hands of the Labor Committee, and Considerant's subcommittee, and into those of a new special committee, which he was able to dominate even more effectively than the Labor Committee.[54] After this events moved swiftly. On June 15 Michel Goudchaux, the former minister of finance and an ally of Falloux, gave a speech in the Assembly declaring that "the National Workshops must disappear . . . immediately, in the provinces as well as Paris." On June 19, speaking in the name of the new special committee, Falloux again scathingly attacked Trélat on the floor of the Assembly and called for the immediate application "of effective measures." Falloux then proposed a bill, adopted the following day, that in essence empowered his own special committee to draw up a definitive plan for the dissolution of the workshops if the Executive Commission failed to act. But on June 21 the Executive Commission finally did act. Capitulating to the demands of the National Assembly and Falloux's special committee, the Executive Commission issued an order compelling unmarried members of the National Workshops to join the army or else face dismissal. This order was published in the *Moniteur officiel* of June 22; the following day a working-class revolt of unprecedented scope was under way in Paris.[55]

What was Considerant's role in these events, beginning with the creation of the Labor Committee and culminating with the tragic *dénouement* of the June days? As a member of the Labor Committee's subcommittee on the National Workshops, Considerant was—at least until May 30—well placed to lead the resistance to Falloux. Apart from his joust with Rondeau on May 29, though, his role was relatively modest. For two weeks he participated actively in the work of the Labor Committee, but generally his interventions had to do with matters of detail. As a rule he took positions that would require the softening, or gradual implementation, of any decree leading to the dissolution of the National Workshops, but he did not question the necessity for dissolution.

Does this mean that Falloux was correct in claiming in his memoirs—written forty years after the events and with his customary lack of candor—that Considerant and Beslay actually supported his efforts to hasten the dissolution of the National Workshops?[56] Hardly. What is clear is that Considerant felt himself isolated within the Labor Committee and that his efforts to widen the debate over the National Workshops to include some discussion of workers' rights evoked no positive response. Failing to elicit such a response, he confined himself for the most part to commenting on matters of detail. What is also clear from a study of the sources is that between June 3 and June 20 Considerant took no part at all in the debates concerning the National Workshops either in the Assembly or in committee. Indeed, he does not even appear to have been present. How are we to explain Considerant's absence in such a crucial period? Was it due to sickness? In a letter of June 8 to Proudhon, apologizing for his failure to study Proudhon's proposal for a *banque d'échange,* Considerant described his health as "not very sound just now."[57] The next day he asked for a temporary leave of absence from the Assembly, noting in his request that "due to illness" he had been "prevented for several days from participating in the work of the Assembly."[58] But if Considerant was sick, he was apparently not too sick to write articles and hold meetings at the rue de Beaune, or to attend the meetings of the Constitutional Committee during this period.

So again, how are we to explain Considerant's absence? It would seem that his most powerful motive was quite simply despair—the sense that nothing he might do or say about the National Workshops could possibly make any difference. Considerant was in fact very much involved in the work of the Labor Committee during the last two weeks of May, the period in which his subcommittee was active. After May 30, though, with the voting of the law on the National Workshops, the work of his subcommittee was over; and when the issue was raised again two weeks later, he was not asked to serve on the new special committee. By that time it was clear that there was no role to play for the conciliator that Considerant hoped to be.

v

There was nothing in Paris's past to equal the ferocity of the fighting that marked the workers' revolt that began on June 23, 1848, the day after the publication of the order abolishing the National Workshops. The "June Days," as they became known, were all over by noon of June 26, but in the course of those four days a battle was fought in the streets of Paris that left at least four thousand dead and culminated with the arrest of some fifteen thousand insurgents.[59]

The June Days left a scar in the memory of almost everyone who lived through them. One reason for this was the sheer magnitude of the event. Some fifty thousand men and women, the whole of eastern Paris it seemed, took arms against the government; and the force deployed against them was, by the end of the fighting, at least twice as large. What made the June insurrection unforgettable, though, was what almost all contemporaries took to be its class character. It was not a conflict between opposing political factions; it was in Tocqueville's words "the revolt of one whole section of the population against another." When the fighting began, republicans found themselves allied with royalists against an army of the dispossessed. This was an army without leaders or any discernible support from the socialists and radical republicans who had for years been identifying themselves with the cause of "the people." Tocqueville's words are familiar, but they are again worth quoting: "The insurgents were fighting without a battle cry, leaders, or flag, and yet they showed wonderful powers of coordination and a military expertise that astonished the most experienced officers." The war itself, according to Tocqueville, was "a class struggle, a sort of 'servile war.'"[60]

If the insurgents had a unity born of desperation, the government's supporters were divided in their motives. This is not to say that they disagreed about goals. They were all fighting to defend the republic and the authority of the National Assembly. What distinguished democrats and conservatives was rather the ambivalence of many of the former and the single-mindedness of the latter. For the majority of the members of the National Assembly, as for most conservatives and moderates outside the Assembly, the June insurrection posed no difficult choices. They knew where they

stood. Tocqueville, for example, recognized that the insurgents were motivated by ideals, by "a sort of revolutionary religion . . . that our bayonets
and our cannon will not destroy." Nonetheless, there was absolutely no
doubt in Tocqueville's mind about what needed to be done: the insurrection
had to be crushed. Others on the right were cruder in their appreciation of
the insurgents' motives and behavior. During and after the fighting, respectable journals portrayed the insurgents as "cannibals," "savages," and
"lepers" whose social ideal could be summed up in the words "pillage and
rape." Shortly after the end of the fighting, the writer Ximénès Doudan
could describe the military dictatorship of General Eugène Cavaignac as "a
pearl of great value compared to the possibility of being devoured one day
or another by the packs of wild beasts that howled around all the houses of
Paris two weeks ago." For Doudan and many other conservatives, the insurgents could scarcely be represented as human beings; they were better
described as "menacing animals thirsting for an impossible well-being."[61]

For democrats in and out of the Assembly, on the other hand, the June
insurrection was the occasion of deep and painful soul-searching. They had
long been arguing that the political system of the July Monarchy was un-
just because it excluded and oppressed "the people," and they believed—or
had come to believe—that only under the institutions of a democratic republic would the people attain full freedom and dignity. Yet they were confronted in June with an insurrection in which the people were seeking to
overthrow the republic that had been established in their name. Finally, almost all of them reacted in the same way, joining their National Guard units
or supporting the declaration of a state of siege or otherwise identifying
with the government. The comtesse Marie d'Agoult, who was closely tied
to many of these democratic republicans, gave eloquent expression to their
dilemma—and their choice—in her *Histoire de la Révolution de 1848*.

> The most convinced republicans, men who throughout their lives had
> fought for the progress of democratic ideas, men like Guinard, Bixio,
> Dornès, Clément Thomas, Edmond Adam, Charras, Charbonnel,
> Arago, were persuaded this time that the people, in revolting against
> the national representation, would destroy, along with law and right,
> the republic and perhaps the state itself in their calamitous triumph.
> Thus with broken hearts but firm resolve, they went off to fight this
> strange enemy whose emancipation had been the goal of their efforts
> for more than twenty years.[62]

The ultimate success of the repression, according to Marie d'Agoult, lay
not only in the vastly superior firepower at the disposal of the government

but also in the fact that the government was still able to enlist on its side people inspired by the republican ideal.

The position of the Fourierists in June was in many respects similar to that of the democratic republicans. The Fourierists, though republicans of recent date, had come to identify their aspirations for social change with the republic's survival, and their response to the insurrection was marked by an ambivalence similar to that felt by the republicans. As one of the Fourierists wrote on June 25, the birth process of the republic was "bloody" and "painful," yet it offered the promise "for France, for Europe, for humanity, of an era of peace, association, and veritable fraternity." The republic could not be abandoned or overthrown, because it was through the republic that the new social world would come into being.[63]

The ambivalence of the Fourierists with regard to the June insurrection comes through most clearly in their treatment of the insurgents themselves. Repeatedly in the numbers of *Démocratie pacifique* that appeared immediately after the June Days one finds the insurrection described as having two faces. Among the insurgents there were "men depraved by the habit of crime," "foreign mercenaries," and the "hired agents of odious pretenders." A "greater number" of the insurgents were honorable men and women, however, "unemployed workers unable to feed their families and preferring death by gunfire to the slow agony of hunger." The description in these articles of the causes of the June insurrection is similarly ambiguous. Workers are depicted as worn down by poverty, hunger, and by "an industrial crisis that was the final legacy of the monarchy." All of this made them vulnerable to "criminal intrigues" and "perfidious seductions." They were easily manipulated. What they needed was to transcend class hatred, to recognize that civil war solved nothing and that only the republic could "place a balm on the wounds" suffered by both sides.[64]

Finally, the Fourierists, like almost all the other republicans, came down firmly in support of the repression. They sympathized with the insurgents' pain, but condemned their actions. They opposed the proclamation of a state of siege, but once it was declared they gave their support to Cavaignac. Forced to choose between the republic and the rebellious people, they chose the republic. Still, the role played by Considerant over the course of the insurrection differed from that played by most republicans. For if he supported military action against the insurrection, he was also one of the very few members of the National Assembly who spoke out repeatedly for gestures and policies of conciliation.

Considerant's most dramatic attempt at conciliation came in the National

Assembly on the night of June 23, at a time when barricades had risen all over the east of Paris but Cavaignac's troops were not yet fully engaged. In a voice that Louis Blanc later described as "almost pleading," Considerant urged the Assembly to issue a proclamation calling on the insurgents as "brothers" and as "victims of a fatal misunderstanding" to lay down their arms. Many of the insurgents had been "misled," he insisted, and a concilatory proclamation might go far toward "reestablishing peace in the blood-stained streets" of the capital. But Considerant's references to the insurgents as "brothers" and "victims" and his reaffirmation of their right to work drew howls of protest from the Assembly. "Order!" people shouted with what Tocqueville remembered as "a sort of fury." "You have no right to talk like that until after the victory."[65]

Considerant continued, asking that the president of the Assembly, Sénard, appoint a committee to consider, and possibly revise, his proclamation. Sénard (who had already made a reputation for himself as a tough prosecutor of working-class rebels at Rouen) sarcastically declined the honor of naming representatives "to negotiate with the rebellion" ("pactiser avec l'émeute"). "I have shown the proclamation to about twenty of my colleagues," Considerant went on. "They have all approved of it. All of them believe, as I do, that at this terrible moment a word from the National Assembly would do more to repress or dissipate the rebellion than armed force itself." A chorus of protest greeted this assertion, but Considerant pressed on. He was not asking the government to withdraw its troops and guns. He was simply asking the Assembly to consider whether a few words from it might not have "immense power in bringing these unfortunate misguided people back into line." At this point shouting began from all sides. A voice was heard above the tumult: "You call assassins 'unfortunate misguided people'!" The shouting grew louder. Considerant remained at the rostrum, but his voice could no longer be heard.[66]

Later that evening Considerant's proposal was taken up again by the fiery democrat Marc Caussidière, who urged the reading of a conciliatory proclamation in working-class quarters by torchlight that very night. Offering himself as a hostage to the rebels, Caussidière guaranteed that the bloodshed could be brought to an end. He too was shouted down.

The following day Considerant made another attempt at conciliation. The Assembly had just voted to declare a state of siege and to place all executive powers in the hands of General Cavaignac. (Considerant was one of just sixty representatives voting against the state of siege; others in the ill-assorted group of sixty included Tocqueville, Odilon Barrot, and Jules Grévy.) Considerant then rose to call on the Assembly to draft a proclamation of its own to accompany the declaration of a state of siege—a proclamation expressing its desire for a return to peace and mutual respect. "Armed with words of peace," he declared, "we will all go forth to calm the civil war. For my part I am ready to go out among the insurgents bearing words of peace in the name of the National Assembly, but I will never consent to be the missionary solely of the state of siege." At this point Considerant was interrupted with shouts of "It's too late!" His voice shaking with emotion, he shouted back: "If you don't take this measure, you'll be letting Paris burn."[67]

Paris did not burn. But during the course of June 24 the fighting took on a new savagery. Once vested with full powers, Cavaignac went on the offensive. By midmorning he had begun a systematic cannonade of the centers of the insurgency. The government troops were soon reinforced by trainloads of National Guards and volunteers from the provinces eager to join the action. By nightfall the tide of battle had turned. The insurgents were gradually pushed back into tight pockets of resistance—the Clos Saint-Lazare, the Faubourgs Saint-Antoine and Saint-Denis, the areas around the Place de la Bastille and the Hôtel de Ville. Yet they fought on desperately. In the Faubourg du Temple a large detachment of troops under Lamoricière was pinned down for an hour on the morning of the twenty-fifth by a few snipers in a building near the Château d'Eau. Resistance remained fierce around the Place de la Bastille and the Hôtel de Ville. It was not until midmorning on June 26 that the last shots were exchanged in the Faubourg Saint-Antoine. Finally, at eleven twenty, Sénard brought word to the Assembly that the rebels had capitulated unconditionally.

It was at this point, after the insurgents had laid down their arms, that the real massacre began. Probably no more than four or five hundred of them had been killed in the course of the streetfighting, but by Georges Duveau's estimate more than three thousand were killed by the Mobile Guards, the National Guards, and the regular army after the fighting had stopped. Men were shot because they had gunpowder on their hands, because they looked menacingly at their captors, because they were dressed like workers. Describing one such incident in his novel *Education sentimental,* Flaubert (or his narrator) went on to reflect on the fury of the National Guards.

> By and large, they were merciless. Those who hadn't taken part in the fighting wanted to distinguish themselves. It was an explosion of fear. They took revenge at one and the same time for the journals, the clubs, the demonstrations, the doctrines, for everything that had been exasperating them for the past three months.

In the end, wrote Flaubert, both sides sank to "an equality of brutishness, a common level of bloody atrocities," and what was left was an enduring legacy of hatred.[68]

Flaubert's novel was published twenty-one years after the June Days, but a similar sense that the violence of June would leave a lasting legacy can be found in numerous contemporary writings. On July 1, 1848, for example, the young Ernest Renan wrote that "the atrocities committed by the victors" in June "take us back in a day to the period of the wars of religion." The June Days had culminated in arbitrary military rule and "a real Terror," when "something hard, fierce, inhuman" entered "people's habits and speech."

> People on the side of "order," those who are called *honnêtes gens,* want nothing but grapeshot and fusillades. The death penalty has been done away with; they are substituting massacre. The bourgeois class has proved that it was capable of all the excesses of our first Terror, with an added degree of reflection and selfishness. And they believe that they will always be victors. When is the day of reprisals coming?

Nevertheless, Renan added, the victory of the army, the National Guard, and the bourgeoisie was not a bad thing, "for the triumph of the insurrection would have been even worse."[69]

When one considers the verdicts on the June Days left by democrats and socialists, one finds a similar sense of horror at the brutality of the repression. For some of them this was enough to destroy whatever hopes they had placed in the republic. In the aftermath of June, for example, George Sand could write that she no longer believed in a republic that began by killing its proletarians. The Christian democrat Lamennais lamented that the republic was now morally dead. "What we see is assuredly not the republic . . . but around its bloodstained tomb, the saturnalia of reaction."[70]

Others on the left deplored the violence but, like Renan, found it necessary. To them the June insurrection had threatened to bring civil war and anarchy and to undermine the foundations of society. From this perspective, which was that not only of moderate republicans but also of Louis Blanc and many others, General Cavaignac was the defender of popular sovereignty and the savior of the republic; however, many who believed in the necessity of repression were fearful of its consequences. Charles Beslay, for example, described the crushing of the June insurrection as a "necessary victory but a sad one." As Beslay put it, "This social war, which left a river of blood between the bourgeoisie and the people, opened up only the most ominous perspectives. Everyone felt that this victory, indispensable though it was, solved nothing, and that the struggle between capitalists and laborers, far from subsiding, was only becoming more bitter and widespread."[71]

Considerant also believed in the necessity of the repression but was horrified by its brutality. When the killing went on after the surrender of the insurgents, he did all he could to denounce, and bring an end to, the atrocities committed by the Mobile Guards. In a distraught letter dated June 28, he went directly to Cavaignac, arguing that the only way to end the killings would be to get the Mobile Guards out of Paris.

> My dear Cavaignac: Anger is extreme in the faubourgs. The most appalling rumors are circulating on the fate of the prisoners held in the cellars of the Hôtel de Ville, the Tuileries, etc. and about executions in the Luxembourg Palace, on the banks of the Seine, beneath the Palais de l'Assemblée, etc. You must absolutely give orders and issue proclamations that will calm down exaggerated rumors.
>
> The workers are above all indignant about the Mobile Guards, who have to be gotten out of Paris (put them in the forts or elsewhere) to prevent the masses of assassinations that would otherwise be inevitable.
>
> Enclosed are two documents concerning two arrests. Please take a look at them.
>
> *A toi de coeur,*
> V. Considerant

Although Considerant had voted against the proclamation of a state of siege, he had confidence in Cavaignac. By way of a postscript, he added that he supported, and had in fact "launched," Cavaignac's candidacy for the presidency of the republic. "It is, I believe, the only way the republic can save itself."[72]

Three days after writing this letter, Considerant published a long article in *Démocratie pacifique* in which he tried hard to find salutary "lessons" that might be learned from the June Days by all sides. The most obvious lesson for the left, he maintained, was that revolutionary dictatorship could not be imposed on France. In less than three days 60,000 provincials had descended on Paris to participate in the crushing of the revolt. "If the insurrection had lasted a week, 500,000 National Guardsmen from the provinces would have come to crush it." Thus the "mad artisans of conspiracy" were deluding themselves if they believed that a "democratic, fraternal, and social republic" could be founded by force and "in the blood of their brothers."[73]

There were also lessons to be learned by the victors. They and their political economists would have to recognize that large industrial cities, which were periodically full of unemployed workers, were the natural breeding grounds of insurrection. Until something was done about the condition of these workers, and the causes of their unemployment, they would continue to pose a threat to society's existence. Considerant also noted that many members of the working classes actually helped their National Guard units to put down the insurrection. In the provinces, the National Guard was composed largely "of *citoyens en blouse,* laborers with callused hands." In Paris the members of "well-organized National Workshops" (Considerant specifically mentioned the harness-makers directed by Captain Durand) either sat out the insurrection or fought against it in the ranks of the National Guard. The conclusion he drew from this—and from the role played by the proletarian members of the Mobile Guard in repressing the insurrection—was that workers who had been given work, organized, and decently fed were not necessarily enemies of the social order. "There is only one means," he wrote, "to save order and society: give the assurance of work, guarantee existence for the disinherited masses by means of a productive job."

In his review of the lessons to be learned from the June Days, Considerant had some words of criticism for his own journal, *Démocratie pacifique,* for nurturing "revolutionary illusions," which, together with hunger and "ardent passions," were so many "powder kegs" in the midst of the extremes of wealth and poverty in Paris. However, he directed much more forceful and pointed criticism against Falloux and his allies, whom he saw as the real instigators of the revolt. He conceded, as he had in the discussions within the Labor Committee, that the National Workshops were "a disheartening evil." Nonetheless, he insisted, they were "an evil that must be remedied." The great need was to create jobs and give productive work to unemployed workers, not simply disband the workshops. It was the haste of men like Falloux and Goudchaux, and their call for immediate dissolution, that transformed the workers into "a formidable army of insurrection and revolt." In Considerant's eyes the June insurrection was, or should have been, above all a lesson for "these *violent* friends of moderation and order."

Finally, Considerant argued, there was a great lesson to be learned by "intriguers" for the various pretenders—legitimist, Orleanist, Bonapartist. This lesson was that the only alternative to republican government in France was civil war. In June both sides had fought to the cry of "Vive la République!" In sowing hatred and war within the republic, the pretenders were not preparing the way for a new monarchy; rather they were preparing "the ruin of the country, the destruction of property, the murder, the suicide of France."

Considerant's personal identification with the republic had not been shaken by June. Unlike Lamennais, he continued to believe that republican government ("founded on the broadest possible democratic base") was the only conceivable framework for healing conflicts that threatened to tear French society apart. He ended his article with an appeal to mend fraternal bonds.

> Let us calm people's feelings, let us get rid of their hatreds, let us re-solve their problems, let us love one another, above all let us love the common people who suffer so much, who nourish us by their labor, and whom the old society has left a prey to poverty and ignorance and so easily liable to all sorts of incitements and all sorts of suspicions. Let us labor, let us labor ardently, let us labor in harmony at the task of union, of redress, of fraternity! . . . Let all hands prepare to be clasped and to labor together for the happiness of the native land we share.

It was not at all clear, however, even as Considerant wrote these words, that appeals to unity, fraternity, and peaceful democracy would have any more resonance in July 1848 than they had had on the night of June 23 when Considerant had been shouted down on the floor of the National Assembly by a majority that wanted to crush the insurrection and not to negotiate with it.

10

Reaction and Renewal

The 1848 revolution did not come to an end with the crushing of the June insurrection. The summer and fall of 1848 were, to be sure, a period of fierce reaction; and the election of Louis-Napoleon Bonaparte as president of the Second Republic in December 1848 can be seen as a repudiation of a republican movement that had no more appealing a candidate to offer than Eugène Cavaignac, the "butcher of June." Yet Louis-Napoleon's overwhelming victory in the presidential elections reinforced a tendency that had already begun to manifest itself in French political life. This was the emergence of an organized left, the alliance of republicans and socialists that became known as the *démoc-soc* movement. This movement was to gather strength in the winter and spring of 1849, and in the legislative elections of May 1849 *démoc-soc* candidates received over two million votes, 35 percent of the total, establishing the movement as a major force in French politics. Considerant did not formally ally himself with the *démoc-soc* movement until after the May 1849 elections, but in the fall of 1848 he was attending its banquets and meetings and working closely with its leaders. As the movement gathered strength, his own positions became increasingly radical. The socialist whose moderation had been noted by Odilon Barrot and Alexandre Marie in the early days of the Second Republic and who had sought to play the role of conciliator in June had become by May 1849 one of the most outspoken and influential leaders of the left.[1]

I

The reaction of the summer of 1848 had been under way ever since the massive conservative victory in the April elections. Only in the aftermath of the June days, however, did the reaction become fully self-conscious. Within a few days after the end of the fighting, the National Assembly took a series of measures intended to crush all vestiges of radicalism in France. On June 26 the Assembly voted to create a fifteen-member Investigating Committee to study the causes and punish the instigators of both the June insurrection and that of May 15. This committee, led by Odilon Barrot, did not include a single representative from Paris, and its members were described with an ironic wink by the *Revue des deux mondes* as "not generally distinguished by a very long-standing republican fervor."[2] On June 27, in a session lasting until after midnight, the Assembly voted that all rebels captured with arms in hand should be subject to immediate deportation. The efforts of Pierre Leroux and Marc Caussidière to make distinctions among prisoners or to delay sentencing were shouted down.

Finally, on June 28, the Assembly adopted a resolution that gave almost hysterical expression to the main themes of the reaction. In it, the June insurrection was described as the work of "madmen who, without principles, without a flag, seem to have armed themselves only for massacre and pillage."

> Family, institutions, liberty, fatherland, all were stricken in the heart, and under the blows of these new barbarians the civilization of the nineteenth century was threatened with destruction. But no! Civilization cannot perish! No! The republic, a work of God, the living law of humanity, the republic will not perish. This we swear by all of France, which rejects with horror those savage doctrines in which the family is only a name and property is only theft.[3]

The "savage doctrines" here alluded to as underlying the June revolt were clearly Proudhon's critique of property and the Fourierist attack on the family.

In the immediate aftermath of the June insurrection, little attention was paid to the social problems that had prompted the uprising. Instead, the June insurrection was attributed to the plots of conspirators and the proliferation of radical ideas, and these were blamed on the complete freedom of the press and of assembly that had prevailed since February. In July and August the National Assembly voted to place limits on both the freedom of the press and the right of assembly. On July 28 the Assembly passed a bill, introduced by Sénard, placing political clubs under close regulation. And on August 9 and 11, the Assembly voted to reestablish the *cautionnement* for the political press, with the result that many modestly funded radical newspapers were forced to suspend publication permanently. "The poor man's press is dead," announced Proudhon in transforming his daily, *Le Représentant du peuple*, into a weekly. When Lamennais published the final issue of his newspaper, *Le Peuple constituent*, on August 11, it was bordered in black and carried the headline: "Silence to the Poor!"[4]

The response of the Fourierists to all these measures was equivocal. They criticized acts of "vengeance" against the insurgents, and on July 2 they called on journalists to stop running horror stories on atrocities allegedly committed during the insurrection. They also opposed the prolongation of the state of siege, and on August 4 Considerant published a strong critique of the report of the Investigating Committee, which he described as a "pathetic indictment crammed with servants' gossip." Yet, in the immediate aftermath of the insurrection, Considerant and his colleagues were careful to keep their distance both from the insurgents and from the few socialists, like Proudhon and Pierre Leroux, who attempted to defend the insurgents from what Proudhon described as the "calumnies of the reaction." Indeed, *Démocratie pacifique* supported deportation for insurgents captured with arms in hand and lavished praise on Cavaignac for his "noble words" and "strength of character" in the struggle against the "menacing sedition" and "odious plots" of the "madmen" and "conspirators" of June. In an article published on July 1, Considerant chastised the rebels, asserting that the "madmen" who had attempted to establish a "fraternal, democratic, and social republic . . . by force and in the blood of their brothers" would have to learn "the terrible lesson taught them by Paris and the provinces." Thus, there was some justification in Proudhon's fiercely sarcastic attack on Considerant a few months later: "Monsieur Considerant and his fellow sectarians deny any kind of solidarity with the 'savages' who in June, without thinking of their households and families and while showing respect for property, rose up against a civilization that is starving them."[5]

Considerant's response to the legislation on political clubs was no more vigorous. He spoke at length in the Assembly on points of detail and against several amendments that would have made the law even more restrictive than Sénard's original bill. Like almost everyone else on the left, however, he made no significant objection to the legislation and did not question the assumptions on which it was based. He conceded that since political clubs could be "centers of danger and disorder," they were in need of careful regulation. He explained his support of Sénard's bill on the ground that a free republic needed protection from "excesses resulting from the abuse of freedom." Considerant's position on the press legislation of August restoring the *cautionnement* was only slightly bolder. He voted against the legislation, but in doing so he took pains to affirm the need to curb the "excesses" of the press with other kinds of sanctions.[6]

So after failing in his self-appointed role as conciliator during the June insurrection, Considerant spent the ensuing weeks distancing himself from the insurgents and attempting to balance his muted criticism of the reaction with warnings against excess and anarchy. During the summer and fall of 1848, as the National Assembly occupied itself with the revision of the initial draft of the constitution, Considerant did speak forcefully on the right to work; he also spoke in support of a law limiting working hours and a proposal to nationalize the railroads. However, he intervened rarely in the discussion of major constitutional questions, and he generally voted to accept the watered down or conservative formulations that the Assembly kept producing. He believed that a flawed or imperfect constitution was the best that could be expected under the circumstances and would serve as a starting point for democratic reform. As he wrote at the end of the year: "We have a constitution that is, after all, republican and much more democratic than any constitution that has ever been applied in this imperfect world. It contains the seeds of the extension of the revolution to the social sphere, and it will lend itself to progress by the normal means of amendment."[7]

It was in the late summer and early fall, during the course of the debate on the constitution, that the reaction of 1848 acquired organization and outreach. Its center was the so-called Committee of the rue de Poitiers, a group of prominent conservatives who had begun to meet regularly in a building on the rue de Poitiers shortly after May 15. Its leaders were monarchists of different factions, such as Berryer, Falloux, Molé, de Broglie, and Thiers. One of the committee's tasks was to coordinate the legislative initiatives and activities of conservatives. The committee also played an important role in orchestrating the "red scare" that was a pervasive feature of French public life in the second half of 1848.[8]

The campaign against socialism and communism organized by the Committee of the rue de Poitiers had both a popular and a sophisticated dimension. First, there was a popular campaign, which began with a fund drive (conceived by Adolphe Thiers) intended to make possible the flooding of the countryside with crudely written brochures and pamphlets warning peasants and other small property owners of the threat posed to their property and their welfare by "the reds." By the fall of 1848 this popular campaign was well under way. A typical specimen of the genre was the *Cathéchisme républicain* cited by the vicomte d'Arlincourt in a brochure published in August 1848. "What is fraternity?" asked the republican. "The need generally felt by the poor to plunder the wealth of the rich and, if necessary, to kill him." "What is the laborer?" "A worker who is paid and who does not labor." [9]

Most of these pamphlets attacked socialism and communism in general, but others sought to ridicule the major socialist leaders. Proudhon was a favorite target of criticism. He was a sinister or satanic presence in numerous brochures and pamphlets; he was even lampooned on stage in vaudevilles like "Property Is Theft, a socialist folly in three acts and seven tableaux," in which he appeared as a bespectacled serpent in the Garden of Eden. Considerant, too, figured in this literature. He appeared in several brochures subsidized by the Committee of the rue de Poitiers, notably Gustave Claudin's "Interview of Voltaire and Considerant in the Waiting Room of Purgatory." [10]

Along with the wave of cheap brochures, the attack on socialism and communism was carried on, at a slightly higher level, in literary and political journals with intellectual pretensions. Between July and November of 1848, for example, the *Revue des deux mondes* ran a series of articles aimed at "bringing the public back to its senses by combating the circulation of false ideas." In a putative "History of the Idea of Work," Saint-Marc Girardin ridiculed the national workshops as one of the "slothful and well-remunerated dynasties that thronged out of the fecund flanks of the proclamation of February 25" and sarcastically characterized the socialist ideal as the triumph of "a sovereign and lazy people, having its own civil list, supported by the state, entertained by the state." In a critique of the ideas of Louis Blanc, Benjamin Delassert warned against the "thousand disguises" that could be adopted by communist theories and that had been "repelled with horror" by sensible people whenever they had appeared in their "hideous nudity." "Woe unto us," Delassert concluded, "if, in more or less disguised form, communism, socialism, or what are known as humanitarian doctrines begin to take over our laws of finance." In a long and enthusiastic review of Adolphe Thiers's *De la propriété*, Albert de Broglie sounded an even more dire warning: "Until recently the right of property has in a sense served to illuminate all political discussions; everything else referred back to this fundamental right. Since February 24 the skyline has been shaking; it is the earth's axis that is bending." [11]

If any one individual can be said to have orchestrated the red scare of 1848, it was Adolphe Thiers. His *De la propriété* was the fullest and most influential, though hardly the best informed, statement of the case against socialism. It was Thiers also who took the lead in the parliamentary attack on socialism, which came to a head in September with the bitter debate over the right to work. In a long and caustic speech characterized by what Considerant described as Thiers's habitual "oratorical impertinence," Thiers argued that society had always rested on three basic principles: property, liberty, and competition. The interaction of these three principles was the cause of progress; and prosperity was a function of the degree to which property was respected in any society. Of course, there never was, and never would be, a society in which all people were equally prosperous. Some degree of suffering would always be the lot of ordinary people. Thanks to the interplay of property, liberty, and competition, however, the laboring classes were now better off than they had ever been. Did the socialists dispute this fact? Did they believe it possible to reduce the workers' suffering through the reorganization of society and the redistribution of wealth? Were their plans to be taken seriously? Thiers repeatedly posed these questions; and in the most provocative portion of his speech he reviewed what he described as the fundamental propositions of the four main schools of socialism and communism. Actually, what he offered was caricatures of the views of Cabet, Louis Blanc, Proudhon, and Considerant. (In this scheme, Considerant's system was identified with the right to work.) These caricatures were accompanied by a repeated challenge. What practical remedies did the socialists have to offer to the problems of poverty, unemployment, and crime? "You accuse the old political economy and the old statesmen of not having improved the lot of the people. I ask you again: what means do you propose?"[12]

Victor Considerant had not initially planned to take part in the debate on the right to work. He was suffering from a chest cold and a sore throat and had difficulty speaking. But after listening to Thiers's glib provocations, he found it impossible to remain silent. In a hoarse voice he told the Assembly that he could not share Thiers's optimism for the state of society and the condition of the working class. "I find that the present system of social organization must be reshaped from top to bottom," he began, immediately provoking what the stenographer described as a "prolonged interruption." But he continued:

> I believe, gentlemen, that a society with . . . such a small number of rich people and such a large number of people enduring hardship or poverty is a badly organized society, a society in which something is missing. I believe that a society in which the principle of competition . . . con-

stantly works to produce disasters and ruins, a society in which accounts are settled every ten years or so by industrial crises that cover the field of production and distribution with ruins and bankruptcies, I believe, I say, that from an industrial standpoint this society is badly organized.

I believe that a society in which a proletariat and pauperism develop in direct proportion to the production of wealth and the development of industry is badly organized. And the result of this is that today the wealthiest nations, the nations that have gone the farthest down the road of industrialism, are those that you can see covered with the largest number of the poor, of proletarians, and of the starving.[13]

Considerant went on to respond to Thiers's challenge. Thiers had asked the socialists what practical solutions they had to offer. Considerant's answer was that he had a plan, a theory of social organization, the application of which would bring an end to the ills of contemporary society. Obviously this plan could not be spelled out rapidly in a single extemporaneous speech.

Do you believe that from this rostrum it is possible for me to make you witness, in a sense, the constitution of a new world? (*Agitation.*) Do you believe that one can, at this rostrum, set forth the elements of a whole science and transform this auditorium into a classroom? (*Yes! Yes!—No!*)

What Considerant proposed was that the Assembly allow him to use the relatively intimate quarters of the old Chamber of Deputies rather than the cavernous new National Assembly to give a detailed presentation of his theory in four evening sessions. These would not be regular sessions of the National Assembly but rather voluntary sessions open to all representatives. After setting forth the theory, Considerant would present a detailed plan for its implementation.[14]

At this point the Assembly, which had already grown restive, frequently interrupting Considerant, exploded in what he later described as a "tempest" of exclamations, catcalls, and sarcastic comment. "Instead of four days, take six to create your new world," shouted one representative. "Let's have advertising and competition," added another. For some time the president of the Assembly was unable to restore order. Finally he announced that there would be no discussion of Considerant's proposal since the National Assembly was a legislative body and not a classroom. Although Considerant had been at the rostrum for little more than ten minutes, he was exhausted. His voice was gone for two days and he was left with an inflammation of the chest that lasted a month.[15]

This joust with Adolphe Thiers was, unfortunately, one of Considerant's best publicized appearances before the National Assembly. It made him, for a short time, an object of mirth in the popular press. The next day conservative journals were full of witticisms about the "secret" Considerant proposed to reveal and about his "success" in discrediting the doctrine of the right to work. To the once liberal *Constitutionnel*, Considerant's speech was a "gasconade" and to the Catholic *Univers* it was simply laughable. In the memoirs of contemporaries Considerant was sometimes described as having fallen into a "trap" set by Thiers. He himself denied this, claiming that his request for the opportunity to outline his theory in four sessions was shrewdly designed to keep him out of Thiers's clutches. As he wrote a few weeks later:

> To prove that I was speaking seriously and that I was not a fool, ready to fall unsuspectingly into a trap, I specified the conditions for a fair debate, a serious examination. I did not agree to a parliamentary joust in which no one listens to you and you are systematically interrupted, in which at least two hundred out of the seven or eight hundred members of the audience . . . drown out your voice by striking paper knives, write letters, talk, laugh, gossip, make paper birds, pay absolutely no attention to you, and then judge you afterward. I'm not that stupid!

Just a few months later, Considerant was to have the very experience he described here.[16]

II

If the period from July to December 1848 was a period of reaction, it was also, as we now know, a period of renewed radical activity and organization.[17] It was a period marked by the emergence of the *démoc-soc* movement. The creation of this movement was an attempt to overcome the long-standing divisions of the left—the mutual antagonisms of radical republicans, Blanquists, and socialists of various schools—and also the sense of isolation and discouragement that each of these groups felt in the aftermath of the June insurrection. The whole French left had been compromised in the eyes of much of the Parisian working class by their failure to support the insurrection, and in the eyes of conservatives who blamed them for inciting the insurrection.

The propaganda of the conservative "party of order," which culminated in the well-orchestrated red scare of the summer and fall of 1848, did something to drive the left back together. The main impetus for the development of a new coalition on the left, however, came from the radical republicans and their leader, Ledru-Rollin. Recognizing the need for a united opposition to the continuing conservative reaction, Ledru-Rollin and his followers organized a banquet campaign in the fall of 1848. Their aim was to ally radical republicans and socialists around a common program of social reforms and a conception of republican government as necessarily entailing social reform. The campaign's opening event was a huge banquet held at the Châlet of the Champs Elysées on September 22, to mark the fifty-sixth anniversary of the founding of the First Republic. Over five hundred people attended, and among them were almost a hundred members of the National Assembly, including Considerant. Speeches and toasts were given by Ledru-Rollin, Etienne Cabet, and Audrey de Puyraveau. According to *Démocratie pacifique*, Ledru-Rollin "electrified" the crowd with an "admirable" speech, the banquet was "full of animation and cordiality," and all agreed that "the only means of salvation for the republic" was "to rally round the principles of social democracy." [18]

Although Ledru-Rollin stressed his support for the right to work on September 22, he hesitated to call himself a socialist. Other speakers that evening were bolder. In a widely reprinted toast, Etienne Cabet insisted that the words "republic," "democracy," and "socialism" all meant "essentially the same thing." Several weeks later, at the second great banquet of the season, the radical lawyer d'Alton-Shée maintained that republicanism and socialism were inseparable parts of the society that the left hoped to create. "The republic is the form," he announced, "socialism is the essence." [19]

The banquets continued throughout the fall and winter. Many were held in November as the left tried—without much success—to agree on a single candidate for the presidential elections on December 10. Like other socialists and radical republicans, Considerant and the Fourierists were unable to make a clear choice. From the beginning they mistrusted Louis-Napoleon Bonaparte, even though he had once been a reader of *Démocratie pacifique*. By early November they were describing him as a creature of the Party of Order and his candidacy as a "trial balloon" floated by the monarchists of the Committee of the rue de Poitiers. They also rejected Cavaignac because he seemed to lack a deep commitment to social reform. In the end the Fourierists supported Ledru, but it was only a week before the election that they gave his candidacy their complete and unambiguous support as "the proper rallying point for all democratic socialists." [20]

The massive victory of Louis-Napoleon Bonaparte in the presidential elections of December 10 was seen by Marx as a "peasant insurrection," and many historians have argued that the most striking feature of the election returns was the success of Louis-Napoleon's candidacy in rural France. But what was the significance of the peasant vote? Was it a vote for order on the part of conservative peasants led on by local notables? Or was it, as Marx suggested, a confused but powerful gesture of protest against the establishment and its candidate, Cavaignac? To this question, which continues to divide historians, Considerant's answer was clear. He saw the election as, above all, a repudiation of Cavaignac, whose "deplorable" policies had made possible the advance of reaction, and of "the purely formalistic republicans" of the *National*. In Considerant's view "immense masses of republicans" had preferred to take their chances on Louis-Napoleon rather than risk the possibility of Cavaignac's election. To be sure, Louis-Napoleon's intentions were a mystery, but that did not trouble Considerant. If Louis-Napoleon's policies as president were democratic, he would receive the support of the democratic left. If, as was far more likely, his policies were retrograde, his popularity wouldn't last. As president he was sure to be surrounded by all sorts of "monarchical intriguers," who would in all likelihood wind up compromising both him and each other. What the left needed in these circumstances was discipline, self-restraint, and organization. "Let us take a position within the terrain of legality and the constitution," Considerant wrote shortly after the election.

> Let us unite to defend that position intrepidly, to develop its democratic, social, and popular implications. Let us get ready to form a Great Opposition, united by principles and acting as one. . . . Let us proscribe violence. Let us know how to restrain hotheads. Let us concentrate on legal agitation, that is to say agitation by ideas, by enlightenment, by the education of the people.[21]

In fact, the Great Opposition had already begun to form. During the election campaign radicals had created two organizations, both designed to coordinate the efforts of republicans and socialists and to win support for their ideas among rural voters in particular. The first of these organizations, Solidarité républicaine, was essentially a campaign organization with its headquarters in Paris and branch offices in some sixty-two of France's eighty-six departments. Led by the radical journalist Charles Delescluze, the printer Martin Bernard, and the former *compagnon* Agricole Perdiguier, Solidarité républicaine has been described as "the first French attempt to establish an organized national political party."[22] Its aim was to bring together all republicans who desired social reform within a national political organization and thus to "constitute on a solid and durable foundation the great party of the democratic and social republic." Less than two months after the presidential elections (in which it supported Ledru-Rollin), it was outlawed by the government. By that time, though, it had established a network of some 350 provincial affiliates, many of which continued to function as local electoral committees supporting *démoc-soc* candidates in the national legislative elections of May 1849.[23]

The second important *démoc-soc* organization was the Propagande démocratique et sociale européene. This was a journalistic clearinghouse conceived in October 1848 by Gabriel Mortillet to centralize the dissemination of radical propaganda and to encourage its diffusion throughout the countryside. Works disseminated by the Propagande included theoretical and topical pieces by established socialist authors like Considerant, Pierre Leroux, and Etienne Cabet—sometimes these were newspaper articles reprinted as small brochures or broadsides—and also songs, engravings, portraits, and caricatures that could serve the cause, as well as statuettes, medallions, and even pipes bearing the features of leading socialists and republicans. All of these were purchased wholesale from the publisher or producer and then sold to peddlars and provincial booksellers at a modest markup.[24]

Considerant was not a member of either of these organizations, but he had good working relations with both. His biography and portrait were included in brochures distributed by the Propagande démocratique et sociale, as were pamphlets consisting of extracts from his longer works.[25] His speeches and articles were reprinted in *démoc-soc* newspapers, and *Démocratie pacifique* in turn published articles condemning the government's moves against Solidarité républicaine in late January. Somewhat later— probably in March—*Démocratie pacifique* joined with seven other *démoc-soc* newspapers to create a Comité de la presse démocratique et sociale. At the same time Considerant was collaborating with leading republicans like Ferdinand Flocon, Joseph Guinard, and David d'Angers in the running of a Society of Friends of Democratic Poland, which he helped create on November 30, 1848.[26] Finally, on April 28, 1849, Considerant's links with the *démoc-soc* movement were formalized as he received the endorsement of the Comité démocratique-socialiste des élections as a member of its official slate of candidates in Paris for the May 13 legislative elections.[27] Henceforth Considerant was a leader of the organized left.

III

Considerant's most ambitious effort to put the events of 1848 in broad perspective and to situate himself with regard to the emerging *démoc-soc* coalition was a book published in December 1848, immediately after the presidential elections, and written in great haste during the fall. *Le Socia-*

lisme devant le vieux monde, ou le vivant devant les morts was organized around an elaborate rhetorical figure evoking the decomposition of the political world and the efforts of "the dead" to govern and influence events. At the outset the ghostly voice of Guizot is heard, speaking from "the grave" of exile, and then the narrator comments: "I know of no more irrefutable testimony than these voices which come out of the ground, than this funereal illusion which makes intelligent people take the memory of past events for living realities, thus rendering them impervious to any idea that belongs to a stratum later than their own." [28] To the modern reader this title and the ghostly imagery of the opening section irresistibly recall the initial sections of Karl Marx's *Eighteenth Brumaire of Louis Bonaparte*, with its walking specters, its conjuring up of the dead, and its memories that weigh on the living. Yet despite the similarity in imagery, Considerant's theme was different from that of Marx. For Marx, inherited memories and conceptions inevitably clouded the vision of all contemporaries with regard to the realities of their own time. The peasantry and emerging proletariat were still as much in the thrall of historical memories as were the bourgeoisie and the landed aristocracy. It was only through a process of struggle and necessary defeat that the peasantry and the proletariat would work their way free of the weight of the past. In Considerant's more simplistic vision, on the other hand, the dead weight of the past was only felt by certain groups—those who identified themselves with the elements of a political world that was in a state of decomposition. These were Considerant's "dead"—the legitimists and Orleanists of the rue de Poitiers, the dynastic opposition under the July Monarchy, the formal republicans of the *National*, all those who sought their political ideals in an exhausted past. The "living" were those—above all the socialists—who were able to recognize and identify themselves with the new social and political order that was struggling to emerge.

Running through all of *Le Socialisme devant le vieux monde* was this fundamental contrast between the old and the new, the dead and the living. There was the old, dying world of egoism, exploitation, and slavery, a world of warring interests in which human relations were based on force or the threat of force. Then there was the new, emerging world of socialism, a world not of war but of peace, not of force but of law and love, and a world in which exploitation and wage slavery would be replaced by the social emancipation of the proletariat. Considerant asserted that history had reached a turning point. It was "one of those great *époques palingénésiques*," he wrote, borrowing the term made popular by Ballanche, in which the old world must inevitably give way to the new. The change had all the necessity of a natural process. It was no more possible for states or leaders to prevent a "radical renewal of European society" than for parents to keep their children from passing through puberty, or for the ice not to melt in spring. The only question was whether the changes that would inevitably take place would be peaceful or violent.

The great change to come was the social emancipation of the proletariat. Considerant warned that any attempt to prevent the working classes from claiming their rights would eventually lead to a "horrible" civil war beside which "the bloody insurrection of June will only have been a FIRST PRELIMINARY SKIRMISH." What were the causes of the June insurrection? The radical press and the revolutionary clubs had played a role, he conceded, in creating a climate of discontent. More important was the provocation contained in the dissolution of the national workshops. But the principal causes of the June insurrection lay deeper. Like the excesses and follies of the first French Revolution, the June uprising could be explained as a reaction to "the blind resistance of the men of the Old Regime to reforms whose time had come."[29]

Considerant's point was that the revolution was not over. The revolutionary movement begun in 1789 had not been completed with the acquisition of political rights by adult males. Thus, he argued, "the revolution will remain PERMANENT until the organization of a society capable of substituting . . . association for fragmentation, cooperation for struggle, peace for war, the freedom of all for the slavery of the many, generalized wealth for all forms of poverty."[30]

The term that Considerant used to characterize the new society that would inevitably emerge out of the revolutionary struggle was "socialism." This word had been a part of his vocabulary since 1838.[31] It is worth noting, though, how vague—and apparently willfully vague—he was in using it. What did Considerant mean by socialism? He himself posed this question early in his book, only to answer that socialism was "not a fixed doctrine" but rather an "immense, irresistible aspiration" toward the emancipation of workers from the wage system and the establishment of a harmonious and peaceful society. Indeed, he insisted that the movement for workers' emancipation was only "the first formulation of the socialist aspiration." The fuller and more complete formulation would define the goal of socialism in terms that applied to all members of society. Socialism in these broader terms would seek

> the amelioration of the condition of ALL through the establishment of fraternal and harmonic relations between all classes; through the free

and voluntary association of capital, labor, and talent; through the indefinite growth of public wealth; through the multiplication and universalization of property and education; through the good and free combination of all social forces; through the free development and useful employment of all the human faculties in the attainment of the public happiness and the individual and collective perfection of the species.

Far from being the ideology of a class, socialism for Considerant was, in its fullest formulation, universal in its aspirations.[32]

If socialism sought to create a new world, Considerant stressed that it had its roots in the old. In historical terms the struggle for socialism could be seen as the last in a series of struggles of oppressed groups. The emancipation of the slave had produced the serf, and the emancipation of the serf had produced the bourgeoisie and the proletariat. The bourgeoisie, socially emancipated by wealth and education, had completed its emancipation through the conquest of political rights, which Considerant saw as occurring with the extension of the suffrage in 1830. The proletariat had won political emancipation with the establishment of universal male suffrage in February 1848. What remained was the struggle for the social emancipation of the proletariat, the wage worker's struggle to free himself from dependence on the owners of the instruments of labor and to win for himself a just share in the fruits of his labor.

Considerant stressed that there was more to socialism than the emancipation of the working class. The "higher" goal of socialism was the establishment of "a society of peace, harmony, and collaborative effort, the fusion and accord of all social forces and all classes." Considerant argued that the roots of this larger vision were to be found in Christianity. The teaching of the Gospels, the vision of a kingdom of God that would one day be established on earth, the preaching of the Apostles and of the early Church fathers—these were the authentic sources of the socialist ideal in its broadest and richest sense. The original Christians had striven to create a new world of peace and harmony out of the disparate and conflicting elements of the societies they knew. Their vision of this new world had rapidly become a part of the shared consciousness of humanity; it had been weakened during the period of medieval barbarism, but had been reawakened by the *philosophes* and by "the sublime enthusiasms" of the French Revolution.[33]

Considerant saw socialism as the heir of *both* the Christian and revolutionary traditions. In language reminiscent of his contemporary Michelet, he identified socialism with the struggles and aspirations of all humanity. "Socialism today," he wrote, "is humanity which labors, which suffers, which groans, which thinks, and which wishes to be free, rich, moral, and happy." Finally, and again like Michelet, Considerant turned to geological imagery to give his ideas full expression. Socialism, he asserted, was more than an ideology, more even than an aspiration; it was "the burning lava of humanity steeped for five thousand years in the furnace of progress," and erupting now to flow into "the great mold that God [had] prepared for it"— the mold of "the universal people."[34]

Having attempted to characterize the ideals and aspirations of modern socialism in the broadest possible terms, Considerant devoted the greater part of his book to a discussion of the various socialist schools, doctrines, and thinkers, from Babeuf to Proudhon. He noted that, contrary to the claims made by socialism's critics, very few of the leading socialist thinkers sought the abolition of the family system, and that some (like himself) were defenders of private property. He stressed the importance of Christian ideals and values for most contemporary socialists. At the same time he emphasized his own distance from a literal and dogmatic adherence to all of Fourier's ideas.

In his long review of the different socialist *écoles*, Considerant posed the question: What were the conditions for the *ralliement*, the unified action, of all socialists? He argued that it was important for the members of the different schools both to respect the differences that separated them and to seek common ground on which to build an alliance. But there were two points on which he was adamant. First, he argued strongly against those like Cabet who claimed that the establishment of a socialist society would require the abolition of private property. Second, he rejected violence as a means for the establishment of the good society. He believed the two were related.

> Property is too deeply rooted in human nature as a principle, too lively, too energetic, and too powerful as an interest and an institution, to be suppressed peacefully. It is thus certain that if its suppression were the formal and necessary condition for the solution of the social problem . . . this problem would be difficult to resolve in any other way than through a great civil war culminating with the crushing of the property-owning party.[35]

Considerant vehemently rejected the idea that socialists must be prepared to arm themselves for an inevitable class struggle. He believed that only a nonviolent and nondogmatic socialism could play the unifying and conciliatory role that he regarded as necessary. Socialism would not become "a narrow and violent party," he wrote.

> It will remain the great and irresistible aspiration of our time, the great current of sentiments and ideas summoned to give substance to philos-

ophy, democracy, and Christianity, to realize their high ideals. . . . And socialism would only be Anti-socialism if it did not possess that power to socialize, to conciliate, and to bring universal union.[36]

Defining socialism in the broadest possible terms, Considerant was convinced that "today socialism is everywhere," that it was taking possession of public opinion and the minds of the common people, that it had become part of the air people were breathing. He could argue that socialism was "stronger" than the ideologies of the political establishment. Some people believed that socialism had lost ground with the defeat of the "brutal and blind insurrection of June" and the failure of the National Assembly to include the right to work in the Constitution. On the contrary, he claimed, socialism had made "enormous gains." It had even gained in the Assembly. "Socialism is stronger than you," he addressed the Party of Order. "It is living and you are dead."[37]

Where did the strength and vitality of socialism lie? In what sense could Considerant argue that socialism was "living," the leaders and ideologies of the establishment dead? His main point was that the socialists possessed a vision and a "faith" consistent with the direction of history, whereas their enemies persisted in seeking to breathe life into old social forms. The Party of Order had no understanding of the needs and passions of modern society and "the ideas that were developing within it." The socialists, on the other hand, grasped the emerging "idea" and had faith in the future. "Socialism has faith in the new society," he wrote, "in the young society which it carries in its loins and which it loves with a devoted and maternal love." Considerant conceded that in its vagaries and hatreds, socialism could become "criminal"—as indeed it had in the June insurrection, but "its hatreds, its violence, and the very energy of its revolts" proved that it was alive. The defeat of June was salutary in teaching the working class that there was nothing to gain from violence. "Strong as [socialism] is," wrote Considerant, "master as it is of the future, it is by calm, by reason, by ideas, and not by brutal force that it must conquer men's minds and organize the new society."[38]

What is most striking about Considerant's argument is its radically idealistic form. He did not speak of socialism as an expression of the emerging industrial society but of the new society as an emanation of the socialist idea. He wrote that "socialism has faith . . . in the young society which it carries in its loins." Conversely, he asserted that what triumphed with the crushing of the June insurrection was not an idea but interests, and that interests without a unifying idea quickly come into conflict and destroy each other. He told his adversaries that because they were inspired only by interests and not by an idea or a faith, they were as good as dead. "Without an idea and without faith, you are only pure interests, facts, crumbling aggregations of dead matter." The premise that underlay all this was made explicit in Considerant's insistence on the shaping and life-giving role of ideas in history: "The ideas that are emerging are the vivifying forces of nations, just as in spring sap is the vivifying force of nature. Nothing resists it."[39]

If Considerant occasionally used biological imagery to characterize the faith of "the living," his analysis of the predicament of "the dead" was worked out in terms of zoological and geological metaphors. Obeying an impulse similar to that of Marx in his writings on 1848, Considerant treated the representatives of the Party of Order as a species that had outlived its time. They were the "fossils of political evolution," the "petrifications of pure politics," "political crustaceans" whose scales had rendered them impervious to the rays of enlightenment.[40] In substantive terms Considerant made two main points in his analysis of "the dead." First, the material forces at their disposal—their armies and their National Guard—could no longer be relied on in an age of universal suffrage: "An army in a democratic republic, an army that votes, is an army that has the right to think" and to question its superiors. Second, the moral force available to his adversaries was nonexistent. They had neither unity nor good faith. The disputes of Orleanists, Legitimists, and Bonapartists within the Committee of the rue de Poitiers mirrored conflict within the Party of Order as a whole. And what was the Party of Order but a discordant assemblage of "frustrated ambitions, extinct factions, blindnesses, ill-concealed hatreds, fears, more or less slickly and tortuously contrived intrigues . . . discredited elements that hold each other in contempt."[41]

On the individual level, Considerant saw Adolphe Thiers as exemplifying the moral emptiness of "the dead." In his view, Thiers was a man whose values and qualities of mind were antithetical to those of "the living." He was "materialism incarnate, theoretical and practical fatalism, the absolute negation of the ideal." He was a man who did "not understand how the words faith, hope, and charity could belong to the political and social language of a great people." A man endowed with an almost unlimited capacity for self-esteem, he was never so satisfied with himself as when he was giving cynical expression to his contempt for "principles" and "rights" and to his "horror" of progress, innovation, and anything related to the ideal. The one thing Considerant found difficult to understand when confronted by the "fatalistic and atheistical thought" of a man like Thiers was what this cynic hoped to accomplish in politics through the exercise of power.

Considerant addressed the question to Thiers and, through him, to all "the dead."

> Ah! If I had, as you do, a soul made arid and dried up by the cold wind of skepticism, if I believed in nothing, in nothing! if my heart was hermetically sealed, as yours are, against any faith, any hope, any work of social charity, then, God is my witness, I would immediately abandon this arena of cries and dust where your shrill voices are yelping. I would go live in some isolated place where you can't get newspapers, and I would plant potatoes in a little garden and quietly go fishing and do what I could to make life better for a few poor peasants.

Considerant could not understand what "directionless souls" like Thiers thought they were doing "in the midst of the struggle for a new life." [42]

Considerant concluded his book by addressing a few words to his allies, the radical republicans, or Montagnards (also known as "the Mountain"). He noted that the "odious" red scare of the summer and fall had focused as much on the "red republicans" as on the socialists. While recognizing "the deviations and extravagances" of certain "zealots," he went to the defense of the Montagnards as a group.

> The majority of the representatives who are referred to by the unfortunate and anachronistic name of Montagnards are good-hearted men, men full of good sentiments and the love of humanity. They are passed off as bloodthirsty tigers, but they all voted for the absolute abolition of the death penalty. They form a party that has the temperament and fiery ardor of youth, with its rages and its often unthinking outbursts. They lack maturity; they are not yet a party that could govern, I agree, but they are animated by good, by excellent desires. [43]

Considerant noted with approval the socialist professions of faith of many Montagnard leaders during the fall banquet campaign. This was "a sign of intelligence and insight." He urged them to study works by socialist writers and to urge their followers to do likewise. For there was work to be done.

> The task of the first revolution was to destroy the old order. The task of the present revolution is to organize the new order. Let us have an end to the formulas, the tone, and the violent behavior of '93. Serious study concerning the future must replace the memories of the past. If the conversion of the Mountain has this good influence on the eager young minds whom it represents and who trust it, then it will have earned the praise of France and of humanity. [44]

Considerant wrote these words in November 1848, a few weeks before the presidential elections. The triumph of Louis-Napoleon in these elections was to drive him still closer to the Montagnards and to strengthen his commitment to the *démoc-soc* movement.

IV

Considerant's concern with bringing together the socialists and his rapprochement with the Montagnards disturbed many of his old Fourierist colleagues, who felt he had become so caught up in national politics that he was neglecting the affairs of the Ecole. As his close friend, the Catholic Fourierist Désiré Laverdant, warned him, there was a danger that he might become trapped by his active participation in the *démoc-soc* alliance. "And then, obliged to make concessions and sacrifices, as you have already done in appearance, and no longer being free in your movements, you run the risk of compromising your future, that of the cause, and that of humanity." [45]

This criticism was apt. Ever since the February Revolution, Considerant had been absorbed by national politics. He had become so preoccupied with the work of the National Assembly that he had little time for anything else. He had played no role in the Fourierist political club, and in October 1848, when a Fourierist Congress was held to consider the prospects for a practical "realization" of Fourier's ideas, he gave the welcoming address but did not participate in the work sessions. [46] Early in 1849 he wrote occasional articles for *Démocratie pacifique*, taking critics to task for ill-informed attacks on Fourier's ideas, and in January and February much of his energy was devoted to a bitter polemic with Proudhon concerning the significance of the June Days. [47] His main concern during the first months of 1849, however, was with political matters—notably the threat posed to the existence of the republic by the presidency of Louis-Napoleon Bonaparte.

The threat was real. The cabinet formed by Louis-Napoleon after his election as president did not include a single republican. Instead, it was dominated by royalists from the Committee of the rue de Poitiers, notably the Orleanist Odilon Barrot and the legitimist comte de Falloux; and there were widespread fears that an attempt would soon be made to overthrow the republic. During the first weeks of 1849 almost every issue of *Démocratie pacifique* carried an article defending the constitution, the republic, or the National Assembly against the maneuvers of Falloux, Barrot, Interior Minister Léon Faucher, or Louis-Napoleon. By the end of January, when troops were brought into Paris on the pretext of preventing possible rioting, Considerant had become convinced that Louis-Napoleon was plotting a coup d'état.

In this context, fearing for the survival of the republic, Considerant made one more effort to get a hearing from the National Assembly. On April 13 he requested permission to speak the following day. Noting that both society and the Assembly itself were deeply divided, he said he wished to propose some means of healing those divisions and, as he put it dramatically, of "saving society."[48] The following day, April 14, Considerant appeared before the Assembly with four legislative proposals and a speech, which it took him almost three hours to deliver, even in a radically truncated form.

The most important of Considerant's four proposals would have authorized the government to turn over to the Fourierists a parcel of land "either in the forest of Saint Germain, or anywhere else near Paris" to serve as the site for "the foundation by degrees of a societary community." A second proposal renewed Considerant's call for a new cabinet position, a Ministry of Progress, to examine and test propositions of social reform. His other two proposals were both related to a plan designed to facilitate the issuing of low-interest government loans to needy farmers and artisans. One called for a new system of drawing up deeds and mortgages and the other for the creation, throughout France, of "chambers of agriculture and industry" that would represent farmers and industrial producers just as chambers of commerce represented business interests.[49]

In support of these proposals Considerant had prepared a very long speech, which he began to read to the Assembly. His aim, he announced, was to explain the nature of socialism—first socialism in general, and then his own particular brand of socialism—and the resources it offered to a government interested in restoring calm and prosperity to a troubled society. He planned to begin with an account of the vices of the present economic and social system and a demonstration of the process by which a new "industrial feudalism" had grown out of the system of free competition. He then planned to discuss the new credit system implicit in his proposal for chambers of agriculture and industry, a system that would also involve the creation of a vast network of "territorial banks." Finally, he planned to discuss Fourier's utopian vision—the ideal community that would enable human beings for the first time to combine their own powers with those of nature in making the earth the place of happiness and abundance it was always meant to be.

Unfortunately, Considerant's speech did not go according to plan. One problem was its length. He announced at the outset that he would make cuts and summarize portions of his prepared text, but he asked that the whole be reproduced in the *Moniteur*. This produced objections, and one representative shouted sarcastically that Considerant should just have the speech printed up and distributed. "We have better things to do than listen to the reading of a book." Considerant's main problem, however, was that he was simply unable to communicate with the Assembly. He was unable to impress an unsympathetic and inattentive audience or to carry them away on the waves of rhetoric that had magnetized audiences on his speaking tours of the provinces. From the beginning he was defensive and apologetic, both about the length of his speech and about its content, and when he adopted the exalted tone that friendly audiences at Fourierist banquets found so inspiring, he was greeted with laughter and sarcasm. "I propose to you," he intoned, "the opening, without further delay, on this earth, for France, for Europe, for all of humanity, and for the life of humanity, of the era of integral and universal harmony. . . . It is the kingdom of God that I ask you to make at last a reality." But then he was interrupted: "Spare us all that. Don't speak of the kingdom of God. Speak of your own kingdom."

In the face of the laughter and heckling, Considerant did not lose his dignity, but his self-confidence collapsed. He practically begged the Assembly to hear him out.

> Gentlemen, you have attacked socialism a hundred times from this rostrum. . . . You have a hundred times challenged us to come here and answer your criticism with practical proposals. And now that I have completed a serious piece of work, a piece of work in which I communicate ideas that are not familiar to you [*Audience: "Oh! Oh!"*] but ought to be . . . you don't listen to me, you don't take me seriously. When your orators are at the rostrum, I listen to them; for once you ought to do the same for me!

Considerant did get to the end of his speech, but not before most of the Assembly had walked out and he himself had been reduced to a state of exhaustion.

In the discussion that followed his speech, Considerant received the support of the Montagnard Félix Pyat and the socialist Pierre Leroux. Leroux argued eloquently that while the socialists began with different assumptions, they sought a common goal, and that fire and sword would not suffice to suppress their ideas. To Considerant's chagrin, though, the most memorable intervention was that of a representative named Desjobert, who provoked hilarity among those who remained in the hall by reading excerpts from what he described as "the chastest passages" on marriage in Fourier's *Théorie des quatre mouvements*.[50]

This confrontation with the conservative majority of the National Assembly was, unfortunately, Considerant's single greatest moment of notoriety as a public figure. The next morning almost all of Paris's daily newspapers had something to say about it. Predictably, many journals of the left were sympathetic. Proudhon's *Le Peuple* regretted that the Assembly had not taken seriously Considerant's "challenge" to the government, and Eugène Bareste's *La République* observed that the money requested by Considerant for a socialist community would be better spent than "the sums extravagantly squandered" on repressive measures since June. On the other hand, Adam Mickiewicz wrote a long article in his *Tribune des peuples* criticizing Considerant's whole effort to win over "exploiters" and "oppressors" by the force of his arguments. The Fourierist system would remain "an empty utopia," he wrote, as long as its spokesmen kept seeking to transform the world "without offending anyone."[51]

Conservative journals commented derisively on Considerant's performance. *Le Siècle* asserted that the National Assembly's day had been "wasted," and *La Patrie* argued that the Assembly and the public had been the victims of "a veritable mystification." Similarly, the Bonapartist *Le Dix-Décembre* offered what Considerant's collaborators described as no more than "unintelligent pasquinades against socialism." Lamartine probably spoke for many when he wrote in his *Le Conseiller du peuple* that the month of April had been "ill-fated" for the two main socialist sects—the Fourierists and the followers of Proudhon. Proudhon's People's Bank had failed, and Fourierism had drifted off "into the realm of chimeras" with Considerant's speech before the National Assembly. The English humor magazine, *Punch*, was blunter, smirking that Considerant's "four-hour" speech had "killed" socialism in France.[52]

Well before April 14, Considerant had already become a preferred target of political satirists and cartoonists in the popular press. In February *Le Charivari* had published Daumier's famous cartoon showing him in the pose of a crouching anti-lion and endowed with a Fourierist *archibras* (a tail with an eye at the end) "seeking to Phalansterize all the members of the National Assembly." Considerant's journalistic wars with Proudhon had been followed by more cartoons by Cham, Bertall, and others depicting the two socialists as dogs and cats fighting for the bones of the old social order. But the speech of April 14 was the occasion for a new volley of cartoons in which Considerant was shown exposing his Fourierist tail to the National Assembly, expounding his theories to housewives, and even digging for gold in California.[53]

What made Considerant the butt of ridicule in April 1849 was, in part, his failure to adapt his message to his audience. He spoke to the Assembly in the tones of a true believer—a man confident that "the *école* to which I belong carries in its loins the salvation, the liberty, and the happiness of the world." Even if he had made more modest claims, though, he would not have been taken seriously. After the June insurrection, his program of peaceful democracy had lost its political meaning. Likewise, as Mickiewicz pointed out, his long-standing faith in the power of rational argument and appeals to a common good had become almost grotesquely irrelevant in the prevailing climate of reaction and social conflict. Considerant himself seems to have had some sense of this, for near the end of his speech he launched a warning. If European conservatives ignored his message of peace and reason, the year 1850 would bring "from one end of Europe to the other . . . the apocalypse of the old world and the drowning of the debris of this old world in a sea of fire and blood."[54] Considerant had not abandoned his vision of peaceful democracy and class reconciliation; most of his speech discussed its implementation. But he had begun to take seriously the possibility that significant social change would require violence.

V

In the days that followed his speech before the National Assembly, Considerant and his colleagues tried to put the best face on matters. On April 17 they produced a special supplement to *Démocratie pacifique* containing the text of the speech as recorded in the *Moniteur officiel*, with all the interruptions. It began with a statement protesting the "sustained inattention and preconceived scorn" of the Assembly and appealing for vindication "to the tribunal of all intelligent and good-hearted men of Europe." Shortly thereafter Considerant's much longer written text was published in a cheap popular edition designed to promote his candidacy in the May 13 legislative elections.[55]

Preparations for these elections had been going on since the middle of March; and Considerant had decided early on to present himself as a candidate again both in Paris and in the Loiret. On April 28 his candidacy in Paris was formally endorsed by the Democratic-Socialist Election Committee; and since his commitments as a representative made it difficult for him to travel to the Loiret, he seems to have decided this time to make his major effort in Paris.

The legislative election campaign of May 1849 was very different from that of the preceding year. The elections of April 1848 had taken place in great confusion, but in 1849 there were two clear political groupings— each with its own electoral committees, lists of candidates, and national program. On the left were "the reds," the *démoc-socs* who, after the out-lawing of Solidarité républicaine, had created other electoral committees and campaign organizations, notably the Parisian Democratic-Socialist Election Committee and the Democratic and Social Press Committee (to which *Démocratie pacifique* belonged). Their program, which was drawn up by Félix Pyat, called for the right to work, free and obligatory primary education, lower taxes, and cheap credit for small farmers through the creation of agricultural banks. On the right was the "Party of Order," which included conservatives of all stripes—legitimists, Orleanists, Bonapartists, and conservative republicans—as well as the vast majority of practicing Catholics. It was held together by the Committee of the rue de Poitiers with its Electoral Union and its departmental committees. Its chief political leaders were Thiers and Falloux, but its moral leader was comte Charles de Montalembert, who, in an appeal to the voters of the Doubs, defined the basic themes of the campaign as the right saw them. Against "the new barbarism that wild reformers are preparing for us," Montalembert asserted, it was necessary to raise the three great barriers of religion, family, and property.[56]

One of the most striking features of the election campaign of May 1849 was the renewal and intensification of the red scare that had already acquired momentum in the presidential campaign of the previous fall. Again the Committee of the rue de Poitiers attempted to flood the countryside with antisocialist literature. Within a few days in April, over 200,000 francs were raised to subsidize the printing and distribution of works such as Jean Sabbatier's *Petite conversation entre M. Gaspard, maître d'école, et J. Blaise, vigneron, à la sortie de la grande messe*, the *Lettre aux habitants des campagnes*, a brochure written collectively by members of the Committee of the rue de Poitiers, and *Les Rouges jugés par eux-mêmes*, in which Considerant, Proudhon, and Cabet, among others, were judged and found wanting. A particularly influential specimen of the genre was Jean Wallon's *Les Partageux*, a collection of dialogues in which the common sense of an old peasant, le père François, repeatedly triumphed over the shallow and sinister views of a communist, a socialist, and a Montagnard.[57]

In their efforts to combat the attacks of the right, the *démoc-socs* sought to address the grievances of the peasants more effectively than they had the previous year. Considerant's proposals for agricultural credit and Proudhon's Banque du peuple were just two of many efforts by socialists to find new ways of providing the peasants with the cheap credit they so desperately needed. *Démoc-soc* propaganda also addressed more specific grievances of the peasants, such as the demands for the elimination of the salt tax and for the restoration of traditional forest rights. They also sought to produce popular works of their own that would find a large audience in the countryside. To a large extent they were successful. Pierre Joigneaux's journal, *La Feuille du village*, which circulated widely in central and eastern France, turned out to be extremely influential, and Félix Pyat's *Toast aux paysans de la France*, which warned peasants against the blandishments of royalists and priests, was published as a broadside and sold hundreds of thousands of copies at two and a half centimes apiece.[58]

As election day approached, it became clear that the *démoc-socs* were having success not only with the peasants but also with officers and enlisted men in the army. In response, the government began to intervene actively in support of the right. *Démoc-soc* electoral meetings were broken up; newspapers were seized; and functionaries unwilling to cooperate with the government were dismissed. At the same time, Interior Minister Léon Faucher outlawed organizations—even cooperative bakeries—thought to be centers of political agitation and ordered the publication of false police reports to discredit the left. Faucher even had the cry "Vive la République démocratique et sociale!" declared unconstitutional. By the beginning of May the situation was further complicated by the bitter dispute between left and right concerning the French military intervention against the Roman republic. Three days before the election the situation had become so tense that the editors of *Démocratie pacifique* could declare: "We are on the eve of civil war."[59]

Not surprisingly, the elections resulted in a massive conservative victory on the national level: 450 out of 750 seats in the new Legislative Assembly went to candidates of the Party of Order. The big losers in the election were the moderate republicans, who had dominated the Constituent Assembly. Their number was reduced to fewer than 100; and many of their leaders—Lamartine, Marie, Marrast, and Sénard among others—were not reelected. As for the *démoc-socs*, the results for them were in some ways extremely encouraging. They won close to 200 seats and received 2,360,000 votes, more than 35 percent of the total. Furthermore, in addition to running strongly in Paris, *démoc-soc* candidates were successful in Lyon, Alsace, and over two dozen rural departments of the Center and Southeast of France. The *démoc-soc* appeal to the peasantry had been heard; and against the self-described "France honnête" of the West, North, and Southwest, there now emerged a "France rouge" concentrated in the Center and the Southeast.[60]

Considerant shared in the victory. Although narrowly defeated in the Loiret—missing reelection there by fewer than 500 votes—he was successful in Paris, where he received 110,127 votes, placing him eighteenth among twenty-eight successful candidates. The support of radical democrats affiliated with the Mountain had clearly been important to him; and when the Legislative Assembly first met on May 28 Considerant joined them. Formally identifying himself with the Mountain, he became a regular participant in their meetings at 6, rue du Hasard. He had been unwilling to join the Mountain during the lifetime of the Constituent Assembly, but now the situation had changed. There was no longer any point in attempting to play the role of mediator. The left had to close ranks. A "war" now pitted "the forces of social democracy" against "the forces of aristocracy," and Considerant felt "absolutely bound to participate in the struggle."[61]

From its opening session, the atmosphere that reigned in the Legislative Assembly was indeed that of war. Despite its massive victory, the Party of Order was disturbed by the victories of the Montagnards—and especially by their success among the peasants and the military. Fearful that these two "anchors of mercy" might snap in the storm, conservatives were gripped, according to Tocqueville, by "a terror so profound that I can only compare it to that which followed February." The head of the ministry, Odilon Barrot, later spoke with horror of some of the newly elected representatives as "socialists emerging from the lowest depths of society." At the same time the radicals took heart from the results, which were much less a defeat for them than for the moderate republicans. Tocqueville could write that on returning to Paris for the opening of the Legislative Assembly after several weeks in Germany, he found the political scene completely changed. In the new Assembly, he wrote, "one felt one was breathing the air of civil war. Speech was abrupt, gestures violent, phrases extravagant, and insults outrageous and direct." The legislature was now meeting in the Old Chamber of Deputies, which had been built to accommodate 460 members, not the 750 new representatives. "So," wrote Tocqueville, "we were pressed up against one another, despite the loathing that kept us apart." A confrontation seemed imminent, and an issue to fight over already existed in the form of the military expedition that had been sent to Italy by the Constituent Assembly in April with the avowed purpose of preventing Austrian intervention in republican Rome.[62]

11

June 13, 1849

The Roman Republic came into being in February 1849, slightly more than two months after rioting had driven Pope Pius IX out of the Vatican and into exile. The republic's life span was less than five months, and during much of that period it was under attack by French forces seeking to restore the Pope. The Romans resisted bravely, however, and republicans and revolutionaries all over Europe took up their cause. For the Pope, republican Rome became "a den of wild beasts, crammed full of men of all nations who, being apostates or heretics or teachers of Communism and Socialism . . . strive to teach and disseminate errors of every description." For Giuseppe Mazzini, who emerged as its leader, the Roman Republic was, on the other hand, "the holy ark" of the "redemption" of the Italian nation.[1]

I

After his flight from Rome in late November 1848, Pius IX had taken refuge in the Neapolitan border town of Gaeta. From there, in January 1849, he appealed to Catholic Europe for help in restoring his temporal power. At Rome, in the meantime, a constituent assembly was elected, and on February 9, 1849, the Roman Republic was proclaimed. Even before the arrival of Mazzini on March 5, major reforms were undertaken. Church properties were nationalized and old church buildings made over into housing for

246

the poor. Censorship was abolished, the Inquisition suppressed, and clerical control of the university brought to an end. Soon Mazzini was expounding to the Roman Assembly his doctrine of a Third Rome, the Rome not of the emperors or the Pope but of the people.[2]

But the Roman Republic never had more than a precarious existence. By the end of March 1849, Austria, Naples, and Spain were all preparing to use force to restore papal rule in Rome. The French government also began to discuss intervention to keep the Austrians out of Rome and to ensure that the Pope, once returned to his capital, would maintain the secular institutions introduced in the spring of 1848. On April 16, the French National Assembly, by a large majority, voted to send a French expeditionary force to Rome. The head of the ministry, Odilon Barrot, presented this intervention as an attempt at mediation between the Pope and his rebellious subjects, whom the French would "protect" against Austrian designs. From the beginning, though, it was clear that the French troops could be used against the Roman Republic. As Considerant wrote on April 18, explaining his refusal to vote credits, the measure was actually "a carte blanche accorded to MM. Barrot, Léon Faucher, and Falloux in favor of the restoration of the Pope." Sending French troops to Rome would also play into the hands of the Austrians, Considerant argued, by allowing them to concentrate their own troops on the repression of the newly declared Hungarian Republic. "It's a question for France," he wrote, "of serving as Austria's policeman in Italy, bringing about or helping to bring about counterrevolution in Rome, restoring the Pope to his temporal power, and extricating Austrian troops from Italy to give them the opportunity to go fight the Hungarians." In all of this Considerant saw only "counterrevolution, the violation of the Constitution, the shame and debasement of France."[3]

The commander of the French forces, General Nicolas Oudinot, landed at Rome's port, Civita Vecchia, on April 24 with 10,000 men. Meeting no initial resistance, he set out for Rome (in the words of a British agent) "full of vain anticipation of a glorious reception." In fact, the Romans were determined to defend their city against all invaders. Although their military position initially seemed hopeless, it improved on April 27 with the arrival of 1,200 of Garibaldi's followers and 600 Lombard volunteers under Colonel Luciano Manara. Then, on April 30, as Oudinot attempted to force his way into the city, he was suddenly attacked on the flank by Garibaldi's troops and forced to retreat to Civita Vecchia.[4]

Oudinot's unexpected and humiliating defeat created what amounted to a constitutional crisis in France. On May 7, just a week before the legislative elections, the Constituent Assembly passed a resolution effectively forbidding the French expeditionary force to attack Rome. The following day, however, the pro-government journal *La Patrie* published a bellicose letter from Louis-Napoleon to Oudinot: "Our soldiers have been received as enemies; our military honor is at stake. I shall not allow it to be stained. You will not lack reinforcements."[5] And reinforcements were sent. During the month of May, while a young French diplomat, the future canal builder Ferdinand de Lessups attempted to reach a negotiated settlement with the Romans, the French tripled their garrison and supplied it with enough food and artillery to mount a prolonged siege.

In the meantime Considerant emerged as a leading critic of the government's Roman policy. On May 8 *Démocratie pacifique* published a fierce attack on the "odious politics" of the ministry, which had "torn up the Constitution and dragged the French flag in blood and mud." The following day at the Assembly, Considerant introduced a resolution signed by fifty-nine representatives in which Louis-Napoleon and his ministers were accused of having violated the article of the Constitution committing the republic to respect the liberties of all nations. This resolution soon became a bill, submitted jointly by Considerant and Ledru-Rollin, calling for an "act of accusation" against Louis-Napoleon and his ministers. This bill was voted down on May 11, but it did receive the support of 138 representatives as against 388 opposed.[6]

The crisis reached a head at the end of May when, defying the Assembly's resolution, the government secretly sent Oudinot orders to attack Rome. The attack began on June 3, as French troops occupied Roman outposts on the right bank of the Tiber. This time the Roman position was indeed hopeless. Fighting heroically, the Romans under Garibaldi managed to hold out for a month. Rumors of the French attack on Rome began to circulate in Paris on June 6, but only on the evening of June 9 did the news receive official confirmation. Although the attack was welcomed by conservative Catholics and by most of the parliamentary majority, many moderate republicans felt stunned and betrayed, and members of the government found themselves in a difficult position. Alexis de Tocqueville, who was appointed foreign minister on the same day as the attack and who was obliged to assume responsibility for the Roman expedition, did so reluctantly. In public he supported the expedition, but in his *Souvenirs* he characterized the attack on Rome as an act of "flagrant disobedience to the injunctions of a sovereign assembly . . . and in contradiction to the terms of the Constitution." As for the left, it reacted predictably with consternation and anger. There were protests and calls to action from the Democratic Socialist Committee of the Seine, the radical clubs, workers' trade societies, the Montagnard Society of the Rights of Man, and the moderate republican Friends of the Constitution. In the Assembly, Ledru-Rollin announced an interpellation, which quickly became a bill of impeachment signed this time by 148 representatives.[7]

II

Considerant and the Fourierists were at the center of the agitation protesting the attack on Rome. On June 10 and 11, *Démocratie pacifique* published lead articles denouncing the attack as a violation of the constitution, which expressly forbade the use of French military force "against the liberty of any people." On the morning of June 11, Considerant presided at the offices of *Démocratie pacifique* over a meeting of radical journalists with a group that called itself the Committee of Twenty-five. (Its members were representatives of the Democratic Socialist Committee that had drawn up the radical slate for the May elections.) All agreed that there had been a violation of the Constitution, but the point of the meeting was to determine the form that protest should take. The members of the Committee of Twenty-five maintained that the people of Paris were ready for an armed uprising and proposed that representatives of the Mountain should take the lead, withdrawing to a stronghold—a Mount Aventine—in the east of Paris. Considerant, on the other hand, spoke for a powerful street demonstration. Warning that even that might end in violence, he urged that all elected representatives make their protests in the National Assembly and not on the streets. Considerant was followed by Emile de Girardin, the editor of the popular daily *La Presse* and a moderate republican who had moved into the radical camp during the constitutional crisis. Girardin warned that after the June insurrection of the previous year and in a time of cholera, the Paris population would not be likely to support any sort of armed insurrection. He went on to argue with great eloquence for a strictly peaceful demonstration and an appeal to the president to reverse government policy.[8]

Considerant left the meeting at *Démocratie pacifique* around noon and hurried to a meeting of representatives of the Mountain, which had been called to make plans for the afternoon's session of the Legislative Assembly. He brought with him four hastily drafted resolutions to be issued by the radical opposition if and when the conservative majority in the Assembly rejected the motion of impeachment to be made by Ledru-Rollin. These resolutions specified that immediately following the vote, the opposition deputies should announce that the Constitution had been violated and declare the people, National Guard, all state functionaries, and members of the army released from their oath of obedience to the executive power. Proclaiming themselves the only legal representatives of the people, the members of the opposition would then declare themselves a rump assembly by right of Article 68 of the Constitution.[9]

Considerant's idea was that these resolutions should be issued by the Mountain *within* the National Assembly. Later he wrote that he did not conceal from himself the likelihood that he and his colleagues would be immediately arrested. He was in fact inviting arrest. It seemed vital to him, though, that the Mountain's protest be made within the National Assembly and in such a manner that no one could accuse the Montagnards of plotting the Assembly's forcible overthrow. In associating themselves with a demonstration outside the Assembly—even a peaceful demonstration, Considerant argued—"we could easily be made to look like seditious rebels."[10]

The leader of the Mountain, Ledru-Rollin, was unfortunately not as concerned as Considerant with niceties of appearance and principle. That very afternoon, in his interpellation of the prime minister, Odilon Barrot, he used language that fatally compromised Considerant's proposed strategy. "The Constitution has been violated," proclaimed Ledru-Rollin in presenting his bill of impeachment. "We shall defend it by all possible means, even by force of arms." In making this statement Ledru-Rollin was widely assumed to be speaking for the Mountain as a whole. "Yet," as one of its members later pointed out, "the Mountain had not been consulted and had not authorized the great orator to make imprudent and rash commitments." In fact, nothing could have been better suited than this threat of armed rebellion to discredit the Mountain—to make its members seem like rebels rather than defenders of the Constitution.[11]

That evening, after the discussion of Ledru-Rollin's bill of impeachment had ended inconclusively, approximately 150 members of the Mountain crammed into the meeting rooms of its parliamentary caucus on the rue du Hasard. They were joined by a number of prominent radical journalists and by delegates from the Committee of Twenty-five. The latter, together with a group of radical representatives, argued forcefully that the time was ripe for armed insurrection. Others, including Considerant, warned that a call to arms would fail to attract support from a population weakened by cholera and still recovering from the effects of the June Days. After Ledru-Rollin's speech, however, it was difficult to turn back, and many of those who had objections seem to have kept them to themselves. Writing about the meeting a few months later, Considerant recalled that there was no serious discussion of alternative courses of action and that virtually the whole meeting was given over to the discussion and drafting of a statement to be given to the journals.[12]

On June 12 the Legislative Assembly concluded its discussion of Ledru-Rollin's bill of impeachment by decisively voting down the measure. It was a strange discussion. The presence of a huge police guard and large crowds in the area immediately around the Assembly created an ominous and somewhat unreal atmosphere within. Stranger still, however, was the character of the debate. The spokesmen of the Mountain—including Ledru-Rollin—were cautious and hesitant, as if they feared the impending conflict. When asked whether the left accepted responsibility for the appeal to arms, Ledru-Rollin was silent and left it to Pierre Leroux to reply that he and his friends appealed to reason, not arms. Tocqueville, who spoke for the government, later observed that the leaders of the Mountain,

> who were more used to talking than fighting and more passionate than resolute, showed on that day, for all the intemperance of their language, a sort of hesitation that they had not shown the day before. After having drawn their swords half-way, they seemed to want to sheathe them again. But it was too late; the signal had been given by their friends outside [the Assembly], and from then on they were no longer directing events but were being led.[13]

It was already nine thirty in the evening when the session of the Legislative Assembly was finally adjourned. At that point most of the members of the Mountain made their way from the Palais Bourbon to the offices of *Démocratie pacifique* on the rue de Beaune. (They believed that their normal meeting place on the rue du Hasard was no longer safe.)[14] There they were joined by members of the Committee of Twenty-five and various working-class radicals. Their ostensible purpose was to work out a plan of action for the following day. Most of those who attended this final meeting were already committed to participation in some sort of organized extraparliamentary protest demonstration. Some had already drafted calls to arms, but there was still no general consensus on the form the protest would take. Judging from the evidence available to us, the argument that was later to be made by the government prosecutor—that this was the last in a series of meetings devoted to planning an armed insurrection—seems ludicrously wide of the mark. The whole problem with the actions taken by the Mountain on June 13, 1849, is that they were *not* planned but improvised on the spur of the moment.[15]

The discussions of the night of June 12 in the offices of *Démocratie pacifique* did not focus on the planning of an insurrection but on whether or not there should be an insurrection at all.[16] Several representatives, including Martin Nadaud and Victor Baudin (who was to be shot on a barricade protesting the coup of Louis-Napoleon on December 2, 1851), argued that a call to arms was folly because the vast majority of Parisians did not understand the constitutional issues and would not rise up. However, Michel de Bourges, a lawyer and a gifted orator, argued passionately and persuasively that the population was ready and that the army could be won over. A proposal that the Mountain meet in rump session in a hall on the rue Saint-Martin in the east of Paris was rejected. Then Ledru-Rollin, Considerant, and Félix Pyat were named to draft a proclamation in the name of the Mountain. In this proclamation they accused Louis-Napoleon of having violated the Constitution in making war on the Roman Republic, and they charged that the majority in the National Assembly had become "accomplices" in the president's "crime." "In this situation, what should the minority do?" they asked.

> After having protested within the Assembly, the minority can do no more than remind the people, the National Guard, the army, that Article 110 confides the safeguarding of the Constitution and the rights that it guarantees to the protection and patriotism of all the French.
> People, the supreme moment has come! All these acts betray a great system of monarchical conspiracy against the republic. The hatred of democracy, which is poorly hidden on the banks of the Seine, is freely bursting forth on the banks of the Tiber.
> In the struggle pitting the people against kings, the government has sided with the kings against the people.
> Soldiers. . . . National Guardsmen. . . . Let us all rally to the cries of: "Long live the Constitution!" "Long live the Republic!"[17]

This proclamation, which was distributed to the press at one o'clock in the morning, *was* a call to revolution, but of course it said nothing at all about the form the popular demonstration should take or the role to be played by the representatives themselves.

Considerant left two accounts of this nocturnal meeting at the offices of *Démocratie pacifique*. In his published account, written just a few days later, he noted that the meeting did not finally break up until after three o'clock in the morning but that many of the representatives had in fact departed even before the distribution of the proclamation at one o'clock. Considerant himself stayed until the bitter end. By his own account he continued to argue to anyone who would listen that the representatives should remain in the National Assembly while a peaceful demonstration was being organized. Having issued a call to revolution, they should wait for the popular voice to be heard. In his published account, Considerant noted that "at three o'clock in the morning" his views "seemed to have won over those who were still present." But, he added, "the issue remained a matter of personal opinion. We started discussing things again; we separated, wearied by fatigue, and nothing was decided at the meeting except for the declaration given to the journals at one o'clock in the morning." In an unpublished statement on the events, written four months later, Considerant insisted even more emphatically on the Mountain's inability to formulate any coherent plan of action for June 13.

> On the evening of the twelfth and down until one o'clock in the morning the people meeting at *Démocratie pacifique* discussed and drew up a second manifesto, which appeared in the newspapers on the thirteenth. By one o'clock in the morning many representatives had left. No decisions of any sort were taken. I continued to uphold my opinion in diverse conversations until three o'clock. But no resolution, no more mine than anyone else's, was even put to discussion; and nothing, absolutely nothing, had been decided on any sort of mode of action when people left to go to the demonstration.

It would be hard to make clearer the lack of planning and preparation for the *journée* of June 13.[18]

III

On the morning of June 13, four proclamations were posted along the streets of Paris and published in the radical newspapers. The first was the proclamation of the Mountain that Ledru-Rollin, Considerant, and Félix Pyat had handed over to the press during the night. It was signed by 122 members of the Mountain. The second, signed by the press and school committees, the Committee of Twenty-five, and the Luxembourg delegates, portrayed a revolution already in progress.

> The National Guard is rising!
> Workshops are closing!
> Let our brothers in the army remember that they are citizens, and that as such the first of their duties is to defend the Constitution.
> Let all the people rise up!

The third proclamation, issued by the moderate republican Amis de la Constitution, called upon the people of Paris to join a "grand and calm demonstration" to protest the violation of the Constitution. And the fourth, signed by the delegates of the Fifth Legion of the National Guard, called on all members of the National Guard to meet at 11 AM at the Château d'Eau, in the heart of working-class Paris, "in uniform, but without arms, to march to the Legislative Assembly to remind it of the respect due to the Constitution, the defense of which is entrusted to the patriotism of all citizens." [19]

Many contemporaries were later to criticize the organizers of the June 13 demonstration for insisting that the participants come unarmed. "I found it absurd to convoke *without arms* citizens who were bound to come in conflict with armed soldiers," wrote the Montagnard Sébastien Commissaire. "That meant exposing them to the possibility of getting massacred without any chance of defending themselves." For Karl Marx the insistence on an unarmed demonstration was one sign, among many, of the petty bourgeois character of the June 13 insurrection's leadership. Modern historians, on the other hand, including some writing from within Marxist perspectives, have been less categorical in their treatment of the *journée*. In his lucid and careful study of June 13, Bernard Moss argues that, taken as a whole, the proclamations issued that day constituted a call for armed rebellion and that "most radicals" expected armed units of the National Guard and the army eventually to intervene. For Moss the call to arms was not spelled out, but it was clearly implied. [20]

Be this as it may, there can be no doubt about Considerant's position. He was unalterably opposed to an armed demonstration. When he was asked, early in the morning of the thirteenth, for his views on the matter, his reply was emphatic: "No arms! For the love of God and the Constitution, no arms! What we need is an imposing and peaceful demonstration. Arms will ruin everything." [21] Apparently Considerant was counting on the moral pressure created by a massive and peaceful popular demonstration together with the principled refusal of the Montagnard representatives to countenance the violation of the constitution. What he failed to recognize was that Ledru-Rollin's threats (plus the calls to arms of his allies) had created a situation in which the Mountain had lost the moral high ground and could now easily be accused of seditious plotting.

Insofar as there was any plan for June 13, it was for the members of the Mountain not to participate in the great popular demonstration. They had agreed to meet in the morning at their headquarters on the rue du Hasard, and it was assumed that they would make their way from there to the National Assembly to await the demonstrators. As for the demonstration itself, it began at about eleven thirty at the Château d'Eau. A crowd estimated at between twenty and thirty thousand formed rows of twenty abreast and began marching down the boulevards toward the Madeleine.

At the head of the procession were Etienne Arago, the former foreign minister Jules Bastide, a number of prominent republicans, and a few Montagnard representatives such as Pierre Malardier. Immediately behind them was an honorary contingent of radical exiles including Alexander Herzen and possibly Karl Marx. Then came about five thousand members of the National Guard, in uniform but unarmed, and many more workers and students. The demonstrators shouted "Long live the Constitution!" and "Long live the republic!" A large crowd of spectators lined the boulevards. Although few of them joined the line of march, they waved and cheered as the demonstrators began to sing the Marseillaise. "At that moment," recalled Alexander Herzen,

> there was really something grand about the demonstration. As we slowly moved down the boulevards all the windows were thrown open; ladies and children crowded at them and came out on the balconies; the gloomy, alarmed faces of their husbands, the fathers and proprietors, looked out from behind them, not observing that in the fourth stories and attics other heads, those of poor seamstresses and working girls, were thrust out—they waved handkerchiefs, nodded and greeted us.[22]

All went well until the marchers reached the rue de la Paix, near the spot where Garnier's Paris Opera was to rise two decades later. There they were met by three columns of troops and cavalry under General Changarnier. Without even ordering the crowd to disperse, Changarnier commanded his troops to charge. They did so, cutting the procession in two, isolating the leaders, and pushing the followers back down the boulevard toward the working-class quarters from which they had come. Some demonstrators tried to argue or plead with the soldiers, but they were pushed aside or knocked to the ground. "The dragoons in a frenzy fell to riding down people," Herzen wrote, "striking them with the flat of their swords and using the edge at the slightest resistance." A few shouts of "Aux armes!" were heard as the demonstrators dispersed, but the only response was the slamming of doors and the closing of shutters. Likewise a few feeble attempts were made to form barricades with the chairs and tables of nearby cafés. But these were quickly destroyed by Changarnier's troops. This was the end of the peaceful demonstration.[23]

During the morning, while the popular demonstration was running its course, the Montagnards gathered at their headquarters on the rue du Hasard. Anxiously they waited for news about the demonstration and about the reaction of the Parisians to their proclamation. By late morning pledges of support had come in from some National Guard units and from the Society of the Rights of Man. Initial reports also indicated that the demonstration was going to be sizable, but by midday it was clear that there would be no general rising of the Paris population. As Considerant put it later, the attitude of ordinary Parisians seemed to be that it was "up to the constitutional representatives and the National Guard to make the protest." The common people were "not getting involved."[24]

Around one o'clock, feeling they had to take some new initiative, the Montagnard representatives decided to march together to the Conservatoire des Arts et Métiers in the heart of working-class Paris, where, it was rumored, the sixth legion of the National Guards under Colonel Forestier was waiting for them. It is not entirely clear why the Montagnards took this decision. Did they see the Conservatoire des Arts et Métiers as a stronghold—a "Mount Aventine"—from which to direct a true armed insurrection? Were some of them so caught up in the mythology of the French Revolution that they imagined that the Conservatoire might serve them as a "new Jeu de Paume"? Were they simply looking for a refuge—a safe place from which to plan their next move? The latter seems most likely.[25]

What was Considerant's position at this critical juncture? No doubt he was as confused and uncertain as the other Montagnards. Probably his decision to accompany some of them to the Conservatoire was motivated more by feelings of human solidarity than by any sort of rational calculation.[26] It is clear, in any case, that by proceeding not to the National Assembly but to the Conservatoire des Arts et Métiers, the Montagnards were doing just what Considerant had warned against earlier. They were allowing their protest to assume a form that would make it easy for the government and the parliamentary majority to depict them not as defenders of the Constitution but as instigators of civil war.

On their way to the Conservatoire des Arts et Métiers, the group of Montagnard representatives stopped at the Palais Royal (then known as the Palais National) to pick up an armed escort from the artillery legion commanded by Colonel Joseph Guinard, who had been a Montagnard representative in the Constituent Assembly. There they learned that Changarnier had crushed the popular demonstration. None of them had expected the demonstration to be so swiftly and decisively crushed. Guinard was as shocked as they were. Reluctant now to order his men to escort the representatives, Guinard agreed to ask them to do so as a matter of personal conscience.[27]

Leaving the Palais Royal, the representatives marched three and four abreast with columns of Guinard's artillerymen on either side. In front were Ledru-Rollin, Guinard, and the venerable republican Jean-Marie Joseph Deville. Right behind them came Considerant, marching arm in arm with François Rattier and Jean-Baptiste Boichot, radical junior army officers elected to the Legislative Assembly by vote of the soldiers. In all there were no more than sixty representatives of the people, three hundred artillerymen, and a crowd of about a thousand civilians.[28] Considerant recalled later that, as they moved through the center of Paris toward the eastern working-class districts, they were greeted by shouts of "Vive la Montagne!" They tried to drown out these shouts, however, with cries of "Vive la Constitution!" and "Vive la République Romaine!" "We kept telling each other," wrote Considerant, "that our role for this day was traced, that there was nothing to discuss, that we ought to avoid any call to arms, that we should place ourselves at the head of the demonstration and face, if necessary, the blows of bayonets and rifle fire."[29]

The procession arrived at the Conservatoire at around two fifteen. Forcing their way into the courtyard, the representatives and artillerymen—a crowd of about four hundred in all—were met by the director of the Conservatoire, Claude Pouillet, who later left a vivid picture of the intruders.

> I saw before me . . . a group of representatives wearing their sashes and all the formal dress of office. Behind them, filling the first courtyard, I saw the red plumes of the National Guard artillery, their hats and caps bearing the sign of the level, the symbol of the Society of the Rights of Man. Above all that a disorderly forest of bayonets was shaking.[30]

Pouillet went on to offer an account of his ensuing conversation with Ledru-Rollin.

> "What do you want?"
> "A refuge."
> "This establishment is the refuge of science and peace, not of war. Go elsewhere with your banner."
> "We are being beaten and cut down in the boulevards and the streets."
> "The Conservatory will not save you; it will be fatal to you."
> "In the streets we will be massacred."
> "Here you will be surrounded, assailed from all sides without any means of defending yourselves."
> "Time is passing. We want a place to talk. Have you a room for us?"
> "You have forced your way in. Alone against you and your army, I have only my words with which to oppose you. If you don't believe me, if you cannot see the danger you are in here, come and I will open up a room for you.[31]

When the amphitheater that Pouillet made available to them proved unsatisfactory, the representatives forced their way into another room, the Salle des Filiatures. This became their headquarters for the next half-hour.

So far as it is possible to reconstruct what went on in the Conservatoire des Arts et Métiers between about two thirty and three thirty on the afternoon of June 13, the scene seems to have been one of almost total chaos. At the outset there may have been as many as sixty representatives present, but there was no leadership and no organization, and the National Guard units that had been expected were nowhere in sight. Witnesses remembered Michel de Bourges looking like Marat with his head wrapped in a bandanna while he drafted a proclamation, and Ledru-Rollin was described as "worried . . . gesticulating . . . looking like a sick man."[32] Considerant, who seems to have been calmer, could not get more than half a dozen people to listen to him at a single time. Afterward he painted a picture of complete confusion.

> Minutes passed. Nothing happened. People conversed in groups of two, three, six; they came and went; but there was not a single general discussion, not a single decision taken in common. A few individuals shouted, "Aux armes!" asking for cartridges and for the order to build barricades. At the same time people kept running up to newcomers asking for news. People kept on waiting, but the National Guards from the demonstration did not come.[33]

On Considerant's initiative, emissaries were sent out to get information and to find out why Colonel Forestier's Sixth Legion of the National Guard had not arrived. Others left to seek reinforcements from nearby National Guard units and from the mayor of Belleville.

Afterward claims were made that a call to arms was hastily drafted at the Conservatoire—by Ledru-Rollin or possibly Michel de Bourges—and sent out to be published by Proudhon's journal *Le Peuple*. According to one account (that of Sébastien Commissaire) the decision to issue the call was made by a spontaneously formed triumvirate consisting of "the three most influential figures" in the Conservatoire—Ledru-Rollin, Michel de Bourges, and Victor Considerant. This call to arms does *not* seem to have been simply fabricated by the government in order to discredit the Mountain: at three in the afternoon a copy was in fact delivered to Alfred Darimon at the offices of *Le Peuple* by a friend of Ledru-Rollin. However, it is most unlikely that Considerant had anything to do with drafting it, and it is not at all certain that Ledru-Rollin wrote it. Considerant at any rate was unequivocal. "I did not see the proclamation said to have been seized," he wrote shortly afterward, "and I swear, having always been beside Ledru-Rollin or near him, that he did not see it either."[34]

As time passed, Considerant became increasingly anxious about the position into which the representatives had put themselves. It was as if they had created a trap and walked right into it. "I was not slow in understanding," he wrote later, "that we were going to be surrounded, captured, taken for rebels guilty of insurrection." A conversation with Pouillet, who was desperately trying to persuade the intruders to leave the Conservatoire, reinforced Considerant's fears. "Several times," he wrote, "I expressed the opinion that we should leave and go look for [the remnants of] the demonstration on the boulevards or the National Guard in the sixth arrondissement." But then, when he had finally won over his colleagues and just as they were preparing to leave, shots rang out and a large contingent of regular army troops entered the courtyard.[35]

As the government troops moved forward, the representatives, artillerymen, and National Guards inside the Conservatoire made no effort either to resist or to escape. "There was so little thought of flight," one of the Montagnards said later, "that we all went up to the troops, Ledru-Rollin at our head. The artillerymen waved their rifles in the air and cheered for the republic and the constitution."[36] The government soldiers continued to advance, however, and the group inside the building was forced backward into the large reception room of the Conservatoire. Considerant later wrote that "from the moment the troops entered, we considered ourselves to be prisoners," but the confusion and noise were so great that he could not hear the orders given by the officers.[37]

At this point Ledru-Rollin tried to speak to the commanding officer, but the officer disregarded him and shouted at the representatives: "Line up against the wall; you're going to be shot." As the representatives were pushed against the wall, one of them climbed up on a table and tried to give a speech. The captain, whom several witnesses described as in a drunken rage, grabbed him by his official sash and pulled him down, saying that he did not recognize that badge of authority. What followed is best described in Considerant's own words:

> Suddenly some of the soldiers in the first section retreated two paces and crossed their bayonets, while others, who had doubtless misunderstood the command, raised their rifles and took dead aim at us. I thought we were going to be shot right there. However I couldn't figure out the motive, since they didn't shoot while entering the first courtyard. Some of the people next to me, in the first row, dropped to

the ground. I got down just as they did. Then in an instant I got up and crossed my arms, looking right into the muzzles of the guns. Behind me people were for the most part standing firm.[38]

At this point apparently a superior officer came running up and ordered the troops to lower their guns. Considerant did not see the officer or hear the order, but the next thing he knew, some of the demonstrators were smashing the long French windows that opened onto the garden of the Conservatoire and trying to make their escape. He himself, and many of the other representatives, made no effort to escape.

A few minutes later, without a word of explanation, the soldiers began to withdraw from the Conservatoire. In the confusion most of the demonstrators left in the building managed to escape through the garden and over the walls. Soon only a few artillerymen and a dozen or so representatives remained. As they began to discuss what to do next, they suddenly heard the main gate of the Conservatoire swing shut. "Outside in the street a portion of a company of National Guards was standing," Considerant wrote later. "At its right stood a citizen out of uniform, about fifty-five years old with a calm and mild appearance. He told us politely that we were not going to get out." By this time the others had disappeared, and only Considerant, Ledru-Rollin, Martin Bernard, and Guinard were left. "Look," said Considerant, "this building has other exits and we are its masters. Why shouldn't we see about getting out? Let's take a look at the garden." The group of four was heading toward the garden when a secretary appeared and told them that one of the garden doors was open. They found it and walked out.[39]

No sooner were Considerant and his friends out in the street than they found themselves again in danger. They were recognized, cheered, and followed by the people of this working-class quarter. "Three times I was obliged to dismiss a compromising escort," Considerant recalled, "and twice we had to change direction or retrace our steps in order not to run into cordons of troops."

Just then a boy of fifteen or sixteen approached Considerant. Taking him by the hand, the boy peered into his face with an expression of devotion and shrewdness that Considerant was never to forget. "Will you trust me?" he asked. "Follow me. Come." The boy led Considerant into an alley. Then he took off his shirt and his dirty old gray hat and gave them to Considerant. "Quick, put them on," he said, "and you can go anywhere." But Considerant said he didn't want to wear a disguise. "Well then," said the boy, "let's go inside somewhere. In this quarter we're all friends." The boy knew what he was talking about, for Considerant was taken in at the first door they tried.[40]

From his hiding place in the quartier du Temple Considerant wrote a quick note to his wife at the rue de Beaune and gave it to the boy. On the boy's return Considerant sent him off again with notes to his friends from *Démocratie pacifique*. Within a few hours he learned that an order had been issued for his arrest. He also learned that, at about six o'clock, a battalion of National Guards had entered and sacked both his apartment and the offices of *Démocratie pacifique* on the rue de Beaune.

> I learned about the invasion of *Démocratie pacifique,* the destruction of our workshops, the breaking up of our printers' fonts and cases, the dispersion of the type, and the friendly visits made to my apartment by some crazy people without a search warrant who shouted at my wife and mother-in-law as they searched all the rooms: "We're looking for a man, and when we find him we'll tear him into bits and pieces."[41]

Unfortunately the comings and goings of Considerant's young messenger attracted attention. A man was heard on the street threatening to denounce his neighbors for harboring a criminal, so Considerant left. Having done so, he found that he could not get back to the rue de Beaune. For the moment at least Paris was cut in two. Thus he made his way to the house of a friend in the eastern part of the city. There he learned that a state of siege had been declared and that orders were being issued for the arrest of fifty-four Representatives of the People. The Mountain had been decimated.

IV

The events of June 13, 1849, have been exhaustively documented, so it is not hard to follow Considerant's trail during the days leading up to June 13; however, we know little about his movements thereafter.[42] Apparently he remained in Paris for three weeks. Unable to return home, he was sheltered by friends. A key benefactor seems to have been an old friend and comrade from the Ecole Polytechnique, Pierre-Dominique Bazaine-Vasseur, the brother of the future Marshal Bazaine. An engineer who had supervised the construction of several major French railroad lines, this Bazaine served the Second Republic as general secretary of the Railroad Section of the General Council of Bridges and Roads. Saluted by a Fourierist as "the devoted friend who saved [Considerant] in 1849," Bazaine may have been the person who gave shelter to Considerant during these weeks, and it was almost certainly he who arranged to get him the false passport and other papers he needed to leave France.[43]

During his first week in hiding Considerant remained indoors. He spent most of his time writing—in white heat—the narrative and justification of his role in the events of June 13 that was published in Brussels in early July under the title *Simples explications à mes amis et à mes commettants*. Once this was finished, he continued to lie low while false papers were being obtained for him, but he surfaced occasionally to spend an afternoon fishing incognito under the bridges of the Seine. This was possible because, having shaved off the magnificent *moustaches gauloises* that were his trademark, he was not easily recognizable—even by those who knew him well.

Finally, early in July, armed with a passport identifying him as Louis Bernard Dauphin, a traveling salesman from the Jura, Considerant simply took the train from Paris to Brussels. He was apparently accompanied on that trip by three other *proscrits* of June 13, Ledru-Rollin, Martin Bernard, and Etienne Arago, each of whom was also armed with a false passport.[44] It was almost ten years before Considerant again set foot on French soil, and over twenty before he could again call France his home.

V

The affair of June 13, 1849, came to be regarded as one of the great fiascoes in the history of the nineteenth-century French left. During the six months that followed the election of Louis-Napoleon as president, the left had been gaining strength both in the country at large and in the National Assembly. Democrats had won victories in by-elections; they had developed a peasant policy; and they had won over 35 percent of the vote in the legislative elections of March 1849. They were still far from achieving a parliamentary majority, but they had begun to establish themselves in a large part of rural France. Thus liberals and radicals throughout France were cheered by the election results.

At just this moment in England, John Stuart Mill could express delight that "the number of the Montagne or red republican party (who are now all socialists) have increased fourfold." Mill was suspicious of some of the leaders of the French left—notably Proudhon, whom he described as a "firebrand" and "the most mischievous man in Europe," but he found "a great source of hope for France" in the fact that "the most powerful and active section of the socialists are the Fourierists headed by Considerant, who are much the most sensible and enlightened both in the destructive, and in the constructive parts of their system, and are eminently pacific."[45]

At this point, however, with so many hopes invested in them, the leaders of the Mountain went outside the Assembly and threatened insurrection, appealing for popular support for an ambiguously defined mass demonstration. Did they seek to overthrow the Legislative Assembly? This aim was clearly implied in Considerant's proposal that the members of the opposition declare themselves a rump assembly. However, Considerant was also adamant in his rejection of the use of force. He seems to have assumed that if the Mountain took its stand in defense of the Constitution, popular support would come spontaneously and the challenge to the authority of the Legislative Assembly could be sustained without the use of force. But of course support did not come. If June 1848 had been a revolt of the masses without leaders, June 1849 was (as Marx and others noted) a revolt of leaders without masses.

As a result of June 13, the leadership of the Mountain was so easily dispersed and decimated that it was as if they had fallen into a trap. In fact, there was no trap. By threatening violence but planning only for a peaceful demonstration, they had set themselves up for failure. Whereas Considerant later spoke of June 13 as "a pacific, constitutional, and legal insurrection against the violators of the Constitution," Marx could deride the actions of the left as typical of petty bourgeois half-heartedness:

> If the Mountain wished to triumph in parliament, it should not have called to arms. If it called to arms in parliament, it should not have acted in parliamentary fashion on the streets. If the peaceful demonstration was seriously intended, then it was folly not to foresee that it would be given a warlike reception. If a real struggle was intended, then it was a queer idea to lay down the weapons with which it must be waged.

Similarly Proudhon could write derisively of the June 13 demonstration as "inopportune, politically inept, [and] badly led." Alexander Herzen, who participated in the street demonstration, could leave an unforgettable picture of the revolutionary "choristers" of June 13 who boasted of the fact that they "had no plan." As Herzen caustically summed up their strategy: "Inspiration was to descend upon them as the Holy Ghost once descended upon the heads of the apostles. There was only one point on which all were agreed—*to come to the meeting-place unarmed.*"[46]

If contemporaries on the left believed that the Mountain had fallen into a trap on June 13, right-wing observers were convinced that the "insurrection" was the outcome of a carefully laid plot against the government and that the attack on Rome gave the plotters the "pretext" they needed. This was the prosecution's argument in the trial of the Montagnards that finally took place in October.[47] In the immediate aftermath of June 13, though, what the right found most noteworthy was the farcical conclusion of the *journée*. For weeks right-wing journals were full of stories concerning the inglorious manner in which the leaders had allegedly saved themselves. The chief butt of these stories was Ledru-Rollin, and the press had a field day speculating as to how this portly politician could ever have escaped, as was reported, via a transom. But Considerant, too, had been compromised. Some of his supporters found it hard to believe that he could have actually participated in this challenge to the authority of the Legislative Assembly of which he was himself a member. More generally, many Fourierists who had already been complaining about the politicization of the movement saw the events of June 13 as the logical outcome of the *démoc-soc* alliance, and some of them were bitterly angry at Considerant.[48]

Echoes of the split within the Fourierist movement concerning Considerant's political activity can be found in the defensive tone of a printed letter sent out by the Conseil de direction of the Ecole Sociétaire on June 21. Although the authors of this letter did not in any way criticize Considerant (or François Cantagrel or Allyre Bureau, who had also participated in the June 13 events), their carefully chosen phrases did seem to be responding to anticipated criticism.

> In our epoch of general transformation, it is impossible to remain isolated from political agitation. Never to compromise ourselves in defending the rights of citizens or the independence of nations, to take refuge in the most technical parts of Phalansterian theory while the European Revolution is going on—these are commitments we never made and could never have kept. Such conduct would have isolated us in France.

The remaining Fourierist leaders argued that they had had no choice— moral or political—but to support the movement of protest against the government's Roman expedition, but they hesitated to say what the outcome might be. "The future will tell," they wrote, "if we gained or lost through our involvement in political debates."[49]

Considerant's initial assessment of the significance of June 13 was much more unambiguously positive than that of his Fourierist colleagues. In a long article written less than a month after the events, he argued that although June 13 was obviously "a blow" to the left in general and to the Fourierists in particular, its long-term consequence would be to leave the Fourierists "much stronger" than before. How could the Fourierists have possibly *gained* anything from the events of June 13? Considerant's view was that they had now acquired "the solid sympathy of everyone in France and in Europe who belongs to the party of the future and of the people."[50]

For a long time, Considerant explained, the Fourierist movement had suffered from its own isolation and from the fact that its ideas had been presented to the public in a way that seemed "too scientific," too far ahead of the time. The main result of the previous year and a half had been to end that isolation—to give the Fourierist movement a relatively wide base of support among "the intelligent and healthy section of the bourgeoisie." No longer "an isolated *école*," the Fourierists were now "a major element in the liberating movement" that embraced the entire democratic and socialist left. How had this been possible? Considerant described the Fourierists' abandonment of narrow and sectarian propaganda and their active participation, after June 1848, in the *démoc-soc* alliance as wise tactical moves that gave their ideas a resonance previously lacking. Yet in Considerant's view the central reason for the improved prospects of Fourierism was the fact that events since February 1848 had dramatically served to expose the "illusory" character of the republican faith in universal suffrage.[51]

In outlining his position, Considerant recalled an argument that he and Godefroy Cavaignac ("the real Cavaignac") had had in 1831. When Considerant had insisted on the necessity of proposing economic and social initiatives to deal with the social question, Cavaignac had replied that "universal suffrage is fecund by itself. All the necessary solutions will emerge spontaneously from its womb." This statement by Cavaignac epitomized, in Considerant's view, "the illusion in which the whole party of simplistic republicans was long steeped." What were the results of universal suffrage, though? Here Considerant replied sarcastically:

> Universal suffrage has given us the Constituent and Legislative Assemblies. The Executive Commission, the dictatorship of Cavaignac, the presidency of M. Louis Bonaparte, the ministries of Falloux-Faucher-Barrot and Barrot-Falloux-Dufaure, the two states of siege, and the reaction have all emerged from the womb of universal suffrage. What lovely solutions to social questions![52]

The collapse of what Considerant called "simplistic republicanism," together with the fact that the Fourierists had played an important role in the *démoc-soc* coalition, had gained them both a larger following and a sort of moral authority that they had not previously enjoyed.

> The Ecole Sociétaire is today at the forefront of the democratic movement as it was at the forefront of the socialist ideas that have transformed Europe from top to bottom in the past eighteen years. [Our

Ecole] has acquired moral authority and the sympathy of the masses. The time of trials is also the time of proofs. . . . For us the moment has come. Today we have only to speak to be listened to sympathetically and, as a consequence, understood and followed. Twenty years of labor and of dedication have prepared the way for us.[53]

Finally, Considerant believed that the great benefit of June 13 was that it gave moral authority to the losers. Because their cause was just, because they had been defeated while defending the constitution, they now had "only to speak to be listened to sympathetically."

How wrong Considerant was. Not only was he exaggerating the power of ideas and moral convictions to move people to action; he was also ignoring or minimizing the *equivocal* character of the role he and his allies had played on June 13. Yes, their enemies had supported an unconstitutional attack on the integrity of the Roman Republic. Considerant and his allies were defending a good cause. However, they had sought to challenge their enemies by taking to the street, by threatening to bring down the Legislative Assembly, the ministry, the government (it wasn't clear) through the use of (in Ledru's words) armed force. The equivocal character of the protest itself made it difficult for Considerant and the Montagnards to hold the moral high ground they sought to claim.

Considerant's response to all this would probably have been, first of all, to concede that Ledru-Rollin was wrong to threaten violence and, secondly, to argue that in any case violence was not necessary. The violation of the Constitution and of the basic respect owed by one republic to another was so evident that the rational and moral citizens of the Second French Republic could not fail to support the Mountain. This faith in the basic rationality and goodness of the majority, which had led Considerant to call the June Days of 1848 a "misunderstanding," received a greater blow on June 13, 1849.

1. Salins in the romantic period. The town in the time of Considerant's youth, protected by its two forts, Fort Belin on the left and Fort St. André on the right. Engraving by Boullenier. Photo by University of California at Santa Cruz Photographic
Services.

2. Clarisse Vigoureux. Oil portrait by Jules Laure. AN 10AS 35 (1). Photo by Service Photographique des Archives Nationales.

3. Julie Vigoureux. Self-portrait in charcoal, probably dating from the years when she and Considerant first knew each other. Photo courtesy of Musée Historique du Palais Granvelle, Besançon.

4. Victor Considerant with Julie and Clarisse
Vigoureux. Julie is on the right with light hair.
Pen and ink sketch in a letter from Considerant
to Clarisse Vigoureux, October 8, 1835. Photo
by University of California at Santa Cruz Photographic Services.

5. Charles Nodier's salon at the Bibliothèque de l'Arsenal. Considerant was a habi-
tué of this salon, which was a gathering place for writers and artists from Franche-
Comté and a focal point of the romantic movement in France. Engraving by Tony
Johannot. Photo by University of California at Santa Cruz Photographic Services.

6. Charles Fourier. Lithograph by Cisneros after the portrait by Gigoux. Photo from Cabinet des Estampes, Bibliothèque Nationale.

7. Just Muiron in old age. AN 10AS 35 (2). Photo by Service Photographique des Archives Nationales.

JOURNAL DE L'ÉCOLE SOCIÉTAIRE

FAISANT SUITE AU JOURNAL

LE PHALANSTÈRE ou LA RÉFORME INDUSTRIELLE (1832-1834).

LA

PHALANGE

JOURNAL DE LA SCIENCE SOCIALE

DÉCOUVERTE ET CONSTITUÉE

PAR

CHARLES FOURIER.

Industrie, Politique, Sciences, Art et Littérature.

TOME I.

IDÉE D'UN PHALANSTÈRE.

Habitation d'une PHALANGE de 400 à 500 familles associées en fonctions de
Agriculture, ménage, fabriques, éducation, art, sciences, etc.;
Remplaçant, dans l'ORDRE SOCIÉTAIRE, les 400 à 500 constructions incohérentes,
maisons, masures, granges, étables, etc.,
d'une bourgade de 1800 à 2000 habitants dans l'ORDRE MORCELÉ actuel.

PARIS

AU BUREAU DE LA PHALANGE, RUE JACOB, N° 54.

1836-1837

8. Victor Considerant's design for a Phalanstery. *La Phalange,* volume 1, 1836. Courtesy of Kress Library, Harvard University. Photo by Harvard University Library Reproduction Services.

9. A Fourierist Phalanx, about 1845. The main building, or Phalanstery, still looks rather like the Palace of Versailles, as it did in Considerant's earlier image. Now, though, it is surrounded by symbols of modernity—a factory, a smokestack, a railroad train (in the distance), and a side-wheeler steamboat. Note the Gothic church just beyond the Phalanstery. At this time, many Fourierists were eager to emphasize the harmony between Fourierism and Christianity. Charles Fourier is seated on the bench in the lower righthand corner, a benign and paternal presence. Lithograph by Proudhomme after a drawing by Charles Daubigny. Photo by Harvard University Library Reproduction Services. By permission of the Houghton Library, Harvard University.

10. A fifty-franc share in the Joint Stock Company for the Spread and Realization of the Theory of Charles Fourier, made out to Félix Beuque of Lyon, brother of Aimée Beuque. AN 10AS 29 (2). Photo by Service Photographique des Archives Nationales.

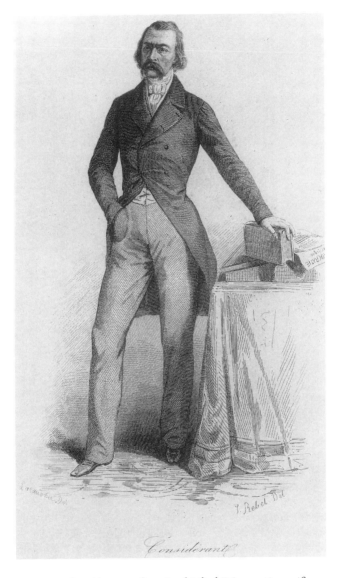

11. Victor Considerant, editor-in-chief of *Démocratie pacifique*.
Engraving by Lacauchie and Rebel. Photo courtesy of Roger-
Viollet.

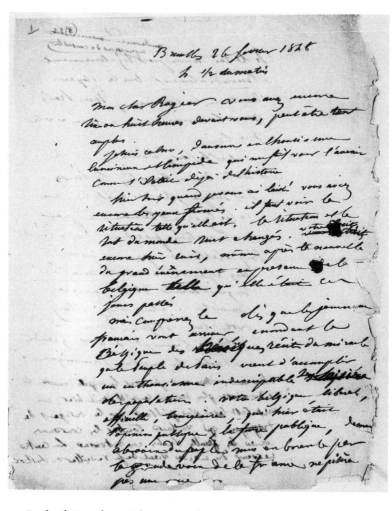

12. Draft of Considerant's letter to Belgian Interior Minister Charles Rogier, Brussels, February 26, 1848, 4:30 AM. Considerant had just learned of the February Revolution in Paris. He tells his friend that monarchy is finished in Belgium and all of Europe. He describes himself as "calm, in a state of luminous and limpid enthusiasm" that permits him "to see the future as if it were already history." AN 10AS 28 (8). Photo by Service Photographique des Archives Nationales.

13. French National Assembly in 1848. The Assembly met in a huge, barnlike hall that had been hastily constructed in a courtyard of the Palais Bourbon. Adjacent to the old Chamber of Deputies, the new hall had to accommodate an Assembly of almost nine hundred *représentants du peuple.* This illustration gives some sense of the cavernous nature of the hall and the problem any speaker must have had in making himself heard. Engraving by Edouard Renard. Photo courtesy of Roger-Viollet.

14. "The Carnival of Ideas" by Bertall. *Le Journal pour rire*, October 14, 1848. In this cartoon, which appeared during the period of reaction between the June insurrection and the election of Louis-Napoleon Bonaparte as president of the republic on December 10, 1948, Considerant is depicted, along with Proudhon, Cabet, Leroux, and Louis Blanc, as a carnival barker hawking his nostrum for "assured happiness." To leave no doubt about his own opinion of the schemes being advertised, Bertall includes at the far end of the line of salesmen the figure of Robert Macaire, the shyster and con man brought to life on the French stage by Frédéric Lemaître. Photo by University of California at Santa Cruz Photographic Services.

Charles Fourier believed that in the happy and harmonious societies of the future the human body would undergo a series of striking physical changes. Men and women would grow seven feet tall and live to the age of 144. They would acquire replaceable teeth, more refined senses, and the ability to breathe under water. The most remarkable physical change that Fourier predicted was the growth of a new member, a long tail with a small hand at its extremity. This tail, or *archibras*, would serve as both a tool and a weapon, and it would render life immensely more interesting and exciting for its possessors.

Although Fourier lovingly described in his manuscripts "the precious attributes of this member without which the human body is truly stunted," he never referred to it in print. His followers were equally circumspect. When in the aftermath of the Parisian insurrection of June 1848 they published Fourier's manuscript on "The Regeneration of the Human Body," they simply omitted the passage describing the *archibras*. They were too late, however. Word of this remarkable Fourierist prophecy was already out.

French journalists seem to have discovered Fourier's *archibras* around 1840. Enough had been said about it by 1843 that Balzac could include it in his *Monographie de la presse parisienne* as one of the "extravagances" of contemporary social thought with which "the Wag, second variety of minor Parisian journalist," could earn ten francs a day entertaining his readers. The "Fourierist tail" had also entered the oral tradition. In his *Souvenirs de jeunesse*, the Alsatian republican Auguste Scheurer-Kestner recalled that in 1842, when Victor Considerant came to Mulhouse to lecture, so much had already been said at the family dinner table about the Fourierist tail that he and his brother (aged nine and eight) fully expected Considerant to have one himself. "We saw looming up in our home a sort of giant with long mustaches, eating and drinking like a normal person. As for his tail, we walked round and round him, but we couldn't find it."

It was during the Second Republic that the Fourierist tail became permanently associated with Victor Considerant. Like Proudhon, Pierre Leroux, and several of the other socialist leaders, Considerant was the target of numerous cartoonists in 1848 and 1849. In the cartoons of Daumier, Bertall, Cham, and many others, Considerant was represented as a tall, thin man with flowing hair and *moustaches gauloises*—normal in all respects except one: a long tail extended out from under his coat, and at the end of that tale was a large round eye. The eye was the cartoonists' invention—not Fourier's and certainly not Considerant's—but it became a permanent feature of Considerant's tail. In the cartoons reproduced here we see the eye eyeing Considerant, we see Considerant using his extra eye to keep a close watch on his enemy, Adolphe Thiers, and we see the tail put to practical use in helping a Californian Considerant mine gold. All of this was irritating to Considerant at the time, but in his more serene old age he was simply amused. As he told an interviewer at the age of eighty-two, "None of this keeps the grain from growing or socialism from advancing."

CONSIDÉRANT,
représentant du peuple et du phata tère.

Considérez *Considérant,*
Considérant qu'on considère;

Considéré *Considérant,*
Considérant vous considère.

15. Victor Considerant, Representative of the People. Considerant is shown astride a pail of milk. The pail reads: "Sea of milk. Read Fourier." This is an allusion to Fourier's prophecy that in the era of "Full Harmony" the sea's salt water would become a sweet-tasting drinkable fluid. Cartoon by H. Emy, *Le Journal pour rire*, November 4, 1848, reprinted in *Bêtisorama ou le socialisme, le communisme, le fouriérisme et les autres folies de notre époque* (Paris, 1849). Photo by Harvard University Library Reproduction Services. By permission of the Houghton Library, Harvard University.

VICTOR CONSIDERANT.

Dessiné d'après nature à la tribune le jour mémorable où orné de tous les attributs d'un disciple de Fourrier, et prenant la pose de l'anti-lion, il chercha à phalanstériser tous les membres de l'assemblée nationale.

16. Considerant addressing the National Assembly, September 13, 1848. The caption reads: "Victor Considerant. Drawn from nature at the rostrum on the memorable day when, endowed with all the attributes of a disciple of Fourrier [sic], and striking the pose of an *anti-lion*, he seeks to phalansterize all the members of the National Assembly." Lithograph by Daumier. Photo by University of California at Santa Cruz Photographic Services.

M. Victor Considerant ayant la chance de se voir tout à coup gratifié d'une organisation phalanstérienne avant les temps prédits par Fourier!

17. Considerant sprouts a "Fourierist tail" before the time predicted by Fourier. Cartoon by Cham (Amédée de Noé), *Folies du jour. Caricatures politiques et sociales*, Paris, 1849, p. 8. Photo by Harvard University Library Reproduction Services. By permission of the Houghton Library, Harvard University.

Les Phalanstériens trouvant moyen d'utiliser leur queue en Californie pour l'extraction des blocs d'or.

18. Considerant uses his tail to mine gold in California. Cartoon by Cham, *Coups de crayon*, Paris, 1849, p. 5. Photo by Harvard University Library Reproduction Services. By permission of the Houghton Library, Harvard University.

M Victor Considérant profitant de son organisation phalanstérienne
pour surveiller M. Thiers de sa place.

19. The tail enables Considerant to keep a watchful eye on his enemy, Adolphe
Thiers. Cartoon by Cham, *Folies du jour. Caricatures politiques et sociales*, Paris,
1849, p. 8. Photo by University of California at Santa Cruz Photographic Services.

Proudhon et Considerant savent fort bien qu'ils ne peuvent se digérer ni l'un ni l'autre, et pourtant ils cherchent à se dévorer mutuellement.... Étrange aberration sociale ! ! !

20. Considerant and Proudhon fight it out. The caption reads: "Proudhon and Considerant know very well that neither one can digest the other. Nonetheless each seeks to devour the other. . . . A strange social aberration!!" Cartoon by Bertall, *Le Journal pour rire,* February 24, 1849, reprinted in *Bêtisorama.* Photo by Harvard University Library Reproduction Services. By permission of the Houghton Library, Harvard University.

LA MONTAGNE, ASSEMBLÉE NATIONALE.

1 Pierre Bonaparte.
2 Théodore Bac.
3 Ledru-Rollin.
4 Félix Pyat.
5 Lamennais.
6 Démosthènes Olivier.
7 Flocon.
8 Marc Caussidière.
9 Mathieu de la Drôme.
10 F. V. Raspail.
11 Armand Barbès.
12 T. Lagrange.
13 Martin-Bernard.
14 Baune.
15 Duvignier.
16 Pelletier.
17 Greppo.
18 Victor Considérant.
19 Albert.
20 Proudhon.
21 Louis Blanc.
22 Schœlcher.
23 A. Guinard.
24 David d'Angers.
25 Louisy Mathieu.
26 James Demontry.
27 Germain Sarrut.
28 Pierre Leroux.
29 Etienne Arago.
30 Audry de Puigraveau.

A Lyon, chez Pézard J. Edit, rue de l'Humanité 2. — Dépot.

21. Thirty leading members of the Mountain in the Constituent Assembly, 1849. This lithograph probably dates from the first months of 1849. It includes Considerant, even though he did not formally identify himself with the Mountain until after the legislative elections of May 1849. Photo courtesy of Roger-Viollet.

22. The *Journée* of June 13, 1849. Ledru-Rollin harangues the crowd in front of the Conservatoire des Arts et Métiers. There is a more substantial working-class presence in the crowd than most of the sources suggest. Wood engraving from *L'Illustration*. Photo by University of California at Santa Cruz Photographic Services.

23. Considerant in exile. Oil portrait by Amédée Bourson painted in Brussels, probably not long before Considerant's departure for Texas, c.1854. Photo courtesy of
Musée Historique du Palais Granvelle, Besançon.

24. Broadway in 1850. The carriages and fine ladies in hoop skirts contribute to a rather genteel image of the city, but the buildings were all part of the city as Considerant first saw it: Astor House, one of America's first luxury hotels, on the right; P. T. Barnum's museum with its illustrated billboards on the left; Trinity Church (the spire in the distance); and St. Paul's Chapel (the columned façade). Lithograph by Deroy, after August Köllner. Eno Collection, Miriam and Ira D. Wallach Division of Art, Prints and Photographs, The New York Public Library. By permission of The New York Public Library.

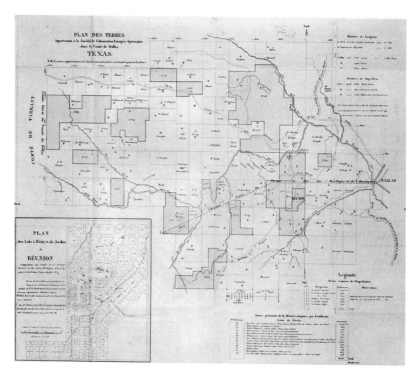

25. Reunion, Texas, about 1856, showing the landholdings and building sites at Reunion. The colony was located on a bluff overlooking the Trinity River in what is now West Dallas, between Westmoreland and Hampton roads. Map issued by the European-American Colonization Society in Paris. Photo by Harvard University Library Reproduction Services. By permission of the Houghton Library, Harvard University.

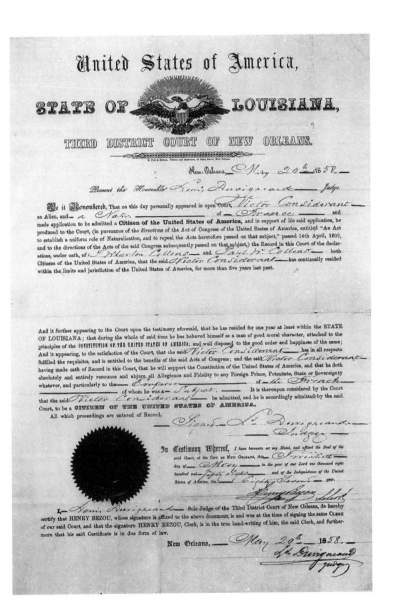

26. Considerant's U.S. citizen's papers issued at New Orleans, May 20, 1858. The document includes several false statements concerning the length of Considerant's residence in the United States and Louisiana. AN 10AS 29 (2). Photo by Service Photographique des Archives Nationales.

27. The Considerants' house along the San Antonio River near the Mission la Concepción just outside San Antonio. This was their home throughout most of the 1860s. This drawing by James Wells Champney originally appeared in *Scribner's Magazine* in the early 1870s and was later published in Edward S. King, *The Great South* (Hartford, Ct., 1875), 156. Photo by University of California at Santa Cruz Photographic Services.

Agave Consideranti (au tiers de grandeur naturelle).

28. Considerant's cactus, the *Agave Consideranti,* which he probably found near Monterrey (Nuevo Léon) on his trip through northern Mexico in 1863. Considerant brought one of these cacti back to France and exhibited it at the annual meeting of the Société Centrale d'Horticulture de France in 1872. From E.-A. Carrière, "Agave Consideranti," *Revue horticole,* 47 (1875), 427–430. Photo by University of California at Santa Cruz Photographic Services.

29. Considerant on his return to France in 1869. Considerant's "Fourierist tail" is not forgotten. Having acquired the properties of a hose, it waters the tree of liberty. Caricature by Job in André Gill's satirical journal *L'Eclipse,* October 3, 1869. Photo by University of California at Santa Cruz Photographic Services.

30. Considerant in his seventies. This may be the photograph
he sent to Désirée Véret, who asked for another with a less
"heartbroken expression." Cabinet photograph. AN 10AS 34.
Photo by Service Photographique des Archives Nationales.

31. Considerant in the Texan-Mexican garb of his last years. Wood engraving based on a *carte de visite* photograph. Photo by University of California at Santa Cruz Photographic Services.

ᶜTOR CONSIDÉRANT DANS SON CABINET DE TRAVAIL. — (Dessin d'après nature de M. MOULIGNIÉ

(Le Monde Illustré du 6 Janvier 1894.)

32. Considerant in his study. Lithograph based on a drawing by Moulignié, published in *Le Monde illustré,* January 6, 1894, shortly after Considerant's death. AN 10AS 29 (3). Photo by Service Photographique des Archives Nationales.

12

Belgian Exile

In June 1849 Considerant was still just forty years old. His life was not yet half over. His role in French public life, however, was finished. Ahead of him lay twenty years of exile and an even longer period of retirement in France after that. He was not, of course, in any position to know the future; like many other socialists and republicans who took the road to exile between 1848 and 1851, Considerant did not expect the Party of Order to remain in power for very long. He said so bluntly in a letter to the French foreign minister, Alexis de Tocqueville, written shortly after his arrival in Brussels. Although he was writing to ask a favor, he could not resist taunting Tocqueville:

> You will last for two or three months perhaps, and the pure Whites who will follow you are good for six months at the longest. Both of you, it is true, will have completely deserved what you will infallibly get sooner or later. But let us talk no more politics and respect the very legal, loyal, and Odilon Barrotesque state of siege.[1]

Tocqueville cited this letter in his *Souvenirs* of 1848 as an example of the "natural querulousness and conceit" of the Montagnards. What it more obviously expresses is the strength of Considerant's faith in the ultimate triumph of his cause.

The same tone of assurance pervaded Considerant's first public statement on the meaning of the failed insurrection of June 13. This was the pamphlet entitled *Simples explications à mes amis et à mes commettants*, which he wrote while still in hiding and published in Brussels on July 5. Ever since the French Revolution, he argued, a "new world of justice and liberty" had been emerging invincibly out of the old world of privilege, oppression, and exploitation. A "necessary and irresistible transformation" was taking place, which the privileged classes were powerless to halt. In the context of this great historical movement, the defeat of June 13 was simply a momentary reverse, a "little accident of the struggle." Humanity was marching toward "radiant horizons." He could write that he had never felt within himself "a faith more luminous" or "a certainty more calm, more limpid, and more complete" in the imminent triumph of "the holy cause."[2]

Considerant was never entirely to lose this confidence in the future, although the grounds for his optimism were to change, as was his conception of the distance to be traveled to reach the "radiant horizons." In the meantime, however, he had to deal with the practical problems of exile.

I

One consequence of the reaction that began in France with the crushing of the June 1848 insurrection was the massive exodus of radical republicans and socialists forced into exile in England, Switzerland, or Belgium. Many of these exiles had played important roles in the political and cultural life of their countries. Once abroad, however, they were, as two American historians have put it, "reduced to the status of journalists without newspapers, speakers without rostrums, politicians without parties, and patriots without a country."[3]

Along with London and Geneva, Brussels had one of the most important communities of French political exiles in the mid-nineteenth century. Proudhon, Victor Hugo, Edgar Quinet, and Etienne Arago were among the best known of the French republicans and socialists to seek refuge in the Belgian capital during the years 1848–1852, but the events of June 13, 1849, and especially December 2, 1851, brought many other French radicals to Belgium in search of political asylum. Some of these refugees became permanent residents of Brussels, joining the French exile community, which gathered regularly in the cafés lining the passage Saint-Hubert. For many more, Brussels was only a way station on the road to a permanent place of exile. Some, like Ledru-Rollin, Louis Blanc, and Armand Barbès, were denied the right to settle anywhere in Belgium; others like Considerant himself were assigned to provincial towns, but only on condition that they report regularly to the Belgian authorities.[4]

The Belgian government's reluctance to give asylum to all who sought it is not hard to understand. Neither the Belgian monarchy nor Belgian independence were well established; both had come into being only in 1830. The Belgian government was justifiably wary about the intentions of both the French government and the radical opposition in France. In late March 1848, in the so-called Risquons-Tout affair, French radicals including Caussidière and possibly Ledru-Rollin and Charles Delescluze had attempted to foment a republican insurrection in Belgium. This was a fiasco, and in 1849 a repeat seemed hardly likely. Nonetheless, the Belgian authorities remained suspicious of all radicals, and many of those who were allowed to reside in Belgium were placed under police surveillance and denied the right to publish or to participate in public meetings.

Considerant had good reason to hope for special treatment at the hands of the Belgian authorities. Unlike most political refugees, he had a wide circle of friends and admirers in Belgium, many of them known to him since the time of his great lecture series at Brussels in 1845. Some, like Philippe Bourson, the liberal editor of the official government newspaper, *Le Moniteur belge*, were influential members of the Belgian establishment. Of course Charles Rogier, an old friend if no longer a close one, was a member of the government. Considerant had his mail held for him by Bourson, and he probably spent some time with the Bourson family on his arrival at Brussels. However, it was to Rogier that he went to make arrangements concerning his future and also that of his companions in exile, Ledru-Rollin, Martin Bernard, and Etienne Arago.[5]

What Considerant learned in talking to Rogier was that his companions would not be granted political asylum. Ledru-Rollin in particular was "too troublesome a fish" for the government.[6] Considerant himself was to be granted asylum in Belgium—provided he kept a low profile. A year later, in a bitter letter to Rogier, Considerant recalled their first conversation in July:

> Your first words upon my arrival in Belgium were fine and friendly: "I was expecting you. I've talked things over with my colleagues. I don't wish a representative, you above all, to be troubled here." That was the old Rogier. Then the timorous, uncertain equivocator had to add: "Be prudent. Don't attract attention. . . ." and other advice which was just as useless for a man whom you know to be respectful of the proprieties, reluctant to make a spectacle of himself, and completely unconspiratorial.[7]

Considerant found Rogier's language insulting, but he promptly accepted the offer of political asylum with the understanding that he would find a place to live somewhere in the countryside in French-speaking Belgium.

After about a week in Brussels, Considerant left for the resort of Spa, where he planned to spend some time with Alexandre Delhasse, a retired geology professor who with his brother Félix had been one of the most ardent Fourierists of the 1840s.[8] On the way, Considerant spent several days exploring the Ardennes, taking lodgings in the village of Coo in the province of Liège, visiting the Cascade de l'Emblève, doing a little writing and a lot of fishing, and looking in the area around Malmédy and Stavelot for a place where he, Julie, and her mother might settle down. He needed tranquillity and, as he wrote later, it was exhilarating for him to wander footloose in the Ardennes. "The mountains, which I hadn't seen for a long time, gave me the wanderlust, to which I gave in, recognizing in myself a real need for fresh air, rain, sunshine, and movement."[9]

On July 19 Considerant arrived at Spa. He was still traveling under a false name, though now it was not Dauphin but Saisenay. (This was the name of a village in the Jura, not far from Salins.) A few days later he received the visit of the police commissioner of Spa, who politely asked to see his papers. Considerant replied that his papers were in Brussels but that Delhasse and others could vouch for him. The commissioner seemed satisfied, but Considerant soon discovered that both he and his comrade François Cantagrel (who had also fled to Belgium after June 13) had been placed under police surveillance.[10] He was furious. He immediately fired off a bitterly sarcastic letter to his "friend," the "timid and timorous" minister of the interior, Charles Rogier. "I am not just anybody," he wrote. "I am known and, I dare say, respected and even loved by many people in Belgium." Boasting that he could, if need be, produce "a thousand" letters of reference—including, he was sure, one from Rogier himself—Considerant observed that in Belgium, as in most other European countries, foreigners were naturally outside the law. Still he believed that he and Cantagrel had the moral right to protest special police surveillance. He told Rogier that he would prefer a formal notice of expulsion rather than endure petty and unreasonable harassment by the Belgian police.[11] In fact, Considerant was not expelled, but he was to undergo much more harassment.

While staying at Spa with Alexandre Delhasse, one of Considerant's tasks was to find a place to live suitable for Julie and Clarisse Vigoureux. He quickly ruled out Spa, which he described to Julie as "expensive and boring." For a while he thought of Charleroi, where he had cousins, whom he visited in late August; a police report on August 27 noted his presence at Charleroi and warned that his purpose was probably "to foment disturbances" among the democrats of the area. (In fact, he spent most of his time at Charleroi fishing.) Finally he settled on Laroche, an "isolated little hole" in the Ardennes about fifty kilometers south of Spa. By the end of August he had found an inn there where the three of them could stay comfortably and economically for a month while looking for a permanent residence. Early in September he set out to meet Julie and Clarisse Vigoureux at the frontier.[12]

As a result of the events of June 13, Considerant still enjoyed some notoriety in Belgium: his movements were news. On September 7, journals in Brussels and Liège informed their readers that two days earlier Considerant had been seen traversing the town of Saint-Hubert "in the company of two ladies" in a carriage "laden with trunks and packages." In a register that he had been given to sign he had identified himself as "Victor Considerant, représentant du peuple," and had melodramatically given his domicile as "Everywhere, except France."[13]

The month that Victor, Julie, and Clarisse Vigoureux spent together at Laroche turned out to be a very happy time for them all. Clarisse, who had fallen into a state of deep depression after Victor's flight, now, for the first time since June, began to talk about the future with some optimism. As for Julie, she had never really felt at home in Paris, and she left the capital without regret. She was delighted to be reunited with her husband and even more delighted that for the first time in years she had him to herself. As her cousin, Clarisse Coignet, put it later, the "storms" that marked Victor's public life during their years together in Paris had made it impossible for Julie to "possess" him fully and had left her in a state of more or less permanent anxiety as she watched him exhaust himself in journalism and political struggle. "Here at least she [could] devote herself fully to his needs," knowing that her efforts would make a difference.[14]

For his part Victor was still optimistic about the future, and he claimed to have no regrets about the past. "One doesn't regret having done one's duty," he wrote his brother Gustave in September. At the same time, in a long article in *Démocratie pacifique* explaining why he did not intend to return to France to face trial, he restated his faith that humanity would ultimately reach the promised land of socialism. He recognized that this would take time and struggle. For the moment he was content to lie low in the Ardennes and regain his strength. If he sometimes referred to Laroche as a backwater, in writing his brother he described it in almost idyllic terms. "Right now we are perched in a mountain village in the middle of the Ardennes with great rocks and deep valleys and clear and limpid lakes . . . with lots of trout, like those of our Jura." In fact, Considerant's main activity during this period seems to have been trout fishing.[15]

II

Considerant originally planned to stay at Laroche through the end of the year. In mid-October, however, he moved back to Brussels. He wanted to be in closer communication with Paris while the trial of the participants in the June 13 "conspiracy" was going on. On October 13, the first day of the trial, he, Julie, and Clarisse Vigoureux took up residence at 11, place des Barricades, in Brussels. This stay in Brussels began inauspiciously. Considerant's first letters to Paris were full of complaints about the "detestable" dinner hours at Brussels, the poor tobacco, his headaches, his spleen, his inability to work.[16] In fact, he seems to have fallen into a state of lethargy and depression connected with feelings of anger and frustration and perhaps also guilt provoked by the trial at Versailles.

Considerant had already explained publicly his reasons for refusing to return to France to face trial. He saw no purpose in allowing himself to be judged by a government whose legitimacy he denied. Nevertheless it was painful for him to sit helplessly by in Brussels while friends like Allyre Bureau were facing their accusers and while he himself was being judged *in absentia*. In the end Bureau was acquitted. Considerant's own conviction, which was announced on November 15, could not have come as a surprise. Indeed, his spirits seem to have improved as soon as the trial was over.

Considerant's stay in Brussels lasted until April 1850. For these six months he was closely involved in the life of the radical emigré community in Brussels and was in daily contact with François Cantagrel. At the same time he cemented ties with a number of Belgian radicals who were to remain his friends for the rest of his life. One of these was the lawyer Adolphe Demeur, who was, over the next forty years, often to serve as Considerant's host during his visits to Brussels. Another was the army officer Hippolyte Colignon, a professor of artillery at the Belgian Ecole Militaire who became notorious in Belgian military circles both for his close relations with Considerant and as "the chief of the democrats in the army." Considerant, Colignon, Cantagrel, and others often met at a café in Brussels, the Café des Trois Suisses, which became an important rendez-vous for French and Italian political refugees.[17]

Considerant's regular meetings with Colignon and others soon became known to the Belgian police, and on March 1, 1850, the minister of justice asked the administrator of public security to have Considerant placed under special surveillance. In addition to publishing political articles in *Démocratie pacifique,* some of which were reprinted in the Belgian press, Considerant was behaving in provocative ways, the minister noted: "I am informed that Monsieur Considerant regularly frequents the Café des Trois Suisses near the theater, and that he talks very freely there about the political affairs of France and Belgium." Shortly thereafter Considerant received word from Charles Rogier that his continued presence in the Belgian capital had become an embarrassment. "The minister told me that I was a nightmare for him," wrote Considerant sarcastically to Allyre Bureau. "I am denounced every day as a terrible danger to him, to the king, and to his august family."[18] At about the same time Considerant wrote a long letter to "His Excellency, my friend, the brave minister of the interior," making fun of his timorousness while sarcastically reviewing the charges against him:

> I'm a great criminal. After having tried to overthrow the government of the Republic of France and having rebelled against a constitution for which I voted, I received the hospitality of Belgium. How did I express my gratitude to this country? By the blackest acts of ingratitude.
>
> First of all, under the false pretext of a love of mountains, clear streams, and fishing, I ran around Luxembourg trying to sound out the population and to ready them for a French and demagogical invasion. That's been proved.
>
> When I came back to Brussels in the winter, I made use of my anarchic pen to declare war [against Belgium]. . . . I organized meetings of workers at Charleroi. I harangued them. I stirred up their evil passions. . . .
>
> At Brussels I'm a notorious habitué of the Café des Trois Suisses. I gather crowds of workers there. I carry on inflammatory conversations at the café and I play chess—a game of perfidious and revolutionary symbolism that is no more than a permanent conspiracy against kings and queens. . . . I'm living on the place *des Barricades!* Isn't that pretty significant.

As hardened a criminal as he was, Considerant did not wish to be "a ceaseless and cruel nightmare" for Rogier. He had resolved to spare his old friend further pain by leaving Brussels in early April instead of waiting for the mild weather that May would bring. All he asked was permission to reside in Bouillon rather than returning to Laroche.

> I would be most happy to return to Laroche, but, *monsieur le ministre,* Laroche is the most out-of-the-way village in the Ardennes. My wife, who is almost always sick, and her aged mother still merit some consideration from my heart of stone. People have spoken to me of Bouillon as a small town sheltered from the north wind, receiving the warm rays

of the sun, and being the Nice or the Iles d'Hyères of Belgium. Bouillon also possesses a river, the Semois, which is rich in trout and even salmon, and by dint of pretending to be a passionate fisherman, I have wound up by getting hooked.

Considerant knew that there would be an objection to Bouillon: it was near the French frontier. Therefore he gave his word that he would abstain from all forms of provocative behavior and would seek to establish "no criminal relations" with the "reds" of France.[19]

In the end Considerant was given what amounted to a temporary residence permit in Bouillon. Barely a week after his arrival there on April 3, though, the administrator of public security was addressing new complaints to the minister of justice about Considerant's writings and his unwillingness "to enjoy Belgian hospitality in silence." The reports on Considerant submitted by the police chief at Bouillon showed no cause for alarm, and he himself claimed that he was careful to receive no compromising visitors. But on May 16 the French Ministry of Foreign Affairs made a formal request that Considerant be assigned another residence farther from the French frontier. The Belgian authorities immediately ordered Considerant to return to Laroche or face expulsion. One week later he was back in Laroche.[20]

Considerant hoped that his return to Laroche would put an end to his surveillance by the police. On the contrary, he was now placed under closer watch than ever; and the *bourgmestre* (mayor) of Laroche was ordered to submit a report on him every two weeks. This was more than he could stand. He dispatched a "last" angry letter to Rogier, denouncing his former friend's "lack of character," his "chronic indecision," his "incurable weakness," and his "miserable habits of fluctuation and maneuvering." The result of all this, he observed bitterly, was that the real head of the political police in Belgium was not Rogier, the interior minister, but rather his subordinate Hody, "the laughable counterfeit" of the French police chief Carlier, "who has brought to Laroche all the informer's tricks that his master uses at Paris." Considerant angrily criticized the methods of the Belgian police.

> To place me under surveillance in Laroche, the capital of brambles and briars, is just too much! All I do is work in my room until three o'clock; at four I go fishing, and I don't come back until bedtime. . . . This sort of surveillance goes beyond the ordinary limits for the police and reaches new heights of stupidity, grotesquery, and comedy.

What Considerant found particularly infuriating was that even his acquaintances at Laroche were placed under surveillance. One of them was an "inoffensive and taciturn" young road surveyor named Roger whom Considerant sometimes took fishing.

> He dines at our inn. He is my only companion, if I except a few children to whom I give fish-hooks and who are very fond of me. Well, I hadn't been here a week when we learned that an order had been given to four policemen . . . to keep watch on this functionary because of his relations with me.

Considerant made fun of the policemen who were so marginally literate that "it took them three quarters of an hour to read my residence permit." He would have been even more amused if he could have read the reports sent regularly to the Administration of Public Security by Goedert, the commander of the police brigade in Laroche. These reports made Considerant seem like a country gentleman on an extended vacation. It appeared that Considerant spent "whole days fishing, from morning til night," that he was "very moderate in conversation at his hotel and at dinner," that his conduct was "irreprehensible[sic]."[21]

Another view of Considerant from this period reinforces our image of the man as leading a life of leisure in which fishing loomed larger than politics. Clarisse Coignet, who visited Victor, Julie, and her aunt Clarisse several times during these years, described them as leading an "errant" life and spending time in "the prettiest spots in the Walloon countryside." Ordinarily they looked for "the most cheerful sites, near some affluent of the Meuse, and they made themselves at home there in a rustic inn without worrying about the lack of ease and comfort." Clarisse Vigoureux, who was already in her sixties, did not find this new life easy to adapt to, but she never complained. For his part "Victor hardly noticed" his mother-in-law's discomfort, and "Julie worried only about Victor."[22]

In her biography of Considerant, Clarisse Coignet went on to describe a fishing expedition on which she and Julie accompanied Victor.

> I can still see them setting out at daybreak. . . . Victor, in country clothing, his knapsack on his back, his rod on his shoulder, leads the way; and his wife and I follow him courageously, often for hours on end, across hills and fields. A peasant accompanies us, carrying the fishing tackle and our lunch. We stop at the banks of a stream or river at a carefully chosen spot. While the fisherman gets to work, Julie and I settle down at a little distance so as not to distract him. Julie takes out her sketchbook and her crayons and I my tapestry, and our chatter doesn't stop. Toward midday the peasant, who has gone off in search of wild berries and dry wood, comes back loaded down and lights the fire. Victor comes back to us gloriously with a full net and describes to us excitedly the events of

his fishing. The poor fish are thrown living into the frying pan; a flavorful tea, eggs, and fruit make up the rest of the most succulent of meals.[23]

Not all of Considerant's fishing expeditions were as idyllic or as carefully planned as this. More typical perhaps is his account of a "successful" three-day trip in the region of Saint-Hubert in late November 1850.

> For three days I wandered through the mire and the hedges of Saint-Hubert, through terrible sloughs and peat-bogs, with the water above my knees, a bitter wind, and often rain on my back. The first day I caught twenty-two trout; but the second, on the advice of a peasant who sent me to "the best spot," I floundered in the worst mud you can imagine and caught only five trout. Still I was happy to have gotten those, because in this out-of-the-way place I could still get them fried in a peasant hovel and eat them with a piece of bread I'd brought along in my basket. What a cursed place in winter are these swamps of the Haute Ardenne![24]

As Considerant described this trip to his friend Allyre Bureau in Paris, he couldn't resist adding that he would like to see "the National Assembly and Monsieur 'Poleon" wandering through the same swamps.

Quite apart from the November fishing trips, life at Laroche was hard in winter. Thus in mid-December, and with permission of the authorities, Victor, Julie, and Clarisse Vigoureux moved to the city of Namur, where they took up residence at 846, rue de Fer, in the heart of the old city. Not long after his arrival Considerant wrote that he found Namur "much more pleasing than Brussels" and that he expected the police would leave him alone now. He was wrong. By the beginning of February his old enemy Hody, the administrator of public security, was again complaining about him to the minister of justice. Considerant was "discussing his principles with many people," wrote Hody, "even with army officers," and there was no reason why the government should tolerate such behavior on the part of socialists "who are particularly dangerous when they have a golden tongue." A few days later Hody instructed the royal prosecutor in Namur to threaten Considerant with expulsion unless he ceased talking politics at the Namur Casino. But Considerant knew the threat was hollow. He had highly placed friends not only in Brussels but also in Namur. Thus he could write the Parisians in February that the royal prosecutor of Namur had been "mortified" by the whole affair and had written the minister of justice that most of the charges against him had been invented by the government's informers. "I am pretty certain that nothing will come of this business and that

Hody, the Belgian Carlier, will once more have to swallow the rage he feels toward me."[25]

Although most of the charges against Considerant were indeed false, or greatly exaggerated, it is true that he rarely bothered to get official permission for his trips. In mid-February 1850 he took a brief unauthorized trip to Brussels to arrange for the publication and distribution of his brochure, *La Solution, ou le gouvernement direct du peuple*. Again in late June he took an unauthorized trip with Cantagrel and Adolphe Demeur through the Ardennes, along the valley of the Ourthe, to fish and also to look for a house where he, Julie, and her mother could spend the summer. Hody regarded both these trips as highly suspicious, and after the second he wrote the minister of justice urging that Considerant be placed in internment or else expelled.

> This gentleman does not stand on ceremony and he does just what he wants; he doesn't even deign to tell us where he is going or to ask if we approve of his peregrinations. I have a strong suspicion that he has taken trips to France. In my opinion it is time to put a stop to Monsieur Considerant's free and easy ways by assigning him a fixed residence or by inviting him, if he does not wish to undergo internment, to do his fishing somewhere else.

Fortunately for Considerant, other members of the government did not share Hody's views; and "the Belgian Carlier" was again left to suffer in silence.[26]

At the end of July 1851, Considerant, his wife, and mother-in-law finally did move out to the country to spend the rest of the summer in a rented cottage in the tiny village of Bomal, at the junction of the Ourthe and Aisne rivers. The fishing was excellent and the setting stunning: a short walk from the cabin gave Victor and Julie a spectacular view of the valley of the Ourthe and the ruined château de Logne. There was no way to heat the cottage, however, and in September the cold weather forced the three to move just upriver to Barvaux. This was a village of 1,200 inhabitants that Considerant described as "not at all picturesque" but possessing amenities not to be found in Bomal—a few stores, an inn where meals were served, and a house to rent with a wood stove. "Next to Bomal," Considerant wrote, "Barvaux is a capital." The Considerants were to stay there for the next sixteen months.[27]

Considerant's difficulties with the police did not end when he moved to Bomal. In September 1851, reports (later proved false) reached the Belgian

Foreign Ministry that Considerant was making "frequent trips to Sedan with the aim of establishing relations with the workers' associations of that city." At about the same time his enemy, Hody, attempted unsuccessfully to have him interned at Turnhout, a town near the Dutch border, far from any railroad line where no French was spoken. Once the Considerants were established in Barvaux, however, police surveillance proved to be relatively discrete. The *bourgmestre* of Barvaux simply noted Considerant's visitors and occasionally informed Hody that Considerant was "always present in the commune . . . tranquil . . . and spends much of his time fishing."[28]

During his sixteen months at Barvaux Considerant regaled the Parisians with stories of his prowess as a fisherman—of "fourteen, fifteen, sixteen pounds of fish" caught in "less than two hours." His only noteworthy contact with the authorities at this time was an amusing exchange of letters with a Baron Van der Skalen, the inspector of streams and forests for the *arrondissement* of Marche. In April 1852 Considerant got the "disastrous news" that all fishing was to be forbidden in the Ourthe during April and May. Thereupon he wrote a comic twelve-page letter of protest to Van der Skalen, calling the ban on fishing a "coup d'état, an aquatic December 2," and asking that an exception be made for fly fishermen. In his gracious reply the baron refused but added that "if you handle a fly rod as skillfully as you handle a pen, trout and other fish must rarely get away from you."[29]

Just a few weeks after this exchange Considerant was visited by an American Fourierist, Albert Brisbane. Although this visit certainly did not cause Considerant to lose all interest in trout fishing, it did mark the beginning of a new period in Considerant's life when trout fishing was no longer so absorbing a preoccupation.

III

During the first three years of his exile, Considerant's main activity (apart from fishing!) was writing. He went through periods of depression when he was incapable of any serious intellectual work; and he sometimes complained, especially during his first six months in Belgium, of being unable even to hold a pen in his hand. Yet by the beginning of 1850 he had begun to establish a regular rhythm of work; and during the next two years he produced three substantial brochures and a whole series of essays and articles, most of which he sent to the Parisian Fourierists for publication in *Démocratie pacifique*. Along with these articles went a steady stream of letters exhorting, criticizing, and advising his colleagues of the rue de

Beaune about everything from the rental of his Paris apartment to questions concerning the journal's layout and type faces.

These years were in fact difficult ones for *Démocratie pacifique*. Shut down after June 13, 1849, it reappeared in late August. Shortly thereafter, new censorship laws were voted, and the journal was seized on October 23, 1849, and again on May 15, 1850. Each seizure brought heavy fines. By May 1850 the journal's financial situation was so bad that its editors had to stop publication for two months. When *Démocratie pacifique* reappeared in early August 1850, it was as a weekly rather than a daily—and in Considerant's opinion a rather dull one at that. During its last fifteen months of publication its editors gave up trying to reach an audience outside the Fourierist movement. At the end, which came with Louis-Napoleon's coup of December 2, 1851, *Démocratie pacifique* had become no more than the organ of a movement.

Considerant was deeply unhappy about the narrowing of the scope—and audience—of *Démocratie pacifique*. He had no objection to the existence of a special doctrinal journal, but he felt that such a journal should be a supplement to, not a substitute for, a more popular daily with a relatively large circulation. What he found most disturbing, however, was that, whatever audience his colleagues were trying to reach, their journalism was dull and uninspired. His letters to Paris included harsh criticism not only of the writing in *Démocratie pacifique* but also of the design, layout, and even typography. The tiny headlines and fine print gave the paper what he described scornfully as "the look of a provincial newspaper" seeking to cut costs by using every inch of available space.[30]

One constant bone of contention between Considerant and his colleagues was the editorial treatment given to his own essays and articles. They complained that he ignored the constraints they labored under in producing the journal. His articles contained passages likely to provoke the government censors; and his prose was often too colloquial, lacking "dignity and measure in expression."[31] Conversely, what upset Considerant was that his colleagues could not understand that he often *intended* to violate rules and adopt colloquial turns of phrase. Instead, they sought to cleanse and even to "castrate" his prose, making corrections that were motivated by what he regarded as intolerably narrow notions of literary propriety.[32]

The work that caused the most trouble between Considerant and his colleagues was a long brochure written at Laroche during the summer of 1850. *Les Quatre crédits, ou 60 milliards à 1½%*, set forth in popular terms a new system for making low-interest loans readily available to producers from all strata of society. Considerant had already described this system in the published text of his speech of April 14, 1849, to the Constituent Assembly. Here he cast his exposition in the form of a dialogue featuring a motley cast of characters including a Marquis de Bric-à-brac, the Père Girod (a peasant farmer from the Jura), and "the socialist." In the course of the dialogue, which was punctuated by the increasingly enthusiastic out-pourings of a chorus of proprietors and producers, the initially skeptical men of wealth were won over by the articulate socialist and the plain-speaking Père Girod. In adopting this mode of presentation, Considerant was influenced by the efforts of contemporaries such as Pierre Joigneaux to reach a wide audience in rural France through the use of dialogue, slang, and dialect. But Considerant's use of these devices was crude—even by contemporary standards—and there was, as his colleagues complained, an "air of charlatanism" not only in his catchy subtitle but in his whole mode of presentation.[33]

Considerant recognized his limitations as a popular writer, but he did not accept the criticism of his colleagues. He saw their concern with correct style as one expression of a fundamental timidity and fearfulness. Borrow-ing a term popularized by Victor Hugo and then applied by Marx and many others to the timorous majority that controlled the National Assem-bly in 1850, Considerant characterized the editors of *Démocratie pacifique* as "Burgraves."[34] Like the hereditary German lords portrayed by Hugo, and like the conservative leaders of the National Assembly, the editors of *Démocratie pacifique* were afraid of everything new, unusual, or popular. They clung to narrow conventions and established traditions. Considerant, on the other hand, saw himself as a democrat seeking a mode of expression consistent with his ideological commitment. As he wrote Allyre Bureau in November 1850:

> I still have so little of the Burgrave in me that, for the time being, I beg my dear Burgraves of *Démocratie pacifique* to stop inflicting Burgra-vian corrections on my articles. . . . You keep stubbornly depriving my form of features that are peculiar to it. When I use an expression that is familiar, popular, trivial if you like, it is certain that I am aware of it and that I am using it on purpose. It is my character and my theory to make use of such language in the most serious articles. I detest stuck-up people and the refined genre, and I do not aspire to the Academy. This is a weakness, no doubt, but that's the way it is. For my familiari-ties, and even the brutalities of style scattered here and there in my work, are on my part a protest against refinement. What's more, I claim that these familiarities constitute a good democratic seasoning, and that they are pleasing to those whom I wish to please. Be as classical, pure,

solemn, and academic as you like. I don't find fault with that. But I intend to be free to do things my way.

Considerant insisted that he did not object to changes made when the threat of censorship was real. However, he wanted to present himself to the world not in sanitized prose but with "my mustaches, my warts, my facial hair, and my balls."[35]

Considerant's criticism of his "Burgrave" colleagues focused on questions of substance as well as style. In his letters from Belgium, he repeatedly criticized them for the timidity of their views, the modesty of their goals, and their lack of self-confidence. According to Considerant the Parisian Fourierists were too apologetic, too prone to self-criticism. They suffered from a "malady" that he characterized (in a term borrowed from Fourier) as "the love of self-scorn." They could not recognize or take pride in their own accomplishments. In particular, they regarded themselves as failures because they had not, through their propaganda and their publications, managed to swell the ranks of "pure-blooded Phalansterians." What they failed to recognize was that they had played a significant role in stimulating the rise of a more diffuse socialism. Vast numbers of people were now passionately concerned with finding solutions to "the social question"; sooner or later these people would embrace the Fourierist answer, for there was no other. Fourier's doctrine was in fact the "scientific" socialism to which the present "vague and multiform" socialism would necessarily lead.[36]

In his writings of the early 1850s, Considerant reaffirmed his optimism about the course of contemporary history. One of the most forceful of these writings was a brochure entitled *La Dernière Guerre et la paix définitive en Europe*, which Considerant wrote in March 1850. The main argument of this brochure was familiar. The old feudal, aristocratic, and monarchical order was doomed. A new democratic order based on industry, commerce, and labor was emerging irresistibly. This new order would substitute the spirit of fraternity for the spirit of war, liberty for conquest, association for despotism. The process of transformation would probably require violence and bloodshed. The next war, which would be the last, would no doubt be fought with guns and swords like all the others, but "the decisive artillery" in this final conflict would be "principles, sentiments, and ideas." And there could be no doubt about the outcome. The principles of fraternity, liberty, and association would constitute the basis of the new democratic and socialist order.[37]

In Considerant's private correspondence for this period one encounters the same tone of steadfast and stubborn optimism. Particularly interesting here is a letter written to Gustave Tandon in March 1851 and subsequently published in *Démocratie pacifique*. Tandon was about to embark on a tour of the provinces in the hope of rekindling the energies of provincial Fourierists. "Ah! I would very much like to take this tour with you," wrote Considerant.

> If only I could see them face to face, shake their hands, respond to their fears and complaints, and wave the Phalansterian flag before them. That flag will soon be victorious, even though there are some who, lacking a long enough and wide enough view, seem to be giving up out of fatigue and the withering away of faith and hope. I am sure of victory. Everything is so well prepared; the destruction of the old world is so complete. . . .
> There is one thing I would like you to see that our friends are imbued with. I would like them to have, as I have, a deep, clear, certain sense of our strength, of the invincible necessity of the imminent coming of our idea, of the dazzling and triumphant realization of the Phalanx of Harmony in the field of contemporary history.[38]

This confidence in the "imminent coming of our idea" had withstood the defeats of June 1848 and June 1849, but it was to be tested even more severely in the 1850s.

IV

During his years of exile in Belgium, Considerant may have been frustrated by his inability to participate in the editing of *Démocratie pacifique* and the day-to-day activities of the Fourierist circle at Paris. He was not isolated, however, from the debates and activities carried on within the wider circle of the French left during this period. He had been preceded on the road to exile by Louis Blanc, Caussidière, and Cabet; and by the end of 1849 almost as many of the leaders of the French left were to be found in exile as in France. Most of them shared Considerant's belief that their exile would be only temporary; many were involved in efforts to prepare the way for a triumphal return to France. In London both Louis Blanc and Ledru-Rollin were publishing journals and trying to create a united front among exiled radicals. Blanc was writing voluminously on recent history in an effort not only to justify his own role in 1848 but also to trace out the path to socialism. Considerant's exile was less active than this. Nonetheless, he kept in touch with some of the Londoners, warning Ledru-Rollin against supporting conspiratorial efforts in France, and writing a furious twenty-five-page reply to one of Mazzini's "antisocialist manifestos" of

1852. He also associated himself with a few collective *démoc-soc* projects such as the *Almanach républicain démocratique* for 1850.[39] In that same year, 1850, Considerant was also involved in a major political debate within the French left over "direct government."

The idea of direct government—direct participation by citizens in the legislative process without recourse to any form of representation—has long been a strand within the democratic tradition. In its modern formulation its roots go back at least as far as Rousseau with his critique of representative institutions and notion of a general will. Sovereignty cannot be delegated, Rousseau argued, and representative government invariably leads to the atrophy of citizenship. Those who attempt to implement theories of popular sovereignty through the election of representative assemblies are deluding themselves. In fact, the Englishman is free only on the day when he casts his ballot and not during the periods when he is represented by a member of parliament.[40]

This critique of representative government came to have particular resonance in Europe during the period of reaction that began in the summer of 1848. The verbosity and indecisiveness of the Frankfurt parliament did nothing to enhance the reputation of representative institutions in Germany. In France the record of the National Assembly was scarcely more encouraging. After voting emergency powers to Cavaignac in June 1848 and drawing up a conservative constitution in the fall, the French National Assembly then violated both the spirit and the letter of that constitution by sending troops to Italy to destroy the Roman Republic. Finally, in May 1850, the Assembly passed a new electoral law disenfranchising two and a half million working-class voters.

For many on the French left this electoral law of May 31, 1850, was the last straw. It offered a vivid demonstration of the fundamentally antidemocratic character of an assembly of representatives elected by universal male suffrage. In attempting to explain the passage of this law and, more generally, to make sense of the failures and defeats of 1848–1850, socialists and radical republicans began increasingly to assert that "the people" had been betrayed by their elected representatives. To establish genuinely democratic government, they argued, it would be necessary to do away with representative institutions and to create a system within which citizens would be constantly involved in the making and execution of the law. What this implied in concrete terms was a system of government in which all important decisions were taken by referendum or initiative.

The vogue of the idea of direct government was short-lived. The first pamphlets on the subject by Rittinghausen and Considerant were published in the fall and winter of 1850. Rejoinders by Proudhon, Ledru-Rollin, Emile de Girardin, Louis Blanc, and many others quickly followed. The discussion ended abruptly in December 1851, however, with the coup d'état of Louis-Napoleon Bonaparte. By overthrowing the Second Republic, Louis-Napoleon rendered the left-wing critique of its institutions moot; his subsequent massive victories in the plebiscites of December 21, 1851, and November 21, 1852, demonstrated that the failure of the republican and socialist left was not merely a matter of a faulty electoral system. For a short time, however, the left looked on the system of direct government as a panacea, and Considerant himself played an important role in promoting the idea.[41]

Prior to the February Revolution, Considerant had already displayed some interest in the critique of traditional systems of representative government. In the fall of 1846, during discussions of the reorganization of cantonal government in Switzerland, he published an open letter to the members of the Great Constituent Council of Geneva demonstrating "mathematically" the weakness of traditional systems of representation and proposing a "new" system of proportional representation.[42] It was only in 1849, though, that Considerant began to think seriously about the system of direct government. In his campaign that spring for election to the Legislative Assembly, his platform included a demand for direct democracy. Then in exile, in the spring of 1850, he met a young German radical named Moritz Rittinghausen, a former member of the Frankfurt parliament from Cologne, who had become a champion of direct democracy. According to Rittinghausen's system, there would be no national parliament. Rather, all important issues would be put to the vote of the nation, which would itself be divided into sections of a thousand citizens each. In September 1850 and at Considerant's behest, Rittinghausen's treatise on direct democracy was published in installments in *Démocratie pacifique.*[43]

In December 1850, Considerant published a seventy-two–page brochure containing his own version of direct democracy, *La Solution, ou le gouvernement direct du peuple.* Addressing himself to democrats, he argued that the idea of direct government could become a natural rallying point for the whole democratic left. Sixty years earlier democracy had made its "first serious explosion." Since then Europe had been caught up in the struggle between feudalism and democracy, between the spirit of authority and the spirit of liberty and equality. France had been affected more than any other nation by the new spirit: "The French are the people in whose consciousness the notion of political liberty is incarnated to the highest degree." The result, he argued, was that the French people could no longer be governed by a power external to themselves. After the February Revolution, when France "felt itself for a moment in possession of its right, of the principle of its sovereignty," it had become "absolutely ungovernable."[44]

Considerant went on to characterize the confusion that existed in France concerning the concept of popular sovereignty. Under the July Monarchy the argument had been made that the nation had "delegated" its sovereignty to the House of Orléans. Under the Second Republic, the sovereign people delegated its sovereignty to an elected national assembly. Considerant maintained that both forms of delegation could more properly be described as abdication. In electing a constituent, and then a legislative, assembly, and in endowing that assembly with its own sovereignty, the French people had in effect created a new authority external to itself, a new monarchy. The fiction was that since it consisted of elected representatives of the people, the National Assembly was simply an embodiment of the popular will. This fiction was exploded for good, however, with the passage of the electoral law of May 31, 1850, which deprived almost a third of the "sovereign" people of the right to vote.

Considerant asserted that, far from being a misfortune, the new electoral law would teach democrats a salutary lesson.

> The law will teach the people that when one delegates one's sovereignty to representatives, one becomes no more than the most humble subject of these representatives. The representatives become the actual sovereign, and they do so even when they write at the beginning of the constitution this fine joke: "Sovereignty resides in the totality of the citizens, and no fraction of the people can lay claim to the exercise of sovereignty without violating the constitution."[45]

All modern constitutions paid lip service to the principle of popular sovereignty, but to delegate it to representatives was in fact to give it up.

At the center of Considerant's brochure were his proposals for a system of direct legislation that would give real substance to popular sovereignty. What he had in mind can probably best be described in modern terms as a system of government by referendum or initiative. Any proposition supported by 500,000 citizens would be put to a vote by the nation as a whole. Citizens would meet regularly in their communes to discuss and vote on all propositions. If the commune was large, it would be divided into sections. The section meetings would be open to adults of both sexes, as would the right to vote. Each section would have a president, two secretaries, and four "scrutineers" to count and validate the votes. When votes were counted, the results would be forwarded to the department, and the department would forward its count to Paris. The sum of all the people meeting in all the sections would comprise the "general assembly," and its will, as determined by majority vote, would be sovereign.[46]

Near the end of his brochure, Considerant attempted to respond to objections that might be made to the idea of direct legislation. Some would surely argue that the whole scheme was hopelessly impractical, that there never could be a whole nation of legislators. To this Considerant replied that impossibility had "never prevented anything from happening," that the history of human progress was "an immense tissue of realized impossibilities." However impractical it might seem, direct legislation must be tried because it was the only means by which popular sovereignty could be made a reality. Furthermore, in a certain sense the task of legislation would be enormously simplified by the new system. Nine-tenths of the work of existing legislative bodies was devoted to "the fabrication of repressive laws" required by the perpetual revolutionary ferment of the nineteenth century. The establishment of real popular sovereignty would bring an end to the struggle for control of the state, and the result would be to focus attention on the serious task of social reform.[47]

It might still be argued that even a truly sovereign people could not do everything themselves, that they would need help in the day-to-day exercise of their sovereignty. Considerant's reply was that there was nothing to prevent them from appointing an administrative commission to help with the execution of laws. So long as such a commission functioned "under the eyes of the people," it need not be feared. Considerant wrote that the sovereign people could also elect public officials who would be responsible to the general assembly. Unfortunately, he said nothing about how such officials would be kept from exceeding their mandate and using their power for private purposes.[48]

Considerant's discussion of direct legislation was in many respects stunningly brief and simplistic. His discussion of possible objections did not get to the heart of any real issue, and he ignored or avoided most of the truly problematic dimensions of the topic, treating sovereignty and democracy as transparent concepts, ignoring the question of the rights of minorities, and assuming that the will of "the people" could be unambiguously elicited by majority vote. There was little in Considerant's text of Rousseau's awareness of the difficulties inherent in any attempt to give substance to popular sovereignty. On one topic, however, he did go deeper: the role of a free press in fostering the discussion necessary to create an informed citizenry. In order for direct government to work, Considerant insisted, complete freedom of discussion and information would have to be guaranteed. He stipulated that the media of communication should be free of censorship, *cautionnement,* and special taxes and that newspapers and journals should be circulated free of charge by the national postal service.[49]

The most striking feature of Considerant's text, however, lies not in any of the details but rather in the general sense of confidence in the future that radiated from the work as a whole. Toward the end Considerant struck a note both hopeful and mystical:

> Rivers flow, the sea rises, the earth turns. Who will stop them? . . . The advance of history is as irresistible as the advance of cosmological forces. Humanity is more than a river, more than a sea, more than an earth. It is God unfolding. For three centuries humanity has been advancing discernibly toward democracy, that is to say, toward its political liberty, toward its autonomy, toward the full possession of itself.[50]

After more than a year of exile Considerant's hopes were undimmed.

Considerant's brochure on direct government was neither original nor profound. He conceded that he owed many of his ideas to Moritz Rittinghausen, and his exposition of direct democracy was followed by others that delved more deeply into the problematic aspects of the concept. Still the brochure was relatively widely read—it went through four editions in as many months—and it aroused strong feelings. Some of Considerant's closest political allies, like the Belgian Fourierist Hippolyte Colignon, found the scheme "neither practical nor desirable." Others outside the movement, however, such as George Sand, were intrigued by the brochure. Half a century later it was still being cited appreciatively by critics of representative democracy such as the socialist Jean Allemane and the sociologist Robert Michels.[51]

From very different perspectives, Pierre-Joseph Proudhon and Louis Blanc both took the trouble to publish extensive criticisms of Considerant's ideas. Proudhon argued against Considerant that the abolition of representative assemblies would only be a half-measure. The point was to abolish *all* government. In practice, wrote Proudhon, the system of direct government would lead, as it had during the French Revolution, to the concentration of power in the hands of committees and clubs. Proudhon described direct government as "the stairway to dictatorship." For Louis Blanc, on the other hand, writing from within the Jacobin and centralizing tradition, the trouble with direct government was that it led not to dictatorship but to anarchy. Drawing on a much deeper knowledge of Rousseau than Considerant possessed, and also on more extensive reflection on the history of political thought, Louis Blanc criticized Considerant's notions of sovereignty, delegation, and democracy and challenged the notion that "a blind multitude, which often does not know what it wants," could make its own laws.[52]

Considerant did not publish a reply to the criticisms of Proudhon and Louis Blanc, but a long letter to Ledru-Rollin early in 1851 gave him the opportunity to restate the assumptions that underlay his enthusiasm for the idea of direct government. In it, Considerant urged Ledru-Rollin to distance himself from conspiratorial activity aimed at overthrowing the Second Republic or its president, Louis-Napoleon. The best strategy in Considerant's opinion was to rally democratic forces around the idea of direct democracy and wait for the presidential elections of 1852. "Don't count on any decisive action by the Mountain," he advised Ledru-Rollin. "Strength lies in ideas and feelings, in the spontaneity of the democratic principle whose historical moment has come. It is to encourage the development of this invincible spontaneity that we must work." The day would soon come when oppressive state power would wither away, when there would be "no power outside the people."[53] It was in the light of this faith in the primacy of ideas in history, and in the spontaneous and necessary emergence of "the democratic principle," that Considerant's enthusiasm for direct government burned bright.

V

The coup d'état of Louis-Napoleon Bonaparte on December 2, 1851, brought about a radical change in the French political landscape, altering permanently the hopes and expectations of the entire French left. Those like Considerant who had already been driven into exile were as much affected as were radicals who remained in France. Until December 2, some grounds remained for believing that exile wouldn't last. For three years the left and right had struggled for control of the French countryside, and at the beginning of 1851 the outcome still hung in the balance. Among republicans and socialists hope was high that the presidential elections of 1852 would bring one of their own to power. As we have seen, Considerant shared this hope; like many others he believed that the left should unite behind the candidacy of Ledru-Rollin. "You are the rallying point for 1852," he wrote Ledru in January 1851, adding that as the bearer of "the democratic idea," Ledru had with him "the wind, the rising tide, the great current of history."[54]

The coup of December 2 and of Louis-Napoleon's massive victory in the plebiscite held three weeks later not only crushed the hopes of emigrés for a quick return to France and sent a large new cohort of radicals into exile;

it also destroyed the illusions of many republicans and socialists concerning the will of the people and the efficacy of universal suffrage and called into question their faith that history was on their side. For a few like Proudhon the result was at least temporarily to provoke a turn to Bonapartism. For many others December 2 brought exile, disillusionment, and the end of participation in French political life. Some maintained their faith in exile. Victor Schoelcher could write from London in 1852 that "December 2 is an accident, unhappy and dismal, but it is only an accident. The revolution is not finished." Yet Schoelcher, like Louis Blanc and Ledru-Rollin, was not to return to France until 1870. Still others did not leave France but fell silent and went into virtual retirement after 1851 like Philippe Buchez, or underwent a sort of "internal exile" like the socialist Constantin Pecqueur, who refused to swear the oath of allegiance to Louis-Napoleon that his job as librarian at the National Assembly required and continued to write voluminously but published virtually nothing during the entire Second Empire.[55]

For Considerant the main significance of the December 2 coup d'état was not that it called into question his basic optimism about the ultimate triumph of "the democratic idea." He never lost this faith. What December 2 did do, however, was make him rethink how this triumph might be brought about. In short, the coup destroyed Considerant's hopes concerning the usefulness of a political coalition with the republican left and drove him back to the idea of a Fourierist communitarian experiment.

Considerant had, as we know, given lukewarm support to most of the efforts at a Fourierist *essai* undertaken in the 1840s. He feared that the failure of such efforts might fatally compromise the whole Fourierist movement, and he believed that the resources available to the movement were better employed in subsidizing a newspaper. To be sure he had always conceded that the ultimate goal was the establishment of a model community, which would vindicate Fourier's theory.[56] Still, until 1852 Considerant responded skeptically or evasively to all attempts to focus the movement's energies and resources on an immediate effort at community building. This was true even after June 13, 1849. The following winter, when urged to appeal for funds for a trial Phalanx, he was incredulous: "But aren't you afraid that this appeal will sound like a joke at the present time?" When Just Muiron made a similar proposal in 1850, Considerant could barely conceal his amusement: "He believes himself perfectly capable, deaf and old as he is, to found a Phalanstery just as you would swallow an egg."[57]

With the coup of December 2, which decimated what was left of the *démoc-soc* movement in France and brought the permanent suspension of

Démocratie pacifique, Considerant had a change of heart. As he later put it, he was forced by circumstances to "recognize that for the Ecole *any* sort of activity was preferable to a prolongation of absolute inaction." In his correspondence with the Parisians in 1852 we find him insisting that the great task was now to get support for a practical communitarian experiment. He drew up stipulations concerning the conditions that would have to be met. At the same time he responded by letter to proposals coming from Fourierists in France. In August 1852, for example, he exchanged letters with Auguste Savardan, a doctor from Chapelle-Gaugain, who wanted to purchase what was left of the old Fourierist Phalanx at Condé-sur-Vesgre and convert it into an orphanage run on Fourierist principles. Considerant thought the idea was silly. In his comments to Savardan he was relatively tactful, but in writing to Bureau he spoke of the proposal as "about as childish as they come, no pun intended." The key consideration for Considerant was that any proposal for a practical application of Fourier's ideas should be sufficiently attractive in itself to interest outsiders and thus serve as a rallying point for talent, labor, and capital.[58]

In his own thinking Considerant initially focused on Switzerland as a likely site for a venture in applied Fourierism. As early as 1846 he had told the president of the Council of State of Lausanne that "in view of the obtuseness and the harassment of the government of Louis Philippe, it may well be that the first Phalanstery will rise on the banks of Lake Geneva and not on those of the Seine."[59] In April 1852 he wrote Allyre Bureau that two big advantages of Switzerland were its stability and its liberal traditions. The following month the American Fourierist Albert Brisbane came to visit the Considerants at Barvaux. Brisbane had already spent some time in Paris, where he got the Fourierists excited about the prospects for establishing a community in America. In Barvaux, Brisbane continued to talk up America, while Considerant, in turn, tried to interest Brisbane in a Swiss venture.[60]

By the fall of 1852 Considerant was still not committed to any particular project. But then in November, almost casually, on the spur of the moment, he decided to accept Brisbane's long-standing invitation to come to America to explore the possibilities for a communitarian experiment there. As he wrote Bureau:

> Brisbane is pressing me to leave with him for America. In fact a two month's voyage can't do any harm, and a reconnoitering of that country just might be useful. Thus I have pretty well decided to go to Liverpool on December 1 to join him. Besides I am leaving without fuss, and I'll be back before people know I've gone.[61]

Considerant did leave for the United States with Brisbane on December 1 on the luxurious new paddle-wheel steamship, the *Arctic*. But he traveled under his middle name, as "Prosper" Considerant, in order to avoid publicity. He was still so doubtful that America would offer a site for an *essai* that he brought with him the draft of his proposal for Switzerland, thinking to finish it at sea and send it back to France from New York. Within a few weeks after his arrival in America, however, all his ideas on the subject had changed.[62]

PART IV

Texas

13

Discovering America

The United States, at the time of Considerant's arrival, was a nation on the move. In the 1840s the trickle of pioneers who had crossed the Mississippi during the previous decade became a great restless horde moving west in search of good farmland, freedom, profit, a better life, and (after 1848) gold. During the later 1840s, immigrants also arrived in unprecedented numbers from Ireland, England, and Germany, the Irish crowding into the big cities and factory towns of the Northeast, and the Germans often moving on to the Midwest to set up farms or to seek work as artisans in cities like Cincinnati, St. Louis, and Milwaukee. The rate of immigration, which had increased fitfully in the 1830s, began to soar after 1845, tripling between 1845 and 1850. At the same time, and partly due to the influx through immigration of a huge cheap labor force, industrial output took off. Between the mid-1840s and mid-1850s, the United States underwent one of the most remarkable periods of growth in its history. Every economic indicator moved ahead: manufacturing, grain and cotton production, population, railroad mileage, sales of public land.

The most dramatic indication of increased mobility, and one of the main causes of economic growth, was the rise of the railroad. Work on the Baltimore and Ohio Railroad, the first to be built in America for passengers and freight, had begun in 1828. Boston and Albany were connected by railroad in 1842, Boston and New York only in 1849. By 1850, however, there were already 10,000 miles of track in the United States. In the next five years railroad mileage doubled, and a network of new lines began to spread west of the Alleghenies, transforming agriculture, consumption patterns, and urban life. In 1845 Chicago had been a muddy frontier station, smaller than Nauvoo, the Mormon settlement on the Mississippi. Ten years later it was the terminal for 2,200 miles of railroad track, a vast commercial center, and, as the home of the McCormick reaper, the capital of the American farm machine industry.

As striking an image of modernity and movement as was the steam locomotive, transportation in America in 1852 was still largely based on water. After twenty-five years the Erie Canal remained the most important commercial artery in America. Because the new railroad lines were still poorly coordinated, anyone who wanted to travel rapidly toward the West in 1852 had to do so mainly by steamboat. This was in fact the golden age of steamboat travel, the age of the great races up and down the Mississippi and even across the Atlantic. The *Arctic*, the luxurious steam-powered paddle-wheeler that brought Considerant to America in December 1852, had, a few months earlier, made a record crossing of the Atlantic, in just under ten days.

So the steamboat, like cotton, was still king. Not until the generation after the Civil War did the railroads catch up with the steamboats and trade seek an outlet by rail to the Atlantic seaboard instead of flowing down the Mississippi to New Orleans. In the America that Considerant first encountered, the river valleys were the great regions of growth, and the passenger list of a river boat was a microcosm of the nation, including (in Herman Melville's words) "fine ladies in slippers and moccasined squaws; Northern speculators and Eastern philosophers; English, Irish, German, Scotch, Danes; Santa Fe traders in striped blankets, and Broadway bucks in cravats of cloth of gold," soldiers and religious fanatics, teetotalers and drunkards, "men of business and men of pleasure; parlor men and backwoodsmen; farm-hunters and fame hunters; heiress hunters, gold-hunters, buffalo-hunters, bee-hunters, happiness-hunters, truth-hunters, and still keener hunters after all these hunters."[1]

I

Considerant's ship entered New York harbor on the night of December 14, 1852. He debarked the next morning and was driven up Broadway past St. Paul's Church and past the great tourist attraction of the period, P. T. Barnum's museum, to the Hotel of Europe at the corner of Houston and Crosby streets. He had time that morning to walk around the city—to explore a bit of lower Broadway and to begin to take the measure of the island that Walt Whitman (then a journalist in Brooklyn) was soon to celebrate as his Manahatta—"city of hurried and sparkling waters! city of spires and masts!" with its "high growth of iron" and its "numberless crowded streets."[2]

Considerant's first impression was one of delight and sudden comprehension. He wrote later that "two hours of strolling in the streets of New York" had given him a more vivid sense of America than had all his readings. He was overwhelmed by the sheer vitality of New York and the spectacle of the diverse energies at work in the city. Trying to characterize his first reactions later, he adopted the language of romantic—almost vitalistic—science. He marveled at the spectacle of "human spontaneity at work in a field without limits," at the "unbelievable quantity of social labor" put out by individuals who were "ceaselessly erupting volcanoes of molecular activity." He had the sense of entering a world in which the powers of the individual, repressed within the confining structures of European society, had been unleashed. The energy and the creativity of American society were so insistently evident on the streets of New York—"staring you in the face, shouting in your ears, tearing at you, jostling you"—that the newly arrived European had to recognize that he had "set foot in a new world."[3]

In his writings Considerant had for some time been contrasting the decadence and corruption of Europe with images of youth, energy, and vitality, which he identified with democracy. It is hardly surprising that he was rapidly seduced by America. A week after his arrival he wrote Allyre Bureau jubilantly that he was glad he had come and that he was now aware that America offered "enormous resources" to anyone interested in radical social experimentation. "People here display a sociability much more active and emotional than in Europe," he wrote. "Civilization here is still civilization, no doubt, but instead of stagnating it advances like a great river and does not present obstacles to real progress." It now seemed to Considerant that the Bonapartist regime was well established in France and that for the next "eight or ten years" there might be little that Fourierists could do in Europe. In that case, he asked, wouldn't it make sense for "a part of the Phalansterian hive in Europe" to emigrate, if only temporarily, and see what could be done in America—"this beautiful, large, magnificent, and free country"? Adopting Biblical imagery, Considerant added that the departure from France need last only as long as Napoleon's dictatorship. It would be the Fourierists' period of "Egyptian servitude"—after which time they could "return to the banks of [their own] River Jordan," the Seine.[4]

Although Brisbane had business of his own to attend to after their arrival, Considerant quickly fell in with Brisbane's associates on the *New York Tribune*. He received his mail at the *Tribune* and went by its offices on Ann Street on his first day in New York to pay a call on its founder and editor, Horace Greeley. The next day Greeley ran an article on Considerant, introducing him to the American public as "the most eloquent expounder of the doctrine of Associative Life and Industry and the leader of the Phalansterian School of France up to the time of its dispersal by force in June 1849." Considerant, wrote Greeley, had come "to spend a few months travelling in the United States, with a view to observe here the results of democratic self-government and industrial freedom."[5] Shortly thereafter Considerant was invited to a monthly gathering of New York journalists, and soon other newspaper articles appeared "singing," as he put it, "my political and rustic virtues."[6] Soon he became acquainted with a number of figures in the New York journalistic and literary world, several of whom (Charles Dana, George Ripley, and Parke Godwin, as well as Brisbane and Greeley) had played significant roles in the American Fourierist movement of the 1840s. Ripley, the leader of the Fourierist community at Brook Farm, was now working for Greeley as the literary editor of the *Tribune*. Dana, also a Brook Farmer, was now Greeley's chief editorial assistant.[7]

Considerant's chief contact in New York City was, of course, Albert Brisbane, who had persuaded him to make the trip. Brisbane had a reputation in New York as an eccentric. Here is how Walt Whitman described him in a little portrait gallery of figures one might encounter on Broadway in the mid-1850s:

> A tall, slender man, round-shouldered, chin stuck out, deep-set eyes, sack-coat. His step is quick, and his arms swing awkwardly, as if he were trying to knock his elbows together behind him. Albert Brisbane, the socialist; the capitalist, too—an odd circumstance for a radical in New York! Somehow or other he always looks as if he were attempting to think out some problem a little too hard for him.[8]

To Considerant, Brisbane was a fascinating figure, not so much for what made him unusual as for what he had in common with other Americans. He seemed to typify the restlessness and ceaseless movement that Considerant now saw as one of the Americans' most fundamental traits. During his brief stays in New York he was constantly changing his lodgings, and more often than not he was on the road. As Considerant wrote Julie, "Brisbane has spent twenty-five years, one might say, on railroad trains and steamers. His real domicile is much more on highways and rivers than in his little village [of Batavia]." Brisbane was hardly unique. Reporting to Julie that Brisbane's brother had sold his house on a whim and moved out of it in twenty-four hours, Considerant commented, "Americans are really amusing and strange. They are no more tied down within their societies, in spite of the apparent solidity of their houses, than the original inhabitants of America were tied down under their tents."[9]

Brisbane's fluent French greatly simplified Considerant's relations with him, Considerant's English at this point being virtually nonexistent. He had at one time studied the language, and in his twenties he read it well enough to make a study of Robert Owen's writings in the original.[10] However, he had never had occasion to speak English, and he had trouble writing even brief thank you letters in that "cursed language." Still George Ripley could write of Considerant two weeks after his arrival that he was "devoting himself assiduously to learning English" and "getting on famously" in his social relations. Presumably his natural warmth and spontaneity compensated for his lack of knowledge of the language and enabled him to make himself more or less understood from the outset.[11]

Considerant was eager to see America, but Brisbane, his guide, had business to attend to in January and February. Thus, after two weeks in New York City, Considerant accepted an invitation from Brisbane's friend, Charles Sears, to spend a few weeks at the North American Phalanx in Red Bank, New Jersey. He needed to digest his initial impressions, make travel plans, and improve his English. The North American Phalanx seemed a good place to do all these things. Founded in 1843, it was the longest-lived of all the Fourierist communities in America and the only one still active of the two dozen established during the heyday of American communal experimentation in the mid-1840s.[12]

The American Fourierists at Red Bank were delighted at Considerant's visit. On January 3, 1853, Charles Sears welcomed him effusively, urging him to "consider our association as your proper home during your stay in this country." A few days later a banquet was held in Considerant's honor with numerous toasts and dancing that went on through much of the night. To one French observer the atmosphere that evening was one of "serenity" and "constant felicity" rather than "mad gaiety," but Considerant's first assessments of the quality of life at the North American Phalanx were much more reserved. Soon he was writing Julie about "the debility, the poverty, and the paralysis of this poor Phalanx." In his view this "trans-Atlantic child of Fourier's thought" was a sickly infant bearing little relation to its illustrious father. "Passionate harmony seems much more to be in a coffin here than in a crib. It is cold, frozen, dead." Still, Considerant observed, the

North American Phalanx was a good vantage point from which to form a critical assessment of the communal experiments undertaken in America in Fourier's name.[13]

Considerant spent about six weeks at the North American Phalanx. During this time he helped organize work groups attempting to clean up and improve the shabby grounds of the Phalanx.[14] He worked hard on his English, and after two weeks he could boast that he had already completed the equivalent of half a year's school work. In due course he also came to appreciate certain aspects of the life of the Phalanx. He liked the absence of constraint in its social relations, and he was charmed by seeing young men and women act as waiters at one meal while being served at the next. He was particularly impressed by the role played by women in both the work groups and the general meetings. "The industrial and social equality of the sexes [was] established there almost spontaneously," he wrote later. In general, Considerant believed that the modest successes of the North American Phalanx showed that the American character ("the cold and reserved nature and the more reasonable than passionate sociability of the North Americans") was better adapted to certain rudimentary forms of association than that of hot-blooded Latins. Still, on balance, Considerant's impressions of the North American Phalanx were negative. After an evening's conversation with Charles Sears at the end of January, he wrote Julie that under the right leadership, great things might have been done at Red Bank, but Sears and his collaborators seemed "tired and discouraged." A year later, in summarizing his impressions, Considerant wrote: "Vitality, zest, attraction to work were totally absent. Individual spontaneity, that powerful characteristic of the American populations, which serial organization can alone maintain and develop within an association, tends visibly to lose its strength here. Association was vegetating rather than thriving."[15]

In mid-February Considerant moved back to New York City. After a few days in his hotel on Houston Street, he moved into cheaper bachelor's quarters in a house shared with two Belgians and a Frenchman. He continued to take English lessons, now with Brisbane's wife, and for the next six weeks he made New York City his base for several trips up and down the East Coast. A visit to Washington in late March proved disappointing: in the midst of the "battles and intrigues" surrounding the end of a congressional session and the beginning of the new presidential administration of Franklin Pierce, he found it difficult to get attention—especially since Brisbane was unable to accompany him as interpreter and guide.[16] A two-week trip to Massachusetts in mid-March fascinated Considerant, though. He was intrigued by the new textile towns of Lawrence and Lowell, whose "fabulously rapid" growth was a tribute to the "practical genius of American industrialism." Lawrence especially was "an ensemble of buildings comparable to nothing in Europe." In Boston Considerant was warmly received by James T. Fisher, a merchant active in American Fourierist affairs. Fisher introduced Considerant to many of his friends, including the former Brook Farmer John Dwight and Dr. William Francis Channing, son of the famous preacher, William Ellery Channing, and a cousin of William Henry Channing, a leading American Fourierist. Months later Considerant recalled with pleasure the group of Boston Fourierists "who received me so fraternally and so warmly . . . and whose memory has a cherished place in my heart."[17]

Although Brisbane would not stay in one place for very long, he and Considerant found time for several long talks, both at Red Bank and in New York City, during the first three months of 1853. Brisbane proposed that they should collaborate on a daily journal devoted to propagating the doctrine in America. Considerant, however, insisted that the time for such a journal was over, that the pressing need now was to unite people around "practical realities." The two also considered the possibility of purchasing land in Ohio or Illinois and creating "rival agricultural squadrons" that would engage in large-scale corn or wheat farming, but this idea was rejected, as was that of attempting to breathe life back into the North American Phalanx.[18]

Considerant and Brisbane gradually established an area of agreement. Both were attracted to the idea of some sort of practical communal experiment on which Americans and Europeans might collaborate. They eventually agreed in ruling out the North, East, and Midwest as areas for settlement. Land in these areas was expensive, and the long winters forced people into a state of isolation not conducive to experiments in communal living. On the other hand, both Considerant and Brisbane came to believe that the vast empty spaces of the American West, where land was abundant and cheap, might be well suited to a communal experiment. They apparently knew nothing about the disastrous efforts of Etienne Cabet's Icarians to establish a community in Texas in 1848. What did excite them was the example of the Mormons: "With a baggage of retrograde and absurd ideas, a bizarre mixture of Mohammedanism, patriarchy, and Biblical theocracy, but thanks to a certain dose of truly socialist solidarity, the Mormons have in a few years attained a state of unbelievable prosperity."[19] So excited were Considerant and Brisbane by the Mormons' success and the rapid population growth in other parts of the American West that they talked of the possibility that European socialists might establish a state of their own in the West, where Fourier's ideas and those of other socialists might be given limited, practical applications. Considerant was initially eager to see a more thoroughgoing application of Fourier's theory, but eventually the two compromised. What they would seek in America was a site for the "creation of a social milieu freely open to all progressive ideas, where convinced Phalansterians might in particular propose the organization of integral serial harmony."[20]

Early in April 1853, Considerant wrote a long letter to Allyre Bureau that gives some sense of his state of mind just before his departure for the West. There was no question, he said, of "abandoning our flag and our cause in Europe." The question was whether *some* of the Fourierists should participate in an effort at community-building in America. Considerant now answered this question in the affirmative. He had become convinced that America was destined to become the source and center of the world's progress; the best Europe could hope for would be to stagger from crisis to crisis. He raised the possibility of founding a "socialist state" in the West (analogous to the Mormons' Utah Territory) within which an "integral Phalansterian community" might serve as a central rallying point. As old Europe teetered between anarchy and despotism, such a state could exercise a powerful attraction on "the living elements of progress and liberty" in Europe. So Considerant urged his friends in Paris to study English. For his part, he would carefully investigate the options open to the Fourierists in America. On his return they could all meet in Belgium and he would present his views and conclusions. He now thought that he would favor "a gradual and well-organized movement of emigration to America of a part of our forces."[21]

II

On April 6, 1853, Considerant left New York City. He planned to meet Albert Brisbane at his home in Batavia, New York, and then to set out on a trip by train and steamboat as far as Little Rock. From there they would travel by horseback into North Texas to explore the land beyond the Red River, which informed travelers had recommended to them. On his way to Batavia, Considerant visited John Humphrey Noyes's Oneida Community in upstate New York. There he made inquiries concerning the day-to-day functioning of the community, exchanged views with an Oneida Indian leader named David Johnson, and impressed his hosts with his prowess as a trout fisherman. Despite what they described as "his imperfect understanding of the English language," he won everyone over with his exuberant curiosity, his capacity for wonder, and his sheer vitality.[22]

Arriving in Batavia on April 10, Considerant found that Brisbane still had unfinished business to attend to in New York City. Brisbane took him on a hasty tour of Buffalo and Niagara Falls. Then, while Brisbane briefly returned to New York City, Considerant went back to Niagara Falls to admire that "Wonderfull Werck of the Nature" (Considerant dixit) in a more leisurely fashion than was possible with Brisbane. Viewing the falls from a narrow, suspended footbridge, he shouted his greetings to Julie and his Parisian friends, but the crashing of the falls drowned out his voice, and the winds carried his greetings away to Ontario.[23] On April 23 he was still a tourist, describing to Julie his encounters with Indian squaws who came to Buffalo to sell pins and pottery. "I look at them with a great deal of curiosity, but on their side the sight of my mustache (a phenomenon unknown in this area) causes even more surprise. I probably seem more savage to them than they seem to me."[24]

Finally Brisbane rejoined Considerant, and on the morning of April 27 the two friends left Buffalo by steamboat for Cleveland and then Canton, Ohio. Considerant was so excited that, as night fell that first day, he couldn't sleep. He stayed on the bridge, watching the stars and listening to the call of the night birds from the shores of Lake Erie. It had been cold, and that afternoon huge blocks of ice could be seen on the lake. When they arrived at Canton the next day, though, spring had arrived. The flowers and trees were in bloom; the sun was warm; and birds were everywhere, displaying a more powerful "ardor for work and love" than Considerant had ever witnessed in Europe. He himself felt vivified. At Canton they were met by Elijah P. Grant, a Yale-educated lawyer and "pure-blooded Phalansterian" who took them fishing for "chubs," perch, and sunfish. Then they proceeded by train to Alliance, Ohio, and from there via newly laid track to Wellsville on the Ohio River. Considerant spent most of the trip outside on the train's platform, looking out at the freshly cleared farmland. As the flatland gave way to rolling hill country, parts of it reminded him of valleys in the Ardennes. Much of it, however, was like nothing Considerant had ever seen before, and he felt himself for the first time a witness to a primal struggle in which the farmland became a "battlefield on which the American pioneers savagely fought with the savagery of nature."[25]

Considerant's first glimpse of the "beautiful, broad" Ohio River came at Wellsville. It was a moving sight for him because he remembered well that almost forty years earlier, after the restoration of the Bourbons, his father had spoken of quitting France and settling with a group of friends on the banks of the Ohio. At Wellsville Considerant and Brisbane boarded a huge steamboat with smoke belching from four stacks and glided down the Ohio to Wheeling in Virginia, "the land of slavery and tobacco." In Wheeling they spent the night in a dingy hotel that was not at all to Brisbane's taste but that fascinated Considerant because it was something totally new.

On May 2, after a "superb" voyage down the Ohio, they arrived at Cincinnati, where they were again welcomed by long-standing Fourierists. One of them, Benjamin Urner, "who frequently conversed with the souls of the dead," attempted (without success) to put Considerant in touch with his parents and Charles Fourier.[26] Another old Fourierist, living in a cabin in the woods outside Cincinnati, was the architect Colombe Gengembre. Twenty years earlier Gengembre had been involved in the first communal venture at Condé-sur-Vesgre. (Fourier himself did not appreciate Gengembre's excessively "civilized" architectural ideas.) In 1849 Gengembre had become disgusted with Europe and had emigrated with his family to the United States. Now at the age of sixty-five he was living happily with his wife and her sister in a cabin that he and his two sons had built in a week on the banks of the Ohio. Considerant was delighted to see his old friend again and charmed by his cabin, which he baptized a "Gengembre Box."[27] "Like the immense majority of the Europeans whom I met in America," he wrote later, Gengembre "never ceased blessing the inspiration that brought him there. 'Get all our friends to come to America,' he kept telling me. 'Here we can and will easily accomplish great things.'"[28]

Considerant and Brisbane spent four or five days in Cincinnati. His friends there publicized his visit, and for a moment he became a local celebrity. He described his reception to Julie with amused detachment:

> The celebrated Considerant being a European animal, a very curious specimen in the American West . . . Phalansterians, socialists, wits, and phrenologists all want to see him. He has to pay calls, receive visitors, speak English, take tea, taste the local wine, the famous Catawba, which isn't worth a damn and has a long way to go before it's drinkable.[29]

Considerant was fascinated by Cincinnati, which was by then a prosperous and fast-growing city of well over 100,000 inhabitants. When Charles Dickens had visited Cincinnati a decade earlier, he had been charmed by its "intelligent, courteous and agreeable populace," its "clean houses of red and white," and its "well-paved roads, and foot-ways of bright tile." What impressed Considerant was something more specific. This was the way the economic life of the city was organized around supplying and outfitting settlers on their way west. To his eyes, Cincinnati was an "arsenal for interior colonization." Just as an army in the field had its supply depots and bases of operation, Cincinnati with its huge warehouses and stores was a base and supply center for the conquest of the new lands to the west. This was important to Considerant because it suggested to him that the material problems confronting community builders in America might be less overwhelming than he had initially feared. "Here at Cincinnati I have understood the colonization of America," he wrote his friends in Paris. "You can understand here why it is easier to create a city or a state in America than to start the smallest enterprise in France."[30]

On May 7 Considerant and Brisbane traveled downriver from Cincinnati to Patriot, Indiana, where they spent several days with an old friend of Brisbane's who was a great admirer of Considerant. This was John Allen, a former Unitarian minister who had joined the Brook Farm community and become a talented Fourierist lecturer and a founder in 1846 of the American Union of Associationists. Allen had moved west late in 1847, at a time of flagging hopes for American Fourierists. In 1849 his wife, Ellen Lazarus, the sister of the socialist mystic Marx Edgeworth Lazarus, had given birth to a baby boy, whom the couple had christened Victor Considerant Allen. At the time of Considerant's visit his namesake was four years old and "an adorable child" who "carries these three names well and properly." Considerant was delighted to meet both the boy and his parents; and the night of his arrival he proudly sent Julie a lock of the blond hair of this little boy, "who chirps like a bird, who doesn't cry when he hurts himself, and who has just this minute brought me a chain he made out of dandelion stems."[31]

From Patriot, Indiana, Considerant and Brisbane continued downriver by steamer. They descended the Ohio to Cairo, Illinois, and then followed the Mississippi south to Napoleon, Arkansas. While changing steamers at Napoleon, Considerant encountered a caravan of Choctaw Indians. He wrote Julie that his "soul was touched" by the condition to which "these poor former masters of the country" had been reduced, and he reflected on the fact that at this point only the introduction of a system of "attractive labor" could prevent "the destruction of these unfortunate races." Sailing up the Arkansas River, Considerant and Brisbane arrived at Little Rock on May 15. They had originally planned to spend several days in Little Rock to buy horses and supplies and then to set out on horseback for the Red River. They were disappointed to find that a stagecoach now made regular runs along their planned route. In a letter to Paris, Considerant thundered his discontent: "A diligence when we were going to buy horses and begin our expedition into the virgin land of civilization. We've been robbed."[32]

So they continued west on another steamer, the *Franklin Pierce*, bound for Van Buren and Fort Smith, planning to set out from there by horseback for Texas. In his letters to Julie and Allyre Bureau, Considerant set down his impressions of the trip. As they got ever closer to the last outposts of civilization, he was amazed by the elegance of the steamer's furnishings and service: "rugs everywhere . . . ice in the drinking water . . . meals worthy of New York with sardines, stews, jams, and two or three sorts of cream . . . men in silk vests, women in silk or muslin dresses." At the same time he was astonished by the depth of "the sentiment of equality" among the steamer's crew, one of whom settled a quarrel with the captain with "a magnificent punch in the authority's face, which drew blood." Considerant was also greatly impressed by the independence of the children, who were allowed to run free at an early age, and by the fact that women could travel alone without fear.[33]

The *Franklin Pierce* stopped for a few hours at Van Buren, Arkansas, before proceeding on to Fort Smith. Although the stop was brief, Considerant had time to meet a young doctor from Salins who had emigrated in 1851 and was now selling drugs and practicing medicine in the back country. He also encountered a band of Osage Indians in full native dress who had come two hundred miles to demand retribution from the courts for horses stolen from them by white settlers. Their determination, erect carriage, and faces "full of expressiveness and grandeur" left a deep impression on him—a deeper impression than that made by George Catlin's troops, which he had seen in Paris in 1845.[34] The next morning, May 18, Considerant and Brisbane debarked at Fort Smith. There they bought horses and saddles and made inquiries concerning the next stage in their journey, the two-hundred-mile trip on horseback through Indian territory to Preston, Texas. The following day, toward midafternoon, they set out from Fort Smith.

III

Both in his letters and in the formal account of his trip published a year later, Considerant asserted that the crucial part of the trip—and his real venture into the unknown—began when he and Brisbane set out on horseback from Fort Smith on the long trek through Indian Territory to the Red River. The terms in which he described this part of the trip were already in his mind before it began. They were the terms of Charles Fourier's stage-theory of history, in which an initial age of edenic delight was followed by a period of material backwardness and psychic inertia called Savagery. This was followed by the even more lugubrious periods of Patriarchy, Barbarism, and Civilization. According to Fourier's historical timetable, it was only after the fall of Civilization that humanity would begin to progress through several transitional periods to the eventual establishment of full Harmony. Drawing on this scheme, Considerant wrote Allyre Bureau from Fort Smith on May 18: "Tomorrow: passage from Civilization to Savagery."[35]

When he later came to write a carefully contrived account of his travels, Considerant played on the contrast between Civilization and Savagery, depicting himself as having passed, within the space of two hours, from civilization into a primal state:

> It is impossible to traverse more brusquely three social periods. At two o'clock we were still in the pleasant city which has grown up at the base of Fort Smith: there were houses painted white or in red brick, surrounded by verdant verandahs and separated by flower gardens; wide and perfectly aligned streets; stores of all sorts; ladies in muslin dresses; children all dressed up playing with their parasols; lawyers, doctors, goldsmiths, watchmakers, and three or four big steamboats tied up at the quay on the Arkansas River: a whole young, alert, and prosperous civilization.—Less than two hours later our horses were having the utmost difficulty in extricating themselves from the mire, the dead branches, the half-rotten tree trunks through which we were laboriously following a sort of trail through the primitive forest under a cover so thick that it already seemed like night along the swampy bottom of the Poteau River. It was wild nature in all its purity; the somber, silent, virgin solitude and its rough perfumes; the luxuriant and thick vegetation of the masses of tree branches and gigantic creepers that were strangling the big trees and catching them up in inextricable webs; generations of plants rising, without any interruption of time and space, out of the centuries-old debris of dying and dead generations all heaped together. We were alone, and for the first time we had reached the bosom of those untamed energies at the beginning of all things natural. It was superb!

This passage, which is written in Considerant's most luxuriant mode of high lyric evocation, is of course much more than a dramatic application of Fourier's historical theory. It represents an attempt on his part to communicate his own sense of having returned, as he slogged through "the soggy bottom land of the Poteau River," not merely to a primal realm but to the source of nature itself. The language has echoes of both Rousseau and Spinoza, but the central aspirations are Faustian. Like Faust, Considerant seeks to find "the secret force that hides in the world and rules its course." And he now believes that it is near.[36]

It was dark when Considerant and Brisbane finally arrived at the Indian village of Choctaws Agency (later: Scullyville). There they dined on cornbread, raw onions, and "a blackened object" that turned out to be "fish, burned to a crisp on the outside and perfectly raw inside." For eight days Considerant and Brisbane continued riding southwest through Indian Territory. After the first night they slept under the stars and dined on "raw fish, wild turkey, wild pigeons, and undercooked cornbread and other primitive foods." The second night out Considerant went to sleep exhausted and running a high fever. He had thoughts of turning back and wondered if his motives in undertaking the trip were anything more than curiosity or "a puerile amour-propre." Brisbane urged him to keep going, however, and suggested that his exhaustion might be due less to any organic cause than to the change in diet and the fact that he had not ridden a horse for fifteen years. He was right.[37]

By Considerant's own account, the turning point of his trip through Indian Territory came on the fourth day, when he and Brisbane left behind the tangled forests and muddy rivers of the Ouachita Mountains and came out into a land of open, rolling hills and wide horizons. A great valley stretched before them, and on either side "rich prairies, rising in elegant undulations, stretched out toward lines of wooded mountains, green near us and blue in the distance, which framed the landscape." This was the high basin of the Red River. To Considerant it was inviting, even edenic, country—not at all the "sad and monotonous" prairie that he had expected to find in the American West. "We rode ten or eleven leagues a day," he wrote his friends in Paris, "without ceasing to imagine that we were in the middle of perfectly maintained English parks." What especially impressed Considerant about this strangely beautiful land was that it seemed to be wonderfully adapted to the eye, and to the needs, of man. As he wrote his friends:

> We have been overwhelmed by the richness and fertility of these immense solitudes. Nature here is magnificent, all ready to receive man, fertile, healthy, friendly. In three month's time and work one could have everything essential and necessary to life. It's superb. It's a rude Eden waiting to be transformed without trouble, without difficulty, into a harmonic Eden. And all along the way people have told us that Texas is even richer and more fertile.

In the more carefully studied prose of *Au Texas*, Considerant evoked the same setting in erotic imagery. Nature in this corner of Indian Territory was seductive. "Primitive earth" was a woman, extending a "sweet and majestic invitation" to social man. Considerant wrote that both he and

Brisbane were overwhelmed by a sense of new possibilities. Reflecting on what might come of the "betrothal" of the earth and the free, harmonized labor of social man, they were struck as if by a "sudden revelation of Destiny."[38]

Finally, on their eighth day out of Fort Smith, the travelers reached the Red River. Their first night on Texas soil was spent in less than edenic conditions in the rough river town of Preston. A contemporary described Preston as a town of "bad repute . . . a collection of low groggeries and a few stores, lining the high bluff bank of the river." But Considerant was still in Eden.[39]

Considerant's exploration of Texas with Brisbane lasted about six weeks —from late May to early July. Setting out from Preston for Gainesville, they were initially accompanied by a guide, a Captain Bolen, whom Considerant described as having "spent fifteen or twenty years roaming the area and fighting Indians." With Bolen they reconnoitered the uninhabited Cross Timbers region of North Texas for about a week. Then they rode south toward what was then the village of Dallas (population 500). Stopping at a cabin along the Trinity River, they learned of a Frenchman who "kept a saloon and taught school" at Dallas. This turned out to be Adolphe Gouhenant, a former follower of Etienne Cabet. Accused of treason by Cabet when his attempt to establish a settlement in Texas failed, Gouhenant had been left behind when Cabet led his followers to Nauvoo, Illinois. He had subsequently made a new life for himself, buying land and establishing an "Arts saloon" on the main square in Dallas. (This was not a bar but an art gallery and photography studio, which also served as a "combination church, Masonic lodge, dance hall, and law court.")[40]

The next day Gouhenant sat Considerant down under a cottonwood tree on the banks of the Trinity River and told him the story of his life as a follower of Cabet. His ties with the Icarian leader dated back to 1843, when he had stood trial for participation in an Icarian secret society. Acquitted with Cabet's help, he had subsequently been placed in charge of the "advanced guard" of seventy-five colonists sent by Cabet to Texas in 1848. This first group of Icarian settlers received inadequate support and finished by arriving at their destination only a few weeks before they were required to have completed work on the buildings and other improvements necessary for them to lay claim to the land. Cabet had apparently made Gouhenant the scapegoat for his own failures. Still, Gouhenant had survived and, to a degree, prospered.[41]

Gouhenant's account of the failure of the first Icarian community in Texas was fascinating to Considerant not only because it made a remarkable story but also because he believed it contained an important lesson. Any successful attempt at settlement, he concluded, would require extremely careful planning as well as an advance guard given ample time to prepare the site before the settlers arrived. Considerant also reflected on the extraordinary ups and downs of Gouhenant's career. In 1848 he had been "sacrificed, slandered, and crushed" by Cabet, and two years later he was still skinning deer and trying to make a living on the sale of their hides. But now, in 1853, Gouhenant had become "the proprietor of a dozen lots of land in the town of Dallas" and had established a successful business. Only in America, Considerant believed, was such a rapid change of fortunes a relatively commonplace occurrence.[42]

After a few days in Dallas, Considerant and Brisbane moved on to Fort Worth, which they used as a base for two weeks while exploring land along the west fork of the Trinity River and one of the sources of the Brazos River. Fort Worth was then little more than a military post, established to protect a few ranchers from Indian attacks. Its commander, Brevet Major Hamilton W. Merrill, was a native of Brisbane's home town of Batavia, and he received the travelers royally. Considerant was now euphoric. He wrote delightedly to his friends in Paris of Merrill's hospitality and of his pleasure at sleeping once again in bedsheets and eating meals with fresh meat and wine served on linen tablecloths. Later in his published account of the trip he was equally enthusiastic about the fertility of the soil and the temperate climate of North Texas—and even the absence of weeds in the vegetable garden at Fort Worth.[43]

By the middle of June all of Considerant's doubts about Texas had been dispelled, and his tone in writing the Parisian Fourierists was that of a man who had undergone a religious revelation. "Friends," he wrote, "I'm telling you the truth. I've seen the light." Until reaching Texas, he had been moved by logic and curiosity, but he had not been inspired. Now he no longer hesitated.

> When you know what this region has to offer, what one can do here, with what *facility* one can in five years create immense wealth here and in seven years at the most establish a harmonically organized community (it is integral harmony that I'm talking about), you will say as I do that it would be a folly and a crime to continue to wait in Europe while the movement atrophies.

There was no time to waste. Within two years the price of land around Fort Worth would increase ten times. So money should be raised immediately—enough to purchase 250 to 300 square leagues of land in the vicinity of Fort Worth. To make this possible, it would of course be necessary to rekindle the energies of the European Fourierists. "As soon as I get back," wrote Considerant, "we must without wasting any time about it hold meetings with our influential friends, revive a monthly journal, and reorganize the movement in Europe by giving it the practical goal of establishing a community in Texas."[44]

Considerant went on to outline his own plans for the next few weeks. He had accepted Major Merrill's offer of a military escort for a trip down the Brazos River. He and Brisbane would quit the escort around Waco and then ride south alone to Austin. There they would sell their horses and begin the long trip home. He was now ready to return for he believed that his job in Texas was essentially done. "I have all the elements necessary for a report and for the drafting of the project that we will draw up together." He would begin to write this report on the boat trip home. Speed was necessary. "We have two years at most to take possession of the land we need here."[45]

Considerant's return took longer than he anticipated. A mild attack of yellow fever obliged him to undergo treatment for two weeks in New Orleans. There he made contact with members of the French community, including a number of former followers of Etienne Cabet as well as "Elie, a professor of chemistry, and a few other Phalansterians." He had never met the Fourierists before, but they greeted him like an old friend; and he was left with the conviction that if a communitarian experiment could be initiated in Texas, it would not be hard to create a supportive Fourierist center at New Orleans. By late July he was ready to move on. Warnings concerning low water on the Ohio River convinced him to return to New York by way of the ocean (and Havana) rather than by riverboat. He was disappointed to miss his *"brave ami"* John Allen and his wife, and the young Victor Considerant Allen. Nonetheless, as he boarded ship at New Orleans, his hopes were high. "My friends," he wrote the Parisians, "I tell you that the future which we have been pursuing for twenty-five years, the glorious transformation of the world . . . is now within our grasp." He insisted that the time of sacrifice and suffering was over. "We can in very little time create a half-paradise for ourselves, and just a few years later we can call forth from this half-paradise a full and radiant Paradise." He reminded his friends of how modest his own hopes had initially been. "It was in Texas, only in Texas, that I was converted and edified, that my view became clear, that I saw the light."[46]

IV

Considerant's effusive letters and reports from America met a mixed response in Paris. Many Fourierists wanted to believe, and share, his hopes concerning a communitarian venture in Texas, and almost everyone admired him, but a number had doubts about his judgment, and some were alarmed by his religious language and his talk of a "conversion." Emile Bourdon, for example, wondered whether the Fourierists could ever raise the capital or acquire the knowledge necessary to establish a successful colony in Texas. If so, he wrote, their efforts would need to be tempered by an "English" caution that he, for one, did not detect in Considerant. They would need to be "cool, calculating, and persevering," and they would need to plan for all contingencies so as not to be "destroyed by unforeseen events." "If we get carried away by enthusiasm at the beginning," wrote Bourdon, "we shall fail." [47]

Considerant had anticipated these objections, but his letters to Paris from New York and then Belgium continued to employ the "enthusiastic" language of a religious convert. We are entering "the promised land," he wrote from New York on August 9. Describing North Texas as "the flower of the United States, the pearl of the world, blessed ground," he expressed the hope that the Phalansterians might "make themselves the masters" of a part of this territory before it had been "deflowered" by settlers and speculators. In his letters to Julie his language was more restrained but no less optimistic. The idea of establishing a community in the American West was "not at all utopian," he wrote Julie from New York. "The Mormonts [sic] with their absurd ideas" had already created a territory that would soon be "flourishing." There was nothing to prevent the Fourierists from "proceeding better and faster in opening up in the West and the Southwest a protected area [champ d'asile] for American and European socialism." [48]

Considerant finally left New York on August 13 on a steamship bound for Liverpool. In his last letter to Julie from the United States, he complained that there was as yet "no electric telegraph at the two ends of which we might talk." He wouldn't have needed such a contrivance for long, though. By August 30 he had reached Ostende, and three days later he was back in Barvaux with Julie. Eager to share news of his trip with those he cared for, he summoned his sister Justine and his brother Gustave to Belgium; his letter to them after the visit shows that he remained ecstatic about prospects in Texas. He wrote that he looked forward to the day, not far distant, when they would all be together in Texas, "living in liberty and breathing the joy that must emanate from the cradle of a society which is just, worthy, radiant, and liberating." He went on to assert that "all the conditions of a great success are gathered together under the clear sky beneath which I traveled this summer."[49]

On his return to Belgium, Considerant's two great concerns were to meet with as many of the Parisian Fourierists as possible and to write up a report on his trip. At once he began urging the Parisians to come and see him at Barvaux.[50] At the same time he set to work on the book that was to be published under the title *Au Texas*. Between September 1853 and March 1854, he worked hard at the book, seeking not merely to describe what he had seen and done in Texas but also to convey to his readers his own conviction that the good society for which they had all been striving could and would take root in Texas soil. As he wrote, he kept in close contact with the Parisians, requesting books and maps, sending installments of the manuscript, responding to their questions and criticisms, conveying detailed instructions on editorial matters and typography, and complaining about their tardy responses, their absorption in the contemporary vogue of table-turning and the occult, and his own isolation. By January the isolation had become troubling enough to him that he sought official authorization to live in Brussels. This was granted. (One of the arguments Considerant used was that his current activities were hardly threatening to the Belgian or French state since his goal was now to promote an exodus of radicals from Europe.) Thus in mid-January he, Julie, and her mother moved into an apartment at 32, rue de la Machine Hydraulique, in the Belgian capital.[51]

Back in Brussels, Considerant stuck to the pattern of his days in the countryside. He wrote until midafternoon, then had lunch and relaxed for the rest of the day. Only now his relaxation took the form not of solitary fishing expeditions but of evenings of chess and talk at a café on the passage Saint-Hubert or the place de la Monnaie. He also gave informal nightly English lessons to a few émigrés, and dined regularly with fellow exiles like Cantagrel and Belgian friends such as Félix Delhasse, Adolphe Demeur, and Philippe Bourson. His relations with the Bourson family were particularly close: their little boy Eugène was like a son to Victor and Julie, and their twenty year-old daughter Amédée painted what remains one of the best portraits of Victor.[52]

If Considerant was loved and admired by close friends like the Boursons, he made a different impression on some of his more casual acquaintances within the French exile community. The radical journalist and art critic, Théophile Thoré, for example, left a picture of Considerant as a man strangely detached and phlegmatic. Meeting him at a dinner with Cantagrel, Delhasse, and others, Thoré was stunned by Considerant's apparent levity.

As he wrote in his journal afterward: "Not a word about France, about the Revolution, about social ideas, not even about Fourierism. He speaks of *rattlesnakes!*" After dinner, Thoré went on, things got even worse. Considerant pulled out his pipe and began, to his own great admiration, blowing smoke rings. "Look, there's a good one!" he would say. "Look at that one!" Then he sat down to play chess with his host.[53]

It is hard to know what to make of an anecdote like this. From Thoré's radical republican perspective, Considerant's behavior indicated a fundamental lack of seriousness, commitment, gravity. Considerant, of course, was no more sympathetic to republican gravity than to the gravity of the "Burgraves" of *Démocratie pacifique*. He may have simply been tired. In any case, it is clear that many of the mundane aspects of the venture in Texas did not interest him. In writing the Parisians, for example, he insisted that it was up to them to handle the financing of any new community. As he informed Allyre Bureau in a typically brusque and peremptory letter:

> Instead of [playing at] table-turning, you would do better to hold a meeting of six or eight of the practical fellows in your group and discuss seriously the question of the terms to offer on capital invested in the Texas project. My business is colonization and the establishment of activities on the new social terrain. But the question of the offers to make to capital to get the whole thing started is a matter of ordinary business, of civilized transactions.[54]

Considerant was not going to involve himself in civilized transactions.

There was one "practical fellow" in the Fourierist camp whom Considerant did contact personally. This was Jean-Baptiste Godin, a successful stove manufacturer from the Aisne who had a long-standing interest in Fourier's ideas and who was later to become famous as the founder of the Familistère of Guise. In January 1854, Considerant wrote Godin asking for his advice concerning the terms to be offered to investors. Godin replied at length, offering sound and specific advice together with a set of proposed statutes. In particular, he insisted on the need to minimize the conflict between labor and capital so as to avoid creating "a new Ireland in Texas." Godin also had some doubts about the climate in Texas, and he worried about problems that might arise if the administration and the colony itself were separated by an ocean. Still, he was hopeful. Some problems could be overcome, he believed, by "placing the seat of the administration in the heart of the colony itself" and by "offering the colonists the opportunity to become shareholders in the Society of Colonization."

In the end, very little of Godin's advice was taken. If it had been, the outcome might have been different.[55]

V

Au Texas. Rapport à mes amis, appeared at the beginning of May 1854. As the subtitle suggests, it was initially intended to be a "report" to friends and fellow travelers on Considerant's trip to Texas. "My account is not a book addressed to the public," he wrote in February. "It is . . . an intimate and in a sense confidential communication to friends of the Phalansterian cause."[56] What Considerant offered his friends was far from a simple narrative, though, and the "report" had multiple dimensions. On one level it was the record of a spiritual odyssey, the account of a journey to the Promised Land in which Considerant cast himself in the role of Moses. "The redeeming idea is slumbering in its Egyptian captivity," he wrote. "Let it awaken. Believe in it, and the Land of Realization, the sacred ground, is yours." From a different perspective, *Au Texas* can also be seen as a piece of promotional literature in an emerging tradition of American boosterism. As such, it gave an extravagantly rosy picture of the opportunities awaiting settlers and investors in Texas. It painted Texas as "the pearl of the thirty-two states of the Union," a land of rich soil, pleasant winters, and abundant harvests. Drawing on his observations, his reading, his conversations with Major Merrill at Fort Worth, and, it would seem, his fantasies, Considerant boasted that in no other part of America was rainfall more reliable than in Texas. Even poverty assumed a different character in Texas than in old Europe. "Poverty in Texas is not an old poverty," he wrote, "a resigned and static poverty, a normal condition." Rather it was "a momentary transition, a beginning, a point of departure. Comfort and wealth come right on its heels."[57]

If Considerant sought to arouse interest in the new Phalansterian Promised Land, his report also included the detailed description of a plan to establish a colony in Texas. What is striking about this plan, however, is how little it owed to the ideas of Charles Fourier. Nowhere in the book did Considerant use the terms "Phalanx" or "Phalanastery." On the contrary, he warned his readers against any premature attempt to create a Fourierist community in Texas. "Although the ultimate goal . . . of the Phalansterians is indeed the experimentation of their social method," he wrote, "[they] should beware of seeking to employ it at the outset . . . as a means of colonization." It would be wiser, he advised, to begin by employing "the simplest and most practical means," which implied "the avoidance of any preconceived system." [58]

What Considerant proposed was the creation of a colonizing company— an "agence de colonisation"—which would initiate and supervise the initial phases of settlement. It would be run as a joint-stock company capitalized at five million francs. Its main tasks would be to purchase land in North Texas, then recruit and hire an advanced guard of about 150 American pioneers to clear fields, plant crops, and build temporary lodging. Meanwhile the colonizing company in Europe would be negotiating with groups of prospective settlers. These settlers would purchase the improved land from the company, and it would arrange their transportation to Texas. Once they arrived, they would be free to organize their collective life as they pleased. Although some would follow Fourierist principles, other methods of communal organization should also be represented. The aim was to permit the testing of Fourier's ideas against those of other social theorists. Confident that Fourier's theory would eventually be vindicated, Considerant's initial goal was to create in America a "great protected area freely open to all forms of progressive thought." [59]

Why was Considerant so reluctant to call for an immediate effort to build a Fourierist community in Texas? Presumably because he did not think it would work under frontier conditions and in a strange country. He said as much in his text when he criticized the "illusions" of those who wished to proceed immediately to the "realization." Under the best of circumstances, he argued, the creation of an experimental Fourierist community would not be easy. There was no point in compounding the problems of the "realization" with those created by resettling hundreds of Europeans in the American wilderness. Far better to separate the tasks of the pioneer and the community builder. The creation of a "champ d'asile" open to all progressives would facilitate this separation, and it would have the added advantage of drawing on a much wider range of talents and energies than could be tapped by an appeal to Fourierists alone. [60]

Au Texas concluded with an appeal for support. There was an immediate need for capital, since the value of land in Texas was rising rapidly. Traditionally, the cheapest and easiest way to buy Texas land had been through the purchase of "headrights"—small land grants originally made by the Republic of Texas to volunteers who fought against Mexico in the War of Texan Independence. Now, though, even these headrights were rising in price. There were rumors that a railway line would soon be laid across North Texas, and this would surely increase prices further. Considerant also asked all those who might consider emigrating to Texas to declare themselves. Farm laborers, carpenters, and cooks would be particularly useful at the outset, but in the long run there would be a place for artisans of all sorts, clerks, metal workers, and even glassmakers.[61]

On its appearance in early May 1854, *Au Texas* was not placed on public sale. Rather it was sent out free of charge (with requests for contributions) to friends of the Fourierist movement. Most of the work of circulating the book in France was done by Allyre Bureau and the Fourierists at Paris. At Considerant's behest, Bureau sent a hundred copies to Brisbane for distribution in America and ten copies for Muiron to distribute in Besançon. From Brussels, Considerant himself sent out copies to his brother Gustave in Angers, to his sister Justine in Beaufort, to friends in Salins, and to foreign intellectuals such as Moritz Rittinghausen in Cologne and August Cieszkowski in Berlin.[62]

The response came quickly, and it was overwhelmingly positive. One of the first to reply was Just Muiron, who wrote on May 11 that he found Considerant "a more elegant, eloquent, solid, and seductive writer" in *Au Texas* than in his earlier work. "I am just as pleased as I can be. My hope and my faith . . . are redoubled." Two days later Godin wrote Considerant that his "doubts and fears about the climate, the healthiness and the security" of Texas had vanished. Oscar Koechlin of Mulhouse was even more enthusiastic. "I have received Considerant's report," he wrote, "and read it with great pleasure. What warmth of style, what soundness and grandeur of ideas and conception! What faith! What enthusiasm! It is sublime. It is practical. Considerant, this time you've hit the nail on the head. You have discovered the true way of the future. Lead us. We will follow you." What these letters suggest is that in the barren political landscape of the early Second Empire the Fourierist faith continued to live an underground existence in France and that Considerant's "rapport" had called it back to life. By providing a focus for the energies of his friends and followers, Considerant had reawakened the hopes that they had long ago placed in him and in their cause.[63]

Within a few weeks it was clear that the response would exceed Considerant's wildest hopes. The Fourierists' Paris office was deluged with letters of support and pledges of money totaling hundreds of thousands of francs. By early June a hundred offers of participation had been received, and by mid-August the number had reached two hundred. They came not only from France but also from Belgium and Switzerland, from both the young and the old. Some offers were received from artisans and skilled laborers, but a larger number of prospective colonists were clerks, functionaries, and professional people with little experience of physical labor. There was Bessard, for example, a thirty-nine-year-old notary's clerk who described himself as a lover of hunting, fishing, and gardening, and Perrot, a sixty-two-year-old music teacher who would be accompanied by his wife and three daughters, and the widow Jayter of Paris, "almost sixty but in very good health."[64]

A few of those excited by *Au Texas* were non-Fourierists like Louis Krolikowski, the former editor of Etienne Cabet's journal *Le Populaire*, who were attracted by Considerant's idea of creating a "champ d'asile" for radicals of all persuasions. But the vast majority of the most enthusiastic readers were Fourierists who wanted to see the prompt application of Fourier's ideas and had little interest in Considerant's broader proposal. The problem was that Considerant had so eloquently (not to say extravagantly) described the opportunities awaiting settlers in Texas that his warnings about the difficulties of the task and the need to avoid sectarian dogmatism were simply not heard.

The enthusiasm of the response to *Au Texas* took Considerant by surprise. He did not expect it would be so easy to get support for any sort of colonization project in Texas. Once he had this support, he was not exactly sure what to do next. He found himself unable to answer his readers' queries; and for more than a month he even stopped writing to Bureau and the other Fourierists in Paris. He realized that a company would have to be organized and statutes drawn up. First, though, he needed to consult with would-be investors and colonists. In June he summoned Godin to Brussels for discussions, and in July he talked over the project with the wealthy American expatriate Marcus Spring. Early in June he wrote the Belgian authorities formally requesting permission to travel to Switzerland to meet with his supporters there. He also began meeting regularly with François Cantagrel to work at drawing up a set of statutes for what they were soon calling the "Société de Colonisation."[65]

In early August Considerant finally drafted a general reply to the readers who had answered his call. This letter, which was written in his most exalted, most Biblically prophetic manner, was published in a second edition of *Au Texas*. "To all of you," he wrote, "who in isolation could believe that the springs of our faith have dried up . . . I can now say: 'Rejoice . . . the waters have again begun to flow in abundance. . . . The sacred flame is burning.'" He concluded with a fantasy of his own death in which he described the Texas colonization project as a "legacy" to his followers and to a suffering humanity. "If I should die tonight, my profound conviction is that I would be leaving you less—much less—for the future of our cause, and for our own collective future, if I left you the treasures of the Rothschilds or all the gold in California."[66]

On August 11, two days after Considerant wrote these lines, a bizarre series of events took place. Police agents entered his apartment looking for firearms and he was taken off to jail, accused of having participated in a plot against the Belgian government. The evidence against him turned out to be the flimsiest imaginable. The police had intercepted letters appearing to link Considerant with individuals making large purchases of arms and also with a "Monsieur Sanders," an exalted republican from Liège who was accused of having manufactured bombs to be used against Leopold I or Napoleon III. The truth of the matter was that Considerant had simply placed orders for hunting rifles for his own use, for his brother, and for the use of American friends including John Allen and Hamilton Merrill, the commander of the army garrison at Fort Worth. Eventually he managed to explain things to the satisfaction of the Belgian police, but not before he had spent nine days in solitary confinement.[67]

On his release, Considerant immediately drafted an account of his arrest and imprisonment in a pamphlet entitled *Ma Justification*. In this pamphlet, which took him just nine days to write and see through the press, he sought not only to justify himself before the court of public opinion but also to show with what contempt the rights of law-abiding citizens were now treated in Belgium. *Ma Justification* purported to be more than a personal apology; it was also an indictment of European justice at the moment when he and his followers were "on the eve of quitting the old European society to found, in our splendid wilderness, a New Society, radiant with Youth, Wealth, Justice, and love." Considerant also used the brochure as an opportunity to bring his plans for Texas to the attention of Belgians. Already, he boasted, 600,000 francs had been pledged, and large numbers of artisans, farmers, engineers, doctors, and professors were ready—"perhaps even a bit too ready"—to emigrate. Furthermore, it was "infinitely likely" that the government of Texas would concede to the group "free of charge" a territory "roughly equal in size to a French department or a province." Considerant concluded, in a phrase that did not endear him to his European socialist comrades, that the existing sovereigns of Europe had nothing to fear from an enterprise the consequence of which would be "to sweep out of Europe many socialists of all persuasions."[68]

Ma Justification gave Considerant a chance to deploy his talents as a publicist; and it may have served a useful purpose in explaining the circumstances of his arrest to his bewildered followers. But not all of them appreciated the pamphlet. To a man of action like Godin it seemed a frivolous diversion. "I see with the deepest regret," wrote Godin, "that you are clinging to the illusion that, at this time, one can influence people effectively through writings. That time is over: today we need acts, facts, movement, material accomplishments." Considerant was not troubled by this criticism. In his reply he declared breezily that Godin was "the best of men and the most solid of Phalansterians," adding that the statutes for the Colonization Society were almost ready for publication.[69] There is a sense in which Godin's words were wasted, however. Considerant was not about to become a man of action in Godin's sense. Writing—and talking—had always been, and would remain, the ways Considerant was best able to influence the world.

VI

On September 26, 1854, the Société de colonisation européo-américaine au Texas formally came into being. Godin, Bureau, and Ferdinand Guillon all came to Brussels to join Considerant and Cantagrel to sign the official document. It was voluminous. Including eighty-seven articles, the statutes for the Colonization Society have been described by Arthur Bestor as "the most complicated set of by-laws ever drafted for a communitarian experiment."[70] The society's goal, according to the statutes, was to make possible "the realization of the plan of colonization proposed and described" in *Au Texas*. Specifically, the society undertook to purchase land, prepare it for settlement, buy livestock and tools, and provide transportation to America for groups of colonists. The financial arrangements and many of the administrative details were to be handled by a board of directors with offices at 2, rue de Beaune, in Paris. Godin, Bureau, and Guillon were named directors; they were to serve as the effective leaders of the Ecole Sociétaire in France. It would be their responsibility to publish a *Bulletin* concerning the activities of the society, call meetings of its shareholders, and oversee the activities of the executive agent in Texas.[71]

The executive agent was, of course, Considerant. Receiving an annual salary of $1,200, he was to direct operations in Texas. As Godin put it, he was "the soul of the enterprise," but the more practical directors would take care of the details. There was also to be a council of supervisors, whose five members would be elected by the shareholders. The shareholders would meet regularly in general assemblies open to all investors who had purchased shares with a total value of at least $125 or 675 francs.

In a commentary circulated along with the statutes, Considerant emphasized that the task of the Colonization Society was to purchase land and to aid in the process of settlement but not to engage in any kind of social experimentation. He clung to his vision of creating in Texas a "champ d'asile" open to radicals of all persuasions. He conceded that some of the would-be shareholders had already made clear their preference for the establishment of a Fourierist Phalanx, but he argued for a slower, more gradual approach and an appeal to a wider public. Colonization, he asserted, would in and of itself increase the value of any land purchased by the society. It would yield profits for both settlers and shareholders. In an apparent effort to reassure those who might regard his proposal as sanctioning vulgar speculation in Texas real estate, Considerant specified the exact proportion of profits to go to labor, capital, and talent. In invoking the familiar Fourierist triad, however, he stressed the profit motive. The creation of a free area for progressive social experimentation was not conceivable, he argued, without capital and competition. He emphasized the difference between Fourier's ideas and those of utopian communists like Cabet. Fourierists criticized the abuses of capital, he wrote, but their goal, unlike that of the communists, was the creation of a form of association in which capital and labor could be reconciled.[72]

The statutes of the Colonization Society were published in November 1854, along with Considerant's commentary, in an expanded second edition of *Au Texas*. The response to this was if anything even more enthusiastic than that provoked by the first edition. By the end of 1854, 1,291,446 francs had been pledged, and Allyre Bureau could announce that a total of 7 million or 8 million francs was expected and that the number of would-be colonists now reached "at least 2,500."[73] The vast majority of respondents wanted to join an association based on Fourierist principles; very few accepted Considerant's contention that colonization and social experimentation should be kept distinct.

This desire to move rapidly to the practical realization of Fourier's theory had long been widespread within the Fourierist movement. It had lain behind the complaints about Considerant's political activities in 1848 and 1849 and about his coolness in the 1840s to the projects of *réalisateurs* like Arthur Young and Arthur Bonnard. One of these practical Fourierists who was still active in the 1850s was Dr. Auguste Savardan, whose proposal to create a Fourierist orphanage at Condé-sur-Vesgre had been discouraged by Considerant. Although Savardan occasionally grumbled about Considerant's "peremptory and overbearing personality," he, like many others, was captivated and inspired by the eloquence of *Au Texas:*

> With his stirring prose, with the precision of his affirmations about the beauty of the climate, the miraculous fecundity, and the extremely low price of the land, [Considerant] had aroused in my mind, as in so many others, the mirage of the rapid establishment of the city of our dreams, the magnificent Phalansterian city.

What excited Savardan was not Considerant's proposal for a "champ d'asile" open to all progressives, but rather the description of Texas as a magnificent site for the establishment of a Fourierist Phalanx. He wrote Considerant urging "the immediate constitution" in Texas, if not of a full-scale Phalanx, then at least of an "administrative center" organized according to Fourier's ideas.[74]

At the end of August 1854, Savardan traveled to Brussels to make his case to Considerant in person. He was shocked by what he regarded as Considerant's casual attitude toward preparations. Later he recalled that he came upon Considerant stretched out on a sofa and smoking his pipe, and that during their conversation Considerant seemed more interested in blowing perfect smoke rings than in listening carefully to his proposals. In any case, Savardan presented himself as someone who could lead the first cohort of settlers. His group would perform the functions of the pioneers: they would prepare the land and welcome newcomers. At the same time, they would create the rudiments at least of a common life by constructing and operating a communal kitchen and restaurant, a library, a school, an infirmary, a bathhouse, a laundry, and a general store. These facilities would be open to all members of the community and would be paid for by the users in proportion to their use. Once this partial realization of Fourierist principles had been achieved, Savardan argued, then the Colonization Society could occupy itself with the purchase of land and the other functions Considerant had in mind.[75]

Considerant's initial reaction to Savardan's proposal was evasive, and he made no reference to it in the by-laws adopted in September. The response to the publication of the by-laws was so emphatically favorable to some sort of experiment in association, however, that Considerant was obliged to reconsider his position on the role a Fourierist association might play in the initial phases of settlement. In late October he met with the directors in Brussels and reached a verbal understanding on the principles of a "provisional agreement" intended to serve as the charter of a "Phalansterian Society" to exist autonomously on the territory to be purchased by the Colonization Society. This smaller society, which would offer welcome and temporary lodging to subsequent groups of settlers, would be run, in some respects at least, as a Fourierist association.[76]

In early November, just a few days after his meeting with the directors in Brussels, Considerant traveled to Switzerland to make contact with his supporters there and also to see his friends and relatives from Franche-Comté one last time. Since he could not enter France, his sisters Justine and Julie and his friends from Salins, Auguste and Mariette Thiébaud, met him in Geneva. He also visited the Swiss Jura, where he met with people interested in organizing groups of artisans and laborers for eventual emigration to Texas. His talks with members of the community of watchmakers at Lôcle were especially productive; and from Neuchâtel, where he stayed with the former *représentant du peuple*, Jean-Baptiste Victor Versigny, he wrote jubilantly to his associates in Paris of the possibility of a massive migration of Swiss watchmakers to America. Three days in Geneva and one in Annecy, where he met with the exiled novelist Eugène Sue, only reinforced his enthusiasm. "All by itself," he wrote, "our Swiss contingent would make up a good core group for colonization."[77]

On his return to Brussels in mid-November 1854, Considerant again had to confront the question of the Fourierist association desired by Savardan and many others. During his absence the directors had written Savardan to enlist his aid in drafting a new set of by-laws for the proposed "Phalansterian Society." For more than a month Considerant and his associates considered the matter; and there was some discussion of it at the first general assembly of shareholders held in Paris on December 26. It was only a few days later in Brussels, where Considerant and Cantagrel were joined by Bureau, Godin, Savardan, and the Swiss Fourierist Karl Burkli, that a formal agreement was reached and a new set of by-laws adopted.[78]

According to the provisional agreement drawn up in late December, the new Phalansterian Society would serve two functions. First, it would contribute to the work of colonization by providing a center in which arriving colonists might find "temporary lodging, information, provisions, a friendly population, and everything necessary to facilitate the definitive establishment of a settlement, whatever form it might take." Second, the elements of collective organization that it embodied (for instance, the communal kitchen and dining room) would make of it "a first step on the road that leads to integral association." In commenting on this proposal in an addendum to the second edition of *Au Texas*, Considerant noted that he himself shared the widespread desire to create some sort of genuine association in Texas. It is possible that in writing this he had in fact convinced himself that the provisional agreement was consistent with what he had wanted all along. To a detached observer, though, it would seem that the attempt to create any kind of Fourierist association at the outset was exactly what Considerant had been warning against in the first edition of *Au Texas*.[79]

One other issue considered at the meeting in Brussels was the timetable for emigration and the composition of the departing groups. In *Au Texas* Considerant had been adamant about the dangers of impatience. He had warned against the belief in the "immediate realization" of the ideal, and he had insisted on the need to avoid any precipitous departure of would-be colonists. His original proposal had in fact called for an advanced guard of about 150 pioneers—most of them Americans—to spend as much as a year preparing the site prior to the arrival of groups of settlers. In accordance with this plan, François Cantagrel had sailed for America in October with the intention of meeting up with John Allen in Cincinnati and proceeding to North Texas to select a site and recruit laborers.[80] Much of this was called into question, though, by the adoption of the provisional agreement, which suggested that a group of European Fourierists would take over the functions of the avant-garde. The whole situation was further complicated by the fact that some Europeans, notably a group from Louvain, were determined to leave as soon as possible for Texas, regardless of the instructions of Considerant and the directors. Considerant did his best to dissuade them, and he raised the whole issue of the timetable for emigration at the meeting in Brussels in late December.[81]

This meeting was attended by several individuals who had been given the responsibility of organizing and leading groups of emigrants—notably Savardan and Karl Burkli of Geneva. Exactly what was decided at the meeting is not clear. Considerant subsequently claimed only that he had made "some choices from among the candidates for emigration," while insisting that none should leave until he gave the signal.[82] According to Savardan, however, each of the group leaders presented to Considerant a list of the names of all the would-be emigrants in his group, and these lists were "attentively examined, discussed, and determined by him and by us." Savardan, whose account says nothing about an agreement on the timing of departures, conceded that "at the moment of the departures, these lists were somewhat exceeded." He claimed, however, that the directors had accepted all additions. In the end, close to 150 French, Swiss, and Belgian emigrants were to depart for Texas during the winter of 1855. If the question of who authorized these departures is hard to resolve, one thing is clear: Considerant's original plan to separate the tasks of the pioneer and the community builder was now a dead letter. Jean-Baptiste Godin wrote to Cantagrel on February 3: "Plans have changed. It is no longer with American pioneers that the preparation of the terrain will take place. The colonizing wave is pushing us here, and Europe is going to furnish the first colonists needed to get things started."[83]

The discussion over the statutes and forms within which the emigration to Texas would take place did not prevent Considerant from pushing ahead with plans for his own departure. In the last two months of 1854, his letters to Allyre Bureau and the others at the rue de Beaune were a litany of requests for clothing, tobacco, hammocks, maps, seeds, plant cuttings, and books. Clearly he did not plan to be returning soon. He took with him as many of his most precious possessions as he could gather. Above all, he took his most prized books—his vellum-bound copy of Fourier's *Traité*, and his inscribed copy of the *Introduction à la science sociale* by Amédée Paget, whose death ten years earlier had been a blow that still caused pain.

Considerant also said his good-byes. The trip to Switzerland gave him the chance to see his sisters and a few old friends for the last time. Others he wrote. One lovely farewell letter, addressed to Eugène Bourson, the young son of his Belgian friend Philippe Bourson, is worth quoting in part:

> Soon you will come join us in Texas. You must become an engineer, proficient in theory and skillful in practice, so that you are competent in many different areas and are not obliged to spend your whole life below-decks on a ship. A military ship is, after all, only a floating prison. But you will be free on the Phalansterian ships which float over there under the bright sun with their flags rippling in the wind. And then sometimes you will . . . run and hunt in the woods, spending your time with your friends, and sometimes you'll make great sea voyages. You'll see how happy you will be.[84]

The great Fourierist exodus to America was going to take place under the very conditions Considerant had warned against. Still, he was hopeful. He could picture his group arriving like a Phalansterian ship, flags flying and the crew warmed by the radiant Texas sun. In the first days of January, as he addressed his comrades for the last time prior to his departure, he seemed to have no doubts or reservations.

> Time is pressing. Some have already reached Texas and others are at sea. The year 1855 is beginning, and we are beginning our first campaign with it. The living spirit of humanity is in us. God will protect our work! I am leaving, friends, and I will wait for you on the immaculate ground in which we have to sow liberty, science, and love."[85]

14

A Texas Utopia

In *Au Texas* Victor Considerant talked about the state of Texas as if it were
his own personal discovery. In fact, by 1854 Texas had long been a focal
point for the hopes and dreams of restless, dissatisfied, or simply ambitious
Europeans. There was nothing new about the extravagance of Considerant's language or his paeans to the soil and climate of Texas. Indeed, the
European fascination with Texas went back to the period of Spanish rule. In
1817 the Napoleonic general Charles Lallemand brought two boatloads of
retired soldiers to Galveston Island in hopes of creating a sanctuary where
veterans of the Grand Army might find a new life as *soldats-laboureurs*.
"Le Champ d'Asile," as it was called, never amounted to much, but thanks
to the poetry of Béranger, the fiction of Balzac, and the work of many other
novelists, poets, and painters, a legend was created that continued to haunt
the French imagination twenty years later.[1]

In 1842 a group of German noblemen led by Prince Carl of Solms-Braunfels founded the Adelsverein, a society for the protection of German immigrants in Texas. Their dream to create a feudal German state in Texas was
doomed from the start, but their efforts culminated in the founding of cities
like New Braunfels and Fredericksburg and in the establishment of a lasting
German presence in West Texas. Finally, during the period of Texas inde-

pendence (1836–1845), the distribution of huge land grants led to the emergence of a new class of capitalist entrepreneurs like the Frenchman Henri Castro, the founder of Castroville, Texas, who dreamed of making fortunes by transporting and settling colonies of immigrants. Castro's wealth didn't last, but Castroville did; and the brochures published by its founder helped create an image of Texas as a bountiful land whose fertile and well-watered soil awaited only the efforts of hard-working European farmers to make it yield rich harvests.[2]

Alongside the political refugees, idealistic noblemen, and capitalist entrepreneurs, there was another group of Europeans for whom Texas was the object of rich and alluring fantasies. These were the utopian socialists. In 1828, after disappointments at New Harmony, Indiana, Robert Owen negotiated with the Mexican government for the grant of an immense domain located in the provinces of Coahuila and Texas. In the end, the Mexican Congress failed to approve the land concession, but Owen continued to nurse the dream of a Texas community and apparently communicated it to Etienne Cabet later.[3]

Cabet's ill-fated attempt to create an Icarian colony in Texas has already been mentioned. In articles in his weekly *Le Populaire* and in several brochures published in 1847 and 1848, Cabet celebrated the climate, soil, rainfall, and general salubrity of Texas. On February 3, 1848, an Icarian "advance guard" led by Adolphe Gouhenant sailed from Le Havre with the intention of readying land for the arrival of a second wave of settlers. The land acquired by Cabet in signing a spectacularly unfavorable contract with the Peters Company of Cincinnati turned out to be arid and far from any navigable river. It suited Cabet, however, to accuse Gouhenant of having been charged by "the Jesuits" with the "infernal mission" of destroying the colony.[4]

Considerant, we know, heard Gouhenant's side of the story from his own lips in 1853. In his youth he had also surely heard talk of the "Champ d'Asile" from his father, whose dreams of emigrating to the banks of the Ohio may well have been inspired by stories about Lallemand's venture. Considerant may not have known much, before 1853, of the German communities in Texas or of Castroville. However he was, or at least he claimed to be, aware of many other ventures in emigration to the New World, some of which had resulted in "serious defeats, sad failures, or total catastrophes."[5] He felt confident of his ability to avoid the errors and illusions of his predecessors. This confidence was to be shaken, however, within weeks of his arrival in America.

I

On the evening of January 15, 1855, Victor and Julie Considerant and Clarisse Vigoureux sailed for New York abroad the steamer *Union*.[6] When they docked at New York on February 4, Considerant's hopes were as high as ever, but he soon made a series of discoveries that left him sick and demoralized. First, the Texas state legislature had closed off a large amount of land to settlement and development. A railroad line was to be built through North Texas, and until the route was determined a wide strip of land was being placed in reserve. As a result, the territory around Fort Worth that he had explored in 1853 and chosen as the ideal site for a community was closed to settlement. There were, to be sure, rumors that the reserve would soon be lifted, but these rumors made it harder to buy land. Settlers were simply moving in and establishing themselves on lands within the reserve, and land not in reserve was rapidly being bought up by both pioneers and speculators.

Another disappointment for Considerant was the project's failure to attract significant American support. During his trip through the West in 1853 he had been exhilarated by the interest shown by individual American Fourierists, not only at the North American Phalanx but also in Boston, New York, and Cincinnati. It turned out, however, that the American Fourierist movement, so vigorous in the 1840s, had exhausted itself. There were individual gestures of sympathy and support. James T. Fisher of Boston and Benjamin Urner of Cincinnati served as American agents for the project and raised some money selling Fourierist tracts. A former Brook Farmer, John Allen, agreed to help recruit American laborers and oversee their work. Brisbane, Urner, Marx Lazarus, Thomas Durant, and Nicholas P. Trist all bought stock or made contributions to the venture. In October 1854, Brisbane published a much abridged translation of *Au Texas* under the title *The Great West*. And in August 1855 a group of American Fourierists from New York and Pennsylvania formed the Texas Emigration Union to publicize the project and recruit colonists. In the end, all these efforts made little difference. Apparently no more than two dozen Americans actually joined the community in Texas, and the attempt to raise money from American Fourierists was a dismal failure. Even Brisbane contributed only seven thousand of the twenty thousand dollars he had initially pledged. Worse yet, in June 1855 he was already circulating plans for a rival Fourierist community to be composed exclusively of wealthy Americans.[7]

A final cause for discouragement on Considerant's part was the hostility of the Texas press toward his plans, once they became known. At the time of his first trip he had been overwhelmed by the warmth and hospitality of the Texans he met and by their sympathetic interest in his project, but when he returned a year and a half later conditions had changed. With the rapid increase of immigration into Texas, a powerful nativist or "Know-Nothing" movement had emerged in the state. This movement was actually national in scope, and its roots lay in the anti-foreign parties and movements that had arisen in New York and Boston in the 1840s. However, the hatred of Catholics and suspicion of foreign radicals characteristic of early urban nativism found an echo in the rural South and Southwest of the mid-1850s, where they were reinforced by the fear that foreigners—especially radical foreigners—were likely to be Abolitionists.[8]

The Know-Nothing movement enjoyed only a brief period of influence in American political life, but Considerant's arrival happened to coincide with the height of the movement's popularity. Not surprisingly his plans, as they were explained to the American public in Brisbane's abridged translation of *Au Texas*, aroused bitter opposition from the Know-Nothings and their sympathizers. Just two weeks after Considerant's arrival, the *Texas State Gazette* of Austin published a long editorial deploring Considerant's plan to establish "a colony of socialists" in Texas.

> We are always pleased to have industrious immigrants come among us. Plenty of work can be found by mechanics and laborers, and there is room in all our towns for more enterprising merchants and business men. There is one class, however, that we are opposed to, and have no disposition to hold out to them inducements to settle among us. This class is of that Propagandist school which in France and in parts of the United States, has and is seeking to sap the foundations of society. The socialist desires to destroy individual rights in property; and, if he is not a very intelligent and moral man—a rare thing—we may have in him a neighbor who will rob and plunder us whenever he can get the chance; for he holds it as a primary principle in his creed, that no individual has a right to accumulate property for himself, and all above what is necessary to sustain him belongs to the rest of society. . . . Again, the socialist is an *abolitionist* everywhere. He would not be less opposed to slavery by living in Texas than in France or in Ohio. It is part of his creed. Now, we are told that John Allen, of Ohio, and Mons. Victor Considerant, propose bringing out from France to western Texas a colony of socialists. This move, for the purpose of building up a sect opposed to our political institutions, may well be regarded with jealousy, and the founders may rely upon it that they will not be suffered to tamper with our institutions. . . . We note this advent of socialism in Texas as foreboding us no good; and we wish them to have a fair understanding before they reach our soil, that as a political sect, our whole people are against them.[9]

This editorial was widely circulated and applauded not only in numerous letters to the editor of the *Texas State Gazette* but also in editorials published elsewhere in papers ranging from the *Texas State Times* to the *Washington Sentinel*.

Not all Texas newspapers were hostile to Considerant's project. The *Dallas Herald,* the *Northern Standard,* and the *Galveston News* were all relatively sympathetic. Nonetheless, before leaving New York Considerant felt obliged to write a thirty-eight-page pamphlet, *European Colonization in Texas: An Address to the American People,* which described the aims and benefits of a European settlement in Texas in a way calculated both to disarm his Know-Nothing critics and to attract American investors. Unfortunately, this pamphlet did nothing to mollify the critics, and it passed largely unnoticed by investors.

Considerant later wrote that these reverses did not in themselves destroy his confidence. It was only later, when he learned that two groups of emigrants led by Savardan and Burkli and including women, children, and old men, had sailed for America without waiting for his authorization, that he fell to the ground, "beaten, crushed, a living cadaver."[10] Yet he did get sick shortly after his arrival, and he apparently fell into a state of depression that left him feeling that the weight of the world had fallen on him.[11]

Convinced that the success or failure of the venture now depended entirely on him, Considerant remained on the East Coast during February and March of 1855, writing his *Address to the American People* and seeking support for his project. He discussed its prospects with members of the North American Phalanx, with Boston Fourierists like James Fisher, with the still unknown young journalist Frederick Law Olmsted, and even with a figure out of the past, the philanthropist Arthur Young, whom he met in New York City on February 12. A week later he traveled to Washington to seek help from Texas congressmen in obtaining a land concession or at least in circumventing the newly imposed restrictions on settlement. There he was joined by his friend, the architect César Daly, whose English was fluent and who had come to America to help get the colony established. In Washington, Considerant and Daly were received courteously by several legislators (including a former governor of Texas), but all they obtained were vague promises that the reserve would eventually be lifted and assurances that attractive sites could be found elsewhere in Texas.[12]

Unable to obtain the land he wanted in North Texas, Considerant began in March to consider the southern part of the state. At that very moment, however, and unknown to Considerant, his collaborator François Cantagrel was buying unrestricted land in North Texas, though at a much higher

price than Considerant had hoped to pay.[13] Cantagrel, who had sailed for
New York on October 3, 1855, accompanied by a young Belgian medical
student named Roger, had traveled by steamboat and horseback to Texas by
roughly the same route that Considerant and Brisbane had taken eighteen
months earlier. At Patriot, Indiana, Cantagrel had been joined by John
Allen and a small group of American laborers including Arthur Lawrie.[14]
Arriving in Dallas on December 29, Cantagrel discovered that the area
around Fort Worth was now restricted and that the unrestricted lands in
Cooke County north of Fort Worth, which Considerant had praised, had
been claimed by settlers and speculators.[15] After some further investiga-
tions along the West Fork of the Trinity River above Fort Worth and along
the Clear Fork of the Brazos, Cantagrel traveled to Austin to consult land
surveys. In mid-February he returned to Dallas, where he had already seen
some attractive land. Shortly thereafter, while Considerant was in Washington talking to Texas congressmen, Cantagrel purchased 2,436 acres of
land located along the bluffs overlooking the West Fork of the Trinity River
just three miles southwest of the village of Dallas.[16]

So it was that a site for the community was finally selected just a short
distance from Dallas. Setting up their headquarters in a cabin by the river,
Cantagrel, Roger, and John Allen bought several pair of oxen and hired local laborers and carpenters from Dallas to bring trees out of a cedar forest
on the property and start the work of building. By the middle of April,
when Considerant had only just embarked from New York by steamer for
New Orleans, Cantagrel had assembled a labor force of about twenty, and
they were working with an energy and speed that later arrivals like Alexandre Raisant and the Polish engineer Kalikst Wolski found impressive.[17]

The site chosen was near the top of a bluff overlooking the Trinity River.
It was dotted with outcroppings of white limestone; and although the quality of the soil was poor, small trees, vines, and buffalo grass grew abundantly, creating an illusion of fertility. The first buildings were simple log
cabins, but Cantagrel also got work started on a large central building of
rough-sawed cedar logs and hand-hewn limestone rocks, which would
house dormitories, a communal kitchen, and a dining room. Plans were
drawn up for a director's house and for separate bunkhouses; large tracts on
the hillside were laid out for vineyards and orchards; and the valley land
was divided into separate fields. The name given to the settlement was
Reunion.[18]

News that the Colonization Society had actually acquired land in Texas
reached Considerant a few weeks before his departure from New York,
but the same news did not reach Paris until April 20, 1855. (It took at least

six weeks for a letter to travel between Paris and Dallas, and three months for an exchange to take place.) By that time, and even though they had no fixed destination, over a hundred would-be colonists were en route to Texas. Two groups, totaling almost fifty people, had sailed just prior to Considerant. Then on February 28 a boatload of forty-three colonists left Le Havre for New Orleans under the leadership of Dr. Savardan. On April 12 another group of twenty-seven Swiss led by Karl Burkli of Zurich sailed out of Bremen. Ironically, although the Parisian directors were well aware of the dangers of premature emigration, they authorized these last two departures without hesitation, and in May they could write optimistically of further sailings in the fall.[19]

Considerant finally left New York on April 14. Traveling with him were his wife and her mother, the architect César Daly, and two other Frenchmen, Maguet and Willemet, whom Considerant had met at the North American Phalanx. When the group arrived in New Orleans on April 28, Dr. Savardan and his party were already there. Savardan found Considerant "preoccupied, care-worn, sad," still showing signs of the illness that had laid him low in New York, and in no condition to discuss practical matters.[20]

Two years later, when Savardan was writing his own account of the "wreck" of the community at Reunion, he reflected on the responsibilities of the man he had called the "new Moses." Considerant had, in his view, shown "great weakness" from the time of his arrival in New York.

> Forgetting the conditions of time and number that he had himself set, and losing control at the first hint of a miscalculation, he gave way and broke down into a state of complete discouragement. Since that time none of us has seen him without the more or less pronounced symptoms of this sickness. Like some other sick people, he loved to describe its effects to anyone who would listen.

Savardan went on to observe that he saw little of Considerant during the week that they were both in New Orleans. Considerant seemed to be avoiding him and his group of emigrants; when they left for Galveston, Considerant booked passage for his party on a different steamship. "We observed in him," wrote Savardan, "without being able to explain it at that time, a disdain, a pronounced repugnance to the majority of the emigrants who had come to him so trustingly and who counted so firmly on his leadership." Actually Considerant's aloofness may be explained in part by the fact that, in addition to being sick and tired, he wanted to spend his time in New Orleans with his host, Jules Juif, who was a cousin of Julie's and an old friend. It is true, however, that Considerant did eventually come to feel an almost visceral repugnance toward most of the colonists. The first and strongest object of his dislike was Savardan himself, who emerges from his own book as a self-important, punctilious, and splenetic busybody and who clearly came to symbolize for Considerant a kind of narrowness and conventionality that he hoped he was leaving behind when he came to the United States.[21]

Considerant's party reached Galveston on May 8, a few days after Savardan with his large group of colonists. On his arrival, Considerant was interviewed by a journalist from the Galveston *Civilian,* and he had the opportunity to restate the message of the brochure he had published before leaving New York. The main goal of the French colonization project, he asserted, was not to subvert American institutions but to demonstrate to European workers the results that might be yielded by "peaceful work . . . under a system of free and democratic institutions." He then went on to describe in glowing terms the contribution his group could make to the life of Texas. Their aim was not merely to engage in farming but to "perfect agriculture," "establish factories," and collaborate on the improvement of roads and rivers and on "the construction of the railroads that will one day cross the whole country." In the slightly more distant future, Considerant predicted, his compatriots would establish a university in Texas, "a university in which English and French literature, the arts, physics, mechanics, and the sciences will be taught by men of recognized learning."[22]

After several days in Galveston, Considerant's and Savardan's parties went on—again by separate steamboats—up Buffalo Bayou to Houston, where a small farm had been purchased to serve as a way station for colonists and as a nursery for plants brought from Europe. In Houston both groups had to pause for a week to make ready for the arduous overland journey of 250 miles from Houston to Dallas.

In *Au Texas* Considerant had asserted that water was abundant in Texas and that its larger rivers were navigable much of the year. In fact, the Trinity River was already almost dry. Thus, all the goods and supplies brought from France or purchased in New Orleans and Houston had to be loaded on rented carts and covered wagons. Livestock had to be purchased—oxen to haul the wagons, and horses to round up the oxen each morning—and teamsters had to be hired to drive the oxen. Savardan later noted bitterly that, as the leader of a large group, he was responsible for making all these arrangements while Considerant, who was responsible only for his family and a few friends, occupied himself in Houston mainly with the purchase of saddle horses and two handsome gray mares to pull a "joli char-à-bancs" purchased for him in Cincinnati. To make matters worse, Considerant's group simply left when they were ready, without even offering to accompany or help Savardan's group.[23]

An episode that took place in Houston provides revealing insight into the developing antagonism between Considerant and Savardan. The two had been invited to dine at the house of a well-to-do Texan, and Considerant sat down at the dinner table with his hat on and his coat off. Savardan felt obliged to lecture him about proper table manners, which prompted Considerant to reply that he "needn't have bothered to come to the land of liberty" if it meant "putting up with such constraints." This was not the end of Savardan's unhappiness with Considerant's table manners: at Reunion, he complained, Considerant seemed to prefer the company of some of the crudest and least educated individuals, and his language and manners were even worse than theirs. "At Reunion," he recalled, "every day we saw . . . Monsieur Considerant sit down and sit his ladies down at the dinner table next to working people, with his elbows on the table, his hat on his head, and his pipe in his mouth."[24]

Considerant's group arrived at Reunion on May 30, two weeks ahead of Savardan's. Considerant found that morale was good and that the laborers working under Cantagrel's direction had started to build housing for the community. They were not prepared, however, to provide anything but the most primitive accommodations for the seventy additional colonists who were on their way. Three large bunkhouses had now been built out of stone and log, each with some private rooms in the rear for couples and single women and a dormitory for men at the front. They had long sloping shingled roofs, and a porch in front of each building served as a dining area. Considerant, who was not happy with them, called them "mastodons."[25]

Both Considerant and Cantagrel agreed that since at the outset the colonists were going to have to live off food and supplies purchased in Houston or Dallas, it would be wise to eat as frugally as possible. Thus for the first weeks the colonists dined with monotonous regularity on coffee and bread and occasional cornmeal pancakes in the morning, a lunch of weak bouillon and boiled beef (which Savardan later described as more often rancid than not), and in the evening leftovers from lunch. They rarely ate vegetables, and the only amenities were an occasional cup of tea and a small glass of whiskey ceremoniously poured out in the evening to each adult. By midsummer, however, the menu had become a little more varied, as hunters began to bring in game from the woods and fields below the town site. At the same time the purchase of cows, pigs, and goats permitted the colonists to enjoy what one of them described as "a host of little treats which were lacking at the start, such as butter, cheese, etc."[26]

During the early part of the summer the colonists devoted themselves to construction, to planting vegetables, and to establishing small herds. They soon realized, however, that in the absence of cities, markets, and even roads, there was no point in trying to establish the sorts of workshops and industries with which most of them were familiar. There was no market for even the most basic of manufactured goods. The town of Dallas was still little more than a dot on the map: its population in 1855 had not yet reached four hundred, and it was only incorporated the following year. Under the circumstances, tanning and distilling were the only industries that could amount to anything.[27]

It was clear that once roads were built and a railroad line established across North Texas, economic growth would be rapid. (For this reason speculators had already bought up much of the available land in the area.) In the meantime, the only profitable farm work seemed to be stock raising and vegetable farming. The latter was difficult, however, because, as Kalikst Wolski put it, "the sun, so beneficent in other countries, burns mercilessly in Texas." The only way of getting many vegetables to grow was to plant them between rows of corn, which provided shade and helped the soil to hold its moisture. Much of the colonists' capital was spent on the acquisition of livestock. Almost everyone was also asked to lend a hand in the fields and gardens or to help with the work of construction. Those, like the Belgians Cousin and Roger, who were suited neither for carpentry nor for farming, waited on table and helped with the preparation of meals.[28]

The working day was long. Since it was impossible to work outdoors during the heat of the day, the colonists had to get up before dawn and work until seven in the evening with a three- or four-hour siesta at noon. Until the arrival of Savardan's group, morale remained high, and most of the colonists accepted the routine uncomplainingly. "Here everyone does what is needed," a young Belgian wrote back to his parents.

A professor of music (M. Steere) hews stone with his friends MM. Danton, Johnson, etc. A former Unitarian minister (M. Allen) goes out at four o'clock in the morning to herd the cattle and plant sweet potatoes, peas, and beans with me. The same Allen kills the beef cattle and skins them, etc. Roger carries wooden shingles on his back across a Mexican rope bridge to the West Fork. Then he goes off on horseback to buy provisions from the local farmers and comes back at a good trot with a basket full of six or ten dozen eggs . . . without breaking a single one. Cousin bakes the bread and pours the whiskey twice a day. There are all sorts of things to be done. As for me, I've already helped out in the kitchen, in the garden. I spent three days plowing a cornfield, and I water the sweet potatoes, which I'll dig up after having helped plant them.[29]

Other colonists were not so delighted with the organization of work at Reunion. There were complaints about waste and mismanagement and about the incompetence of the ministers, musicians, and medical students in the performance of their assigned tasks. Despite the complaints, though, there were moments during the first few months when the whole community came together happily and harmoniously. Such at least is the impression one gets from letters published in the *Bulletin de la Société de Colonisation*—letters describing celebrations on July 4 and July 14, and dancing on Sundays after dinner, in an outdoor amphitheater decorated with bouquets and garlands of flowers.[30]

It was Julie Considerant who created this amphitheater, which Wolski described in his recollections as an "improvised salon."

> Not far from the dwelling houses of Reunion colony was to be found a small piece of woods, overgrown with cedars, whose green branches made a curiously pleasant contrast with the yellowness all around that came from the hot sun. This little place Madame Considerant transformed into a kind of salon, and here she received all the colonists who, after the exhausting labors of the day, wished to get away and enjoy absorbing ideas exchanged among themselves.

Long afterward Wolski fondly remembered the coolness of the spot, its "rug of natural green," the music of the birds, and the lighting provided by the moon and the stars. "Instead of a sofa and armchairs," he wrote, "hammocks were hung from tree to tree," which spared the colonists "the unpleasant visits of snakes, always crawling in uncounted numbers everywhere in this region." Here, Wolski wrote, a "select company of Reunion colonists" would gather after nine in the evening. The long midday siesta "permitted us the luxury of reveling in the marvelously beautiful nights beneath the Texas sky, in an enlightened and congenial company." The talk, which was sometimes erudite but more often "of a light and witty nature," sometimes went on until one or two in the morning.[31]

By the middle of July 1855, with the arrival of the groups led by Savardan and Burkli, the population of Reunion reached about 130. At this point serious problems began to emerge within the community. One of the chief problems was simply that the newcomers were exhausted and in many cases bitterly disappointed from the moment of their arrival. After an ocean voyage of at least six weeks and an arduous three- or four-week trip in covered wagons through dry creek beds, burned forests, and waterless prairies, they arrived at Reunion to find primitive accommodations, bad food, oppressive heat, springs running dry, and rattlesnakes.

The summer of 1855 was, in fact, one of the hottest and driest in memory: rivers and springs dried up prematurely, crops failed to mature, and prices rose. Since the planting at Reunion had gotten under way late, and since the colonists had in any case planted many crops not native to the area, Reunion was especially hard hit by the drought. "The garden is a complete failure," wrote one colonist in early July, "because we planted everything two months too late, and because this is a year of unprecedented drought." [32] Some wheat had been harvested, and there was still hope for late plantings of corn and sweet potatoes, but the rest was lost; and in the fall these late plantings, too, were ravaged as hordes of grasshoppers and caterpillars descended on Reunion, devouring everything in their path.

In the month of August everything went wrong. First, the colony's principal spring went dry, and water had to be hauled in from a distance. Then the merchant in Dallas who had been the colonists' chief supplier warned them that he would soon be out of salt and sugar. There was now so little water on the prairies that the ox-drawn wagons that normally brought supplies from Houston to Dallas could no longer make the trip. Not surprisingly, with food and water running short and the new arrivals exhausted by the rigors of the trip, a number of colonists fell sick. In early August two people died: Vézian, an ex-army officer of just twenty-five; and Rupert, a journalist of Swiss origin. In the last two weeks of August there were two more deaths; and Kalikst Wolski noted in his journal that a tailor named Maguet was "busy stirring up our colonists against Dr. Savardan, claiming that it is he who is the chief cause of our misfortunes, that he does not know how to treat disease." [33]

In the face of all these difficulties many of the colonists lost courage. In July the Belgians and some of the French began to feud; and there were conflicts, too, between different groups of immigrants. Dr. Savardan's group of forty-three colonists began, almost immediately after their arrival in mid-June, to complain loudly about the food, the quality of their accommodations, and the chaotic organization of work within the community. By Savardan's own account, his group soon fell "almost completely into disgrace," serving as the target of a "running fire of slanderous taunts" from the Belgians. On the other hand, the smaller group of Swiss under Karl Burkli, who arrived on July 5, were highly respected by the rest of the community, but they were so dissatisfied with Considerant's leadership that, within six months, most of them had left. [34]

Throughout all of this the main problem confronting Considerant and his associates was that, far from being self-supporting, the community was living off its capital. By August a substantial herd had been established— eighty beef cattle, thirty milk cows, twenty pigs—and the community managed to set up its own butcher shop at a time when the village of Dallas had none. The colonists could also boast that they had placed four hundred acres of land under cultivation and established an elaborate irrigation system including three hundred meters of zinc pipe. But the system was worthless when their springs were running dry; and they had no more to show for their efforts than a little grain and a few plates of radishes. They still had to buy almost all their food, except for meat, at Dallas. Even though they now had a sawmill, lumber and other building materials had to be purchased at Dallas, or else carted in at great expense from Houston.[35]

In due course, Considerant believed, the capital investments already made would bear fruit. In the worst case, the land's value would increase dramatically once Dallas was connected by rail with the rest of the country. Eventually it would certainly be possible to realize a profit on the money invested in Reunion. In the short run, though, Considerant knew that the community would continue to absorb vast amounts of capital. Thus he saw himself as confronted by a hard choice. He could either withdraw support from the colony or else maintain that support and allow the capital to dissipate.

Considerant was unable to make this choice. Instead, he fell silent and, in effect, retreated to his hammock. For six months after his arrival at Reunion he did not send a single letter to the directors at Paris, allowing Cantagrel and Savardan to handle all communications. Later he wrote that the only acceptable course of action would have been to send nine-tenths of the colonists back to Europe—at the expense of the society if necessary—and simply write off the losses of the first year. But this could only have been done, he believed, if he had been confident of his ability to "limit the disastrous effect that such an act would have produced both in Europe and at Reunion itself."[36] He possessed no such confidence.

Finally Considerant adopted a compromise solution. In his capacity as Executive Agent of the Colonization Society—and without consulting the directors in Paris—he devised a plan that would place limits on the support given to Reunion by the Colonization Society. Creating an autonomous Society of the Proprietors of Reunion, he ceded to it the "domain of Reunion," consisting now of 12,286 acres of land. The Colonization Society then bought 400 shares in the Proprietors' Society for $30,000 and received the right to half its profits. The other half was to be divided among the colonists, who were also to receive a daily wage ranging from 4½ to 8½ francs

($.90–1.65) depending on the kind of work they did. But they were only to receive one-third of this wage in tokens good for purchases at Reunion's store. The rest would be withheld by the Proprietors' Society and converted into shares to be credited to the account of each worker.[37]

The Proprietors' Society was formally constituted on August 7, 1855, with Cantagrel as director and a council of administration hand-picked by Considerant. At that time there were 128 colonists at Reunion, but only 95 of them joined the new association. The other 33 chose to leave. A dozen bought land and set about creating a village of their own, Mutuelle, to the west of Dallas on the road to Fort Worth. Some of the defectors were quick to let the directors in Paris know what they thought about the ineptitude and "unbelievable incapacity" of Considerant's leadership. As for Considerant himself, he had now become sick and embittered by the whole experience, aware of his responsibilities but at the same time unable either to write to the directors at Paris or to deal with the colonists he had brought to Texas. Later, when Savardan suggested that he raise the salary actually paid to the colonists, Considerant apparently replied: "No, not at all, I won't consent to that, because I set the rate on purpose to force them to leave if they don't know how to live on it."[38]

Considerant's rapid disenchantment with the whole venture, his exhaustion, and his inability to exercise real leadership are evident in most of the existing descriptions of life at Reunion during its first year. But the most vivid picture is certainly that of his enemy, Dr. Savardan, whose *Naufrage au Texas* includes the following account of a meeting of the council of administration:

> The director, M. Cantagrel, came to the meeting with all the questions concerning the Colony formulated in advance, and he called for solutions. In considering each question M. Roger rarely failed to raise endless objections and to make personal criticisms and sly insinuations. . . . M. Considerant, the President of the Council, was reclining in one of his two hammocks. Around him the councilors were sitting on the ground or on logs as in an Indian powwow. M. Cousin was lying in the other hammock, and from time to time he would pass a match to his master to keep the eternal fire burning in his pipe. Nonchalantly stretched out as they were, those two seemed to be trying to justify the term of "loaf-ansterians" [*fainéanstériens*] that someone had created for them in a moment of spite.[39]

In some other accounts of Reunion Considerant appears in a better light. The general impression one gets, however, is that he had completely lost control of the situation, that he had fallen into a state of mental and moral collapse. He said as much himself in the extraordinary apology he wrote two years later under the title *Du Texas*. There he described himself as a passive spectator and Reunion as a sort of monster that had come into being despite his efforts.

> I dragged around until autumn witnessing the spectacle, which was heartbreaking for me, of this strange "colonization" which replaced what I had thought was to be done in Texas. All the time I had before my eyes this hideous bastard, this fatherless monster, or rather this child of too many fathers which . . . I was supposed to treat as if it were my legitimate child.[40]

II

In October 1855 Considerant abruptly left Reunion to go to Austin. He was motivated primarily, no doubt, by the desire to get away from the "heartbreaking spectacle" that confronted him at Reunion, but his ostensible purpose was to seek the support of members of the Texas state legislature for a land grant to his Colonization Society. Since his English was still rudimentary, he asked his friend Roger, the Belgian medical student, to come along as his interpreter. Shortly after his arrival at Austin, Considerant made the acquaintance of a French-born Texas state senator who had a law practice in San Antonio. This was A. Supervielle, whom Victor described to Julie as "a fine, good-hearted man . . . who will be a great help to us if there is something to be done here."[41] Supervielle did put Considerant in touch with other legislators, and in due course Considerant obtained verbal expressions of support from a majority of the legislature's Committee on Public Lands. Still, he was not very hopeful of winning a vote in the legislature as a whole. Too many land grants had already been made to speculators who proved to be more interested in turning a quick profit than in attracting settlers to Texas. The legislature had become reluctant to award land grants to anyone claiming to promote immigration. Of course, it didn't help that the prospective immigrants in this case were socialists and abolitionists.[42]

In December Considerant was joined in Austin by the architect César Daly and the accountant Amédée Simonin. Simonin had been sent to Texas by the directors to keep an eye on Considerant and to find out what was going wrong with Reunion. He kept a diary during this period, and the picture of Considerant that emerges from this diary is of a sullen, uncommunicative, deeply depressed individual. At times it seemed to Simonin that Considerant was like an old man falling into senility before his eyes. "His brain is giving way under the weight of responsibility," wrote Simonin on January 21, 1856, "and he is paralyzed by terror in thinking of the activity that he ought to deploy in order to make things happen." At other times Simonin tried to explain Considerant's gloom and inertia in terms of the influence on him of his Belgian friends, those "two icicles" Roger and Cousin.

> Roger and Cousin have none of the qualities that Considerant needs in his friends. He has spent his life among warm-blooded, warm-hearted, and affectionate people who constantly let him know how they feel. He should have fallen in and established ties here with true and devoted friends, friends full of warmth and generosity. His nature is so good and so delicate that he gives way to the impressions he receives from the people, things, or objects that surround him. He needs to have around him warm people whose affection and devotion he can count on. For no one is more sensitive than he to the signs and marks of true devotion and true affection.[43]

Others who met Considerant in Texas were less understanding. To an American named Renshaw, for example, whose son James had come to Reunion from the North American Phalanx, Considerant was not only an incompetent leader; he was also guilty of bad faith in his dealings with his associates in Europe. He was not only "incapable of running an undertaking"; he was also "morally sick."[44]

Both César Daly and Amédée Simonin spoke English fluently, and they were able to widen Considerant's contacts with members of the Texas state legislature, but by this time Considerant no longer hoped for much from Austin, at least in the near future. He began to look in other directions—particularly toward West Texas. His friend Supervielle, who represented Bexar County in the State Senate, had spoken encouragingly of great tracts of land that might be bought for a reasonable price in the hill country west of San Antonio. There the population was ethnically mixed—"Germans, Mexicans, and a few American frontiersmen"—and was likely to be much less hostile to a group of "foreign socialists" than the population around Dallas. One of these tracts that Considerant found especially appealing was located along the Sabinal River in what was then called Uvalde Canyon, about eighty miles west of San Antonio. In early February, at the end of the legislative session, Considerant set out for San Antonio with Supervielle and Daly to inspect this property and to inquire, more generally, into the availability of land in the region west of San Antonio.[45]

Considerant spent about six weeks in San Antonio—from early February until mid-March. During this time his morale and his health improved.

The highlight of his trip was what he described as "a nice, invigorating little expedition" on horseback into Uvalde Canyon. It was only an initial tour of reconnaissance, but nearly everything he saw and learned about the canyon was encouraging. On his return to San Antonio he described it enthusiastically to the directors in Paris as "a miniature Alsace . . . a charming valley . . . watered from one end to the other by the Sabinal," whose "waters are the clearest and most freely flowing you can imagine." To his wife he wrote that it might be possible to buy all of Uvalde Canyon in one or two quick purchases. "If it is as easy to buy it all as I've been told, we shouldn't hesitate to buy at the price I've heard quoted, if only as a good investment of the funds of the Society." A few months later he was describing it to Julie simply as "a real little paradise."[46]

Considerant was back at Reunion by March 24. Not long after his return rumors began to spread among the colonists that he was making plans to dissolve the Proprietors' Society and sell its land in small parcels.[47] These rumors were not very wide of the mark. Considerant's main concern now was, in fact, to relieve the Colonization Society of the burden of maintaining the community at Reunion. Once this goal had been achieved, then the resources of the parent society could be used to promote a new effort of colonization elsewhere, presumably in Uvalde Canyon. This time, Considerant believed, there would be no question of throwing all the resources of the Colonization Society into a premature attempt at creating a Fourierist association. Instead, by purchasing all of Uvalde Canyon, the Colonization Society would be in a position to open up a vast area to a variety of efforts at community building. Thus, in the spring of 1856, Considerant was still hoping to realize the vision outlined in *Au Texas* and in the original statutes: the creation of a sanctuary for different kinds of radical social experimentation.

A first step in this direction was taken on May 7, when, on Considerant's initiative and against the strong objections of Dr. Savardan and the half-hearted resistance of Cantagrel, the council of administration of the Proprietors' Society voted to allow its members to exchange their shares for land. This opened the way for the establishment of privately owned farms within the community, and it clearly marked the abandonment of the attempt to create anything like a Fourierist association at Reunion. It was for this reason that Savardan opposed the move.

> If, by means of a coup d'état, you now destroy the Proprietors' Society, you will be committing an unjust act and, what's more, you will be making an irreparable mistake. Among the immigrants there are not ten percent who want the property to be broken up, and there are even fewer who could take up and above all maintain the life of settlers.[48]

In Savardan's view Considerant was a "dictator" who was willing to destroy an authentic experiment in Fourierist association simply to engage in land speculation.

Although Considerant had given up on Reunion by the spring of 1856, the material situation in the community was actually in some ways more promising than it had been the previous fall. The winter had been bitterly cold, and a good deal of time had been spent tightening up and insulating the bunkhouses and dormitories that had been hastily constructed the previous summer. New buildings had also been built—a smokehouse, a bakery, and new workshops and storage buildings—and a general store had been established; the herd of cattle had been enlarged; and by the end of March the plowing and planting were well under way. Hunting parties brought in wild game, which, with the addition of a few winter vegetables, made savory hot soups that colonists remembered long afterward. As the days grew longer and warmer, visiting resumed and the colony's morale improved. But in early May disaster struck. A bitter north wind brought a severe frost that ruined the growing crops and gardens. It was so cold that—in May!—the Trinity River froze over for three days. The plowing and planting had to be done all over again, but very little of what was planted in May survived the sun, drought, and grasshoppers of another hot summer.[49]

To complicate the situation still further, six new groups of colonists arrived during the first six months of 1856, bringing the total at Reunion to almost three hundred. Most of these were specialized workers who came with the approval of the directors in Paris, but others came on their own, sometimes bringing with them children and elderly relatives. Even the specialized workers sometimes turned out to be worthless. The gardener Guillier, for example, who had been the director of a nursery in Algeria, refused to run the nursery in Houston because of the danger of yellow fever. Explaining that he had not come to Reunion to work but to direct the work of others, he spent most of his eight months in the community playing the accordion. As for the uninvited arrivals, most of them were Fourierists who had been excited by *Au Texas*, but a few were survivors of failed utopian experiments elsewhere, such as Cabet's Icarian communities at Nauvoo and in Texas.[50]

Considerant himself obviously bore a large share of the blame for these unwanted arrivals. His failure to give clear instructions to the directors in Paris during his first six months at Reunion had placed them in an impossible position. By April 1856 he finally understood that something had to be done to stop the flow of immigrants. He wrote Alexandre Raisant, who ran the little farm near Houston that served both as a nursery for shrubs and seedlings brought from France and as a way station for immigrants, urging him to do everything possible to prevent new arrivals from continuing on their way to Reunion. He also sent his young lieutenant, the Belgian medical student Roger, back to France to explain to the directors that no new immigrants could be accepted. On his way Roger met several parties of would-be colonists—the first in the middle of the prairie between Dallas and Houston, but they had come much too far to turn back.[51]

What these new colonists found on their arrival must have made many of them wish that they had turned back. They had been warned about the material hardships awaiting them. What they could not have been prepared for was the total lack of direction at Reunion and the pervasive atmosphere of acrimony and discouragement. The restaurant and store were still relatively well run, but among the work groups discipline had collapsed. Woodcutters and artisans now spent their days fishing and hunting for their dinner; groups of workers quarreled interminably over the use of a team of horses; and tools, sacks, and saddles lay abandoned in the fields. The whole community was divided into factions whose members spent more time trading insults and accusations than working at their appointed tasks. Considerant and Savardan had become bitter enemies. Cantagrel was accused of mismanaging funds. Ugly rumors were circulating about Julie Considerant. Many of the original members of the community were now complaining openly about her husband's capriciousness and lack of leadership. And Amédée Simonin, the accountant whose diary is a major source for this period, had become convinced that Considerant was no longer in possession of his faculties.[52]

On April 7, 1856, a banquet was held to celebrate the anniversary of Fourier's birth. Speeches and toasts were given, and Considerant regained some of his old eloquence in appealing to the colonists to lay aside their differences. Considerant also took personal responsibility for many of the mistakes that had been made. At the end of his talk there were cheers from some of the colonists, but others were silent. Simonin noted afterward that Considerant himself did not really seem to believe his own hopeful words. No wonder then that he "could no longer electrify" a crowd that just a year earlier "considered him to be a demi-god."[53]

The real problem was that Considerant was no longer capable of acting like a leader—or even of making a decision. Both Simonin and Cantagrel noted that Considerant's mind was becoming increasingly confused, that he was losing his former lucidity. He now spent much of his time writing long and impractical papers on the problems confronting the community—

only to disavow them in the face of objections. He and Cantagrel now began to argue over the possible dissolution of the Proprietors' Society and the privatization of its land and resources. When Cantagrel talked of resigning, however, Considerant's response was to threaten to commit suicide.[54] By the end of April, Considerant had lost the confidence of almost all the members of the community—including some of his staunchest allies. Now a number of the colonists began to leave. A few who could afford it returned to France, and others moved into Dallas to seek work. Simonin the accountant resigned in June; Cantagrel kept talking of returning to France, and Considerant of leaving for West Texas.

Matters finally came to a head in July. Cantagrel, who had been particularly upset by Considerant's reluctance to remunerate colonists leaving the community, at last made good on his threats to quit. On July 6 he resigned as director, announcing his intention to return to Europe. The next day Considerant took over negotiations with the unhappy colonists and reached an agreement that gave them half of the wages previously withheld. This agreement was to be drawn up and signed on the morning of July 8, 1856, but that morning Considerant was nowhere to be found. Julie Considerant remained at Reunion, but her husband was gone, unable to tolerate the situation any longer.[55]

Eighteen months later, writing his own account of the history of Reunion, Auguste Savardan referred to Considerant's departure as a "flight" and attributed it to "the proofs of his inadequacy . . . to the deadly influence of opiates, and . . . to the enervation produced by the constant abuse of tobacco." The charge of drug dependency was not gratuitous; Considerant himself later admitted that he had been taking morphine as a sedative.[56] It is also abundantly clear that Considerant could no longer stand the sight of his fellow colonists at Reunion and that his departure was indeed a flight. Ten weeks later, when negotiations were under way to send someone else from Paris to take charge of Reunion, Considerant wrote his wife from San Antonio: "Let Guillon or Bureau come. I won't have any trouble with either one of them. I'll explain to them my way of looking at things, and they will do whatever they wish in the county of Dallas and the surrounding area. I won't have anything more to do with it."[57] In fact, Considerant had nothing more to do with Reunion. In his future comments on the community his only concern was to see it disbanded as rapidly as possible.

15

Uvalde Canyon

In leaving Reunion on June 8, Considerant's first impulse was to put as much distance as possible between himself and the colony. He did not want to think about it any more. He did not want to hear about it. When he had something to say about it in his letters to Julie, his comments were curt. Seven months later, when he was asked to return to Reunion to preside over its dissolution, he refused outright. If he had to set foot in Reunion again, he said, he would "die." The mere thought of the colony made him "sick in soul and body," and the only thing he could do to avoid succumbing to this malady was to "force [him]self to think about something else."[1]

I

The "something else" that Considerant now clutched at was his plan for the settlement of Uvalde Canyon in West Texas. Shortly after his first trip into the hill country west of San Antonio, he had already written a huge letter to the directors at Paris detailing his views as to the "superb" potential of the valley as a "site for colonization."[2] The interior of the valley, he had written, was a plain (about six leagues long and two leagues wide) gently sloping toward the south. Water from the Sabinal River and the streams that fed into it could be used, he believed, to irrigate ten or twelve square miles of land within the valley. The mountains were sparsely forested and would not yield much lumber. However, other building materials—sand, gravel, building stone—were abundant, and one could use local materials to build houses in the canyon out of concrete, according to the methods perfected by François Coignet.

In his letter to Paris, Considerant went on to evoke the spectacle of a whole set of small industries growing up along the Sabinal River. The river would provide power for a sawmill, for grain mills, and eventually for spinning mills for cotton and wool. Furthermore, given the proximity of the canyon to the gold and silver of Mexico, a watch industry could be more easily established there than at any other point in Texas. Considerant also talked about the possibility of growing grapes in the foothills surrounding the valley, and he claimed that goods and supplies could be hauled into the canyon from the Gulf of Mexico and San Antonio more cheaply and more easily than they could be sent from Galveston and Houston to Reunion.

One of the greatest assets of the new site, moreover, was the fact that the population was far more diverse than in the area around Dallas. "Here already we find in one place a population consisting of up to five different elements: Mexican, American, German, French, and Polish." Considerant noted that the result of this diversity was to render people "more supple and more tolerant" in their thinking and to create a cultural climate in which there was "none of the strict and often narrow uniformity of the pure American element." In San Antonio and throughout West Texas people weren't shocked to find their neighbors dancing and laughing on Sundays. "All languages are spoken," wrote Considerant, "people go to religious services of many different denominations, and Know-Nothingism has little support." It was "incontestable" that, although the Southwest was "under the same political and legal regime" as the rest of Texas, people there were "in fact much freer socially."

According to Considerant's estimates, the entire valley would cost 200,000 francs—including roughly 50,000 francs to be paid to squatters for cabins, fences, plowed fields, and other improvements already made in the valley. Once purchased, the land could then be resold or leased out to settlers in a manner consistent with Considerant's original plan. He would move out to the valley with a small number of reliable men, and together they would set up a supply center, survey the land, and divide it up into sites suitable for different types of colonization. With the help of local laborers—"Mexicans and perhaps a few Germans"—Considerant and his associates would prepare the land for settlement, all the while keeping the

Colonization Society in Paris abreast of developments and indicating the sorts of workers whose presence would be most useful. Colonists who wished to come to Texas would be free to purchase or lease improved or unimproved land as they wished and to try out a variety of different schemes of settlement. "Those who would like to establish individual farms and businesses will be just as free to do that," wrote Considerant, "as those who come here as members of any sort of association." In all cases, the costs incurred in Texas would be borne by the colonists themselves and not by the European shareholders. By thus following his original plan, he believed, it would be possible to avoid the pitfalls that had destroyed Reunion.

It was with this aim in mind—setting up a colonization society consistent with his original plan—that Considerant left Reunion in early June. He first headed for Austin, where he still hoped to get support from the Texas State Legislature. He had given up hope of a free land grant, but he still wanted to incorporate the Colonization Society—as he finally did on September 1, 1856, thanks to the efforts of Supervielle and a few other allies. Within a day or two after the passage of the bill, Considerant left Austin for San Antonio. There his first concern was to organize an expedition along the Nueces and Leona rivers and into Uvalde Canyon. "I want to see the canyon after a long period of drought," he wrote Julie on September 14. "If we find enough water now, we can be sure that at any time the supply will be adequate."[3]

Two weeks later Considerant was back in San Antonio, and he could report that he had now purchased for the Colonization Society seven of the fourteen available parcels of land. The Society now owned almost eighteen thousand acres in Uvalde Canyon. "This valley is a real little paradise," he wrote, adding that there was "much more" wood than he had originally thought and that the supply of water was "most satisfactory." Even in this terribly dry year the water in the Sabinal would have been sufficient "to keep mills running if there were any."[4]

In early October Considerant set out on another expedition into Uvalde Canyon, accompanied this time by a Frenchman from San Antonio "who is taking four wagons and thirty Mexicans into the canyon to gather pecans." The plan was to camp in the canyon for about two weeks. "We will have maps in hand, and this time we will study the terrain carefully enough to know it well." Considerant now regretted that the Colonization Society could not buy all the land at once. "What a good position we would be in if I had not been crushed at the start by the terrible business at Reunion," he wrote Julie. "When I have the whole valley, then we will begin *the way I wanted to begin*."[5]

II

While Considerant was buying up Uvalde Canyon, a general assembly of Colonization Society shareholders met in Paris on September 3 to make decisions on the fate of Reunion. In a report on the community, Allyre Bureau argued that almost all the difficulties at Reunion were due to an irreconcilable conflict between two "tendencies." On the one hand, there were those who favored Considerant's original plan, according to which the Colonization Society should seek to facilitate the initiatives of a variety of different groups. On the other hand, there were those (like Savardan) who identified themselves with the "provisional agreement" of December 1854, which left room for the Colonization Society to give its active support to a Fourierist *essai*. According to Bureau, all "the conflicts, misunderstandings, and discord" at Reunion could be traced back to the basic disagreement. The whole enterprise at Reunion could be seen as "an experimental school" and a source of valuable lessons. Now it was time to bring this particular experiment to an end—to send one of the directors to Texas with the power to dissolve Reunion and to sell off its territory to individual buyers.[6]

This report was unanimously approved by the general assembly; and, in the absence of other volunteers, Bureau himself was chosen to go to Texas to oversee the dissolution of Reunion. On September 30 he and his family left Le Havre by steamer. They arrived in New Orleans at the beginning of December; and finally, on December 23 Bureau reached San Antonio, where he spent two days with Considerant before proceeding to Reunion. Considerant's land purchases in Uvalde Canyon now totaled 23,751 acres (purchased at an average price of about fifty cents an acre); he told Bureau that he was about to conclude negotiations for the purchase of over 10,000 additional acres at prices ranging from eighty cents to a dollar an acre. Unfortunately his purchases had had the effect of driving up prices. After some discussion, therefore, Considerant agreed to make no more purchases for the time being and to let it be known that he had no immediate plans to open up the canyon to colonization. This does not mean that he was abandoning his dreams for Uvalde Canyon. He apparently hoped that by announcing a postponement of colonization he could drive land prices back down.[7]

Considerant was naturally pleased at the decision to dissolve Reunion and at the choice of Bureau as the man to carry out the dissolution. As it turned out, though, Bureau was far too gentle and kindly a person for the job. Within two weeks of his arrival at Reunion, as he attempted to resolve disputes and settle the claims of individuals leaving the colony, he suffered what amounted to a physical breakdown. Thereupon, both Savardan and

Willemain wrote Considerant, urging him to return to Reunion to oversee the liquidation of the colony. Considerant refused. The most he would do was to send Vincent Cousin in his place. He regretted the fact that Bureau was sick, but under the circumstances, he wrote, the people at Reunion should simply act "as if I were dead."[8]

During the first two months of 1857, as Vincent Cousin did his best to sell off land at Reunion and settle the claims of departing colonists, Considerant was more than once asked to return to help liquidate the colony, but he kept refusing. His main concern now was to get his wife and mother-in-law out. He kept up a steady stream of letters to Julie, urging her to join him quickly, and sending detailed instructions about the trip along with requests for winter clothing, fur-lined boots, a spring mattress, his horse's saddle, and extra copies of *Au Texas*. It was only in late February that Julie and Clarisse finally managed to leave Reunion, taking the six-day trip by mail coach from Dallas to San Antonio. But this departure was for good. Neither Julie nor Victor was ever to return.[9]

III

In March 1857 Victor, Julie, and Clarisse Vigoureux set up housekeeping in a rented house in San Antonio, at this time an already old and (by the standards of the American West) remarkably cosmopolitan city. With a population of close to eight thousand, San Antonio was the second largest city in Texas. It had a large population of European, and especially German, immigrants. In fact, in the late 1850s the Germans comprised the largest single ethnic group in the city, outnumbering both the Mexicans and the Anglos. There was also a substantial French community, and the city as a whole was growing rapidly.[10] As Considerant wrote in the summer of 1857: "Within the space of a few months whole quarters of the city have become completely unrecognizable; old parts of the city have been reconstructed and rebuilt; and new quarters have appeared where there were formerly open fields." After Reunion Julie and Clarisse appreciated the bustle and liveliness of San Antonio, but above all they appreciated the chance to be reunited with Victor. As Julie wrote later: "The milder climate, the distance from that wretched Reunion, a few acquaintances, and above all our return to Victor's side after eight months of absence—all these things made our life seem better."[11]

At the end of May, with the coming of warm weather, Victor set out again for Uvalde Canyon, this time accompanied by Julie and Allyre Bureau and an entourage including half a dozen other companions, two

Mexican guides, a wagon train, and a large supply of guns and ammunition.[12] This was Victor's fourth trip into the canyon, but it was the first for both Julie and Allyre Bureau. The fourth day out, as the group made camp at Comanche Prairie not far from the canyon, Victor scrawled a letter in pencil to Clarisse Vigoureux, whom they had left behind in San Antonio.

> Dear mother, your two children are in perfect health. We got here early, about four o'clock in the afternoon, and we found a charming campsite about nine miles from the entrance to the small canyon, which we will reach early tomorrow morning. Can you imagine that the water which we are looking at here, and which would be called a "lake" if we were at Reunion, appeared here just three months ago. Last fall, even after heavy rain, there wasn't anything. . . . We've had fine weather, we've eaten omelettes and partridges, ducks and sauteed peas, all very nicely seasoned. We've even had a few little quarrels to amuse us and to give us an appetite. Le père Bureau is fine and finds that nothing is healthier than life on the prairie. . . . Julie looks like a real Texas wagonmaster with my hat, which has now taken a completely American shape.[13]

Considerant's delight in the expedition is evident, as is his determination to see everything in a good light. But Allyre Bureau seems to have been almost equally delighted.

Although Bureau noted in his journal that forty-four rifles seemed more than enough to protect the expedition from "a few marauding Indians," he enjoyed the trip immensely and was able on his return to send a most enthusiastic report on the canyon back to Paris. Bureau noted that the hillsides were more thickly wooded than Considerant had initially thought and that even after a period of "ruinous drought" there was ample water. While the horses had been grazing on the way in, the canyon itself was rich in grasses. "We could admire the vigorous health and the shiny coats of the livestock in the canyon, contrasting with the exhaustion of the herds we encountered on the way in." Thus, Bureau concluded, "the three elements that are essential to colonization, water, wood, and grass, are all to be found within the canyon even in disastrous years." Bureau added, however, that he and Considerant agreed that it would not be wise to bring colonists into the area until the whole valley had been purchased.[14]

IV

During the fifteen months that followed his abrupt departure from Reunion, Considerant remained in relatively close touch with the directors of the Colonization Society in Paris. Every few months he sent them a long letter describing his explorations, purchases, and hopes concerning the colonization of Uvalde Canyon. The purchases continued as well, despite Considerant's agreement to suspend land acquisition. By September 1857 he could report three new purchases: 5,085 acres of land in a nicely wooded valley to the west of the Frio River fifteen or sixteen miles south of Uvalde Canyon; two big parcels of land in Uvalde Canyon totaling 5,025 acres; and another parcel of 2,302 acres also in the canyon. Considerant had now purchased 44,860 acres in West Texas, and the amount of land owned by the Colonization Society, including the land at Reunion, now totaled 56,669 acres.[15]

In his letters to Paris, Considerant described these new purchases with his customary enthusiasm. The supply of water in the Frio parcel was "superb"; the trees were "the most handsome in the region"—there were "cedars forty feet high" and "as straight as masts"; after logging there would still be "excellent land" that would "have great value in a few years." But all of Considerant's superlatives had now begun to sound a bit hollow to his colleagues both at Paris and at Reunion. There were people at Reunion like Savardan and the family of Allyre Bureau (though not Bureau himself) who had come to detest Considerant as a coward who had created an impossible situation at Reunion and then walked out on it. Others regarded Considerant's efforts to promote Uvalde Canyon as at best a distraction likely to hinder the effort to sell off the land at Reunion. Finally there were those, especially in Paris, who believed that Considerant was becoming addicted to land speculation, while continuing to delude himself with grandiose dreams that would take years to materialize. These skeptics conceded that Uvalde Canyon could eventually become "the principal theater of our movement of colonization," but they insisted that "as long as the interior of Texas is without roads, without easy communications, without markets, we cannot think of developing industry, commerce, or even large-scale farming."[16]

It was to answer these critics and, at the same time, confess his own mistakes and try to build interest in the eventual colonization of Uvalde Canyon that, during the summer of 1857, Considerant wrote an eighty-page brochure, *Du Texas: Premier Rapport à mes amis*. This brochure, which was his first public statement of any kind in almost three years, was a strange piece of writing—at once self-critical and querulous, sincere and hyperbolic, disarmingly frank but also heavy on pathos. The work as a whole conveyed a double message, both about Considerant and about the Fourierist movement. The message about the movement was that although the past three years had been catastrophic, the future was bright. As for Considerant, these three years had been a "hell," a state worse than death, but now he was "resuscitated." He had been crushed by his own failures and by the failure of Reunion; he had become a "breathing cadaver." The "resurrection of our activities" had finally brought him back to life.

Considerant began *Du Texas* with a review of the past. For two years, he wrote, he had looked on while "the greater part of the funds available to the Colonization Society, of which I was the founder and the chief, were swallowed up . . . in operations . . . contrary to the plan proposed by me, adopted by you all." How had this come about? A fundamental problem was the ambiguity created by the acceptance of the "provisional agreement." Closing off the land that he had initially hoped to purchase had also been a major reverse. The "crushing" blow, however, had been the "premature emigration" of scores of would-be colonists who had refused to wait until the signal for departure had been given. What should Considerant have done? In retrospect it was clear that the proper course of action would have been to send back to Europe, at the expense of the Colonization Society, nine-tenths of the original colonists. But he could not bring himself to do this. Nor could he bring himself to confront the situation in any other way. He simply fell silent, ceasing to write the directors in Paris and becoming a passive witness to the collapse of the "fatherless monster" of a colony that he had helped bring into being.[17]

In the second part of *Du Texas*, Considerant described his "resurrection" and the recovery of his hopes. He talked once again about the productivity of Texas agriculture and the excellence of his original plans for a "champ d'asile" open to a variety of modes of settlement and development. He boasted that after three years he had "not a single modification" to make in this plan. He praised Vincent Cousin for his work in subdividing and selling off some of the property at Reunion, and, at the same time, he described the land in Uvalde Canyon in glowing terms. He concluded on a note of high pathos with an extended metaphor likening the sickness and recovery of the Colonization Society to that of his horse Domingo, whom he had recently nursed back to health after a near-fatal illness.

Considerant finished *Du Texas* on August 8, 1857. He immediately sent the manuscript to Paris for publication. It arrived there at the beginning of October. One of the first to read it while it was still in press was the factory-owner, J.-B.-A. Godin, who was now a director of the Colonization Society. On October 13 Godin began a letter to Considerant that is probably indicative of the response of even the most sympathetic of his associates: "I would like to have nothing but encouragement to give you," Godin began, "but

I cannot accept with the necessary enthusiasm the new hope held out by you on your return to our activities." Unfortunately, the situation was no longer that of 1854. "Texas, which you then revealed to us as a promised land, has lost its prestige." As a result of Considerant's overstatements and exaggerations, he too had lost both prestige and credibility. "I note with a certain feeling of fear," Godin wrote, "the ease with which you are able, out there in the wilderness, to resolve in your mind all sorts of problems for which centuries of wisdom have not found easy answers, even in the most advanced civilizations." From Godin's standpoint, Considerant had a naive and exaggerated confidence in the efficacy of planning, science, and rational thinking. What he failed to understand was the importance of the practical knowledge that could only be acquired slowly, through experience and familiarity with particular situations. In Godin's opinion, Considerant also failed to recognize the importance of leadership. "Do you really believe," he asked, "that the most skillfully conceived plan retains any value if a general is not there to resolve the initial difficulties?" Leadership was an essential ingredient in the success of all human enterprises, and one of the main causes of Reunion's collapse was quite simply Considerant's failure to act like a leader.[18]

For a month Godin could not bring himself to finish this letter. Finally in mid-November he returned to it, noting that *Du Texas* had now been circulated among the shareholders "without apparently bringing any significant modification in the dead calm of people's spirits." Godin found that there was little in Considerant's proposals to attract any of the people he wanted to reach.

> The rich will not be very interested in going to take up residence in the log houses or mud huts you speak of. If the rich are not attracted, won't people with limited resources hesitate before embarking on a trip that will cost them almost everything they have? . . . As for workers who have nothing more to offer you than their labor, what will you do with them?

Godin's advice to Considerant was to stop buying land and to start thinking about ways to derive some income from the land that had already been purchased.[19]

Considerant was much too deeply convinced of the value of his proposal to accept Godin's criticism or his advice. He believed it was imperative to buy up the rest of the land in Uvalde Canyon and to raise more money so that the canyon could be settled on a large scale. Despite Godin's blunt criticism of his failure as a leader, Considerant continued to have faith in his

own persuasive powers. Thus, early in the spring of 1858, he decided to return to Europe to plead the case for Uvalde Canyon in person before friends
and colleagues, many of whom had not seen him in nine years.

v

Considerant's trip to Europe in 1858 represented his last effort to play a significant role within the Fourierist movement. The final result was discour-
aging. Nonetheless, he retained enough of his curiosity and responsiveness
to make the trip, at the outset at least, an adventure. He began around
May 10 with a grueling stagecoach ride from San Antonio to the coast. He
then traveled by boat from Port Lavaca to Galveston and on to New Orleans, where he stayed for a few days with members of the local Fourierist
group. These included several old acquaintances of Brisbane's—notably
the federal attorney Thomas J. Durant, who was to serve briefly as Louisiana's attorney general during Reconstruction, and also T. Wharton Collins,
an attorney and city judge, a Fourierist of sorts who was later to become a
Christian socialist writer.[20]

Before leaving New Orleans, Considerant went through the formalities
necessary to acquire U.S. citizenship. He may have believed that traveling
as a U.S. citizen he would find it easier to return to France. He may also
have simply felt that after three years in the United States, it was time. In
any case on May 20, appearing before Louis Duvigneaud, judge of the
Third District Court of New Orleans, Considerant was formally granted
U.S. citizenship.[21] For the rest of his life he was to remain an American citizen and to identify himself as such when signing several of his subsequently published works.

Traveling by boat to Mobile and then by train, Considerant reached New
York in early June. Pausing there for two weeks, he stayed with his old
friend from Lyon, Jules Juif. This gave him time to visit the journalist
Charles Dana and some of his other friends in New York literary and journalistic circles. Dana and George Ripley were now collaborating on a project that was to make them both very rich men, the publication of the *New
American Cyclopedia*. Considerant probably heard all about this. He also
learned from Dana that he might have better luck securing passage to
France if he left from Canada. He quickly found a place on a British steamer
sailing from Quebec on June 19. Less than three weeks later he was back in
Brussels.[22]

Considerant's first impression of the Belgian capital was that little had
changed in the three and a half years since he had left. He wrote Julie that

the merchants with whom they had done their shopping had not moved and that most of their old friends were still there. During his two weeks in Belgium he visited old friends in Louvain, Liège, and even Barvaux, where he and Julie were warmly remembered. Most of his time, however, was spent in Brussels, where he stayed with the lawyer Adolphe Demeur, whose residence at 16, rue de la Régence, served as the Brussels headquarters of the Colonization Society. He also spent several evenings with the family of Philippe Bourson, whose daughter Amédée was now an established artist and whose young son Eugène was now at boarding school. It was Bourson probably who arranged the meeting that took place on July 21 between Considerant and his old compatriot and adversary, Proudhon. Obliged to flee France after the condemnation of his *De la justice dans la Révolution et dans l'église,* Proudhon commented wryly in his journal: "What a meeting! The two socialists, so often the butt of caricatures, meet again in exile."[23]

It had not been clear, prior to his arrival in Belgium, that Considerant would be permitted to enter France. Even though he was now an American citizen, he was still a political criminal in the eyes of the law. In fact, it proved easy for him to obtain the necessary papers through the French embassy in Brussels. On July 23 he boarded a train for Paris. Ironically, the first person he met after crossing the French frontier was his old adversary, Adolphe Thiers. As they waited together on the platform at the Gare de Valenciennes, they talked briefly about what had become of France under Napoleon III. "Ah," commented Thiers, "you are going to find the country greatly changed, much drawn in on itself, very quiet."[24] This was indeed the case, at least as far as Considerant's world was concerned.

While in Paris Considerant stayed at the old apartment on the rue de Beaune. The salon, which had been the center of such animated and intense discussions ten years earlier, was now empty. The dining room, where Victor and Julie had often entertained, had been converted into the office of the Fourierist bookstore. Aimée Beuque, who managed the bookstore and lived in the apartment, was now the heart and soul of what was left of the Fourierist movement. Considerant found her "as young and lively as ever," and just after his arrival he had a good talk with Jules Duval. But his general impression was that the Ecole Sociétaire was dead.[25]

So it was, judging from the account left by Clarisse Coignet, who was in close touch with many of the Fourierists at this time.

> Here and there you could still meet isolated disciples who kept alive the cult of the past and continued to cherish a last hope for the future. . . .

But there was no longer a group resolutely affirming the doctrine, propagating it with pride and passion, sure of the future and of themselves. . . . Often at that time in Paris I invited them to my home and gathered them around my table, those last representatives of an extinct faith. Each one clung to his dream. The old formulas, the old words recurred in their conversation, but like a weakened echo from the past, the words had lost their resonance.[26]

Considerant's faith was not dead, and he had shown in *Du Texas* that he could still write with power and conviction. In one of his first letters from Paris he spoke of himself as having "already rekindled the enthusiasm" of some of his old friends.[27] However, he could do little to alter the general sense of discouragement and resignation.

After two weeks in Paris, Considerant left for the Loire Valley to visit friends and relatives—among them his brother Gustave at Saumur and "le brave père Edel" at Nantes. He wrote Julie on August 12 that he was touched by "the expressions of affection and concern" he had encountered from friends along the way. His goal now, he said, was to try to get in touch with as many others as possible "to make them understand the present situation [in Texas] and to show them that there is nothing risky about our operations." If he could accomplish this, he maintained, then "my voyage will have been worthwhile."[28]

What Considerant really needed to do, however, was not so much rekindle the enthusiasm of his friends as convince the growing number of his critics that another effort of colonization should be made in Uvalde Canyon and along the lines that he had already suggested. His best opportunity to do this came on September 1, when he gave a formal presentation to the annual meeting of the general assembly of the Colonization Society at Paris. Fifty-nine shareholders attended this meeting, including the manufacturers François Coignet and J.-B.-A. Godin and also Dr. Baudet-Dulary, the sponsor of the first Fourierist *essai* at Condé-sur-Vesgre twenty-five years earlier. Considerant spoke to this group in his capacity as executive agent of the Colonization Society in America.

The main point of Considerant's speech was simply that after a "deplorable" beginning, the colonizing effort in Texas was at last on the right track. In the year that had passed since the writing of *Du Texas* the situation had "only improved," and now at last it was possible to establish a "fruitful colonizing operation" of the kind he had initially envisaged. Reviewing the history of Reunion, Considerant noted that success would have required the meeting of three conditions: the process of emigration should have been orderly and carefully phased; the Society should have functioned simply as a clearinghouse for groups of emigrants, without undertaking to sponsor or subsidize any single venture; and the amount of money spent on the purchase of land should have been minimal. The community actually established at Reunion had met none of these conditions. Several hundred immigrants had arrived prematurely, and land of dubious value had been purchased at a high price. In the end the resources of the Colonization Society had been squandered in the attempt to sustain "a crowd of individuals without aptitude for basic agricultural tasks . . . brought together confusedly before the creation of the conditions in which their talents might have been put to use."[29]

Fortunately, Considerant continued, it had been possible to terminate the sponsorship of Reunion before all the capital of the Colonization Society had been dissipated. Now Reunion had been reorganized on a sounder footing. At the same time, with the purchase of the bulk of Uvalde Canyon, the Colonization Society had at last acquired "a territorial base consistent with the true principles of its constitution." The valley, which would soon be owned in its entirety, was fertile, well watered, and situated not far from important trade routes. Furthermore, the success of the neighboring German communities of Fredericksburg and New Braunfels, and the Alsatian town of Castroville—all established in the mid-1840s—demonstrated that the area was one in which Europeans could thrive.

Considerant went on to discuss the benefits that would result from the cooperation of the groups and individuals participating in the colonization of Uvalde Canyon. Property would remain individually owned, but the Colonization Society would facilitate the efforts of separate landowners to establish common herds and cooperatives for the production of milk and cheese. (These would presumably be modeled after the *fruitières* of Franche-Comté.) Fencing, irrigation, and the marketing of goods could also be undertaken cooperatively. The cost of heavy farm machinery could be shared. And the Colonization Society could take the initiative for the creation of a general store, which could serve as "the point of departure for a *comptoir communal* (Fourier's term) offering credit to farmers and artisans and helping them to centralize and rationalize their sales and purchases."

In all of this Considerant's point was that, while respecting the rights of private ownership and individual initiative and without risking the capital of the Colonization Society in subsidizing a single group of settlers, Uvalde Canyon could serve as the theater for a whole series of limited experiments in collective action. Thus, explained Considerant, "we can gradually move to the most advanced forms of social experimentation while proceeding with a great deal of prudence and guiding the process of colonization in a direction in which there are obvious advantages to be gained through collective action."

In Considerant's view none of this represented a departure from the original plan outlined in *Au Texas*. On the contrary, it was just what he had in mind before deviations from the plan had led to "the waste and ruin" of Reunion. Thus, what he proposed to do on his return to America was to buy up the rest of the valley and then make a detailed survey of those areas that would first be opened to settlement. Information would be made available to all prospective settlers concerning the costs of the different types of land, the provisions they would need, and the conditions they would encounter on their arrival. By these means "a kernel of population" could be established in Uvalde Canyon under conditions "quite consistent with those of the original plan."

Considerant concluded by stating that he wished no vote to be taken. He simply wished to inform his friends and colleagues in France as to the situation in Texas. He planned to remain in France for several months, and during this period he would place himself at the disposition of anyone seeking more information. He urged all prospective settlers and investors to contact him, and he reminded his audience that in order to take advantage of the golden opportunity that now existed, a new commitment of energy and capital would be needed.

VI

This speech was Considerant's last attempt to play a guiding role within the Fourierist movement, but it is hard to say just how it was received. The minutes of the general assembly note only that there were a few questions and that Considerant answered them. The initial response was apparently warm and friendly but also noncommittal. As Aimée Beuque put it three weeks later: "Everyone was kind and sympathetic," but there had been "no positive results." [30] The warmth was surely an expression of sympathy for Considerant; however, there was also an underlying skepticism as to his specific proposals. Many of his friends and colleagues had lost confidence in his abilities as a leader. In addition, the financial situation of the Colonization Society was actually much worse than he was willing to admit.

In his speech, Considerant spoke of the main difficulties facing the society as having been overcome and the financial situation as "already almost completely put to right." His assumption was that the increase in the value of land purchased by the Colonization Society would soon be sufficient to compensate for the money lost at Reunion. The problem Considerant ignored, however, was that there was no market for the society's land. To make the land attractive to investors at a time when there was unimproved land for sale all over Texas, it would have to be improved. But improvements would require liquid capital. As Emile Bourdon pointed out in a lucid and grim report to the same general assembly, only 292,000 francs remained in liquid capital, and this would be gone in three years assuming that the society's interest payments and operating expenses remained fixed.[31] If anything at all was to be done in Uvalde Canyon, a new rush of pledges was needed similar to that which had greeted the publication of *Au Texas*.

The pledges never came. Three weeks after the General Assembly, Aimée Beuque was still hopeful, but Considerant himself had already given up. This defeat was crushing. Shortly after the general assembly he went out to the Ville d'Avray to spend a few days with Clarisse and François Coignet, and long afterward Clarisse remembered him at this time as a man consumed by melancholy.

> Victor Considerant had lost nothing of his old grace, his openness, his warm spontaneity, his old powers of seduction. However, nothing could tear him out of his melancholy. This brilliant conversationalist remained silent. . . . His sole distraction was to play with my son, a three-year-old boy to whom he had taken a liking. They spent whole hours together, and for him they were the best hours. One day, seeing him silently stretched out on a divan near the window, his eyes lost in space, I asked him, "What are you doing there, dear Victor? Are you dreaming? Are you letting yourself be distracted?" "It's rather," he answered, "that I'm letting myself die."[32]

Considerant was just fifty years old. He had thirty-five more years to live. But he felt that his life was over. Indeed, his life as a Fourierist, as an actively participating member of the Fourierist movement, was over.

In October Considerant traveled to Franche-Comté to see relatives at Salins and Lons-le-Saunier and to spend a few days at Beaufort in the Jura with his sister Justine's family. Throughout this trip he was under police surveillance, and one of the reports left by the informers who watched him gives a poignant glimpse of him at the train station at Lons-le-Saunier: "He had a sad and beaten-down air about him. When his relatives asked him why, he answered that he was going to leave France, never to see it again."[33]

Back in Paris at the beginning of November, Considerant began to say his good-byes. For a few weeks he also made daily visits to François Coi-

gnet's factory at Saint-Denis, studying the process by which Coignet manufactured a grade of "agglomerated" concrete that was both cheap and
dense enough to use for many different kinds of construction. Apparently
Considerant was still preoccupied by Uvalde Canyon and the need to discover building materials cheap enough to be used in an undercapitalized
development scheme.[34] By the end of the month, however, he had had
enough. He wrote Julie that he was coming home as soon as possible.

> For a long time now we've had the sort of hard, unpleasant weather that
> I don't like at all. It's only by your side that I will find my sun again, sun
> for my body and sun for my heart. I love you with all my heart, and I
> rebel against this absence that has become absurdly prolonged.

It was six weeks, however, before Considerant actually began the long trip
back to America. He really believed that he was leaving France forever, and
there were people to see and purchases to make. His brother Gustave came
to spend a few days with him in December, and he spent much of the rest
of the month sending off packages of supplies, seeds, and plants. On January 8 he wrote a poignant farewell letter to Alphonse Delacroix and his
family. Finally, on January 11, he sailed for New York on the steamship
François Arago. After brief stops in New York and New Orleans, he was
back in San Antonio by the middle of February.[35]

VII

Not long after his return to San Antonio, Considerant wrote the directors
of the Colonization Society that he and Vincent Cousin were about to undertake a full-scale survey of Uvalde Canyon. In fact, they never even
started. A few months later Considerant resigned his position as Executive
Agent of the Colonization Society. In June 1859 an announcement appeared in the Society's *Bulletin* indicating that its resources had shrunk
to the point that it could no longer concern itself with colonization at all.
Henceforth, the Society would be "no more than a simple proprietor of
land, possessing a large number of acres for sale in Texas."[36]

The Colonization Society maintained its shadowy existence for the next
fifteen years. Its remaining members continued to hope that population
growth and the spread of railroad lines would raise the value of the land
enough to compensate for the big losses suffered at Reunion between 1855
and 1857. This never happened. Considerant's friend, François Giraud, who
handled the affairs of the Colonization Society between 1868 and 1875, did
manage to sell off almost ten thousand acres in Uvalde Canyon to some of

the canyon's original white settlers, John Ware, Robert Kincheloe, Gideon Thompson, and Joseph Kelley, but this was the best land in the canyon, and the price paid for it—never more than $1.25 an acre—was just about the same as what Considerant had paid fifteen years earlier. The land around Reunion commanded a somewhat higher price, and about a thousand acres were sold in the early 1870s. The income from all these sales was barely enough to cover the cost of taxes and fees, though. Finally, in April 1875, the Colonization Society was dissolved, and all its remaining landholdings were auctioned off. Most of them were purchased by none other than François Cantagrel. In the end shareholders recovered just 12 percent of their original investments.[37]

Although Considerant's role in the Colonization Society—and in what was left of the Fourierist movement—came to an end in 1859, the Society's long decrepitude and final dissolution must have been a painful reminder to him of how wrong he had been in his faith in land speculation as a medium for accumulating capital destined to promote social change. Considerant was a man of extraordinary recuperative powers, however; and though he bent, he was not broken by the failure of Reunion or by his inability to get support for the colonization of Uvalde Canyon. Nor did these painful experiences cause him to lose hope in America and the role he believed it would play in the eventual establishment of a democratic and socialist world order. Nevertheless, he was numbed and silenced by his experience. It seems to me that the best epitaph for the events just described is to be found, not in Considerant's writings, but in those of his wife. In writing Aimée Beuque a few months after Victor's return to San Antonio, Julie Considerant had this to say:

> I will always hope that we can see each other again on this earth, that some miracle will reunite us. But whatever has been the moral misery in which we have lived, I have never regretted leaving Europe. America is ahead of the other nations and, be sure of this, sooner or later it will be the cradle of future harmonies.[38]

Today, 130 years after the Considerants left America for good, their dreams with regard to "Uvalde Canyon" remain unfulfilled. It never became the agricultural and industrial center that Victor had prophesied. Cotton was introduced into the lower part of the canyon—the region around Sabinal—in the years after the Civil War, and there has always been some ranching in the canyon. Ironically, though, the area's most important contribution to the economy of the hill country west of San Antonio remains the money brought in by hunters, fishermen, and campers attracted, just as

Considerant was, by the "limpid" waters of the Sabinal and the abundant game. Near the north end of the Canyon—about twenty miles north of Sabinal—a town eventually grew up around the store built by Robert Kincheloe in 1873 on land purchased from Considerant. This town, now a center for local tourism and the home of an important producer of bottled water, bears the name "Utopia." By another irony, it owes its name not to Considerant's dreams for the area but rather to the fact that, twenty years later, another settler became enamored of the canyon and convinced of the curative powers of the waters of the Sabinal.[39]

16

San Antonio Farmer

During the 1860s Considerant lived in greater isolation than at any other time of his life. He fell out of touch not only with his former allies within the Fourierist movement but with the whole intellectual and political world that had previously been his element. For two years after his return to San Antonio in February 1859, he and Julie kept in touch with relatives and close friends like Aimée Beuque, but he was never again to have any dealings with François Cantagrel, Auguste Savardan, or most of his other associates at Reunion. And the vote of no confidence that he received in Paris in 1858 estranged him from many of the active Parisian Fourierists. Then in April 1861, with the outbreak of the Civil War, communications with Europe and with the North were cut off. As Considerant put it later, he had left the "stifling" atmosphere of Second Empire France to return to the "solitudes monotones" of Texas, where, "separated from the North by the Civil War . . . I found myself cut off for almost five years from any contact with human beings."[1]

Already well before the outbreak of the war, Considerant had cause to feel isolated, not only from the outside world but also within Texas. In January 1860 the Texas state legislature passed a bill imposing prison sentences on anyone found guilty of publishing, circulating, or receiving writings opposed to slavery. Considerant's friend, the legislator A. Supervielle, wrote him that, given the "fanaticism" and "intolerance" of the legislature, the bill did not surprise him. What did surprise him, however, was that "you, Victor Considerant, the Fourierist, socialist, Manichean, and atheistical leader, were the cause of the bill." Word had spread in the legislature that Considerant was a subscriber to Horace Greeley's *New York Tribune,* and this was regarded in some quarters at least as "a hanging offense."[2]

I

If Texas was not the scene of much significant fighting during the Civil War, the war still had a devastating effect on the life of the state. It left one-quarter of the white males of fighting age dead or disabled, and it dissipated or destroyed almost every form of real wealth except the land itself.[3] The state's entire economy was disrupted by the federal naval blockade established along the Texas coast in the first months of the war. The blockade not only cut off communications with the North and with Europe but also greatly complicated the export of cotton and vastly reduced the flow of manufactured goods into the state. Considerant could write in 1865 that he had "not received a single letter from France since the establishment of the blockade," and his wife could recall at the end of the war that for five years she had to keep mending her husband's clothing and make his shoes herself, since shoes could not be bought.[4]

Conditions in San Antonio were actually better than elsewhere in Texas during the Civil War. With the shift in trade routes caused by the blockade, it became for a time the state's major commercial center. Although close to half the city's population had opposed secession, San Antonio also became the state's military headquarters, and its streets resounded with the noise of marching soldiers during the early days of the war. Considerant himself was apparently offered a commission in the Confederate Army. Unlike some of his compatriots in Texas (such as Xavier Debray, who became a Confederate general), he declined. He detested slavery; and for him the Southern war effort was "a gigantic carnival of Southern rage and stupidity."[5] Throughout the war he kept a low profile, living quietly with his wife and mother-in-law in San Antonio. Their life was not easy. They raised their own food and earned a little money through the sale of flowers and vegetables in San Antonio. At least once during the war Considerant even paid his taxes in kind with a load of sweet potatoes.[6] Their chief diversion was an occasional Sunday afternoon in the new San Pedro Springs Park with its restaurant, German beer gardens, and extraordinary tropical gardens with "many beautiful and wonderful specimen of cacti." Both Victor and Julie loved these gardens, and Victor could speak enthusiastically about the cacti and the profusion of vegetables there.[7]

During the war Considerant went into a kind of intellectual hibernation. He continued to reflect on scientific and political questions that had long interested him, but apart from his wife, he had no one with whom to discuss these matters. Furthermore, there was no way of getting books; and he no longer had access either to French journals or to Greeley's *New York Tribune*. When he was visited in 1861 by a young Mexican admirer, Alberto Santa Fe, who as the author of *Ley del pueblo* was later to become an important early Mexican agrarian socialist, Considerant apparently had nothing to say about his writings or anything else to do with Fourierism. What stuck in Santa Fe's mind, as he recalled the meeting long afterward, was the image of a man "dedicated to botany" whose great occupation was "to collect in his large garden all the varieties of the cactus family."[8]

If the Considerants were poor, theirs was a relatively genteel poverty. They still possessed the carriage they had brought with them to Reunion, though they scarcely used it anymore. They occasionally had household help. And they maintained cordial relations with several leading members of San Antonio's French colony. One of their friends, for example, was the wealthy merchant and cotton broker François Guilbeau, who served for many years as the consular agent for the French government in San Antonio. Born in France in 1813, Guilbeau had lived in San Antonio since 1839. Early on he had established one of San Antonio's first bakeries and an import business specializing in fruit, vegetables, and wine. Two decades later he was the possessor of a splendid formal house with crystal chandeliers, sixteen-foot ceilings, and three large drawing rooms. In the 1850s and 1860s this house served as the French consulate, and Victor and Julie were occasionally invited there for official receptions.[9]

Another friend of Considerant's in San Antonio's French colony was the architect and civil engineer François Giraud. A native of Charleston, South Carolina, and ten years younger than Considerant, Giraud had studied in France before settling in San Antonio around 1847. He was a cultivated man and a talented architect who designed several of San Antonio's most admired religious buildings—churches, schools, and convents—and furnished plans for the reconstruction of the city's most imposing church, San Fernando Cathedral on the Main Plaza. Giraud was elected mayor of San Antonio in the early 1870s. Much earlier, though, while still a young man, he served as the city's first civil engineer. In this capacity he made land surveys that definitively established the city's boundaries and those of its missions. In the 1850s and 1860s he also undertook a number of irrigation studies of the area, and on at least one of these he sought the collaboration of Considerant.[10] We know little of Considerant's other friends during these San Antonio years. One individual with whom he clearly established an enduring relationship was Lorenzo Castro, the foster son of Henri Castro, founder of Castroville. He also had at least occasional contacts with the painter Théodore Gentilz and the merchant Auguste Frétellière, two early settlers of Castroville who had moved to San Antonio around 1850. He was on friendly terms, too, with the contractor Jules Poinsard, who had built the first house the Considerants lived in at San Antonio and who was fascinated by Considerant's accounts of François Coignet's experiments in agglomerated concrete. The only testimony we have of most of these friendships, though, is an occasional comradely salutation or a line or two here and there in Considerant's correspondence.[11]

II

The most significant event in the lives of Victor and Julie Considerant during these years of isolation was the long, slow decline of Clarisse Vigoureux, the woman whom they both called "mother."[12] Julie recalled later that during their first years in Texas that her mother had apparently had several minor strokes; even earlier, in Belgium, she would sometimes faint or fall inexplicably, only to get up and laugh about it. Her health deteriorated during Victor's trip to France in 1858. Still, Julie felt able to leave her mother alone. If she went out for a walk, her mother would go to visit their Mexican landlady, Señora Benito. It was not a problem that the landlady knew no French. "Madame Benito, always gracious and respectful, would say 'Si Señora' to everything my mother said," Julie remembered. Clarisse replied in kind, and both were delighted. Shortly after Victor's return to San Antonio in 1859, however, Clarisse began to act strangely. One day, having gotten her dress soaked and finding herself unable to get it off quickly, Clarisse took a pair of scissors and simply cut it off her body. She also became preoccupied with childhood memories, and she began to act increasingly like a child.

In September 1860, Victor and Julie purchased for $1,500 a large, comfortable cabin about three miles south of San Antonio on the bank of the San Antonio River.[13] It was near the old Spanish mission, the Mission Nuestra Señora de la Purisma Concepcion; and in his letters Considerant simply gave as his address Mission la Concepcion. In moving out to the country with Clarisse Vigoureux (and also Victor's Belgian friend, Vincent Cousin), Victor and Julie hoped to live more frugally than they could in the city. They planned to grow their own food and raise flowers, which Julie would sell in San Antonio. According to Julie's later account, their first months in this new residence were happy ones. They were all glad to get away from the dust of San Antonio, and Clarisse was "enchanted" to live in the countryside again. Even the outbreak of the Civil War didn't much bother them, for the fighting was far away and "everyone thought that in a few months it would all be over."

By the late spring of 1861, though, the little group was in difficulty. None of them was young, and the work of plowing, planting, tending chickens, and fixing up their new house was simply too much for them all. As Julie wrote later, "sickness descended on our house." First it was Cousin who fell sick, then Victor, then finally Julie herself. Clarisse remained relatively healthy, but she could no longer be counted on for anything. So the whole family had to move back to San Antonio to be near a doctor, and they had to have Clarisse placed in what amounted to a nursing home.[14] By midsummer they were all able to return to their cabin, but by then they had lost most of their vegetables, their chicken had wandered off, and Julie's flowers had been ravaged by insects.

Settling back into the cabin on the San Antonio River, the Considerants established friendly relations with several of their neighbors, including a young girl named Christine Bruck who helped them with chores and virtually became a daughter to them. But Cousin's health remained poor, and Clarisse became weaker and more confused every month. So Julie had to run the house for all of them while Victor tried to scratch a living from the soil. Clarisse had good days and bad days. Julie later recalled that occasionally her mother showed signs of energy and decisiveness that surprised them all. Once, for example, when Julie and Victor were debating whether it was worth mending a badly worn pair of pants, Clarisse interrupted. "I'll mend them," she said, and she did it better than "at any other period of her life." According to Julie, Clarisse remained very sociable. She was friendly toward everyone. But her memory became increasingly confused, and Julie found it impossible to talk with her about their friends in France, because whenever she did so, her mother assumed that they were about to leave for France.

In fact, as long as the war went on, there was no way they could even think of returning. It was all they could do to get from day to day. Clarisse was blissfully ignorant of material realities, though. Julie recalled that while "Poland and Italy caused her heart to beat faster," she had no interest in American affairs. "The hardships that we had to bear because of the war passed right over her." When Clarisse saw Julie making shoes for the family because there were none to buy, she gently chided her daughter: "You'd do better to buy shoes." Of course, one of the strangest features of that time, Julie observed, was that "while necessities were virtually impossible to obtain, fashion magazines and luxury goods got through every blockade. At no other time did Southern belles wear more extravagant dresses."

As the war continued, Clarisse became increasingly dependent on Julie. "Although my mother made no demands," Julie wrote, "she became increasingly like a spoiled child with me." Julie found herself constantly waiting on her mother, dressing her, cleaning up after her. In the first years of the war she had been able to let Clarisse roam at will outside their cabin. "I can still see her wandering in the woods and garden," Julie remembered, "talking to the birds, picking flowers, carrying a brood of little chickens in her dress, giving bread to her favorite hen." By the end of the war, however, Clarisse had become almost completely helpless. She was incontinent; she needed to be fed; and at times she was unable to talk. She did indeed become a child again, loving to play with fire and scissors, cutting up her clothes or her hair. Julie feared that someday she might fall into the river and drown. When Julie tried to reason with her, she would take Julie's hands and smile back at her with a look of absolute innocence.

The period that Julie later called "the long twilight" of her mother's life finally came to an end on January 13, 1865, when Clarisse Vigoureux died peacefully in her sleep. They buried her in the middle of the garden, first covering her body with aromatic plants and placing a crown of leaves on her head. The site of her grave, like that of the cabin itself, is now lost, but Clarisse Vigoureux was to remain a vital presence in the lives and memories of both Julie and Victor.[15]

III

In February and March 1863 Considerant took an extended trip through Mexico's northern provinces, traveling as far south as Monterrey. He traveled with his friend François Guilbeau, who was now in business as a cotton broker at the Mexican border town of Piedras Negras, just across the Rio Grande from Eagle Pass. For Guilbeau it was an ordinary business trip, but he may also have wished to meet with the powerful *caudillo*, Santiago Vidaurri, the governor of Nuevo León and Coahuila, to ask for a reduction in the duties levied on the vast wagon trains carrying Texas cotton overland for shipment from Mexican ports. Considerant also hoped to speak with Vidaurri, who on an earlier trip to San Antonio had expressed a desire to meet with "Biktor Consideran, el gran socialista." [16] Considerant's main purpose, though, was simply to see a bit of Mexico and, at the same time, collect rare and unusual species of cactus.

The travelers' route initially took them by carriage to Castroville, past the southern end of Uvalde Canyon and across desolate country to Eagle Pass. Considerant saw some magnificent stands of cactus along the way, but in February it was still too early for the desert flowers to come into bloom. He saw flowers of another kind, however, for all the way to the Mexican border the trail was marked by bits of cotton that had fallen from the overloaded wagons carrying cotton to Mexican ports that were not affected by the Union blockade of Confederate shipping. These little bolls of cotton that marked the trail were, wrote Considerant, "the artificial flowers that King Cotton leaves to mark the new route that he has laid out this year in the direction of Mexico." [17]

Guilbeau stopped at Eagle Pass for almost a week to tend to his business and purchase mules for the trip south to Monterrey. This gave Considerant a chance to explore the country along the Rio Grande and to take note of the "superb pitayas" and other splendid cacti in the region. Still, his strongest impressions were of the poverty and desolation of the frontier. "I'm writing within sight of the Rio Grande and of the Mexican side," he wrote Julie on February 13. "The shacks of Piedras Negras are spread out on the other side of the river, and they don't look like splendid palaces." And a few days later: "We are still here on the enchanting banks of the Rio Grande, i.e., in the middle of sand, drift boulders, and a few scrawny patches of mesquite." [18] The stay at Eagle Pass gave Considerant the opportunity to catch up with his friend Lorenzo Castro, who had taken a job as a customs collector at Eagle Pass to avoid serving in the Confederate army. With the Union blockade of Confederate ports, Castro's job had become an important one, and he found himself being made much of by Texas cotton merchants. "Lorenzo is very nice," Victor wrote Julie. "It amuses me a lot to see how he is now being fawned upon. He can laugh about it with me. All the cotton merchants from San Antonio and elsewhere are just full of attentions for him." [19]

At Monterrey Considerant did manage to meet with Santiago Vidaurri. At that time Vidaurri had assumed control of much of the north of Mexico and was negotiating as a virtually independent sovereign both with the Mexican president Benito Juárez and with officials of the Confederate government in Texas concerning the division of revenues from the cotton trade. At the same time Vidaurri was engaged in a complicated game of diplomacy, trying to maintain the independence of his region as all of Mexico became caught up in the military struggle between forces loyal to Juárez and the expeditionary force commanded by Marshall Bazaine. Eventually Vidaurri was to cast his lot with the French-imposed government of the Emperor Maximilian; and after the fall of Maximilian he was shot by troops loyal to Juárez. In 1863, though, Vidaurri's future was still open.

At their meeting in early March, Vidaurri peppered Considerant with questions about French intentions and especially about the possible willingness of the French to negotiate with Juárez once the Mexican forces had been defeated. Considerant replied that in his view the French would not negotiate with Juárez. He believed that Napoleon III "wished to have Mexico at his disposal." To what end? Considerant doubted that Napoleon himself knew. He added that although Mexico could no doubt easily be conquered by a European power at a time when America was caught up in civil war, he did not believe that France or any other European nation could long maintain control of Mexico. He went on to argue that the best thing any new regime could do for Mexico would be to abolish the "detestable" system of peonage that dated back to the Spanish conquest.[20]

In his letters to Julie from Mexico, Considerant had more to say about the many varieties of cacti and wildflowers that he encountered than about high politics. His subsequent writings show, however, that as he traveled Considerant was attentive to the effect of social institutions and political developments on the Mexican people. He was impressed by the hospitality and warmth of the ordinary Mexicans he met and by what he described as the natural graciousness of the "Mexican race." At the same time he was shocked by the country's poverty and by the institution of peonage, which he described as "simply another form of slavery," a degrading institution compared to which slavery seemed almost a "blessing," a "sweet-smelling flower."[21]

During and after his trip Considerant was also preoccupied by the French military intervention in Mexico. On March 5, 1863, he wrote Julie from Monterrey that reports had just arrived from the south that Puebla was still holding out against the French. Within three months, however, both Puebla and Mexico City had fallen, and the French were masters of Mexico. On his return to San Antonio, Considerant continued to follow events in Mexico closely. He had access to Mexican journals, which enabled him to see through French efforts to justify their military intervention. He knew, too, that France's allies in Mexico were on the whole an unsavory group—"bandits, thieves, assassins, and intriguing Mexican priests, a scum of bandits and Mexican traitors." [22]

Finally, in 1864 and 1865, Considerant began to set down on paper his own reflections on the Mexican situation, which enabled him, as he put it, to scrape away "ten years of rust" from his mind. These reflections took the form of a series of long, almost book-length letters addressed to the principal actors. He began with a critical analysis of peonage, which he apparently sent, or tried to send, to Napoleon III. This was followed by a huge letter to the Emperor Maximilian outlining, and providing a rationale for, the policies that Maximilian would need to follow to win popular support and keep his throne. This letter was never sent, but some of its arguments were restated in another series of letters addressed to Marshall Bazaine, the commander of the French forces. These letters, which were actually sent to Bazaine, as well as to his enemy Benito Juárez and the liberal journalist Francisco Zarco, were published anonymously in Belgium in 1868. [23]

Considerant's main theme was that Mexico's whole social and economic system was corrupted by the institution of peonage and that as long as peonage existed, Mexico was doomed to backwardness and the vast majority of its people to lives of poverty and squalor. The defenders of peonage argued that it was milder than slavery because every year the peon had the right to buy his liberty or change his master. Considerant replied that this was merely a formal right that could be exercised only by peons who were free of debt. In reality, peonage was a hereditary condition. Children were responsible for debts contracted by deceased parents, and the vast majority of peons had fallen permanently into debt to their masters. The situation of the peon, then, was in some ways worse than that of the slave. [24]

Considerant's letters to Bazaine, Maximilian, and the others grew out of "solitary reveries" and his own responses to the bits and pieces of news that reached him in San Antonio. In setting them down on paper he frequently noted that, having "long lost the habit of ordering and formulating" his ideas, he found it hard to stick to the point. Although his original aim had been to call attention to the evils of peonage, Considerant soon found himself launched on a much broader discussion of the French intervention in Mexico—its motives and its opportunities for success. He dismissed as fabrications the pretexts initially invented by the French to justify the intervention—the stories of "atrocious crimes committed against the French people by Juárez or at his instigation." Considerant granted that not all the French motives were base. Napoleon III was inspired in part, he asserted, by the desire to give Mexico "stability, order, a decent administration, and justice." However, the intervention was more obviously inspired by a mixture of less admirable domestic political calculations and grandiose dreams of empire. Napoleon III wished, at one and the same time, to limit the influence of the United States, "to inoculate the continent against the constitutional virus," to create an overseas empire of his own, a "little pendant" to his uncle's Egyptian expedition, and to curry favor with the papacy and with French Catholics by protecting the interests of the Church in Mexico.[25]

Whatever its motives, the most obvious result of the French intervention was to awaken Mexican nationalism. The liberal government of Juárez became a rallying point for national resistance against the foreigner. The intervention came to be seen as a "brutal and sycophantic intrusion" into Mexican affairs—an intrusion accompanied by "imperial luxury, diplomatic indignities, and lying proclamations." Considerant noted that, in fact, Maximilian had proved to be surprisingly liberal once in power. "The Emperor, instead of going along with the reactionaries, the traitors and the allies of the intervention, turned out to be liberal, democratic, national, and he replaced the government overthrown by [French] bayonets only to realize its principles more effectively." Considerant went on to argue that the only way Maximilian could remain in power would be to pursue policies that were "the systematic negation" of the motives that prompted the intervention. Maximilian would have to reject the hopelessly anachronistic European vision of empire. He would have to show himself willing to abandon his crown, announcing that he wished to rule only at the behest of the "spontaneous and freely expressed will of the Mexican people." Above all, he would have to abolish the system of peonage.

IV

Both Considerant's critique of the French intervention in Mexico and his assessment of Maximilian's prospects as emperor rested on an elaborate set of reflections concerning the difference between European and American societies. These reflections were actually an expansion of the ideas about the "old" and the "new" worlds—the world of war and the world of work—that Considerant had already begun to articulate in the 1840s. In his American solitude, however, he had the opportunity to give them fuller development than ever before. He did so especially in a long, rambling essay, "The Comparative State of European Society and American Society," which constituted the third part of his "Letter to Maximilian."[26] In this essay his key distinction was between traditional European societies, which had been formed by war, and modern societies (such as the American), in which work, science, and law were the shaping influences.

Considerant's premise was that warfare had played a fundamental role in the making of European society. Up until the present, he wrote, "the history of Europe has been uninterruptedly unfolded in war." From the "butcheries" of the misnamed Heroic Age of ancient Greece to the commercial rivalries of the Renaissance to the contemporary rumblings of class war and social revolution, European society had been shaped and reshaped by war. A consequence of the importance of warfare in European history was that traditions and memories related to war had an inescapable hold on the minds of Europeans. As Considerant put it: "The European world that was cradled in war, grew up in war, whose every tradition is connected with war . . . whose poetry is but an everlasting song of war, is so full of war and has so glorified it" that, despite the civilized tastes and softened manners of the nineteenth century, the spirit of Europe has been "petrified and brutalized by the superstition of war." [27]

A further legacy of Europe's tradition of warfare, according to Considerant, was the prevalence of monarchical government in Europe. "Monarchy," he wrote, "is the natural and legitimate, or at least necessary, form of government in any society in which war is the principal element." The contemporary European state system was a "monarchico-military empire" that devoured Europe, even in peacetime, through its military spending. There was, of course, one nation in Europe that had limited the powers of its kings and resisted their efforts to give it a permanent army. But this nation, England, was an island and thus protected from the permanent threat of war.

Considerant speculated on the possibility that kings and armies might "by some sleight of hand" be eliminated from the political map of Europe. What would take the place of the monarchico-military state system? His answer was that the warring monarchies of Europe would be replaced by a peaceful European federation—a "United States of Europe." This was precisely the direction in which "the great natural current of modern social interests" was moving the whole world. In the accents of a latter-day Saint-Simonian, Considerant asserted that in the nineteenth century powerful unifying forces had emerged. Science, large-scale production, the accumulation and mobilization of capital, the development of international trade, the creation of "marvelous" new modes of communication and transportation like the railroad, steamship, and telegraph—all of these were forces of peace and unity that would eventually destroy the old monarchical and warlike order. Many of these forces had already been operative at the beginning of the century, and Napoleon might have harnessed them. "Napoleon could have been the Washington of Europe," wrote Considerant. "But he preferred to become a sort of nineteenth-century Charlemagne. The effort was a gross anachronism, and he failed in it."[28]

Considerant conceded that "commonplace minds" would reject his whole line of argument. They would argue that the European monarchies were entrenched and that religious, cultural, and linguistic differences were too great to permit anything approaching European unity. His reply was that the European federation he saw emerging need not involve the abandonment of significant cultural differences or even of political independence. The repressive military actions of Russia in Poland and of Napoleon in all of Europe had led to the destruction of political and cultural autonomy. However, a European federation could promote respect for political, cultural, and religious differences.

In his "Letter to Maximilian," Considerant formulated the law that underlay and explained the transition from warlike monarchy to peaceful federation (just as it explained the transition from feudalism to centralized monarchy). "When institutions have had their time," he wrote, "and when the new needs of society dictate their replacement by a new institution, revolution is inevitable." Modern Europe was marked by a "profound antagonism" between the traditional monarchical political structure and the movement of society and the economy. A new world was emerging—a world organized around productive industrial activity and the assertion of the rights of labor, a world driven by socializing and unifying forces that tended to undermine the military dynasties, the monarchies, that remained in control of material power.

In Europe, Considerant concluded, the struggle between the old and the new was still going on. But in America the issue had already been decided.

> America was founded by and on the modern element. . . . Its constitution did not emerge from civil wars. It is not with war and through war that America grew and took shape. Its kind of war is the war against rude nature, and its kind of conquest is the conquest of the wilderness.[29]

In the modern world, work, science, and law were replacing the feudal and warlike elements of traditional society. And America was the modern state par excellence. For that reason monarchy, which was founded on war, had no place in America.

Considerant's distinction between the European world of war and the American world of work was not gratuitous. It shed light on the power in

Europe of the chivalric tradition and in France of the Napoleonic myth. It has had echoes in American political science in various attempts to derive American exceptionalism from the lack of a feudal past.[30] Still, one can only marvel at Considerant's ability to argue that America was not forged in war, writing, as he was, during the bloodiest war in American history, and standing, as he was, on ground that Americans had wrested from Mexico by war.[31]

V

With the end of the Civil War, the Considerants were at last able to get back in touch with their friends in France. What first broke their isolation, apparently, was a letter to the French Fourierists from Supervielle, describing the pitiful condition to which Considerant and his little family had been reduced. Although the letter has been lost, its "lamentable news" was summarized by Désiré Laverdant:

> Madame Vigoureux has fallen into a [second] childhood. She can no longer even feed herself. Her children are not able to take care of her. Poverty has invaded their home. We had thought that Victor would get along thanks to a small business established with the help of his Belgian friend, Cousin. But Cousin himself is in a state of decrepitude, and Considerant has to provide for the whole group by himself. He has been reduced to working the soil, and you can imagine how hard this must be for a man who is not used to this kind of backbreaking work and who is no longer young. They say that he has changed a lot, that he is crushed, exhausted.[32]

In spreading the news of the Considerants' destitution, Laverdant, together with the faithful Aimée Beuque, set about raising money to be sent to the Considerants in Texas. Finally, by mid-August of 1865, they had collected 3,400 francs, all of which eventually reached Considerant either in cash or in the form of books requested by him.[33]

Judging from the letters that he now began to send to his old friends in France, Considerant had not been crushed by poverty and isolation. The opportunity to renew contact with France seems to have revived his spirits. The money sent by his friends in Paris now enabled him to devote much of his time to reading and writing. There were still numerous household chores to be performed—and his own responsibilities ranged from feeding the chickens to baking the bread,[34] but now he began to fill his letters to Europe with requests for books and journals. He also got back in touch with Albert Brisbane, Horace Greeley, and Charles Dana, and he began to work on essays and articles that might be published in Greeley's *New York Tribune* or the European press. The most substantial of Considerant's writings during this period were the various "letters" on Mexico and on France's Mexican intervention discussed above. During the three years following the end of the Civil War, however, Considerant also wrote a long essay on currency reform in the United States and a series of letters to Ernest Renan on his controversial *Vie de Jésus* as well as many shorter letters and essays on scientific topics.[35]

A first fruit of this renewed activity was a long letter, dated October 11, 1865, and published two months later in the French journal, *La Morale indépendante*, by its addressee, Clarisse Coignet. In this letter Considerant attempted to take stock of his own intellectual evolution, to specify what was left of his lifelong commitment to Fourier's ideas, and above all to characterize his developing faith in science.

> Tomorrow I will be fifty-seven years old. . . . I didn't imagine when I was young that one could ever be that old. . . . I don't know if I am deceiving myself, but I am much inclined to think that nothing will be accomplished, no progress will ever be made . . . without arriving as quickly as possible at the absolute supremacy of *science.*
>
> I certainly don't want to make war on sentiment. A purely rational humanity would be a monster, just as much as would a purely material humanity. I mean that science should become the *only* superior and universal *law.* And by science I mean the truth recognized by an *intelligence guided by strict scientific methods that it has created to govern itself.* Sentiment, imagination, intuition, the soul's ardor may flush or throw out hypotheses as a dog flushes game. But the dog is not the hunter. . . .
>
> In the last analysis there is nothing stable and certain in the world, nothing that has a rightful claim to be a part of the gradually acquired treasure of humanity, that has not passed through the sieve of science, that is not admitted and recognized by science. Science *alone* has the sovereign and supreme trait of *unity.* Everything that is recognized scientifically is *certainly* destined to be accepted universally in the measure that the culture of humanity develops. Everything else, all *dogmas,* all *beliefs* only serve, even with the bravest tendencies to unity, to maintain subversive divisions in humanity. Everything that is not science is hypothesis; science alone is *universally* human; hypotheses are purely personal. . . .
>
> With the development of science in the world and of the *notion of science* in the human mind, there will be an end to the conditions in which any dogma can dominate as a dogma. Science is the Catholicism and the Church against which no other force can prevail. As for me,

I will no longer *affirm* that "attractions are proportional to destinies" because, even if this formula were true, neither I nor anyone else could be scientifically certain of it. I will content myself to *affirm* that in the natural order destinies are proportional to attractions, this alone being certain and scientifically demonstrable. In the current state of human knowledge and of the development of the human mind, there is between these two formulas all the difference of the dogmatic and the scientific. Even though I have always attempted to separate these two domains in my past reflections, I will do so much more strictly now that I am at the end of my career than I did when I was at the beginning.[36]

Science for Considerant had always been the measure of all things. As a young man, he had been drawn to Fourier's doctrine precisely by what he took to be its scientific character. In his writings of the Second Republic he had moved increasingly away from the fundamentals of Fourierism—but without calling into question its status as a science. This letter was as close as he had yet come to disavowing altogether the scientific character of the whole Fourierist project.

The effort to reach a scientific understanding of social problems was evident in everything Considerant wrote during his final five years in America. Even his "Letter to Maximilian" was buttressed, in its fullest versions, by an elaborate set of reflections concerning the "rules" necessary for the development of a science of history and politics. Clearly what Considerant was trying to do in these writings was to work out a general framework within which particular political and social problems, such as those posed by the French intervention in Mexico, could be solved scientifically. Just as clearly, Considerant's conception of science was deeply influenced by what he knew of work in the field of evolutionary biology. It was only in 1867 that he obtained (from Aimée Beuque) a copy of Clémence Royer's translation of Darwin's *Origin of Species*.[37] For several years already, though, it would seem his intellectual preoccupations had been those of a Social Darwinist.

Near the beginning of his essay, "Investigation of Some Rules for the Solution of Problems of General Politics," Considerant described the new science of evolutionary biology as the model on which to found a genuinely scientific understanding of history. "A noble science of wholly modern creation has opened the great history of nature to man." Consulting the geological record, he wrote, we find "a triumph incessantly renewed" of organisms best adapted to survive in changing circumstances. History could be understood in similar terms. Its first cause was "identical with the cause of the development of organic life." The key units of historical development were large groups—tribes, races, nations, federations. These groups "have their own life, like individuals." Thus, "a nation is a real organism," a so-cial organism, or, in a term of Considerant's coinage, a "socio-organism."[38]

Considerant noted that the struggle for survival between social organisms was "going on now, before our eyes, on each of the five continents." The chief conflict was that pitting the "advanced" civilizations against the "barbarous" races, which represented five-sixths of the world's population. "The ultimatum of competition is not only presented to these races," he wrote, "it enfolds them and works upon them irresistibly." These races must rapidly become civilized, or civilization would simply pass them by. "Civilization advances like cholera, only cholera spares many, civilization none."[39]

Despite his grim assessment of the significance of the "civilizing" mission of the "advanced" nations, Considerant's overall view of history was thoroughly optimistic. He believed that sociability was both a distinguishing trait of the human species and the basis on which even richer and more complex forms of collective organization would emerge. "The history of humanity consists in the development of organic forms of social life," he wrote. "Progress is accomplished by the triumph of social forces more fitted to the wants of man, to the expression of his individual and collective life." Ultimately progress would lead to the development of socio-organisms reflective of the unity of the species.[40]

In this light, Europe itself could still be seen as politically backward. Indeed, Considerant argued that within Europe the development of socio-organisms was still at a rudimentary stage, for the nation-state still reigned: the nations of Europe were not yet integrated within a larger federation. "Europe is still an acephalous system," he wrote. It was a system without a head or a brain, and as such "one of the lowest forms of life in the chain of being within the socio-organic realm." Insofar as a European political order existed, it was the result of the unstable equilibrium of various ganglions. There was no controlling intelligence. As a result Europe was undergoing constant crises, periodic convulsions, "veritable epileptic attacks," and these would continue to wrack the body politic until a European federation was formed consistent with the socializing and unifying forces at work in the economic and social spheres.[41]

If scientific history as Considerant understood it studied the struggle for survival of social organisms, it also focused on labor and on the political and social conditions of the laboring classes. Here he argued—as had Marx two decades earlier in *The German Ideology*—that human history was coextensive with the history of productive labor. The moment at which human beings began to emerge from sheer animality was the moment at which they began to transform natural objects for their own purposes. Labor was thus man's "first historical title of nobility." Considerant observed that man's discovery of the value of productive labor was the key to a "great social transformation": the transformation from societies of hunters and gatherers to societies based on farming and stockraising. With the establishment of settled societies, he continued, a change took place in the nature of warfare. Now the victor in war did not slaughter the enemy but enslaved him. Slavery was in fact "the first form of productive labor in primitive society."[42]

From the establishment of the first slave societies down to modern times, labor continued to be performed in conditions that were "painful, repugnant, and even murderous for the worker." Man had not yet completed the transition from an animal existence to a truly human one. Still, the history of labor was the history of the process by which man acquired his humanity. Through labor men wrested a living from nature and created the means to satisfy their desires—"wealth, power, the means of survival and expansion, the refinements and the pleasures of life, social liberty itself." All these goods, which were the fruits of labor, were at the same time the objects of competition; the history of labor itself was "an unrelenting competition for the greatest part of the fruits of labor and the smallest part of its pains." This competition was not destined to last forever, though. Considerant looked forward to a time of "redressement social," when "all traces of animal competition will have disappeared, when every worker will be the proprietor of the whole real value of the product of his labor, when with the elimination of the destructive activity of war society will be no more than an organized and intelligent workshop of production in which each person will work freely" to enrich his own life and that of the collectivity. In such a society a "completely humanized competition" would encourage and inspire workers, and society would be the gainer. This was Considerant's sketch of the fully human existence toward which "the forces and the interest of labor" were leading humanity in the long term.[43]

VI

Considerant's intellectual isolation during the 1860s permitted him to reflect uninterruptedly on fundamental questions and to pursue his ideas back to their logical foundations. Thus his criticism of the French intervention in Mexico led him to seek to define the basic differences between European and American society that made the idea of an American monarchy unthinkable. Similarly, his reflections on social and political issues led him repeatedly back to religion and ethics.

Considerant had long been fascinated by religion. Although strongly, and at times fiercely, anticlerical, he regarded religious belief as something that human beings could not do without and as a potentially powerful source of social cement. Indeed, his last articles in *Démocratie pacifique* had focused on the role played by the Christian religion in creating a consciousness of a common humanity among its believers.[44] The coup of December 2, 1851, and Considerant's emigration had turned his attention to other, more concrete matters, but his interest in religion was rekindled toward the end of the Civil War when he learned of the publication of Ernest Renan's controversial and immensely popular *Vie de Jésus.* Considerant had the book sent from France; and in April 1868 he sent two long letters on it to Renan himself.[45]

Renan's *Vie de Jésus* was one of the great publishing successes of the nineteenth century. Within its first six months of publication over sixty thousand copies were sold. What made the book so provocative to its contemporary readers was its critical analysis of the evidence contained in the Gospels concerning Jesus' life, and its portrait of Jesus not as the son of God but as a "sublime person." All this was fascinating to Considerant. In his letters to Renan, however, he focused more on the book's broader dimensions and its affirmations rather than on what it criticized. "Although your book is a work of scientific-historical research," he wrote, "it is also a work of religious reflection, if only because, in reducing the divine to the human in Christianity, it shows the human in the divine."

Considerant went on to describe to Renan his own impression of the impact that the *Vie de Jésus* must have had in the "asphyxiating" atmosphere of the Second Empire. On his trip to France he had found "liberty suppressed, hope extinguished, and mental life quiescent." The streets of Paris had been full of soldiers and priests, and the only sounds were those of "swords, robes, and money."

> There was the dim light and the foul air of a cellar dug out in some unhealthy spot where the soul of the nineteenth century seemed to live as if this were its normal atmosphere. Now then, your *Jésus* impressed me as having opened up a great hole in the wall through which pure air and light came pouring into the cellar. The bright light and the pure air rendered the inner darkness and the stench *perceptible.*

Considerant saw the *Vie de Jésus* as a deeply subversive book—as a "protest" against the ruling groups and the ruling ideas of the Second

Empire. "You have initiated a movement of protest," he wrote Renan, "against the supremacy of the Praetorian guard of the barracks, the sacristy, and the stock exchange.[46]

There were three respects in which Considerant believed Renan's *Vie de Jésus* to have been a subversive work. First, by showing the strength of the movement Jesus created by preaching peace and fraternity, Renan had effectively demonstrated the weakness of brute force and armaments. Second, Renan had "attacked at its core the texture of superstitions, of materialism and smug idiocy" with which Napoleon III was seeking "to bring the nineteenth century back to a state of fanatical piety" ("réembéguiner le dix-neuvième siècle"). Finally, and most importantly, Renan's *Vie de Jésus* had reawakened generous and idealistic impulses that had long seemed dead in Second Empire France. "In making music on the strings of the human soul that had long been left silent," wrote Considerant, "you have played a melody of pure sentiments, high ideas, and aspirations to liberty and universal justice, which clashed with the music of small change, even that of big money, and which devalued the economic harmonies of orthodox, plutocratic, and right-minded political economy."[47]

What particularly excited Considerant about Renan's *Vie de Jésus* was that it seemed to point the way toward a new understanding of the course of Western religious history. "I believe that with your learning, your serene independence, and the deep love you feel for your subject," he wrote, "you can render still greater services to the history of the human spirit and to its present religious development." In other works Renan could elaborate his "fecund" distinction between Jesus' three different conceptions of the Kingdom of God and could trace the way in which each of them had been developed and altered by the followers of Jesus. He could study the influence on early Christianity of Greek, Roman, and Oriental religious traditions. Finally, he could write the "natural history" of Western Christendom in such a way that supernatural intellectual formulations could be understood in secular and scientific terms. The result of all this would be more than academic; it would constitute an essential contribution to the elaboration of "the true religion of humanity"—a rational and scientific religion built on the critique of Christian dogma begun by the eighteenth-century *philosophes*.[48]

Considerant's letters eventually reached Renan in Paris, and although Renan's reply skirted both the general issues raised by Considerant and his specific points of criticism, it was warm and sympathetic. "To reply to such letters, which constitute a veritable book on the gravest issues, another book would be necessary," wrote Renan. However, Renan added that he had been told that Considerant was planning to return to France before long. "So, if you wish, we can talk at our leisure about these problems, the principal attraction of which is perhaps that they are insoluble and which nevertheless thrust themselves so inescapably on the human mind." Renan then went on to pay tribute to Considerant in terms that must have moved him deeply.

> You have devoted your life to the discussion of social issues, and I understand the interest that the origin of Christianity inspires in you. This great movement was indeed, in a sense, a social event; but it was above all a religious event, and it is precisely for that reason that the element of socialism in it thrived. The solidity of a foundation stands in direct relation to the quantity of dedication, sacrifice, and self-denial that has been placed in its base. Some ancient people believed that, if a building was to endure, a man had to be buried alive in its foundations; that is true enough, at least in the moral order. Temporal interest does not suffice to inspire man to the degree of heroism necessary to create something truly lasting and great. Will idealism be strong enough to accomplish one day what was once accomplished by faith in a material and imminent kingdom of God? It is a fine thing, in any case, to protest in the manner of the Stoics of the ancient world. By your courage and by your life entirely dedicated to the pursuit of what you conceive as the ideal, you belong to the ranks of the noble Phalanx.[49]

Renan was far more skeptical than Considerant about the contribution his own writings might make to the elaboration of "the true religion of humanity," or about the efficacy of any such secular religion. His reply did at any rate show that Considerant was not forgotten at Paris.

If the reading and criticism of Renan's *Vie de Jésus* helped Considerant work out his ideas on a future religion of humanity, another work that was equally important to him in the late 1860s was Alexis de Tocqueville's *Démocratie en Amérique*. During his years in San Antonio, Considerant wrote scores of pages on Tocqueville's great book (many of them within the framework of his "Letter to Maximilian"), and one of his unfulfilled intellectual projects of the 1860s seems to have been an attempt to work out a reassessment of American democracy aimed explicitly at rectifying some of the principal shortcomings in Tocqueville's analysis.

There was much in Tocqueville's portrait of American society that Considerant found incisive and revealing. Tocqueville's fundamental distinction between the Yankee and the Virginian, his discussion of the influence of Puritanism, his analysis of grass-roots political life in the small towns of New England—these were just a few of the elements of *Démocratie en*

Amérique that Considerant found richly suggestive. Considerant was also impressed by the "remarkable clarity" of Tocqueville's discussion of causes. This was, in some respects at least, "scientific history" that sought out the real and material causes of things. Nonetheless, Considerant believed, there was a fundamental problem with Tocqueville's assessment of America. Everything Tocqueville saw, he saw clearly and described vigorously. Yet when Tocqueville sought to get beyond appearances, to penetrate to the core of things, his voice turned mystical and at times deeply fearful. Quoting the famous passage from the introduction to *Démocratie en Amérique* where Tocqueville speaks of the development of equality as a "providential fact," of historical actors as "blind instruments in the hands of God," and of his whole book as "written under the impression of a sort of religious terror" at the irresistible advance of democracy, Considerant comments that the sense of religious terror is invoked frequently throughout Tocqueville's book—that it "darkens" both the book and the soul of the author. "This mind, so penetrating when it is free, appears to be constantly beset by the return of a sort of faith, at once obscure and artificial, in a power which sometimes seems to be the blind *fatum* of the ancients and sometimes a providence which is hardly different." Considerant finds in Tocqueville a "fatal veneration for hidden and mysterious things," which he sees as "the academic and modern form of superstition."[50]

In Tocqueville's view of history, Considerant observes, man is fundamentally passive—the plaything of large forces over which he has no real control. "Instead of seeing in the march of democracy the autonomous, simple, and natural development of *human power*," Tocqueville describes a process of historical evolution determined by "an external, occult, supernatural power against which man can do nothing and which makes sport of his liberty." What Tocqueville refuses to recognize is that democracy can also be seen as the outcome not of some providential decree but of the history of human strivings in the material world. What his great work lacks, in other words, is due attention to "the history of labor and of the condition of laboring people."[51]

Considerant finds Tocqueville's fatalism curious because in many passages Tocqueville shows himself perfectly well aware of the role played by man's strivings. He concludes that Tocqueville's fearfulness and pessimism are the expression not of a deeply held conviction but rather of a capitulation before the conventions of religion and class. The key to the contradictions in Tocqueville's thought, according to Considerant, lies in the fact that his "honest and penetrating genius" was "grafted onto a rather weak temperament" and that in his conception of history Tocqueville was influenced by his peers within the historical school of the Restoration. In the work of these historians, writes Tocqueville (referring presumably to Barante, Thierry, and Guizot), we find a widening of the boundaries of history. Law, liberty, religion, political institutions, and economic interests were all seen as "mutable phenomena" having histories of their own, but the "plebeian question of labor" was not yet judged worthy of a place in history. The whole process of history was seen as ultimately controlled by divine external forces. It was these two weaknesses—the omission of labor and the postulation of a supernatural force defining the march of history—that held back "the investigative genius of Tocqueville. And, Considerant insists, these two "weaknesses" are complementary. If you do not or cannot recognize the role played by human striving in history, you will necessarily have to postulate some sort of external cause.[52]

VII

In the late 1860s, while Considerant was setting down his reflections on Renan and Tocqueville, he also maintained a regular correspondence with friends and relatives in France and Belgium. He had always been particularly fond of his oldest sister, Justine Palas. He husband was dead now, and so was Considerant's unwed sister Julie—she died in 1866, leaving him a small legacy of 2,000 francs. But Justine was well, and her son, Jules Palas, was thriving. After a few years in the imperial navy, he had settled down in the Jura, and Considerant could address him jocularly in 1868 as "sailor at anchor, land owner, and respectable man."[53] During these years Considerant was also in touch with Aimée Beuque, Clarisse Coignet and Désiré Laverdant, and his Belgian friend Adolphe Demeur. From the letters exchanged with all these friends one gains some sense of the Considerants' life during these last years in Texas, and one can also follow their preparations for a return to France.

In the spring of 1867 Considerant was writing his sister Justine about his desire to return to France. His health was not good, and neither was Julie's. He continued to suffer from periodic headaches, and she from recurrent chest colds and other respiratory problems. Considerant also continued to be afflicted by spells of depression. He wrote Justine that "without being what people call sick," he was "absolutely inert," and that his great aim was to pull himself out of "the inertia and ennui that are devouring me."[54] The best remedy, he believed, would be closer contact with his loved ones in France. Ever since the general amnesty of 1859 it had been possible to return. The problem was finding a buyer for his house and land. This proved to be difficult. In December he wrote Aimée Beuque that he hoped to rent his house if he couldn't sell it. He had also settled a dispute concerning a small piece of property he owned in downtown San Antonio. Thus he and Julie could expect to leave Texas with at least a modest nest egg. They would wait until the following spring, however, because "after twelve years in this land of sunshine," they did not wish too abrupt a confrontation with "the hard winter of North America, or even that of Europe."[55]

Considerant's thoughts turned to the journey home. Julie had come to Texas by boat and had seen little of the rest of America. Now he would show her the country, and they would take a steamboat up "the noblest river in the world." France, he knew, would be a very different country from the one they had left, and he rejoiced in the reports that reached him of the development of the workers' movement and the rise of opposition to Napoleon III. The empire was in decline, and perhaps even before their return the emperor would have been dispatched to a Saint Helena of his own.[56]

While Considerant fantasized about the fall of Napoleon III and playfully evoked his return in letters to Adolphe Demeur, he recalled what he was leaving behind. "What wonderful weather," he wrote his nephew at the winter's end. "March 16: roses in bloom, the countryside all dressed in green, the swallows back five days ago, the birds chirping this morning, the fish as fat as pigs. And to think that I can't take our winters back with me to make summers there!" By May 1868 Victor and Julie had done most of their packing and had begun selling off their furniture. Once the warm weather arrived, though, they were reluctant to leave. Why, Victor wrote his sister, should "lizards like us" for whom warmth was a necessity be going back to France? In any case, they still had to sell the house.[57]

In the fall of 1868 they finally found a buyer, one Nicholas Lardner, who offered them $6,600 to be paid in installments over ten years. This was a "pretty good price," Victor wrote later. With a 10 percent down payment, that would give them an income of $600 a year for ten years. He hoped that this would eventually be supplemented by the income from his "little speculation" on property within the city limits. "I am leaving here a few lots in the city that cost me a trifle and that will be worth something in a few years," he told his nephew. In ten years their value might increase ten times. "That's the way people with money get rich in this world."[58]

Having sold the house, Victor and Julie moved back into San Antonio, where they rented a small house until their departure. They now had to say farewell to their friends in the French colony—the merchant François Guilbeau with whom Victor had toured Mexico, the contractor Jules Poinsard, the painter Théodore Gentilz, the merchant Auguste Frétillière, Lorenzo Castro, who was now involved in real estate speculation, and the civil engineer François Giraud, whom Victor had recommended in 1867 as the man best qualified to represent the interests of the Colonization Society in San Antonio. On June 1, 1869, Victor and Julie went to the county clerk's office to sign papers granting the merchant Honoré Grenet power of attorney to collect their mortgage payments and handle their other business affairs.[59] A few days later they left San Antonio for good.

In his last long letter from the United States to his sister Justine, Considerant made it plain that he couldn't wait to return to Franche-Comté. If at all possible, he wrote, he and Julie would be back for the grape harvest. He would fish the trout streams of the Jura; and together he and Julie would explore old haunts. Perhaps they would even travel through the Jura by means of the newly invented velocipede. What a sensation they would create in arriving at Beaufort astride these new two-wheeled vehicles. When they visited Justine, she would serve them all the old Franc-comtois dishes he remembered from childhood—crayfish, ramekin, potato pancakes. "How our mother cooked up all these things. And let's not forget *des atros* [pork fritters]! *Des atros!* Since my childhood I've never seen anything like them, and I think it would bring back my youth to get reacquainted with them."[60]

Victor and Julie reached New Orleans by the beginning of July. There they spent a few days in the city's large French colony with old friends—notably Dr. Louis Louis, a self-taught veterinary whose stay at Reunion had tarnished neither his faith in Fourier's ideas nor his friendship for Considerant.[61] Before continuing on to New York, Considerant gave an interview to a local French-language newspaper: "One thing that makes me happy," he declared, "is that I am leaving the United States purged of the crime of slavery, and I hardly know how to express my joy at seeing newspapers established by people of color in the Deep South, courageously defending the cause of the oppressed."[62]

Considerant's final stay in New York City lasted over a month. This gave him time to see most of his old friends in the city. These included Brisbane, who had been only slightly distracted from his dogged advocacy of Fourierism by a newfound interest in transportation by pneumatic tubes, and Charles A. Dana, who was now at the beginning of a thirty-year career as the influential editor and part owner of the *New York Sun.* Considerant also managed to pay a return visit to the Oneida Community in upstate New York, where he had been warmly received on his first trip to America sixteen years earlier. He was impressed by the growth and prosperity of the community, and he came away with renewed admiration for the spirit of "unity" and "dedication" that reigned among its members. He wrote later that nowhere else had he encountered "a social group as united, as prosperous, as upright, as decent, and as truly Christian in the moral and nobly human sense of the word as the community of Perfectionists in Oneida County, N.Y." [63]

While in New York City Considerant had dinner with Horace Greeley and took the opportunity to urge him to give the editorial support of the *New York Tribune* to the women's suffrage movement. "To have been the first to inscribe on your flag universal suffrage . . . will be one of your glories," he told Greeley. But the suffrage would not be universal as long as half the adults in America were deprived of the vote. Having been a leader in the movement for the enfranchisement of Negroes, who "did not ask" for the vote, Greeley could hardly deny it to women, "who ask for it." Considerant had other advice for Greeley on subjects ranging from the "Greenback Controversy" to the role that a phonetic alphabet might play in the struggle against illiteracy. It would seem that on many of these issues Greeley was a sympathetic interlocutor. At any rate he made space in the *Tribune* for the publication of an article by Considerant restating the views expressed in his 1868 brochure on currency reform. [64]

Shortly before leaving New York Considerant was interviewed by a reporter for Dana's *New York Sun;* and this gave him an opportunity to express, for the last time in America, his views on Europe and America and on the future. "The monarchies of the old world are losing confidence in themselves," Considerant asserted. Europe would soon adopt republican institutions. In due course a Great European Republic would be established; and eventually Europe and the United States would form a union, taking into their hands "the government of the world" and exercising it "in the interests of the people." Would these developments occur peacefully or violently? Would the deepening struggle of labor and capital be resolved without revolution? Considerant argued that only "social science" could provide a peaceful solution to the problem of social reconstruction. Still, he doubted that the remedies of social science would be accepted by either capital or labor. The immediate future might well be bloody. [65] It was with such doubts and uncertainties that Victor Considerant, American citizen, returned to the land of his birth.

PART V

Return

17

Under Two Sieges

Victor and Julie Considerant returned to Paris on September 3, 1869, just twenty years and two months after Victor had gone into exile. During those years France had undergone more profound changes than in any two decades of its history. The nation's industrial production had doubled; its railroad network had quadrupled; and great banking houses like the Crédit Lyonnais and the Crédit Foncier had been established to stimulate economic growth. At the same time a new mass culture was emerging with large-circulation newspapers and the first modern department stores. And the city of Paris had been transformed. In 1859 the old Farmers' General wall around Paris had been demolished and the boundaries of the city enlarged to include seven new arrondissements. In the heart of Paris twenty thousand houses had been destroyed and forty thousand new ones built. Great boulevards had been cut through the old working-class quarters of the city, rents had doubled, and the poor had been driven to the outskirts—to Belleville, Ménilmontant, and La Villette.

Some of these transformations appalled Considerant; some delighted him; all of them left him amazed. When, in due course, he became reacquainted with the French provinces, he found more cause for wonder. The coming of the railroad had changed everything. On his first trip through the North of France, he found Amiens almost unrecognizable. With its "fine views" and "beaux quartiers," it had little in common with the city he remembered from "the era of stagecoaches."[1] Even more striking to Considerant than these physical changes was the extraordinary change in the political climate of France—and especially of its capital. France was no longer the "dim, dead" nation to which he had briefly returned in 1859. Public life was once again intense, and the empire's political opponents were thriving. Beginning with the fiasco of the Mexican intervention, the government had suffered an unbroken string of military and diplomatic reverses; an embarrassing series of scandals had reinforced its difficulties; and a significant parliamentary opposition had emerged.

The big political turning point came in May 1869, just a few months prior to the Considerants' return, when general legislative elections gave over three million votes—40 percent of the total—to opposition candidates. Now a number of Considerant's old friends and allies were members of the Corps Legislatif. The industrialist Frédéric Dorian, who had encouraged Considerant's first efforts to run for the Chamber of Deputies, was now himself a legislator from Saint-Etienne. Wladimir Gagneur, the author of Fourierist brochures on the Fruitières and on credit schemes, had been elected deputy from Poligny in the Jura with the support of the whole liberal opposition. And Dr. Edouard Ordinaire, the Fourierist dissident whose uncle had been a classmate of Charles Fourier, had been elected deputy from Besançon as a staunchly anti-Bonapartist radical republican.[2]

Considerant's return to France also coincided with the awakening of the French labor movement. Only five years earlier, in 1864, Napoleon III had granted French workers the right to strike, and only one year earlier he had given official toleration to trade unions. Already there were a hundred Sociétés Ouvrières in Paris, and twenty or thirty in Lyon, Marseilles, and Rouen. In 1869 a wave of strikes swept across France. Army troops were called in to combat strike movements in Anzin, La Ricamarie, and Decazeville; and in October 1869, just a month after Considerant's return, a confrontation between workers and troops in Aubin culminated in a fusillade that left fourteen workers killed and fifty wounded. At the same time, the French sections of the Workers' International, founded at London in 1864, were growing rapidly. By the summer of 1870 they could claim thousands of members, one of whom was Considerant himself.[3]

The difficulties for the government caused by labor unrest and by the political and diplomatic reverses of the late 1860s were compounded by the effervescence of the press. Laws passed in March and June of 1868 had liberalized controls on the press and on public assemblies. The result was to open an era of tumultuous public meetings and to let loose a flood of new journals, many of them, like Henri Rochefort's *La Lanterne* and Charles

Delescluze's *Le Reveil*, fiercely hostile to the regime. The government now came under furious attack. The new mood of strident, often scurrilous, criticism was expressed most strikingly not in the editorials of the great Paris dailies but rather in the emergence of what one observer described as "the acrimonious, denigrating, ironic *petite presse*, which every day spreads more scorn and calumny on everything that concerns the government." It was not so much by argument as by ridicule, by "perfidious and defamatory slurs," that the men and institutions of the Second Empire were now coming under attack.[4]

I

During their first two weeks in Paris, Victor and Julie had little time to reflect on all these changes. Indeed, they hardly had a moment to themselves. There were poignant reunions with friends, more formal discussion sessions with old Fourierists, and invitations from complete strangers. Considerant found himself a celebrity. Newspapers of all political persuasions —*Le Siècle, Le Figaro, L'Opinion nationale*—printed articles on his return. André Gill's satirical journal *L'Eclipse* ran a full-page caricature of Considerant along with an article recalling his moment of notoriety in 1848. He was described there as one of many "political swallows" returning from exile—a quixotic figure, no doubt deluded in his ideas, but still "a friend of the suffering masses" and deserving of praise for his "humanitarian intentions." Other journals were less sympathetic: the conservative *Figaro* described Considerant as the "high priest" of Fourierism who owed his "considerable fortune" to a legacy from "the Amazon, Princess Belgiojoso." Still others treated him as a curiosity, a ghost from the past, a kind of Rip Van Winkle. That is, in effect, what he was.[5]

After two weeks in Paris the Considerants were ready for the calm of Franche-Comté. So around September 20 they left to visit Besançon and Salins and to spend the harvest season in Beaufort in the Jura with Victor's sister Justine and his nephew Jules. They found Justine in fine fettle—"a hundred times more fit" than they expected—and they delighted in having at last returned "home." The stay in Beaufort gave Considerant time to take stock of his situation, see old friends, and do a little writing. He met with his cousin, the architect Alphonse Delacroix, and with his old comrades from the Ecole Polytechnique, Alphonse Tamisier and Eugène Bossu. He exchanged warm and wry letters with George Sand. He also traded reflections on the progress of direct legislation in Switzerland with Moritz Rittinghausen and negotiated with Albert Brisbane concerning the translation and

publication of his article on the Greenback Controversy.[6] The most important letter Considerant wrote at this time, however, was a long and carefully
considered epistle to Charles Pellarin spelling out his reasons for refusing
to assume once again leadership of the Ecole Sociétaire.

Considerant's letter to Pellarin of November 5, 1869, is a fascinating
document. Not only does it mark his formal separation from the affairs of
the Fourierist movement, it also reflects the bitterness that he continued to
feel about old quarrels. Considerant wrote that he had returned to France
because he needed intellectual nourishment—to "breathe an air agitated
by ideas."[7] But he never intended to take back his position as leader of the
Ecole. He was too old and tired, and he had been leading a solitary and con-
templative life for too long. The only role he felt capable of playing now
was that of an "irregular Cossack, an independent laborer" outside the
movement.

Considerant had other reasons for refusing to reclaim the leadership,
though. Twenty-four years earlier, he recalled, Pellarin had quarreled with
him and had virtually withdrawn from the Fourierist movement. Pellarin's
position was that the Fourierist Ecole had become "an obstacle" to the
spread of Fourier's ideas. Pellarin had protested against Considerant's "monopolistic" pretensions, his attempt to treat Fourier's ideas as "private
property." He had argued that the greatest service the disciples could render their master would be to stop publishing their journals and their popularizations of Fourier's ideas, to break up the Ecole, and to allow Fourier's
books to make their own way in the world.

Pellarin's mistake, according to Considerant, was to believe that public
opinion was as well prepared to assimilate Fourier's ideas as he himself had
been; it was to believe that a reading of Fourier's works "would bring about
the intellectual illumination of the masses" just as rapidly as it had brought
about his own illumination. In fact, wrote Considerant, Fourier *needed* disciples in order to make his ideas accessible. If Fourier had not been "discovered" by Just Muiron, he would have died in oblivion. The historic
achievement of the Ecole Sociétaire was to enable Fourier's ideas to find an
audience and to be taken seriously. This work had been accomplished by the
end of the 1840s. Now Fourier was known; his ideas had become part of the
intellectual landscape of the modern world; and they could be counted on
to "sail safely toward the future" with or without the aid of disciples.

Considerant's letter to Charles Pellarin was a leave-taking of sorts.
Henceforth he had nothing to do with the organization and leadership of
the Fourierist movement or with the publication of its journals. Still, he
regularly attended its banquets and dinners. He remained close to many of

its individual members, and he continued to discuss with some of them the issues raised in the letter to Pellarin, especially the question of the proper attitude to take toward Fourier's ideas. His own view was that Fourierism should be understood critically. It contained elements of science and elements of fiction or poetry. It was now more important than ever, he believed, "to save the *science* in Fourier's thought by separating it from the *poetry.*"[8]

The Considerants returned to Paris toward the end of November. They took up residence in the Latin Quarter, near the Sorbonne. For a few months they lived in rented rooms on the rue de la Sorbonne. Then, the day after Easter 1870, they moved into a small apartment at 48, rue du cardinal Lemoine. This apartment was just a few steps from the Ecole Polytechnique, where Considerant had spent his first years in Paris. It was to be home to Victor and Julie for the rest of their lives.

During the winter and spring of 1870, the Considerants settled into their new lives as Parisians. They lived frugally, subsisting "like birds" on coffee, tea, bread, and milk, Clarisse Coignet recalled, "and only in the evening did they eat a more substantial meal . . . in a little neighborhood restaurant." They had friends in Paris like Aimée Beuque and Clarisse Coignet whom they sometimes invited in for tea and conversation. Occasionally they dined out in style with their old friends, Frédéric and Caroline Dorian, or with Juliette and Edmond Adam. It was through Aimée Beuque that they became acquainted with Juliette Adam. Already on her way to becoming one of the most influential hostesses of the period, the future "Egérie de la République," Juliette Adam was the daughter of a doctor with Fourierist sympathies and an old friend of Aimée Beuque and Alphonse Toussenel. Despite their differences of character and personality, she and Julie liked each other; and for a few years they became good friends.[9]

It was only on April 8, 1870—seven months after his return from France—that Considerant made his first public appearance. The occasion was the annual banquet held by the Ecole Sociétaire to celebrate Fourier's birthday. Pellarin and the other Fourierists had originally asked Considerant to preside. He refused, but he did agree to be a speaker; and his presence helped draw some two hundred people to the restaurant Bonvallet on the boulevard du Temple. According to one participant, it was the most festive banquet in years. The atmosphere was one of warmth and "gentle gaiety," and when the name of Considerant, "the Saint Paul of the Phalansterian doctrine," was mentioned for the first time, there was an "explosion of applause and bravos" that shook the hall.[10]

Considerant's speech was both a celebration of Fourier and an attempt to show the relevance of his ideas to the modern world. He noted recent signs of progress: the abolition of slavery in America and the formation of the Workers' International in Europe. Calling on his familiar geological imagery, he observed that in 1864, and thanks no doubt to "the great calm of nature" in the American West, he had perceived a "shaking" of the European earth. Europe was still caught up in its old dynastic struggles, crushing military budgets, and devastating wars. However, it was now clear that both its monarchies and its armies were monstrous anachronisms—"great reptiles of the Jurassic Period." A "new act of social geology" was about to begin. Europe would acquire a federal constitution. A United States of Europe would soon emerge, and labor would establish little by little "an international understanding with itself."

As the new order took shape, there would be new problems to resolve—problems involving the organization of labor and the restructuring of collective life. It would be necessary to move from a "verbose, confused, ignorant, revolutionary, and declamatory socialism" to a "practical and scientific socialism." At this point Fourier's ideas would come into their own. His thought was an "intellectual California," the riches of which would only become fully evident to future explorers. Thus Considerant concluded by declaring that if time and reflection "have produced some modifications in the forms of my thought, I have wished my first public statement here to be an homage to the thinker who . . . made me what I am."[11]

II

In the spring of 1870 Napoleon III seemed to be recovering from the political setbacks of the previous year. Faced with mounting challenges to his own authority, he had been urged to reverse his liberal reforms of the preceding ten years. But he refused to do so. In December 1869 he called upon the liberal politician Emile Ollivier to head a cabinet supported by a coalition of liberal Bonapartists, conservative Republicans, and a group of old-line Orleanist politicians including the indestructible Adolphe Thiers. Then, in April 1870, as agitation for reform continued, the Ollivier government issued a revised constitution that put together all the liberal reforms made since 1860 and added others. The following month a plebiscite was held on the new constitution. The results seemed to vindicate the Liberal Empire. Although the republican opposition won the cities and over 1.5 million "no" votes in all, the "yes" votes totaled 7.3 million—almost exactly the number of votes cast in approval of Louis-Napoleon's seizure of power eighteen years earlier. Thus in the early summer of 1870 it seemed that Napoleon III had made a recovery. Republicans gloomily predicted a long reign for the Prince Imperial, the economy showed new life, and prices on the Paris stock exchange rose. But then, on July 19, France stumbled into war with Prussia, and six weeks later the Second Empire was dead.

In his writings on the war Considerant was to make much of its origins in the high politics of dynastic rivalry. The point is hard to deny. Whatever else can be said about the roots of the Franco-Prussian War, it is evident that Napoleon III was pushed into this war by the conservative faction at court (including his wife Eugénie), whose members believed that an easy military victory would be the best way to restore the empire's prestige. Thus in the summer of 1870, when Bismarck openly challenged France by proposing a Hohenzollern as a candidate for the Spanish throne—a throne held to be within the French sphere of influence—Napoleon's conservative courtiers pressed him to accept the challenge and to go to war with Prussia. On July 19, after a series of diplomatic blunders, Napoleon III declared war—assured by his minister of war that the French army was ready "down to the last gaiter button."

On July 21, two days after the French declaration of war, Considerant published an article strongly condemning French policies.[12] "A Patriotic Address" consisted of the text of the speech that he would have given in the debate over the declaration of war in the Corps Législatif. It began with a brief and powerful introductory statement. "Two hundred thousand bodies are going to be left on the banks of the Rhine," he wrote. If this "hecatomb" had any purpose at all, it was to gratify the vanity of Napoleon III and "to facilitate the transmission of his crown to his son." The terrible "stupidity" of the war was evident. Less comprehensible was the fact that not a single French legislator had raised his voice in protest.

"There are now two Europes," wrote Considerant at the outset of his imaginary speech, "a Europe of feudal and dynastic interests and the Europe whose interests are those of labor and humanity." On the one side there was the "military Europe" of kings and emperors, and on the other the "peaceful and industrious Europe" of the laboring population. The first—the old Europe of kings—was on the way out, and the second—the new Europe of the working people—was coming into being. Nothing could stop its rise. "I tell you," proclaimed Considerant's legislator, "whether you vote war or impose peace, you will not prevent the disintegration of the old Europe and the rise of the new." The only difference was that with war the birth of the new Europe would be accompanied by "blood, carnage, ruins, hundreds of thousands of human bodies."

Considerant's imaginary speech was a warning to kings and emperors who had traditionally used war to achieve their ends. The war would have unanticipated consequences, he argued. It would call into question the principle of monarchy itself. Already in Germany, France, and Spain "the representatives of labor, the real representatives of the true interests of peaceful, industrious, and confederated Europe," had made their protests heard against the "gigantic atrocity" of this dynastic war. The war had been condemned repeatedly by various sections of the Workers' International. Taking note of this condemnation, Considerant's legislator concluded by announcing his own intention to join the International. Apparently Considerant had already taken the same step himself. On a trip to Brussels in early July he had met with Belgian leaders of the International, and shortly thereafter the Belgian newspaper *L'Internationale* announced his adherence.[13]

"A Patriotic Address" appeared in Louis Ulbach's journal *La Cloche* on July 21. Not surprisingly, it caused problems for Considerant, Ulbach, and his publisher. By Considerant's account, he and the publisher were summoned three times before the Police Court of the Seine to answer charges of "insulting the person of the emperor and inciting hatred and contempt of the Government." Apparently the matter reached the desk of Emile Ollivier: according to his memoirs, he personally ordered the dismissal of the charges against Considerant.[14]

A week after the appearance of his article in *La Cloche,* Considerant wrote a set of predictions concerning the war. There had not yet been significant combat, but already he could write that there were seven chances in ten that Germany would win the war. This was partly owing to the superiority of the German high command and the organization of the German army, but the Germans also had a psychological and political advantage. They had a common goal—the establishment of a nation—whereas the only real French objective was the satisfaction of "personal, dynastic interests." This was abundantly clear from the nature of French propaganda and the hollowness of the appeal to French traditions. "All the feelings stirred up by the pro-war journals," wrote Considerant, "are petty, false, swaggering, inhuman." The old republican and nationalist songs and slogans were being "prostituted" to "purely Bonapartist interests." The result was that "everything rings false, is a parody, and *contradicts* its intended meaning."[15]

In late July, when Considerant wrote these words, some in France already recognized the hollowness of the effort to justify the war against Germany as a continuation of the French Revolution. In a fierce and haunting poem the young Arthur Rimbaud scornfully derided the raising of the "dead of '92 and '93" by Bonapartist propagandists like Paul de Cassagnac.[16] Still, French opinion was behind the war, and enthusiasm rose with the news that on August 2 French forces had captured Saarbrucken from a weak German advance force. This was to prove France's only victory of the entire war. Within a few days the two main French armies—one under the command of Marshal MacMahon and the other under the emperor himself—had suffered major defeats. On August 12 the emperor handed over the supreme command to Marshal Bazaine. Then a disorderly retreat began and the two French armies divided, with MacMahon falling back on Chalons-sur-Marne and Bazaine on Metz. Parisians made ready for a siege. There was still hope that Bazaine's army might regain Paris to participate in its defense, but this hope died on August 17 with the news that Bazaine had been defeated at Gravelotte and was penned in at Metz. The same day General Louis-Jules Trochu was appointed governor of Paris and charged with its defense.

Thanks to the perfection of the telegraph and the emergence of something approaching modern war reporting, Considerant was able to follow military developments closely and to write letters (subsequently published) to Trochu and Adolphe Thiers offering unsolicited military and political advice. From the military standpoint, he argued, it was essential to keep at least one army in the field. Now that MacMahon could no longer join up with Bazaine, he should move into Alsace and attack the invading Prussian forces from behind. Politically, it was time to recognize that the empire was dead, that the war had destroyed the authority and credibility of Napoleon III. "Bonaparte has been expelled from the command of the army," he wrote on August 24. "Now he should be expelled from France." Indeed, nothing would do more to stiffen resistance to the German invaders than the removal of Napoleon III.[17]

Events moved quickly in just that direction. By the end of the month Bazaine's forces were still trapped at Metz while the troops under MacMahon had been caught in the small citadel town of Sedan, sixty miles away. For a few days the French cavalry under Gallifet made a show of resistance. Finally, on September 1, as MacMahon's army disintegrated and Prussian shells tore into what was left of the imperial baggage train, Napoleon III ordered the white flag raised. The following day the emperor met Bismarck to surrender formally with his 104,000 troops. The man whom Considerant described as "His Imperial Mediocrity" was then sent on his way to imprisonment in the Westphalian castle that had once been the seat of his uncle Jerome's kingdom.

III

During the afternoon of September 3, word reached Paris of the German victory at Sedan and the emperor's capitulation. Early the next morning crowds gathered on the boulevards, calling for the proclamation of a republic. By midday they had converged on the Palais Bourbon, where the Corps Législatif had already given up trying to save the empire. Carrying out what had now become a familiar ritual, the crowd then proceeded to escort the republican deputies to the Hôtel de Ville. There, with the tacit support of the stunned Bonapartist majority, the deputies representing Paris proclaimed the republic. Over the protests of radical leaders, the Parisian deputies also constituted themselves as a provisional government, a Government of National Defense, which would carry on the war until national elections could be held. To serve as military commander, the deputies called on the one general whose reputation was still untarnished, Trochu.

Victor Considerant, who was on the boulevards that day, later referred to it as the "superb" *journée* of September 4 and described the Government of National Defense as undeniably legitimate. At its inception, he said, it was the expression of a "unanimous will."[18] Even if something approaching a common revulsion against the Second Empire did exist on September 4, however, the tasks facing the new government were sure to divide its members, particularly with regard to the war. On the one hand, there was Léon Gambetta, the fiery young interior minister, who saw himself as a second Danton, rallying the nation in its hour of need. Also deeply committed to carrying on the war was Considerant's old friend, Frédéric Dorian, the industrialist from Saint-Etienne, who was soon to win enormous popularity through his efforts at organizing the war effort as minister of public works. On the other hand, there was Jules Favre, the foreign minister, whose lavish use of the rhetoric of intransigent revolutionary nationalism masked his covert efforts to reach a settlement with the Germans. Many of the other Parisian deputies had hidden reservations about the war. The position of General Trochu himself was unclear. He was strangely reluctant to pursue the military opportunities that arose; and it seemed to many observers that he had lost hope, that his main concern was simply to put up an honorable show of resistance to the Germans.

From the outset, the Government of National Defense found itself in a difficult position. Not only were its members divided; it also lacked formal legal authority. It was a revolutionary government that owed its existence to the Paris crowd, but it soon found itself at odds with the same crowd. Here again the main issue was the war. Within a few weeks of the establishment of the Government of National Defense, radical journalists like Blanqui, Delescluze, and Pyat were criticizing it for its timidity and its efforts to reach an accommodation with the Germans. "The Government of so-called National Defense has only one thought: peace," wrote Blanqui on September 22. "Not a victorious peace, not even an honorable peace, but peace at any price. That is its dream, its fixed idea."[19]

Why did the government continue to employ the most bellicose rhetoric while covertly trying to make peace with the Germans? To this question lucid contemporaries had a ready answer. The leaders of the Government of National Defense were much more worried about the threat of social revolution in Paris than about the Prussians. As Jules Ferry put it, the exaltation of the struggle against the Germans was a means of channeling or "bridling" the energies of the Parisian poor; by encouraging the "patriotic delirium" of the people of Paris, the Government of National Defense was attempting to maintain the social order—and its own power. The majority of its members understood—and shared—the judgment that Bismarck was reported to have made on them: "You were born in an act of [popular] sedition, and tomorrow you may be overthrown by the populace."[20]

What was Considerant's position in all this? Where did he now stand with regard to the war? With regard to the Government of National Defense? He was in fact close to the center of the action through his personal connections with members of the government. The most important of these was Frédéric Dorian, but other friends, old and new, had assumed important roles in the new regime. The old Fourierist Alphonse Tamisier had been appointed commander of the Parisian National Guard on September 6.[21] Edmond Adam, an influential moderate republican and the husband of Juliette Adam, was made prefect of police on October 8.

It was to Dorian that Considerant wrote, just two weeks after the fall of the empire, to report a great discovery: "I have the absolute, positive, infallible, and superb solution to the present crisis. If you in the government accept it, France can impose peace on Europe and can emerge radiant from its disasters and its shame." But the hour was late. The Germans had virtually encircled Paris. So Considerant begged Dorian to gather "as many members of the Government as possible, and the most open-minded" and to give him half or three-quarters of an hour to set forth his views. "I am not crazy," he added. "I have understood perfectly what has been going on. I have accurately predicted the events of the recent past, and I see things now with the same clarity."[22]

With its tone of urgency and of absolute self-confidence, Considerant's letter was probably no different from dozens of crank letters sent to the

Government of National Defense at this time of crisis. But Considerant was a friend of forty years' standing, and Dorian gave him what he asked for. He arranged a meeting at the Hôtel de Ville between Considerant and "a delegation" of members of the government. We don't know who this delegation included. What we do know is that at the meeting, held on September 19, Considerant read out loud portions of a "letter" that he later published as *La France imposant la paix à l'Europe. Lettre aux membres du gouvernement de la République.*

La France imposant la paix à l'Europe is a curious but oddly powerful text. It is in simplest terms an appeal to the French to give up the armed struggle against Germany, to renounce war as an instrument of policy, and to agree to submit their foreign quarrels to arbitration. All this is framed, however, within a historical analysis of American society and of the republican idea in which Considerant drew on his own experience and observation over the previous twenty years.[23]

Considerant's text began with the same fundamental distinction that had shaped much of his writing on political questions since 1848. Contemporary history could be seen, he asserted, as the struggle of two opposing social orders: the traditional, aristocratic, and militaristic societies of Europe; and the new society, based on labor and law, that was emerging in the United States of America. In an initial section entitled "Incarnation of the New Spirit in American Society," Considerant argued that the federal union of the American states, each with its own legislature and court system but without a standing army, should serve as a model for the future political organization of Europe. He went on to characterize the forces of resistance in Europe to all attempts to replace the existing state system with a general federation of republics. He noted that "the natural and logical political form" assumed by "industrious peoples" was "the juridical or republican form." But he pointed out that in Europe "the civil, juridical, and modern concept of the republic" had become "deplorably mixed up with classical memories and traditions of the historical republics of Sparta and Rome—which were only warrior aristocracies." In the course of the French Revolution the republican idea was further corrupted through its association with French nationalism. As a result, the French republican party had been one of the main participants—along with the Catholic Church, the aristocracy, and the various European royal houses—in the "Great Reaction" of the nineteenth century against the cosmopolitan and universalistic traditions of the Enlightenment.

There were, however, two great forces at work in nineteenth-century Europe to dispel the "backwardness and confusion" created by the Great

Reaction. These were science and large-scale industry, which were transforming the material life of all Europeans and creating a world in which "the interests and consequently the real forces of the old feudal and warlike world" would have "only an artificial existence." Considerant posed a rhetorical question: "Who in Europe in 1870 has a REAL INTEREST in maintaining the vampire of war in the bosom of the [new] industrious Europe?" No one, he answered. Not capitalists, not proletarians, not peasants, bourgeois, savants, artists, merchants—no one except a few dynastic, princely, and military families, the detritus of the old feudal aristocracies, and their hangers-on. These groups stayed in power by promising peace, order, and the muzzling of revolution. The industrious and productive classes of contemporary society had failed to understand that "in taking charge of their own government themselves," they could "maintain order and peace in Europe by themselves, just as the same [classes] maintain[ed] it so easily in America." Why had the industrious classes failed to recognize the connection between republican self-government and peace? Because the spokesmen of the republican idea in France had consistently identified it with armed insurrection, foreign wars, and the brutality of the Terror.

What should the Government of National Defense do in these circumstances? Considerant urged them first of all to recall Thiers, who was then traveling around Europe seeking the aid of foreign powers. France was now a republic, and its representatives should not be asking for favors from the old European monarchies. The government should organize a plebiscite, which would enable France to rise "like Lazarus" from "the rot of its imperial and Bonapartist sepulchre." The resolution to be voted on would include a statement committing France to disarm and to renounce forever the recourse to war. France would "dictate peace" to Prussia by proclaiming its own intent to renounce war unilaterally, "whatever might happen" as a consequence. France would force peace on Prussia, and the rest of Europe, by proclaiming its intent "to renounce war here and now," to renounce "its pomp and ceremony and its fierce glories," to renounce "the vile national vanity based on the superiority of brute force," to renounce "the degradation of the free man into a soldier, into a murdering machine," to renounce "the metamorphosis of workers into disciplined and regimented tigers, killing men on order." Whatever the future might bring, wrote Considerant, no matter how abject the condition to which France might be reduced by "this atrocious imperial war," its people should proclaim by a plebiscite (but this time "a free, enlightened, and truly republican one") their intention to disarm permanently and to assume henceforth a purely peaceful and industrious status.

Considerant's letter to the Government of National Defense also included advice concerning the posture France should assume in peace negotiations with Germany. France should agree to pay reparations, he asserted, but these should be determined by an international tribunal. The French should be prepared to give up territory, too—but only if Alsace and Lorraine (or Nice and Savoie) freely voted to become German (or Italian). If Germany simply took Alsace and Lorraine, France would have to accept the fact, but it could never be forced to recognize the seizure as a transfer of property, since these territories were "not the property of France, but the property of their own populations."

Considerant concluded with a brief discussion of some of the institutional changes he expected to occur in the coming political and social order. The cessation of war implied the abolition of armies, conscription, fortifications, and military budgets. Basing himself on the American model, he also looked forward to the complete separation of church and state. His vision of the future included a thoroughly decentralized France. "Decentralization at all levels: the administrative autonomy of communes, departments, and provinces in the free national hierarchy. . . . No more Parisian dictatorship: reduction of Government-Power to Government-Administration; no other power than the judicial power." These were some of the features of the emerging "universal republic," but Considerant did not go into details. He expected Europe to dictate its own future, and the role he created for himself was that of an outsider. "Messieurs," he concluded, "you are the masters of eloquence. I am providing you with raw ideas. Having lived in the great wilderness of the American prairies, at the farthest frontier of civilization, I have lost the traditions of orderly speech." The Government of National Defense should take his "raw ideas" and give them "the forms of political dignity."

What was the response to this extraordinary letter? The members of the Government of National Defense do not seem to have taken it seriously. Apparently Considerant asked them to have it published. Since they weren't interested, he had it printed at his own expense (along with his earlier predictions on the war and his letters to Trochu and Thiers) in the form of a four-page six-column newspaper. He hired a man to sell copies at fifteen centimes on the streets of Paris. At the same time he sent copies to friends and acquaintances who might help distribute it. A packet of ten copies went to U.S. Ambassador Elihu B. Washburne, who, though a staunch conservative in politics, seems to have liked Considerant. "I hope you will not smell any unamericanism in it," wrote Considerant. More copies went to Clarisse

Coignet, Juliette Adam, Michel Chevalier, Charles-Louis Chassin, André Léo, and many others. What did these people think of the pamphlet? Washburne's letter of acknowledgment was polite and vague: he probably hadn't read it. Chassin found it "remarkable" if somewhat long-winded; and Michel Chevalier, who had been a man of great influence under the empire, wrote that he found the section on America "an imperishable monument." On the streets the pamphlet seems to have sold relatively well for a few days, if only because of its low price and alluring title. In the end, though, no one was persuaded. Long afterward the sympathetic Chassin could sum up the response in these terms:

> Naturally this rational solution to the military problem was treated as a chimera by all the journalists, who did not perhaps even take the time to read it. As for the Government, it didn't know what to make of the harmonic reveries of a Phalansterian visionary, returned from the new world.[24]

During the months of October and November, Considerant made repeated efforts to draw attention to *La France imposant la paix à l'Europe*. He had two editions published and sold on the streets. He also had a form letter to Parisian newspapers printed up and distributed. Signing himself "one of the deans of the Parisian press," he urged other journalists to reprint his text. He said he would not object if they wished to treat him as a madman or a visionary and insisted that he did not seek personal profit. His sole concern was to come to the rescue of his country in its hour of need and to convert a military disaster into a political triumph.[25] At the same time Considerant wrote, and apparently sent, two letters to Bismarck asking the German chancellor to consider the proposals spelled out in his pamphlet, and conjuring up the vision of a future European confederation based on the collaboration of France and Germany.[26]

IV

The vision of the future collaboration of France and Germany was central to another work published at this time in which Considerant had a hand. This was a pair of open letters addressed by Gustave Courbet to the German army and German artists. Although Considerant and Courbet were never particularly close, they had many friends in common (notably Max Buchon and Edouard Ordinaire); and they were of course both natives of Franche-Comté. They may have had some contact in the 1840s before Considerant's exile, and they most certainly spent time together during the fall and winter of 1870. By Courbet's own account, it was "my friend Considerant" who urged him to set his ideas down on paper in October.[27]

Courbet's *Lettres à l'armée allemande et aux artistes allemands* were a mixture of insults and appeals to shared democratic values. "Go back home," Courbet told the German army, "and take a republic back with you." In his second letter Courbet recalled the sense of solidarity he had felt with German artists on his visits to Frankfurt and Munich; then he upbraided them for allowing themselves to be "enrolled in Bismarck's bands," for participating in the siege of Paris, and for supporting the German demand for war reparations. If the Germans wanted an indemnity, wrote Courbet, they could take back to Germany, as trophies of war, stones from the captured cities of Toul and Strasbourg. At the same time they would do well to destroy their own citadels and disband their armies. Then French and Germans could drink together "to the United States of Europe." Courbet's "Letter to German Artists" concluded with a vision—not unlike Considerant's—of a disarmed European federation in which France and Germany would be united, but Courbet gave this vision a symbolic form that was all his own. "Leave us your Krupp cannons," he told the German artists. "We will melt them down together with ours." The last cannon, its barrel in the air, would be "fixed on a pedestal mounted on three cannonballs; and this colossal monument, which we will erect together on the Place Vendôme, will be your column and ours, the column of the people, the column of Germany and France federated forever."[28]

Courbet's *Lettres* appeared in print at the beginning of November. But they were first presented orally at a public meeting—a "soirée littéraire"—organized by Considerant at the Athénée on the evening of October 29. Considerant also spoke that evening, reading a paper entitled "Constitution of the Government of the Universal Republic." In this long, rambling talk, Considerant argued that politics and society should be understood in terms similar to those employed in the physical sciences. His main point, however, was that the French had it in their power to bring a rapid end to the war. All that was needed was "a system of filters" permitting the government to "pass judgment rapidly on inventions, plans of organization, military or political ideas" and "a system of sieves for separating out people of ability from the incompetents." Presumably plebiscites would be a part of this "system of filters," but Considerant did not linger on institutional details. He preferred to evoke the changes that would already have taken place if the energies and the human resources of France had been concentrated, since the fall of the empire, on the sole task of ending the war. The Germans would now be on their way home. Most likely, the political settlement would have included the formation of an "indissoluble fraternal alliance" between the French and German people. How could such an alliance even be thinkable? Because France and Germany, "the two most civilized peoples of Europe," had "every reason to join forces instead of tearing each other apart." Their failure to cooperate could only be the result of "a misunderstanding, an absurdity, an abominable stupidity." And there was "no misunderstanding, absurdity, or stupidity that, attacked by a sufficient amount of intelligence, would ultimately fail to give way."[29]

Considerant's lecture was a remarkably candid expression of rationalist political optimism, and it showed that in some important respects his views had changed little since 1848. Just as in 1848, when he attempted to explain to the National Assembly that the June insurrection was the result of a "misunderstanding," so now he argued that the conflict between "the two most civilized peoples of Europe" could only be a "misunderstanding." What he refused to accept was the possibility that the conflicts of 1848 and 1870 might be beyond rational reconciliation.

How was Considerant's plea for reconciliation received? The question is worth asking because this was one of his very few public appearances of the period—and the only time when he lectured to an audience that did not already share his viewpoint. The answer is that the whole occasion was a fiasco.[30] Courbet turned out to be unable to read by the artificial light in the auditorium and was finally obliged to abandon the podium. When Considerant appeared, he first struck one member of the audience as being "still nimble and vigorous" even though the features of "an *illuminé*" were "barely hidden under his large gray mustache." But Considerant had forgotten his glasses. He was no more able than Courbet to read the lecture he had written out. He borrowed a pince-nez from a member of the audience, but the pince-nez wouldn't stay put: with every contraction of his muscles, it "wriggled and hopped" on the bridge of his nose. The audience laughed. Considerant got angry. He borrowed another pair of glasses, which were more satisfactory, but the audience continued to laugh—now because of the strangeness of his language, "a real hodgepodge in which the Bible, philosophy, history, politics, and social economy were seasoned with an indescribable apocalyptic sauce." Amid the laughter, Considerant continued to read his lecture. "Impassive" to the end, "he didn't spare his audience a single line." But it seems unlikely from the one surviving account of the evening that his plea for the reconciliation of France and Germany was even heard, let alone understood.

V

Two days after Considerant's "soirée littéraire," there was an insurrection in Paris that almost brought down the Government of National Defense. Angered by the news of the apparently treasonous capitulation of Marshal Bazaine with 170,000 troops at Metz on October 27, Parisians were further infuriated by Trochu's failure to support the French troops who had taken Le Bourget from the Germans on the twenty-eighth. The conviction spread that the government and the army high command had no real desire to prosecute the war, that their policies were motivated much more by fear of the Parisian lower classes than by fear of the Germans. At Belleville and in other parts of Paris, crowds gathered shouting, "No armistice!" and "Down with Trochu!" By noon on October 31, the place de l'Hôtel de Ville was packed with demonstrators. Neither the mayor, Etienne Arago, nor General Trochu could persuade the crowd to disperse. Suddenly the iron gates in front of the Hôtel de Ville gave way and the crowd entered the building, trapping the members of the government inside. In the great confusion that ensued, calls for the creation of a new government were mixed with frantic efforts at negotiation. For a few hours the insurrection appeared to be victorious, but by nightfall troops loyal to the Government of National Defense had surrounded the Hôtel de Ville. Some of these troops managed to get inside the building by means of an underground passageway. Scuffling broke out. This was followed by several hours of negotiation, in which a major role was played by the minister of public works, Frédéric Dorian, whose efforts at organizing the defense had made him the only member of the government whom the radicals trusted. Finally an agreement was reached: the government would hold elections immediately and would take no reprisals against the insurgents; in return, the members of the government would be released and the Hôtel de Ville evacuated. At 3 AM the evacuation began. Among the first to leave the Hôtel de Ville were Considerant's friends, Dorian and Tamisier. The former walked out arm-in-arm with Charles Delescluze and the latter with Auguste Blanqui. Four days later, however, and despite its promises, the government began arresting the leaders of this failed insurrection.[31]

The day after the insurrection, Considerant wrote a long, urgent letter to Frédéric Dorian. He began by asserting that the Government of National Defense had now lost all its legitimacy; it had, in a sense, "committed suicide" on October 31 by calling out the troops against a popular insurrection and by reneging on its promise to hold municipal elections immediately. "Your name is *the only one* that now inspires *almost universal confidence*," wrote Considerant. "Consequently you are for the moment all by yourself the real and legitimate government." Considerant argued that to retain the trust of the people Dorian must himself take charge of the defense of Paris.

Trochu's position was now deeply compromised, Considerant argued. He had for a few weeks enjoyed great authority because he had seemed to incarnate the will of Paris to resist the Germans. However, the Le Bourget affair had demonstrated once and for all his inability to organize and direct the defense of Paris. Now it was up to Dorian—not to exercise personal power, like Trochu, but to draw on and coordinate the energies of all of Paris in a way that would make it clear to Parisians that he was their agent. How was this to be done? Dorian could begin by consulting the people of Paris on the organization and direction of their own defense. He could issue a proclamation summoning all citizens with ideas on the subject to meet at the Hôtel de Ville. The object of this meeting would be "to determine the best means of defense" and "to constitute a High Council for the centralization and general direction of the defense." If Dorian acted promptly and resolutely, the organization of the defense of Paris could acquire a spontaneous character that it had never had under Trochu.[32]

Considerant's view of Dorian as the embodiment of the will of Paris to resist the Germans was not unusual at this time. As Jules Ferry put it later, "M. Dorian was the idol of the crowd. . . . His name signified resistance to the bitter end." On October 31 the crowd wanted "to make him dictator." What was remarkable in Considerant's letter, however, was his belief that the collective energies of the Parisians had only to be called upon to assume a productive form—his belief in the spontaneous emergence of a collective will and a collectively elaborated strategy of defense. In this respect his letter was a throwback to the faith of the democratic 'forty-eighters in spontaneous popular action. Remarkable also was Considerant's belief that his friend Dorian might share his ideas. In fact, Dorian had more in common with the other members of the government than Considerant realized. As Dorian himself put it later, "I was more afraid of the Parisians than of the Prussians."[33]

Considerant's naive democratic faith was again evident in a letter he wrote to General Trochu just a week later. Protesting the arrests made after the insurrection of October 31, Considerant reminded Trochu of his stated intention "to govern only by means of moral force." Considerant observed that moral force was "at bottom, the only real force" that the government possessed. For that reason Trochu's position was not only noble but also shrewd. Unfortunately, Trochu was not able to retain "the public trust," which was "the essential condition" for the exercise of moral force.

You have not understood the *elementary* condition of republican government, which is not to lock yourself within the restricted circle of a *personal* government . . . but to call on all the living forces [of society] and to give them the means of manifesting themselves, of coming together, and of selecting from among their accomplishments those which are *the most effective* from the standpoint of the common welfare.

The arrest of participants in the insurrection of October 31, who had ended their occupation of the Hôtel de Ville on the understanding that there would be no reprisals, was, according to Considerant, not only "a huge public error" but also "an act of bad faith" and "abominable cowardice" that seriously compromised government's credibility. The result would be to "encourage the reaction" and to "prepare civil war." [34]

VI

When the siege of Paris began on September 19, few expected it to last into the following year. Not the Government of National Defense, whose members believed that food supplies would last three months at best. And certainly not Bismarck, who had cynically predicted that "a week without *café au lait*" would break the will of the Parisian bourgeoisie. But as winter set in and the siege entered its third month, there was still no end in sight. By mid-November, after the city's supply of horse meat had been exhausted, dogs, cats, rats, and finally zoo animals appeared on restaurant menus and on the dinner tables of those who could afford them. New kinds of bread were devised, one of which was described as tasting of "sawdust, mud, and potato skins." The *Paris Journal* published advice on how to "fish for sewer rats with a hook and line baited with tallow." At the same time, the news from the provinces (brought in by carrier pigeon) was hardly encouraging. Hopes rose briefly when Gambetta's Army of the Loire defeated the Germans at Coulommiers on November 9 and then recaptured Orleans, but it soon bogged down. Trochu's long-awaited "Great Sortie," which began on November 29, proved a failure as well. By early December, as the snow piled up on the streets, Parisians were making firewood of furniture, park benches, and trees in the Bois de Boulogne and wondering whether they could ever last out the winter. [35]

Where were Victor and Julie Considerant in all this? Like other Parisians of limited means, they were necessarily caught up in the day-to-day struggle for survival—the search for coal or firewood, the long waits in line to purchase "siegebread." Their health was poor: Victor took sick several times during the siege. They were also touched by the mood of anxiety and suspicion that could now be felt almost palpably in public places. Victor called it an "epidemic" of fear and mistrust, and Julie felt its effects personally. On September 30, as she asked directions on the rue Mouffe-tard to a store where she could buy milk; Julie Considerant was somehow taken for a German and surrounded by a crowd of angry women shouting, "There's a Prussian woman!" She had to be rescued by the police.[36]

In some respects life went on as before. On October 12 Victor and Julie had a modest celebration for Victor's sixty-second birthday, and on that oc-casion she wrote him a beautiful note that gives us a glimpse of their life together during the siege.

> My good Consi, in this blockaded Paris, for this October 12, 1870, I'm giving you the pauper's gold, flowers from our city walls, the sweet william that I've always loved, and two little cups so that, if God gives us life, we can drink chocolate together. I would also like to give you my heart and its deep affection. But how can one always keep giving something which was given long ago. Long live the universal republic, fraternity, and justice.[37]

During the siege Victor and Julie continued to see old friends. A few of them, like the Dorians and the Adams, were people of great wealth. Al-though Juliette Adam later recalled that during the winter of 1870–1871 dinners were like potluck picnics, it is significant that she and her husband continued to entertain at all, if only on a modest scale. So did the Dorians, who were able even in January to invite the Considerants and Courbet to dinner at their townhouse on the rue Blanche.[38]

During the siege Considerant spent a considerable amount of time as an observer, both of the war effort and of the activities of the radical clubs. On December 10 he received a pass from Dorian's Ministry of Public Works au-thorizing him and Courbet to tour the Mont Valérien fort, one of the vital links in the French system of defense. At the same time he attended the meetings of a number of the clubs that had, as he put it, "sprouted like mushrooms" after September 4. Having joined the International the previ-ous summer, he attended the meetings of his section, now the Section des Gobelins, "eight or ten times during the siege," and he was invited in March to serve on its Comité de Vigilance. He declined. He was impressed by the high level of the discussions in his section, however, and he wrote later that "but for colds and the rigor of the winter . . . I would not have missed a single session."[39]

Considerant also regularly attended the meetings of a club called the Union Républicaine Centrale. This was an organization dominated by old 'forty-eighters such as the socialist journalist Charles Fauvety and the former *représentants du peuple* Louis Vauthier and Dupont de Bussac. It also had room, however, for young radicals influenced by Proudhon. Founded in November 1870, this club lost influence after the March 1871 elections, but during its short life its members argued forcefully in support of working-class demands and for the creation of a municipal council, a Commune, to govern Paris. Considerant was proud of his association with this group, which he described in February as "perhaps the best of all the analogous gatherings in Paris at this time."[40]

In November and December Considerant gave several talks or oral presentations to the Union Républicaine Centrale. In one of them he strongly criticized the Government of National Defense for its failure to institute a system of rationing and price controls. Noting the inequality of Parisians in the face of hunger and disease, Considerant argued that "the supreme condition for the defense" ought to be "the unity and solidarity of the mass under attack." In a besieged city as on a foundering ship, justice and humanity required "the recognition of the equal right of all to the necessities of existence." What the government should have done, therefore, was to announce, at the very beginning of the siege, that it would guarantee to all Parisians "an equal right to a necessary minimum in clothing, lodging, and food."[41]

Considerant no longer enjoyed public speaking. In a letter that winter he described himself as afflicted with the "disease" of *logophobia* or *phraseophobia*. He found himself increasingly intolerant of long-winded oratory, his own included. Yet some of his listeners still found him an impressive speaker. One of them was Edouard Vaillant, the future Communard, who was then serving as a representative of the Central Committee of the Twenty Arrondissements at the meetings attended by Considerant.

> Of all those present, one citizen was particularly noteworthy for his intelligence and good looks. He seemed familiar to me. I soon realized that it was to the caricaturists of 1848 that I owed my recollection of the man. It was Considerant. What he said tallied so well with our feelings, and was so superior to the comments of the opportunist and radical clowns of the reaction that my fellow delegates and I were tempted to say to him: "Come join us. Leave the reactionaries, and let's go together to the Corderie [the meeting place of the International and of the Central Committee of the Twenty Arrondissements]."[42]

Vaillant did not know that Considerant had already joined the International.

VII

On January 3 the Germans began to shell Paris. The bombardment, which went on for four or five hours every night, was to last twenty-three days. By the middle of the month, though, the military situation had already come to seem hopeless to the army and the Government of National Defense, if not to the mass of Parisians. A final sortie, launched on January 19, resulted in heavy casualties among the National Guard units, which participated for the first time in such an action; and many Parisians believed that it had been the government's intention to demonstrate the weakness of the National Guard as a fighting force. Angry and frustrated, radical leaders called for a protest march on the Hôtel de Ville on the twenty-second. This turned into a violent confrontation and an exchange of fire that lasted over fifteen minutes and left half a dozen dead and about twenty wounded on the place de l'Hôtel de Ville. This was the first time during the siege that Frenchmen had fired at, and killed, other Frenchmen.

After the fusillade of January 22, Jules Favre wrote later, "civil war was a few meters away, famine a few hours." Fearing a war on two fronts, the Government of National Defense now took strong action. It issued a series of decrees shutting down radical clubs, banning the journals of Delescluze and Pyat, and ordering the arrest of almost a hundred radical leaders. At the same time the government began talks with the Germans in view of an immediate armistice. On January 28, after five days of negotiations, Jules Favre and Bismarck announced an agreement calling for an armistice of three weeks. During this time national legislative elections were to be held, and the new assembly would meet at Bordeaux to consider the permanent peace terms to be offered by Germany. Meanwhile the French troops in Paris would surrender their arms and the Germans would permit Paris to be resupplied with food.[43]

The measures taken against the clubs, journals, and radical leaders provoked strong protests in Paris. Considerant added his voice to the chorus, beseeching Dorian to disavow such "ignoble" decrees. Nothing came of these protests, but the Parisian response to the armistice was harder to ignore. The news was received in Paris with a mixture of rage and stupor. The general belief was that it was not an armistice but a capitulation, and it was not at all clear that Paris would accept it. Even a moderate like the composer Vincent d'Indy could describe himself as having "literally cried with rage" on hearing the news. Considerant's reaction was calmer and more philosophical. A few days later he wrote his sister Justine that he and Julie had lost weight but not hope. "Let the Prussians go home, let the sun shine again, and let France keep a good republic. On these conditions the adventures of the past five or six months will have been all to the good for France. That's my way of looking at things."[44]

Elections were held on February 8. The "campaign" lasted just eight days, and in the territory occupied by the Germans there was no campaigning at all. Under the circumstances, the real choice seemed to be between a conservative peace or a republican war. The result was a massive conservative victory. Although most of the deputies elected by Paris were republicans or socialists, provincial voters turned, as they usually had in times of crisis, to the old *notables*—royalist and Catholic members of the old landed ruling class.

The election results infuriated the radical republicans in Paris. Not only had the electoral law allocated Paris a mere 6 percent of the deputies, but the system of voting (not by arrondissement but by the city as a whole) also worked to prevent the election of many radical leaders. A chasm was opened between Paris and the provinces, and the first acts of the new Assembly only served to widen it. These included the choice of Thiers as head of the new government, the ratification of a crushing peace treaty, and the passage of laws cutting off the pay of the Parisian National Guard, ending wartime rent controls, and allowing Parisian landlords to demand immediate payment of all uncollected rent. Finally, on March 10, the Assembly adjourned, voting to reconvene ten days later, not in Paris but at Versailles— an appropriate choice since most of its members were royalists.

While the Assembly was establishing itself at Versailles, Adolphe Thiers, the new "chief of the executive power," moved his administrative offices into Paris. He found the city in an angry mood and quickly decided to disarm its National Guard. However, the army bungled its attempt to get large numbers of cannons out of Paris quietly during the night of March 17–18. This provoked rioting that culminated in the lynching of the two generals in command of the operation. Thereupon Thiers abandoned Paris, removing his administration to Versailles. Formal governmental authority remained in the hands of the mayors of Paris's twenty arrondissements; in fact, Thiers' departure left the city in a political vacuum that was filled first by the Central Committee of the Paris National Guard and then by the Paris Commune.

VIII

The Paris Commune of 1871 came into being on March 26 with the election of a new municipal council consisting of a mixed group of Proudhonists, Blanquists, and neo-Jacobins. The election had been called just eight days earlier by the Central Committee of the Parisian National Guard and then hesitantly endorsed by some of the mayors of Paris's twenty *arrondissements*. The Commune was to remain in existence for just seventy-three days, much too short a time to carry out any permanent measures of social reform but long enough to create a myth—the myth of the Commune as the first great workers' revolution, the first attempt on the part of a basically working-class movement to smash the power of the bourgeois state. This myth was to inspire communists, socialists, and syndicalists, and it was kept alive by the annual pilgrimage taken each May 28 to the wall of the Père Lachaise Cemetery, where the last defenders of the Commune were executed. The myth has proved so powerful that it requires a special effort of imagination to think one's way back into the confused political situation of March 1871.[45]

When one does try to grasp the Commune not in the light of the myth but rather in its historical unfolding, the outlines become blurred, for the Communards were united neither by doctrine nor by social origin. More of them were bourgeois intellectuals—journalists, teachers, professional men—than artisans or wage laborers. There was a deep split among them between authoritarian revolutionaries and Proudhonian federalists. And the elections that created the Commune were marked by an abstention rate of over 50 percent. Only in the northeast of Paris, in the working-class quarters of Ménilmontant, Belleville, and La Villette, did participation reach levels exceeding those of the hastily called legislative elections of February, and in the complementary elections held in April, participation collapsed.

One other complicating factor in the period surrounding the elections of March 26 was the role played by moderates, who sought to mediate between the Party of Order encamped at Versailles and the Party of Revolution, which controlled Paris. For a week prior to the elections and for several weeks thereafter, groups and committees shuttled back and forth between Paris and Versailles, seeking to negotiate a settlement that would persuade both Communards and Versaillais to lay down their arms. Ultimately the attempt failed, but that in itself is no reason to discount it, or to follow some historians in echoing the verdict of the Commune's majority that conciliation was a treasonous "mask of reaction."[46]

Victor Considerant remained in Paris throughout the spring of 1871. He was one of the very few "vieilles barbes" of 1848 to join the International; and his sympathies were clearly with the Communards and not the Versaillais. Yet when he intervened publicly in the events of 1871, it was as a conciliator. In the days immediately preceding the election he joined a committee of conciliation seeking to mediate between the legal authorities, the mayors of Paris's twenty arrondissements, and the representatives of the Parisian National Guard. He signed (as did Arthur Ranc, Ulysse Parent, and Georges Avenel) a poster placarded by the committee on the walls of Paris on the night of March 24, urging the mayors to set aside legalistic scruples and sanction the elections. He made the same point at a meeting with the mayors, arguing that "politics is a chess game in which the goal is to win without necessarily slaughtering all one's opponent's pieces" but rather "to find just the right move." [47] After the elections Considerant apparently associated himself with the efforts of the Ligue d'Union Républicaine des Droits de Paris to mediate between Versailles and Paris.[48]

Considerant had initially resisted invitations to stand for election to the National Assembly, and no move was made a month later to place his name in nomination in the Parisian elections of March 26. However, when complementary elections were held on April 16, his name appeared as a candidate for the Municipal Council on lists drawn up by the group La Conciliation par l'Action, and by the radical journals *Le Père Duchêne* and *La Sociale*. Considerant only received a few hundred votes, finishing fourth in a field of four.[49] Still, he continued to intervene in public affairs, more often than not to call for moderation and sobriety. He persuaded Raoul Rigault to have the engineer Emile Allard released from prison, thereby probably saving Allard's life. Then on April 20 he wrote a letter to the members of the Commune of Paris, arguing strongly against the demolition of the Imperial Column on the Place Vendôme. The Commune had voted to destroy the column as a "monument of barbarism," a symbol of a rejected militaristic and imperial past. Considerant urged them to think twice. "Citizens," he wrote, "a great enlightened people does not erase its history any more than it destroys monuments. It leaves those methods to barbarians, it *judges* its history and it *judges* its monuments." In Considerant's eyes the column was a national monument, and Paris had no right to destroy it without the approval of France. What Parisians could properly do was to record their judgment on the monument itself. They could even alter it, substituting a skull for the crowned head and a skeletal hand for Napoleon's scepter. That would be "macabre, imperial, hideous, and superb," better than the act of vandalism that they were considering.[50]

Considerant's major intervention in public life during the brief existence of the Paris Commune was a brochure entitled *La Paix en 24 heures dictée par Paris à Versailles*. Published newspaper-style on both sides of a large folio sheet and sold in the streets for five centimes, *La Paix en 24 heures* was written shortly after the elections of March 26. It was originally meant to be a letter to the editor of the moderate daily *Le Temps*. While writing, however, Considerant fell ill, and when he returned to his letter he found that he could not maintain the "coolness of tone" or the brevity required by *Le Temps*. Finally the letter became a brochure written in the visionary tone of a man absolutely certain of possessing the knowledge his contemporaries needed at "a grandiose and terrible moment."[51]

Considerant began *La Paix en 24 heures* by recapitulating familiar themes. The age of warlike and aristocratic societies was ending, he wrote, and that of peaceful and productive societies was dawning. The Franco-Prussian War might be the last of the great dynastic struggles, because monarchy, aristocracy, and war itself were on the way out. They were the "debris" of a passing era. They were "poisons" that had to be purged from "the social system of modern Europe." Why had they survived so long, though? What could account for the persistence of life in the "old political cadavers" of Bonapartism, royalism, and even republicanism in its narrow and chauvinistic form? In addressing this question Considerant began to explore new territory.

Now there are two Frances, he wrote. Not a red France and a white France but a political France and an apolitical France. Political France consisted of those who had fixed political convictions, whether monarchist or republican. At most it consisted of 2 million citizens. The rest were the 36 million French men and women who made up the passive, inert, ignorant mass of French society. Of their number the 7 or 8 million adult males constituted "the herd of universal suffrage." This huge, inert, and largely rural mass—"the flesh of the social body"—had appeared to act spontaneously only once in the nineteenth century: under "the puerile and absurd impulsion" of the cult of Napoleon.

Why, asked Considerant, was the bulk of the French population so easily led, so caught up in the political illusions kept alive by the leaders of all the old parties, whether Bonapartist, monarchist, or republican? His answer was that the leaders of these parties continued to play effectively on the old reflexes of fear and the desire for security. On most substantive matters their language was as empty as the oratorical posing of Jules Favre, who boasted while he was negotiating a humiliating armistice with the Germans that he would never tolerate the loss of an "inch" of French territory. At bottom, they appealed to the fears of the rural population and their desire for protection.

All this ignorance, all this eloquence, all these dramatic memories, these Roman, Jacobin, and Montagnard memories; the operatic thunderclaps of the orators in the clubs; the threatening tirades; all these wild lightning bolts, all these detestable follies, collected, heaped up, stitched together, constitute the great bogeyman, the Giant Manikin, the Red Scare in other words, with which M. de Falloux, M. Thiers, M. Romieu, and the other politicians of the rue de Poitiers made the Empire of M. Louis Bonaparte.

The peasants believed, and the panic-stricken bourgeoisie could be made to believe, that peace, prosperity, and even survival required a strong centralized state—"a STRONG POWER, the master of everything, controlling everything, and armed to the teeth."

With the crushing German victory, Considerant wrote, "the great centralizing machine" of the state had been broken. Now Adolphe Thiers was attempting to repair it at Versailles. Nonetheless, the French state was only a shadow of its former self. There was no constitution, no shared understanding of rights, duties, and spheres of authority, and this presented Paris—and the rest of France—with a great opportunity. A plebiscite should be held on Paris's independence. Considerant went on to spell out the terms of the plebiscite. Paris should accept the peace treaty negotiated with Bismarck by the National Assembly. It should accept the responsibility of the Assembly to exercise administrative powers. At the same time, however, Paris should deny the Assembly all claims concerning the exercise of national sovereignty. Paris should affirm its own autonomy and declare itself ready to join with other cities, departments, and provinces "to organize a national government on the basis of freely constituted local autonomy." Ten days after the plebiscite, Parisians should gather to elect a new municipal body, "a new Commune," to exercise sovereign power.

What Considerant was calling for, in essence, was a federalist restructuring of French (and European) politics not unlike that advocated by Proudhon's followers within the General Council of the Paris Commune. His insistence on the importance of communal authority as the basis of all social and political reform was, to be sure, consistent with Fourierist traditions, and every line of *La Paix en 24 heures* reflected the faith in direct, plebiscitory democracy that had inspired Considerant since the 1840s. Yet the terms of the plebiscite Considerant proposed were also very close to those proposed by the Proudhonist Pierre Denis in the *Déclaration au peuple français* of April 18, which was in fact the first formal statement of the program of the Paris Commune.

Considerant was, in any case, convinced that his plebiscite was a weapon that would force peace on Versailles. He did not doubt that it would receive massive support in Paris from people of all walks of life. It would constitute a challenge to the authority of the National Assembly and of "His Majesty Thiers, the First Emperor and King of Versailles"—a statement that Paris wished to receive nothing from them, and that it would "henceforth handle its own affairs and freely share, along with the rest of France, responsibility for the general business of the nation." Such a declaration, once endorsed by hundreds of thousands of voters, would force peace on Versailles by destroying the myth that Thiers had invented to justify the civil war that he had started—the myth that Paris was "in the hands of twenty thousand convicts."

Considerant saw another advantage in the plebiscite, though: it would bring an end to "the dictatorship of the present Commune." Criticizing those who had "shamefully slandered" the Paris Commune, Considerant conceded that the Communards had come to exercise a dictatorship—"necessarily a troubled and feverish one, like any dictatorship improvised in a supreme and terrible moment." Once the plebiscite had been organized, he wrote, the dictatorship of the Commune would lose its raison d'être, and the Commune itself would become no more than a simple "provisional municipal administration."

La Paix en 24 heures has sometimes been described as an "endorsement" or "justification" of the Paris Commune.[52] It was. Considerant saw the Commune, even in its existing, imperfect form, as corresponding to the Paris population's legitimate aspiration to self-rule. His comments on the dictatorship of the Commune and his call for new elections were not to the liking of all the Communards, but the majority regarded him as an ally. To Lissagaray he was "the good and visionary Considerant," and to Gustave Lefrançais he belonged among the "esprits d'élite" of the nineteenth century. Jules Vallès published an extract from *La Paix en 24 heures* in his *Le Cri du peuple*.[53] And when Considerant's manuscript was seized in a raid on the publisher, the Council of the Commune moved quickly to have it returned and printed.[54] It went on sale on April 26.

Two days later, in Félix Pyat's *Le Vengeur*, Pierre Denis published a front-page article on Considerant's brochure. Noting that Considerant's predictions on the war had been all too accurate, Pierre Denis was not disturbed by what he described as "the neological, philosophical, cabalistic, and bizarre form" of the brochure. What he did challenge was Considerant's confidence that Thiers and the Versaillais could be persuaded by a mere vote for autonomy on the part of the Paris population. He observed that he had himself proposed a plebiscite a month earlier, when (if accompanied by a display of military force on the part of the Paris National Guard) it might have served to prevent the outbreak of full-scale civil war. Now it was too late for a plebiscite to make any difference. Nonetheless, wrote Pierre Denis, "the vision of Victor Considerant is of an absolute truthfulness when he sees in the present war the final and decisive struggle of an industrious, productive civilization against a military, priest-ridden, political, exploitative civilization, or rather barbarism." It was just because the conflict was so decisive, and because in the long run their cause was doomed, that the Versaillais would refuse any compromise and would attempt to impose their own domination by force.[55]

In the same article, Pierre Denis noted the support now being given to Parisian autonomy by previously moderate or apolitical groups such as the Freemasons and the Ligue d'Union Républicaine. On April 28, Considerant appeared at meetings held by both these groups. He was apparently merely a guest at the meeting of the Venerables of the Parisian Masonic Lodges, where a discussion was held on the Masonic demonstration planned for the next day in support of the Paris Commune.[56] At the meeting of the Ligue d'Union Républicaine des Droits de Paris, however, he gave a speech arguing for Parisian autonomy. His general theme was the importance for France of communal life and local autonomy. "For him as for us," one of his listeners recalled later, "French unity was an unshakable historical fact. But this unity could not be permitted to stifle its own elements, the individual and the commune. It could be reconciled with individual and communal rights, with the liberty of the citizen and the freedoms of the city." Central to Considerant's argument once again were the critique of representative government and the call for a new form of direct, plebiscitory democracy that would free the individual and the commune from the tyranny of both kings and legislatures.[57]

This talk to the Ligue d'Union Républicaine was Considerant's last public appearance during the life of the Paris Commune. By the end of April the Versaillais had taken up positions in the hills overlooking Paris, and their artillery had begun the second bombardment of the city. On May 1, faced with a desperate military situation, the Paris Commune voted to delegate power to a five-member Committee of Public Safety. Now the dictatorship that Considerant feared was indeed in place, and the discussion of social and political questions was indefinitely postponed as the Communards prepared for a second defense of Paris—this time against an army of 130,000 Frenchmen.

On May 4, in Félix Pyat's *Le Vengeur*, an anonymous article appeared attacking the editor of the journal in which Considerant had originally published *La Paix en 24 heures*. Considerant was also taken to task and described as an "old ghost from Texas" whose "superannuated jeremiads" had done harm both to Fourier's reputation and to that of the Paris Commune. Considerant had little respect for the windy Pyat (who was one of the members of the Commune's new Committee of Public Safety), but the attack was painful to him because he admired Pyat's collaborator Pierre Denis. He responded angrily, denouncing the article's "insults" and "calumnies" and describing "the idiotic theory of delegated sovereignty" as "the source of all our misfortunes." Considerant's letter was not published, but it did result in a formal disavowal by Pyat of the article's criticism of "the first and most illustrious disciple of Fourier."[58]

As Considerant defended himself against the attack of *Le Vengeur*, the Versaillais were tightening their grip on the capital. On May 9 they took the fort of Issy and on May 13 that of Vanves. The Communards were reduced to desperate reprisals: the destruction of Thiers's house in Paris, the chapel dedicated to the memory of Louis XVI, and the Vendôme column. Finally, on May 21, after a prolonged and methodical bombardment of the city, the Versaillais broke through the fortifications (which ironically had been built at Thiers's instigation in 1844). During the week that followed, "Bloody Week," the Communards were hunted down like animals; prisoners were shot on both sides; much of Paris was burned; and, in bitter street-by-street fighting, the Commune was crushed.

Considerant, who believed he had something to say to both sides, would dearly have liked to remain active during these last weeks of the Commune's existence, but just as he had fallen sick in June 1848, he was physically incapacitated during much of May 1871. His earlier physical problems were compounded after May 15 by what he later described as a "paralysis" of the right side of his face. We don't know whether this was a stroke, a severe case of Bell's palsy, or something largely psychosomatic. What we do know is that Considerant played no part in Bloody Week, nor in any of the events of the preceding two weeks. The first trace of him in the archives after May 5 comes just a month later, when we find him writing his nephew Jules Palas that he has been sick in bed for twenty days and that he still has no feeling in the right side of his face. "I deplore my condition all the more in that I have never been so eager to enlighten the world about the declarations and foul deeds of the politicians."[59]

In the aftermath of the Commune, Considerant was not himself troubled by the authorities, but many of his friends were. Few were as cynical as Félix Pyat, who, as the end neared, made a fiery speech on the necessity of armed resistance—and then quietly made his way into exile. Considerant's friend Courbet stayed in Paris until the bitter end and then went into hiding—only to be captured by the police on June 7. Another friend, Eugène Bestetti, the secretary of Considerant's section of the International, was arrested during Bloody Week, imprisoned, brought to trial only a year later, and eventually deported. In June and July 1871, Considerant was at last able to play a role—if not in support of the Commune, at least in support of these and other Communards facing trial.[60]

In the case of Courbet, who had been a member of the Council of the Commune and who was later to be held personally responsible for the destruction of the Vendôme column, an elaborate campaign for clemency had to be mounted. Considerant participated in this effort, speaking to Dorian on Courbet's behalf and writing a long and moving letter to the judge who was to hear Courbet's case. "Do you really believe," he asked the judge, "that the government has not already produced enough corpses—corpses of women, corpses of children, corpses of defenseless prisoners of war?"

> The idea of putting that question to you personally came to me when I learned of the arrest of Courbet. If I had not been for more than six weeks suffering from a paralysis of the right side of the face, I would have written you sooner. I don't know if you know Courbet. I who know him can make this deposition: although he has passed the age of fifty, Courbet is, as far *as reason is concerned*, a child of under seven. . . . As for his sentiments and intentions, he tried very hard, for example, to get [Gustave] Chaudey freed, even though he didn't care much for Chaudey as a person. There you have one of his crimes, and I am absolutely certain that he has not committed others.

Whatever Considerant may have actually thought about Courbet's rational capacities and his political judgment—and it is quite possible that he meant exactly what he said—this line of defense seems to have been effective. In the case of Bestetti, Considerant's continuing efforts over a year made little difference.[61] Not all of Considerant's friends supported the Communards. Among the Fourierists, some shared the views of Charles Pellarin, who in the summer of 1871 publicly denounced the "atrocities," "carnage," and "ignoble tyranny" of the Paris Commune. Considerant had other friends who were members of the National Assembly but did not share the punitive zeal of the majority. These included Dorian and Godin and also Alphonse Tamisier, who wrote Considerant from Versailles in July that he was remaining "in the midst of the Merovingians" to do what he could to support policies of moderation.[62]

As for Considerant himself, he had no desire to remain among "the Merovingians." In early June he was already talking of spending a good part of the summer in the Jura, and on June 19 a passport was issued by the U.S. Embassy to "Monsieur Victor Considerant, citizen of the United States," for travel in Switzerland with his wife. In the end it was not until mid-September that Victor and Julie left Paris for Franche-Comté and Switzerland.[63] They were gone for several months. Thus they were far from Paris and Versailles in November when the Communards were executed.

18

Ghost of the Latin Quarter

In October 1871 Considerant turned sixty-three. He still had twenty-two years to live, but he was tired and in poor health. He had, as he often observed, lost the habit of writing and public speaking, and he was conscious of being the relic of another age. There were, it is true, a number of his contemporaries—old 'forty-eighters—who came back now to make new careers for themselves in Third Republic France. His fellow Jurassian, Wladimir Gagneur, was at sixty-four just at the beginning of a twenty-year career in the National Assembly; and Jules Grévy, Gagneur's schoolmate at Poligny and a member of the Constituent Assembly in 1848, was to become president of the Third Republic. Other 'forty-eighters like Louis Blanc, Martin Nadaud, and even François Cantagrel all served—along with the slightly younger Fourierists, Godin and Tamisier—as deputies in the early years of the Third Republic. But Victor Considerant was not about to start a new life. Although his democratic socialism and his views on many specific issues did not put him out of step with the left, his basic assumptions and intellectual style did. He was an idealist in an age of materialism, an internationalist and a pacifist in an age of nationalism and materialism. And although he had a deep respect for scientific knowledge, he couldn't stand the application of that knowledge in positivism and naturalism. His literary hero was not Zola but Hugo.

I

On their return to Paris in late November 1871, Victor and Julie Considerant settled back into their apartment on the rue du Cardinal Lemoine, surrounded by the books, paintings, and memorabilia that Aimée Beuque had safeguarded for them during their years in America. They entertained a little; Julie painted; Victor read omnivorously and audited lectures at the Sorbonne and the Collège de France. In the summers, when the academic year was over, they left Paris for a month or two to visit Considerant's brother at Saumur, or his sister at Beaufort in the Jura, or friends on the Atlantic coast. But they always returned in time for the beginning of the next academic year.

The Considerants' apartment was modest—just two rooms above the shop of a *peintre-vitrier* and looking down on the intersection of the rue Monge and the rue du Cardinal Lemoine. Visitors remembered the clutter of the apartment, the warmth of the Considerants' welcome, and above all Victor's striking appearance. Clarisse Coignet wrote that "in his dark velvet greatcoat and dark pants" and his "broad-brimmed hat and oak cane," he seemed "a traveler from far away in search of unknown shores."

> In his old age he kept his erect and supple posture; his handsome face was now covered with gray hair, and his finely etched features were ennobled by age. There was always a melancholy tinge to his countenance, but it was a resigned and serene melancholy. . . . He would open the door himself and, with the courteous manners of an earlier day, he would lead you into a sitting room strewn with books and papers. On the walls were family portraits, paintings, drawings by Gigoux, landscapes by [François-Louis] Français.

The conversation was "fluent, agreeable, and varied, without a hint of sectarianism." For the Considerants were as familiar with literature and the arts as with social ideas, and Victor was "always reading . . . often late into the night, because he slept very little." [1]

So Considerant's life had come full circle. The Latin Quarter was his home again just as it had been almost a half-century earlier when he entered the Ecole Polytechnique. And he was a student again—a conscientious student who attended lectures faithfully, took notes carefully, and asked questions of his professors. He became friends with several of them —notably the Lamarckian biologist Edmond Perrier of the Muséum d'Histoire Naturelle and the physiologist Balbiani at the Collège de France. With others he initiated scientific correspondences. He sent long letters to the zoologist Lacase-Duthiers concerning his Sorbonne lectures in the academic year 1875–1876 and the social implications of Darwin's work. He also initiated a correspondence with Darwin's first French translator, the anthropologist and philosopher of science Clémence Royer, on the occasion of her Paris lectures in 1884.[2] In his attempt to reach an understanding of Darwin's conceptions of evolution and natural selection, however, Considerant also went directly to the source. His papers include a long and heavily revised draft of a letter to Darwin himself. In it he comments on both *The Origin of Species* and the first volume of *The Descent of Man* and raises questions concerning the importance of maternal—as opposed to sexual—selection.[3]

With his cane, greatcoat, broad-brimmed Mexican-style hat—and persistent questions—this elderly student made a striking impression in the Latin Quarter. To Jules Marcou, who saw the Considerants shortly after their return to France, he looked like a transplanted Texan or Mexican farmer with his sombrero and serape—except that instead of an American flannel shirt "he wore the short one-buttoned cape worn by the romantics of 1830 and artists in their studios." To one of his professors, the philosopher Paul Janet, he was a remnant of a bygone age—an "old medieval student . . . caring only for science and study."[4]

This "old medieval student" did not put his American experience completely behind him, though. He remained in touch with several American friends. Albert Brisbane in particular turned out to be an indefatigable correspondent. For almost ten years Brisbane wrote Considerant regularly, bringing news of his latest inventions, projects, and opinions and urging him not to "bury" himself but to tell the world what he had learned in America. Victor and Julie also kept in contact with friends from San Antonio who sent occasional reports on the city's growth and the doings of its French colony. Thus they learned in 1873 that Lorenzo Castro was building a ranch house on the outskirts of town, that Poinsard was still trying without much success to mix concrete according to Coignet's method, that the Lardners were thriving in the Considerants' old house, and that flowers were blooming on Clarisse Vigoureux's grave. Christine Bruck, the little girl who had lived with them in San Antonio, was a faithful correspondent, and through her letters they could follow her progress from adolescence to marriage to motherhood.[5]

Considerant, who had signed himself "citoyen américain" in his published writings of 1870 and 1871, never ceased to take pride in his American connection. He regarded the victory of the Union in the Civil War as the triumph of the new spirit of industry, freedom, and democracy over the old bellicose, aristocratic, and racist order of the slave South. Having brought a large American flag back to France, he proudly displayed it from his window each July 4 until, on July 4, 1877, he was informed by the police that it was illegal for a private citizen to display a foreign flag in France. Considerant also brought back from America a variety of seedlings and cacti. He had some of the seedlings planted at Condé-sur-Vesgre, but since there was hardly room for the cacti in the Considerants' small apartment, he sold some of them and donated others to the Muséum d'Histoire Naturelle. One of the species he brought back to France was unknown to botanists in Europe. He exhibited it in 1872 at the annual exposition of the Société Centrale d'Horticulture de France, and it was baptized *Agave Consideranti*.[6]

Now that they were back in France, Victor and Julie were able to renew their ties with family members and many of their old friends. Not all of them, to be sure. Victor's unmarried sister Julie had died shortly before they left Texas. Aimée Beuque—Julie's beloved "tante Beuque"—died in September 1871 after a long illness. And Victor and Julie had long since broken off relations with her brother Paul, who still believed that they were somehow responsible for the loss of Clarisse Vigoureux's fortune and for all his other woes. Victor's brother Gustave and his sister Justine were in good health, however, and he and Julie visited them regularly. In his letters to Victor, Gustave continued to fulminate against the Jesuits and royalists who had shortened their father's life and to berate Gambetta and other republican leaders for their willingness to make accommodations with the Vatican. Justine turned eighty in 1874, but she was still going strong. Her son Jules died that year, and Victor's heartfelt letter of condolence shows how deeply attached he was to both his sister and his nephew.[7]

Some of Considerant's friendships did not survive his years in America. He and François Cantagrel were never reconciled after their falling out at Reunion; and the widow of Allyre Bureau never forgave Considerant for his role in bringing her husband to Texas. Nor were Considerant's relations with his devoted friend and admirer Désiré Laverdant always smooth. Shortly after his return from Texas, Laverdant had to warn Considerant that their friendship could not survive if he persisted in making scathing remarks about the Pope and the Virgin Mary in front of Laverdant's wife and nieces. Considerant replied "with a sense of sadness" that they should avoid any discussion of religious and philosophical questions since he regarded Laverdant's views as "a pack of fallacies."[8]

But with most of his friends the renewal of ties was easy. Considerant was quickly back on terms of intimacy with his friends Alphonse and Jenny Delacroix of Besançon, with César Daly, with Franchot and Edel, and with his "dear old friend" from Pouliguen, Benoît, whom he described as "the most tender of brothers." He also continued to have warm and untroubled relations with the army officer Alphonse Tamisier, whom he had known since their student days. In welcoming Considerant back, Tamisier noted with pleasure that Considerant's trials and tribulations in America had not cost him his good humor or his joie de vivre and added that Considerant's return was a "good omen" both for France and for his friends.[9]

Considerant's closest relations at this time were with the family of Frédéric Dorian. Dorian himself died unexpectedly in 1873, just three years after his great days as the organizer of the defense of Paris. However, Victor and Julie kept in touch with Dorian's widow, Caroline, and his daughter, Aline, who was to become one of the great *salonnières* of the Third Republic. Aline Ménard-Dorian was a remarkable woman: plainspoken, immensely energetic, staunchly anticlerical and antimilitarist, passionately interested in politics, she was to be elected vice-president of the Ligue des Droits de l'Homme. She and the Considerants were of one mind on most political questions; and her salon on the rue de la Faisanderie was one place where they always felt at home. Their relationship with that other great hostess of the Third Republic, Juliette Adam, did not endure, however. As her voluminous memoirs make clear, Juliette Adam was a celebrity hunter; and Victor Considerant was now more a relic than a celebrity. Furthermore, she was moving to the right politically. In 1883, when Considerant sent her an article for possible publication in her journal *La Nouvelle Revue*, he did not even receive a reply.[10]

II

During the 1870s, Considerant had several opportunities to return to public life. He was invited to write articles, to run for office, to give public lectures. In 1872 there was talk of his giving a course of lectures in a hall near his apartment. That year he was also invited by Albert Brisbane to help create a monthly journal devoted "not to the reveries of socialism" but to "the exposition of the most advanced ideas on social science." Although he was tempted, Considerant turned down these proposals. The most he felt capable of was "a series of *causeries* with a small number of sympathetic listeners for an audience." Perhaps if some of them could take notes, this would help him clarify his thoughts.[11]

Considerant was particularly eager to reach the young. As he wrote Caroline Dorian in 1874, he wished to find out if "the younger generation today are capable of being magnetized by the high ideas that moved us so powerfully when Dorian and I were young." Considerant gave a few talks on Fourier's doctrine that year before a group of young people and was reasonably satisfied with the result. In 1876 another opportunity arose. He found a group of students including Gustave Geoffroy, the future art critic and biographer of Blanqui, the poet Julien Sermet, and the historian Gabriel Deville, who were willing to participate in a series of "conversations" in which he would lecture on what he called "the science of the moral world" and they would take notes and ask questions.[12]

Considerant's *causeries* met once a week in May and June 1876. About a dozen students participated, and one of them later wrote an account of the experience.

> I went to Victor Considerant's apartment for a few weeks each Thursday evening. . . . I remember well the quartier du Panthéon, the white house on the rue du Cardinal Lemoine, the salon where we gathered. Considerant was sitting in a corner, dressed all in gray, in loose-fitting clothes. His bearing was military, his head small, his mustache long and hanging down at the ends in the gallic style. He was tall, refined; he welcomed us most warmly and seemed alert despite his seventy-one years [sic]. What I also remember very well is the charm of Madame Considerant, her old woman's beauty, her kindly face, and the graciousness with which she offered us tea and cookies.

The student, Gustave Geoffroy, went on to reproduce his notes on Considerant's first talk and to describe the impression it made on him.

> He proposed to discuss with us the final meditations of his life; and certainly now, at a distance, the effort seems even more significant and more noble than I found it then. He proposed to try to expound to us a positive science that he called the science of the moral world.

Two questions stood at the center of Considerant's first lecture, each of them illustrated by an example drawn from recent history. How could a psychological doctrine portraying human beings as motivated primarily by the pursuit of pleasure account for acts of heroism and self-sacrifice such as the suicide of Charles Delescluze after the defeat of the Paris Commune? What grounds could such a doctrine give to criticize the action of General Bazaine, who surrendered his army and betrayed his country while seeking to realize his personal ambitions?[13]

Considerant's talks ended with the coming of summer vacation. In less than two months, however, he apparently managed to cover much of the history of philosophy, focusing especially on the history of different conceptions of pleasure from the Greeks and the Buddhists through Kant,

Schopenhauer, Darwin, and Haeckel. "These lectures contained no great revelation," wrote Geoffroy. What Considerant did offer was a thoughtful self-examination and a summation of his thinking. His "age and experience" gave poignancy to this "effort at self-knowledge, this desire to press on, to keep up with the times."[14]

Through the 1870s and into the 1880s, Considerant continued to read and write, attempting to reconsider his views in the light of recent scientific work and to see how much of the old Fourierism might be left in a modern social science. He rarely spoke about his work, and when he did it was often simply to complain about his "graphophobia"—the "pathological repugnance" that "pen and ink inspired" in him. He was understood to be working on "a sort of philosophical testament," possibly in the form of a series of lectures, that would "summarize the studies and observations of his whole life of work and dedication to an ideal."[15] He never produced such a testament. The most he could write was a series of fragments—letters to eminent scientists and his professors and brief sketches in which he attempted to evaluate Fourier's thought and his own life's work.

Two of these fragments are especially worth discussing because they give us some insight into Considerant's final views. The first is a letter written in May 1880 in response to an appeal for guidance from fifteen young people calling themselves "the Phalansterian group of Marseille." Describing themselves as having "reached the entrance of the temple built by Fourier," they asked Considerant to "take them into the sanctuary." Having read and admired Considerant's work, they "ardently" wished him "to make his voice heard once again."[16] This was a hard invitation to turn down. Considerant wrote, and published, a reply.

> I still think that Fourier made the crucial discovery in the area of social science, and that nothing good or fruitful will be done outside the conception that he has left us. But on the other hand I think that in attempting to revive the active propagation of Fourier's ideas, we must not look for the ruts left by the first [Fourierist] movement and seek to follow the path that we trod fifty years ago.

Any attempt to repeat the work of the original Fourierist movement would be sterile. Considerant argued for "the creation of a new movement, a new school, a new form of propagation . . . based on absolutely scientific foundations."

> I would have made an effort, through lectures, to create a new workshop within which this task might be undertaken, if I had found young

people inclined to help me out. I have not found any up to now. But I have made use of my time in attempting to familiarize myself with modern science.

In 1880 Considerant had still not entirely abandoned the hope of creating a new movement, inspired in part by Fourier's "idea" but resting on up-to-date scientific foundations.[17]

The second fragment, dating from a year or two later, is an unpublished thirteen-page manuscript entitled "Views that I no longer hold, having recognized them to be erroneous." In this manuscript Considerant observed that while meditating on Fourier's work "in the calm of the American prairies," he had come to realize that in its original form Fourier's theory was based on an assumption that could never be proved. This was the assumption of a preestablished harmony, a providential order that, once established, would guarantee the harmony and reconciliation of hitherto conflicting passions and interests. It was the assumption that everything in the world can be understood in terms of "a preconceived plan" in the light of which the desires and "attractions" of every individual were destined for fulfillment and satisfaction. One cannot say, "Attractions are proportional to destinies," Considerant now believed. The only claim consistent with a scientific understanding of the world was the claim that "destinies are proportional to attractions"—that people's fates are in large measure shaped by their inclinations and drives.

Fourier had believed in the existence of a "providential order," a state of "universal harmony" toward which both nature and society were tending. The ultimate reality in his view, the "destiny" of man and the world, was a state of perfect harmony. But this belief was false. Considerant had learned from Darwin that nature was not a realm of order and harmony but one of "perpetual conflict" and "universal strife." Similarly, the social world was a realm of conflict the outcome of which could not be known. Thus Fourierism in its original form was not a science but a faith. This was not to discredit it entirely, however. Like all faiths, true or false, the Fourierist belief in a pre-established harmony had the power to move people, to stimulate them in their search for a better world.[18]

So Considerant came at the end of his life to a view of Fourier's thought not unlike the view of Marxism articulated a quarter-century later by Georges Sorel. Marxism was not a science, Sorel argued, but a faith; and the belief in a general strike that would galvanize the working class and topple capitalism was a myth. Like other political myths, though, it could inspire and even ennoble the people who believed in it, endowing them with a heightened sense of their own collective powers. It could in the end prove to be a self-fulfilling prophecy.[19]

This essay, written a year or two after his wife's death, was in a sense Considerant's obituary of Fourierism. Or at least it was an appreciation of Fourierism that recognized its grave limitations in a scientific age. Considerant made this plain near the end of his essay. It is not regrettable, he wrote, that Fourier's thought was premised on the scientifically untenable belief in a providential order. Without such a belief Fourier could never have given his theory the imaginative coherence, the "prodigieuse intégralité," that it in fact possessed. It is true that the world imagined by Fourier was "100,000 times more beautiful than the real world of the actual creator." But this was not necessarily a flaw. At a moment when science, "having reached the age of maturity, was about to close forever the era of . . . great imaginary systems," it was not a bad thing "for the glory of the human mind" that Fourier's vision emerged. Throughout the Christian era, religion and philosophy had provided a whole series of "pitiful, empty, or childish conceptions of the world in general and of the afterlife in particular." Compared to these "pitiful, incoherent, and arbitrary conceptions," Fourier had offered a vision of the world that was "magnificent" in its reach and its beauty. Its only defect was that it was "not consistent with reality."[20]

III

The relationship between Victor and Julie Considerant deepened as the years passed. They needed each other. He helped her deal with her various physical infirmities, and she helped him get through the long periods of lassitude and depression that came on him especially in winter time. But the relationship was based on more than need. "Rarely have two human beings understood each other better and remained so constantly attached to each other," wrote Jules Marcou. "Although they had no children, the ties that bound them tightened with age and misfortune." A little note that Julie wrote to Victor on his sixty-fourth birthday testifies not only to her beautiful simplicity of expression but also to the depth of their attachment after thirty-four years of marriage: "To Consi. The prairie grass loves each new year. I am the grass on your prairie. Julie Considerant, 12 October, 1872. Paris."[21]

Julie wrote this note at a difficult time. She had long had heart palpitations that made it hard for her to do certain kinds of sustained work. Her symptoms apparently included an irregular and at times much too rapid heartbeat and poor circulation in the arms and legs. In the fall of 1872 these problems were compounded by a "dangerous" bout of pneumonia that lasted three months. Then, in the winter of 1874, her eyesight deteriorated significantly. She was bothered by dark spots and flashes of light, which became so severe that she finally had to give up painting.[22]

Julie coped with all these physical problems without complaint. Victor could write in 1875 that, having quit painting, Julie now joined him regularly in auditing Sorbonne lectures in natural history. "Julie likes these lectures so much," he wrote, "that she can no longer do without them." Still her heart problems persisted, and she was sometimes unable to accompany Victor on his summer trips to the seashore. She did normally go back with him to Franche-Comté, however; and it was there in the summer of 1879, while she and Victor were walking in the woods near his sister's home in Beaufort, that she had a bad fall that left her bedridden for several months. In November she was well enough to accompany Victor on a trip to Brittany, but she was not yet fully recovered. That winter other problems developed. Finally, on the night of April 7, 1880, she died.[23]

Although Julie's death was not unexpected, it left her husband distraught. He managed to write out a brief announcement evoking their forty-three years of marriage and "more than half a century of affection and harmony in life." But at the civil ceremony held in their apartment on Sunday April 11 he was almost mute with grief. There were brief obituaries in many of the Paris journals, but it is a measure of the obscurity into which the Considerants had fallen that most of these confused Julie and her mother, describing Julie as a woman "known in the world of letters" as the author of *Parole de Providence*. In a few of the obituaries some sense was conveyed of the character and personality of this remarkable woman—her love of music, flowers, and birds, her hatred of injustice, her compassion for all of life's victims. A more revealing appreciation of Julie may be found in a letter from her niece Berthe: "My aunt was so good, so brave, and, along with that, so simple in her manners, so kind. It seemed to me that she did the right and good thing naturally, without the least effort."[24]

Victor accompanied Julie's body by train to Besançon, where he had her buried in the Cimitière des Chaprais alongside her sister Claire. He designed her gravestone, on which a large tulip was carved along with words evoking their life's itinerary: "Besançon 1812, Paris, Belgium, Texas, Paris, Besançon 1880." The tulip was Julie's symbol, he explained, "that plant with a straight and bare stem and a triangular flower, which Fourier was right to describe as representing the traits of honesty, truth, and justice."[25] After burying Julie, Victor stayed on in Franche-Comté for almost two months. He didn't want to leave until her gravestone had been carved and put in place, and he had no desire to hurry back to the empty apartment in Paris. So he made a nostalgic visit to his birthplace, Salins; he also went to see his sister Justine in Beaufort. He found her in excellent health at the age of eighty-six. This turned out to be their last meeting. Shortly after his departure, she died of burns suffered in a household accident.[26]

Considerant's stay in Franche-Comté was also the occasion of some very unpleasant business. On August 14, two days after Julie's burial, he received the first in a series of letters from her brother Paul, demanding payment of money he claimed was due him from their mother's estate. Paul's claims were absurd. He wanted retribution for Julie's dowry (which in fact had never been paid), for their mother's contribution to the cost of Victor's education, and even for the furniture that she had brought with her when she came to live with Victor and Julie. It was easy for Victor to rebut these claims—to point out, for example, that neither he nor Julie had ever received "a centime" of the sums agreed upon in their marriage contract and that they had after all taken care of Clarisse Vigoureux for twenty-five years. But having to say all these things poisoned four days for Considerant immediately after his wife's death.[27]

IV

When Considerant returned to Paris after burying his wife, he tried to resume his old daily patterns. He began again to attend lectures at the Sorbonne—those of Fustel de Coulanges in history, for example, and Elme Caro in philosophy.[28] He continued to attend the monthly dinners of the Parisian Fourierists; and he tried to make himself do at least some writing every day. Still, he felt bewildered and only half alive without Julie. The apartment, of course, was full of her paintings, her medallions, and other objects that reminded him of her, but he felt her loss in other, less obvious ways. So much of his life with her had consisted of shared experiences and so many of his responses and judgments had been shaped in conversation with her that he now felt disoriented.

"I've felt listless and exhausted in this poor little lonely apartment," he wrote Caroline Dorian in August 1880. He had no energy, no will power; and he simply could not get used to Julie's absence. He had spent much of his time since his return to Paris cleaning and arranging the apartment. Once the job was done, though, he kept waiting for Julie to appear and take pleasure in his work. It was as if he had to learn over and over again that she would never come back.[29]

A year after Julie's death, Victor went by himself to the annual art exhibition at the Palais de l'Industrie. This was something that he and Julie had always done together. "Ah! What a disappointment!" he wrote the next day:

> We always had the same impressions and almost always the same judgments. Now I feel confused. It seems to me that I don't have any more opinions or judgments. Those little morning trips to the Palais de l'Industrie, walking along the Seine, were always little holidays for us. They made us want to sing; now I want to cry.

Ironically, summers were particularly hard for Considerant. When Julie was alive, summer had been a time of renewed health and energy for both of them. Now the opposite was true. Considerant found himself falling into a "state of physical, moral, and nervous lethargy" each spring with the return of warm weather.[30]

With his wife and sister gone, Victor's brother Gustave was now the only surviving family member of his generation with whom he felt close. But Gustave died in 1886. Thus, during the last years of his life, Considerant was thrown back on his friends for the psychological and practical support that he needed more than ever. His two oldest and closest friends now were Jules Benoît and César Daly. Both of them had been attracted to the Fourierist movement in the 1830s but had gone on to make careers outside the movement, Daly as an architect and the founder of France's most influential architectural journal. Benoît had retired to Pouliguen at the mouth of the Loire, where Considerant visited him at the end of almost every summer in the 1880s. Daly, a man of refinement and cultivation who had stood by Considerant through thick and thin, understood him as well as any of his friends, appreciating his emotional needs and his desire to make contact with the young.[31]

Two other close friends of Considerant during these years were Caroline Dorian and her daughter Aline. They looked after him, inviting him to dinner at the rue de la Faisanderie and for summer visits to their country estate. Considerant, who was touched by their "tender affection," described their letters as "rays of light." His letters to them convey a sense of the loneliness and depression and lack of direction that constantly threatened to overcome him. His physical ailments were many: headaches, fever, rheumatism, arthritis, nervous trembling, unexplained sweating, nightmares. But more difficult to bear were the reminders of Julie's absence, which left him in what he described as an almost constant state of physical and moral enervation.[32]

Although Considerant's letters to the Dorians are full of complaints about his bad health and his worse morale, he could still occasionally rouse himself to inveigh against the short-sightedness and lack of imagination of the leaders of the republican left. He was particularly disappointed in Georges Clemenceau's leadership of "this 'radical' group, which is not radical at all." In his view Clemenceau was "wasting his talent and his future" and misusing "abilities from which I expected much." "It is most unfortunate," he wrote in 1883, "that the progressive republic is so badly served." Two years later the overthrow of the second Ferry ministry following a momentary military reverse in Tonkin was in Considerant's eyes "nothing less than an infamy." "I consider that France has met a disaster, but not in Tonkin," he wrote in April 1885. "The republican majority in the Palais Bourbon has dishonored itself in the eyes of Europe. . . . The Republic will have to be very strong to hold out and remain standing with this kind of supporters."[33]

Considerant's letters to the Dorians also contain a number of comments concerning his reading. He found Lamartine's *Histoire des Girondins*, for example, as relevant to the political situation in 1881 as it had been to that of 1847. "Our republican deputies today should all read the pages on the passionate and blind quarrels of the Montagnards and the Girondins," he wrote, "in order to keep watch against the dissensions that have brought down the best causes." Considerant also commented on Hippolyte Taine's much-discussed *Origines de la France contemporaine*. He had admired Taine's *De l'intelligence*, writing that there had "never been a better account of the mechanism of the intellect, the conditions and the laws of reason, and the method appropriate to the pursuit of truth." As a historian, however, he found Taine inadequate: "To write a history of the French Revolution properly, the intellect must be grafted onto a [notion of] personality and onto an understanding of the larger course of history and of humanity. This is completely lacking in his work."[34]

As he grew older, Considerant became increasingly absorbed in the past. So many of his old friends were gone now that he couldn't prevent his thoughts from turning to them. Julie's sister Claire, who had died at seventeen, was rarely out of his mind for long. Nor were long-dead friends like Amédée Paget and Allyre Bureau. After his return from America the deaths came more rapidly. One of the most painful for him was that of Frédéric Dorian. "I can still see Dorian," he wrote in his eighty-fourth year. "So constant, so reliable, and at the same time so kind and so gay: he was the Prince Charming of our youth." Considerant could not put these friends behind him. "I do not place them in the past," he wrote. "On the contrary, it seems to me that the older I get, the more I cherish my beloved dead."[35]

It was this same preoccupation with the past that caused the elderly Considerant to reflect on the early history of the Fourierist movement and the origins of socialism. One of his unrealized projects was to write a history of socialism. At the age of seventy-seven he did manage to publish an article on the "first phase" of the Fourierist movement. His point was that the utopian socialism of the romantic period was much richer in imaginative power and sociological insight than the radical ideologies of the "bland" Third Republic. What was most striking in the article was his stark contrast between the "ardent" days of his youth and the "anemic" *fin de siècle*.

The period of the later Restoration and the July Monarchy was a "belle époque," wrote Considerant, and "full of good will, broadly humane and generous." These years were "fruitful in new developments in the domains of art and social thought" and "all the high spheres of the intellect." The "brilliant youth" of the century that opened with the French Revolution was now dismissed as "obsolete" by the "wizened pygmies" of the century's "senile" old age. Posterity would take a different view. It would see the early years of the century as compensation for the "bland resignation" of the "bland positivism" of the 1880s, "crawling along to its heart's content under the weight of established facts," and for the "anemic and empty parliamentary groups that are running the government of a somnolent country that they represent only too well." Literary naturalism was a worthy expression of this pitiful *fin de siècle*, and Emile Zola was a "pygmy" next to the "glorious" Victor Hugo.[36]

If Considerant was disappointed by the men and institutions of the Third Republic, its leaders were more indulgent with regard to him. They saw him as a "precursor" who deserved a place in the genealogy that they were constructing for the regime. Thus during the 1880s several efforts were made to honor Considerant for his service to the democratic cause by granting him an official government pension. In July 1880 Minister of Education Jules Ferry, responding to an initiative by César Daly and Eugène Burnouf, offered Considerant an annual life pension of 1000 francs. Two years later Ferry's successor Paul Bert increased the offer to 1500 francs. Considerant's response to these proposals was simple. Observing that the funding for any pension would have to come from taxes imposed in large part on the poorest members of society, he wrote: "I could not accept the favor which has been so kindly offered me without offending the ideas of social justice for which I have been arguing all my life." Like Charles Péguy two decades later, Victor Considerant believed it was better to live for the republic than off it.[37]

A government pension would have made a big difference to Considerant, for he was hardly a rich man. During the 1870s the Considerants' main source of income had been the annual payments of $600 made by the purchasers of their house near San Antonio. But by the time of Julie's death the house was paid off. Thereafter Considerant seems to have lived on small bequests from his two sisters and a larger one from the Fourierist doctor François Barrier. He did own a small amount of real estate—two or three lots—in the city of San Antonio. Hoping that it would rise in value, he had kept it after his return to France. But property taxes seem to have offset any increase in value. When he finally sold the lots in 1883 or 1884, he invested the money unwisely, purchasing shares in a magnesium company in Eubea that he had been offered by his friend, the pioneer of French Sanskrit studies, Eugène Burnouf. These shares soon lost all their value. Considerant was bitter, feeling that he had been deceived by Burnouf, but nothing could be done: the money was gone.[38]

In 1890 another attempt was made to honor Considerant when a group of socialists including the former Communards Léo Frankel, Augustin Avrial, and François Jourde proposed to organize a banquet paying tribute to him as "the dean of French socialists." Again Considerant rejected the proposal. There would be time enough for such celebrations, he observed, "after the construction of the new world." Furthermore, he was not in sympathy with the direction in which French socialism was moving. There was too much squabbling within the socialist movement, too much vain boasting, too much talk of "apocalyptic violence" and "blathering about massacres." All this could only serve the interests of socialism's enemies. It was also evidence of the greater maturity and discipline of the workers' movements and parties of Germany and Belgium. Given these beliefs, Considerant wrote that it would hardly be appropriate for him to accept a public tribute from a group of French socialists.[39]

By his own choice then, Considerant spent his last years distanced not only from the organized Fourierist movement but also from the various contemporary French socialist groups and factions. He was still eager to make contact with young people, but now he lacked the energy even to hold the semi-formal *causeries* that he had organized in the 1870s, and his contacts with students were confined largely to conversations in the cafés of the Latin Quarter. A café on the corner of the boulevard Saint-Michel and the rue des Ecoles, the Café Soufflet, became a second home to him after

Julie's death. There he could be seen, sometimes holding court with groups of students but sometimes also simply playing dominoes or nursing a beer and staring silently off into space.[40]

Among the students who met him at this time, several recorded their impressions. For the Guesdist Alexandre Zévaès, the Considerant of the Café Soufflet was an impressive patriarch, a "magnificent old man." Another young admirer, Paul Muller, who saw Considerant often at the Café Soufflet, long remembered the warmth with which he spoke of his old Alsatian friends and his lecture tours in Alsace in the 1840s. A third student, the future historian of Icarian socialism, Jules Prudhommeaux, left a sadder picture of the aged Considerant.

> The life that he leads is unworthy of him. Often in the student brasseries around the rue Soufflot you can see a silent, dejected, exhausted man with a gloomy look and the drooping mustache of a Gallic chief. He sits there inert for hours on end with his glass of beer and his pipe. To students who ask, initiates reply in a low voice: "That is the person who once was Victor Considerant."

The language might seem excessive, but Considerant himself used similar words in a letter written to Aline Dorian from his post at the Café Soufflet: "To tell the truth, I've been dead for a very long time."[41]

V

During his last years one of the few sources of real pleasure in Considerant's life was provided by his relations with his old friends in Belgium. He had always had a special fondness for Belgians—a fondness undiminished by his difficulties with their government during his first five years of exile. The greatest triumph of all his years as a lecturer was probably the series of lectures he gave in 1845 at Brussels. Several of the friendships he formed at that time—with Philippe Bourson, Adolphe Demeur, and Hippolyte Colignon—were to last for the rest of his life.

Throughout the 1880s Considerant continued to correspond with these Belgian friends and occasionally to visit them. Philippe Bourson died in 1888, but Considerant was no less fond of Bourson's son Eugène and his granddaughter Louise (Loulou), and it was in the warm and lively atmosphere of her young family that he stayed during his last visit to Brussels in November 1891. On this same trip he also spent time with Adolphe Demeur and visited the offices of the Belgian socialist daily *Le Peuple*. In a published interview a journalist for *Le Peuple* reported that "the venerable

French socialist" was unstinting in his "praise of the Belgian socialists, who by their mutual understanding and the practical way they go about preaching socialism to the masses, should, so he says, serve as an example to other peoples."[42]

Not long after Considerant's return from Brussels in December 1891, Demeur wrote that, despite his age, he was planning to run for election to Belgium's Chamber of Deputies in order to support the socialists' campaign for universal male suffrage. "Bravo!" replied Considerant. "I am delighted to see you getting back into harness for this important struggle. For my part I will be happy to think of you as a member of the phalanx that is going to fight this battle that the Belgian Workers' Party has prepared, initiated, and imposed by means of its fine propaganda." The Belgians had organized a "fine campaign," Considerant wrote, which should serve as "a model for our French socialists."[43]

The day after writing this letter Considerant opened his copy of *Le Peuple* to read that Demeur had suddenly and unexpectedly died. He then wrote Demeur's widow a letter of condolence that was also a cry of pain.

> Dear madame, is it true? Is it possible? Oh, my dear little Demeur! Yesterday evening I wrote you with a feeling of keen joy. I rejoiced in the sense of your strength and of your youth. I imagined it would last a long time, and it seemed as though this would prolong a part of my own life even after my death! And then this morning, just now in opening *Le Peuple*, I saw that terrible black mourning border band and his dear name: Adolphe Demeur! Oh! I shed bitter tears with you.[44]

What is remarkable about this letter is not only the expression of grief but also the expression of empathy. This eighty-three-year-old man who spent many of his days in a café staring vacantly off into space was still capable of experiencing his friend's seemingly recaptured energy and youth as if it were his own.

Adolphe Demeur and the Boursons were old friends of Considerant. He had gotten to know them in the 1840s; he had seen much of them during his years of exile in Belgium and had renewed contact with them in 1870. Considerant had one other old friend in Brussels as well whom he had met even earlier. This was Désirée Véret. He had met her in 1832, and then after a few years they had fallen out of touch. The little packet of letters that he received from her in 1890 and 1891 may have meant less to him than the occasional friendly letters he received from "Loulou" Bourson or Adolphe Demeur. To an outsider, however, the letters to Considerant from Désirée

Véret are among the most beautiful and moving documents in the whole Considerant archive.[45]

Désirée Véret was a twenty-two-year-old seamstress when Considerant met her. She was a person of strong emotions, undivided loyalties, and a passionate desire for independence that was never separated in her mind from the pursuit of collective happiness. Turn by turn Saint-Simonian, Fourierist, Owenite, and Communist, she was a seeker who never lost her curiosity about the world or her desire to make it better. Her "Fourierist period" was brief but long enough for Fourier himself to become infatuated with her and to write her a declaration of love—long enough too for her to conceive a passionate but unavowed love for Considerant. In 1890, having outlived her husband and both her sons, she was living alone, half-blind, in Brussels with only her memories for company.[46]

In May 1890 Désirée Véret obtained Considerant's address (probably through his socialist friends in Brussels) and wrote him a brief note: "Does Victor Considerant remember Jeanne-Désirée? If he does, let him write her. She has forgotten nothing, not Fourier, nor the feelings of the youth of 1832. In her voluntary solitude she is living a calm life, her mind and heart filled with memories of her whole passional life." Considerant's reply was affectionate, and it left Désirée Véret touched by "the good memory you have of my character." This was what she wanted to hear, because she had never stopped wondering about something that had passed between them more than half a century earlier. "I have often been sad at heart," she wrote, "in thinking that you must have judged me a loose woman, quick to give herself and quick to leave." But this was not the case.

> I loved you passionately, Victor, but I could never bring myself to give you a word of love or a single caress, even when you held me in your arms, that brief moment when you loved me a little bit. Pride turned me to stone, and I have never forgiven myself.

She went on to explain how she had felt about him and what she had loved in him in that distant past.

> I dreamed of free love, and I knew that your feelings were pledged and the line of your existence was traced out. But I loved you for your apostle's soul, and I linked my soul to yours in the social love that has been the dominant passion of my life, just as it is still the dominant passion of my impotent but fervent old age.

One would like to know how Victor Considerant responded to this evocation of a lost love, which was also in a way a renewed declaration of love, from an eighty-year-old woman, but we have only her letters.[47]

Having unburdened herself, Désirée Véret went on in her subsequent letters to send Considerant clippings from Belgian newspapers and to talk about Belgian politics and her own life, about her days as president of the women's section of the First International in 1866, about her relations with Fourier and with the Irish feminist Anna Doyle Wheeler, "who was a second mother to me." She also talked about Considerant's work, about the "rigidity" of the disciples of Fourier, who appealed to greed and ambition and not to "the feelings of the disinherited," and about the "little scientific utopian journal" that she hoped Considerant would create. But often she returned to herself, to her inner life—her fantasies, her memories of her "amorous youth," and her feelings about Considerant.

> I recognized right away by intuition your defects and your qualities and, in spite of myself, I loved everything about you. Nothing has escaped my memory: from your arrival at Paris in 1832 and your visit with Fugère up until the last time I saw you in 1837 at Robert Owen's rooms in the Hôtel de l'Angleterre.[48]

She asked him for a photograph, which he sent, but she found his expression too sad, too full of discouragement. So she asked for another. She wanted to fix his image in her mind before she went totally blind. What would be best, she said, would be for him to come to Brussels to see her.

Did Considerant ever call on Désirée Véret at Brussels? It does not seem likely. There is no hint of a meeting anywhere in his papers. He did visit Brussels in November 1891, but her last letter to him is dated July 6. In it she explained that she was trying to prepare herself for the onset of total blindness by learning how to get around her small apartment with her eyes closed. At this rate, she added, she might yet acquire "some physical peculiarities" to go along with "the oddness of my brain." She concluded by asking him to "be indulgent to your faithful friend." Probably she died sometime in the late summer or fall of that year.[49]

VI

In June 1891 Considerant gave an interview to the Parisian daily *L'Eclair.* The interviewer reported that he found Considerant "vigorous" despite his advanced age, standing erect and sharp-eyed, his features framed by his flowing hair and his "celebrated mustache." Asked what he thought about the contemporary social movement, Considerant replied that in his view much of modern socialism had been anticipated by thinkers of his generation. He and his contemporaries had been calling for the peaceful and democratic socialization of the means of production since the 1830s. Fourier's critique of "civilized" society had lost none of its relevance. The number of parasites was continuing to rise; "commerce with its many hygienic falsifications" was "flourishing in all its splendor"; "industrial, commercial, and financial feudalism" was extending its long "shadow over consumers and small capitalists"; and the conflict between rich and poor had not abated—only now "the antagonism of interests" was called "the struggle for survival."

If major social reform did not come soon through peaceful means, Considerant declared, revolution would break out. He preferred reform. Thus he applauded the movement for an eight-hour working day as a "splendid" weapon in the "international war against the exploitation of labor." It was "a simple idea that everyone could understand and that should contribute much to our forward progress." However, the reduction of working hours was not an end in itself. "It is not a solution but an excellent preface." In one of his last public statements Considerant gave his support to a reformist movement while specifying, as he had so often before, that it was only a step on the road to a better world.

As he was about to leave Considerant's apartment, the interviewer noticed a faded newspaper cartoon on the wall. It was one of dozens of caricatures published in 1848 and 1849 representing Considerant haranguing the National Assembly or engaged in earnest conversation while a long tail (with an eye at its end) protruded out from under his coat. Considerant explained that this was a reference to one of Fourier's more spectacular prophecies and that in 1848 he was rarely depicted without it. Once it had irritated him, but in his more serene old age he found it amusing. It was no worse than the caricatures of the shaggy-haired Leroux, the fierce child-eating Proudhon, or little Louis Blanc being stuffed into a lady's muff. "None of that is very wicked," he told the interviewer. "None of it keeps the grain from growing or socialism from advancing." [50]

When Considerant gave this interview he was still living in his Parisian apartment. Despite his apparent vigor, though, he needed looking after, and he had begun to spend an increasing amount of time outside Paris with friends—especially at the country estate of César Daly at Wissous or with Auguste Kleine at Laon in the Aisne. Kleine, a government engineer with residences at both Laon and Paris, had an almost filial relation with Considerant and was connected to the Fourierist movement by both conviction and marriage, since his wife was the daughter of François Coignet. [51]

When Considerant was no longer able to live by himself, he asked Kleine to take him in. So it was at Laon that Considerant spent his last two years. He soon became a familiar sight there, dressed in his "broad-brimmed hat and his huge greatcoat," walking unsteadily along the ramparts of the town and near its great cathedral, leaning on the arm of Kleine.[52]

In the fall of 1893 Considerant's health worsened and Kleine brought him back to Paris to his apartment on the avenue de la Bourdonnais. There, on December 27, 1893, in the shadow of the new Eiffel Tower, Considerant died, watched over by Kleine to the last. The cause of death was variously given as an "apoplexie séreuse" and as a "congestion pulmonaire." Whatever the cause, he was ready to die.

Considerant's death did not pass unnoticed. Fairly extensive obituaries appeared in the Parisian dailies. Several hundred people attended the funeral ceremonies held at Kleine's apartment and at the Père Lachaise Cemetery. According to newspaper accounts, their number included the socialists Jean Jaurès, Alexandre Millerand, and Edouard Lockroy, the anarchist brothers Elie and Elisée Réclus, the feminist Paule Mink, the Belgian socialist Louis Bertrand, and Karl Marx's son-in-law Charles Longuet. Many factions of the left, whose bickering had been so distressing to Considerant, came together around his coffin.[53]

The funeral ceremonies began with a reception at Kleine's apartment, where speeches were given by Hippolyte Destrem, representing the Fourierists, and by a feminist named Vincent, who noted that Considerant was the only member of the Constituent Assembly of 1848 who had publicly supported women's suffrage. Then the group of mourners accompanied Considerant's body on the long trip across Paris to the Père Lachaise Cemetery, where there were more speeches by representatives of the Chamber of Deputies and the Conseil Municipal. Then, according to Considerant's wishes, his body was cremated. His ashes were later transported to Besançon to be buried alongside the remains of his wife.[54]

Of all the speeches given at Considerant's funeral, the one most commented on was that of the old Fourierist Hippolyte Destrem, who movingly evoked Considerant's role in the creation of the Ecole Sociétaire in the "happy" and "pure" years from 1832 to 1847. But Destrem said nothing of Considerant's activities during the Second Republic or of his attempt to build utopia in Texas. On the last thirty-five years of Considerant's life his only comment was: "In the second part of your life, dear Considerant, we respected your [desire for] intellectual rest." Destrem added that while Considerant "rested," Fourier's remaining disciples completed his work, with the result that "today nothing more stands in the way of the progressive conquest of the moral and social world" by the Fourierist movement.[55] Considerant, who retained to the last his faith in the ultimate triumph of socialism, would have been more skeptical with regard to the future of Fourierism. He had learned from bitter experience that the obstacles preventing its spread could not be so easily overcome.

CONCLUSION

Considerant's Significance

When he died in 1893, Considerant had been out of the limelight for over forty years. He had outlived almost all his contemporaries; and although some of the ideas he had fought for had been integrated within the socialist and democratic traditions, many of his views now seemed irrelevant and the idiom in which he expressed them hopelessly out of date. A provincial journalist could begin a relatively sympathetic obituary by noting that it would take a real effort of imagination to grasp "the stir and the headway" that Considerant's ideas had made sixty years earlier. Even at that time, observed the journalist, the "famous theory of the four movements" can scarcely have meant much to anyone outside the Fourierist movement. Today, he scoffed, one could hardly expect to get a hearing in a public meeting if he stood up and announced his intention to prove that "attractions are proportional to destinies."[1]

Not all the appreciations of Considerant's life and thought that appeared at this time were equally serene. In the *Journal des débats*, Considerant's death was the occasion for a sermon on the dangers of even the most peaceful and innocent-sounding socialism. His demise, according to the *Débats*, marked the disappearance of "the last vestige of those socialists of 1848, the disciples of Saint-Simon and Fourier, who dreamed of . . . universal peace, fraternity, and equality in some Icarian heaven." Those who knew Considerant vaunted his gentleness, kindness, and persistent enthusiasm. How-

446

ever, in celebrating him, the journalist warned, these people were making an "inoffensive little saint" out of "this patriarch of socialism, this precursor of Jules Guesde." The correct lesson to be drawn from Considerant's life was that "theorists of his sort innocently load arms that more militant individuals turn against society." Considerant's true colors were shown, the journalist concluded imaginatively, in June 1848, when, "under the pretext of conciliation," he "took the side of the insurgents against the army."[2]

On the other side of the ideological spectrum, the socialist Jean Allemane, founder of the Parti ouvrier socialiste révolutionnaire, described Considerant's long life as a standing reproach to a Third Republic that had "become as dissolute as a monarchy"—a republic whose leaders had "their snouts in the trough" and their ears attuned to "the insipid flattery" of the empire's former servants. Celebrating Considerant as a "brilliant" journalist and a "valiant champion of socialism," Allemane singled out for particular praise Considerant's conduct on the fateful *journée* of June 13, 1849. His reward for defending the constitution "against the cowardly repressors of the Assembly" was twenty years of exile. Nonetheless, his lifelong fidelity to his convictions made his life worth meditating upon in "a time of moral mud" and "fashionable servility" and failing republican institutions.[3]

If Considerant's obituary was sometimes written as a cautionary tale, more often he was treated simply as a "precursor"—a writer and activist whose labors under the July Monarchy and the Second Republic helped pave the way for socialism, democracy, or the women's suffrage movement. Thus while he had a place in the genealogy of socialism constructed in the late 1870s by the reformist socialist Benoît Malon, he was hailed by Marxists like Henri Brissac as a "great apostle" and "tireless fighter" for socialism who had offered an alternative to "the gangrened milieu" of the July Monarchy but who unfortunately never reached a correct understanding of the genesis, functioning, and imminent demise of capital.[4]

Considerant also figured, and continues to figure, in genealogies of republicanism and democratic socialism. As Michel Vernus has recently reminded us, the ideals of the republic and of socialism were inseparable for the mature Considerant. Through his steadfast advocacy of "peaceful democracy," Considerant played a role in acclimatizing in France "a democratic and republican system based on right and law." At the same time, writes Vernus, Considerant stands at the beginning of a long line of French democratic socialists running to Jaurès, Léon Blum, and Mitterrand. Although he dedicated *Destinée sociale* to Louis Philippe, Considerant played an important role in the creation of the *démoc-soc* movement of 1848–1849. And his final writings of 1870–1871 can be seen as part of a continuing effort to define the elements of a nonviolent, gradualist socialism based on respect for the autonomy of local groups and local government.[5]

The assessments of Considerant that appeared immediately after his death situated him within different contexts and genealogies, but almost everyone agreed in characterizing him as a relic of a bygone age—a quintessential "vieille barbe" of 1848. He had already been described in these terms over twenty years earlier on his return from America. This was also the language of a lengthy report on Considerant submitted for unknown reasons to the Paris prefect of police in 1876: "M. Considerant is a sincere enthusiast with too rich an imagination and with the ability to inspire people by his speech. He is one of the most original types of that generation of dreamers and utopians who made up the various socialist schools during the reign of Louis Philippe." Obituaries of Considerant in this vein came from a variety of sources. One of the most surprising may be found in a private letter written in 1894 by the pretender to the throne of France, Philippe, comte de Paris. In this letter to his friend Jules Marcou, the grandson of Louis Philippe described Considerant as

> a type that is absolutely lost today: the dreamer who believes it possible to reshape all of society solely by means of speech, by his reasoning, and by the example of his private virtues, who is almost indifferent to the political form of the government, and who rejects the use of force as a means of bringing about the triumph of his system. You don't meet people like that anymore. Above all you don't meet a man who is perfectly honorable and disinterested in private life, who will die poor after having devoted all his energies and all his intelligence to the realization of his visions.

Today, wrote the comte de Paris, personal ambition was the driving force in politics. Parties and ideologies were "springboards" for careerists, and the contrast between these people and Considerant was "sadly instructive."[6]

These images of Considerant as a "type" or representative of a bygone age—a man of uncommon private virtue and "too rich an imagination," a dreamer who thought that good arguments were all it would take to transform society—have endured. He has gone down in history as a kind of generous Don Quixote of early socialism—a dreamer with a naive faith in people's ability to live for each other and a man whose private virtues were evidence of the sincerity, if not the wisdom, of his convictions. The picture is not an unattractive one. Yet if one looks at Considerant's life and writing with an unsentimental eye, one sees a record that is mixed at best. One sees two significant achievements, but also two huge failures.

Considerant's achievements can be briefly summarized. He did more, first of all, than any other individual to put Fourier's ideas (or a somewhat muted version of them) on the map of nineteenth-century social and intellectual history. Hubert Bourgin's verdict of almost a century ago can still stand. Considerant's *Destinée sociale* was the first exposition of Fourierism that was relatively widely read, and in his subsequent writings Considerant consolidated his position as Fourier's most influential interpreter. Most historians today would dispute Bourgin's claims concerning the fidelity or even the adequacy of Considerant's rendering of Fourier's ideas. However, there is no denying that Considerant's efforts, both as a writer and as a political activist, gave Fourier an influence in the 1840s that he would not otherwise have had.

Considerant's second and greater achievement was to play a major role in the creation of what came to be known as "socialism." As a politically engaged journalist, and as the author of the *Manifeste de la Démocratie pacifique* and *Le Socialisme devant le vieux monde*, Considerant made a contribution to the development of socialist ideology that this book has attempted to characterize. As a political activist and organizer he also participated in the creation of an organization—including a shareholding company, a publishing house, a speakers' bureau, and one of the first socialist daily newspapers—that anticipated, and in some respects influenced, the development of socialist party organizations of the late nineteenth century.

Along with these achievements, however, Considerant's career was tarnished by two great failures. The first was the role that he played in the *journée* of June 13, 1849. Here his failure was one of leadership: he was unable to act decisively when the peaceful demonstration he had helped plan threatened to assume a violent character. Once Ledru-Rollin had publicly threatened to use force, if necessary, to protest the French military intervention in Rome, the government had the pretext it needed to crush the "insurrection" and to decimate the leadership of the left. In retrospect it seems clear (as things usually do in retrospect) that after Ledru-Rollin's speech, Considerant would have been well advised either to withdraw from the leadership of the demonstration or to insist that all the representatives remain in the National Assembly while the demonstration was being organized. If he did neither, it was because he did not wish to abandon his friends and allies. The consequences of his inaction were disastrous, though, both for himself and for his friends and followers.

Considerant's second great failure came in Texas in 1855. Here again the main problem was a failure of leadership, a failure to act decisively when his plans began to go awry. To begin with, he did not supervise closely enough the process by which the first groups of emigrants to Texas were selected. When too many came too soon, he should have either sent them back or at least made some effort to halt the departures. Instead, paralyzed by despondency, he retreated to his hammock. For six months after his arrival at Reunion he did not send a single letter to the directors in Paris. A year later, when his belated efforts to take control of the situation were frustrated, he simply abandoned the community, destroying whatever was left of his influence and credibility as a leader.

So Victor Considerant's career was punctuated by two spectacular reverses. The first brought an end to his public career in France when he was only forty-one years old. The second terminated his role as leader of the Fourierist movement. These were not, of course, merely personal failures. In both cases Considerant took others down with him. In the first case, the responsibilities were shared: many others, notably Ledru-Rollin, were also to blame for the debacle of June 13, 1849. In the second case, that of Texas, Considerant's personal responsibility was clear. In a broader sense, however, both of Considerant's failures were part of a shared experience. For a whole generation of republicans and romantic socialists, the defeats of 1848 to 1851 served to shatter the hope that the world might be remade through politics, that the coming of democracy would lead to a new age of individual regeneration and social harmony. Considerant had shared this hope, and for him both the crushing of the June 13 demonstration and the failure of the community at Reunion were heavy blows from which he never fully recovered.

How did Considerant respond to the collapse of his dreams and of the whole democratic and socialist left after 1848? He did not, like Louis Blanc, devote himself to endlessly replaying the events of 1848, trying to explain where things had gone wrong and why. Nor did he follow the ebullient, resourceful, immensely energetic Proudhon in pursuing new lines of inquiry and trying to adapt himself rapidly to a changed world. Rather, like many of his other contemporaries, he fell silent. This man who had lived by and through his pen for twenty years virtually stopped publishing for the fifteen years that followed the appearance of the second edition of *Au Texas*. For a decade, as he struggled to make a living in Texas, he hardly touched pen to paper. Then, toward the end of the Civil War, having reestablished contact with Europe, he began to write again. But from the late 1860s on almost everything he wrote took a new form: the letter.

Over the years, several of Considerant's friends and acquaintances noted in him a particularly strong need to address himself in writing or in speaking to a responsive and sympathetic audience. He was not one who thrived on argument and confrontation; when speaking in public before a hostile audience, or when surrounded by cool and indifferent people, he became tongue-tied and inarticulate. When he could sense the interest and sympathy of an audience, though, he was capable of rising to heights of eloquence.[7]

Considerant had such an audience in the 1830s and 1840s. In his articles in *La Phalange* and *Démocratie pacifique*, as in his lectures in Brussels, Strasbourg, and Geneva, he expressed himself fluently and articulately, confident of his ability to persuade his audience and to stir its emotions.

After 1848 Considerant lost his audience. The lecture tours were over, and so was the natural and easy rapport between the journalist and his readers. *Le Socialisme devant le vieux monde*, written in the fall of 1848 and published just after the election of Louis-Napoleon Bonaparte as president of the Second Republic, was the last work in which such a rapport existed. During the next few years almost everything that Considerant wrote consisted of "reports" not intended for general circulation but aimed explicitly at the narrower circle of friends of the Fourierist movement. Significantly, when he began writing again, after the long silence of the late 1850s and the early 1860s, most of what he wrote took the form of letters. Some of these letters were a hundred pages long. Most of them were addressed to individuals—Bazaine and Juárez, Maximilian and Napoleon III, Trochu and Bismarck, Renan, Darwin, and U. S. Grant. Some were addressed to groups—the Government of National Defense of 1870, and the admiring Marseille "Phalansterians" of 1880. In all of these letters, Considerant knew exactly whom he was addressing, and his writing was generally an attempt to persuade a specific reader by establishing common ground.

This effort to establish common ground, to speak to shared concerns and elicit a general good, was, of course, just what had characterized Considerant's popularizations of Fourier and his other writings on social questions during the July Monarchy. It was, more broadly, what had characterized the work of many of his contemporaries in the early socialist movement. After June 1848 and December 1851, however, common ground was hard to find. Thus, like many of his contemporaries, Considerant fell silent. In the long twilight of his career, no longer confident of his ability to establish any kind of rapport with a general audience, he limited himself to efforts to reach individuals. On the few occasions when he did write for a general audience in 1870 and 1871, he chose, not surprisingly, to identify himself as a complete outsider: "Victor Considerant, visionnaire et citoyen américain."

What about the content, rather than the form, of Considerant's later writing? Did he break new ground in any of these last works? Or did he only succeed in reiterating familiar themes? In the writings on America and Mexico, he certainly addressed a number of new problems, such as the question of peonage and the role of the history of labor in the larger scheme of human history. His critique of Tocqueville and his letters to Renan represented a genuine effort to keep up to date, and he was obviously intrigued by the challenge of working out a scientific understanding of human history on the basis of the new science of evolutionary biology. Significantly, however, he never came close to finishing his response to *Démocratie en Amérique* or his proposed treatise on history and evolution. All he left was fragments.

In his writings of 1870 and 1871, Considerant had some new ideas about direct democracy and a possible federalist restructuring of European politics. In his very last writings he was also blunt about the limitations of Fourier's thought in a scientific age. Still, all things considered, one is struck by how much Considerant repeated himself as he grew older. The central theme in his later writings—the contrast between the old warlike Europe of kings and emperors and the emerging world of work and productivity— had been a vital part of his intellectual baggage ever since the 1840s. In the end, it would seem that Considerant, like most of the rest of us, was intellectually very much a creature of the years in which he reached maturity. His final musings are fragmentary and inconsistent, but the general impression they convey is that, despite his belief in Progress, he was indeed out of place in the "senile" old age of the nineteenth century, with its "bland" positivism, "pitiful" literary naturalism, and "anemic and empty" parliamentary groups. For all his efforts to keep up to date, he was and remained a humanitarian idealist and a romantic socialist of the 1840s.

ABBREVIATIONS

ADL   Archives du départment de la Loire (Saint-Etienne)

AGR MJ PE   Archives Générales du Royaume (Bruxelles). Ministère de la Justice. Police des Etrangers.

AMG AAC   Archives du Ministère de la Guerre (Vincennes). Archives administratives. Célébrités.

AN   Archives Nationales (Paris)

APP   Archives de la Préfecture de Police de la Seine

BHVP   Bibliothèque Historique de la Ville de Paris

BMB   Bibliothèque Municipale de Besançon

BMS   Bibliothèque Municipale de Salins

BN NAF   Bibliothèque Nationale (Paris). Nouvelles Acquisitions Françaises

BP   *Bulletin phalanstérien* (1846–1850)

BSCEAT   *Bulletin de la Société de Colonisation Européo-Américaine au Texas* (1860–1875)

CF   Charles Fourier

CV   Clarisse Vigoureux

DP   *La Démocratie pacifique* (1843–1851)

DS	*Destinée sociale*, 3 vols. (Paris, 1834–1844).
ENS AVC	Ecole Normale Supérieure. Archives Victor Considerant.
IFHS	Institut Français d'Histoire Sociale (Paris)
JC	Julie Considerant (née Vigoureux)
PhJ	*La Phalange. Journal de la science sociale* (1836–1843)
PhR	*La Phalange. Revue de la science sociale* (1845–1849)
PS	*Principes du socialisme. Manifeste de la démocratie au XIXe siècle* (Paris, 1847).
RI	*La Réforme industrielle ou le Phalanstère* (1832–1834)
RSA	Russian State Archives of Social-Political History (Moscow)
SVM	*Le Socialisme devant le vieux monde* (Paris, 1848)
VC	Victor Considerant

NOTES

1. Benoît Malon, *Histoire du socialisme depuis ses origines probables jusqu'à nos jours* (Lugano, 1879).

2. Pierre Leroux, *La Grève de Samarez*, 2 vols. (Paris, 1863), 1: 255. Leroux's article "De l'individualisme et du socialisme," *Revue encyclopédique*, 60 (October 1833), 94–117, was actually published only in mid-1834. In reprinting this text in 1845, Leroux noted that he had initially distanced himself from socialism and that he had "always opposed absolute socialism." During the early 1840s, he added, the term had taken on a broader sense that he could identify himself with: "For a few years now people have gotten used to calling 'socialist' all thinkers interested in social reforms, all those who criticize and reject individualism, all those who speak under different terms of social providence, of the solidarity that joins together not only the members of a state but the whole human race" (*La Revue sociale* 1, no. 2 [November 1845], 19–22). Among those who used the term *socialiste* prior to Pierre Leroux was the Fourierist Charles Pellarin in *RI*, 15 (April 12, 1833), 174. See Jacques Gans, "L'Origine du mot 'socialiste' et ses emplois les plus anciens," *Revue d'histoire économique et sociale*, 30 (1957), 79–83.

3. The characterization of French romantic socialism offered here is based primarily on my own study of and reflection upon the primary sources. Secondary works that I have found particularly helpful include Alexandrian, *Le Socialisme romantique* (Paris, 1979); Paul Bénichou, *Le Temps des prophètes. Doctrines de l'âge romantique* (Paris, 1977); David O. Evans, *Le Socialisme*

romantique. Pierre Leroux et ses contemporains (Paris, 1948); Maxime Leroy, *Histoire des idées sociales en France*, 3 vols. (Paris, 1947–1954); and Auguste Viatte, *Les Sources occultes du romantisme*, 2 vols. (Paris, 1928). I have found all of Paul Bénichou's work on the history of French romanticism immensely stimulating.

4. Alphonse de Lamartine, "Des Destinées de la poèsie" (1834), in Gustave Lanson (ed.), *Méditations poétiques*, 2 vols. (Paris, 1915), 2: 422.

5. The blending of science and religion was one of the great themes in Victor Considerant's 1848 writings. In *Le Socialisme devant le vieux monde*, for example, he could refer to Christianity as "the good socialism that is at once scientific and evangelical," adding, "this time, science enlightening sentiment, we shall have the New Heavens and the New Earth" (*SVM*, 198). On this issue, see Gareth Stedman Jones, "Utopian Socialism Reconsidered: Science and Religion in the Early Socialist Movement," unpublished paper, especially p. 15.

6. Given this view of the origins of socialism, I find it misleading to argue, as some do, that early French socialism had "its roots in the revolution of 1789" and that "its moral precepts were those of the Revolution, liberty, equality and fraternity." Paul Corcoran, *Before Marx: Socialism and Communism in France, 1830–48* (London, 1983), 1. The Chapelier Law banning workers' associations was the direct outcome of 1789; the two major early French socialists, Saint-Simon and Fourier, were no friends of equality, and their understanding of liberty was very different from that of the French revolutionaries.

7. Louis Reybaud, cited by Jean Bruhat, in Jacques Droz (ed.), *Histoire générale du socialisme* (Paris, 1972), 1: 511; Malon, *Histoire du socialisme*, 241, 249.

8. Alexandre Erdan, *La France mistique. Tableau des eccentricités religieuses de ce temps*, 2 vols. (Paris, 1855). On the *vieilles barbes* of 1848, see Maurice Agulhon, *Les Quarante-huitards* (Paris, 1975), 10–11; and Auguste Vermorel, *Les Hommes de quarante-huit* (Paris, 1869).

9. Friedrich Engels, *Socialism: Utopian and Scientific*, in Robert C. Tucker (ed.), *The Marx-Engels Reader*, 2nd ed. (New York, 1978), 687–690.

10. Karl Marx and Friedrich Engels, *Manifesto of the Communist Party*, in Tucker, *Marx-Engels Reader*, 499.

11. G. D. H. Cole, *A History of Socialist Thought*, 5 vols. (New York, 1967), 1: 68; George Lichtheim, *The Origins of Socialism* (New York, 1969), 32, vii.

12. Stedman Jones, "Utopian Socialism Reconsidered," 3–4.

13. VC, *DS*, 2: lxxvii.

14. Jules Michelet, *Histoire de France*, Préface de 1869.

CHAPTER 1

1. Three outstanding works of erudition that have greatly helped me to understand the milieu out of which Victor Considerant came are Michel Vernus, *La Vie comtoise au temps de l'ancien régime (XVIIIe siècle)*, 2 vols. (Lons-le-Saunier, 1983–1985); Eldon Kaye, *Les Correspondants de Charles Weiss*

(Longueuil, Quebec, 1987); and Marcel Vogne, *La Presse périodique en Franche-Comté des origines à 1870*, 7 vols. (Besançon, 1977–1979). Each of these works offers much more than the title suggests. See also Lucien Febvre, *Histoire de Franche-Comté* (Paris, 1930).

2. Gaston Coindre, *Le Vieux Salins. Promenades et causeries* (Besançon, 1912); Just Tripard, *Notices sur la ville et les communes du canton de Salins, suivies de biographies salinoises* (Paris, 1881), 251–266; Max Buchon, "Le Matachin," *Revue des deux mondes*, 2nd ser. (June 15, 1854).

3. Michel Vernus, "Un libraire jurassien à la fin de l'ancien régime. Jean-Claude Considerant, marchand libraire à Salins (1782)," in *Société d'émulation du Jura. Travaux présentés . . . en 1979 et 1980* (Lons-le-Saunier, 1981), 133–167; Georges Gazier, "Jean-Baptiste Considerant de Salins (1771–1827)," *Mémoires de la société d'émulation du Doubs*, 8th ser., 3 (1908), 359–380.

4. Jean-Claude Dubos, "Les Origines de Victor Considerant et de son épouse Julie Vigoureux," unpublished paper; Archives Nationales (AN), Fonds Considerant, 10AS 29 (3), "Correspondance de famille."

5. VC to Paul Vigoureux, March 24, 1826, AN 10AS 28 (6).

6. "Correspondance de famille," AN 10AS 29 (3).

7. Jean-Baptiste Considerant to Suzanne Considerant, 27 fructidor [1798], AN 10AS 29 (3).

8. Gazier, "Jean-Baptiste Considerant"; Kaye, *Les Correspondants de Charles Weiss*, 138–140; Tripard, *Notices sur la ville de Salins*, 553–554; Emile Fourquet, *Les Hommes célèbres et les personnalités marquantes de Franche-Comté* (Besançon, 1921), 293; *Les Tablettes franc-comtoises*, 1, no. 22 (May 6, 1827).

9. Gazier, "Jean-Baptiste Considerant," 363–364.

10. Charles Weiss, *Journal*, edited by Suzanne Lepin, 4 vols. (Paris, 1972–1997), 2: 103; Charles Nodier, J. Taylor, and Alphonse de Cailleux, *Voyages pittoresques et romantiques dans l'ancienne France. Franche-Comté* (Paris, 1825 [sic for 1827]), 164.

11. Weiss, *Journal*, 2: 103; Nodier, *Voyages pittoresques*, 164. See also VC to CV, "dimanche soir" [1825], Bibliothèque Municipale de Besançon (BMB) Ms Z464.

12. Jean-Baptiste Considerant to Suzanne Considerant, February 25, 1829, AN 10AS 29 (3).

13. Jean-Baptiste Considerant to Victor Thelmier, May 17, 1814, Archives Municipales de Besançon (AMB) Ms 1419P no. 17, also in Gazier, "Jean-Baptiste Considerant," 380.

14. Jean-Baptiste Considerant to Victor Thelmier, November 27, 1824, AMB Ms. 1419P, no. 112; Pierre Haubtmann, *Pierre-Joseph Proudhon. Sa vie et sa pensée (1809–1849)* (Paris, 1982), 67–69; VC, *Destinée sociale* (DS) (Paris, 1838), 2: lv–lvi. See also Gaston Bordet's excellent *La Grande Mission de Besançon: janvier–février 1825* (Paris, 1998).

15. Clarisse Coignet, *Victor Considerant. Sa vie et son oeuvre* (Paris, 1895), 2.

16. VC to Victor Thelmier, May 31, 1828, in Emile Ledoux, "Victor Considerant. Trois lettres inédites. Notes sur sa jeunesse," *Mémoires de la société d'émulation du Doubs*, 8th ser., 3 (1908), 386; VC, DS, 2: 275.

17. Ledoux, "Victor Considerant," 383n.; E. Delacroix, "Notice sur M. Delly, Professeur de mathématiques spéciales à Besançon," *Mémoires et comptes rendus de la Société d'émulation du Doubs*, 1(1841), 68–69.

18. Ledoux, "Victor Considerant," 383n. VC to Jenny Delacroix, January 23, 1878, collection of Robert Guillaume, copy kindly provided by Jean-Claude Dubos.

19. Alphonse Tamisier to VC, May 24, 1878, AN 10AS 42 (2). Another student at the Collège royale de Besançon at this time, just one year behind Considerant, was his future antagonist, Pierre-Joseph Proudhon. According to Proudhon, they had no contact. See J.-A. Langlois (ed.), *Correspondance de P.-J. Proudhon*, 14 vols. (Paris, 1875), 2: 23.

20. My account of Clarisse Vigoureux's discovery of Fourier is based largely on an untitled twenty-one-page manuscript in her hand in the Archives Victor Considerant (AVC) at the Ecole Normale Supérieure (ENS), carton 9 (I, 1). For a thoughtful and well-informed biographical essay on Clarisse Vigoureux, see Jean-Claude Dubos's preface to his edition of CV, *Parole de Providence* (Seyssel, 1993), 7–90. The complicated financial affairs of Joseph Gauthier, leading to his ruin and that of Clarisse Vigoureux in 1840, are masterfully untangled in Jean-Claude Dubos, "Une famille de maîtres de forges: les Gauthier," *Bulletin de la Société d'Agriculture, Lettres, Sciences et Arts de la Haute-Saône*, new ser., 17 (1984), 61–114. See also Janine Joliot, "Clarisse Coignet, cousine des Considerant. Une adolescence fouriériste," *Académie des sciences, belles-lettres et arts de Besançon. Procès-verbaux et mémoires*, 185 (1982–1983), 253–274.

21. CV, untitled manuscript on Fourier, ENS AVC carton 9 (I, 1).

22. VC, quoted in Just Muiron to CV, May 15, 1852, ENS AVC carton 3 (XI, 1). For Considerant's letters to Clarisse Vigoureux, see AN 10AS 28 (6) and (7), and ENS AVC carton 2 (I, 4 and 5).

23. Clarisse Coignet, *Mémoires*, 4 vols. (Lausanne, 1899–1903), 1: 114, 237–238; Joliot, "Clarisse Coignet," 258–259; VC, "Un Pressentiment," *Revue des deux mondes* (October 1831), reprinted in *Cahiers Charles Fourier*, 7 (1996), 7–13. The story does not identify the characters except to say that the young man is seventeen years old and preparing for the Ecole Polytechnique and the young woman, who is sixteen, is the wife of his uncle. Jean-Claude Dubos argues convincingly that in its broad outlines the story is a "barely disguised autobiography in which Considerant revealed . . . one of the most painful episodes of his youth." Jean-Claude Dubos, "Victor Considerant nouvelliste: 'Un pressentiment' (1831)," *Cahiers Charles Fourier*, 7 (1996), 15–20.

24. Gazier, "Jean-Baptiste Considerant," 376–379; Kaye, *Les Correspondants de Charles Weiss*, 139–140.

25. VC to CV, March 22, 1826, AN 10AS 28 (6).

26. For the orations delivered at Jean-Baptiste Considerant's funeral by

Father Racle and Dr. Broye, see AN 10AS 29 (3), and *Les Tablettes franc-comtoises,* 1, no. 22 (May 6, 1827).

27. On the Ecole Polytechnique, see Gaston Pinet, *Histoire de l'Ecole Poly-technique* (Paris, 1887); Gaston Pinet, *Ecrivains et penseurs polytechniciens* (Paris, 1902); *Ecole Polytechnique. Livre du Centenaire, 1794–1894,* 3 vols. (Paris, 1895); and Terry Shinn, *L'Ecole Polytechnique, 1794–1914. Savoir scientifique et pouvoir social* (Paris, 1980).

28. In addition to the works cited above, see Adeline Daumard, "Les Elèves de l'Ecole Polytechnique de 1815 à 1848," *Revue d'histoire moderne et contemporaine,* 5 (1958), 226–234.

29. VC to Thelmier, May 31, 1828, in Ledoux, "Victor Considerant," 386.

30. VC to CV, January 20, 1828, AN 10AS 28 (6). Claire Vigoureux died at the age of seventeen on January 15, 1827, just a year before this letter was written. In 1838 Considerant was to marry her younger sister Julie. Copies of Claire's birth and death certificates were carefully preserved among Considerant's papers until his death. AN 10AS 29 (1).

31. VC to CV, January 2, 1827, BMB Ms Z 464. Considerant does not say, but quite likely it was from Clarisse Vigoureux that he borrowed the money he needed to attend Polytechnique.

32. Pierre Chalmin. *L'Officier français de 1815 à 1870* (Paris, 1957), 170; VC to Charles Magnin, n.d. [1828], Bibliothèque Municipale de Salins (BMS); VC to Thelmier, May 31, 1828, in Ledoux, "Victor Considerant," 386.

33. VC to CV, July 15 [1828], ENS AVC carton 2 (I, 4).

34. François-Augustin Gréa, a lawyer, was mentioned in 1806 in a list of "the sixty proprietors of the Jura most distinguished by their wealth and by their public and private virtues," cited in Jean-Claude Dubos, "Les Origines de Victor Considerant." On Desiré-Adrien Gréa, see Jonathan Beecher, *Charles Fourier: The Visionary and His World* (Berkeley, 1968), 163–164, 381–382, 464, and *passim.*

35. On Emmanuel Jobez and his family, see Christiane Claerr-Roussel et al., *Les Forges de Syam (Jura)* (Paris, 1996), 3–10. On Considerant's relations with Jobez and Gréa, see VC to CV, June 1828 and July 15 [1828], ENS AVC carton 2 (I, 4). On July 15 Considerant wrote: "My free days are just as pleasant as they could be. Very often I go to visit your deputy [Jobez] and his family. I am treated like a nephew there." See also Jean-Luc Mayaud, *Les Patrons du Second Empire. Franche-Comté* (Paris, 1991), 130–136, for a rich and well-informed article on Alphonse Jobez (the son of Emmanuel) and his role in the establishment of "un fouriérisme de notables" in Franche-Comté during the July Monarchy. On Gréa's offer to subsidize Victor's education, see Jean-Baptiste Considerant to Gréa, August 18, 1825, declining the offer. Collection of Henri de Boissieu (Rotalier). My thanks to M. de Boissieu and to Jean-Claude Dubos for making a copy of this letter available to me.

36. VC to CV, July 15 [1828], ENS AVC carton 2 (I, 4). On the Nodiers and their Sunday evenings at the Bibliothèque de l'Arsenal, see Michel Salomon, *Charles Nodier et le groupe romantique* (Paris, 1908), 116–224.

37. On Charles Magnin, see Kaye, *Les Correspondants de Charles Weiss*, 298–301, and Jean-Jacques Goblot, *La Jeune France libérale. Le Globe et son groupe littéraire* (Paris, 1995), 53, 531–534, 580, and *passim*. Magnin's papers at the Bibliothèque Municipale de Salins include eleven letters from Considerant written between 1827 and 1851.

38. VC to Magnin, August 20, 1829, BMS. On Considerant's relations with Bugeaud and Soult, see his file at the Archives du Ministère de la Guerre at Vincennes, Archives administratives, Célébrités (AMG AAC), especially VC to Soult, May 5, 1832, and Bugeaud to Marshal Maison, September 14, 1835. See also letters of Bugeaud to VC, AN 10AS 36 (12).

39. F. A. Hayek, *The Counter-Revolution of Science* (Glencoe, Ill., 1952), 105–116.

40. Considerant graduated sixty-ninth in a class of 123. At the end of his first year his rank was fifty-seventh out of 127. Ledoux, "Victor Considerant," 385.

41. VC to Thelmier, February 21, 1830, in Ledoux, "Victor Considerant," 388. On the Ecole d'application de Metz, see Frederick B. Artz, *The Development of Technical Education in France, 1500–1850* (Cambridge, Mass., 1966), 259–261.

42. *Daniel Tyler: A Memorial Volume* (New Haven, 1883), 10–11. VC to Paul Vigoureux, September 28, 1829, AN 10AS 28 (6).

43. VC to CV, January 26 or 27, 1829, ENS AVC carton 2 (I, 5); VC to Thelmier, February 21, 1830, in Ledoux, "Victor Considerant," 388.

44. VC to Thelmier, February 21, 1830, in Ledoux, "Victor Considerant," 389; VC to CV, February 8, 1830, in Nicolas Marsollier, "Victor Considerant dans les débuts de l'Ecole Sociétaire à travers quelques lettres inédites," Mémoire de maîtrise d'Histoire et de lettres modernes, Université d'Angers (1991), 87, 226; VC to Magnin, August 20, 1829, BMS.

45. VC to Magnin, February 6, 1830, BMS; VC to CV, May 3, 1830, and June 11, 1830, AN 10AS 28 (7).

46. Henry Contamine, "La Révolution de 1830 à Metz," in Comité français des sciences historiques, *1830: Etudes sur les mouvements liberaux et nationaux de 1830* (Paris, 1932), 55–63; VC to CV, August 3, 1830, and August 4, 1830, AN 10AS 28 (7).

47. VC to CV, August 13, 1830, and October 7, 1830, in Marsollier, "Victor Considerant," 230–236; VC to Marshal [Soult?], draft, September 30, 1830, AN 10AS 28 (7).

48. VC to CV, October 7, 1830, and December 10, 1830, BMB Ms Z463; VC to Magnin, February 9, 1831 [not 1830], BMS. On Fourier's lecture, see Beecher, *Charles Fourier*, 407–408.

49. VC to Julie Vigoureux, May 1, 1832, ENS AVC carton 9 (III, 1); VC to CV, February 15, 1831, ENS AVC carton 2 (I, 5).

50. VC to Thelmier, December 14, 1831 [not 1832], in Ledoux, "Victor Considerant," 390. On the Association Nationale, see Gabriel Perreux, *La Propagande républicaine au début de la Monarchie de Juillet* (Paris, 1930), 5–6;

and Paul Thureau-Dangin, *Histoire de la Monarchie de Juillet*, vol. 1 (Paris, 1888), 415–416.

51. The Institut Barbet, which was founded in 1825, later became one of the most famous Parisian preparatory schools for students seeking to enter the *grandes écoles*, such as Polytechnique and the Ecole Normale Supérieure. On its founder, Jean-François Barbet (1799–1880), see the *Dictionnaire de biographie française*, vol. 5 (Paris, 1951), 278–279, and Richard Moreau, "Jules Marcou (1814–1898)," in *Procès-verbaux et mémoires de l'Académie de Besançon*, 190 (1992–1993), 163–167. Although Considerant's stint as a teacher at Barbet's institute was brief, the two remained in touch for almost fifty years. Considerant's papers include a letter of condolences for his wife's death written in a quavering hand on April 10, 1880, and signed "ton vieil ami Barbet," AN 10AS 29 (1). See also Ledoux, "Victor Considerant," 390n., and Sébastien Bottin (ed.), *Almanach du commerce de Paris . . . 1829* (Paris, 1829), 139–140.

52. VC to Thelmier, December 14, 1831, in Ledoux, "Victor Considerant, 390–391.

53. Antoine Fontaney, *Journal intime*, edited by René Jasinski (Paris, 1925), 4–5 (August 21, 1831); VC to CV, September 11, 1831, AN 10AS 28 (7); Fonds "phalanstérien" d'André Morlon, Bibliothèque Municipale de Nevers, Ms 1364, in Guy Thuiller, *Les Manuscrits et les dessins de la Bibliothèque de Nevers* (Nevers, 1992), 126; Henri Delprat to VC, August 6, 1836, AN 10AS 37 (7).

54. VC, "Un Pressentiment." This story is not mentioned by any of Considerant's biographers, and I have not found any reference to it in his papers. It was discovered by Jean-Claude Dubos, who republished it, with an introduction, in the *Cahiers Charles Fourier*, 7 (1996), 7–20. For the description of "Un Pressentiment" as a "charming" story, see Fontaney, *Journal Intime*, 61 (October 28, 1831).

55. Corps royale du génie, Rapport particulier sur M. Considerant, Metz, September 10, 1831, signed Cournault, Colonel du régiment; note added by a general: "This officer is returning from leave in connection with the Associations. He shows little zeal in his activities." AMG AAC, Dossier VC.

CHAPTER 2

1. Beecher, *Charles Fourier*, 71–72.

2. Charles Fourier (CF), *Oeuvres complètes*, 12 vols. (Paris, 1966–1968), 6: 47. See also Beecher, *Charles Fourier*, 220–240.

3. CF, "Lettre au Grand Juge," published by Jean-Jacques Hémardinquer in *Le Mouvement social*, 48 (July–September 1964), 60. See also Beecher, *Charles Fourier*, 55, 65–67.

4. CF, *Oeuvres complètes*, 7: 432–435.

5. CF, *Oeuvres complètes*, 6: 206–214.

6. Virtomnius [Just Muiron], *Les Nouvelles transactions sociales, religieuses et scientifiques* (Paris, 1832), 146–150.

7. CV, untitled manuscript, 21 pp., ENS AVC carton 9 (I, 1). See also Beecher, *Charles Fourier*, 158–163.

8. VC to Paul Vigoureux, May 24, 1826, 13 pp., AN 10AS 28 (6).

9. VC to Magnin, August 20, 1829, 8 pp., BMS.

10. Jules Lechevalier, *Etudes sur la science sociale* (Paris, 1834), 15. VC to CV, July 15 [1828], ENS AVC carton 2 (I, 4).

11. VC to Deleuze, December 18, 1826, in *Les Annales franc-comtoises*, new ser., 7 (1895), 363. On Considerant's interest in Owen, see the large envelope of reading notes on works by and about Owen in AN 10AS 26 (29). See also VC to Magnin, August 20, 1829, p. 2, BMS. On the Saint-Simonians, see VC to CF, September 7, 1831, ENS AVC carton 2 (I, 5).

12. Comte LeCamus, *Mémoires du vicomte Armand de Melun*, 2 vols. (Paris, 1891), 1: 48. VC to CF, September 7, 1831, AN 10AS 28 (7).

13. VC, "Le Nouveau monde industriel et sociétaire de M. Charles Fourier," *Le Mercure de France au XIXe siècle*, 28 (March 13, 1830), 477–490.

14. CF to the editors of the *Mercure de France*, December 20, 1831, draft, AN 10AS 16 (42).

15. VC to CV, August 7, 1831, BMB Ms Z464.

16. VC to CF, September 7, 1831, AN 10AS 25 (3bis); VC to CV, September 11, 1831, AN 10AS 28 (7); VC to CF, September 24, 1831, ENS AVC carton 2 (II, 2).

17. VC to CV, November 13, 1831, AN 10AS 28 (7). On the Saint-Simonians, see Sébastien Charléty, *Histoire du Saint-Simonisme* (Paris, 1931); Robert B. Carlisle, *The Proffered Crown: Saint-Simonianism and the Doctrine of Hope* (Baltimore, 1987); and Henry-René d'Allemagne, *Les Saint-Simoniens, 1827–1837* (Paris, 1930).

18. Charles Pellarin, *Notice sur Jules Lechevalier et Abel Transon* (Paris, 1877); Henri Louvancour, *De Henri Saint-Simon à Charles Fourier. Etude sur le socialisme romantique français de 1830* (Chartres, 1913).

19. VC to CV, September 11 and November 13, 1831, February 27, 1832, AN 10AS 28 (7); VC to CV, December 3, 1831, BMB Ms Z463; VC to CF, December 7, 1831, and January 5, 1832, AN 10AS 25 (3bis); VC to CV, December 15, 1831, BMB Ms Z417; VC to [?], February 10 [1832], BMB Ms Z417; VC to Paul Vigoureux, March 24, 1832, BMB Ms Z417.

20. VC to CF, January 5, 1832, 10AS 25 (3bis); Beecher, *Charles Fourier*, 419, 433.

21. VC to Julie [Vigoureux], May 1, 1832, ENS AVC carton 9 (III, 1); VC to Paul Vigoureux, March 24, 1832, BMB Ms Z417; VC, *DS*, 1: 465; VC to Marshal [Soult], May 5, 1832, AMG AAC, Dossier VC. Considerant's dossier at the AMG also includes endorsements of his request by General Pajol and Marshal Soult.

22. *La Réforme industrielle ou le Phalanstère* (*RI*), 1, no. 1 (June 1, 1832), 2.

23. VC to CV, June 18, 1832, BMB Ms Z417; VC to CV, July 4, 1832, BMB Ms Z463.

24. VC to Marshal Soult [July 1832], in *RI*, 1, no. 10 (August 2, 1832), 84–86. VC to Lechevalier, July 19, 1832, AN 10AS 28 (7).

25. *RI*, 1, no. 6 (July 5, 1832), 55; "Conçernant l'administration du journal *Le Phalanstère*," AN 10AS 25 (12). See also Beecher, *Charles Fourier*, 435.

26. Lemoyne to Transon, March 16, 1833, AN 10AS 39 (10).

27. VC to CV, September 27, 1832, BMB Ms Z463.

28. Anonymous letter [signed "J . . ."] to CF, July 24, 1833, AN 10AS 40 (5); VC to Gréa, October 10, 1833, AN 10AS 28 (7).

29. *RI*, 1, no. 1 (June 1, 1832), 7; *RI*, 1, no. 8 (July 19, 1832), 69; *RI*, 1, no. 15 (September 7, 1832), 132.

30. VC to CV, November 23, 1832, AN 10AS 28 (7). See also VC to CV, September 27, 1832, BMB Ms Z463.

31. CV to CF, December 3, 1832, AN 10AS 25 (3bis).

32. CF, "Les Alliés dangereux," *RI*, 2, no. 13 (March 29, 1833), 149.

33. VC to CV, August 15, 1833, AN 10AS 28 (7). See also VC to CV, August 12, 1833, BMB Ms Z464.

34. VC to Julie [Vigoureux], May 1, 1832, ENS AVC, carton 9 (III, 1).

35. VC to CV, September 27, 1832, BMB Ms Z463. VC to Devay, October 13, 1832, Archives of La Colonie, Condé-sur-Vesgre. On the "Societary Colony" of Condé-sur-Vesgre, see Gabriel Vauthier, "Un Essai de Phalanstère à Condé-sur-Vesgre," *La Révolution de 1848*, 21 (February 1925), 327–344, and 22 (April 1925), 417–432; Desroche, *La Société festive*, 220–235; and Beecher, *Charles Fourier*, 454–471.

36. *RI*, 1, nos. 25 and 26 (November 15 and 22, 1832). Italics added.

37. *RI*, 1, no. 26 (November 22, 1832), 217.

38. VC to CV, September 27, 1832, BMB Ms Z463; VC to CV, November 23, 1832, AN 10AS 28 (7).

39. *RI*, 1, no. 29 (December 13, 1832), 245, and 2, no. 1 (January 4, 1833), 3.

40. *RI*, 1, no. 30 (December 20, 1832), 254.

41. *RI*, 2, no. 12 (March 22, 1833), 143–144; *RI*, 2, no. 11 (March 15, 1833), 132.

42. Baudet-Dulary to Devay, "Confidential," February 7, 1833, Archives de la Colonie, Condé-sur-Vesgre; accounts for the Société de Fondation, AN 10AS 19 (2).

43. *RI*, 2, no. 22 (May 31, 1833), 264; "Acte de Société de la Colonie Sociétaire de Condé-sur-Vesgre," *RI*, 2, no. 24 (June 14, 1833), 277–280; CF to Muiron, March 9, May 2, and July 10, 1833, in Charles Pellarin, *Charles Fourier, sa vie et sa théorie*, 2nd ed. (Paris, 1843), 244–245.

44. *RI*, 2, no. 29 (July 19, 1833), 333; Fugère to VC, May 27, 1836, AN 10AS 38 (7); VC to Pellarin, July 18, 1833, AN 10AS 28 (7). On the general gloom at Condé, see also Vinçard aîné, *Mémoires épisodiques d'un vieux chansonnier saint-simonien* (Paris, 1878), 158–160.

45. Baudet-Dulary, "Rapport à l'assemblée générale de la Colonie sociétaire

de Condé-sur-Vesgre, September 22, 1833," *RI*, 2, no. 36 (November 13, 1833), 396.

46. VC to CV, August 12, 1833, BMB Ms Z464; CF in *RI*, 2, no. 33 (August 16, 1833), 372; VC to CV, August 15, 1833, AN 10AS 28 (7).

47. Baudet-Dulary, in *RI*, 2, no. 36 (November 16, 1833), 396.

48. Baudet-Dulary to shareholders in the Colonie sociétaire, April 15, 1836, AN 10AS 31 (1).

CHAPTER 3

1. VC to Gréa, October 10, 1833, AN 10AS 28 (7).

2. VC to Gréa, October 10, 1833, AN 10AS 28 (7).

3. VC to Gréa, October 10, 1833, AN 10AS 28 (7), is the source of all quotes in the preceding five paragraphs.

4. VC to Gréa, October 10, 1833, AN 10AS 28 (7). On Lydie Vassal Roger, see her correspondence with Fourier, AN 10AS 25 (3), and see the fascinating account of her spiritual peregrinations in "Mémoires inédits d'Hippolyte Auger (1810–1869)," in *Revue retrospective*, 13 (July–December, 1890), esp. 166–178, and 14 (January–June, 1890), esp. 140–144, 171–172.

5. VC to CV, October 28, 1833, AN 10AS 28 (7).

6. VC to CV, December 17, 1833, BMB Ms Z463. See also Charles Pellarin to CV [December 12, 1833], BMB Ms Z464. For lengthy *comptes rendus* of Considerant's lectures, see *L'Impartial* (Besançon) (December 6, 9, 13, 14, and 15, 1833).

7. Just Muiron to CV, December 27, 1833, AN 10AS 40 (5). See also Charles Weiss, *Journal*, ed. Suzanne Lepin (Paris, 1991), 17.

8. VC to CV, December 30, 1833, AN 10AS 28 (7).

9. VC to CV, March 4, 1834, AN 10AS 28 (7).

10. VC to CV, April 6 and May 1, 1834, AN 10AS 28 (7).

11. VC, "Plan d'attaque. Tableau des journaux, 1ère Division. *Destinée sociale*," ENS AVC carton 8 (I, 2). For the list of subscribers and the distribution of copies, I am grateful to Jean-Claude Dubos for providing me with a copy of a document from the Sainte-Agathe family archives: "Etat des 300 premiers exemplaires de *Destinée sociale* laissés par Victor Considerant, le 27 octobre, 1834."

12. On the sales of *Destinée sociale*, the editors of *La Phalange* noted that eight hundred copies were sold or distributed prior to the publication of volume 2 in 1838, *PhJ*, 2nd ser., 1, 866. This was a respectable figure, although Dommanget exaggerates in describing it as "remarkable" for a theoretical work. Maurice Dommanget, *Victor Considerant, sa vie, son oeuvre* (Paris, 1929), 17. For Considerant's response to the "vieux tonnerre enrhumé" of Pope Gregory XVI, see *PhJ*, 2nd ser., 1, no. 13 (November 10, 1836).

13. Weiss, *Journal*, 3: 67 (entry for September 28, 1834). Among the pre-publication subscribers to *Destinée sociale* were former Minister of Justice Joseph Courvoisier, future deputies Auguste Demesmay and Auguste Parandier, future mayor of Besançon Léon Brétillot, postal inspector Raymond de Ray-

mond, banker Alfred Marquiset, as well as various painters, professors, and businessmen. "Etat des 300 premiers exemplaires de *DS*," Sainte-Agathe family archives. Interestingly, Pellarin described Parandier as an "absurd and nitpicking" critic of Considerant's lectures the previous December. See Pellarin to CV [December 12, 1833], BMB Ms Z464.

14. VC to CV, September 10, 1835, BMB Ms Z463.

15. Considerant's dossier at the Archives du Ministère de la Guerre at Vincennes includes an unsigned memorandum dated November 18 [1835] arranging a conversation on his case between General Schramm and Marshal Maison and adding: "Not very long ago the marshal extended the furlough of M. Considerant against the opinion of the bureau. This furlough will now last until April 1, 1836." See also Bugeaud to Maison, September 14, 1835, as quoted in chapter 8, note 26, of this volume, and VC to Maison, September 22, 1835, both in AMG AAC, Dossier VC.

16. AMG AAC, Dossier VC. Considerant's resignation was finally and formally accepted August 16, 1836.

17. VC to CV, April 6, 1834, and March 4, 1836, AN 10AS 28 (7); Tamisier to VC, August 5, 1836, AN 10AS 40 (2); Muiron to VC, March 9, 1836, and Muiron to CV, February 25, 1836, and March 17 [1836], AN 10AS 40 (5).

18. Muiron to CV, March 17 [1836], AN 10AS 40 (5).

19. VC, "Discours prononcé au Congrès historique, le 11 décembre, 1835," in Charles Dain, VC, and Eugène d'Izalguier, *Trois discours prononcés à l'Hôtel de Ville* (Paris, 1836), 51.

20. VC, *Trois discours*, 48.

21. VC, *Trois discours*, 83, 159.

22. VC, *Trois discours*, 90.

23. *L'Univers religieux* (December 12, 1835), cited in *Trois discours*, 149; letters of Muiron to CV, December 27, 1835, January 6, 11, and 24, 1836, AN 10AS 40 (5); drafts of CF to *Gazette de France*, December 1835, AN 10AS 19 (3), and AN 10AS 20 (7).

24. VC to CF [December 1835], ENS AVC carton 2 (II, 1); Edmond Vidal to VC [1837], AN 10AS 42 (7); Hugon Roydor, August 27, 1837, in *Correspondance harmonienne*, 2 (September 1, 1837), 12.

25. VC to Prefect of Police [March 18, 1836], ENS AVC carton 4 (VI).

26. VC, *Débâcle de la politique en France* (Paris, 1836). Most of the copies of the first edition had been burned in a warehouse fire not long after publication.

27. Muiron to CV, December 27, 1833, AN 10AS 40 (5). See also Muiron to CV, October 30, 1834, February 8, 1835, and January 24, 1836, AN 10AS 40 (5).

28. Muiron to CV, February 8 and 22, 1835, AN 10AS 40 (5).

29. Muiron to VC, February 28, 1836, AN 10AS 40 (5); Muiron to CV, September 25, 1836, AN 10AS 40 (5), including a "Tableau de tous ceux auxquels l'envoi du projet d'union a été fait"; Muiron to CF, July 24, 1836, AN 10AS 40 (5).

30. CF to Muiron, draft, August 26, 1836, AN 10AS 16 (42). For Conside-

rant's response, see Muiron to VC, August 14, 1836, AN 10AS 40 (5). VC to CV, August 3, 1836, AN 10AS 28 (7).

31. Muiron to VC, August 14, 1836, AN 10AS 40 (5).

32. VC to Muiron (and also Pellarin and Hippolyte Renaud) [late August 1836]. This letter is signed by Eugène d'Izalguier, Charles Dain, and Amédée Paget as well as Considerant. It is docketed by Muiron "received at Besançon September 2, 1836," AN 10AS 28 (4).

33. CV to Muiron, draft [August 1836], ENS AVC carton 9 (I, 1).

34. Muiron to CV, September 25, 1836, AN 10AS 40 (5). Gagneur to VC, August 13, 1836, AN 10AS 38 (9).

35. Brac de La Perrière, Morellet, and Reydor to VC, September 10, 1836, AN 10AS 41 (11).

36. VC to JM, undated draft [September 1836], AN 10AS 28 (4). "Projet de circulaire" in Muiron's hand, October 10, 1836, and Muiron to VC, July 12, 1837, AN 10AS 40 (5). Emile Poulat, "Sur deux textes manuscrits de Fourier," in Henri Desroche et al., *Etudes sur la tradition française de l'association ouvrière* (Paris, 1956), 10–11.

37. VC, *Débâcle de la politique*, 79.

38. Muiron to VC, March 9, 1836, AN 10AS 40 (5). For the contribution of Clarisse Vigoureux, see VC to Jaenger, September 20, 1838, BN NAF 22,050, and VC to Frédéric Dorian, February 15 and March 13, 1836, Archives du département de la Loire (ADL) 1 J 771. Muiron got loans of 8,500 francs from Mlle. Appoline Bruand and 5,000 francs from a Mlle. Ducreux. See Muiron to CV, September 25, 1836, AN 10AS 40 (5). Mlle. Bruand, the sister of Muiron's deceased colleague, the subprefect Joseph Bruand, had previously provided loans necessary for the publication of Fourier's *Traité d'association domestique-agricole* (1822) and his *Nouveau monde industriel* (1829).

39. VC, "Déclaration," *PhJ*, 1, no. 1 (July 10, 1836), col. 10; Jaenger to VC, July 28, 1836, AN 10AS 39 (4); Pouliguen to VC, October 14 and September 15, 1836, AN 10AS 41 (8); Prévost to VC, October 14, 1836, AN 10AS 41 (9); Renaud to VC, August 11, 1836, AN 10AS 42 (15).

40. VC to CV, October 6, 1836, AN 10AS 28 (7).

41. VC to de Molien, August 5, 1836, Bibliothèque Nationale, Nouvelles Acquisitions Françaises (BN NAF) 1302. *Lettre confidentielle aux membres de la réunion du 31 juillet* (Paris, August 1837), 14–15. Copy of this brochure in ENS AVC carton 11 (II).

42. VC, "A Nos Amis des départements," *PhJ*, 1, no. 5 (August 20, 1836).

43. VC, "Appel pour la réalisation de la théorie sociétaire," *PhJ*, 1, no. 30 (July, 1837), 972–976. Livre de comptes: crédit de 10,000 francs, ENS AVC carton 2 (V, 1). Muiron to Jaenger, March 25, 1845, BN NAF 22,050; Muiron to VC, July 12, 1837, AN 10AS 40 (5); Lacoste to VC, July 14, 1837, AN 10AS 39 (7); Emile Poulat, "Ecritures et traditions fouriéristes," *Revue internationale de philosophie*, 16, no. 60 (1962), 225; Poulat, "Sur deux textes," 11–12.

44. Constantin Prévost, "Lettre aux partisans de la théorie de Ch. Fourier,"

June 8, 1837, AN 10AS 36 (9), in Poulat, "Sur deux textes," 12. See also Prévost to VC, October 14, 1836, AN 10AS 41 (9).

45. *Aux Phalanstériens. La Commission préparatoire de l'Institut Sociétaire* (Paris, August, 1837), Institut Français d'Histoire Sociale (IFHS) 14AS 6–8, pp. 2–8. See also Muiron to CV, August 15, 1837, AN 10AS 40 (5).

46. VC, Supplément to *PhJ*, 1, no. 30 (July, 1830), IFHS 14AS 6–8; Poulat, "Sur deux textes," 11–12.

47. Poulat, "Sur deux textes," 13; *Aux Phalanstériens. Compte rendu de la Réunion du 31 juillet*, 23. For Fourier's criticism of Prévost's letter, see AN 10AS 12 (8), and *Lettre confidentielle aux membres de la réunion du 31 juillet*, 20–23.

48. *Aux Phalanstériens, Compte rendu de la Réunion du 31 juillet*, 23–29.

49. *Aux Phalanstériens, Compte rendu de la Réunion du 31 juillet*, 27–28.

50. For Fourier's complete text, see AN 10AS 22 (1), published in Poulat, "Sur deux textes," 14–15.

51. *Lettre confidentielle aux membres de la réunion du 31 juillet en réponse à une brochure intitulée "Aux Phalanstériens,"* 5–6, ENS AVC carton 11 (II).

52. Pellarin, *Fourier*, 285–291.

53. In 1829, Fourier wrote Muiron of his intention to leave his manuscripts to him. In the spring of 1837, when it became apparent that Fourier did not have much longer to live, Clarisse Vigoureux got him to sign a statement (written in her hand) renewing his bequest to Muiron. Then, after Fourier's death, Muiron signed documents sharing his right of ownership with Considerant and Madame Vigoureux. For a clear and careful account of these events, emphasizing the manipulation of Fourier by his disciples, see Pierre Mercklé, "Le Testament perdu de Fourier," *Cahiers Charles Fourier*, 6 (1995), 31–45.

54. Complaints about Catholic burial cited in Poulat, "Ecritures," 229; letters of Pouliguen and Benoît to Fourier, cited in Bourgin, *Victor Considerant*, 42; quote from letter to VC signed by Blanc, Barbier, Bing, Chapelain, and Michelot, AN 10AS 30 (1), cited in Poulat, "Deux textes," 17.

55. Edouard Ordinaire, "A M. Victor Considerant et aux partisans de l'Ecole Sociétaire," April 1, 1838, cited in Poulat, "Deux textes," 17; Jaenger to VC, October 15, 1837, AN 10AS 39 (4).

56. Scarpédon [pseudonym of J.-J. Reverchon], letter of January 2, 1840, published in *Correspondance harmonienne*, 31 (February 2, 1840), cited in Desroche, *La Société festive*, 249. On the later history of the Fourierist dissidence, see Poulat, "Ecritures," 221–233.

57. Edouard Ordinaire to VC, January 21, 1844, in Desroche, *La Société festive*, 250.

CHAPTER 4

1. Contrat de mariage, Victor Considerant and Julie Vigoureux, registered by Fourchy, notaire à Paris, February 16, 1838, AN 10AS 29 (1). The specification that the dowry was not to become joint property was included at Victor's

insistence. The marriage contract also stipulated that in five years he was to receive twenty thousand francs from his mother-in-law. Owing to the bankruptcy of Julie's uncle, this sum was never paid.

2. VC to Jaenger, September 20, 1838, BN NAF 22,050.

3. VC to Jaenger, September 20, 1838, BN NAF 22,050.

4. Clarisse Coignet, *Mémoires*, 4 vols. (Lausanne, 1899–1903), 1: 237.

5. Coignet, *Mémoires*, 2: 51–56.

6. Charles A. Dana, *The Harbinger*, 8 (November 4, 1848), 5. I am grateful to Carl Guarneri for sending me a copy of this article.

7. Coignet, *Mémoires*, 2: 27–33. Clarisse Coignet, *née* Gauthier (1823–1918), was the daughter of Julie Considerant's uncle, Joseph Gauthier. After her father's bankruptcy in 1840, she found work as a teacher in England and converted to Protestantism. In 1850 she married François Coignet, a manufacturer of Fourierist sympathies. In later life she collaborated on several important journals (*La Morale indépendante, La Revue bleue*), was a leading advocate of a secular educational system, and wrote numerous works on education and on the history of French Protestantism. Her *Mémoires*, published privately in four volumes, are a wonderful source for the history of Fourierism, the republican opposition to Napoleon III, and the role played by the French Protestant elite in the campaign for a secular educational system. See the excellent article by Janine Joliot, "Clarisse Coignet, cousine des Considerant. Une adolescence fouriériste," *Académie des sciences, belles-lettres et arts de Besançon. Procès verbaux et mémoires*, 185 (1982–1983), 253–274.

8. Coignet, *Mémoires*, 2: 30–31.

9. VC to Allyre Bureau, June 12, 1852, ENS AVC carton 8 (II, 1). Muiron's natural daughter, Rosa, married Hippolyte Becquet on April 21, 1852. See François Lassus, "Introduction," in Jean-François Muiron, *Le Paillard septuagénaire, ou Chansons sur ma vie* (Paris, 1988), 49.

10. François Cantagrel, dedication to *Le Fou du Palais Royal* (Paris, 1841); Désiré Laverdant, *Socialisme catholique. La déroute des Césars* (Paris, 1851), introduction; Gabrielle Rey, *Le Fouriériste Allyre Bureau (1810–1859)* (Aix-en-Provence, 1962).

11. VC to CV, June 9, 1828, ENS AVC carton 2 (I, 4); Jules Benoît to VC, February 7, 1838, AN 10AS 36 (4); Désirée Veret, veuve Gay, to VC, 1890–1891, AN 10AS 42 (8).

12. Marie Mennessier-Nodier, *Charles Nodier. Episodes et souvenirs de sa vie* (Paris, 1867), 306; Michel Salomon, *Charles Nodier et le groupe romantique* (Paris, 1908), 202–203; Antoine Fontaney, *Journal intime*, edited by René Jasinski (Paris, 1925), 4–5 (August 21, 1831); VC to CV, September 11, 1831, AN 10AS 28 (7); P. de Lallemand, *Montalembert et ses amis dans le romantisme* (Paris, 1927), 275–276; Alexandre Dumas, *Mes Mémoires* (Paris, 1986), 779–780; Jacques Van der Linden, *Alphonse Esquiros. De la Bohème romantique à la république sociale* (Paris, 1948), 124–125.

13. Madame [Virginie] Ancelot, *Les salons de Paris. Foyers éteints* (Paris, 1858), 130–132, 134, and *Un Salon de Paris de 1824 à 1864* (Paris, 1866), 100,

108; Honoré de Balzac, *Correspondance*, 5 vols. (Paris, 1960–1969), 4: 178–179, 192–193, 195–198, 636–640, 645–647, including letters from VC to Balzac of September 14, 1840, and December 27, 1843; Camillo Cavour, *Diari (1833–1856),* edited by Alfonso Bogge, 2 vols. (Rome, 1991), 1: 630. My thanks to Marc Vuilleumier for this reference.

14. Gérard de Nerval, "Les Prophètes rouges," *L'Almanach cabalistique pour 1850, Oeuvres de Gérard de Nerval,* vol. 2 (Paris: Bibliothèque de la Pléiade, 1961), 1226. See also Claude Pichois and Michel Brix, *Gérard de Nerval* (Paris, 1995), 102, 248–249; and F. J. Fornasiero, "'La Treizième revient': la passion 'grandiose et pivotale' de Fourier dans *Les Chimères* de Gérard de Nerval," *Cahiers Charles Fourier,* 7 (1996), 21–36.

15. Edgard Pich, *Leconte de Lisle et sa création poétique* (Lyon, 1975), 51. On Leconte de Lisle's early Fourierism, see Pich, *Leconte de Lisle,* 34–53, and Jean-Paul Sartre, *The Family Idiot,* translated by Carol Cosman, vol. 5 (Chicago, 1993), 321–328, 362.

16. William Fortescue, *Alphonse de Lamartine: A Political Biography* (London, 1983), 112–116; Lamartine to VC, June 24, 1843, AN 10AS 39 (7), and VC to Lamartine, June 12, 1842, in private collection, and June 12, 1843, in V. de Lamartine (ed.), *Lettres à Lamartine* (Paris, 1892), 201–202; Beth Archer Brombert, *Cristina: Portrait of a Princess* (New York, 1977), 65, 75, 95; letters exchanged by VC and Cristina Belgiojoso, AN 10AS 28 (8), 10AS 29 (2), and 10AS 36 (4); Roger Pierrot, *Honoré de Balzac* (Paris, 1994), 402.

17. Coignet, *Mémoires,* 2: 32–33.

18. In the vast literature on manic-depressive disorders I have found the following to be particularly helpful: Frederic K. Goodwin and Kay Redfield Jamison, *Manic-Depressive Illness* (New York, 1990); and Kay Redfield Jamison, *Touched with Fire: Manic-Depressive Illness and the Artistic Temperament* (Toronto, 1993).

19. Coignet, *Mémoires,* 1: 114–115; and Coignet, *Vie de Considerant,* 26.

20. Coignet, *Mémoires,* 1: 114.

21. Coignet, *Mémoires,* 1: 61. On Joseph and Virginie Gauthier, see Coignet, *Mémoires,* 1: 31–70, and Joliot, "Clarisse Coignet," 254–264.

22. VC to CV, "mardi au soir" and "mercredi" [October 1–2, 1828], AN 10AS 28 (6).

23. Justine Demesmay to JC, collection of about 160 letters, mostly undated but dating from 1820s to 1870s, AN 10AS 37 (8). Aimée Beuque to JC, August 10, 1854, AN 10AS 36 (5); Marie Mennessier-Nodier to JC, three letters, AN 10AS 41 (1); Coignet, *Mémoires,* 1: 242.

24. VC to his sisters, June 9, 1839, AN 10AS 28 (7); JC to VC [1842], ENS AVC carton 13 (II, 8).

25. VC to JC, July 24, 1858, AN 10AS 28 (9); letters of Christine Evers (*née* Bruck) to VC and JC, 1878–1880, AN 10AS 38 (6), and BMB Z418; Jean-Claude Dubos, "Préface" to CV, *Parole de Providence,* 77, 90. See also letter to JC from "your dear little friend Ida," March 6, 1872, AN 10AS 42 (15).

26. VC to Eugène Bourson, September 29, 1854, in Louis Pierard and Marc-

Antoine Pierson, *Belgique, terre d'exil* (Brussels, n.d.), 36–37; Marie Mennessier-Nodier to JC, March 26, 1842, AN 10AS 41 (1).

27. JC to VC, August 16, 1842, AN 10AS 42 (10).

28. Jules Marcou, "Notice biographique sur Victor-Prosper Considerant," *Le Salinois*, 5 (February 4, 1894).

29. "Arrogant posturing": Baudet-Dulary, letter of September 8, 1837, in *Correspondance harmonienne*, 3 (October 1, 1837). Financial problems: VC to Jaenger, September 20, 1838, BN NAF 22,050.

30. VC to Jaenger, September 20, 1838, BN NAF 22,050. In fact, neither Victor nor Julie Considerant received any part of her dowry. Clarisse Vigoureux's fortune vanished in 1840 with the bankruptcy of her brother, Joseph Gauthier.

31. Sherman Kent, *Electoral Procedure under Louis Philippe* (New Haven, 1937), 26; Christopher Johnson, *Utopian Communism in France: Cabet and the Icarians, 1839–1851* (Ithaca, 1974), 30; Justine Pallas to VC, April 8, 1842, AN 10AS 42 (15); VC to Frédéric Dorian, February 7, 1839, ADL 1 J771; Auguste Bouchot to VC [1839], AN 10AS 36 (8).

32. Just Muiron to VC, March 9, 1836, AN 10AS 40 (5); Paul Vigoureux to VC, August 17, 1836, AN 10AS 42 (11); VC to Frédéric Dorian, February 7, 1839, ADL 1 J771.

33. On elections under the July Monarchy, Kent, *Electoral Procedure*, is reliable but narrowly institutional. I have learned much about the way elections were actually run from André-Jean Tudesq, *Les Grands Notables en France (1840–1849)*, 2 vols. (Paris, 1964), 2: 853–895 and *passim*, and from two great unfinished novels: Stendhal, *Lucien Leuwen* (1834–1835), and Honoré de Balzac, *Le Député d'Arcis* (1842–1843). Balzac's novel, published in part in 1847 as *L'Election*, dealt with the election campaign of 1839.

34. H. A. C. Collingham, *The July Monarchy: A Political History of France, 1830–1848* (London, 1988), 212–217; *Journal des débats*, March 1, 1839, cited in Collingham, *July Monarchy*, 216.

35. Collingham, *July Monarchy*, 215–216.

36. VC, "La Paix ou la guerre. A la France et aux électeurs," *PhJ*, 2nd ser., 2, no. 28 (February 15, 1839), 449–464.

37. "Candidature de M. Considerant à la députation," *PhJ*, 2nd ser., 2, no. 28 (February 15, 1839), 404; Jaenger to VC, February 9, 1839, and February 12, 1839, AN 10AS 39 (4); VC, "Intelligence et bonne foi de certains journaux," *PhJ*, 2nd ser., 2, no. 29–30 (March 24, 1839), 496–499; *Le National* (February 7, 1839).

38. Letters of VC and Charles Pellarin to Frédéric Dorian, February 1839, ADL 1 J778; Muiron to Frédéric Dorian, February 23, 1839, ADL 1 J779; VC, *"A MM. les électeurs du collège de Montbéliard"* (February 27, 1839); Weiss, *Journal*, 4: 70; VC to JC, March 1, 1839, BMB Ms Z417.

39. VC to JC and CV, March 3, 1839, BMB Ms Z417. See also VC to JC, March 2, 1839, BMB Ms Z417.

40. Justine Demesmay to JC, March 26, 1839, AN 10AS 37 (8); VC to JC and CV, March 3, 1839, BMB Ms Z417.

41. Obituary of Joseph Gauthier, probably by Just Muiron, *L'Impartial de Besançon* (September 24, 1847); Dubos, "Une Famille de maîtres de forge," 61–114; Joliot, "Clarisse Coignet," 254; Coignet, *Mémoires*, 1: 25–36, 2: 5–6.

42. Paul Vigoureux to VC, October 6, 1881, AN 10AS 42 (11); Dubos, "Une Famille de maîtres de forges," 86–103. Arthur Louis Dunham, *The Industrial Revolution in France, 1815–1848* (New York, 1955), 85–91, 119–149, still provides a useful introduction to the history of the French iron industry during the July Monarchy. But see also Bertrand Gille, *La Sidérurgie française au XIXe siècle* (Geneva, 1968), as well as the more specialized studies by Jean Girardot, *L'Industrie du fer en Franche-Comté* (Besançon, 1962); Gabriel Pelletier, *Les Forges de Fraisans. La Métallurgie comtoise à travers les siècles* (Dole, 1980); and Christiane Claerr-Roussel et al., *Les Forges de Syam (Jura)* (Paris, 1996).

43. Paul Vigoureux to VC, October 6, 1881, AN 10AS 42 (11); Dubos, "Une Famille de maîtres de forge," 86–91, 96–99.

44. Dubos, "Une Famille de maîtres de forges," 89–91; VC to M. Rigaud, draft, November 7, 1840, AN 10AS 28 (7).

45. Dubos, "Une Famille de maîtres de forges," 91–92; VC to JC and CV [December 18, 1840], AN 10AS 28 (7); VC to JC, December 19 and 27, 1840, BMB Ms Z417. VC to JC, December 21 [1840], BMB Ms 464.

46. Dubos, "Une Famille de maîtres de forges," 92–93; Justine Demesmay to JC, January 16, 1841, AN 10AS 37 (8); VC to General Boileau, Commander of the Ecole Polytechnique, draft, n.d., AN 10AS 28 (8); VC to General [?], draft, n.d., ENS AVC carton 2 (I, 12); Coignet, *Mémoires*, 2: 52.

47. Coignet, *Mémoires*, 2: 53; Dubos, "Une Famille de maîtres de forges," 99; Joliot, "Clarisse Coignet," 266–267. For Paul Vigoureux's endless complaints, see his letters to VC in AN 10AS 42 (11), and see Janine Joliot, "Un Salon républicain sous l'Empire et les débuts de la Troisième République," *Procès verbaux et mémoires de l'Académie de Besançon*, 186 (1984–1985), 72–76.

48. Gabriel Vauthier, "Arthur Young et la Colonie sociétaire de Cîteaux, 1841–1844," *La Révolution de 1848*, 23 (1926), 771–780; letters of VC to Young, AN 10AS 28 (8); letters of Young to VC and others, AN 10AS 42 (13). For Young's "subscription" of 350,000 francs, see Young to VC, December 27, 1841, AN 10AS 42 (13).

49. Young to VC, November 23, 1841, AN 10AS 42 (13); Bourgin, *Fourier*, 483; *Acte de Société pour la propagation et la réalisation de la théorie sociétaire* (June 15, 1840), i–xxi; "Système des développements de l'Ecole sociétaire," *La Phalange. Revue de la science sociale* (PhR), 1 (1845), xxx.

CHAPTER 5

1. Claude Bellenger, et al. (eds.), *Histoire générale de la presse française*, 4 vols. (Paris, 1969), 2: 120. On French journalism during the July Monarchy,

see Bellenger, 2: 91–146, 173–203, and Charles Ledré, *La Presse à l'assaut de la monarchie, 1815–1848* (Paris, 1960). Tudesq, *Les Grands Notables en France,* includes a mine of information on many of the aspects of the culture and politics of the July Monarchy considered in this chapter.

2. VC to CV, October 6, 1836, AN 10AS 28 (7); Bourgin, *Victor Considerant,* 73; *Appel aux lecteurs de la Phalange* (Paris, March 17, 1843), 5.

3. *PhJ,* 3ʳᵈ ser., 1, no. 1 (September 2, 1840), 3.

4. *Appel aux lecteurs de la Phalange,* 14; *Démocratie pacifique (DP),* 1, no. 1 (August 1, 1843), 7. According to Ledré, *La Presse,* 244, the circulation of *DP* in 1845 was 2,247. Using the same sources (the AN's monthly records of the number of copies submitted for the *timbre*), Bellenger, *Histoire générale,* 2: 146, gives the figure of 1,665 copies as the average press run for 1846. The circulation of *DP* was thus about half that of the republican *National* or Cabet's *Le Populaire* and roughly comparable to that of the democratic *Réforme.*

5. VC, "Justification des horreurs de la guerre d'Afrique!!" *DP,* 5, nos. 22, 24 (July 22 and 24, 1845); "L'Agitation," *DP,* 6, no. 69 (March 10, 1846); "Sursum corde," *DP,* 6, no. 70 (March 11, 1846); "Seul moyen de salut de la cause polonaise," *DP,* 6, no. 75 (March 16, 1846); "Pourquoi nous défendons l'Irlande et O'Connell," *DP,* 1, nos. 84, 87 (October 23, 26, 1843).

6. Collingham, *July Monarchy,* 169–185; Ledré, *La Presse,* 170–195, 244; Fortescue, *Lamartine,* 118.

7. *Statuts de la Société pour la transformation de la Phalange en journal quotidien* (Paris [1843]), 8, article 2, cited in Bourgin, *Considerant,* 75.

8. *Bulletin phalanstérien (BP),* 2 (September 14, 1846), 10, 14–15. Of the 250,000 francs in costs for 1845, 58,000 went for paper and printing, 48,000 for the salaries of writers, editors, and an office staff of ten, and 33,000 francs for the purchase of feuilletons, stock market reports, and transcripts of parliamentary debates. Other expenses included 27,000 francs for mailing and 41,000 francs for the government *timbre.*

9. *BP,* 1 (July 1846), 3, and 2 (September 14, 1846), 19. "*La Démocratie pacifique* à la presse," *DP,* 6, no. 81 (March 22, 1846).

10. "*La Démocratie pacifique* à la presse," *DP,* 6, no. 81 (March 22, 1846); "Ecole Sociétaire. Situation de la rente de l'Ecole et de la Librairie phalanstérienne," *DP,* 7, no. 152 (December 27, 1846); *BP,* 2 (September 14, 1846), 13, and *BP,* 4 (June 25, 1847), 54.

11. VC, report to the General Assembly of July 12, 1846, *BP,* 2 (September 14, 1846), 16. "Système des développements de l'Ecole sociétaire," *PhR,* 1 (1845), xliii.

12. Jules Duval, "Progrès de la cause sociétaire en 1846," *DP,* 6, no. 11 (January 11, 1846).

13. *Catalogue raisonné de la Librairie Sociétaire* (Paris, 1845); Michel Vernus, *Victor Considerant, 1808–1893. Le Coeur et la raison* (Dole, France, 1993), 115–123.

14. "Ecole Sociétaire. Situation de la rente de l'Ecole et de la Librairie phalanstérienne," *DP,* 7, no. 152 (December 27, 1846); *BP,* 4 (June 25, 1847), 63.

15. Coignet, *Victor Considerant*, 31; "Banquet anniversaire de la naissance de Fourier," *DP*, 8, no. 84 (April 8, 1847); "Statistique des banquets phalanstériens," *DP*, 8, no. 129 (May 30, 1847).

16. Marcou, "Notice biographique," *Le Salinois* (February 4, 1894).

17. Coignet, *Mémoires*, 2: 51.

18. The Hôtel Mailly-Nesles, with entrances at both 2, rue de Beaune, and 29, quai Voltaire, was a building rich in literary associations. Marie d'Agoult had lived there a few years earlier; Voltaire had died just next door in 1778; and Alfred de Musset's residence in the 1840s was two doors down at 25, quai Voltaire. *Guide littéraire de la France* (Paris, 1964), 11–12.

19. Charles Dana [Letter from Paris], July 12, 1848, in *The Harbinger*, 7, no. 14 (August 5, 1848), 109. My thanks to Carl Guarneri for sending me copies of this article and of the letter cited in note 20.

20. James T. Fisher to John S. Dwight, August 9, 1849, Dwight Brook Farm Papers, Boston Public Library, Ms. E.4.1. no. 69. Margaret Fuller to W. H. Channing, May 7, 1847, in Robert N. Hudspeth (ed.), *The Letters of Margaret Fuller* (Ithaca, 1987), 271.

21. Considerant's speaking tours were given extensive coverage in *La Phalange* and, under the rubric "Mouvement phalanstérien," in *Démocratie pacifique*. I am most grateful to Marc Vuilleumier for sending me substantial notes and copies of archival material concerning Considerant's lectures and travels in Switzerland. On Considerant's Swiss tours, see also James Guillaume, *L'Internationale. Documents et souvenirs (1864–1878)*, vol. 1 (Paris, 1903), 90; and Marc Vuilleumier, "Weitling, les Communistes allemands et leurs adeptes en Suisse. Quelques documents (1843–1847)," *Cahiers Vilfredo Pareto. Revue européenne des sciences sociales*, 11, no. 29 (1973), esp. 56–58, 96–100.

22. *Journal de Lille*, cited in *DP*, 7, no. 11 (July 12, 1846).

23. Vuilleumier, "Weitling en Suisse," 56–58, 96–100.

24. "Expositions phalanstériennes. A Lausanne—M. Considerant," *DP*, 7, no. 78 (October 2, 1846); Coignet, *Mémoires*, 2: 34; *Journal de Genève*, cited in *DP*, 7, no. 97 (October 24, 1846).

25. On Considerant's lectures at Brussels, see *DP*, 5, nos. 126, 131, 132, and 136 (November 3, 8, 9, and 13, 1845), and Ernest Discailles, "Le socialiste français Victor Considerant en Belgique," *Bulletin de l'Académie royale des sciences, des lettres et des beaux-arts de Belgique*, ser. 3, 29 (1895), 711–718.

26. For a brief overview of Belgian Fourierism, see John Bartier, "Le Socialisme utopique en Belgique de 1830 à 1848," in Maurice Agulhon et al., *1848. Les Utopismes sociaux* (Paris, 1981), 255–258. On Charles Rogier, see Ernest Discailles, *Charles Rogier (1800–1885) d'après des documents inédits*, 4 vols. (Brussels, 1893–1895); and Discailles, "Considerant en Belgique," 708–711. The Papiers Charles Rogier at the Archives Générales du Royaume (AGR) at Brussels include seven letters from Considerant to Rogier, 1839–1847. My thanks to Hans Moors for helping me come to an understanding of Rogier and nineteenth-century Belgian liberalism.

27. VC to Rogier, copy, June 6, 1850, AN 10AS 26 (10). See also VC to

Rogier, February 28, 1847, AGR Papiers Rogier, dr. 209, and see Considerant's praise of Rogier's role in the development of a national railroad system in Belgium: "Retards du gouvernement dans l'exécution des chemins de fer," *PhJ*, 3rd ser., 6, no. 30 (September 7, 1842), 491–492.

28. Ducpétiaux to VC, July 7, 1843, and September 21, 1843, AN 10AS 38 (2). The Ducpétiaux file at AN 10AS 38 (2) includes a dozen letters to Considerant and Cantagrel dating from 1841 to 1847. On Ducpétiaux, see Roger Aubert, "Ducpétiaux," in *Biographie nationale*, vol. 32, supp. 4 (Brussels, 1964), cols. 154–175; Félix Delhasse, "Ecrivains belges. M. Edouard Ducpétiaux," *Revue trimestrielle*, 7 (1855), 204–228; John Bartier, "Le Socialisme utopique," 255–256.

29. "Deuxième réunion des électeurs du 10e arrondissement," *PhJ*, 3rd ser., 6, no. 5 (July 10, 1842), 68–76; VC to Lamartine, June 12, 1842, asking for "un billet d'usage confidentielle" supporting him, private collection.

30. Désiré Laverdant to JC, July 10 [1842], BMB Ms Z418; VC to JC, July 14 [1842], BMB Ms Z417.

31. VC and Perreymond, "De l'unité administratif du département de la Seine," *DP*, 1, nos. 82, 103, 110 (October 21, November 11 and 18, 1843). On the electoral meetings, see *DP*, 1, no. 119 (November 27, 1843), and *Le Siècle*, 8, no. 324 (November 25, 1843). On the Conseil Général de la Seine, see Philippe Vigier, *Paris pendant la monarchie de juillet (1830–1848)* (Paris, 1991), 139–155.

32. *DP*, 1, no. 119 (November 27, 1843), summarizes journalistic comment about Considerant's candidacy. On the Legitimists' *politique du pire*, see Claude-Philibert Bartelot, comte de Rambuteau, *Mémoires* (Paris, 1905), 295. Election results in *DP*, 1, no. 121 (November 29, 1843).

33. Peaulejeune and Jules Benoît to VC, cited in Bourgin, *Victor Considerant*, 88. See also Lamartine to VC, December 9, 1843, AN 10AS 39 (7), and Muiron to VC, January 3, 1844, ENS AVC carton 13 (II, 2), and Rondel Van Davidson, *Did We Think Victory Great? The Life and Ideas of Victor Considerant* (Lanham, Md., 1988), 130.

34. Patricia O'Brien, "L'Embastillement de Paris: The Fortification of Paris during the July Monarchy," *French Historical Studies*, 9, no. 1 (Spring 1975), 63–82; VC, "Les Fortifications de Paris. La Question militaire et la question politique," *DP*, 2: no. 69 (March 9, 1844), and "Discussion sur les fortifications de Paris," *DP*, 2: no. 70 (March 10, 1844). See also *PhJ*, 3rd ser., 1, no. 7 (September 16, 1840), 121–124; and see VC's articles in *PhJ*, 3rd ser., 2: nos. 12, 13, 14 (January 27, 29, 31, 1841), and *DP*, 1, no. 56 (September 25, 1843), and *DP*, 4, nos. 72, 91, 125 (March 13, April 1, May 5, 1845).

35. VC, *Déraison et dangers de l'engouement pour les chemins de fer* (Paris, 1838), 7, 10. For an initial version of this pamphlet, see *PhJ*, 1st ser., 2: nos. 15 and 16 (August 1 and 15, 1838), 225–252. VC, "De la discussion des tracés des chemins de fer," *DP*, 2, no. 161 (June 9, 1844). This article, and its continuation in *DP*, 2, no. 162 (June 10, 1844), consists of excerpts from a report by VC to the Conseil Général. It was published separately as *Chemins de*

fer, ligne de Paris à Lyon et de Paris à Strasbourg. Rapport fait au Conseil municipal de Paris sur le tracé de Paris a Strasbourg (Paris, 1844). "Acts of extreme immorality . . ." is from VC, "Vendra-t-on la France?" *DP,* 2, no. 164 (June 12, 1844).

36. VC, "Vendra-t-on la France?" *DP,* II, no. 164 (June 12, 1844).

37. For a sampling, see Desroche, *Société festive,* 217–218, 236–240. For an excellent survey of the twenty-five Fourierist communal experiments initiated in North America during the same period, see Carl J. Guarneri, *The Utopian Alternative: Fourierism in Nineteenth-Century America* (Ithaca, 1991).

38. [VC], "Système des développements de l'Ecole sociétaire," *PhR,* 1 (1845), vii, viii, xv. See also VC to Young, draft, November 6, 1841, AN 10AS 28 (8).

39. Jules Duval, "Au docteur Charles Pellarin," *La Science sociale,* 2 (1869), cited in Desroche, *Société festive,* 250. See also Duval's letters of 1844 and 1845 to VC, criticizing the vagueness and the lack of practicality of the reforms proposed in *Démocratie pacifique,* AN 10AS 38 (5); and see Guy Thuillier. *La Bureaucratie en France au XIXe et XXe siècles* (Paris, 1987), 390–393.

40. Young to VC, cited in Bourgin, *Fourier,* 482.

41. Letters of VC to Young, AN 10AS 28 (8), and Young to VC, AN 10AS 42 (13). See also Bourgin, *Victor Considerant,* 61–62.

42. Gabriel Vauthier, "Arthur Young et la Colonie sociétaire de Cîteaux, 1841–1844," *La Révolution de 1848,* 23, no. 113 (December 1925), 771–780; Pierre Lévêque, *Une Société provinciale: La Bourgogne sous la monarchie de juillet* (Paris, 1983), 539–541; Patrick Henrard, "Du monastère au phalanstère: La Colonie sociétaire de Cîteaux (1841–1846)," unpublished paper (1994).

43. Arthur Young, sample membership form in the Association Domestique, Agricole et Industrielle de Chateaux-les-Cîteaux [1841], AN BB18 1399 (dr. 4092). This dossier at the Archives Nationales, consisting largely of correspondence between the ministers of justice and the interior, gives a fascinating picture of the (sometimes exaggerated) fears of authorities (both local and national) as Arthur Young's plans unraveled.

44. Drafts of about two dozen letters from VC to Young, March 1841–May 1842, AN 10AS 28 (8); *PhJ,* 3rd ser., 4, no. 48 (December 19, 1841), 783–784.

45. "Etat de la situation actuelle de l'établissement de Cîteaux," in Ministre de l'Intérieure to Garde des Sceaux, January 12, 1843, AN BB18 1399 (dr. 4092).

46. VC to *Spectateur de Dijon,* in *DP,* 6, no. 24 (January 24, 1846).

47. Fernand Rude, "Les Fouriéristes lyonnais et la colonisation de l'Algérie," *Cahiers d'histoire,* 1 (1956), 41–63; David Prochaska, "Fourierism and the Colonization of Algeria: L'Union Agricole d'Afrique, 1846–1853," *Proceedings of the First Annual Meeting of the Western Society for French History* (March 14–15, 1974), 283–302.

48. François Barrier, *Union agricole d'Afrique. Nouveau système de colonisation de l'Algérie* (Lyon, 1846), in Rude "Les Fouriéristes lyonnais," 56, 59.

49. For Lamoricière and Soult, see Rude, "Les Fouriéristes lyonnais," 60. Prosper Enfantin, "Nouvel essai de colonisation," *L'Algérie, courrier d'Afrique,*

d'Orient et de la Mediterranée, 3, no. 164 (April 22, 1846), in Rude, "Les Fouriéristes lyonnais," 61.

50. VC, "Le Principe sociétaire en Afrique," *DP,* 6, no. 140 (May 31, 1846). See also VC, "Le Principe sociétaire en Afrique," *DP,* 6, no. 133 (May 24, 1846).

CHAPTER 6

1. For *"socialistes,"* see VC, *DS,* 2 (1838), xxxix; VC, *Déraison et dangers de l'engouement pour les chemins de fer* (Paris, 1838), 7; and [VC] in *PhJ,* 3rd ser., 6, no. 118 (March 31, 1843), 1925. Considerant had his "Manifeste politique et social de la *Démocratie politique"* reprinted in 1847 as *Principes du socialisme. Manifeste de la démocratie au XIXe siècle.* Although before 1847 Considerant generally used the term *socialiste* to refer to the ideas of others, he was in 1842 sarcastically described by Proudhon as a "profound *socialiste"* who timidly practiced Fourier's principle of *"écart absolu."* Pierre-Joseph Proudhon, *Avertissement aux propriétaires* (Paris, 1938), 215.

2. VC, "Sur l'état actuel des esprits en France. Appel aux hommes sincères de tous les partis," *PhJ,* 1, no. 2 (July 20, 1836).

3. VC, *DS,* 1: 91.

4. VC, *DS,* 1: 78–83, 87.

5. VC, *DS,* 1: 89–90.

6. VC, *DS,* 1: 92.

7. VC, *DS,* 1: 57–61.

8. VC, *DS,* 1: 100–102.

9. VC, *DS,* 1: 408.

10. VC, *DS,* 1: 387, 423–424, and see 1: 134–136, 214, 430.

11. VC, *DS,* 1: 388, 389, and [VC], *Immoralité de la doctrine de Fourier* (Paris [1841]), 24–29.

12. VC, *DS,* 1: 458–462, and VC, *Description du Phalanstère et considérations sociales sur l'architectonique* (Paris, 1848), 39–43.

13. VC, "Première condition de légitimité d'une doctrine sociale," *PhJ,* 1, no. 9 (October 1, 1836), 275.

14. VC, "Première condition," *PhJ,* 1, no. 9 (October 1, 1836), 279.

15. VC, *DS,* 2: xx, 18.

16. VC, "Absurdité de l'engouement du public pour les chemins de fer," *PhJ,* 2, no. 15 (August 1, 1838), 229.

17. VC, *DS,* 1: 125.

18. VC, "Presse parisienne," *PhJ,* 1, no. 1 (July 10, 1836), 14.

19. VC, *DS,* 1: 145–207.

20. VC, *Principes du socialisme. Manifeste de la démocratie au XIXe siècle* (Paris, 1847), 1.

21. VC, *PS,* 2.

22. VC, *PS,* 4–5.

23. VC, *PS,* 5–6.

24. VC, *PS*, 6–7. See also *DS*, 1: 190–194.

25. VC, *PS*, 9, 11, 20.

26. VC, *PS*, 8.

27. VC, *PS*, 13–14.

28. VC, "Première condition," *PhJ*, 1, no. 9 (October 1, 1836), 277–278.

29. VC, *DS*, 2: xviii–xxii.

30. VC, *DS*, 2: 28; VC, *De la politique générale et du rôle de la France en Europe. Suivi d'une appréciation de la marche du gouvernment depuis juillet 1830* (Paris, 1840), 157; *DS*, 2: 9.

31. VC, *DS*, 1: 51.

32. VC, *DS*, 2: 265–266; and [VC], *Immoralité de la doctrine de Fourier*, 24–38.

33. Honoré de Balzac, *Autre étude de femme*, in Hayek, *Counter-Revolution of Science*, 224. See also Armand Cuvillier, *Hommes et idéologies de 1840* (Paris, 1956), 233; Vernus, *Victor Considerant*, 110.

34. VC, *DS*, 1: 290. See also David W. Lovell, "Early French Socialism and Politics: The Case of Victor Considerant," *History of Political Thought*, 13, no. 2 (Summer 1992), 258.

35. Considerant sometimes referred to Robert Owen and Etienne Cabet as communists of a "peaceful" variety. Normally, though, his use of the term implied coercion and revolution.

36. VC, *PS*, 18–19, 45. See also VC, *DS*, 1: 323–368, 403–405; and VC, *Contre M. Arago . . . suivie de la théorie du droit de la propriété* (Paris, 1840), 50–51, 58–59, 64.

37. VC, *Exposition abrégée du système phalanstérien de Fourier* (Paris, 1845), 3; VC, *DS*, 1: 409n. "*La propriété composée*" was property subject to multiple claims by a variety of types of "owners." In some of his paeans to this form of property, Considerant suggests (with an assurance that has an eerie resonance in post-Soviet times) that such vices as theft can be abolished by decree: "As property passes to the *mode composé* and becomes owned by everyone, shareholders and workers alike, theft is abolished; because you cannot steal from yourself." VC, *DP*, 1: 404. See also VC, *Théorie du droit de propriété et du droit du travail* (Paris, 1839).

38. VC, *DS*, 1: 290, 293.

39. According to Fourier's system of remuneration, each member of a properly organized association would receive an annual dividend based on his or her contribution in work, capital, and talent. Five-twelfths of the surplus produced by the association would go to labor, four-twelfths would serve as interest on invested capital, and three-twelfths would go to "talent"—that is, the more skillful and experienced members of the association. See CF, *Oeuvres complètes*, 6: 303–323, and Beecher, *Charles Fourier*, 279–280.

40. VC, *Exposition abrégée*, 90–91; VC, *DS*, 1: 93.

41. VC, *DS*, 1: 295–296.

42. VC, *DS*, 1: 296; VC, *Exposition abrégée*, 90.

43. VC, *Description du Phalanstère*, 23. See also VC, *DS*, 1: 29, 308.

44. VC, *DS*, 2: 15–31, 121. All of *DS*, volume 3, is devoted to a discussion of the educational groups and methods of the Phalanx.

45. VC, *Description du Phalanstère*, 57.

46. VC, *Description du Phalanstère*, 57–58.

47. VC, *Description du Phalanstère*, 67–69. See also VC, *DS*, 2: 76–77, and VC, *Description du Phalanstère*, 93.

48. VC, *DS*, 2: 120, 87. See also CF, *Oeuvres complètes*, 6: 52.

49. VC, *DS*, 2: 106, 121–135.

50. VC, *DS*, 2: 105, 288–289, 325.

51. VC, *DS*, 2: 105.

52. VC, *DS*, 2: 105.

53. Anonymous letter to VC, Liège, February 2, 1848: "I was not at all satisfied with yesterday's lecture. You weighted the scales too much in favor of women by arguing that they are the mistresses of men in love, and you seemed to approve that man should yield to woman." BMB Ms Z417.

54. VC, *DS*, 2: 350; VC, *Description du Phalanstère*, 32; VC, "L'Avenir," *DP*, 13: 52–67 (July 27–November 9, 1851).

55. VC, *DP*, June 20, 1844, as cited in Davidson, *Did We Think Victory Great?* 71.

56. VC, *SVM*, 113–114; *DS*, 1: 214–215. See also *DS*, 1: 216.

57. VC, *Contre M. Arago*, 12.

58. CF, *Oeuvres complètes*, 12: 624, and 10: *Publication des manuscrits* (1851), 222; Louis Blanc, *Organisation du travail* (Paris, 1839).

59. VC, *Contre M. Arago*, 49–64; VC, "Théorie du droit de propriété," *La Phalange*, 2 (May 1839), 590ff., 626ff. See also Paul Bastid, *Doctrines et institutions politiques de la Seconde République*, 2 vols. (Paris, 1945), 1: 63–64.

60. VC, *De la politique générale et du rôle de la France en Europe* (Paris, 1840); VC, *Bases de la politique positive* (Paris, 1841), 18–19. On the influence of Polytechnique, see Hayek, *Counter-Revolution of Science*, 105–188.

CHAPTER 7

1. Bertall, "La Foire aux idées," *Le Journal pour rire*, 37 (October 14, 1848). See Illustration 14.

2. Daniel Stern [Marie d'Agoult], *Histoire de la Révolution de 1848*, 2nd ed., vol. 1 (Paris, 1862), 37n.

3. On the Saint-Simonians, see Sébastien Charléty, *Histoire du Saint-Simonisme* (Paris, 1931); Henri-René d'Allemagne, *Les Saint-Simoniens, 1827–1837* (Paris, 1930); Robert Carlisle, *The Proffered Crown: The Saint-Simonians and the Doctrine of Hope* (Baltimore, 1987).

4. CF, *Pièges et charlatanisme des deux sectes Saint-Simon et Owen* (Paris, 1831); VC, *DS*, 1: 163n, 2: x; VC, *SVM*, 34–37; VC, *PS*, 46.

5. VC to CV, October 7, 1830, BMB Ms Z463.

6. On Buchez, see François-André Isambert, *De la Charbonnerie au Saint-*

Simonisme. Etude sur la jeunesse de Buchez (Paris, 1966), and *Buchez ou l'âge théologique de la sociologie* (Paris, 1967); Armand Cuvillier, *Un journal d'ouvriers, l'Atelier,* 2nd ed. (Paris, 1954), and *Hommes et idéologies de 1840,* 7–144.

7. *PhJ* (March 10, 1837), and *L'Atelier* (July 1846), both cited in Cuvillier, *Hommes et idéologies de 1840,* 106; VC, *SVM,* 69. It was for just such traits that Balzac's character, Daniel d'Arthez, who may have been modeled on Buchez, was admired by his fellow members of the "musico-philosophic and religious *cénâcle* of the rue des Quatre Vents." Honoré de Balzac, *Les Illusions perdues,* edited by Antoine Adam, 2nd ed. (Paris, 1961), xxiv, 224–242.

8. VC, *SVM,* 71–73.

9. Cuvillier, *Hommes et idéologies de 1840,* 104–105, 88; VC, *SVM,* 73.

10. VC, *SVM,* 78.

11. On Pierre Leroux I have found the following works especially useful: David Owen Evans, *Le Socialisme romantique. Pierre Leroux et ses contemporains* (Paris, 1948); Jean-Pierre Lacassagne, *Histoire d'une amitié. Pierre Leroux et George Sand* (Paris, 1973); Armelle Le Bras-Chopard, *De l'égalité dans la différence: Le socialisme de Pierre Leroux* (Paris, 1986); Jacques Viard, *Pierre Leroux et les socialistes européens* (Avignon, 1982).

12. Abel Transon, "Doctrine d'association de M. Charles Fourier," *Revue encyclopédique,* 53 (February 1832), 271–300, and "Exposition succincte de la théorie sociétaire," *Revue encyclopédique,* 54 (May 1832), 290–323. Pierre Leroux, "Lettres sur le fouriérisme," published in eight installments in *La Revue sociale,* 1, no. 9 (June 1846), through 2, no. 7 (April 1847).

13. VC, *SVM,* 95.

14. VC, *SVM,* 95.

15. John F. C. Harrison, *Quest for the New Moral World: Robert Owen and the Owenites in Britain and America* (New York, 1969), remains a sound and reliable survey of Owen's thought, his life, and the communitarian movement that he initiated. On Owen's relations with Fourier and the Fourierists, see Henri Desroche (ed.), "Owenisme et utopies françaises," special issue of *Communautés. Archives internationales de sociologie de la coopération et du développement,* 30 (July–December, 1971); Jacques Gans, "Les Relations entre socialistes de France et d'Angleterre au début du XIXe siècle," *Le Mouvement social,* 46 (January–March 1964), 105–118; and Beecher, *Charles Fourier,* 364–371.

16. VC to CV, May 5, 1829, BMB Ms Z417; VC, "Notes sur Owen," AN 10AS 26 (29); Jacques Gans, "Robert Owen à Paris en 1837," *Le Mouvement social,* 41 (October–December 1962), 35–45.

17. VC, *SVM,* 32; VC, *DS,* 1: 356.

18. VC, *SVM,* 32–33.

19. VC, *SVM,* 33. On Cabet, see Christopher H. Johnson, *Utopian Communism in France: Cabet and the Icarians, 1839–1851* (Ithaca, 1974); and Jules Prudhommeaux, *Icarie et son fondateur Etienne Cabet* (Paris, 1907).

20. VC, "Pour en finir avec M. Cabet," *DP,* 7, no. 135 (December 6, 1846).

21. VC, "Pour en finir avec M. Cabet." For a detailed account of relations between Fourierists and Icarians, see François Fourn, "Icariens et Phalanstériens: regards croisés entre 1845 et 1849," *Cahiers Charles Fourier* 10 (1999), 35–57.

22. The literature on Proudhon is immense. The works I have found most useful are Pierre Haubtmann, *Pierre-Joseph Proudhon. Sa vie et sa pensée (1809–1849)* (Paris, 1982), and *Pierre-Joseph Proudhon. Sa vie et sa pensée (1849–1865)*, 2 vols. (Paris, 1988); Henri de Lubac, *Le Drame de l'humanisme athée* (Paris, 1944); Daniel Halèvy, *La Jeunesse de Proudhon* (Paris, 1913), *La Vie de Proudhon* (Paris, 1948), and *Le Mariage de Proudhon* (Paris, 1955); Edouard Dolléans, *Proudhon* (Paris, 1948); and, in English, Robert L. Hoffman, *Revolutionary Justice: The Social and Political Theory of P.-J. Proudhon* (Urbana, 1972); and K. Steven Vincent, *Pierre-Joseph Proudhon and the Rise of French Republican Socialism* (New York, 1986).

23. Pierre-Joseph Proudhon, *Avertissement aux propriétaires, ou lettre à M. Considerant* (Paris, 1938), 247. On the problem of Fourier's influence on Proudhon, see Fernand Rude, "Proudhon et Fourier," in Henri Lefebvre et al., *Actualité de Fourier* (Paris, 1975), 33–35; and Jean-Paul Thomas, "Proudhon, lecteur de Fourier," *Les Travaux de l'Atelier Proudhon*, vol. 3 (Paris, 1986).

24. Pierre-Joseph Proudhon, *Deuxième Mémoire sur la propriété* (Paris, 1938), 120; Proudhon, *Avertissement aux propriétaires*, 213; Proudhon, *Carnets*, vol. 1 (Paris, 1960), 180.

25. Proudhon, *Avertissement aux propriétaires*, 203–217; Thomas, "Proudhon, lecteur de Fourier," 4–6. In the midst of his vituperation, Proudhon occasionally paused to pay tribute to Considerant's gifts as a journalist. See, for example, Proudhon, *Deuxième Mémoire*, 116: "Of all our active journalists none seems to me more fertile in his resources, more rich in his imagination, more abundant and varied in his style than M. Considerant."

26. Proudhon, *Avertissement aux propriétaires*, 181, 204; Proudhon, *Deuxième Mémoire*, 116; Thomas, "Proudhon, lecteur de Fourier," 6–7, 10–12.

27. Proudhon, *Avertissement aux propriétaires*, 184–185, 247.

28. VC, *SVM*, 99–106, quoted passage is 102.

29. VC, *SVM*, 105.

30. VC, "Pour en finir avec M. Proudhon," *DP* (February 10, 1849). See also Considerant's other contributions to this exchange: "A M. Proudhon," *DP* (February 4, 1849), "Réponse de M. Proudhon à M. Considerant et replique," *DP*, supp. (February 18, 1848), and "Pour se défaire du socialisme," *DP* (February 22, 1849). For a brief review of the several debates between Considerant and Proudhon, see Hartmut Stenzel, "Remarques sur la discussion entre Proudhon et les fouriéristes," in Maurice Agulhon et al., *1848. Les Utopismes sociaux* (Paris, 1981), 181–189.

31. The essential work on Flora Tristan remains Jules-L. Puech, *La Vie et l'oeuvre de Flora Tristan* (Paris, 1925). But see also Susan K. Grogan, *French Socialism and Sexual Difference: Women and the New Society, 1803–1844* (London, 1992), 155–191.

32. Flora Tristan to CF, October 11, 1835, in Flora Tristan, *Lettres*, edited by Stéphane Michaud (Paris, 1980), 57. CF, *OC*, 1: 132–133.

33. Tristan to VC [August 1836], in *PhJ*, 6 (September 1, 1836), 180–182. See also Tristan, *Lettres*, 62–63.

34. VC to Tristan [August 1836], in *PhJ*, 6 (September 1, 1836), 182–188; Tristan to VC, July 26, 1837, AN 10AS 42 (15). See also Tristan, *Lettres*, 64, 71.

35. Tristan, *Lettres*, 79; VC to Tristan, April 5, 1838, in Stéphane Michaud, "Flora Tristan: trente-cinq lettres," *International Review of Social History*, 24, pt. 1 (1979), 98; Puech, *Flora Tristan*, 236, 314–317.

36. VC, commentary, *PhJ*, 3rd ser., 6, no. 118 (March, 1843), 1925–1926. Excerpts from *L'Union ouvrière* appeared in this number of *La Phalange* and in that of March 29.

37. Puech, *Flora Tristan*, 140. This letter was reprinted in *L'Union ouvrière*, 2nd ed. (Paris, 1844), xiv.

38. Flora Tristan, *Le Tour de France*, edited by Jules-L. Puech (Paris, 1973), 24–25.

39. VC, obituary of Flora Tristan, *DP*, 3, no. 141 (November 18, 1844); Puech, *Flora Tristan*, 283.

40. P. V. Annenkov, *The Extraordinary Decade: Literary Memoirs* (Ann Arbor, 1968), 165; Eduard Gans, *Rückblicke auf Personen und Zustände* (Berlin, 1838), in André Liebich, *Between Ideology and Utopia: The Politics and Philosophy of August Cieszkowski* (Dordrecht, 1979), 122; Arnold Ruge, *Zwei Jahr in Paris. Etudien und Erinnerungen*, 2 vols. (Leipzig, 1846), 1: 4ff.

41. Isaiah Berlin, *Karl Marx*, 4th ed. (Oxford, 1978), 61. For a suggestive overview, see Lloyd S. Kramer, *Threshold of a New World: Intellectuals and the Exile Experience in Paris (1830–1848)* (Ithaca, 1988), 15–57.

42. Jacques Grandjonc, *Marx et les communistes allemands à Paris, 1844* (Paris, 1974), 12.

43. On Jan Czynski (1801–1867), see Michael D. Sibalis, "Jan Czynski: Jalons pour la biographie d'un fouriériste de la Grande Emigration polonaise," *Cahiers Charles Fourier*, 6 (1995), 58–84.

44. André Liebich (ed.), *Selected Writings of August Cieszkowski* (Cambridge, England 1979), 22; and Liebich, *Between Ideology and Utopia*, 113–128. For the Polish context, Andrzej Walicki, *Philosophy and Romantic Nationalism: The Case of Poland* (Notre Dame, 1994), is excellent.

45. VC to CV, September 19, 1831, in BMB Ms Z463; VC, "L'Agitation," *DP*, 6, no. 69 (March 10, 1846); VC, "Sursum corda," *DP*, 6, no. 70 (March 11, 1846); VC, "Seul moyen de salut de la cause polonaise," *DP*, 6, no. 75 (March 16, 1846). See also articles in *DP* (March 16 and 22, 1846) on VC's activities in support of the Poles. On VC's role as treasurer of the Société des Amis de la Pologne démocratique in 1848 and 1849, see AN 10AS 31 (6). See also Stanislas Worcell to Berryer, October 28, 1848, AN 10AS 42 (12). On VC and Poland generally, see Marsollier, *Victor Considerant*, 95–99.

46. Edmund Silberner, *Moses Hess. Geschichte Seines Lebens* (Leiden,

1966), 152, 162–163; Ruge, *Zwei Jahre in Paris*, 107–108; "Correspondance particulière. Allemagne," *DP*, 1, no. 79 (October 18, 1843).

47. Ruge, *Zwei Jahre in Paris*, 103–107. See also Gutzkow, *Briefe aus Paris*, extracts in *PhJ*, 3rd ser., 6, no. 54 (November 2, 1842), 885–887; and Emile Bottigelli, "Les 'Annales franco-allemands' et l'opinion française," *La Pensée*, 110 (1963), 47–66.

48. Letter signed Arnold Ruge and "Charles Marx," *DP*, 1, no. 133 (December 11, 1843), 3.

49. David Gregory's claim that Marx "visited the offices of *Démocratie pacifique*" late in 1843 and "probably made [Considerant's] acquaintance" rests on several dubious assumptions and is not supported by evidence. David Gregory, "Karl Marx and Friedrich Engels' Knowledge of French Socialism in 1842–43," *Historical Reflections / Réflections historiques*, 10, no. 1 (Spring 1983), 168. 180. On Marx's sixteen months in Paris, see Grandjonc, *Marx et les communistes allemands à Paris, 1844*; Kramer, *Threshold of a New World*, 120–125; and Auguste Cornu, *Karl Marx et Friedrich Engels*, 4 vols. (Paris, 1955–1970), 2: 229–338, 3:1–86.

50. Alexandre Zévaès, *De l'introduction du Marxisme en France* (Paris, 1947), 36n.

51. Karl Marx, "Der Kommunismus und die *Augsburger Allgemeine Zeitung*," *Rheinische Zeitung* (October 16, 1842), in Karl Marx and Friedrich Engels, *Werke*, vol. 1 (Berlin, 1957), 160–165.

52. VC, "Manifeste politique et sociale de la *Démocratie pacifique*," *DP*, 1, no. 1 (August 1, 1843).

53. Gregory, "Marx and Engels' Knowledge of French Socialism," 180–184. See also Rondel V. Davidson, "Reform versus Revolution: Victor Considerant and the *Communist Manifesto*," *Social Science Quarterly*, 1008, no. 1 (June 1977), 74–85; and Samuel Bernstein, "From Utopianism to Marxism," *Science and Society*, 14, no. 1 (Winter 1949–1950), 58–67.

54. W. Tcherkesoff, *Pages of Socialist History: Teaching and Acts of Social Democracy* (New York, 1902), 56–57; Georg Brandes, *Ferdinand Lassalle* (New York, 1925), 115. See also Georges Sorel, *La Décomposition du Marxisme* (Paris, 1908), 32; and Morris R. Cohen, *The Faith of a Liberal* (New York, 1946), 111.

55. VC, *Principes du socialisme. Manifeste de la démocratie au XIXe siècle* (Paris, 1847).

56. D'Agoult, *Révolution de 1848*, 1: 378–383, 2: 37–42; Louis-Antoine Garnier-Pagès, *Histoire de la Révolution de 1848*, 8 vols., 2nd ed., vol. 3 (Paris, 1866), 48; Bastid, *Doctrines et institutions*, 1: 63–64, 129–131. Rémi Gossez, *Les Ouvriers de Paris* (Paris, 1967), 10–12.

57. Johnson, *Utopian Communism*, 260–263; Oscar Hammen, "1848 et le 'Spectre du Communisme,'" *Le Contrat social*, 2 (1958), 199–200. My own readings suggest that what made the "specter of communism" especially frightening to landowners was not so much the prospect of a mass uprising as

the fear of the seizure of property that would follow the establishment of a communist regime.

58. VC, *Trois discours*, 83; VC, *DS*, 2: xli–lxxxvi; VC, *PS*, 63–64. For a fuller discussion, see Beecher, "Fourierism and Christianity," 394–395.

59. Henri Brissac, "Victor Considerant," *La Revue socialiste*, 19 (January–June, 1894), 73; VC to Gréa, October 10, 1833, AN 10AS 28 (7).

CHAPTER 8

1. VC to Paul Vigoureux, May 24, 1826, AN 10AS 28 (6).

2. VC to Charles Magnin, August 20, 1829, BMS; VC to Paul Vigoureux, May 24, 1826, AN 10AS 28 (6).

3. VC, *DS*, 2: ii (1838).

4. VC, *DS*, 2: ii, lxxxvi. It should be noted that the effort to "disguise the science"—to strip the theory of its most eccentric aspects—did not begin with Considerant. In his later works, Fourier himself made a concerted (though never very successful) effort to present his ideas in a form that he thought would be acceptable to the public. Already in 1819 he was speaking of the need to simplify and even "mutilate" his doctrine by "stripping down or castrating" his theory of association; in 1824 he wrote Just Muiron that he would henceforth practice "dissimulation" in order to make his doctrine accessible. See Beecher, *Charles Fourier*, 173–175, 177, 374–375.

5. VC to the editor of *Le Franc-comtois*, July 21, 1842, in *PhJ*, 3rd ser., 6, no. 10 (July 22, 1842).

6. VC, *Bases de la politique positive. Manifeste de l'Ecole sociétaire fondée par Fourier* (Paris, 1841), 49–50.

7. Davidson, *Did We Think Victory Great?* 66. Vernus also sees Considerant as moving toward "an increasingly pronounced *Fourierist revisionism*" after 1840. Vernus, *Victor Considerant*, 68.

8. VC, *Bases de la politique positive*, 94.

9. Guarneri, *The Utopian Alternative*, 241.

10. VC to Pellarin, draft, November 5, 1869, AN 10AS 28 (5); Charles Pellarin, *Essai critique sur la philosophie positive. Lettre à M. E. Littré* (Paris, 1864), 320; Tristan to VC, October 29, 1843, in Tristan, *Lettres*, 191; Laverdant to VC, n.d. [1843–1845?], BMB Ms Z418.

11. See chapter 4, section I.

12. Alphonse Toussenel, *Les Juifs rois de l'époque. Histoire de la féodalité financière*, 2nd ed., 2 vols. (Paris, 1847), "Préface," cited in *DP* (January 31, 1847).

13. Emile Lehouck, *Vie de Charles Fourier* (Paris, 1978), 228–229. See also Michel Nathan, *Le Ciel des fouriéristes* (Lyon, 1981), 23, for the contrast between the "mellifluous demonstrations," "solemn lyricism," and "prudishness" of Considerant and his colleagues and the playfulness, audacity, and provocations of Fourier.

14. Lehouck, *Vie de Fourier,* 228; Poulat, "Ecritures et traditions fouriéristes," 228–229. For the restitution of the passages cut from Fourier's *Nouveau monde industriel* and for commentary, see Michel Butor's edition of this work (Paris, 1973). It was only in 1967 that Simone Debout-Oleskiewicz established the text of the *Nouveau monde amoureux* and published it as volume 8 in the Editions Anthropos twelve-volume edition of Fourier's works. See her preface to Charles Fourier, *Oeuvres complètes,* 12 vols. (Paris, 1967), 7: vii–cxii.

15. VC to CV, December 10, 1830, BMB Ms Z463; VC, *DS,* 1: 34, 32.

16. VC, *Débâcle de la politique en France,* 18.

17. VC, *DS,* 1: 263; *DP* (November 27, 1843); VC to Lamartine, June 12, 1843, Mme. Valentine de Lamartine (ed.), *Lettres de Lamartine, 1818–1865* (Paris, 1892), 201.

18. VC, *Bases de la politique positive,* 39n. See also VC, "Pourquoi le radicalisme social de Fourier se rallie à l'ordre politique établi," *PhJ,* 2nd ser., 2, no. 47 (December 1, 1839).

19. VC, *PS,* 53 (Considerant's italics). See also Lovell, "Early French Socialism," 266.

20. VC, "Les Eventualités de la régence," *DP,* 2, no. 36 (February 5, 1844).

21. VC, *PS,* 50. See also Considerant's September 1847 "Avertissement" to the second edition of *DS* (Paris, 1848), 1: xi–xii.

22. Dommanget, *Victor Considerant,* 128–129.

23. VC, *PS;* VC, *DS,* 2nd ed. (Paris, 1847), 1: vii; VC, "Mort de M. le duc d'Orléans," *DP,* 6, no. 7 (July 15, 1842), 97–99.

24. VC, *DS,* v–vi.

25. On the French conquest of Algeria, see C. Schefer, *La Politique coloniale de la Monarchie de Juillet: l'Algérie et l'évolution de la colonisation française* (Paris, 1928); and A. T. Montagnon, *La Conquête de l'Algérie: 1830–1871* (Paris, 1986). VC to CV, October 7, 1830. VC to CV, October 7, 1830, BMB Ms Z463.

26. Bugeaud to Marshal Maison, September 14, 1835: "Captain Considerant has had since 1831 a series of unpaid leaves, which he has requested in order to devote himself to a philanthropic project that I regard as impracticable owing to the tendencies of the human heart. But the theory behind this project holds out seductive promises for the future of humanity. Only a noble and generous heart, like that of this officer, could become impassioned by this theory; and that is why I have taken a lively interest in him." AMG AAC, Dossier VC. See also in the same dossier, VC to Marshal Soult, May 5, 1832, and VC to Maison, September 23, 1835. On Bugeaud, see Antony Thrall Sullivan, *Thomas-Robert Bugeaud: France and Algeria, 1784–1849* (Hamden, Ct., 1983); and Jean-Pierre Bois, *Bugeaud* (Paris, 1997). Another highly placed supporter of Considerant was General Pierre-Claude Pajol, a Bisontin who had been a schoolmate of Fourier. On VC's letter to Soult of May 5, 1832, Pajol added the endorsement: "I beg the Marshal to kindly grant the request of M. Considerant."

27. Bugeaud to VC, September 25, 1842, in J. Prudhommeaux (ed.), "Une Lettre du Général Bugeaud," *La Révolution de 1848,* 5, no. 29 (1908), 770. See

also letters of Bugeaud to VC, AN 10AS 36 (12). On the evolution of Bugeaud's attitude toward the colonization of Algeria, see Sullivan, *Bugeaud*, 74, and Tudesq, *Grands notables*, 2: 812.

28. VC, "Le Maréchal Bugeaud," *DP*, 1, no. 12 (August 12, 1843).

29. Charles Pellarin, "Reprise du système guerroyant en Algérie," *DP*, 2, no. 59 (February 28, 1844); VC, "Justification des horreurs de la guerre d'Afrique!!" *DP*, 5, no. 24 (July 24, 1845). See also *DP* 5, nos. 22 and 25 (July 22 and 25, 1845).

30. VC, *A MM. les électeurs de l'arrondissement de Montargis*, August 8, 1846.

31. Bourgin, *Victor Considerant*, 90; Vernus, *Victor Considerant*, 102. Considerant's showing in 1846 was better than in his previous attempt at the Chamber of Deputies in the IXe *arrondissement* in Paris in April 1844, when he received just 34 of the 581 votes cast.

32. On the economic crisis of 1846–1847, see Roger Price, *The French Second Republic: A Social History* (Ithaca, 1972), esp. 82–94; Collingham, *July Monarchy*, 360–362; and the now classic work of Ernest Labrousse (ed.), *Aspects de la crise et de la dépression de l'économie française au milieu du XIXe siècle* (Paris, 1956).

33. Tudesq, *Grands notables*, 2: 926–965.

34. Alexis de Tocqueville, *Souvenirs* (Paris, 1942), 27; Karl Marx, *The Class Struggles in France (1848–1850)* (New York, 1964), 36.

35. Jules Duval, "Notre Programme," *DP*, 7, no. 17 (July 19, 1846); Charles Pellarin, "Petit avis électoral d'un non-électeur," *DP*, 7, no. 23 (July 26, 1846); "Petition pour la réforme électorale," *DP*, 7, no. 87 (October 12, 1846).

36. VC in *Journal du Loiret* (November 24, 1847), extract in AN BB30 296. See also Tudesq, *Grands notables*, 2: 969.

37. Fourteen chapters of Antony Méray's novel *La Part des femmes* had appeared in *Démocratie pacifique* by the beginning of July 1847, when government censors seized three issues of the newspaper. The first two issues included sections of the novel in which the hero goes to bed with a young woman. The third was an article deploring the state's double standard with regard to the crimes of the rich and those of the poor. See A. Colin, "Les Deux catégories de délits," *DP*, 8, no. 159 (July 4, 1847); and VC, "Trois saisies en cinq jours!" *DP*, 8, no. 160 (July 5–6, 1847). See also Jann Matlock, "The Politics of Seduction: Trying *Women's Share*," in *Scenes of Seduction: Prostitution, Hysteria, and Reading Difference in Nineteenth-Century France* (New York, 1994), 220–247.

38. Ordonnance de saisi par le Procureur du Roi, July 4, 1847, ENS AVC carton 3 (IV, 3); "Opinion de la presse sur notre saisie," *DP*, 8, no. 162 (July 8, 1847); "Procès de la *Démocratie pacifique* pour la *Part des femmes*," *DP*, 9, nos. 53 and 54 (August 30–31 and September 1, 1847); "La *Démocratie pacifique* devant le jury," *DP*, 9, no. 59 (September 6–7, 1847); "Acquittement de la *Démocratie pacifique*," *DP*, 9, no. 60 (September 8, 1847).

39. VC, "La Décadence sociale," *DP*, 9, no. 10 (July 11, 1847).

40. VC, "Une Société qui tombe," *DP*, 9, no. 46 (August 22, 1847).

41. VC, "Oui, vous êtes responsables!" *DP,* 9, no. 47 (August 23–24, 1847).

42. The proceedings of the *cour d'assises* for September 7 are reprinted in a long supplement to *DP,* 9, no. 60 (September 8, 1847).

43. *Le Commerce* (September 8, 1847), cited in *DP,* 9, no. 61 (September 9, 1847). This issue of *DP* includes selections from five "independent journals" concerning the acquittal.

44. VC, "De la moralité de l'affaire Praslin," *DP,* 9, no. 58 (September 5, 1847).

45. "Compte-rendu du banquet réformiste de Saint-Quentin du 19 septembre, 1847," *DP,* 9, no. 71 (September 23, 1847), supp.; "Banquet réformiste de Montargis," *DP,* 9, no. 124 (November 24, 1847). See also *Journal du Loiret* (November 24, 1847), extracts in AN BB30 296; VC to Bureau, November 22, 1847, ENS AVC carton 2 (I, 6), and VC to Bureau, November 27, 1847, ENS AVC carton 9 (III, 3).

46. Proudhon, *Carnets,* 2: 201, 296.

47. In the elections of November 1847, the electoral college of Montargis gave Victor Considerant, "candidat de l'opposition," 102 votes as opposed to 276 for the incumbent conservative deputy. In 1846 Considerant had received 91 votes out of a total of 419 cast. *Le Salinois* (November 27, 1847), cited in Vernus, *Victor Considerant,* 102.

CHAPTER 9

1. Among the general histories of the Second Republic, I have found particularly valuable Maurice Agulhon, *The Republican Experiment, 1848–1852* (Cambridge, England, 1983), and Roger Price, *The French Second Republic: A Social History* (Ithaca, 1972). Despite Henri Guillemin's addiction to conspiracy theories, I have also learned much from his spirited *La Première Résurrection de la République* (Paris, 1967), as well as from T. J. Clark's superb *The Absolute Bourgeois: Artists and Politics in France 1848–1851* (London, 1973), and his *Image of the People: Gustave Courbet and the 1848 Revolution* (London, 1973). Among histories written by contemporaries, Daniel Stern (pseudonym of comtesse Marie d'Agoult), *Histoire de la Révolution de 1848,* 2nd ed., 2 vols. (Paris, 1862), is, in my judgment, the richest and most searching. Louis-Antoine Garnier-Pagès, *Histoire de la Révolution de 1848,* 10 vols. (Paris, 1860–1871), is useful on questions of detail.

2. Marx, *Class Struggles in France,* 42.

3. "Propagande phalanstérienne, Victor Considerant à Liège," *DP,* 10, nos. 38, 41, 44 (February 13, 17, 20, 1848); Discailles, "Considerant en Belgique," 719–722; André Cordeweiner, *Etude de la presse liégoise de 1830 à 1850 et répertoire générale* (Louvain, 1972), 106–107.

4. VC to members of the Société d'Emulation de Liège, February 25, 1848, published in *L'Eclair* (Liège), February 28, 1848; and *DP,* 10, no. 55 (March 2, 1848).

5. On Rogier's ministry and the political situation in Belgium, see Brison D.

Gooch, *Belgium and the February Revolution* (The Hague, 1963). For this section, see also Discailles, "Considerant en Belgique," 719–727.

6. VC to Rogier, February 26, 1848, 1 AM and 4:30 AM, in Discailles, "Considerant en Belgique," 723–726. The first letter bears a cryptic annotation in Rogier's hand: "Lettre curieuse reçue à une heure du matin et à laquelle il n'a pas été donné suite." Hasty drafts of both letters are preserved in Considerant's papers: the first in pencil, AN 19AS 26 (38), and the second in hurriedly blotted ink, AN 10AS 28 (8) (see Illustration 12).

7. Friedrich Engels, article in *Deutsche-Brusseler-Zeitung*, February 27, 1848, in Oscar J. Hammen, *Red '48ers: Karl Marx and Friedrich Engels* (New York, 1969), 196.

8. J. Dhont, "La Belgique en 1848," in *Actes du Congrès historique de la Révolution de 1848* (Paris, 1848), 115–131; Gooch, *Belgium and the February Revolution*, esp. 26–36, and 52–69; Hammen, *Red '48ers*, 195–197.

9. Minutes of Les Socialistes Unis, March 2–May 24, 1848, AN 10AS 31 (3). The club soon changed its name to Club des Républicains socialistes. It initially met at the Fourierist headquarters at 2, rue de Beaune. As of April 12, however, its meeting place was changed to the main hall of the Institut de France. Its presidents were Allyre Bureau and Charles Brunier. Considerant, occupied by his own political activities and ambitions, played no role in its sessions.

10. Allyre Bureau, "Concert de tous les socialistes," *DP*, 10, no. 49–50 (February 25, 1848), "numéro spécial, 7 heures du soir."

11. François Vidal, "La République de 92 et celle de 1848," *DP*, 10, no. 49–50 (February 25, 1848), "numéro spécial, 7 heures du soir." According to Emile Thomas, *Histoire des ateliers nationaux* (Paris, 1848), this text had great influence. See also Paul Bastid, *Doctrines et institutions politiques de la Séconde République*, 2 vols. (Paris, 1945), 1: 130.

12. VC, "Le Ministère du Progrès," *DP*, 10, no. 54 (March 1, 1848); VC to Société démocratique de l'arrondissement de Montargis, *DP*, 10, no. 58 (March 5, 1848).

13. VC, *SVM*, 92.

14. VC, *La Dernière guerre et la paix definitive en Europe* (Paris, 1850), 10.

15. VC, *SVM*, 88–90.

16. *Moniteur universel*, March 13 and 22, 1848, in *DP*, 10, nos. 70 and 91 (March 17 and April 8, 1848); Georges Cahen, "Louis Blanc et la Commission du Luxembourg," *Annales de l'Ecole Libre des sciences politiques*, 12 (1897), 187–225, 362–380, 459–481; Louis Blanc, *La Révolution de février au Luxembourg* (Paris, 1849); d'Agoult, *Histoire de la Révolution de 1848*, 2: 39–54; Leo A. Loubère, *Louis Blanc* (Chicago, 1961), 79–86.

17. VC, "Avertissement de l'éditeur," in abbé [Jacopo] Leone, *Conjuration des jésuites. Publication du plan secret de l'ordre* (Paris, 1848), a26.

18. On the election campaign in the Loiret, see Fernand Dieudonné, "Les Elections à la Constituante de 1848 dans le Loiret," *La Révolution de 1848*, vol. 2 (1905–1906), 281–313; vol. 3 (1906–1907), 79–90; and Christiane Marcilhacy,

"Les Caractères de la crise sociale et politique de 1846 à 1852 dans le département du Loiret," *Revue d'histoire moderne et contemporaine*, 6 (1959), 5–59.

19. Dieudonné, "Les Elections dans le Loiret," 289–290; Georges Weil, *Histoire du parti républicain en France (1814–1870)* (Paris, 1928), 220.

20. Considerant, *SVM*, 122–123.

21. Dieudonné, "Les Elections dans le Loiret," 306.

22. *Le Loiret* (April 13 and 18, 1848), in Dieudonné, "Les Elections dans le Loiret," 309; VC to Edouard Charton, April 11, 1848, Bibliothèque Municipale d'Auxerre Ms 333; VC to editor of *Le Loiret*, May 10, 1848, in *DP*, 10, no. 123 (May 11, 1848).

23. Dieudonné, "Les Elections dans le Loiret," 79–90; *DP*, 10, no. 124 (May 12, 1848), supp. In Paris, where about 100,000 votes would have been necessary for election, Considerant received 28,673.

24. Prosper Mérimée to Madame de Montijo, May 6, 1848, and Mérimée to Madame de Boigne, May 5, 1848, in Prosper Mérimée, *Correspondance générale*, edited by Maurice Perturier, vol. 5 (Paris, 1946), 307, 303–304; Tocqueville, *Souvenirs*, 133–134; and James Pope-Hennessy, *Monckton Milnes: The Years of Promise, 1809–1851* (New York, 1955), 283–284.

25. VC to editor of *Le Loiret*, May 10, 1848, in *DP*, 10, no. 123 (May 11. 1848).

26. D'Agoult, *Histoire de la Révolution de 1848*, 2: 213; Tocqueville, *Souvenirs*, 108–109.

27. Garnier-Pagès, *Histoire de la Révolution de 1848*, 10: 46–48.

28. VC, *Les Quatre crédits ou 60 milliards à 1 1/2 pour-cent* (Paris, 1851), 134–135.

29. My account of the *journée* of May 15 is based especially on Tocqueville, *Souvenirs*, 117–127; d'Agoult, *Histoire de la Révolution de 1848*, 2: 240–278; Guillemin, *La Première Résurrection de la République*, 333–352; and Garnier-Pagès, *Histoire de la Révolution de 1848*, 9: 83–266.

30. VC, articles on Poland in *DP*, 10, no. 63, 69 (March 10, 16, 1846). For a substantial account of the meeting of May 11, see *Journal des débats* (May 13, 1848). "De la manifestation en faveur de la Pologne," *DP*, 10, no. 127 (May 15, 1848).

31. Guillemin, *La Première Résurrection de la République*, 352.

32. *Le Moniteur* (May 16, 1848), in *DP*, 10, no. 129 (May 17, 1848).

33. "Une Révolution manquée," *DP*, 10, no. 128 (May 16, 1848).

34. VC, *La Solution, ou le gouvernement direct du peuple*, 4th ed. (Paris, 1851), 28.

35. Bastid, *Doctrines et institutions politiques de la Seconde République*, 1: 234–279.

36. Tocqueville, *Souvenirs*, 161–175. See also Odilon Barrot, *Mémoires posthumes*, 4 vols. (Paris, 1875), 2: 315–379; Paul Bastid, *Un Juriste pamphlétaire. Cormenin, précurseur et constituant de 1848* (Paris, 1948), 199–231; Garnier-Pagès, *Histoire de la Révolution de 1848*, 10: 334–370; and André Jardin, *Alexis de Tocqueville, 1805–1859* (Paris, 1984), 396–399. The principal

source for the deliberations of the Constitutional Committee, however, are the *procès-verbaux* of its meetings, AN C 918. These have now been published in full in Alexis de Tocqueville, *Oeuvres complètes*, vol. 3, *Ecrits et discours politiques* (Paris, 1990), 55–164.

37. Tocqueville, *Souvenirs*, 161.

38 Barrot, *Mémoires posthumes*, 2: 330. See also Aimé Cherest, *La Vie et les oeuvres de A.-T. Marie* (Paris, 1873), 174–175, for a similar appreciation of Considerant by the minister of public works. After condemning "the brutal, mindless, vain, ignorant socialism . . . which only dreams and promises chimeras," Marie goes on to associate Considerant with a more "high-minded, generous, and prudent socialism" whose leaders understood "the necessity of postponing until calmer times the practical realization of ideas that needed a better cultivated soil in order to grow. M. Considerant was one of these leaders. He explained his position frankly to me one day when he came to see me at the Ministry of Public Works."

39. "Procès-verbaux de la Commission de la Constitution de 1848, séance du 15 juin," in Tocqueville, *Ecrits et discours politiques*, 3: 146. See also Garnier-Pagès, *Histoire de la Révolution de 1848*, 10: 358.

40. Draft of a proposed decree to be issued by the National Assembly with a note by VC: "submitted May 15 at 1 o'clock at the desk of the President of the Assembly." ENS AVC carton 8 (I, 2). "Procès-verbaux de la Commission de la Constitution de 1848, séance du 23 mai," in Tocqueville, *Ecrits et discours politiques*, 3: 71, 74. See also Garnier-Pagès, *Histoire de la Révolution de 1848*, 10: 343–345.

41. "Procès-verbaux de la Commission de la Constitution de 1848, séance du 13 juin," in Tocqueville, *Ecrits et discours politiques*, 3: 141; VC, *SVM*, 117–118. See also Garnier-Pagès, *Histoire de la Révolution de 1848*, 10: 366.

42. George Sand to *La Réforme*, reprinted in *La Voix des femmes* (April 10, 1848), and cited by Michèle Riot-Sarcey, *La Démocratie à l'épreuve des femmes. Trois figures critiques du pouvoir, 1830–1848* (Paris, 1994), 326–327; d'Agoult, *Histoire de la Révolution de 1848*, 2: 35–36; [VC], *Immoralité de la doctrine de Fourier*, 24–31. For a skeptical view of the contributions of the Fourierists to the women's suffrage movement, which does not, however, mention this gesture by Considerant, see Riot-Sarcey, *La Démocratie à l'épreuve des femmes*, 207, 234, 337, and *passim*.

43. Joseph Benoît, *Confessions d'un prolétaire* (Paris, 1968), 163.

44. Tocqueville, *Souvenirs*, 203. Tocqueville's portrait of Falloux is penetrating and subtle, but see also d'Agoult, *Histoire de la Révolution de 1848*, 2: 359–364. On Falloux's role on the Labor Committee, see Donald McKay, "Le Vicomte de Falloux et les Ateliers nationaux," *La Révolution de 1848*, 30, no. 144 (March–May 1933), 30–42.

45. For the following, I have relied not only on the published *Procès-verbaux du Comité de travail à l'Assemblée constituante de 1848* (Paris, 1908), but also on the actual stenographic record of the committee in AN C 928. The published *procès-verbaux* are so terse as to be seriously misleading at times,

and there is no way of accurately characterizing the interventions of a particular committee member without going to the *minutes sténographiés*, which exist for eleven of the committee's sessions. Donald McKay's article, cited above, and his book *The National Workshops: A Study in the French Revolution of 1848* (Cambridge, Mass., 1933), have also been a great help to me in my effort to untangle the webs spun by Falloux.

46. McKay, *National Workshops*, 77, 89, 108; Garnier-Pagès, *Histoire de la Révolution de 1848*, 9: 80–81; *Procès-verbaux du Comité du travail*, 3; comte de Falloux, *Mémoires d'un royaliste*, 2 vols. (Paris, 1888), 1: 339.

47. Minutes sténographiés provenant du Comité du travail, séance du 25 mai, AN C 928; *Procès-verbaux du Comité du travail*, 13–14; McKay, *National Workshops*, 109–111.

48. Minutes sténographiés, séance du 25 mai, AN C 928.

49. Falloux, *Mémoires*, 1: 339.

50. Minutes sténographiés, séance du 25 mai, 30, AN C 928. *Procès-verbaux du Comité de travail*, 14, gives a most inadequate summary of Considerant's remarks.

51. Minutes sténographiés, séance du 29 mai, 12–13.

52. Minutes sténographiés, séance du 29 mai, 15, 17.

53. *Compte rendu des séances de l'Assemblée nationale constituante*, vol. 1 (Paris, 1849), 505–506.

54. McKay, *National Workshops*, 122.

55. McKay, *National Workshops*, 120–135.

56. Falloux, *Mémoires*, 1: 328, 333. Beslay's memoirs are vague and unhelpful on this issue. See Charles Beslay, *Mes Souvenirs: 1830–1848–1870* (Paris, 1874; reprinted Geneva, 1979), 180–181, 220–224.

57. VC to Proudhon, June 8, 1848, published in *DP*, 13, no. 153 (June 9, 1848).

58. *Compte rendu des séances de l'Assemblée nationale constituante*, 1: 734.

59. There is no single authoritative monograph on the June Days. Charles Schmidt, *Les Journées de juin 1848* (Paris, 1926), and Georges Duveau, *1848: The Making of a Revolution* (New York, 1968), 133–156, are lucid narratives based on wide reading in the sources. D'Agoult, *Histoire de la Révolution de 1848*, 2: 372–469, is the best detailed contemporary account. Price, *The French Second Republic*, 155–192, and Frederick de Luna, *The French Republic under Cavaignac: 1848* (Princeton, 1969), 128–173, are well informed if now somewhat dated critical surveys. Mark Traugott, *Armies of the Poor: Determinants of Working-Class Participation in the Paris Insurrection of June 1848* (Princeton, 1985), makes a major contribution to our understanding of the June Days and sheds light on a wider range of issues than its subtitle suggests.

60. Tocqueville, *Souvenirs*, 135.

61. Tocqueville, letter of July 21, 1848, in McKay, *National Workshops*, 150. The "cannibals," "savages," and "lepers" are from *Le Constitutionnel* for June 27 and 28, 1848, and from *La Mode* for June 29, 1848. These texts are reprinted in Maurice Agulhon (ed.), *Les Quarante-huitards* (Paris, 1975), 168.

Ximénès Doudan to Madame Auguste de Stael, July 16, 1848, in Jacques Suffel (ed.), *1848. La Révolution racontée par ceux qui l'ont vue* (Paris, 1848), 526–527.

62. D'Agoult, *Histoire de la Révolution de 1848*, 2: 399.

63. "Songeons à l'avenir," *DP*, 17, no. 169 (June 25, 1848).

64. "Appel aux représentants du peuple," *DP*, 17, no. 172 (June 28, 1848); "Comment prévenir la guerre civile," *DP*, 17, no. 174 (June 30, 1848). It is not clear that these articles are by Considerant.

65. "Séance du 23 juin, 1848," *Compte rendu des séances de l'Assemblée nationale constituante*, 2: 177; Louis Blanc, *Histoire de la Révolution de 1848*, 2 vols. (Paris, 1870), 2: 154; Tocqueville, *Souvenirs*, 139; d'Agoult, *Histoire de la Révolution de 1848*, 2: 410–411. For the text of Considerant's proclamation, see *DP*, 17, no. 174 (June 30, 1848), and d'Agoult, *Histoire de la Révolution de 1848*, 2: 592–593.

66. "Séance du 23 juin, 1848," *Compte rendu des séances de l'Assemblée nationale constituante*, 2: 178–179.

67. "Séance du 24 juin, 1848," *Compte rendu des séances de l'Assemblée nationale constituante*, 2: 189; and *DP*, 17, no. 169 (June 25, 1848).

68. Gustave Flaubert, *L'Education sentimentale* (Paris, 1961), 337–338.

69. Ernest Renan to Henriette Renan, July 1, 1848, in Francis Mercury, *Renan* (Paris, 1990), 235–236.

70. George Sand, in Jean Dautry, *1848 et la IIe République* (Paris, 1957), 203; Félicité de Lamennais in *Le Peuple constituant* (July 11, 1848), in Pierrard, *L'Eglise et les ouvriers en France*, 157.

71. Beslay, *Souvenirs*, 194.

72. VC to Cavaignac, June 28, 1848, BHVP Ms 1056 (ff. 39–40). In this letter, preserved among Cavaignac's papers, Considerant used the familiar "tu." He did not know Cavaignac well, but they were both graduates of the Ecole Polytechnique and Considerant had once been close to Cavaignac's older brother, the republican Godefroy Cavaignac.

73. All citations in this paragraph and the next four come from VC, "Leçons pour tous et à tous," *DP*, 17, no. 175 (July 1, 1848).

CHAPTER 10

1. On the rise of the *démoc-soc* movement I have found the following works particularly valuable: Edward Berenson, *Populist Religion and Left-Wing Politics in France, 1830–1852* (Princeton, 1984); Maurice Agulhon, *La République au village* (Paris, 1970), and *Les Quarante-huitards* (Paris, 1975); and Clark, *Image of the People*, esp. 86–112.

2. *Revue des deux mondes* (August 5, 1848), in Guillemin, *La Première Résurrection de la République*, 456.

3. "Séance du 28 juin, 1848," *Compte rendu des séances de l'Assemblée nationale constituante*, 2: 238, in de Luna, *The French Republic under Cavaignac*, 152.

4. De Luna, *The French Republic under Cavaignac,* 203–210; Pierrard, *L'Eglise et les ouvriers en France,* 156–157.

5. "Appel aux représentants du peuple" and "Assemblée Nationale," *DP,* 17, no. 172 (June 28, 1848); "Appel aux amis de l'humanité," *DP,* 17, no. 176 (July 2, 1848); VC, "Folie et vertige," *DP,* 17, no. 209 (August 4, 1848); Proudhon, in *Le Représantant du peuple* (July 6, 1848); VC, "Leçons pour tous et à tous," *DP,* 17, no. 175 (July 1, 1848); *Messieurs Considerant et Proudhon jugés par eux-mêmes* (Paris, 1849), 12.

6. "Séance du 25 juillet, 1848," *Compte rendu des séances de l'Assemblée nationale constituante,* 2: 650; "Assemblée Nationale. Les Clubs," *DP,* 17, no. 200 (July 26, 1848); "Législation de la presse," *DP,* 17, no. 212 (August 7, 1848). See also Peter Amann, *Revolution and Mass Democracy: The Paris Club Movement in 1848* (Princeton, 1975), 315–320.

7. VC, "Position faite au parti démocratique par l'élection de M. Louis Napoléon," *DP,* 17, no. 337 (December 13, 1848). For a clear overview of Considerant's contribution as a member of the Constituent Assembly, see Davidson, *Did We Think Victory Great?* 159–176.

8. On the Comité de la rue de Poitiers, see Garnier-Pagès, *Histoire de la Révolution de 1848,* 10: 44–46; de Luna, *The French Republic under Cavaignac,* 190–191; and especially Tudesq, *Les Grands Notables en France,* 2: 1094–1096, 1141–1144.

9. Vicomte d'Arlincourt, *Dieu le veut!* in Guillemin, *La Première Résurrection de la République,* 465.

10. Guillemin, *La Première Résurrection de la République,* 465; Gustave Claudin, *Mes Souvenirs: Les Boulevards de 1840–1870,* 3rd ed. (Paris, 1884), 79.

11. All citations in this paragraph are from Guillemin, *La Première Résurrection de la République,* 464–465.

12. "Séance du 13 septembre, 1848," *Compte rendu des séances de l'Assemblée nationale constituante,* vol. 3 (Paris, 1850), 994. The principal interventions in the debate over the right to work are reprinted in Joseph Garnier (ed.), *Le Droit au travail à l'Assemblée nationale* (Paris, 1848); for Thiers's speech and Considerant's reply, see 188–224.

13. "Séance du 13 septembre, 1848," *Compte rendu des séances de l'Assemblée nationale constituante,* 3: 1003.

14. "Séance du 13 septembre, 1848," *Compte rendu des séances de l'Assemblée nationale constituante,* 3: 1004–1005.

15. "Séance du 13 septembre, 1848," *Compte rendu des séances de l'Assemblée nationale constituante,* 3: 1004–1005. VC, SVM, 54, and see also 51–53, 58–59, and 71–72.

16. *DP,* 17, no. 149 (September 15, 1848), contains a selection of contemporary press comments on Considerant's speech, from which the citations in this paragraph are drawn. Other contemporary accounts include Claudin, *Mes souvenirs,* 78; Barrot, *Mémoires posthumes,* 2: 415; and Léonard Gallois, *Histoire de la Révolution de 1848,* 4 vols. (Paris, 1851), 4: 147. For Considerant's comments, see SVM, 52–53.

17. For this section I have drawn upon Agulhon, *The Republican Experiment, 1848–1852*, 60–73; Berenson, *Populist Religion and Left-Wing Politics*, 74–126; Roger Magraw, *A History of the French Working Class*, 2 vols. (Oxford, 1992), 1: 131–184; and John Merriman, *The Agony of the Republic: The Repression of the Left in Revolutionary France, 1848–1851* (New Haven, 1978).

18. Berenson, *Populist Religion and Left-Wing Politics*, 76; *DP*, 17, no. 257, 258 (September 23, 24, 1848).

19. Cabet and d'Alton-Shée, cited in Berenson, *Populist Religion and Left-Wing Politics*, 77–78.

20. Reydor to VC, July 21, 1836, AN 10AS 41 (11): "I urge you to send the journal (for two or three months) to Prince Louis-Napoleon Bonaparte at Arenenberg in the canton of Thurgovia (Switzerland). It's worth trying: I have already had the opportunity to write him and to direct his attention to social science." "L'Enigme napoléonienne," *DP*, 17, no. 262 (September 28, 1848); "M. Louis Napoléon et la rue de Poitiers," *DP*, 17, no. 298 (November 7, 1848); "Les Candidats républicains," *DP*, 17, no. 301 (November 10, 1848); "La Politique du général Cavaignac," *DP*, 17, no. 327 (December 3, 1848); "Sauvons le pays!" *DP*, 17, no. 294 (November 2, 1848).

21. Marx, *Class Struggles in France*, 71; Agulhon, *The Republican Experiment, 1848–1852*, 72; VC, "Position faite au parti démocratique par l'élection de M. Louis Napoléon," *DP*, 17, no. 337 (December 13, 1848).

22. Berenson, *Populist Religion and Left-Wing Politics*, 85. See also Claude Latta, *Un Républicain méconnu. Martin Bernard, 1808–1883* (Saint-Etienne, 1980), 163–166, 299–304.

23. Berenson, *Populist Religion and Left-Wing Politics*, 85–95; Marcel Dessal, *Un Révolutionnaire jacobin, Charles Delescluze, 1809–1871* (Paris, 1952), 93–120; Price, *The French Second Republic*, 202–203, 230, 250.

24. Berenson, *Populist Religion and Left-Wing Politics*, 78–85.

25. See, for example, *L'Apocalypse ou la prochaine rénovation démocratique et sociale de l'Europe*, par Victor Considerant, Représentant. Se trouve à la librairie socialiste phalanstérienne, quai Voltaire, 25, et à la Propagande Démocratique et sociale, rue Coquillière, 25 bis [1849], BN Lb55 834. This is a two-page brochure, sold at one centime and extracted from *Socialisme devant le vieux monde*. The portrait of "the Mountain" reproduced here (Illustration 21) is another example of the kind of material distributed by the Propagande. See also Charles Joubert, *Biographies et portraits d'après nature des candidats socialistes du département de la Seine* (Paris). A la propagande démocratique et sociale, 1849. Considerant is here described (p. 8) as endowed with "a mathematical and practical mind" and as "an ardent and conscientious defender" of the "interests of democracy and socialism."

26. On the press committee, see *Procès des accusés du 13 juin 1849* (Paris, 1849), 26. On the Society of Friends of Democratic Poland, of which Considerant was treasurer, see *DP*, 17, no. 350 (December 29, 1848), and the dossier in AN 10AS 31 (6).

27. *DP*, 18, no. 123 (May 6, 1849); *La Vraie République* (April 29, 1849). For the program of the Comité, see Latta, *Claude Bernard*, 177–179.

28. VC, *SVM*, 2.

29. VC, *SVM*, 4, 5.

30. VC, *SVM*, 9.

31. On Considerant's early uses of the terms *socialistes* and *socialisme*, see Chapter 6, note 1.

32. VC, *SVM*, 28, 19.

33. VC, *SVM*, 23.

34. VC, *SVM*, 30.

35. VC, *SVM*, 125.

36. VC, *SVM*, 126.

37. VC, *SVM*, 132–133.

38. VC, *SVM*, 134–135.

39. VC, *SVM*, 135, 136.

40. VC, *SVM*, 145.

41. VC, *SVM*, 159, 163.

42. VC, *SVM*, 167, 168.

43. VC, *SVM*, 201.

44. VC, *SVM*, 202

45. Laverdant to VC [May 1849], AN 10AS 39 (8).

46. See the folder "Congrès phalanstérien de 1848–1849. Travaux du Comité de réalisation," AN 10AS 30 (6). Considerant's speech on October 15, 1848, is summarized in the *procès-verbal* for the opening session. The congress was subsequently divided into four study groups, or "commissions," and their meetings went on into March 1849. Considerant does not appear to have attended any of the subsequent meetings. For a list of the eighty-eight delegates who attended the opening meeting, see ENS AVC carton 2 (IX, 2).

47. See Considerant's criticism of *Le Siècle* in "A MM. Louis Perrée et Chambolle," *DP*, 18, no. 55 (February 24, 1849). Considerant's articles against Proudhon include "Pour en finir avec M. Proudhon," *DP*, 18, no. 41 (February 10, 1849); "Réponse de M. Proudhon à M. Considerant, et réplique," supplement to *DP*, 18, no. 49 (February 18, 1849); "Pour se défaire du socialisme," *DP*, 18, no. 53 (February 22, 1849).

48. "Assemblée Nationale. Séance du 13 avril, 1849," *DP*, 18, no. 101 (April 14, 1849).

49. Citations in this paragraph and the three following are all from "Assemblée Nationale. Séance du 14 avril, 1849," reprinted from the *Moniteur* as a supplement to *DP*, 18, no. 104 (April 17, 1849).

50. "Assemblée Nationale. Séance du 14 avril, 1849," *DP*, 18, no. 102 (April 15, 1849).

51. Adam Mickiewicz, in *La Tribune des peuples* (April 15, 1849), and in his *La Politique du XIXe siècle* (Paris, 1870), 234–250. The rest of the press comment is from "Les Journaux et le Phalanstère" in *DP*, 18, no. 103 (April 16, 1849).

52. Lamartine, in *Le Conseiller du peuple*, 1 (1849), 77; Anon., "Socialism

on Its Last Legs," *Punch, or the London Charivari*, 16 (1849), 185. Other comments are from "Les Journaux et le Phalanstère," *DP*, 18, no. 103 (April 16, 1849).

53. Insofar as Considerant's name meant anything to the general public two or three decades later, it was largely thanks to these cartoons. For a sampling, see Illustrations 16–20.

54. "Assemblée Nationale. Séance du 14 avril, 1849," *DP*, 18, no. 102 (April 15, 1849).

55. VC, *Discours prononcé à l'Assemblée constituante dans la séance du 14 avril 1849* (Paris, 1849), 173 pp.

56. For the Montalembert quote and much of the preceding paragraph, see Pierre Pierrard, *1848 . . . les pauvres, l'évangile et la révolution* (Paris, 1977), 90–94.

57. Bastid, *Doctrines et institutions politiques*, 2: 204–209; Berenson, *Populist Religion and Left-Wing Politics*, 138–140, 216–218.

58. Roger Magraw, "Pierre Joigneaux and Socialist Propaganda in the French Countryside, 1849–1851," *French Historical Studies*, 10 (Fall 1978), 599–640; George Fasel, "The Wrong Revolution: French Republicanism in 1848," *French Historical Studies*, 8 (Fall 1974), 654–677; Peter McPhee, "The Crisis of Radical Republicanism in the French Revolution of 1848," *Historical Studies*, 16 (1974–1975), 71–88.

59. Bastid, *Doctrines et institutions politiques*, 2: 208–209; *DP*, 18, no. 116, 125 (April 29, May 10, 1849).

60. Jacques Bouillon, "Les Democrates-socialistes aux élections de 1849," *Revue française de science politique* (1956), 70–95; Pierrard, *1848 . . . les pauvres, l'évangile et la révolution*, 200–210; Clark, *Image of the People*, 86–87; Tudesq, *Les Grands notables en France*, 2: 1212–1226.

61. VC to Barral, June 1851, AN 10AS 28 (9): "On the day when the reaction began officially and formally to exercise power in France, i.e., after the election of the Legislative Assembly, I enrolled myself in the Mountain, which I had not previously wished to join. Why? Because I now envisioned a war that could only end with a decisive victory for all the forces of social democracy arrayed against all the forces of aristocracy, and I felt absolutely bound to participate in the struggle."

62. Tocqueville, *Souvenirs*, 180, 194; Barrot, *Mémoires posthumes*, in Bastid, *Doctrines et institutions politiques*, 2: 210.

CHAPTER 11

1. Christopher Hibbert, *Garibaldi and His Enemies* (Boston, 1965), 49, 42.

2. Roland Sarti, *Mazzini: A Life for the Religion of Politics* (Westport, Ct., 1997), 139. On the Roman Republic and the background to the French Roman expedition, William L. Langer, *Political and Social Upheaval, 1832–1852* (New York, 1969), 428–450, offers a good brief overview. See also Harry Hearder, *Italy in the Age of the Risorgimento* (London, 1983), 96–119, 202–207; Denis

Mack Smith, *Mazzini* (New Haven, 1994), 64–76; and E. E. Y. Hales, *Pio Nono* (Garden City, N.Y., 1962), 87–140.

3. VC, "L'Abstention," *DP,* 18, no. 105 (April 18, 1849).

4. Langer, *Political and Social Upheaval,* 442.

5. *La Patrie* (May 8, 1849), in Coignet, *Victor Considerant,* 54.

6. VC, "La France Trahie," *DP,* 18, no. 125 (May 8, 1849); VC, "Proposition de mise en accusation du Président de la République," 2 pp., draft dated May 9, 1849, ENS AVC carton 8 (II, 2); "Assemblée Nationale. Séance du 9 mai," *DP,* 18, no. 127 (May 10, 1849); "Acte d'accusation," *Procès des accusés du 13 juin 1849* (Paris, 1849), 25.

7. Paul Raphael, "Les Républicains modérés et la journée du 13 juin 1849," *La Révolution de 1848,* 20 (1924–1925), 43–51; Tocqueville, *Souvenirs,* 193; Bernard H. Moss, "June 13, 1849: The Abortive Uprising of French Radicalism," *French Historical Studies,* 13 (Spring 1984), 401–402. The article by Moss (390–414 in its entirety) is the best study in any language of the *journée* of June 13.

8. "Déclaration," *DP,* 18, no. 158 (June 10, 1849); "La Constitution et l'expédition de Rome," *DP,* 18, no. 159 (June 11, 1849); *Procès des accusés du 13 juin 1849,* 32, 93, 103, 106–108; "Haute Cour de Justice séant à Versailles. Affaire du 13 juin. Acte d' accusation," in *DP,* 18, no. 213–215 (October 14–16, 1849); Moss, "June 13, 1849," 402; Alfred Darimon, *A travers une révolution (1847–1855)* (Paris, 1884), 155–157.

9. VC, *Journée du 13 juin. Simples explications à mes amis et à mes commettants* (Paris, 1849), 23–27.

10. VC, *Simples explications,* 28–29; "Haute Cour de Justice séant à Versailles. Affaire du 13 juin. Audience du 7 novembre 1849," in *DP,* 18, no. 237 (November 8, 1849). In a written statement dated October 19, 1849, Considerant specified that although he was able to present his draft decree to the representatives of the Mountain on June 11, there was no time for discussion. "I lost no opportunity to try to convince my political friends of the need to adopt this project. What is certain is that due to the pressure of circumstances, the project could not even be placed under discussion." ENS AVC carton 8 (II, 1).

11. "Assemblée législative. Séance du 11 juin 1849," *DP,* 18, no. 160 (June 12, 1849); Sébastien Commissaire, *Mémoires et souvenirs* (Lyon, 1988), 232. Tocqueville, *Souvenirs,* 194, called Ledru-Rollin's speech a "call to civil war."

12. Commissaire, *Mémoires et souvenirs,* 232–234; Darimon, *A travers une révolution,* 157–158; Moss, "June 13, 1849," 403–404; VC, statement dated October 19, 1849, ENS AVC carton 8 (II, 1).

13. "Assemblée législative. Séance du 12 juin 1849," *DP,* 18, no. 161 (June 13, 1849); Tocqueville, *Souvenirs,* 195.

14. Commissaire, *Mémoires et souvenirs,* 236.

15. "Acte d'accusation," *Procès des accusés du 13 juin 1849,* 36; Darimon, *A travers une révolution,* 159–160; Moss, "June 13, 1849," 404. Bernard Moss's solid and thoughtful article has been a great help to me in my own efforts to grapple with the primary sources, but my impression from a study of

these sources is that he (like the government prosecutor) overestimates the consensus on armed insurrection.

16. For the fullest firsthand account of this meeting, see Commissaire, *Mémoires et souvenirs*, 236–239.

17. This proclamation was published in *Démocratie pacifique*, June 13, 1849, as well as five other radical journals. The text was reprinted in *Procès des accusés du 13 juin 1849*, 37. See also Félix Pyat, *Lettres d'un proscrit*, 2 vols. (Paris, 1851), 2: 103, for the (dubious) claim that the proclamation was actually drafted by someone else and that he, Ledru Rollin, and Considerant merely went over it with the author,

18. VC, *Simples explications*, 28–29, and statement dated October 19, 1849, ENS AVC carton 8 (II, 1). The manuscript statement was apparently written to refute the attempt of the government prosecutor to demonstrate that June 13 was the outcome of a conspiracy seeking to overthrow the government and the Legislative Assembly. In my view, the statement is entirely credible.

19. All four proclamations are reprinted in *Procès des accusés du 13 juin*, 37–39. See also Commissaire, *Mémoires et souvenirs*, 240–243; and Moss, "June 13, 1849," 404–405.

20. Commissaire, *Mémoires et souvenirs*, 243; Marx, *Class Struggles in France*, 97–100, and *The Eighteenth Brumaire of Louis Bonaparte* (New York, n.d.), 46; Moss, "June 13, 1849," 405.

21. VC, *Simples explications*, 32.

22. Alexander Herzen, *My Past and Thoughts*, 4 vols. (New York, 1969), 2: 679.

23. Moss, "June 13, 1849," 406; Herzen, *My Past and Thoughts*, 2: 679; Gustave Lefrançais, *Souvenirs d'un révolutionnaire* (Paris, 1972), 94.

24. VC, *Simples explications*, 31.

25. Alvin R. Calman, *Ledru Rollin and the Second French Republic* (New York, 1922), 380–381. For the "new Jeu de Paume," see Amédée de Saint-Ferréol, *Mes Mémoires*, 5 vols. (Brioude, 1887–1893), 2: 192. See also Moss, "June 13, 1849," 406.

26. On this point Considerant's own narrative is vague and unhelpful. See *Simples explications*, 30–31.

27. Calman, *Ledru-Rollin*, 381; "Acte d'Accusation," *Procès des accusés du 13 juin 1849*, 46; VC, *Simples explications*, 31–32; Alexandre-Auguste Ledru-Rollin, *Le 13 juin* (Paris, 1849), 17; Moss, "June 13, 1849," 409.

28. Estimates of the number of Montagnard representatives actually participating in the march to the Conservatoire range from sixty in Calman, *Ledru-Rollin*, 382, and sixty to eighty in Arthur Ranc, *Souvenirs — Correspondance, 1831–1908* (Paris, 1913), 47, to thirty in Moss, "June 13, 1849," 406, and fifteen in Darimon, *A travers une révolution*, 162. The "Acte d'accusation" in *Procès des accusés du 13 juin 1849*, 46, mentions a witness who counted fifty-three representatives, but it estimates twenty-five to thirty as the number who stayed in the procession to the end.

29. VC, *Simples explications*, 33.

30. Claude Pouillet, *Le Conservatoire des Arts et Métiers pendant la journée du 13 juin 1849* (Paris, 1849), 5.

31. Pouillet, *Le Conservatoire*, 5–6.

32. On Michel de Bourges, Saint-Ferréol, *Mes Mémoires*, 2: 193. On Ledru-Rollin, see the testimony of Pouillet's secretary, Louis Dupin, in *Procès des accusés du 13 juin 1849*, 236.

33. VC, *Simples explications*, 37.

34. VC, *Simples explications*, 35. For a critical review of the evidence (though not Damiron) that concludes against the authenticity of the call to arms, see Calman, *Ledru-Rollin*, 384–386. See also Commissaire, *Mémoires et souvenirs*, 245–246; and Damiron, *A travers une révolution*, 163–166.

35. VC, *Simples explications*, 38–39; Pouillet, *Le Conservatoire*, 14–15. Pouillet, who was a Franc-comtois like Considerant, was subsequently fired for his alleged misconduct in allowing the Montagnards to enter the Conservatoire. See Philippe Pluvinage, "Quelques épisodes de la carrière d'un grand physicien franc-comtois: Claude-Servais-Mathias Pouillet (1790–1868)," *Mémoires de la Société d'Emulation du Doubs*, new series, 26 (1984), 59–68.

36. Deville in Calman, *Ledru-Rollin*, 388–389. See also VC, *Simples explications*, 39.

37. VC, *Simples explications*, 40.

38. VC, *Simples explications*, 40–41. See also Calman, *Ledru-Rollin*, 389–390.

39. VC, *Simples explications*, 42–45. The staff member who helped Considerant and his friends escape was Louis Dupin, the secretary of the director, Claude Pouillet. See his testimony in *Procès des accusés du 13 juin 1849*, 235–242. Despite conclusive evidence to the contrary, rumors persisted for years that the portly Ledru-Rollin had had to make his escape by wriggling through a transom.

40. VC, *Simples explications*, 45–47.

41. VC, *Simples explications*, 48–49.

42. Some information may be found in VC to Bureau [August 1849], 12 pp., ENS AVC carton 9 (II, 1). There is an account of Considerant's hiding and escape from France in Redelia Brisbane (ed.), *Albert Brisbane: A Mental Biography* (Boston, 1893), 315. This compilation by Brisbane's widow of her husband's notes and jottings is notoriously unreliable, and the account of Considerant's escape is placed in the aftermath of December 2, 1851, not June 13, 1849. But some of the details (which probably come from Considerant's reminiscences to Brisbane) are perfectly consistent with information from other sources.

43. It was Désiré Laverdant who described Bazaine as "the devoted friend who saved the fugitive in 1849." Laverdant to Jaenger, April 1, 1852, BN NAF 22,050, reproduced in part in Paul Muller, "Victor Considerant après le coup d'état," *La Révolution de 1848*, 10 (1913–1914), 435. On Pierre-Dominique Bazaine-Vasseur (1809–1893), see *Dictionnaire de biographie française*, 5 (1951), 1017.

44. The four entered together on July 4. VC to Félix Delhasse, July 5, 1849, in Discailles, "Victor Considerant en Belgique," 729. Latta, *Martin Bernard*, 190–191, describes Martin Bernard as traveling with Ledru-Rollin and Etienne Arago but not Considerant.

45. J. S. Mill to Henry Samuel Chapman, May 28, 1849, in *Collected Works of John Stuart Mill*, vol. 14 (Toronto, 1972), 33–34.

46. VC, *Simples explications*, 56; Marx, *Eighteenth Brumaire*, 46; Pierre-Joseph Proudhon, *Confessions d'un révolutionnaire* (Paris, 1929), 330; Herzen, *My Past and Thoughts*, 2: 676.

47. "Acte d'Accusation," *Procès des accusés du 13 juin 1849*, 17–41.

48. See, for example, Laverdant to VC, July 22, 1849, AN 10AS 39 (8); François Coignet to Parisian Fourierists, July 8, 1849, AN 10AS 37 (4); Krantz to Bureau, May 11, 1850, AN 10AS 39 (5); Paul Muller, *La Révolution de 1848 en Alsace* (Paris, 1912), 182. Even in America W. H. Channing complained that the Fourierist movement had been "compromised by its friends" (*The Spirit of the Age* [August 11, 1849], 89–90), while John Dwight was insisting, in the wake of June 13, that "We are not Red republicans" (*Boston Daily Chronotype*, August 23, 1849), both cited in Guarneri, *The Utopian Alternative*, 339.

49. Conseil de direction de l'Ecole Sociétaire to Fourierists, June 21, 1849, ENS AVC carton 9 (II, 2).

50. VC, "A l'Ecole Sociétaire. Appel de Réorganisation," draft of seventeen folio pages, dated August 8, 1849, "on the Rhine" [sic] and followed by a two-page statement by François Cantagrel, ENS AVC carton 9 (I, 1). A slightly revised version of this article was published in the *Bulletin phalanstérien*, 11 (September 8, 1849), 123–127.

51. VC, "A l'Ecole Sociétaire," 13, and *Bulletin phalanstérien*, 126.

52. VC, "A l'Ecole Sociétaire," 3, and *Bulletin phalanstérien*, 123.

53. VC, "A l'Ecole Sociétaire," 10, and *Bulletin phalanstérien*, 125.

CHAPTER 12

1. Tocqueville, *Souvenirs*, 198.

2. VC, *Simples Explications*, 8, 52, 67. This pamphlet first appeared as a supplement to Félix Delhasse's journal, *Le Débat social*, July 5, 1849. It was then published separately in both Brussels and Paris.

3. Howard C. Payne and Henry Grosshans, "The Exiled Revolutionaries and the French Political Police in the 1850's," *American Historical Review*, 68, no. 4 (July 1963), 954.

4. Amédée Saint-Ferréol, *Les Proscrits français en Belgique, ou la Belgique contemporaine vue à travers l'exil*, 2 vols. (Paris, 1871).

5. One of the principal sources for this chapter is the voluminous police dossier on Considerant kept by the Belgian Ministry of Justice. Considerant was under police surveillance throughout his five years of political exile in Belgium, and the dossier consists of hundreds of pieces. See Archives Générales du Royaume (Brussels), Ministère de la Justice, Police des Etrangers. Dossiers

individuels 36,486. (Referred to henceforth as AGR MJ PE 36,486.) An important published source is Ernest Discailles, "Le Socialiste français Victor Considerant en Belgique," *Académie royale des sciences, des lettres et des beaux-arts de Belgique. Bulletins de l'Académie*, 3rd ser., 29 (1895), 705–748. Although Discailles does little with the police archives, he publishes much of Considerant's correspondence with Charles Rogier, Félix Delhasse, and others.

6. VC to JC and CV, August 9, 1849, AN 10AS 28 (8).

7. VC to Rogier, June 6, 1850, AN 10AS 26 (10). See also VC to Rogier [July 1849], ENS AVC carton 9 (III, 3); and VC and Cantagrel to Brunier or Bourdon, August 1849: "Rogier était un brave homme. Ce n'est plus qu'une citrouille."

8. On Alexandre Delhasse, see the obituary in *DP*, 19, no. 83 (March 25, 1850), and his letters in AN 10AS 37 (7); and J. Kuypers, *Buonarroti et ses sociétés secrètes* (Brussels, 1960), 128–129, 135.

9. VC to Bureau [September 1849], ENS AVC carton 9 (II, 1); Commissaire de Police de Spa to Administrateur de la Sûreté Publique, July 21, 1849, AGR MJ PE 36,486. See also VC to JC, July 19, 1849, BMB Ms Z464.

10. Considerant believed the police commissioner had made him "the object of an experiment." In fact, the minister of justice had given orders that Considerant be placed under surveillance. AGR MJ PE 36,486.

11. VC to Rogier, draft [late July 1849], ENS AVC carton 9 (III, 3).

12. VC to JC [August 1849], AN 10AS 28 (8); Chef des gendarmes à Charleroi to Administrateur de la Sûreté Publique, August 27, 1849, AGR MJ PE 36,486; VC to Parisian Fourierists, August 30, 1849, AN 10AS 28 (8).

13. *La Tribune* (Liège), September 7, 1849, transcribed by John Bartier. *Journal de Bruxelles*, September 7, 1849, cutting in AGR MJ PE 36,486.

14. Coignet, *Victor Considerant*, 70; and Coignet, *Mémoires*, 174.

15. VC to Gustave Considerant, September 26, 1849, ENS AVC carton 9 (III, 3); VC, "Irons-nous à Versailles?" *DP*, 18, no. 195 (September 26, 1849).

16. VC to Brunier, October 4, 1849, AN 10AS 28 (8); reports of Bourgmestre de Laroche, October 8, 1849, and Administrateur de la Sûreté Publique, October 13, 1849, AGR MJ PE 36,486.

17. On Hippolyte Colignon (1813–1891), see the substantial obituary in *L'Indépendance belge*, 72, no. 182 (July 1, 1891). For the Café des Trois Suisses, see Louis Hymans and Jean-Baptiste Rousseau, *Le Diable à Bruxelles*, 4 vols. (Brussels, 1853), 1: 70–71.

18. Administrateur de la Sûreté Publique to Ministre de la Justice, March 1, 1850, AGR MJ PE 36,486; VC to Bureau, March 1850, AN 10AS 28 (9).

19. VC to Rogier, draft, March 23, 1850, AN 10AS 28 (9). Portions published in Discailles, "Considerant en Belgique," 733.

20. This paragraph is based on an abundant series of reports and dispatches in AGR MJ PE 36,486. See especially Administrateur de la Sûreté Publique to Ministre de la Justice, April 12, 1850; French Ministre des Affaires Etrangères to Belgian Ministre de la Justice, May 16, 1850; and the correspondence be-

tween the authorities at Bouillon and the Administrateur de la Sûreté Publique, April 2–May 23, 1850. See also VC to Rogier, draft, June 6, 1850, AN 10AS 26 (10).

21. VC to Rogier, copy, June 6, 1850, AN 10AS 26 (10); Goedert, Brigadier commandant de la Brigade des gendarmes de Laroche to Administrateur de la Sûreté Publique, June 4, July 12, August 10, September 9, December 17, 1850, AGR MJ PE 36,486.

22. Coignet, *Victor Considerant,* 69–70.

23. Coignet, *Victor Considerant,* 70–71.

24. VC to Bureau, November 27, 1850, AN 10AS 28 (9).

25. VC to Parisian Fourierists, December 24, 1850, ENS AVC carton 9 (III, 5); Administrateur de la Sûreté Publique to Ministre de la Justice, February 3 and 14, 1851, and to Procureur du Roi, February 7, 1851, AGR MJ PE 36,486; VC to Parisian Fourierists, February 20, 1851, ENS AVC carton 8 (II, 1).

26. Demeur to Bureau, June 23, 1851, AN 10AS 37 (7); VC to JC, June 20, 1851, AN 10AS 28 (9); Administrateur de la Sûreté Publique to Ministre de la Justice, July 12, 1851, AGR MJ PE 36,486. This last is published in Hubert Wouters, *Documenten betreffende de geschiedenis der arbeidersbeweging (1831–1853),* 3 vols. (Louvain, 1963), 2: 848.

27. Legros, Brigadier Commandant de la Brigade de Gendarmerie à Durbuy to Administrateur de la Sûreté Publique, August 1, 1851, AGR MJ PE 36,486; Xavier Olin, "Une Excursion dans les Ardennes," *Revue trimestrelle* (Brussels), 11 (1856), 244–268; VC to Amédée Guillon, September 1851, ENS AVC carton 2 (I, 3).

28. Ministre des Affaires Etrangères to Ministre de la Justice, September 9, 1851; Administrateur de la Sûreté Publique to Ministre de la Justice, September 10, 1851; Bourgmestre de Barvaux to Administrateur de la Sûreté Publique, December 13, 1851, May 22, 1852, and November 26, 1852, AGR MJ PE 36,486.

29. VC to Namèche Despierreux, March 22, 1852, Bibliothèque Municipale d'Orléans, Ms 1502–1508; VC to Baron Van der Skalen, twelve-page draft [April 11, 1852], ENS AVC carton 9 (I, 1); Van der Skalen to VC, April 13, 1852, AN 10AS 42 (7).

30. VC to Parisian Fourierists, June 14, 1850, ENS AVC carton 8 (II, 1); VC to Bureau, January 11, 1851, ENS AVC carton 9 (III, 3).

31. Undated statement to VC signed by nine editors of *DP,* AN 10AS 36 (9).

32. VC to Bourdon, April 1, 1850, AN 10AS 28 (9).

33. On the charges of "charlatanism," see Considerant's comments in *Les Quatre crédits, ou 60 milliards à 1 1/2 pour cent* (Paris, 1851), v. On Joigneaux and his enormously popular journal, *La Feuille du village,* see Roger William Magraw, "Pierre Joigneaux and Socialist Propaganda in the French Countryside, 1849–1851," *French Historical Studies,* 10, no. 4 (Fall 1978), 599–640.

34. Hugo's play, *Les Burgraves,* was produced in 1843. Marx's Burgraves were "the Orleanist and Legitimist party leaders, the Thiers, the Berryers, the

Broglies, the Molés." See his *Eighteenth Brumaire*, 59. When Marx's work appeared (spring 1852), this usage of the term was already common coin. See Odilon Barrot, *Mémoires posthumes*, 4: 2.

35. VC to Bureau, November 21, 1850, AN 10AS 28 (9). See also VC to [Bureau?], February 8, 1851, ENS AVC carton 2 (I, 3).

36. VC to "Burgraves en conseil," June 30, 1850, AN 10AS 28 (9).

37. VC, *La Dernière Guerre et la paix définitive en Europe* (Paris, March 20, 1850).

38. VC to Tandon, copy, March 25, 1851, AN 10AS 28 (9). Excerpts published in *DP*, 13, no. 44 (June 1, 1851).

39. VC to Ledru-Rollin, draft (January 11, 1851), AN 10AS 28 (9); Ledru-Rollin to VC, February 4 [1851], AN 10AS 39 (7). VC to Mazzini, draft [April 1852], ENS AVC carton 8 (I, 1) and another draft in carton 8 (I, 2), both responding to Mazzini's articles in *La Nation* (Brussels), March–April, 1852. See Denis Mack Smith, *Mazzini*, 85–89. *Almanach républicain démocratique pour 1850*. Rédigé par les citoyens Arnaud (de l'Ariège), Barbès, Louis Blanc, Blanqui, Considerant. . . . (n.p., n.d.).

40. Rousseau, *Le Contrat social*, book 3, chapter 15.

41. On the debate over direct government, see Marcel David, "Le 'Gouvernement direct du peuple' selon les proscrits de la Seconde République," in Association française des historiens des idées politiques, *Actes du XIe colloque d'Aix-en-Provence (21–22 septembre, 1955), La Pensée démocratique* (Aix-Marseille, 1996). See also the introduction by Aimé Berthod to the Rivière edition of Proudhon, *Idée générale de la révolution au XIXe siècle* (Paris, 1923), 56–63; and Bernard Voyenne, *Le Fédéralisme de P-J Proudhon* (Paris, 1973), 109–115.

42. VC, *De la sincérité du gouvernement représentatif ou exposition de l'élection véridique. Lettre adressée à messieurs les membres du Grand Conseil Constituant de l'Etat de Genève* (Geneva, October 26, 1846). See also VC, *Les Quatre crédits*, 140.

43. M. Rittinghausen, "La Législation directe par le peuple, ou la véritable démocratie," *DP*, 13, nos. 6, 7, 8 (September 8, 15, 22, 1850). This work was also published separately as a forty-eight-page brochure by the Librairie phalanstérienne.

44. VC, *La Solution, ou le gouvernement direct du peuple* (Paris, 1850), 8. This work first appeared in *DP*, 13, nos. 16, 17, 19 (November 17 and 24, December 8, 1850), under the title *La Solution, c'est le gouvernement du peuple par lui-même*.

45. VC, *La Solution*, 17–18.

46. VC, *La Solution*, 19–20, 25, 64.

47. VC, *La Solution*, 47.

48. VC, *La Solution*, 50–52.

49. VC, *La Solution*, 25.

50. VC, *La Solution*, 67.

51. Colignon to VC, January 23, 1851, AN 10AS 37 (4); George Sand to

Emile Aucante, January 10, 1851, in George Sand, *Correspondance,* edited by Georges Lubin, vol. 10 (Paris, 1973), 27; Jean Allemane, "Victor Considerant," *Le Parti ouvrier* (December 30–31, 1893); Robert Michels, *Political Parties* (New York, 1959), 23–40.

52. Proudhon, *Idée générale de la révolution,* 213–232; Louis Blanc, *Plus de Girondins* (Paris, 1851), 22–45.

53. VC to Ledru-Rollin, draft [January 11, 1851], AN 10AS 28 (9); see also Ledru-Rollin's reply, February 4 [1851], AN 10AS 39 (7). Ledru-Rollin himself made two contributions to the public debate over direct government: "Plus de président, plus de représentants," *La Voix du proscrit* (February 16, 1851), and "Du Gouvernement direct du peuple," *La Voix du proscrit* (April 5, 1851).

54. VC to Ledru-Rollin, draft, AN 10AS 28 (9). See also Ledru-Rollin to VC, February 4 [1851], AN 10AS 39 (7).

55. Pierre-Joseph Proudhon, *La Révolution sociale démontrée par le coup d'état du deux décembre,* edited by Aimé Berthod (Paris, 1936); Pierre Haubtmann, *Pierre-Joseph Proudhon. Sa Vie et sa pensée, 1849–1865,* 2 vols. (Paris, 1988), 1: 151–160; Victor Schoelcher, *Histoire des crimes du deux décembre* (London, 1852), 17, in Payne and Grosshans, "The Exiled Revolutionaries," 956; Jacques Thbaut, "A Propos du centenaire de la mort de Constantin Pecqueur (1887–1997). Jalons pour une biographie scientifique," in *1848. Révolutions et mutations au XIXe siècle,* vol. 3 (1987), 67–82.

56. See, for example, VC, address to Congrès Phalanstérien, October 15, 1848, in *Bulletin phalanstérien,* 10 (November 30, 1848), 100: "The supreme goal of all the efforts of the Ecole is to arrive at the experimental proof of Fourier's theory."

57. Considerant's incredulous reply cited in Brunier to colleagues, December 20, 1849, AN 10AS 37 (2). Comment on Muiron in VC to Bureau, August 22, 1850, AN 10AS 28 (9).

58. VC, *Au Texas,* 2nd ed. (Brussels-Paris, 1855), 5; VC to Bureau, March 7, 1852, ENS AVC carton 8 (II, 1); VC to Savardan, August 24, 1852, and Savardan to VC, August 30, 1852, copies, AN 10AS 31 (4); VC to Bureau [August 1852], ENS AVC carton 8 (II, 1).

59. Quoted in VC, "A l'Ecole Sociétaire. Appel de Réorganisation," August 8, 1849, ENS AVC carton 8 (I, 1).

60. Guillon to VC, December 30, 1851, AN 10AS 38 (16); VC, *Au Texas,* 6–7.

61. VC to Bureau, November 20, 1852, AN 10AS 28 (9).

62. VC to JC, November 30, 1852, AN 10AS 28 (9); VC, *Au Texas,* 9.

CHAPTER 13

1. Herman Melville, *The Confidence-Man: His Masquerade* (Evanston, 1984), 9.

2. Walt Whitman, "Manahatta," *Leaves of Grass* (Boston, 1899), 360–361.

3. VC, *Au Texas,* 2nd ed. (Brussels-Paris, 1855; reprint ed. Philadelphia, 1975), 9–10.

4. VC to Bureau, December 22, 1852, ENS AVC carton 8 (II, 1).

5. *New York Daily Tribune* (December 16, 1852), in Russell M. Jones, "Victor Considerant's American Experience (1852–1869)," *French-American Review* 1, no. 1 (Winter 1976), 65. Jones's article is based on massive and careful research and offers a lucid narrative of this whole period in Considerant's life. It has been a great help to me in my own work on this chapter and the two that follow.

6. VC to Bureau, December 22, 1852, ENS AVC carton 8 (II, 1). See the *New York Daily Tribune,* December 22, 1852, for "Victor Considerant," translated from the *Allgemeine Zeitung* of New York.

7. Ripley speaks of meeting Considerant in Ripley to James T. Fisher, December 27, 1852, J. T. Fisher Papers, Massachusetts Historical Society, Boston. On Ripley, see the excellent biography by Charles Crowe, *George Ripley: Transcendentalist and Utopian Socialist* (Athens, Ga., 1967). On Dana, whom Considerant had already met in 1848 when Dana was covering events in Paris for the *Tribune,* see Janet E. Steele, *The Sun Shines for All: Journalism and Ideology in the Life of Charles A. Dana* (Syracuse, 1993); and James Harrison Wilson, *The Life of Charles A. Dana* (New York, 1907). Parke Godwin, who had been a major American exponent of Fourier's ideas in the 1840s, was assistant editor for his father-in-law William Cullen Bryant's *New York Evening Post* and (from 1853) co-editor of the influential *Putnam's Monthly.* All these men turned relatively conservative after 1850. For larger contexts I have found helpful Edward K. Spann, *The New Metropolis: New York City, 1840–1857* (New York, 1981), and Thomas Bender, *New York Intellect* (Baltimore, 1987).

8. Walt Whitman, "Street Yarn," *Life Illustrated* (August 16, 1856), reprinted in Walt Whitman, *New York Dissected* (New York, 1936), 129.

9. VC to JC, March 9, 1853, and April 5, 1853, AN 10AS 28 (9).

10. See the large packet of Considerant's reading notes on Owen in AN 10AS 26 (29).

11. VC to Fisher, March 31, 1853, and Ripley to Fisher, December 27, 1852, Fisher Papers.

12. On the North American Phalanx, see Carl J. Guarneri, *The Utopian Alternative: Fourierism in Nineteenth-Century America* (Ithaca, 1991), 179–218, 321–328, and *passim.* Guarneri's book is a marvelously rich and thoroughly reliable guide to the history of all aspects of American Fourierism. I have profited greatly from it.

13. Charles Sears to VC, January 3, 1853, AN 10AS 41 (13); Emile Chevalier, article from *Le Courrier des Etats-Unis,* cited in *Bulletin du Mouvement Sociétaire en Europe et en Amérique,* 32 (November–December, 1860), 257; VC to JC, January 3, 1853, ENS AVC carton 2 (I, 3).

14. Charles Sears to [?], April 22, 1853, AN 10AS 31 (5).

15. VC, *Au Texas*, 12–15; VC to JC, January 26, 1853, ENS AVC carton 2 (I, 3).

16. VC to Bureau, April 4, 1853, ENS AVC, carton 8 (II, 1).

17. VC, *Au Texas*, 16; W. F. Channing to VC, April 3, 1853, AN 10AS 37 (3); VC to Fisher, August 11, 1853, Fisher Papers; Guarneri, *The Utopian Alternative*, 337, 371, 440.

18. VC, *Au Texas*, 17–18; Guarneri, *The Utopian Alternative*, 250.

19. VC, *Au Texas*, 19.

20. VC, *Au Texas*, 20.

21. VC to Bureau, April 4, 1853, ENS AVC carton 8 (II, 1).

22. J. R. Miller, "M. Considerant,—Trout Fishing, etc.," *The Circular* (Oneida Community), 2, no. 43 (April 13, 1853).

23. VC to Bureau and colleagues, April 21, 1853, ENS AVC carton 8 (II, 1).

24. VC to JC, April 23, 1853, AN 10AS 28 (9).

25. VC to JC, May 3, 1853, AN 10AS 28 (9); VC, *Au Texas*, 26. In *Au Texas*, Considerant gives his departure date as April 30, but in his letter to Julie it is April 27. On E. P. Grant, who in 1844 founded the short-lived and undercapitalized Ohio Phalanx, see Guarneri, *The Utopian Alternative*, 156, 387.

26. VC to JC, May 3, 1853, AN 10AS 28 (9).

27. VC to JC, May 3, 1853, AN 10AS 28 (9); VC, *Au Texas*, 27. On Gengembre (also spelled Gingembre), see Beecher, *Charles Fourier*, 461, 465–467, and the (amusing) letters of his son H. P. Gengembre to VC, April 12, 1855, and to Amédée Simonin, April 18, 1855, Simonin Papers, Library of Congress, Manuscript Division, Ms. 18,160.

28. VC, *Au Texas*, 27.

29. VC to JC, May 7, 1853, AN 10AS 28 (9).

30. Charles Dickens, *Pictures from Italy and American Notes for General Circulation* (London, 1966), 347–349; VC, *Au Texas*, 27–28; VC to Bureau and colleagues, May 3, 1853, ENS AVC carton 8 (II, 1).

31. VC to JC, May 7, 1853, AN 10AS 28 (9). The ink of Considerant's letter has browned and the paper is brittle, but the lock of Victor Considerant Allen's hair, which is still tucked between the sheets of paper, is as fresh as ever. On John Allen, see Lindsay Swift, *Brook Farm*, reprint ed. (New York, 1961), 176–177, 181–184; Charles Crowe, *George Ripley*, 191, 204, 206, 217; Guarneri, *The Utopian Alternative*, 238–244, 330–331, and *passim*.

32. VC to JC, May 13 [1853], BMB Z417; VC to Bureau and colleagues, May 15, 1853, ENS AVC carton 8 (II, 1).

33. VC to Bureau and colleagues, May 17, 1853, ENS AVC carton 8 (II, 1).

34. VC to Bureau and colleagues, May 18, 1853, ENS AVC carton 8 (II, 1); and for the Catlin reference, Jones, "Considerant's American Experience," 79–80.

35. Fourier, *Oeuvres complètes*, 1: 33–37, 52–72; Beecher, *Charles Fourier*, 319–329; VC to Bureau and colleagues, May 18, 1853, ENS AVC carton 8 (II, 1).

36. VC, *Au Texas*, 30–31. Since this passage obviously resists fluent translation, I might note the French for the next-to-last sentence: "Nous étions seuls, et pour la première fois au sein de ces énergies indomptées de la nature naturante." The term "la nature naturante" refers to Spinoza's conception of nature as the cause of all phenomena. The reference to *Faust* is to lines 384–385 of part 1.

37. VC, *Au Texas*, 31–32. VC to Bureau and colleagues, May 27, 1853, ENS AVC carton 8 (II, 1).

38. VC, *Au Texas*, 34–35. VC to Bureau and colleagues, May 27, 1853, ENS AVC carton 8 (II, 1).

39. VC, *Au Texas*, 36–37. On Preston, W. B. Parker, *Notes Taken during the Expedition Commanded by Capt. R. B. Marcy, U.S.A., through Unexplored Texas in the Fall of 1854* (Philadelphia, 1856), 72, in William J. Hammond and Margaret F. Hammond, *La Réunion: A French Settlement in Texas* (Dallas, 1958), 40, 137.

40. VC to Bureau and colleagues, May 27, 1853, ENS AVC carton 8 (II, 1); Hammond and Hammond, *La Réunion*, 40; Jones, "Considerant's American Experience," 80; A. C. Greene, *Dallas: The Deciding Years* (Austin, 1973), 11.

41. Considerant's long and detailed narrative, apparently intended for publication, of his encounter with Gouhenant may be found in AN 10AS 28 (9). It is not dated and the pages are marked pp. 3–8. See also VC to Paris colleagues, June 14, 1853, ENS AVC carton 8 (II, 1); and Jules Prudhommeaux, *Icarie et son fondateur Etienne Cabet* (Paris, 1907), 217–235. On Gouhenant, see *Procès du Communisme à Toulouse* (Paris, 1843), 52–53.

42. VC to Paris colleagues, June 14, 1853, ENS AVC carton 8 (II, 1).

43. VC to Paris colleagues, June 14, 1853, ENS AVC carton 8 (II, 1); VC, *Au Texas*, 45–46, 295; VC, *The Great West: A New Social and Industrial Life in Its Fertile Regions* (New York, 1854), 10–11, 12–15.

44. VC to Paris colleagues, June 14, 1853, ENS AVC carton 8 (II, 1).

45. VC to Paris colleagues, June 14, 1853, ENS AVC carton 8 (II, 1).

46. VC to Paris colleagues, June 14, 1853, ENS AVC carton 8 (II, 1). VC, *Au Texas*, 305.

47. Bourdon to [?], August 25 [1853], ENS AVC carton 4 (VI).

48. VC to Paris colleagues, August 9, 1853, ENS AVC carton 8 (II, 1); VC to JC [August 1853], AN 10AS 28 (9).

49. VC to JC [August 1853], AN 10AS 28 (9); VC to Justine Pallas and Gustave Considerant, October 28, 1853, ENS AVC carton 8 (III, 1).

50. VC to Paris colleagues, September 5, 1853, ENS AVC carton 8 (II, 1).

51. VC letters to Paris colleagues, November 1853–February 1854, AN 10AS 28 (9); Ministre des Affaires Etrangères to Ministre de la Justice, January 26, 1854, AGR MJ PE 36,486; VC to JC, January 12, 15, 16, 1854, AN 10AS 28 (9).

52. On the Bourson family, see John Bartier, *Libéralisme et socialisme au XIXe siècle* (Brussels, 1981), 373–374, 489; Bartier's *Naissance du socialisme*

en Belgique. Les Saint-Simoniens (Brussels, 1985), 27; and the substantial collection of letters from the Boursons to Considerant in AN 10AS 36 (8).

53. Théophile Thoré, "Notes et souvenirs," *Nouvelle revue rétrospective,* 9 (July–December, 1898), 321.

54. VC to Bureau, February 12, 1854, AN 10AS 28 (9).

55. Godin to VC, February 4, 1854, in Marie Moret, veuve Godin (ed.), *Documents pour une biographie complète de J-B-A. Godin,* 3 vols. (Guise, 1897–1910), 1: 315–324. See also Godin to Cantagrel, April 23, 1854, *Documents,* 336–337.

56. VC to Paris colleagues, February 2, 1854, AN 10AS 28 (9).

57. VC, *Au Texas,* 82, 57, 68.

58. VC, *Au Texas,* 89–90.

59. VC, *Au Texas,* 114.

60. VC, *Au Texas,* 117.

61. VC, *Au Texas,* 167–170, also 77, 127.

62. Muiron to CV, May 19, 1854, BMB Z418; VC to Bureau, May 12, 1854, AN 10AS 28 (9); Jones, "Considerant's American Experience," 83. See also Rey, *Le Fouriériste Allyre Bureau,* 383–384.

63. Muiron to Bureau, May 11, 1854, AN 10AS 40 (7); Godin to VC, May 13, 1854, in Moret, *Documents,* 1: 345; Koechlin to Parisian Fourierists, May 15, 1854, AN 10AS 39 (5). For a fuller account of the response to *Au Texas,* see Jones, "Considerant's American Experience," 87–89.

64. Bureau to Cantagrel, August 19, 1854, AN 10AS 36 (12); Rey, *Le Fouriériste Allyre Bureau,* 387–389.

65. VC and Cantagrel to Bureau, June 26, 1854, AN 10AS 28 (9); Marcus Spring to Fisher, October 2, 1854, Fisher Papers; VC to Administrateur de la Sûreté Publique, July 9, 1854, AGR MJ PE 36,486. In this letter Considerant expressed the hope that he, Julie, and her mother would be on their way to the United States by "the first week of September." He was duly issued a passport for Switzerland on July 22, 1854, AGR MJ PE 36,486.

66. VC, *Au Texas,* 171–178.

67. For a selection of police documents and official correspondence relative to this affair, see Hubert Wouters (ed.), *Documenten betreffende de geschiedenis der arbeidersbeweging (1853–1865)* (Louvain, 1966), 8–27. See also affidavit from Hamilton W. Merrill, Brevet major, U.S. Army, August 6, 1854, AN 10AS 41 (13); and VC, *Ma Justification* (Brussels, 1854).

68. VC, *Ma Justification,* 43–44.

69. Godin to VC, September 2, 1854, and VC to Godin [September 1854], in Moret, *Documents,* 1: 357, 359. See also *Au Texas,* 180.

70. Arthur E. Bestor, Jr., "Victor Considerant, First Communitarian," Paper delivered at the annual meeting of the American Historical Association, December 28, 1948, 8, Bestor Papers, University of Illinois.

71. "Statuts de la Société de colonisation européo-américaine au Texas," in VC, *Au Texas,* 239–276.

72. VC, *Au Texas*, 250–256, 304–308; Jones, "Considerant's American Experience," 91–92.

73. *Bulletin de la Société de colonisation européo-américaine au Texas* (*BSCEAT*), 1 (January 1855), 3.

74. Auguste Savardan, *Un Naufrage au Texas* (Paris, 1858), 19–20. See also Savardan, *Asile rural des enfants trouvés* (Paris, 1848).

75. Savardan, *Un Naufrage au Texas*, 20–21, 121–122; Jones, "Considerant's American Experience," 93.

76. VC to Bureau, October 17 and 21, 1854, AN 10AS 28 (9); VC, *Au Texas*, 313.

77. VC to Paris colleagues, November 8, 1954, AN 10AS 28 (9); VC to JC, November 14, 1854, BMB Z417; VC to Jules Marcou, October 31, 1854, Houghton Library, Harvard University, 6 Ms Fr 235 (23).

78. Savardan, *Un Naufrage au Texas*, 22; VC, *Au Texas*, 313–315.

79. VC, *Au Texas*, 315. See Cantagrel to Emile Bourdon, March 6, 1856, AN 10AS 37 (2), which suggests that Considerant knew very well that the provisional agreement would destroy all his plans: "At the time of Considerant's arrival here the damage was already done. We didn't do it; we simply suffered its consequences. In signing the by-laws for Reunion, Considerant merely resigned himself to participating in an attempt to carry out the provisional agreement. In doing so, he kept repeating, 'They ruined my plan. I'm being forced to begin at the point where we wanted to end. I'm being forced to do precisely what I predicted would destroy the society if it were done.'"

80. VC, *Au Texas*, 117, 118, 129, 184; VC, *The Great West*, ii.

81. VC, *Du Texas. Premier rapport à mes amis* (Paris, 1857), 7; Savardan, *Un Naufrage au Texas*, 22–23.

82. VC to JC, October 1, 1856, AN 10AS 28 (9); Rey, *Le Fouriériste Allyre Bureau*, 428. See also VC to JC, December 3, 1855, AN 10AS 28 (9): "Contrary to all my instructions, we were stuck with 150 people when I had said and repeated that we had to progress very slowly and begin with 20 selected Europeans at most."

83. Savardan, *Un Naufrage au Texas*, 23; Godin to Cantagrel, February 3, 1855, in Moret, *Documents*, 1: 413. See also VC, *Du Texas*, 8.

84. VC to Eugène Bourson, September 29, 1854, in Louis Pierard and Marc-Antoine Pierson, *Belgique, terre d'exil* (Brussels, n.d.), 36–37.

85. VC, *Au Texas*, 324.

CHAPTER 14

1. René Rémond, *Les Etats-Unis devant l'opinion française, 1815–1852*, 2 vols. (Paris, 1963), 1: 31–99; Kent Gardien, "Take Pity on Our Glory: Men of Champ d'Asile," *Southwestern Historical Quarterly*, 87, no. 3 (January 1984), 241–268; Ronald Creagh, *Nos Cousins d'Amérique* (Paris, 1988), 228–236.

2. Terry G. Jordan, *German Seed in Texas Soil* (Austin, 1966); Rudolph Leopold Biesele, *The History of German Settlements in Texas, 1831–1861*

(Austin, 1930); Prince Carl von Solms-Braunfels, *Texas, 1844–1845,* translated by Oswald Mueller (Houston, 1936); Bobby D. Weaver, *Castro's Colony: Empresario Development in Texas, 1842–1865* (College Station, Tx., 1985), 78, and *passim;* Julia Nott Waugh, *Castro-Ville and Henry Castro, Empresario* (San Antonio, 1934).

3. Robert Owen, *Memorial of Robert Owen to the Mexican Republic and to the Government of the State of Coahuila and Texas* (Philadelphia, 1828); Wilbert H. Timmons, "Robert Owen's Texas Project," *Southwestern Historical Quarterly,* 52 (1949), 286–293; Harrison, *Quest for the New Moral World,* 168.

4. See Chapter 13, section III. Jules Prudhommeaux, *Icarie et son fondateur, Etienne Cabet* (Paris, 1926), 212–235; Robert P. Sutton, *Les Icariens: The Utopian Dream in Europe and America* (Urbana, Ill., 1994), 43–60.

5. VC, *Au Texas,* 105. For a rich sampling of recent and ongoing work on the Fourierists' colony in Texas, see "Autour de la colonie de Réunion, Texas," a special issue of the *Cahiers Charles Fourier,* 4 (1993). In this issue the articles bearing directly on the subject matter of this chapter are: Carl J. Guarneri, "Réunion, Texas, post scriptum ironique au fouriérisme américain" (13–27), James Pratt, "Jeudi 22 décembre 1854: Les Premiers Fouriéristes foulent le sol du Texas" (28–39), Jonathan Beecher, "Une Utopie manquée au Texas: Victor Considerant et Réunion" (40–79), Bruno Verlet, "Les Fouriéristes au Texas. Du rêve à la réalité" (80–101), and Michel Cordillot et al., "Au Texas: Aperçus biographiques sur quelques membres de la colonie de Réunion" (102–128). For a solid analysis of the reasons for the failure of the colony, see Rondel Van Davidson, "Victor Considerant and the Failure of La Réunion," *Southwestern Historical Quarterly,* 76, no. 3 (January 1973), 277–296. Two books have been written on Reunion: Hammond and Hammond, *La Réunion,* and George H. Santerre, *White Cliffs of Dallas: The Story of La Réunion, the Old French Colony* (Dallas, 1955). Both books are based on original research, and the Hammonds' work is good on the attitude of Texans with regard to Reunion, but both also are flawed by major errors and should be used with caution.

6. Bourdon to Paris colleagues, Ostende, January 16, 1855, AN 10AS 31 (4); and Police at Ostende to Administration de la Sûreté Publique, Brussels, January 16, 1855; AGR MJ PE 36,486. All the published sources describe Considerant as having embarked from Le Havre. In fact he was unwilling to ask the government of Napoleon III for permission to enter French territory.

7. Guarneri, *Utopian Alternative,* 331; VC, *Du Texas,* 5–6.

8. On the Know-Nothing movement, see Ray Allen Billington, *The Protestant Crusade, 1800–1860: A Study of the Origins of American Nativism* (Gloucester, Mass., 1963), 380–436; and Tyler Anbinder, *Nativism and Slavery: The Northern Know Nothings and the Politics of the 1850s* (New York, 1992).

9. *Texas State Gazette* (February 17, 1855), in Hammond and Hammond, *La Réunion,* 68.

10. VC, *Du Texas,* 5–9.

11. Savardan, *Naufrage au Texas,* 29, 46; BSCEAT, 2 (May 2, 1855), 1; James T. Fisher to Simonin, May 25, 1855: "I am especially interested to hear

of Considerant's *health*, which was not good when he left here." Simonin Papers, Mss. 18,160.

12. VC, *European Colonization in Texas: An Address to the American People* (New York, 1855), 21; BSCEAT, 2 (May 2, 1855), 1–2; Laura Wood Roper, *FLO: A Biography of Frederick Law Olmsted* (Baltimore, 1973), 104. On César Daly, see Richard Becherer, *Science Plus Sentiment: César Daly's Formula for Modern Architecture* (Ann Arbor, 1984).

13. Savardan contends (*Naufrage au Texas*, 31) that Considerant hurried Cantagrel into the choice of a site for the colony. Savardan neglects to point out another, more compelling reason for making a rapid choice: his own group of forty-three colonists had sailed from Le Havre on February 28, 1855, without waiting to learn whether a site had in fact been selected.

14. V. E. Gibbens (ed.), "Lawrie's Trip to Northeast Texas, 1854–1855," *Southwestern Historical Quarterly*, 48 (October 1944), 238–253.

15. VC, *European Colonization in Texas*, 17–18; Hammond and Hammond, *La Réunion*, 95.

16. BSCEAT, 2 (May 2, 1855), 1; Gibbens, "Lawrie's Trip"; Moret, *Documents*, 1: 420–427. By October, land purchases totaled 12,926 acres (5,31 hectares).

17. BSCEAT, 3 (June 13, 1855), 1–2. The memoirs of Kalikst Wolski are an important source for the history of Reunion's first year. Throughout his stay at Reunion he remained on friendly terms with Victor and Julie Considerant, and he gives a picture of them and of the life of the community that is radically different from that of Savardan. See Marion Moore Coleman (ed. and trans.), "New Light on La Reunion: From the pages of *Do Ameryce i w Ameryce*," *Arizona and the West*, 6, no. 1 (Spring 1964), 41–68, and 6, no. 2 (Summer 1964), 137–154.

18. BSCEAT, 2 (May 2, 1855), 2–3; 3 (June 13, 1855), 1–2; 4 (August 6, 1855), 1–6; Santerre, *White Cliffs*, 47–51.

19. BSCEAT, 2 (May 2, 1855), 1–3; Jones, "Considerant's American Experience," 125.

20. Savardan, *Naufrage au Texas*, 40.

21. Savardan, *Naufrage au Texas*, 46.

22. Unsigned article, "Les Socialistes français au Texas," in the *Galveston Civilian*, reprinted in BSCEAT, 4 (August 6, 1855), 6.

23. Savardan, *Naufrage au Texas*, 47. What Savardan failed to point out was that Considerant's entourage included a sixty-three-year-old woman in poor health (Clarisse Vigoureux) and a newborn child (the Cantagrels' daughter), neither of whom could have withstood the long, grueling trip that Savardan's group took.

24. Savardan, *Naufrage au Texas*, 47.

25. Savardan, *Naufrage au Texas*, 140; BSCEAT, 4 (August 6, 1855), 2, 5–6.

26. Jean Louckx, letter of June 24, 1855, in BSCEAT, 5 (October 8, 1855), 7; Savardan, *Naufrage au Texas*, 57; Wolski, "New Light on Reunion," 143–144.

27. Since Dallas was not incorporated until 1856, the early population figures are approximate. According to W. P. Webb (ed.), *Handbook of Texas*,

2 vols. (Austin, 1952), 1: 456, the population of Dallas in 1851 was 163. By 1860 it was about 775.

28. Wolski, "New Light on Reunion," 142, 145.

29. AVC ENS carton 4 (VIII), text published in *BSCEAT*, 5 (October 8, 1855), 8, with proper names given only as initials. For working hours and distribution of tasks on two particular days, see *BSCEAT*, 4 (August 6, 1855), 7, for the working day of June 22, 1855, and AVC ENS carton 2 (XIII, 2) for May 16, 1855.

30. *BSCEAT*, 5 (October 8, 1855), 7–8.

31. Wolski, "New Light on Reunion," 146–147

32. Letter of Vrydagh in *BSCEAT*, 5 (October 8, 1855), 7.

33. Wolski, "New Light on Reunion," 150–151.

34. Savardan, *Naufrage au Texas*, 83–85; Wolski, "New Light on Reunion," 149–150.

35. *BSCEAT*, 6 (December 18, 1855), 5–8.

36. VC, *Du Texas*, 12.

37. *BSCEAT*, 5 (October 8, 1855), 1–6.

38. Savardan, *Naufrage au Texas*, 110; *BSCEAT*, 5 (October 8, 1855), 1–2, 5.

39. Savardan, *Naufrage au Texas*, 120–121.

40. VC, *Du Texas*, 13.

41. VC to JC, November 9 or 10 [sic], 1855, and February 3, 1856, AN 10AS 28 (9).

42. VC to directors, November 28, 1855, extracts in *BSCEAT*, 7 (February 29, 1856), 2. See also Savardan, *Naufrage au Texas*, 155–158.

43. Amédée Simonin, *Journal*, January 23, 1856, Simonin Papers, Mss. 18,160.

44. Renshaw, cited in Simonin, *Journal*, February 15, 1856.

45. VC to JC, December 3, 1855, and February 3, 1856, AN 10AS 28 (9). See also Savardan, *Naufrage au Texas*, 159–161.

46. VC to Directors, March 11, 1856, extracts in *BSCEAT*, 12 (November 14, 1856), 40; VC to JC, March 6 [1856], and October 1, 1856, AN 10AS 28 (9).

47. Simonin, *Journal*, April 3 and 15, 1856; Savardan, *Naufrage au Texas*, 173–176.

48. Savardan to VC, April 17, 1856, extracts in Savardan, *Naufrage au Texas*, 177; *BSCEAT*, 10 (August 8, 1856), 21–22.

49. *BSCEAT*, 7 (February 29, 1856), 6–7; 8 (May 3, 1856), 1; 9 (June 17, 1856), 18; Moret, *Documents*, 1: 580–582; Savardan, *Naufrage au Texas*, 178–179; Santerre, *White Cliffs*, 62–63.

50. Moret, *Documents*, 1: 576–579; Savardan, *Naufrage au Texas*, 172–173, 247–248; Wolski, "New Light on Reunion," 147–148.

51. Simonin, *Journal*, April 24, 1856; Savardan, *Naufrage au Texas*, 165–166.

52. Simonin, *Journal*, April 16, 19, 21, and 27, 1856; Cantagrel to Bourdon, March 6, 1856, AN 10AS 37 (2).

53. Simonin, *Journal,* April 7, 1856; Savardan, *Naufrage au Texas,* 175.

54. Simonin, *Journal,* April 6, 15, and 16, and May 1, 1856.

55. Savardan, *Naufrage au Texas,* 182–185; Rey, *Allyre Bureau,* 470–471.

56. Savardan, *Naufrage au Texas,* 186; VC, *Du Texas,* 10.

57. VC to JC, September 14, 1856, AN 10AS 28 (9).

CHAPTER 15

1. VC to JC, February 8 and 11, 1857, AN 10AS 28 (9).

2. This long letter, dated March 30, 1856, is largely reprinted, together with a briefer letter dated March 11, 1856, in "Détails sur la vallée d'Uvalde, dite Canon d'Uvalde," *BSCEAT,* 12 (November 15, 1856), 40–43. Citations in the next four paragraphs are from this source. "Uvalde Canyon" cannot be found on any map today; it is now known as Sabinal Canyon. The name "Uvalde Canyon," which also appears in Frederick Law Olmsted, *Journey through Texas: A Saddle-trip on the Southwestern Frontier* (Austin, 1962), seems to have fallen out of use very quickly.

3. "Situation en Amérique," *BSCEAT,* 12 (November 15, 1856), 37–39; VC to JC, September 14, 1856, AN 10AS 28 (9).

4. VC to JC, September 28 and October 10, 1856, AN 10AS 28 (9).

5. VC to JC, October 1, 1856, AN 10AS 28 (9).

6. Allyre Bureau, report to shareholders, September 3, 1856, in *BSCEAT,* 11 (September 13, 1856), 29–30.

7. "Situation en Amérique," *BSCEAT,* 14 (May 5, 1857), 53.

8. "Situation en Amérique," *BSCEAT,* 14 (May 5, 1857), 53–54. Savardan, *Naufrage au Texas,* 205; VC to JC, February 8, 1857, AN 10AS 28 (9).

9. VC to JC, December 1, 9, 20, 21, and 30, 1856, and February 8 and 11, 1857, AN 10AS 28 (9). Savardan, *Naufrage au Texas,* 210, gives the family's date of departure from Reunion as February 23, 1857. I can find no evidence to support Davidson's claim (*Did We Think Victory Great?* 270) that the Considerants remained at Reunion until the spring of 1859.

10. Wheeler, *To Wear a City's Crown,* 35–46, 109–113, 125–127, 141–158; Olmsted, *Journey through Texas,* 79–90.

11. VC, *Du Texas,* 32; JC to Aimée Beuque, April 17, 1865, ENS AVC carton 9 (III, 2).

12. Rey, *Allyre Bureau,* 491–493.

13. VC to CV, May 28, 1857, ENS AVC carton 2 (I, 6).

14. Rey, *Allyre Bureau,* 492; report of Allyre Bureau on Uvalde Canyon, *BSCEAT,* 16 (September 7, 1857), 72–73.

15. "Situation en Amérique," *BSCEAT,* 17 (January 1858), 77.

16. VC to directors, September 26, 1857, in *BSCEAT,* 17 (January 1858), 77; "Situation en Amérique," *BSCEAT,* 13 (December 31, 1856), 46.

17. VC, *Du Texas,* 3, 12, 13, 58.

18. Godin to VC, October 13, 1857, in Moret, *Documents,* 1: 624–626.

19. Godin to VC, November 15, 1857, in Moret, *Documents,* 1: 627.

20. On Durant, see Joseph G. Tregle, Jr., "Thomas J. Durant, Utopian Socialism, and the Failure of Presidential Reconstruction in Louisiana," *Journal of Southern History*, 45 (November 1979), 485–512. On Collens, see Robert C. Reinders, "T. Wharton Collens: Catholic and Christian Socialist," *Catholic Historical Review*, 52 (July 1966), 212–233. For a fascinating discussion of New Orleans Fourierism in the broad context of the antebellum South, see Guarneri, *The Utopian Alternative*, 261–263.

21. Citizenship papers of Victor Considerant signed by Louis Duvigneaud, Judge of the Third District Court of New Orleans. Signing as witnesses, T. Wharton Collens and Paul W. Collens swore (falsely) that Considerant had been a resident of the United States for the previous five years and of Louisiana for the previous year. AN 10AS 29 (2). See illustration 26.

22. VC to JC, May 13, 16, and 26, and June 3 and 5–6, 1858, AN 10AS 28 (9). VC to JC, June 19, 1858, ENS AVC carton 2 (I, 6). Perry Miller, *The Raven and the Whale* (New York, 1956), 341.

23. VC to JC, July 7 and 24, 1858, AN 10AS 28 (9); VC to Vincent Cousin, July 10, 1858, AN 10AS 28 (9). Proudhon, *Carnets*, July 21, 1858, in Klaus Herding, *Courbet: To Venture Independence* (New Haven, 1991), 236.

24. VC to Renan, in Coignet, *Victor Considerant*, 88. Apparently it was Odilon Barrot, of all people, who helped smooth Considerant's way into France. See VC to JC, July 7, 1858, AN 10AS 28 (9).

25. VC to JC, July 24, 1858, AN 10AS 28 (9).

26. Coignet, *Victor Considerant*, 88.

27. VC to JC, July 24, 1858, AN 10AS 28 (9).

28. VC to JC, August 12, 1858, ENS AVC carton 2 (I, 6).

29. Citations in this paragraph and the next five are from "Résumé des communications faites par M. Considerant," September 1, 1858, *BSCEAT*, 19 [December 1858], 90–93.

30. Aimée Beuque to JC and CV, September 20, 1858, AN 10AS 36 (5).

31. Emile Bourdon, "Rapport de la gérance," *BSCEAT*, 19 [December 1858], 90–93.

32. Coignet, *Victor Considerant*, 88–89.

33. Procureur générale de Besançon to Garde des Sceaux, October 18, 1858, AN BB30 421 (dr. 1655).

34. VC to his sisters, November 2, 1858, AN 10AS 28 (9).

35. VC to JC, November 25, 1858, AN 10AS 28 (9); VC to Alphonse Delacroix, January 8, 1859, collection of Robert Guillaume.

36. *BSCEAT*, 20 (June 20, 1859), 105, 102.

37. For a record of the land sales and of Giraud's tenure as director of the Société de Colonisation, see *BSCEAT*, 32–39 (1868–1875), *passim*. On the purchasers of the land, see Morris H. Breazeale, "The Magic Canyon Comes of Age," *Utopia Centennial Souvenir Booklet* (Uvalde, Tx., 1952), 33–47. This booklet also includes brief biographical sketches of Ware, Kincheloe, Thompson, and Kelley. See also the brief "History of Utopia and Sabinal Canyon," in Annalee Wentworth Burns, *Yesteryears* (Uvalde, Tx., 1978), 4–7.

38. JC to Aimée Beuque, July 6, 1859, ENS AVC carton 4 (VIII).

39. Charles Clay Doyle, "Utopia, U.S.A.," *Moreana* (1976), 154–155; Mrs. W. L. Ames, "How Utopia Got Its Name," *Utopia Centennial Souvenir Booklet*, 2. I want to thank Annalee Burns for her guidance on the early history of Utopia, Texas.

CHAPTER 16

1. VC to Ernest Renan, April 1, 1868, *La Revue*, 3rd ser., 15 (August 1, 1901), 225.

2. Supervielle to VC, January 30, 1860, AN 10AS 31 (4).

3. T. R. Fehrenbach, *Lone Star: A History of Texas and the Texans* (New York, 1968), 354–358, 394. But see Kenneth W. Wheeler, *To Wear a City's Crown: The Beginnings of Urban Growth in Texas, 1836–1865* (Cambridge, Mass., 1968), 150ff. My main guides to Texas history during the Civil War have been Fehrenbach, *Lone Star*, 327–408; Wheeler, *To Wear a City's Crown*; Ernest Wallace, *Texas in Turmoil: The Saga of Texas, 1849–1875* (Austin, 1965), 76–138; and Walter L. Buenger, *Secession and the Union in Texas* (Austin, 1984). Like everyone interested in Texas history, I have benefited greatly from D. W. Meineg, *Imperial Texas: An Interpretive Essay in Cultural Geography* (Austin, 1969).

4. VC, *Mexique. Quatre lettres au Maréchal Bazaine* (Brussels, 1868), 60; JC to Aimée Beuque, April 17 [1865], ENS AVC carton 9 (III, 2).

5. Wheeler, *To Wear a City's Crown*, 151–153; Marcou, "Notice biographique," *Le Salinois* (February 18, 1894); VC to Renan, April 1, 1868, *La Revue*, 3rd ser., 15 (August 1, 1901), 225.

6. Receipt for tax payment, Daughters of the Republic of Texas Library, The Alamo, San Antonio. Information kindly communicated to me by Bruno Verlet, letter of February 15, 1993.

7. VC, *Du Texas*, 41. On San Pedro Spring Park in Considerant's time, see Olmsted, *Journey through Texas*, 156; Cecilia Steinfeldt, *San Antonio Was: Seen through a Magic Lantern* (San Antonio, 1978), 199–205. The Considerant archives include an early photograph of the tropical gardens in San Pedro Springs Park almost identical to that reprinted in Steinfeldt, *San Antonio Was*, 205.

8. Alberto Santa Fe, introduction to the Spanish translation of Eugene Nus, *Choses de l'autre monde: Cosas del otro mundo* (Mexico City, 1897), iv–v. On Alberto Santa Fe, see John M. Hart, *Anarchism and the Mexican Working Class, 1860–1931* (Austin, 1978), 69–73, 77.

9. On François Guilbeau, see Frederick C. Chabot, *With the Makers of San Antonio* (San Antonio, 1937), 263–264; Dorothy Steinbomer Kendall and Carmen Perry, *Gentilz, Artist of the Old Southwest* (Austin, 1974), 29, 37; August Santleben, *A Texas Pioneer: Early Staging and Overland Freighting Days on the Frontiers of Texas and Mexico* (Washington, D.C., 1910), 25–27, 74–76,

and *passim;* VC, *Du Texas,* 38; Savardan, *Naufrage au Texas,* 261; Betje Black Klier, "Des Fouriéristes au Texas: La Famille Considerant à San Antonio," *Fremch Review,* 68, no. 6 (May 1995), 1038–1039.

10. On François Giraud (1818–1877), see Chabot, *Makers of San Antonio,* 264, and Charles Ramsdell, "The Legacy of F. Giraud," *Texas Parade* (April 1968), 32–34.

11. See especially Amauntrez [?] to VC, May 19, 1875, AN 10AS 36 (1), a long letter bringing Considerant up to date on the doings, and the health, of his San Antonio friends: "Frétellière, Gentilz, and, in a word, our whole French colony are turning gray but are in excellent health." See also Lorenzo Castro to VC, August 15, 1886, ENS AVC carton 13 (II, 4). On Poinsard, see VC, *Du Texas,* 46–47. On the French colony at San Antonio during these years, see Kendall, *Gentilz,* 3–49, and Klier, "Des Fouriéristes au Texas," 1035–1050.

12. This section is based largely on a single document, the extraordinary letter written by Julie Considerant to Aimée Beuque on April 17, 1865, describing the decline and death of Clarisse Vigoureux. This letter, from ENS AVC carton 9 (III, 2), is published by Jean-Claude Dubos in his edition of Clarisse Vigoureux, *Parole de Providence* (Seyssel, 1993), 70–78.

13. Deed Records, vol. S 1, pp. 472–273, Office of the County Clerk, Bexar County, Texas, in Jones, "Victor Considerant's American Experience," 148.

14. Julie's account, on which all of this is based, does not specify the nature of the illnesses she and Victor and Cousin suffered. She only says that she was bedridden for three weeks and that "Dr. Sherman and arsenic saved me."

15. For a notarized copy of Clarisse Vigoureux's death certificate, see Archives du Département du Doubs E20 346.

16. Supervielle to VC, December 6, 1859, AN 10AS 31 (4). On Vidaurri, see Ronnie C. Tyler, *Santiago Vidaurri and the Southern Confederacy* (Austin, 1973).

17. VC to JC, February 13, 1863, AN 10AS 28 (10). On Eagle Pass and its role in the cotton trade during the Civil War, see Jesse Sumpter, *Paso del Aguila: A Chronicle of Frontier Days on the Texas Border* (Encino, 1969).

18. VC to JC, February 13, 1863, AN 10AS 28 (10); VC to JC, February 16, 1863, BMB Z417.

19. VC to JC, February 16, 1863, BMB Z417.

20. VC, *Mexique,* 10, 73–75. See also Tyler, *Santiago Vidaurri,* 98–128, and Silvio Zavala, "Victor Considerant et le problème social au Mexique," *Revue historique,* 239 (January–March 1968), 19–28.

21. VC, *Mexique,* 17, 33.

22. VC to JC, March 5, 1863, AN 10AS 28 (9); VC, *Mexique.* 64. On the French intervention, see Jack Autrey Dabbs, *The French Army in Mexico, 1861–1867* (The Hague, 1963).

23. VC, "Lettre à Maximilien sur la Doctrine de Monroe et la politique américaine," ENS AVC carton 8 (I, 3), and ENS AVC carton 6 (III, 1). There is also an English version in carton 6: although somewhat shorter, it still runs to

eighty-six pages! Fragments of the "Lettre à Maximilien" may also be found in AN 10AS 27 (1) and ENS AVC carton 9 (I, 1). For a draft of Considerant's letter to Napoleon III, see ENS AVC carton 9 (I, 1).

In June 1865 Considerant wrote the liberal Mexican journalist Francisco Zarco, trying to enlist his help in contacting Bazaine. VC to Zarco, June 9, 1865, draft, ENS AVC carton 9 (I, 1). The letters to Bazaine are dated May 15, May 23, and June 2, 1865, and June 29, 1867. Considerant apparently sent copies to friends in Brussels, where they were published anonymously in January 1868 as *Mexique. Quatre lettres au Maréchal Bazaine*. In March 1868 Considerant sent two copies of the published version to Francisco Zarco, asking him to forward one to Juárez. See VC to Zarco, March 15, 1868, and VC to Juárez, December 14, 1867, ENS AVC carton 9 (I, 1).

24. VC, *Mexique*, 50.

25. VC, *Mexique*, 63, 82–85.

26. VC, "Etat comparé de la société européenne et de la société américaine," 18 leaves, each with four pages of text, numbered 30–47, ENS AVC carton 6 (III, 1). Same in AN 10AS 27 (1), pp. 98ff. Fragments in ENS AVC carton 8 (I, 3).

27. VC, "Lettres à Maximilien," pt. III, ENS AVC carton 9 (I, 1), p. 53, and ENS AVC carton 6 (III, 1), p. 35.

28. VC, "Lettre à Maximilien," pt. III, ENS AVC carton 6 (III, 1), p. 37.

29. VC, *Mexique*, 115–116.

30. For example, Louis Hartz, *The Liberal Tradition in America* (New York, 1955).

31. I am grateful to Carl Guarneri for his thoughtful comments on my "American" chapters and especially for comments bearing on this section.

32. Laverdant to Jaenger, April 8 [1865], BN NAF 22050, published in part by Paul Muller in *La Révolution de 1848*, vol. 10 (1913–1914), 436.

33. "Souscription Victor Considerant," May 24–August 15, 1865, Aimée Beuque, treasurer, ENS AVC carton 13 (VI, 1). See also Laverdant to VC, undated letters, AN 10AS 39 (8).

34. VC, *Mexique*, 79.

35. VC, *Three Hundred Millions of Dollars Saved in Specie by the Meaning of a Word: Letter to Secretary McCullogh* (New York, 1867). This sixteen-page brochure is dated "La Conception, near San Antonio, Texas, July 1867." The copy in Harvard's Widener Library is inscribed to Senator Charles Sumner by Thomas J. Durant.

36. VC to Clarisse Coignet, October 11, 1865, in Coignet, *Victor Considerant*, 90–92.

37. Aimée Beuque to VC, January 20, 1867, AN 10AS 36 (5).

38. VC, "Letter to Maximilian" (English version), ENS AVC carton 6 (III, 1), pp. 29–32. The "Investigation" was part II of the fullest version of the "Letter to Maximilian."

39. VC, "Letter to Maximilian" (English version), ENS AVC carton 6 (III, 1), p. 34.

40. VC, "Letter to Maximilian," (English version), ENS AVC carton 6 (III, 1), pp. 34, 56.

41. VC, "Lettre à Maximilien," ENS AVC carton 6 (III, 1), p. 42.

42. VC, "Lettre à Maximilien," ENS AVC carton 6 (III, 1), pp. 30–32.

43. VC, "Lettre à Maximilien," ENS AVC carton 6 (III, 1), p.34.

44. VC, "L'Avenir," published in installments in *Démocratie pacifique*, August 3–November 9, 1851. See especially the installment of August 10.

45. Considerant wrote at least four letters on the *Vie de Jésus*. Three (dated April 1, 2, and 14, 1968) were published as "Autour de la Vie de Jésus" in *La Revue*, 38, no. 15 (August 1, 1901), 225–244. A fourth letter of thirteen folio pages, dated May 13, 1868, exists in draft form, AN 10AS 28 (3). Renan only received the first two.

46. VC, "Autour de la Vie de Jésus," 232.

47. VC, "Autour de la Vie de Jésus," 232–233.

48. VC, "Autour de la Vie de Jésus," 234.

49. Renan to VC, December 11, 1868; VC, "Autour de la Vie de Jésus," 244.

50. VC, "Lettre à Maximilien," pt. III, "Etat comparé de la société européenne et de la société américaine, . . . *La Démocratie en Amérique* de Tocqueville prise pour point de départ," ENS AVC carton 6 (III, 1), pp. 30–47. For the Tocqueville passage, see *De la Démocratie en Amérique*, 2 vols. (Paris, 1951), 1: 5–6.

51. VC, "Lettre à Maximilien," ENS AVC carton 6 (III, 1), pp. 45,30.

52. VC, "Lettre à Maximilien," ENS AVC carton 6 (III, 1), pp. 46a, 45.

53. VC to Justine Pallas, April 6, 1867, ENS AVC carton 8 (II, 1); VC to Jules Pallas, March 16, 1868, AN 10AS 28 (10).

54. VC to Justine Pallas, April 6, 1867, ENS AVC carton 8 (II, 1).

55. VC to Aimée Beuque, December 3, 1867, ENS AVC carton 2 (I, 5).

56. VC to Aimée Beuque, December 3, 1867, ENS AVC carton 2 (I, 5); VC to Jules Pallas, March 16, 1868, AN 10AS 298 (10); Adolphe Demeur to VC, December 12, 1867, AN 10AS 37 (7).

57. VC to Jules Pallas, March 16, 1868, AN 10AS 28 (10); VC to Justine Pallas, July 27, 1868, AN 10AS 28 (10).

58. Copy of bill of sale, October 1, 1868, AN 10AS 31 (4); VC to Jules Pallas, February 7, 1869, AN 10AS 28 (10).

59. VC to Aimée Beuque, December 3, 1867, ENS AVC carton 2 (I, 5); Deed records, vol. 20, p. 622., Office of the County Clerk, Bexar County, Texas, in Jones, "Victor Considerant's American Experience," 149. On Grenet and Frétellière, see Chabot, *Makers of San Antonio*, 262–263.

60. VC to Justine, Jules, and Laure Pallas, February 7, 1869, AN 10AS 28 (10). *Des âtros* were a kind of fritter made of pork giblets. *Le ramequin* was a Saint-Claude fondue made with Comté cheese and white wine. Paul Duraffourg et al., *Glossaire du parler haut-jurassien* (Saint-Claude, 1986), 27. My thanks also to Gaston Bordet and Michel Vernus for sharing with me their culinary and philological expertise.

61. Michel Cordillot, "Les Derniers fouriéristes français aux Etats-Unis,"

Luvah, 16 (February 1989), 104; and Cordillot, "Au Texas: aperçus biographiques," 117–118.

62. *La Tribune de la Nouvelle Orléans*, July 10, 1869, in Alexandrian, *Le Socialisme romantique* (Paris, 1979), 210.

63. Unfinished draft of a lecture apparently to be given at the Académie des sciences morales et politiques, c.1880, AN 10AS 26 (4), pp. 5–6. See also James B. Herrick to VC, August 30, 1869, AN 10AS 31 (5), and *Oneida Circular*, 6, no. 20 (August 2, 1869), 157.

64. Considerant's dinner conversation with Greeley can be reconstructed from partial drafts of letters (in English) to Greeley, AN 10AS 28 (10). See also VC, "Permanent Reform in the Currency," *New York Tribune* (September 1, 1869).

65. *New York Sun*, weekly edition (August 25, 1869). My thanks to Jerilynn Marshall of the Newberry Library for sending me a typescript of this article.

CHAPTER 17

1. VC to JC [July 1870], BMB Z417.

2. On the launching of Dorian's political career, see Ronald Aminzade, *Ballots and Barricades: Class Formation and Republican Politics in France, 1830–1871* (Princeton, 1993), 139, 164–170. On Gagneur and Ordinaire, see the good biographical notices in Maitron, *Dictionnaire biographique*, 2: 223, 3: 164.

3. For Considerant's membership in the International, see below, note 13.

4. Claude Bellanger et al., *Histoire générale de la presse française*, 4 vols. (Paris, 1969), 2: 352. See also Alain Dalotel, Alain Faure, and Jean-Claude Freiermuth, *Aux Origines de la Commune. Le Mouvement des réunions publiques à Paris 1868–1870* (Paris, 1980).

5. Newspaper clippings in APP Ba 1,017 and in AN 10AS 29 (1); *L'Eclipse*, 2: 89 (October 3, 1869), signed "Cousin Jacques" (see illustration).

6. VC to Aimée Beuque, September 30, 1869, BMB Z417; VC to George Sand, November 1, 1869, BHVP G 3868; George Sand to VC, November 5, 1869, AN 10AS 41 (3); George Sand, *Correspondance*, vol. 21 (Paris, 1986), 697–698; Alphonse Delacroix to VC, October 1, 1869, AN 10AS 37 (7); Alphonse Tamisier to VC, October 10, 1869, AN 10AS 42 (2); VC to Rittinghausen, draft, October 24, 1969, ENS AVC carton 2 (I, 12); Brisbane to VC, numerous letters, September–December 1869, AN 10AS 36 (11).

7. Quotations in this paragraph and the two following are from VC to Pellarin, draft, November 5, 1869, AN 10AS 28 (5).

8. VC to Désiré Laverdant, Easter 1870, AN 10AS 28 (12). Considerant's emphasis.

9. Clarisse Coignet, *Victor Considerant*, 97; Juliette Adam to JC, June 28, 1871, AN 10AS 36 (1); Aimée Beuque to VC, September 2, 1869, and to JC, October 7, 1869, AN 10AS 36 (5). Juliette Adam, *Mes Premières Armes littéraires*

et politiques (Paris, 1904); Sylvie Aprile, "Le République au Salon: Vie et mort d'une forme de sociabilité politique (1865–1885)," *Revue d'histoire moderne et contemporaine*, 38 (July–September 1991), 473–487; Marie-Therèse Guichard, *Les Egéries de la République* (Paris, 1991), 12, 15–19, 23–49.

10. *La Science sociale*, 4, no. 8 (April 16, 1870), 113. This was the largest crowd at the Fourierists' annual banquet since the glory days of the movement at the end of the July Monarchy. In 1847, 900 *convives* had attended the Paris banquet; by 1865 the number had dropped to 65.

11. *La Science sociale*, 4, no. 8 (April 16, 1870), 117–120.

12. "Un Discours patriotique," dated July 14, *La Cloche* (July 21, 1870), reprinted in VC, *Prédictions sur la guerre. La France imposant la paix à l'Europe* (Paris, 1870), 2.

13. *L'Internationale* (Brussels), July 31, 1870, in Maitron, *Dictionnaire biographique*, 5: 163. The archives of the Paris Prefecture of Police also include a police report dated July 29, 1870, which includes "Victor Considerant, publiciste" among eighty-two dues-paying members of the International's Pantheon section. APP Ba 439, pièce 5171.

Considerant's meeting with the Belgian leaders of the International was not an unqualified success. According to a Belgian police report dated July 7, 1870, Considerant spent much of the meeting arguing for an international system of phonetic spelling! Hubert Wouters (ed.), *Documenten betreffende de geschiedenis der arbeidersbeweging ten tijde van de 1e Internationale (1866–1880)*, vol. 1 (Louvain, 1970), 356–357.

14. Summons to VC, Police correctionalle, Département de la Seine, July 20, 1870, AN 10AS 29 (1); VC to Désiré Laverdant, July 22, 1870, AN 10AS 28 (12); Emile Ollivier, *L'Empire libéral. Etudes, récits, souvenirs*, vol. 13 (Paris, 1908), 248.

15. VC, "Prévisions et prédictions sur la campagne avant l'ouverture," dated July 28, were later published in *La France imposant la paix à l'Europe*, 1.

16. "Morts de Quatre-vingt-douze," in Arthur Rimbaud, *Oeuvres complètes* (Paris, 1954), 63.

17. VC to General Trochu, August 24, 1870, and VC to Thiers, August 28, 1870, published in *Prédictions sur la guerre*, 1–2.

18. VC to General Trochu, draft, November 7, 1870, ENS AVC carton 9 (III, 3).

19. Auguste Blanqui, *La Patrie en danger* (September 22, 1870), in Henri Guillemin, *L'Héroïque Défense de Paris (1870–1871)* (Paris, 1959), 170.

20. Jules Ferry and Jules Favre, quoted in Guillemin, *L'Héroïque Défense*, 138, 124. The view that the fear of social unrest in Paris was the underlying determinant of the policies (and the saber-rattling oratory) of the Government of National Defense is developed at length and with great verve by Guillemin throughout his ironically titled *L'Héroïque Défense de Paris*.

21. There is a good notice on Tamisier in Maitron, *Dictionnaire biographique*, 3: 431.

22. VC to Dorian, September 17, 1870, ADL 1 J 772.

23. All citations in this paragraph and the four that follow are from *La France imposant la paix à l'Europe*, 3–4.

24. VC to Elihu Washburne, undated draft with a list of copies sent to others, ENS AVC carton 2 (I, 10); Washburne to VC, September 26, 1870, AN 10AS 29 (1); Michel Chevalier to VC, October 17, 1870, ENS AVC carton 13 (I, 1); Charles-Louis Chassin, "La République de 1870. Extrait des mémoires d'un homme inutilisé" (unpublished), Papiers Chassin, BHVP Ms. 1398, tome IV, vol. I, fol. 29–32.

25. VC to Parisian editors, draft, ENS AVC carton 2 (I, 1). AN 10AS 27 (11) includes seven mimeographed copies of this letter. In November Considerant wrote several letters to the prefect of police protesting the harassment of his salesman by the police. See drafts dated November 15 and November 19, 1870, ENS AVC carton 2 (I, 10), and AN 10AS 28 (11).

26. VC to Bismarck, October 12, 1870, two drafts, AN 10AS 27 (11) and two copies AN 10AS 29 (1); VC to Bismarck, October 13, 1870, five drafts of a second letter, AN 10AS 27 (11).

27. *Lettres de Gustave Courbet à l'armée allemande et aux artistes allemands: Lues à l'Athénée dans la séance du 29 octobre 1870* (Paris, 1870), 4. The question of Considerant's relations with Courbet has been opened up in a fascinating way by Paul Crapo in two articles: "Courbet's Artistic and Political Activities in the Fall of 1870," *Proceedings of the Annual Meeting of the Western Society for French History*, 17 (1990), 319–329, and "Courbet, Considerant et l'Année Terrible, 1870–1871," in press. I am grateful to Professor Crapo for sending me a copy of the second article prior to its publication and for generously sharing with me photocopies of several of his principal sources.

28. *Lettres de Gustave Courbet*, 14–15.

29. VC, "Constitution du gouvernement de la République universelle," AN 10AS 26 (32). Internal evidence (dating, implied audience) suggests that this manuscript of twenty folio pages was in fact the text of Considerant's talk at the Athénée.

30. This paragraph is entirely based on a single eyewitness account of the "soirée littéraire" by one A. Bauche, a syrup manufacturer: "Une Page d'histoire" (written in 1877), BHVP Ms. 1118, fol. 88–98. This text was discovered by Paul Crapo, to whom I am greatly indebted for sending me a photocopy. Given Bauche's tone—consistently one of bemused raillery—it would be good to have the account of a more sympathetic observer. It is clear, in any case, that the evening was a disaster.

31. My account of the abortive insurrection of October 31 is based largely on Guillemin, *L'Héroïque Défense de Paris*, 316–392. Stéphane Rials, *Nouvelle histoire de Paris, de Trochu à Thiers* (Paris, 1985), 158–166, offers another useful overview, and Gustave Lefrançais, *Souvenirs d'un révolutionnaire* (Paris, 1972), 324–331, gives the perspective of an insurgent.

32. VC to Dorian, November 1, 1870, ADL 1 J 772. Considerant's emphasis.

33. *Commission parlementaire d'Enquête sur le 18 mars. Dépositions*, 1: 430, 525, quoted in Guillemin, *L'Héroïque Défense de Paris*, 341, 342.

34. VC to Trochu, November 7, 1870, ENS AVC carton 9 (III, 3). In fact, Trochu's position was not far from Considerant's. Here are the terms in which he explained to Prefect of Police Edmond Adam his reluctance to use force against the insurrectionists of October 31: "We are a government created by public opinion, and we cannot seek support outside of it. We do not have the right to do so. . . . Our only weapon is moral force." Juliette Adam, *Le Siège de Paris. Journal d'une Parisienne* (Paris, 1873), 199.

35. I have taken details on the siege of Paris from Alistair Horne, *The Fall of Paris: The Siege and the Commune, 1870–1871* (Garden City, 1965), esp. 192–211 and 229–246; George J. Becker (ed. and trans.), *Paris under Siege, 1870–1871: From the Goncourt Journal* (Ithaca, 1969); and Adam, *Le Siège de Paris*. The judgments and commentary in all these works should be corrected by Rials, *De Trochu à Thiers*, 187–217.

36. VC, "Au rédacteur," *Le Temps*, October 3, 1870, xerox kindly communicated by Paul Crapo. See also Rials, *De Trochu à Thiers*, 207–208.

37. JC to VC, October 12, 1870, AN 10AS 29 (1).

38. Adam, *Le Siège de Paris*, 358; Courbet to Dorian, January 5, 1871, in Petra ten-Doesschate Chu (ed.), *Letters of Gustave Courbet* (Chicago, 1992), 402. The papers of Frédéric Dorian also include numerous letters from Considerant at this time, offering advice, making requests, and arranging meetings. See "Lettres de Victor Considerant à Frédéric Dorian (Siège de Paris, 1870–1871)," ADL 1 J 772 (1)-(9).

39. Laissez-passer, BHVP, Ms. 1131, fol. 221, cited in Crapo, "Courbet's Artistic and Political Activities," 320; Jules Hamet to VC [March 1871], cited in Dommanget, *Victor Considerant*, 191. Comments on his section of the International in VC to Leblond, draft, July 9, 1871, ENS AVC carton 8 (III, 1).

40. VC to Alexandre Rey, February 3, 1871, ENS AVC carton 8 (IV, 1). On the Union Républicaine Centrale, see Bernard Noel, *Dictionnaire de la Commune*, 2 vols. (Paris, 1978), 2: 266; Jean Dautry and Lucien Scheler, *Le Comité central républicain des vingt arrondissements de Paris* (Paris, 1960), 130–131n; and Martin Philip Johnson, *The Paradise of Association: Political Culture and Popular Organizations in the Paris Commune of 1871* (Ann Arbor, 1996), 92, 94, 122.

41. Draft of notes for a talk to the Union Républicaine Centrale, n.d., AN 10AS 26 (41).

42. Edouard Vaillant, "Considerant," *Le Parti socialiste*, 107 (October 8–15, 1893), in Maurice Dommanget, *Edouard Vaillant, un grand socialiste, 1840–1915* (Paris, 1956), 423–424.

43. For a full and richly sardonic account of the negotiations, see Henri Guillemin, *La Capitulation* (Paris, 1960).

44. VC to Dorian, January 24, 1871, ADL 1 J 772 (7): "I went to your place yesterday, dear Dorian, to ask you sadly in the name of what interest—divine

or human—you allowed your name to be placed at the bottom of that rotten proclamation." Vincent d'Indy, quoted in Rials, *De Trochu à Thiers*, 219. VC to Justine Pallas, February 4, 1871, ENS AVC carton 8 (IV, 1).

45. My own understanding of the Paris Commune has been influenced first of all by the work of Jacques Rougerie, notably *La Commune. 1871* (Paris, 1988), *Paris Libre 1871* (Paris, 1971), and the collective work edited by Rougerie, *Jalons pour une histoire de la Commune* (Paris, 1973). Other works that I have found valuable include Stewart Edwards, *The Paris Commune* (New York, 1973); Prosper-Olivier Lissagaray, *Histoire de la Commune de 1871* (Paris, 1983); Rials, *De Trochu à Thiers*, 249–514; and Kristin Ross, *The Emergence of Social Space: Rimbaud and the Paris Commune* (Minneapolis, 1988).

46. Philip J. Nord, "The Party of Conciliation and the Paris Commune," *French Historical Studies*, 15, no. 1 (Spring 1987), 1–35. See also Jeanne Gaillard, *Communes de province, Commune de Paris 1870–1871* (Paris, 1971), 161–164, and Rials, *De Trochu à Thiers*, 292–300. For the endorsement of the view that "conciliation is treason," see Jean Bruhat, Jean Dautry, and Emile Tersen, *La Commune de 1871* (Paris, 1960), 228.

47. Edmond Lepelletier, *Histoire de la Commune de 1871*, 3 vols. (Paris, 1912), 2: 365. See also William Serman, *La Commune de Paris* (Paris, 1986), 242. Ranc and Parent were both elected to the Commune but resigned early in April. For the text of the poster, see Firmin Maillard (ed.), *Elections des 26 mars et 16 avril 1871. Affiches, professions de foi, documents officiels, clubs et comités pendant la Commune* (Paris, 1871), 90. Considerant's comments at the meeting with the mayors were repeated a month later in a speech to the Ligue d'Union Républicaine des Droits de Paris. Minutes of the Ligue d'Union Républicaine des Droits de Paris. Séance du 28 avril 1871, Floquet Papers, AN 49AP 1.

48. Founded at the beginning of April by a number of mayors and ex-deputies (including Clemenceau, Floquet, Corbon, and Lockroy), the Ligue d'Union Républicaine des Droits de Paris was one of the most important of the groups seeing conciliation. See André Lefèvre, *Histoire de la Ligue d'Union républicaine des droits de Paris* (Paris, 1881); and Nord, "The Party of Conciliation," 8–16.

The Ligue d'Union Républicaine was not the same as the Union Républicaine Centrale, of which Considerant was an active member. Considerant did give a speech at a meeting of the Ligue d'Union Républicaine on April 28, where he described himself as "happy to find himself in the midst of political brothers." In this speech he also described himself as having presented his plebiscite on the independence of Paris "to some members of the Ligue," Floquet Papers, AN 49AP 1. Otherwise his connection with the Ligue seems to have been limited. His name does not appear in the papers of the Ligue at the BHVP Ms 1147–1148.

49. Maillard, *Affiches, professions de foi*, 44, 186–188, 223; Coignet, *Victor Considerant*, 95.

50. Paul Milliet, "Les Milliet. Une famille de républicains fouriéristes," in

Cahiers de la Quinzaine, 13, no. 7 (1911), 46. VC to the Commune of Paris, April 20, 1871, published in VC, *La Paix en 24 heures dictée par Paris à Versailles* (Paris, 1871), 2.

51. Citations in this paragraph and the seven that follow are all from *La Paix en 24 heures dictée par Paris à Versailles*. This pamphlet of two folio pages was originally published in two installments in Alexandre Rey's journal *La Nation souveraine*.

52. Dommanget, *Victor Considerant*, 192–195.

53. Lissagaray, *Histoire de la Commune*, 243; Gustave Lefrançais, *Etude sur le mouvement communaliste* (Neuchâtel, 1871), 147, in Dommanget, *Victor Considerant*, 198; "La paix en 24 heures," *Le Cri du peuple*, April 28, 1871.

54. Georges Bourgin and Gabriel Henriot (eds.), *Procès-verbaux de la Commune de 1871. Edition critique*, 2 vols. (Paris, 1924), 1: 324; Notice signed A[lexandre] R[ey], *La Nation souveraine*, April 22, 1871; Dommanget, *Victor Considerant*, 198.

55. Pierre Denis, "La Paix en 24 heures," *Le Vengeur*, April 28, 1871.

56. Archives du Grand-Orient, BN cote 1632, Vol. II, cited in Maitron, *Dictionnaire biographique*, 5: 163. The Venerables voted 8–6 against the demonstration, but it took place anyway.

57. Lefèvre, *Histoire de la ligue d'Union républicaine*, 174–175. See also Minutes of the Ligue d'Union républicaine des droits de Paris, Séance du 28 avril, 1871: "Citizen Considerant . . . says that French unity is a fact independent of any kind of communal autonomy, an undeniable fact. Free the commune from kings with one head or eight hundred heads; let's have authorities to serve us and not to oppress us. As for the plebiscitory form . . . it is today the only means of bringing all of Paris together in a single thought and of answering Versailles, which treats us as foreigners and as looters." Floquet Papers, AN 49AP 1.

58. Junior [pseudonym], "Le Réveil d'Epiménide," *Le Vengeur*, May 4, 1871; unsigned statement in *Le Vengeur*, May 6, 1871; VC to Pyat, draft, May [5], 1871, AN 10AS 26 (41).

59. VC to Jules Pallas, June 5, 1871, ENS AVC carton 8 (II, 2). See also VC to Dorian, June 6, 1871, ADL 1 J 772 (8).

60. On Courbet, see Jack Lindsay, *Gustave Courbet: His Life and Art* (Bath, 1973), 241–280; and Jacques Rougerie (ed.), *Procès des communards* (Paris, 1964), 74–79. On Bestetti, see Jean Allemagne, *Mémoires d'un Communard. Des barricades au Bagne* (Paris, 1907), 16, 137–138.

61. On Courbet, see VC to Leblond, draft, June 27, 1871, AN 10AS 28 (11), and Courbet to Dorian [mid-June 1871], in Chu, *Letters of Gustave Courbet*, 421–422. Arguments similar to Considerant's were advanced by Dorian, Etienne Arago, and others at Courbet's trial. On Bestetti, see letters of Bestetti and his wife to VC, 1871–1872, AN 10AS 36 (4), and VC to Leblond, draft, July 9, 1871, ENS AVC carton 8 (III, 1).

62. Charles Pellarin, "Préface" dated August 1871 to *Vie de Fourier*, 5th ed. (Paris, 1871), v–vi. Tamisier to VC, July 7, 1871, AN 10AS 42 (2).

63. VC to Jules Pallas, June 5, 1871, ENS AVC carton 8 (II, 2). U.S. Passport no. 1894 issued to VC, July 19, 1871, and countersigned by the mayor of Besançon and the president of the Société Helvétique de Besançon, September 19, 1871, AN 10AS 29 (1).

CHAPTER 18

1. Coignet, *Victor Considerant*, 97.

2. Clémence Royer to VC, 4 letters [March 1884], AN 10AS 41 (11); VC to Clémence Royer, drafts of two letters, March 2 and 12, 1884, AN 10AS 28 (12). A rather misleading picture of this correspondence emerges from Geneviève Fraisse, *Clémence Royer. Philosophe et femme de sciences* (Paris, 1985), 74. Fraisse writes that Royer "enjoyed catching in a flagrant act of misogyny an old Fourierist, Victor Considerant, who thought he was doing a good thing in lavishing her with advice on the running of her lectures." Considerant did indeed criticize the length and delivery of Royer's lectures and even her dress. However, his comments on the substance of her lectures were sufficiently thoughtful that she could write that "the interest you take in all of this . . . consoles me for encountering so much indifference."

3. Coignet, *Victor Considerant*, 98; VC, drafts of letters to Lacase-Duthiers, 1875–1876, AN 10AS 27 (20), and ENS AVC carton 8 (III, 2). VC to Charles Darwin, 21 pages, draft, April 11, 1872, AN 10AS 27 (15). I have found no record of a reply.

4. Jules Marcou, "Notice biographique sur Victor-Prosper Considerant," *Le Salinois*, 7 (February 18, 1894); Paul Janet, "La Philosophie de Charles Fourier," *Revue des deux mondes*, 35 (October 1, 1874), 619–645.

5. Letters of Brisbane to VC, AN 10AS 36 (11). Finally, in 1877, Brisbane settled in Paris with his new wife and for a few years became a mainstay of the aging Fourierist group. Amauntrez [?] to VC, May 19, 1875, AN 10AS 36 (1); letters of Christine Evers, *née* Bruck, to VC and JC, 1877–1878, BMB Z418, and 1879–1880, AN 10AS 38 (6).

6. Report of police officer Rousseau, July 4, 1877, APP Ba 1,017, "Dossier de Victor Considerant"; E.-A. Carrière, "Agave Consideranti," *Revue horticole*, 47 (1875), 427–430.

7. AN 10AS 42 (11) includes both Paul Vigoureux's admiring early letters to VC and the venomous correspondence of his later years. Some of the history of the conflict is rehearsed, from Considerant's perspective, in VC, drafts of letters to the notary Brusset, April 16–20, 1880, ENS AVC carton 8 (IV, 1), carton 10 (VII), and carton 9 (I, 1). See also VC to Aimée Beuque, April 14, 1869, BMB Z417. Letters of Gustave Considerant to VC, AN 10AS 29 (3). VC to Justine, veuve Pallas, December 7, 1874, ENS AVC carton 8 (III, 1).

8. On Considerant's break with Cantagrel, see VC to Talon, April 22, 1882, ENS AVC carton 9 (III, 3): "When one has been as strongly and profoundly linked as I was with him and when a long rupture has occurred, it seems to me that it is better to remain apart rather than to seek a rapprochement that could

not establish the kind of relations that exist in old memories." See also Cantagrel to Talon, April 27, 1882, ENS AVC carton 9 (III, 2): "Considerant is right about the idea of a rapprochement, which could not take place without an explanation that would explain nothing and that would be as painful for him as for me." For Considerant's difficulties with Laverdant, see Désiré Laverdant to VC, n.d., AN 10AS 39 (8), and VC to Laverdant, July 22, 1870, AN 10AS 28 (12).

9. Tamisier to VC, October 10, 1869, AN 10AS 42 (2). On Benoît, see VC to Caroline Dorian, August 4, 1880, ADL 1 J 773 (7).

10. Letters of VC to the Dorian family, ADL 1 J 770–773. For a vivid sketch of Aline Menard-Dorian and her household in later years, see the memoirs of her grandson, Jean Hugo, *Le Regard de la mémoire* (Avignon, 1983), 11, 125, 147, 215, 275–277, 284–285. On Juliette Adam's failure to reply, see VC to Caroline Dorian, August 30, 1883, ADL 1 J 773 (18).

11. Brisbane to VC, November 29, 1872, ENS AVC carton 8 (II, 2); VC to Cohadon, December 25, 1872, AN 10AS 28 (12).

12. VC to Caroline Dorian, July 12, 1874, ADL 1 J 733(3); Gustave Geoffroy, "Un Cours libre de Victor Considerant," *La Société nouvelle*, 10, no. 1 (January 1894), 36–44.

13. Geoffroy, "Un Cours libre de Victor Considerant," 36–44.

14. Geoffroy. "Un Cours libre de Victor Considerant," 44. See also Geoffroy, "Préface," to Julien Sermet, *Les Courtes joies. Poèsies* (Paris, 1897), vi.

15. VC to Jules Pallas, December 25, 1872, AN 10AS 28 (12); L. H., obituary of Julie Considerant, *Le Journal à un sou* (April 14, 1880), ENS AVC carton 13 (V, 4).

16. Le Groupe phalanstérien de Marseille to VC, March 14, 1880, AN 10AS 40 (1).

17. VC, "Lettre au phalanstériens de Marseille," May 15, 1880, *Revue du mouvement social*, 1 (August 1880), 269–271, full text in Vernus, *Victor Considerant*, 277–278.

18. VC, "Des vues que je ne soutiendrais plus aujourd'hui, les ayant reconnues pour erronés," ENS AVC carton 2 (I, 7). See also AN 10AS 26 (30).

19. Georges Sorel, *Réflexions sur la violence* (Paris, 1950), 167–220.

20. VC, "Des Vues que je ne soutiendrais plus aujourd'hui," ENS AVC carton 2 (I, 7).

21. Marcou, "Notice biographique," *Le Salinois*, 5 (February 4, 1894); JC to VC, October 12, 1872, ENS AVC carton 8 (III, 1).

22. VC to Laure Pallas, July 13, 1874, ENS AVC carton 9 (III, 3); VC to Justine Pallas [1875], ENS AVC carton 4 (V, 1).

23. VC to Justine Pallas [1875], ENS AVC carton 4 (V, 1). VC to Caroline Dorian, May 14, 1880, ADL 1 J773 (6), and July 12, 1874, ADL 1 J 773 (3).

24. A dozen obituaries of JC, April 11 and 12, 1880, ENS AVC carton 13 (V, 4), and carton 11 (I, 1). For the ceremony, see the obituary signed L. H. in *Le Journal à un sou*, April 14, 1880, in ENS AVC carton 13 (V, 4). *Le Figaro* went a step further in confusion, describing Victor Considerant as a former

Saint-Simonian! Berthe Bernard, *née* Considerant (the daughter of Gustave), to VC, April 20, 1880, AN 10AS 29 (1).

25. VC to Caroline Dorian, May 14, 1880, ADL 1 J 773 (6). See also VC to Talon, June 1, 1880, ENS AVC carton 9 (III, 3).

26. VC to Talon, June 1, 1880, ENS AVC carton 9 (III, 3); VC to Caroline Dorian, May 14, 1880, ADL 1 J 773 (6); Marcou, "Notice biographique sur Considerant."

27. Paul Vigoureux to VC, twelve letters, 1880–1883, AN 10AS 42 (11); VC to Brusset, notaire, drafts and fragments of a long letter, April 16–20, 1880, ENS AVC, carton 8 (I, 2) and (IV, 1); carton 9 (I, 1); carton 10 (VII).

28. VC to Caro, February 16, 1884, AN 10AS 28 (1). Considerant describes himself as attending the "fine history lectures" of Fustel de Coulanges "with passionate assiduity." See VC, "Critique de l'oeuvre de Fourier et de sa première école," *Revue du mouvement social,* 6 (March 1885), 49.

29. VC to Caroline Dorian, August 4, 1880, ADL 1 J 773 (7).

30. VC to Caroline Dorian, May 10 [1881], ADL 1 J 773 (24), and November 3, 1882, ADL 1 J 773 (11).

31. Considerant's last letter from Gustave dates from 1882. For letters to VC from Jules Benoît and his brother, see AN 10AS 36 (4). For letters from César Daly, see AN 10AS 37 (6), and ENS AVC carton 8 (I, 2). See especially Daly to VC, September 14, 1883: "Mon vieux cher, tu n'est pas un parasseux: tu es un *concentré* et tu te concentres de plus en plus."

32. Correspondence of VC with the Dorians, ADL 1 J 770–773. See especially VC to Caroline Dorian, November 3, 1882, and November 14, 1884, ADL 1 J 773 (11) and (20).

33. VC to Caroline Dorian, December 2, 1883, and April 10, 1885, ADL 1 J 773 (16) and (23). See also Considerant's caustic response to the proposal of a "Comité radical antiopportuniste" to place his name on their list of candidates for the National Assembly: "No one takes a more strongly critical view than I of the campaign of division, intransigence, and implacable hostility led, within the republican party, by certain leaders and journals of anti-opportunist radicalism." VC to Perchet, September 29, 1885, copy in collection of Robert Guillaume.

34. VC to Aline Dorian, December 17, 1881, ADL 1 J 770 (3). See also VC to Taine, draft, September 15, 1880, ENS AVC carton 2 (I, 2).

35. VC to Aline Dorian, May 12, 1892, ADL 1 J 770 (16).

36. VC, "Critique de l'oeuvre de Fourier et de sa première école," *La Revue du mouvement social,* 6 (1885), 1–8, 47–54, 93–105, 140–149; quotes from 1–8.

37. Paul Bert to VC, December 30, 1881, and draft of VC to Paul Bert, January 2, 1882, AN 10AS 29 (1); VC to M. et Mme. Burnouf, draft [1880], ENS AVC carton 2 (I, 2).

38. Considerant's sister Julie, who died in 1866, left him 2000 francs. See VC to Justine Pallas, April 6, 1867, ENS AVC carton 8 (II, 1). His sister Justine left him a life annuity of 400 francs on her death in 1880. See Sachon, notaire,

to VC, June 4, 1880, AN 10AS 29 (1). On Dr. Barrier's bequest of 10,000 francs, see Maréchal to VC, August 1, 1870, AN 10AS 40 (1). Considerant's efforts to sell his properties in San Antonio are described in VC to Talon, copy, April 22, 1882, ENS AVC carton 9 (III, 3), and VC to Caroline Dorian, July 16, 1883, ADL 1 J 773 (12). On Considerant's purchase of shares in the Compagnie générale des Magnésies naturelles d'Eubée and his subsequent falling out with Burnouf, see their acrimonious exchange of letters in ENS AVC carton 13 (II, 7).

39. Form letter on preparations for a banquet honoring Victor Considerant, "the doyen of French socialists," signed by "socialists of various groups and schools," including Avrial, Boiron, Frankel, Jourde, Fernand, Maurice, Monprofit, Raymond, and César Daly, AN 10AS 29 (1); Aubry to VC, October 22, 1890, AN 10AS 36 (1); Daly to VC, November 2, 1890, AN 10AS 37 (6); VC to Raymond, draft, October 21, 1890, AN 10AS 28 (10).

40. On the Café Soufflet as a center of left-wing discussion and agitation in the 1870s and 1880s, see Jacques Droz (ed.), *Histoire générale du socialisme*, vol. 2 (Paris, 1874), 143.

41. Alexandre Zévaès, *De l'introduction du Marxisme en France* (Paris, 1947), 36n; Paul Muller, *La Révolution de 1848 en Alsace* (Paris, 1912), 182; Jules Prudhommeaux quoted in Desroche, *Société festive*, 169–170; VC to Aline Dorian [c.1890], ADL 1 J 770 (12).

42. Loulou Bourson to VC, December 27, 1891, AN 10AS 36 (8); letters of Demeur to VC, AN 10AS 37 (7); interview with VC in *Le Peuple. Organe quotidien de la démocratie socialiste*, 7, no. 319 (November 15, 1891), cutting in ENS AVC carton 1 (I, 1).

43. VC to Adolphe Demeur, May 26, 1892, in Piérard and Pierson, *Belgique, Terre d'exil*, 38–39.

44. VC to Madame Demeur [May 27, 1892], collection of Luc Somerhausen, copy made by Professor John Bartier. My thanks to Madame Bartier for allowing me to see her late husband's transcription of this letter.

45. Letters of Désirée Véret, veuve Gay to VC, 1890–1891, AN 10AS 42 (8). This extraordinary collection of a dozen letters is the main source for the next four paragraphs. We do not have copies or drafts of Considerant's replies.

46. On Désirée Véret, see Michèle Riot-Sarcey's excellent *La Démocratie à l'épreuve des femmes. Trois figures critiques du pouvoir, 1830–1848* (Paris, 1994), and her article "Lettres de Charles Fourier et de Désirée Véret, une correspondance inédite," *Cahiers Charles Fourier*, 6 (1995), 3–14. See also the remarkable evocation of Désirée Véret's correspondence with Considerant in the epilogue to Jacques Rancière, *La Nuit des prolétaires* (Paris, 1981), 432–440.

47. Désirée Véret to VC, May 5 and June 21, 1890, AN 10AS 42 (8).

48. Désirée Véret to VC, October 2–4, 1890, AN 10AS 42 (8).

49. Désirée Véret to VC, July 6, 1891, AN 10AS 42 (8).

50. VC, "L'Opinion d'un Pholanstérien [sic] sur le socialisme moderne," *L'Eclair*, 4, no. 925 (June 17, 1891), in ENS AVC carton 1 (I).

51. Toward the end of his life, Considerant sometimes referred to Kleine in

his correspondence as "my son." He did not legally adopt Kleine, but he did make Kleine his heir, leaving him the huge collection of Fourierist letters and manuscripts on which this study (like many others) is based. In calling Kleine "my son," Considerant was following a practice he also adopted with regard to his "mother" Clarisse Vigoureux and his "daughter" Christine Bruck.

52. Coignet, *Victor Considerant*, 99; *Le Libéral de Vervins*, December 31, 1893, cutting in ANS AVC carton 13 (V, 4).

53. Police report on Considerant's funeral ceremonies, APP Ba 1,017. Obituaries of VC, cuttings from *Le Journal des débats*, *L'Illustration*, *La Liberté*, *Le Matin*, *La Paix*, *La Justice*, *Le Rappel*, *Paris*, *Le Figaro*, *L'Epoque*, and *Le Petit Moniteur universel* (all of Paris); also *Le Peuple* (Bruxelles) and *The London Daily Telegraph*, as well as ten French provincial journals, AN 10AS 29 (3), and ENS AVC carton 13 (V, 4).

54. Obituaries of VC, AN 10AS 29 (3), and ENS AVC carton 13 (V, 4). Kleine to Mme. Bourson, December 27, 1893, RSA *fond* 251, *opis* 1, *delo* 86. See *Le Journal des débats*, December 28, 1893, on Considerant's "great aversion to burial."

55. Hippolyte Destrem, "Dernier adieu à notre cher Considerant," *La Revue socialiste*, 19 (January–June 1894), 77–79.

CONCLUSION

1. *Le Phare de Dunkurque*, December 31, 1893, ENS AVC carton 13 (V, 4).

2. *Le Journal des débats*, December 28, 1893, AN 10AS 29 (3).

3. Jean Allemane, "Victor Considerant," *Le Parti ouvrier* (December 30–31, 1893), 1. My thanks to Donald Reid for this reference.

4. Malon, *Histoire du socialisme*, 105–108; Brissac, "Victor Considerant," *La Revue socialiste*, 19 (January–June, 1894), 73–77.

5. Vernus, *Victor Considerant*, 212–216.

6. A. Marseille, "Rapport sur Victor Considerant," 5 pp., APP Ba 1,017. Philippe, comte de Paris to Jules Marcou [1894], in Richard Moreau, "Jules Marcou (1824–1898) ou 'le diable au corps,'" *Académie des sciences, belles-lettres et arts de Besançon et de Franche-Comté. Procès-verbaux et mémoires*, 290 (1992–1993), 188–189.

7. Coignet, *Victor Considerant*, 24–25, 44–46; Amédée Simonin, *Journal*, January 23, 1856, Simonin Papers, Library of Congress, Manuscript Division, Mss. 18,160.

BIBLIOGRAPHY

This bibliography includes works both by and about Victor Considerant and works relevant to the larger contexts within which I have attempted to situate him. The listing of Considerant's manuscripts and unpublished letters is as complete as I could make it, but so much new material has come to light in recent years that there is every reason to suspect there will be more discoveries. The listing of Considerant's published writing does not include the hundreds of articles he published in the various Fourierist journals and in the Fourierist daily newspaper *Démocratie pacifique.* Nor does it include Considerant's numerous electoral manifestoes or all of the extracts from his writings that were published separately as brochures and broadsides. Still, it is substantial enough, I believe, to convey some sense of the vast range of Considerant's output as writer, journalist, and political *militant.* The listing of contextual works is highly selective and limited, by and large, to works that have been of special value to me. A much fuller range of citations is included in the footnotes.

PRIMARY SOURCES
Manuscripts and Letters

ARCHIVES SOCIÉTAIRES (ARCHIVES NATIONALES 10AS)
This is the essential manuscript source for the study of both Victor Considerant and the Fourierist movement ("Ecole Sociétaire"). It is divided into two sections. The Fonds Fourier (10AS 1 to 10AS 25) consists of manuscripts and personal papers left by Fourier at the time of his death. It includes drafts of his

major works and of his vast unpublished *Grand traité*, numerous fragments and drafts of letters, and several hundred letters addressed to Fourier. The Fonds Considerant (10AS 26 to 10AS 42) consists of Victor Considerant's personal papers, his manuscripts and correspondence, as well as six cartons of papers relating to the Ecole Sociétaire and seven cartons of letters exchanged by members of the Ecole, classified alphabetically.

At Considerant's death in 1893 the entire archive passed into the hands of his heir, Auguste Kleine, the director of the Ecole des Ponts-et-Chaussées. In 1922 Kleine deposited the papers at the Centre de Documentation Sociale created by Celestin Bouglé at the Ecole Normale Supérieure. During World War II the papers were transferred to the Bibliothèque de Documentation Internationale Contemporaine, and they were finally deposited at the Archives Nationales in 1949. Edith Thomas then drew up an inventory of the whole archive, which was published in 1991 by Françoise Hildesheimer. See Edith Thomas, *Fonds Fourier et Considerant. Archives Sociétaires. 10AS Inventaire* (Paris, 1991). Although this inventory includes a number of minor errors of attribution, transcription, and dating, it is still a most useful *instrument de travail*.

Fonds Considerant

10AS 26 and 10AS 27. Manuscripts of Considerant.

10AS 28. Letters of Considerant.

10AS 29. Personal papers of Considerant.

10AS 30. Fourierist organizations and activities.

10AS 31. Fourierist communities: Condé-sur-Vesgre, Cîteaux, Algeria, Texas.

10AS 32. Librairie des Sciences Sociales: subscriptions, accounts, 1870–1884.

10AS 33. Papers and notes by various Fourierists.

10AS 34 and 10AS 35. Photographs.

10AS 36—10AS 42. Fourierist correspondence, organized alphabetically.

Other Considerant material at the Archives Nationales includes letters from Considerant in the Fonds Laurentie (372 AP 11) and the Archives du Théâtre Italien (F21 1114 [3]).

ARCHIVES VICTOR CONSIDERANT. ECOLE NORMALE SUPÉRIEURE

When the Considerant papers were moved from the Ecole Normale Supérieure to safer quarters during World War II, thirteen boxes of manuscripts, letters, and accounts were inadvertently left behind. It was only in the early 1970s that their whereabouts became known and they were made available to scholars. In 1974 a provisional inventory was drawn up by Vincent Prieur. In 1994 Pierre Mercklé completed a fuller and more accurate inventory, which is now available to scholars working with these papers. Most of the cartons contain a miscellany of letters, accounts, bills, receipts, and cuttings. The listing that follows is limited to items relevant to this study.

Carton 1. Miscellaneous brochures, articles, newspaper cuttings.

Carton 2. Letters and manuscripts of Considerant. Accounts, minutes of meetings.

Carton 3. Manuscripts and notes of Fourier, letters of Muiron, receipts, contracts.

Carton 4. Considerant: reading notes, cuttings, drafts of letters and articles.

Carton 5. Brochures published by Considerant and others.

Carton 6. Drafts of Considerant's "Letter to Maximilian" (1865). Bills and receipts.

Carton 7. Considerant's notes and papers from the Ecole du Génie at Metz (1829–1830).

Carton 8. Considerant: manuscripts, drafts of articles, and letters (esp. 1850–1880).

Carton 9. Considerant: drafts of articles and letters. Manuscripts of Clarisse Vigoureux.

Carton 10. Considerant: lecture notes from Metz. Cuttings and maps.

Carton 11. Miscellaneous brochures, printed articles.

Carton 12. Considerant: lecture notes from Metz (1829–1830).

Carton 13. Fourierist correspondence, accounts, printed brochures.

CONSIDERANT PAPERS. BIBLIOTHÈQUE
MUNICIPALE DE BESANÇON

A carton of Fourierist correspondence containing about 500 letters (including almost 150 from Considerant) appears to have been removed from the Considerant archive sometime in the late nineteenth or early twentieth century. It remained in private hands for several generations and constituted the principal source for the *mémoire de maîtrise* by Nicolas Marsollier, *Victor Considerant dans les débuts de l'Ecole Sociétaire à travers quelques lettres inédits* (Université d'Angers, 1991). The bulk of the collection was subsequently purchased by the Bibliothèque Municipale de Besançon, where it is now available to scholars under the following *cotes:*

Ms Z417. Letters from and to Considerant (108 letters from Considerant).

Ms Z418. Letters from and to Clarisse Vigoureux. Letters from Jean-Baptiste Considerant, Julie Considerant, Just Muiron, Désiré Laverdant, and many others.

Ms Z463. Letters from Considerant to Clarisse Vigoureux (23 letters).

Ms Z464. Letters from Considerant to Clarisse Vigoureux and Julie Considerant (26 letters).

The Bibliothèque Municipale de Besançon also possesses a substantial collection of letters from Considerant's father, Jean-Baptiste Considerant, to Victor Thelmier, together with three letters from Considerant to Thelmier (Ms 1419). See also letters of Considerant to Proudhon (Ms 2948), to Philippe Bourson (Ms 2980), and to Charles Weiss (Ms 1903).

OTHER MANUSCRIPT HOLDINGS

Archives de la Préfecture de Police de Paris. Considerant's dossier (Ba 1017) consists of 28 items covering the period 1869–1893. Dossier Ba 1035 ("Banquets phalanstériens") also includes some information on Considerant.

Archives du département de la Loire (Saint-Etienne). The papers of Frédéric Dorian and his family include 70 letters from Considerant to the Dorians (1835–1893).

Archives du département de la Seine et de la Ville de Paris. Letter of Gigoux with endorsement by Considerant [D. 4AZ 1034 (VR2)].

Archives du département du Jura (Montmorot). Letter of Considerant to quaestor of National Assembly, 1848 (ADJ 1 J340).

Archives Générales du Royaume (Brussels). Two sources of Considerant material: The Papiers Charles Rogier (nos. 173, 208, 209) include 7 letters to Rogier from Considerant, 1839–1847. Ministère de la Justice. Police des Etrangers. Dossiers individuels no. 36486 is a huge file on Considerant consisting of several hundred documents and letters relating to his surveillance by the Belgian police, 1849–1854.

Archives Historiques de la Guerre (Vincennes). Considerant's dossier in the Ministère de la Guerre, Archives administratives. Célébrités, consists of 12 items, including letters about Considerant from Bugeaud and Maison and from Considerant to Soult and Maison. Considerant also figures in the Régistre des élèves de l'Ecole Polytechnique, vol. 5 (1820–1830), 239.

Biblioteka Jagiellonska (Krakow). Letter of Considerant to Pitois. Radowitz autograph collection, 6114.

Bibliothèque de l'Arsenal (Paris). Letters and documents pertaining to Considerant in Fonds d'Eichthal (Ms. 14804), Fonds Lacroix (Ms. 9623), and Collection Luzarche (Ms. 7053–7055).

Bibliothèque de l'Histoire de la Ville de Paris. Its collections include letters of Considerant to George Sand (G3648), Jules Michelet (vol. 36), Eugène Cavaignac (Ms 1056), and to the *Moniteur officiel* (Ms 1044). Some material in the Courbet Papers (Ms 1131) and the Chassin Papers (Ms 1398) relates to Considerant.

Bibliothèque de l'Institut de France (Paris). The Fonds de la Bibliothèque Lovenjoul, Chantilly, includes four letters of Considerant to Emile de Girardin and one each to Balzac and Sainte-Beuve.

Bibliothèque Municipale d'Auxerre. Letter of Considerant to Charton, 1848 (Ms 333).

Bibliothèque Municipale de Nevers. The Fonds Phalanstérien of André Morlon (Ms. 1364) includes two letters of Considerant.

Bibliothèque Municipale d'Orléans. Letter of Considerant to Namèche Despierreux, 1852 (Ms 1502–1508).

Bibliothèque Municipale de Périgueux. Letter of Considerant to Toussenel (Ms 88).

Bibliothèque Municipale de Reims. Letter of Considerant from Barvaux, 1852.

Bibliothèque Municipale de Rouen. Two letters of Considerant, one to Théodore Lebreton, July 1848 (Ms m267), the other to Sénard, December 1847 (Collection de Blosseville).

Bibliothèque Municipale de Salins. The Fonds Magnin includes 11 letters of Considerant to Charles Magnin and drafts of 4 replies by Magnin.

Bibliothèque Nationale (Paris). Four letters of Considerant in Correspondence of Dr. Jaenger (NAF 22,050). Individual letters to de Molien and Bixio.

Bibliothèque Publique et Universitaire (Genève). Letter of Considerant to Karl Vogt, 1877 (Ms 2188).

Bibliothèque Royale Albert I (Brussels). Archives et Musée de la Littérature. The Fonds Barral includes 4 letters of Considerant to Jean-Augustin and Georges Barral and to M. Faivre (ML 3732 and 3733).

Collection of Jean-Claude Dubos (Besançon). Four letters of Considerant: to de Brack, Matthieu de la Drôme, Geoffroy Saint-Hilaire, and Edgar Quinet.

Collection of Robert Guillaume (Besançon). Five letters of Considerant to Alphonse and Jenny Delacroix, 1859–1885, and one to Perchet, 1885.

Colonie Sociétaire de Condé-sur-Vesgre. Its collection of 72 letters addressed to Joseph Devay includes 2 from Considerant (1832 and 1836).

Houghton Library, Harvard University (Cambridge, Mass.). Letter of Considerant to Jules Marcou, 1854 (6 Ms Fr 235 [23]).

International Institute of Social History (Amsterdam). Two letters from Considerant in Pecqueur Papers, one in Flora Tristan Papers.

Library of Congress. Manuscript Division (Washington, D.C.). The Amédée Simonin Papers (Mss. 18, 160) include 3 letters from Considerant, 1855–1856. Simonin's diary is a fundamental source for the history of Reunion.

Massachusetts Historical Society Library (Boston). The James T. Fisher Papers include 7 letters from Considerant, 1848–1855.

Russian State Archives of Social-Political History (Moscow). Former Central Party Archives. Its rich collection of documents on the history of French socialism includes a file containing 20 letters of Considerant (to Salvandy, Petrus Borel, Bixio, Flocon, Louis Reybaud, Gagneur, etc.) and a corrected manuscript of the *Quatres lettres* to Bazaine on Mexico (*fond 471, opis 1, delo 13*). Richer still in Considerant material is *fond 251, opis 1*, containing letters from Considerant to the families of his Belgian friends, Philippe Bourson (14 letters) and Adolphe Demeur (28 letters).

Considerant's Published Writings

"Le Nouveau Monde industriel et sociétaire de M. Charles Fourier." *Le Mercure de France au XIXe siècle* 28 (March 13, 1830), 477–480.

"Un Pressentiment." *Revue des deux mondes* (October 1831).

Le Comité de Rédaction de la Phalange au partisans de la théorie sociétaire. Paris: Bourgogne et Martinet, [1833].

Destinée sociale. 3 vols. Vol. 1: Paris: Chez les libraires du Palais-Royal, September 1834. Vol. 2: Paris: Bureau de la Phalange, 1838. Vol. 3: Paris: Librairie de l'Ecole Sociétaire, 1844.

Débâcle de la politique en France. Paris: Bureau de la Phalange, 1836. The first printing of this work, titled *Nécessité d'une dernière débâcle politique en France,* was almost entirely destroyed in a fire.

"Déterminer par l'histoire si les diversités physiologiques des peuples sont entre elles comme les diversités des systèmes sociaux auxquels ces peuples appartiennent." In *Trois discours prononcés à l'Hôtel de Ville par MM. Dain, Considerant et d'Izalguier; faisant complément à la publication du Congrès historique.* Paris: P. H. Khrabbe, 1836, 29–108.

Déraison et dangers de l'engouement pour les chemins de fer. Avis à l'opinion et aux capitaux. Paris: Bureaux de la Phalange, 1838. Originally published in *La Phalange* (August 1 and 15, 1838).

La Conversion, c'est l'impôt. A MM. les Membres de la Chambre élective, par un ancien député. Paris: H. Delloye, 1838.

La Paix ou la guerre. A la France et au corps électoral. Paris: Bureau de la Phalange, 1839. Extract from *La Phalange* (February 15, 1839).

De la politique générale et du rôle de la France en Europe. Suivi d'une appréciation de la marche du Gouvernement depuis juillet 1830. Paris: Bureau de la Phalange, 1840. Part 1 originally published in *La Phalange* (September 1–October 15, 1839).

Contre M. Arago. Réclamation adressée à la Chambre des Députés par les rédacteurs du feuilleton de la Phalange. Suivi de la théorie du droit de propriété. Paris: Bureau de la Phalange, 1840. The second part of this work was republished in 1848 as *Théorie du droit de propriété et du droit au travail.*

Bases de la politique positive. Manifeste de l'Ecole Sociétaire fondée par Fourier. Paris: Bureaux de la Phalange, 1841. A second and greatly enlarged edition was published in 1842. The third edition of 1847 bore the title, "Bases de la politique rationnelle."

Immoralité de la doctrine de Fourier. Paris: Chez les Marchands de Nouveautés [1841].

Exposition abrégée du système phalanstérien de Fourier. Paris: Librairie de l'Ecole Sociétaire, 1841. Originally published in *La Phalange* in 1840, this work consists largely of a journalist's summary of a lecture given by Considerant at Dijon.

De la souveraineté et de la régence. Paris: Librairie de l'Ecole Sociétaire, 1842.

Petit cours de politique et d'économie sociale à l'usage des ignorants et des savants. Paris: Librairie phalanstérienne, 1844. Extract from *Débâcle de la politique en France.*

Chemins de fer, ligne de Paris à Lyon et de Paris à Strasbourg. Rapport fait au Conseil municipal de Paris sur le tracé de Paris à Strasbourg. Paris: Librairie Sociétaire, 1844.

Théorie de l'éducation naturelle et attrayante, dédiée aux mères. Paris: Librairie de l'Ecole Sociétaire, 1844. Extract from *Destinée sociale,* with additions.

Système des développements de l'Ecole Sociétaire. A tous les amis de l'orga-

nisation du travail par l'Association. Paris: Bureau de la Phalange, 1845. Extract from *La Phalange, Revue de la science sociale,* 1, no. 1 (January 1845).

De la sincérité du gouvernement représentatif ou exposition de l'élection véridique. Lettre adressée à Messieurs les membres du Grand Conseil Constituant de l'Etat de Genève. Geneva: G. Fallot, October 26, 1846.

Principes du socialisme. Manifeste de la démocratie au XIXe siècle. Paris: Librairie Phalanstérienne, 1847. This is a reprinting with additions of the "Manifeste politique et social de la démocratie pacifique" first published in *Démocratie pacifique,* 1, no. 1 (August 1, 1843). Three editions were published in 1847, the last followed by *Procès de la Démocratie pacifique.*

Appel au ralliement des socialistes, lettre de M. Rey de Grenoble, communiste, ancien conseiller à la cour royale, aux rédacteurs de la Démocratie pacifique, suivi de Les Deux communismes, observations sur la lettre de M. Rey, par V. Considerant, phalanstérien, membre du Conseil municipal de Paris et du Conseil général de la Seine. Paris: Bureaux de la Démocratie Pacifique, 1847.

Le Socialisme devant le vieux monde, ou le vivant devant les morts. Suivi de "Jésus-Christ devant les conseils de guerre," par Victor Meunier. Paris: Librairie Phalanstérienne, 1848. Two brief extracts were published as broadsides in 1949: *Le Socialisme, c'est le vrai christianisme. Payens, convertissez-vous!* and *L'Apocalypse, ou la prochaine rénovation démocratique et sociale de l'Europe.*

Description du Phalanstère et considérations sociales sur l'architectonique. Paris: Librairie Phalanstérienne, 1848. Extract from *Destinée sociale.*

Réponse de M. Proudhon à M. Considerant et réplique. Examen de la réponse de M. Proudhon, par Victor Considerant. Paris: Lange Lévy, 1849. Supplement to *Démocratie pacifique,* February 19, 1849.

Discours prononcé à l'Assemblée Constituante dans la séance du 14 avril 1849. Paris: Lange Lévy [1849].

Journée du 13 juin 1849. Simples Explications à mes amis et à mes commettants. Paris: Michel Lévy, 1849.

La Dernière Guerre et la paix définitive en Europe. Paris: Librairie Phalanstérienne, 1850. First published in *Démocratie pacifique,* March 27–29, 1850.

La solution, ou le gouvernement direct du peuple. Paris: Librairie Phalanstérienne, December 1850. First published in *Démocratie pacifique,* November 17, 24; December 8, 1850.

Les Quatre crédits, ou 60 milliards à 1 1/2 pour cent. Crédit de l'immeuble. Crédit du meuble engagé. Crédit du meuble libre ou du produit. Crédit du travail. Paris: Librairie Phalanstérienne, 1851. Excerpts published in *Démocratie pacifique,* March 9, 1851.

Ma Justification. Brussels: Librairie Rosez, 1854.

Au Texas. Rapport à mes amis. Paris: Librairie Phalanstérienne, May 1854.

The Great West: A New Social and Industrial Life in Its Fertile Regions. New York: Dewitt and Davenport, 1854.

Au Texas. Deuxième édition. Contenant 1er rapport à mes amis; 2e Bases et

Statuts de la Société de colonisation européo-américaine au Texas; 3e Un Chapître final comprenant, sous le titre de "Convention provisoire," les bases d'une premier établissement sociétaire. Brussels: Au Siège de la Société de Colonisation; Paris: Librairie Phalanstérienne, 1855. This second edition, much fuller than the first and reprinted by Porcupine Press (Philadelphia, 1975) with an introduction by Rondel V. Davidson, is the one cited here.

European Colonization in Texas: An Address to the American People. New York: Baker, Godwin, 1855.

Du Texas. Premier Rapport à mes amis. Paris: Librairie Sociétaire, 1857.

Three Hundred Million Dollars Saved in Specie by the Meaning of a Word. Letter to Secretary McCulloch. New York: New York News, 1867.

Mexique. Quatre lettres au Maréchal Bazaine. Brussels: C. Muquardt, 1868.

Prédictions sur la guerre. La France imposant la paix à l'Europe. Lettre aux Membres du Gouvernement provisoire de la République par Victor Considerant, citoyen américain, ancien représentant du peuple français. Paris: Le Chevalier [1870].

La Paix en 24 heures, dictée par Paris à Versailles. Adresse aux Parisiens, par Victor Considerant, ancien représentant de Paris. Paris: Dubuisson, April 20 [1871].

"La Tombe de Fourier." *Bulletin du mouvement social,* 7, no. 24 (December 15, 1879), 1–2.

"Lettre aux phalanstériens de Marseille." *La Revue du mouvement social,* 1 (August 1880), 269–271.

"Critique de l'oeuvre de Fourier et de sa première école." *La Revue du mouvement social,* 6 (February–May, 1885), 1–8, 47–54, 93–105, 140–149.

"Petite histoire de la féodalité capitaliste." In *Almanach de la question sociale pour 1892,* 43–45.

Posthumous Publication of Works by Considerant

Geoffroy, Gustave. "Un Cours libre de Victor Considerant." *La Société nouvelle,* 10, no. 1 (January 1894), 36–44.

"Autour de la Vie de Jésus (Lettres inédites)." *La Revue,* 38, 3rd ser., 15 (August 1, 1901), 225–244. Considerant's letters to Renan.

Ledoux, Emile. *Victor Considerant. Trois lettres inédites. Notes sur sa jeunesse.* Besançon: Dodivers, 1909.

Lebey, André. "Lettre de Victor Considerant au R. P. Cipoletti." *La Révolution de 1848,* 7 (March 1910), 15–18.

Leuillot, Paul. "Une lettre inédite de V. Considerant au docteur Jaenger." *Revue du Nord* (1950), 355–359.

Dubos, Jean-Claude. "A propos de la publication des manuscrits de Charles Fourier: Une lettre de Considerant à Alexandre Bixio." *Cahiers Charles Fourier,* 1 (1990), 7–10.

Dubos, Jean-Claude. "Victor Considerant nouvelliste: 'Un Pressentiment' (1831)." *Cahiers Charles Fourier,* 7 (1996), 7–20.

Journals on Which Considerant Collaborated

La Réforme industrielle ou le Phalanstère (June 1, 1832–February 28, 1834). Until September 7, 1832, this journal was called *Le Phalanstère*. Weekly until August 16, 1833, then monthly. Until July 1833, Considerant shared chief editorial responsibility with Jules Lechevalier and Abel Transon. Thereafter, Charles Pellarin became managing editor.

La Phalange. Journal de la science sociale (July 10, 1836–July 30, 1843). Second series: three times a month from July 10, 1836, to April 1, 1837; monthly through December 1837; bimonthly from January 1838 through August 15, 1840. Third series: three times a week from September 2, 1840, through July 30, 1843. Considerant was director of *La Phalange* throughout most of its existence.

La Démocratie pacifique (August 1, 1843–November 30, 1851). Daily until May 22, 1850, then weekly. Separate issues of this paper were seized by the government three times in July 1847, and on a few other occasions. Publication was twice suspended for political reasons: from June 13 through August 24, 1849, and from May 23 through August 3, 1850. Considerant was editor-in-chief until June 13, 1849.

La Phalange. Revue de la science sociale (January 1845–December 1849). Monthly, occasionally bimonthly. This was the theoretical journal of the Ecole Sociétaire, and it was in this journal that many of Fourier's manuscripts were published. Considerant was its director.

Bulletin phalanstérien (July 1846–April 27, 1850). A newsletter reporting on the internal affairs of the Ecole Sociétaire. Sent irregularly and free of charge to all subscribers to the Rente de l'Ecole. Considerant was a member of the committee overseeing its publication.

Bulletin de la Société de colonisation européo-américaine au Texas (January 1855–April 1875. Thirty-nine issues, published irregularly under the direction of (at various times) Bureau, Guillon, Godin, Bourdon, and Cantagrel. This journal is a major source both for the history of the Reunion community near Dallas, Texas, and for Considerant's subsequent efforts to find a site and get support for a second communitarian initiative.

SECONDARY SOURCES

Works on Considerant

Abramson, Pierre-Luc. "Victor Considerant et le Mexique." In Daniel Meyren (ed.), *Maximilien et le Mexique (1864–1867)*. Perpignan: Presses Universitaires de Perpignan, 1992, 59–67.

Abramson, Pierre-Luc. "L'Idée démocratique dans 'La Démocratie pacifique,' journal de Victor Considerant." *La Pensée démocratique. Actes du XIe colloque d'Aix-en-Provence (21–22 septembre 1995).* Association française des historiens des idées politiques. Aix-en-Provence: Presses Universitaires d'Aix-Marseille, 1996, 201–206.

Beecher, Jonathan. "Victor Considerant: The Making of a Fourierist." In Richard Bienvenu and Mordechai Feingold (eds.), *In the Presence of the Past: Essays in Honor of Frank Manuel.* Amsterdam: Kluwer Academic, 1991, 93–120.

Beecher, Jonathan. "Une Utopie manquée au Texas: Victor Considerant et Réunion." *Cahiers Charles Fourier,* 4 (1993), 40–79.

Bestor, Arthur E., Jr. "Victor Considerant, First Communitarian." Paper delivered at the annual meeting of the American Historical Association, December 28, 1948. Bestor Papers, University of Illinois.

Bourgin, Hubert. *Victor Considerant, son oeuvre.* Lyon: Imprimeries Réunies, 1909.

Coignet, Clarisse. *Victor Considerant, sa vie et son oeuvre.* Paris: Félix Alcan, 1895.

Collard, Pierre. *Victor Considerant (1808–1893), sa vie, ses idées.* Dijon: Barbier, 1910.

David, Marcel. "Le 'Gouvernement direct du peuple' selon les proscrits de la Seconde République." *La Pensée démocratique. Actes du XIe colloque d'Aix-en-Provence (21–22 septembre 1995).* Association française des historiens des idées politiques. Aix-en-Provence: Presses Universitaires d'Aix-Marseille, 1996.

Davidson, Rondel Van. "Victor Considerant and the Failure of La Réunion." *Southwestern Historical Quarterly,* 76, no. 3 (January 1973), 277–296.

Davidson, Rondel Van. *Did We Think Victory Great? The Life and Ideas of Victor Considerant.* Lanham, Md.: University Press of America, 1988.

Davidson, Rondel Van. "Reform Versus Revolution: Victor Considerant and the Communist Manifesto." *Social Science Quarterly,* 58, no. 1 (June 1977), 74–85.

Discailles, Ernest. "Victor Considerant en Belgique." *Bulletin de l'Académie royale des sciences, des lettres et des beaux-arts de Belgique,* 3rd ser., 29 (1895), 705–748.

Dommanget, Maurice. *Victor Considerant, sa vie, son oeuvre.* Paris: Editions Sociales Internationales, 1929.

Ganzin, Michel. "La Pensée européene de Victor Considerant: Un Prophétisme démocratique." *Actes du Colloque de Nice (17–18–19 septembre 1992).* Association française des historiens des idées politiques. Aix-en-Provence: Presses Universitaires d'Aix-Marseille, 1993, 53–90.

Jones, Russell M. "Victor Considerant's American Experience (1852–1869)." *French-American Review,* 1 (1976–1977), 65–94, 124–150.

Lovell, David W. "Early French Socialism and Politics: The Case of Victor Considerant." *History of Political Thought,* 13, no. 2 (Summer 1992), 257–279.

Marcou, Jules. "Notice biographique sur Victor-Prosper Considerant." *Le Salinois*, 55, nos. 5, 6, 7 (February 4, 11, 18, 1894).

Marsollier, Nicolas. "Victor Considerant dans les débuts de l'Ecole Sociétaire à travers quelques lettres inédites." Mémoire de maîtrise d'histoire et de lettres modernes, Université d'Angers, 1991.

Muller, Paul. "Victor Considerant après le Coup d'Etat." *La Révolution de 1848*, 10 (1913–1914), 435–436.

Riot-Sarcey, Michèle. "A Propos de Victor Considerant en 1848. Victor Considerant en quête d'une 'vérité politique' par 'l'utopie réalisé,'" *Cahiers Charles Fourier*, 10 (1999), 111–120.

Rolland, Patrice. "Considerant et l'Europe," *Il Pensiero Politico*, 31, no. 2 (1998), 321–335.

Vernus, Michel. *Victor Considerant, 1808–1893. Le Coeur et la raison.* Dole, France: Canevas Editeur, 1993.

Zavala, Silvio. "Victor Considerant et le problème social au Mexique." *Revue historique*, 239 (January–March, 1968), 19–28.

Contexts: Franche-Comté and Family

Bichon, Bernard. "Sur le fouriérisme en Franche-Comté dans le Jura pendant la Monarchie de Juillet, Wladimir Gagneur." Mémoire de maîtrise d'histoire, Faculté de lettres, Université de Besançon, 1975.

Bordet, Gaston. *La Grand Mission de Besançon: janvier–fevrier 1825.* Paris: Editions du Cerf, 1998.

Brélot, Claude-Isabelle. *La Noblesse réinventée. Nobles de Franche-Comté de 1814 à 1870.* 2 vols. Paris: Les Belles Lettres, 1992.

Clark, T. J., *Image of the People: Gustave Courbet and the 1848 Revolution.* London: Thames and Hudson, 1973.

Coignet, Clarisse. *Mémoires.* 4 vols. Lausanne: Pache-Varidel, 1899–1903.

Coindre, Gaston. *Le Vieux Salins. Promenades et causeries.* Besançon: Jacquin, 1904.

Cornillot, Marie-Lucie. "La Salle des sociloques comtois au Palais Granvelle de 1948 à 1975. Les portraits: bustes, peintures, dessins." *Académie des sciences, belles-lettres et arts de Besançon. Procès-verbaux et mémoires*, 182 (1976–1977), 75–91.

Dubos, Jean-Claude. "Une Famille de maîtres de forges: les Gauthier." *Bulletin de la Société d'agriculture, lettres, sciences et arts de la Haute-Saône*, new ser. 17 (1984), 61–114.

Dubos, Jean-Claude. "Les Parentés académiques des premiers socialistes comtois: Fourier, Considerant, Proudhon, Just Muiron, Clarisse et Julie Vigoureux." *Académie des sciences, belles-lettres et arts de Besançon. Procès-verbaux et mémoires*, 190 (1992–1993), 27–57.

Dubos, Jean-Claude. "Les Origines de Victor Considerant et de son épouse Julie Vigoureux." Unpublished paper.

Dubos, Jean-Claude. "Clarisse Vigoureux, 'grand honnête homme.'" Preface to Clarisse Vigoureux, *Parole de Providence*. Seyssel: Champ Vallon, 1993, 7–90.

Dubos, Jean-Claude. "Just Muiron et les débuts du fouriérisme à Besançon (1816–1832)." In Maurice Agulhon et al., "Les Socialismes français," *Romantisme*, 24 (1995), 213–221.

Febvre, Lucien. *Histoire de Franche-Comté*. Paris: Boivin, 1912.

Fernier, Jean-Jacques, Jean-Luc Mayaud, and Patrick Le Nouëne. *Courbet et Ornans*. Paris: Herscher, 1989.

Fietier, Roland (ed.). *Histoire de la Franche-Comté*. Toulouse: Privat, 1977.

Fohlen, Claude, et al. *Histoire de Besançon*. 2 vols. Paris: Nouvelle Librairie de France, 1964–1965.

Gazier, Georges. "Jean-Baptiste Considerant de Salins (1771–1827)." *Mémoires de la société d'émulation du Doubs*, 8th ser., 3 (1908), 359–380.

Gazier, Georges. "A propos du centenaire de la mort de Charles Fourier. Le Premier Disciple: le bisontin Just Muiron (1787–1881)." *Académie des sciences, belles-lettres et arts de Besançon. Procès-verbaux et mémoires* (1938), 1–14.

Guibert, Jean-Paul. "Le Fouriérisme et les fouriéristes dans un journal bisontin, l'*Impartial* (1829–1834)." D.E.S. Histoire Contemporaine, Besançon, 1982.

Joliot, Janine. "La Presse à Besançon de 1830 à 1835." D.E.S. Histoire Contemporaine, Faculté de lettres, Université de Besançon, 1955.

Joliot, Janine. "Clarisse Coignet, cousine des Considerant. Une Adolescence fouriériste." *Académie des sciences, belles-lettres et arts de Besançon. Procès-verbaux et mémoires*, 185 (1982–1983), 253–274.

Joliot, Janine. "Un Salon républicaine sous l'Empire et les débuts de la IIIe République." *Académie des sciences, belles-lettres et arts de Besançon. Procès-verbaux et mémoires*, 186 (1984–1985), 53–76.

Kaye, Eldon. *Les Correspondants de Charles Weiss*. Longueuil, Quebec: Le Préambule, 1987.

Mayaud, Jean-Luc. *Les Paysans du Doubs au temps de Courbet*. Paris: Les Belles Lettres, 1979.

Moreau, Richard. "Jules Marcou (1824–1898) ou 'le diable au corps.'" *Académie des sciences, belles-lettres et arts de Besançon et de Franche-Comté. Procès-verbaux et mémoires*, 190 (1992–1993).

Vernus, Michel. "Un Libraire jurassien à la fin de l'ancien régime: Jean-Claude Considerant, marchand libraire à Salins (1782)." *Société d'émulation du Jura. Travaux présentés . . . en 1979 et 1980* (Lons-le-Saunier) (1981), 133–167.

Vernus, Michel. *La Vie comtoise au temps de l'ancien régime*. 2 vols. Lons-le-Saunier: Marque-Maillard, 1983–1985.

Vernus, Michel. "Les Fouriéristes et les fruitières comtoises." *Cahiers Charles Fourier*, 2 (1991), 47–56.

Vogne, Marcel. *La Presse périodique en Franche-Comté des origines à 1870*. 7 vols. Besançon: Imprimerie Néo-Typo, 1977–1979.

Weiss, Charles. *Journal,* edited by Suzanne Lepin. 4 vols. Paris: Les Belles Lettres, 1972- 1997.

Contexts: Socialism and Romanticism

Abensour, Miguel. "L'Utopie socialiste: Une Nouvelle Alliance de la politique et de la religion." *Le Temps de la réflection,* 2 (1981), 61–112.

Agulhon, Maurice (ed.). *Les Quarante-huitards.* Paris: Julliard, 1975.

Agulhon, Maurice, et al. *1848: les utopismes sociaux.* Paris: C.D.U. et SEDES, 1981.

Agulhon, Maurice, et al. "Les Socialismes français 1796–1866. Formes du discours socialiste." Special issue of *Romantisme. Revue du dix-neuvième siècle,* 24 (1995).

Alexandrian. *Le Socialisme romantique.* Paris: Editions du Seuil, 1979.

Alexandrian, et al. "I Socialismi Francesi." Special issue of *Quaderno filosofico,* 11, no. 14–15 (1986).

Beecher, Jonathan. *Charles Fourier: The Visionary and His World.* Berkeley: University of California Press, 1986.

Beecher, Jonathan. "Fourierism and Christianity." *Nineteenth-Century French Studies,* 22, no. 3–4 (Spring–Summer 1994), 391–403.

Bellenger, Claude, et al. *Histoire générale de la presse française.* 4 vols. Vol. 2: *De 1815 à 1871.* Paris: Presses Universitaires de France, 1969.

Bénichou, Paul. *Le Temps des prophètes. Doctrines de l'âge romantique.* Paris: Gallimard, 1977.

Bénichou, Paul. *Les Mages romantiques.* Paris: Gallimard, 1988.

Bénichou, Paul. *L'Ecole du désenchantement.* Paris: Gallimard, 1992.

Benjamin, Walter. *The Arcades Project,* translated by Howard Eiland and Kevin McLaughlin. Cambridge: Belknap Press, 1999.

Berenson, Edward. *Populist Religion and Left-Wing Politics in France, 1830– 1852.* Princeton: Princeton University Press, 1984.

Berenson, Edward. "A New Religion of the Left: Christianity and Social Radicalism in France, 1815–1848." In François Furet and Mona Ozouf (eds.), *The Transformation of Political Culture, 1789–1848.* Oxford: Oxford University Press, 1989.

Bouchet, Thomas, et al. *Fouriérisme, révolution, république. Autour de 1848.* Special issue of *Cahiers Charles Fourier,* 10 (1999).

Bowman, Frank Paul. *Le Christ romantique.* Geneva: Droz, 1973.

Bowman, Frank Paul. "Religion, Politics and Utopia in French Romanticism." *Australian Journal of French Studies,* 11, no. 3 (1974), 307–324.

Bowman, Frank Paul. "Fouriérismes et christianisme: du Post-curseur à l'Omniarque Amphimondain." *Romantisme,* 11 (1976), 28–42.

Bowman, Frank Paul. *Le Christ des barricades, 1789–1848.* Paris: Cerf, 1987.

Carlisle, Robert B. *The Proffered Crown: Saint-Simonianism and the Doctrine of Hope.* Baltimore: Johns Hopkins University Press, 1987

Caron, Jean-Claude. *Générations romantiques. Les Etudiants de Paris et le Quartier Latin.* Paris: Armand Colin, 1991.

Cassagne, Albert. *La Théorie de l'art pour l'art en France chez les derniers romantiques et les premiers réalistes.* Seyssel: Champ Vallon, 1997.

Charléty, Sebastien. *Histoire du Saint-Simonisme.* Paris: Paul Hartmann, 1931.

Clark, T. J. *The Absolute Bourgeois: Artists and Politics in France 1848–1851.* London: Thames and Hudson, 1973.

Desroche, Henri. *La Société festive: du fouriérisme écrit aux fouriérismes pratiqués.* Paris: Editions du Seuil, 1975.

Duroselle, Jean-Baptiste. *Les Débuts du catholicisme social en France, 1822–1870.* Paris: Presses Universitaires de France, 1951.

Evans, David Owen. *Le Socialisme romantique. Pierre Leroux et ses contemporains.* Paris: Marcel Rivière, 1948.

Evans, David Owen. *Social Romanticism in France 1830–1848.* New York: Octagon Books, 1969.

Girard, Louis, et al. *Romantisme et politique 1815–1851. Colloque de l'Ecole Normale Supérieure de Saint-Cloud (1966).* Paris: Armand Colin, 1969.

Goblot, Jean-Jacques. *Aux Origines du socialisme français. Pierre Leroux et ses premiers écrits (1824–1830).* Lyon: Presses Universitaires de Lyon, 1977.

Goblot, Jean-Jacques. *La Jeune France libérale. Le Globe et son groupe littéraire 1824–1830.* Paris: Plon, 1995.

Grogan, Susan K. *French Socialism and Sexual Difference: Women and the New Society, 1803–1844.* London: Macmillan, 1992.

Guillemin, Henri. *La Première Résurrection de la République.* Paris: Gallimard, 1967.

Haubtmann, Pierre. *Pierre-Joseph Proudhon. Sa Vie et sa pensée (1809–1849).* Paris: Beauchesne, 1982.

Haubtmann, Pierre. *Pierre-Joseph Proudhon. Sa Vie et sa pensée (1849–1865).* Paris: Desclée de Brouwer, 1988.

Hayek, F. A. *The Counter-Revolution of Science.* Glencoe: Free Press, 1952.

Hunt, Herbert J. *Le Socialisme et le romantisme en France. Etude de la presse socialiste de 1830 à 1848.* Oxford: Clarendon Press, 1935.

Johnson, Christopher H. *Utopian Communism in France: Cabet and the Icarians, 1839–1851.* Ithaca: Cornell University Press, 1974.

Kramer, Lloyd S. *Threshold of a New World: Intellectuals and the Exile Experience in Paris, 1830–1848.* Ithaca: Cornell University Press, 1988.

Leroy, Maxime. *Histoire des idées sociales en France.* 3 vols. Paris: Gallimard, 1947–1954.

Lichtheim, George. *The Origins of Socialism.* New York: Praeger, 1969.

Louvancour, Henri. *De Henri Saint-Simon à Charles Fourier. Etude sur le socialisme romantique français.* Chartres: Durand, 1913.

Malon, Benoît. *Histoire du socialisme depuis ses origines probables jusqu'à nos jours.* Lugano: Veladier, 1879.

Manuel, Frank E. *The Prophets of Paris.* Cambridge: Harvard University Press, 1962.

Milner, Max. *Le Romantisme, I: 1820–1843.* Paris: Arthaud, 1973.

Mitzman, Arthur. *Michelet, Historian: Rebirth and Romanticism in 19th-Century France.* New Haven: Yale University Press, 1990.

Mitzman, Arthur. "Michelet and Social Romanticism: Religion, Revolution, Nature." *Journal of the History of Ideas,* 57, no. 4 (October 1996), 659–682.

Oehler, Dolf. *Le Spleen contre l'oubli. Juin 1848: Baudelaire, Flaubert, Heine, Herzen.* Paris: Payot, 1996.

Picard, Roger. *Le Romantisme social.* New York: 1944.

Pichois, Claude. *Le Romantisme, II: 1843–1869.* Paris: Arthaud, 1979.

Pichois, Claude, and Michel Brix. *Gérard de Nerval.* Paris: Fayard, 1995.

Pierrard, Pierre. *1848 . . . les pauvres, l'Evangile et la Révolution.* Paris: Desclée de Brouwer, 1977.

Pierrard, Pierre. *L'Eglise et les ouvriers en France (1840–1940).* Paris: Hachette, 1984.

Pilbeam, Pamela M. *Republicanism in Nineteenth-Century France, 1814–1871.* New York: St. Martin's Press, 1995.

Puech, J.-L. *La Vie et l'oeuvre de Flora Tristan (1803–1844).* Paris: Marcel Rivière, 1925.

Prudhommeaux, Jules. *Icarie et son fondateur Etienne Cabet. Contribution à l'etude du socialisme expérimentale.* Paris: Reider, 1926

Rancière, Jacques. *La Nuit des prolétaires. Archives du rêve ouvrier.* Paris: Fayard, 1981.

Rey, Gabrielle. *Le Fouriériste Allyre Bureau (1810–1859).* Aix-en-Provence: La Pensée Universitaire, 1962.

Riot-Sarcey, Michèle. *La Démocratie à l'épreuve des femmes. Trois figures critiques du pouvoir 1830–1848.* Paris: Albin Michel, 1994.

Riot-Sarcey, Michèle. *Le Réel de l'utopie. Essai sur le politique au XIXe siècle.* Paris: Albin Michel, 1998.

Sewell, William H., Jr. *Work and Revolution in France: The Language of Labor from the Old Regime to 1848.* Cambridge: Cambridge University Press, 1980.

Spitzer, Alan B. *The French Generation of 1820.* Princeton: Princeton University Press, 1987.

Stedman Jones, Gareth. "Utopian Socialism Reconsidered: Science and Religion in the Early Socialist Movement." Unpublished paper.

Thibert, Marguerite. *Le Féminisme dans le socialisme français de 1830 à 1850.* Paris: Giard, 1926.

Tudesq, André-Jean. *Les Grands Notables en France (1840–1849).* 2 vols. Paris: Presses Universitaires de France, 1964.

Viard, Jacques, et al. *L'Esprit républicain: Colloque d'Orléans, 4 et 5 septembre 1970.* Paris: Klincksieck, 1972.

Viatte, Auguste. *Les Sources occultes du romantisme.* 2 vols. Paris: Honoré Champion, 1928.

Viatte, Auguste. *Victor Hugo et les illuminés de son temps.* Montreal: L'Arbre, 1942.

Vincent, K. Steven. *Pierre-Joseph Proudhon and the Rise of French Republican Socialism.* New York: Oxford, 1986.

Contexts: Considerant's America

Bender, Thomas. *New York Intellect.* Baltimore: Johns Hopkins University Press, 1987.

Bestor, Arthur. "Albert Brisbane—Propagandist for Socialism in the 1840s." *New York History,* 28 (April 1947), 128–158.

Coleman, Marion Moore (ed. and trans.). "New Light on La Réunion. From the Pages of *Do Ameryce i w Ameryce*" [The memoirs of Kalikst Wolski]. *Arizona and the West,* 6, no. 1 (Spring 1964), 41–68, and 6, no. 2 (Summer 1964), 137–154.

Crowe, Charles. *George Ripley: Transcendentalist and Utopian Socialist.* Athens: University of Georgia Press, 1967.

Davidson, Rondel Van. "Victor Considerant and the Failure of La Réunion." *Southwestern Historical Quarterly,* 76, no. 3 (January 1973), 277–296.

Guarneri, Carl J. *The Utopian Alternative: Fourierism in Nineteenth-Century America.* Ithaca: Cornell University Press, 1991.

Guarneri, Carl J. "Réunion, Texas, post scriptum ironique au fouriérisme américain." *Cahiers Charles Fourier,* 4 (1993), 13–27.

Hammond, William J. and Margaret F. *La Réunion: A French Settlement in Texas.* Dallas: Royal, 1958.

Hayden, Dolores. *Seven American Utopias: The Architecture of Communitarian Socialisme, 1790–1975.* Cambridge: MIT Press, 1976.

Karcher, Carolyn L. *The First Woman of the Republic: A Cultural Biography of Lydia Maria Child.* Durham: Duke University Press, 1994.

Klier, Betje Black. "Des Fouriéristes au Texas: la famille Considerant à San Antonio." *French Review,* 68, no. 6 (May 1995), 1035–1050.

Meineg, D. W. *Imperial Texas: An Interpretive Essay in Cultural Geography.* Austin: University of Texas Press, 1969.

Noyes, John Humphrey. *History of American Socialisms.* New York: Hillary House, 1961.

Olmsted, Frederick Law. *Journey through Texas: A Saddle-Trip on the Southwestern Frontier.* Austin: Von Boeckmann-Jones Press, 1962.

Pettitt, Richard Norman, Jr. "Albert Brisbane: Apostle of Fourierism in the United States, 1834–1890." Ph.D. diss., Miami University (Ohio), 1982.

Pratt, James. "Jeudi 22 décembre 1854: les premiers fouriéristes foulent le sol du Texas." *Cahiers Charles Fourier,* 4 (1993), 28–39.

Reynolds, David S. *Beneath the American Renaissance: The Subversive Imagination in the Age of Emerson and Melville.* Cambridge: Harvard University Press, 1988.

Reynolds, Larry J. *European Revolutions and the American Literary Renaissance.* New Haven: Yale University Press, 1988.

Robertson-Lorant, Laurie. *Melville: A Biography.* New York: Clarkson Potter, 1996.

Santerre, George H. *White Cliffs of Dallas: The Story of La Réunion, the Old French Colony.* Dallas: Book Craft, 1955.

Savardan, Auguste. *Un Naufrage au Texas.* Paris: Garnier, 1858.

Spann, Edward K. *The New Metropolis: New York City, 1840–1857.* New York: Columbia University Press, 1981.

Spann, Edward K. *Brotherly Tomorrows: Movements for a Cooperative Society in America, 1820–1920.* New York: Columbia University Press, 1988.

Verlet, Bruno. "Les Fouriéristes au Texas: du rêve à la réalité." *Cahiers Charles Fourier,* 4 (1993), 80–101.

Wheeler, Kenneth W. *To Wear a City's Crown: The Beginnings of Urban Growth in Texas, 1836–1865.* Cambridge: Harvard University Press, 1968.

INDEX

Victor Considerant is referred to as VC; Julie Considerant is referred to as JC.

Text:	10/13 Aldus
Display:	Aldus
Composition:	G&S Typesetters, Inc.
Printing and binding:	Edwards Brothers, Inc.
Index:	Victoria Baker